GNU/Linux Rapid Embedded Programming

Your one-stop solution to embedded programming on GNU/Linux

Rodolfo Giometti

BIRMINGHAM - MUMBAI

GNU/Linux Rapid Embedded Programming

First published: March 2017

Production reference: 1240317

Published by Packt Publishing Ltd.
Livery Place
35 Livery Street
Birmingham
B3 2PB, UK.
ISBN 978-1-78646-180-3

www.packtpub.com

Credits

Author
Rodolfo Giometti

Reviewer
Luca Zulberti

Commissioning Editor
Kartikey Pandey

Acquisition Editor
Narsimha Pai

Content Development Editors
Juliana Nair
Rashmi Suvarna

Technical Editors
Mohd Riyan Khan
Gaurav Suri

Copy Editor
Dipti Mankame

Project Coordinator
Judie Jose

Proofreader
Safis Editing

Indexer
Pratik Shirodkar

Graphics
Kirk D'Penha

Production Coordinator
Shantanu N. Zagade

About the Author

Rodolfo Giometti is an engineer, IT specialist, GNU/Linux expert and software libre evangelist.

Author of the books *BeagleBone Essentials* and *BeagleBone Home Automation Blueprints* by *Packt Publishing* and maintainer of the LinuxPPS projects (the Linux's Pulse Per Second subsystem) he still actively contributes to the Linux source code with several patches and new device drivers for industrial applications devices.

During his twenty-year+ experience, he, worked with x86, ARM, MIPS, & PowerPC-based platform.

Now, Rodolfo is the Co-Chief at HCE Engineering S.r.l. and he is the Co-Founder of the Cosino Project, which involves new hardware and software systems for the quick prototyping in industry environment, control automation, and remote monitoring.

I would like to thank my wife, Valentina, and my children, Romina and Raffaele, for their patience during the writing of this book. I also give deep thanks and gratitude to the Packt's guys Vivek Anantharaman, who gave to me the opportunity to write this book, and Rashmi Suvarna and Juliana Nair, who supported me in finishing this book (specially to Juliana Nair who spent her nights in editing the book's layout). Many thanks to Luca Zulberti, and Chris Simmonds for their support and effort in reviewing this book so carefully (specially to Luca Zulberti who so carefully re-checked my English, the code, and all circuitries). Also, a big thanks to Mohd Riyan Khan for his patience in adding all my modifications to the final review of this book.

Finally, I cannot forget to thank my parents. Giving me my first computer when I was a child, allowed me to be doing what I do today.

About the Reviewer

Luca Zulberti has obtained a diploma in 2015 in Electronics at ITIS G. Galilei in Livorno, Italy. He is continuing his studies at the University of Pisa in Electronic Engineering class.

In his spare time, he studies several programming techniques and languages. He has fun with several embedded systems and he's interested in Embedded OS development and GNU/Linux programming.

He's member of the Cosino Project on which he writes some articles and projects.

www.PacktPub.com

For support files and downloads related to your book, please visit www.PacktPub.com.

Did you know that Packt offers eBook versions of every book published, with PDF and ePub files available? You can upgrade to the eBook version at www.PacktPub.com and as a print book customer, you are entitled to a discount on the eBook copy. Get in touch with us at service@packtpub.com for more details.

At www.PacktPub.com, you can also read a collection of free technical articles, sign up for a range of free newsletters and receive exclusive discounts and offers on Packt books and eBooks.

https://www.packtpub.com/mapt

Get the most in-demand software skills with Mapt. Mapt gives you full access to all Packt books and video courses, as well as industry-leading tools to help you plan your personal development and advance your career.

Why subscribe?

- Fully searchable across every book published by Packt
- Copy and paste, print, and bookmark content
- On demand and accessible via a web browser

Customer Feedback

Thanks for purchasing this Packt book. At Packt, quality is at the heart of our editorial process. To help us improve, please leave us an honest review on this book's Amazon page at: `www.amazon.com/dp/ASIN/1786461803`.

If you'd like to join our team of regular reviewers, you can e-mail us at `customerreviews@packtpub.com`. We award our regular reviewers with free eBooks and videos in exchange for their valuable feedback. Help us be relentless in improving our products!

Table of Contents

Preface

Embedded computers have become very complex in the last few years and developers need to easily manage them by focusing on how to solve a problem without wasting time in finding good peripherals or learning how to manage them. The main challenge with experienced embedded programmers and engineers is really how long it takes to turn an idea into reality, and we show you exactly how to do it.

This book shows how to interact with external environments through specific peripherals used in the industry. We will use the latest Linux kernel release 4.x and Debian/Ubuntu distributions (with embedded distributions of OpenWrt and Yocto).

The book will present popular boards based on widely used and easily available CPUs on the components market and widely available from different professional boards makers. After a brief introduction of each boards, the book will show how to set up them in order to run a complete GNU/Linux distribution and then getting access to the system console. After that the book will present how to install a complete developing system on each board in order to be able to add developer's programs.

Readers will be able to take their first steps in programming the embedded platforms, using C, Bash and Python/PHP languages in order to get access to the external peripherals. More about using and programming device driver and accessing the peripherals will be covered to lay a strong foundation. The readers will learn how to read/write data from/to the external environment by using both C programs and a scripting language (Bash/Python) and how to configure a device driver for a specific hardware.

The hardware devices used in the book has been chosen in order to cover all possible connection type we can encounter working with an embedded board so you can find I^2C, SPI, USB, 1-Wire, serial, digital and analog devices, etc.

The programming languages used in the book has been chosen according to the rule to find the quickest and easiest solution to solve the current problem, in particular you can find example codes in Bash, C, PHP, Python.

In such chapters were will need to use a daemon, a kernel module or to recompile the whole kernel I've added a short description about what the reader should do and where he/she can get more information regarding the used tools, however some basic skills in managing a GNU/Linux system or the kernel's modules or the kernel itself are required.

What this book covers

This book can be divided into two major parts: the first one, which is introductory to the second one, where you will see how to install the developing systems and the host system and how to get access to the serial console. You'll take a look at some basic bootloader's commands as far as to the C compiler and the cross-compiler and then I'll introduce kernel modules, device drivers and some filesystem internals with a note on the Network File System. Also the machine emulator usage will be presented in order to execute a complete target machine's Debian distribution on a host PC, you'll see the system daemons and script programming in Bash, PHP and Python and then you'll take a look at the flash memories and Linux's Memory Technology Device (MTD) where I'll introduce the JFFS2 and the UBIFS filesystem and two of the most famous embedded distribution used in these days, Yocto and OpenWrt.

Below is a brief introduction of each chapters related to this first part:

Chapter 1, *Installing the Developing System*, will present three of the most used development kits for industrial applications: the BeagleBone Black, the SAMA5D3 Xplained and the WandBoard. After a brief introduction of each boards, we'll see how we can set up them in order to run a complete GNU/Linux distribution. We'll see how to install a complete developing system on each board as far as the host system (even on a virtual machine).

Chapter 2, *Managing the System Console*, will show to setup our developer kits and (in part) the host PC, then we'll go further in exploring the serial console and the shell running in it. In the end a special section will introduce the bootloader commands.

Chapter 3, *C Compiler, Device Drivers, and Useful Developing Techniques*, will focus the readers' attention to the C compiler (with its counter part: the cross-compiler). Then we'll take a look at kernel modules, device drivers and some filesystem internals with a note on the Network File System. In the end we'll see how developers can use an emulator in order to execute a complete target machine's Debian distribution on a host PC.

Chapter 4, *Quick Programming with scripts and system daemons*, will take a look at system daemons (what they are and how to use the most famous and useful ones). Then we'll take a look at script programming by using Bash, PHP and Python languages.

Chapter 5, *Setting up an embedded OS*, will start taking a look at flash memories and the software used to manage them, then we'll present the Linux's *Memory Technology Device* (MTD) and the two major filesystems that can run over them, that is the JFFS2 and the UBIFS. The we'll present two of the most famous embedded distribution used in these days, Yocto and OpenWrt, and how an embedded developer can write an his/her own application and how he/she can add it to them.

The second part then starts in going deeper in presenting all of such peripheral devices that you, as embedded developer, may encounter into your professional life. For each peripheral I'll present where it is available on each embedded kit supported by this book and then how you can get access and use it. For each device kind I'll show to you how you can easily manage it with practical examples.

Below is a brief introduction of each chapters related to the second part:

Chapter 6, *General Purposes Input Output signals - GPIO*, will introduce GPIO lines with a short description and then we'll see where they are physically located in our embedded machines. Then we're going to see in detail how we can get access to these lines in a very simple (but poor efficient) manner and then in a smarter (but a bit more complex) way. In the end we'll cover a rapid introduction of the GPIOs management inside the kernel with IRQ management and LED devices support.

Chapter 7, *Serial Ports and TTY Devices - TTY*, will introduce serial ports, that is one of the most important peripherals class a computer can have (at least a computer used in the control automation industry). After a brief description about what a serial port or a serial device is, we'll see how we can manage them into a GNU/Linux system in order to use a real serial device. Then we'll take a look at a kernel trick useful to communicate between two embedded systems by using a serial line as they were connected by an Ethernet cable.

Chapter 8, *Universal Serial Bus - USB*, will introduce the USB bus, that is a versatile bus, widely used in modern PCs, that allow people to connect an electronic device to a computer: for instance an hard disk, a keyboard or a serial device can be all connected to a computer through the same USB port.

Chapter 9, *Inter-Integrated Circuits - I2C*, will introduce the I^2C bus which is typically used to connect *on-board* devices, that is the main computer with devices whose are all placed on the same board. Several devices use the I^2C bus to communicate with the CPU and in this chapter will give to you a panoramic as wide as possible of them: we'll see several kinds of different devices with different configurations in order to cover as much as possible the combinations offered by this bus.

Chapter 10, *Serial Peripheral Interface - SPI*, will introduce the SPI bus which is another bus kind typically used to connect *on-board* devices as I^2C does. However, and opposed to the I^2C bus, this bus can transfer data at higher rates than I^2C and, since it's full-duplex, data transfer can take place bidirectionally at the same time. Due these features the SPI bus is normally used to implement an efficient data stream for multimedia applications or digital signal processing and/or telecommunications devices and SD cards.

Chapter 11, *1-Wire - W1*, will introduce Ethernet devices whose add the possibility to any equipped device to communicate with other devices even on very long distances. The GNU/Linux based systems offer a really good support of Ethernet devices and their relative networking protocols that's why most of networking devices around the world are based on this technology.

Chapter 12, *Ethernet network device - ETH*, will introduce the one wire bus which is interesting because it permits to communicate with a remote device using only one wire even if at slower rates. This allows to simplify connections between the CPU and its peripherals giving the designer the possibility to have the most economical and simply way to add electronic devices for identification, authentication and delivery of calibration data or manufacturing information to a computer board.

Chapter 13, *Wireless Network Device - WLAN*, will introduce Wireless network devices whose allow the communication between several computers but doing it without using wires. What is really interesting in using these networking interfaces is that a large part of communication protocols used on Ethernet interfaces can be used with these devices too!

Chapter 14, *Controller Area Network - CAN*, will introduce the CAN bus that has been specifically designed to allow microcontrollers, computers and devices to communicate with each other in applications without a host computer by having a message-based protocol. The CAN bus is not so *famous* as Ethernet or WiFi but in the embedded world it is used and is not rare finding SoCs which support it by default.

Chapter 15, *Sound devices - SND*, will introduce sound devices with some possible usages of them till to show to the reader how they can use them in order to generate audio how to implement a simple and low cost oscilloscope.

Chapter 16, *Video devices - V4L*, will introduce common video acquisition devices with some possible usages of them till to show to the reader how they can turn our embedded kits into a surveillance camera or a remote image recorder.

Chapter 17, *Analog-to-Digital Converters - ADC*, will introduce ADCs that can be used to get analogical signals from the environment. The chapter will show how to use them and how to use special software and hardware triggers in order to start conversions at specific timing or when some events occur.

`Chapter 18`, *Pulse-Width Modulation - PWM*, will introduce PWMs that are able to encode a message into a pulsing signal (usually a square waveform) to generate an analog signal by using a digital source, then these messages can be used to control the power supplied to electrical motors or other electronics devices or, as we're going to show into this chapter, to control the position of a servo motor.

`Chapter 19`, *Miscellaneous devices*, will introduce peripherals that can fit in one of the above chapters but that has not reported there for better readability. In this last chapter we're going to present a list of additional peripherals we can encounter into a monitoring or controlling system such as RFID and smart card readers, some digital and analog sensors, GSM/GPRS modem, Z-Wave, etc.

What you need for this book

Following are the requisites for efficient learning.

Software prerequisite

Regarding the software you should have a little knowledge of a non graphical text editor as `vi`, `emacs` or `nano`. Even if you can connect an LCD display, a keyboard and a mouse directly to embedded kits and then use the graphical interface, in this book we assume that you is able to do little modifications to text files by using a text only editor.

The host computer, that is the computer you will use to cross-compile the code and/or to manage your embedded systems, is assumed running a GNU/Linux based distribution. My host PC is running an Ubuntu 15.10 but you can use also a newer Ubuntu Long Term Support (LTS) or a Debian based system too with little modifications or you may use another GNU/Linux distribution but with a little effort from you mainly regarding the cross-compiling tools installation, libraries dependencies and packages management. Foreign systems such as Windows, MacOS or similar are *not* covered by this book due the fact you should not use low technology systems to develop code for high technology system!

Knowing how a C compiler works and how to manage a `Makefile` is required.

This book will present some kernel programming techniques but these must cannot be taken as a *kernel programming course*. You need a proper book for such topic! However each example is well documented and you will find several suggested resources. Regarding the kernel I'd like to state that the version used into this book is 4.4.x.

As a final note I suppose that you known how to connect a GNU/Linux based board on the Internet in order to download a package or a generic file.

Hardware prerequisite

In this book all code is developed for BeagleBone Black board *revision C*, for SAMA5D3 Xplained *revision A* or for the WandBoard *revision C1* (depending on the board used) but you can use an older revision without any issues, in fact the code is portable and it should work on other systems too (but the DTS files whose must be considered apart)!

Regarding the computer peripherals used in this book I reported in each chapter where I got the hardware and where you can buy it but, of course, you can decide to surf the Internet in order to find a better and cheaper offer. A note where to find the datasheet is also present.

You should not have any difficulties in order to connect the hardware presented in this book with the embedded kits since the connections are very simple and well documented. They don't require any particular hardware skills to be performed from you (apart knowing how to use a solder), however having a minor knowledge in electronics may help.

Who this book is for

If you want to learn how to use embedded machine learning capabilities and get access to a GNU/Linux device driver to collect data from a peripheral or to control a device, this book is for you.

If you are interested in knowing how to easily and quickly get access to different computer peripherals in order to realize a functional control or monitor system based on GNU/Linux for industrial applications, this book is for you.

If you have some hardware or electrical engineering experience and know the basics of C, Bash, and Python and PHP programming in a UNIX environment and want using them into an embedded system, this book is for you.

Conventions

In this book, you will find a number of text styles that distinguish between different kinds of information. Here are some examples of these styles and an explanation of their meaning.

Codes and command lines

Code words in text, database table names, folder names, filenames, file extensions, pathnames, dummy URLs and user input are shown as follows: "To get the preceding kernel messages, we can use both the `dmesg` and `tail -f /var/log/kern.log` commands."

A block of code is set as follows:

```
#include <stdio.h>

int main(int argc, char *argv[])
{
    printf("Hello World!\n");

    return 0;
}
```

You should note that most code in this book has 4 spaces indentation while the example code you can find into the files provided with this book on Github or Packt site, has 8 spaces indentation. So the above code will look like as follow:

```
#include <stdio.h>

int main(int argc, char *argv[])
{
        printf("Hello World!\n");

        return 0;
}
```

Obviously they are perfectly equivalent!

Any command line input or output given on one of the embedded kits used in this book is written as follows:

```
root@bbb:~# make CFLAGS="-Wall -O2" helloworld
cc -Wall -O2 helloworld.c -o helloworld
```

Then by looking into the prompt string we can deduce which board we're currently using. I use the string bbb for the BeagleBone Black, a5d3 for the SAMA5D3 Xplained and wb for the WandBoard. However I use the generic string arm when I'm referring a generic embedded kit.

Note also that due space reasons into the book you may read very long commands lines as follows:

```
$ make ARCH=arm CROSS_COMPILE=arm-linux-gnueabihf-
            sama5d3_xplained_nandflash_defconfig
```

Otherwise I have had to break the command line. However in some special cases you can find broken output lines (specially on kernel messages) as follow:

```
cdc_ether 2-1.1:1.0 usb0: register 'cdc_ether' at usb-0000:00:1d.0-1.1
, CDC Ethernet Device, 62:1e:f6:88:9b:42
```

Unluckily these lines cannot be easily reported into a printed book so you should consider them as a single line.

Any command line input or output given on my host computer as a *non-privileged user* is written as follows:

```
$ tail -f /var/log/kern.log
```

When I need to give a command as a privileged user (root) on my host computer the command line input or output is then written as follows:

```
# /etc/init.d/apache2 restart
```

You should notice that all privileged commands can be executed by a normal user too by using the sudo command with the form:

```
$ sudo <command>
```

So the preceding command can be executed by a normal user as:

```
$ sudo /etc/init.d/apache2 restart
```

Kernel and logging messages

On several GNU/Linux distribution a kernel message has the usual form:

```
Oct 27 10:41:56 hulk kernel: [46692.664196] usb 2-1.1: new high-speed USB
device number 12 using ehci-pci
```

Which is a quite long line for this book, that's why the characters from the start of the lines till the point where the real information begin are dropped. So, in the preceding example, the lines output will be reported as follow:

```
usb 2-1.1: new high-speed USB device number 12 using ehci-pci
```

However, as just said above, if the line is still too long it will be broken anyway.

Long outputs, repeated or less important lines in a terminal are dropped by replacing them with three dots . . . shown as follows:

```
output begin
output line 1
output line 2
...
output line 10
output end
```

When the three dots are at the end they mean that the output continues but I decided cut it for space reasons.

File modifications

When you should modify a text file, I'm going to use the *unified context diff* format since this is a very efficient and compact way to represent a text modification. This format can be obtained by using the diff command with the -u option argument.

As a simple example, let's consider the following text into file1.old:

```
This is first line
This is the second line
This is the third line
...
...
This is the last line
```

Suppose we have to modify the third line as highlighted in the following snippet:

```
This is first line
This is the second line
This is the new third line modified by me
...
...
This is the last line
```

You can easily understand that reporting each time the whole file for a simple modification it's quite obscure and space consuming, however by using the *unified context diff* format the preceding modification can be written as follow:

```
$ diff -u file1.old file1.new
--- file1.old 2015-03-23 14:49:04.354377460 +0100
+++ file1.new 2015-03-23 14:51:57.450373836 +0100
@@ -1,6 +1,6 @@
 This is first line
 This is the second line
-This is the third line
+This is the new third line modified by me
 ...
 ...
 This is the last line
```

Now the modification is very clear and written in a compact form! It starts with a two-line header where the original file is preceded by --- and the new file is preceded by +++, then follows one or more change hunks that contain the line differences in the file. The preceding example has just one hunk where the unchanged lines are preceded by a space character, while the lines to be added are preceded by a + character and the lines to be removed are preceded by a – character.

Still for space reasons, most patches reported into this book has reduced indentation in order to fit printed pages width, however they are still perfectly readable in a correct form. For the real patch you should refer to the provided files on Github or Packt site.

Serial & network connections

In this book I'm going to mainly use two different kind of connections to interact with the the embedded boards: the serial console, an SSH terminal and an Ethernet connection.

The serial console, that is implemented over the same USB connection used to power up the board, is mainly used to manage the system from the command line. It's largely used to monitoring the system especially to take under control the kernel messages.

An SSH terminal is quite similar to the serial console even if is not exactly the same (for example kernel messages do not automatically appear on a terminal) but it can be used in the same manner as a serial console to give commands and to edit files from the command line.

In the next chapters I'm going to use a terminal on the serial console or over an SSH connection indifferently to give the most of the commands and configuration settings needed to implement all the prototypes explained in this book.

To get access to the serial console from your host PC you can use the `minicon` command as follow:

```
$ minicom -o -D /dev/ttyACM0
```

Or the next one according to the board and/or the USB-to-Serial adapter used:

```
$ minicom -o -D /dev/ttyUSB0
```

However in `Chapter 1`, *Installing the Developing System*, this aspects are explained and you should not worry about them. Note also that on some system you may needs the root privileges to get access to the `/dev/ttyACM0` device. In this case you can fix this issue or by using the `sudo` command or, better, by properly add you system's user to the right group by using the command below:

```
$ sudo adduser $LOGNAME dialout
```

Then log out and log in again and you should access the serial devices without any problem.

To get access to the SSH terminal you can use the emulated Ethernet connection over the same USB cable used for the serial console. In fact, if your host PC is well configured, when you plug in the USB cable, after a while, you should see a new cable connection with a proper IP address (in case of the BeagleBone Black you should get the address 192.168.7.1, for the SAMA5D3 Xplained the address 192.168.8.1, while address 192.168.9.1 for the WandBoard. See `Chapter 1`, *Installing the Developing System*). Then, for example, I can use this new connection to get access to the BeagleBone Black by using the following command:

```
$ ssh root@192.168.7.2
```

The last available communication channel is the Ethernet connection. It is used mainly to download files from the host PC or the Internet and it can be established by connecting an Ethernet cable to the each embedded kit's Ethernet port and then configuring the port accordingly to the reader's LAN settings.

But it's quite important to point out the you can get connected with the Internet by using also the emulated Ethernet connection over USB presented above. In fact, by using the commands below on the host PC (obviously GNU/Linux based), you'll be able to use it as a router allowing your embedded boards to surf the net as it was connected with its real Ethernet port:

```
# iptables --table nat --append POSTROUTING --out-interface eth1
                       -j MASQUERADE
# iptables --append FORWARD --in-interface eth4 -j ACCEPT
# echo 1 >> /proc/sys/net/ipv4/ip_forward
```

Then, for instance, on the BeagleBone Black I should set the gateway through the USB cable using the following command:

```
root@bbb:~# route add default gw 192.168.7.1
```

Note that the eth1 device is the preferred Internet connection on my host system, while the eth4 device is the BeagleBone Black's device as viewed on my system.

Other conventions

New terms and **important words** are shown in bold. Words that you see on the screen, for example, in menus or dialog boxes, appear in the text like this: "Clicking the **Next** button moves you to the next screen."

Warnings or important notes appear in a box like this.

Tips and tricks appear like this.

Reader feedback

Feedback from our readers is always welcome. Let us know what you think about this book-what you liked or disliked. Reader feedback is important for us as it helps us develop titles that you will really get the most out of.

To send us general feedback, simply e-mail `feedback@packtpub.com`, and mention the book's title in the subject of your message.

If there is a topic that you have expertise in and you are interested in either writing or contributing to a book, see our author guide at `www.packtpub.com/authors`.

Customer support

Now that you are the proud owner of a Packt book, we have a number of things to help you to get the most from your purchase.

Downloading the example code

You can download the example code files for this book from your account at `http://www.packtpub.com`. If you purchased this book elsewhere, you can visit `http://www.packtpub.com/support` and register to have the files e-mailed directly to you.

You can download the code files by following these steps:

1. Log in or register to our website using your e-mail address and password.
2. Hover the mouse pointer on the **SUPPORT** tab at the top.
3. Click on **Code Downloads & Errata**.
4. Enter the name of the book in the **Search** box.
5. Select the book for which you're looking to download the code files.
6. Choose from the drop-down menu where you purchased this book from.
7. Click on **Code Download**.

Once the file is downloaded, please make sure that you unzip or extract the folder using the latest version of:

- WinRAR / 7-Zip for Windows
- Zipeg / iZip / UnRarX for Mac
- 7-Zip / PeaZip for Linux

The complete set of code can also be downloaded from the following GitHub repository: `ht tps://github.com/PacktPublishing/GNU-Linux-Rapid-Embedded-Programming/`. We also have other code bundles from our rich catalog of books and videos available at: `https ://github.com/PacktPublishing/`. Check them out!

For this book the example code files can also be downloaded from the author's Github repository at URL `https://github.com/giometti/gnu_linux_rapid_embedded_programming`.

Just use the following command to get it at once:

```
$ git clone
   https://github.com/giometti/gnu_linux_rapid_embedded_programming.git
```

The examples are grouped according to the chapters name so you can easily find the code during the reading of the book.

Downloading the color images of this book

We also provide you with a PDF file that has color images of the screenshots/diagrams used in this book. The color images will help you better understand the changes in the output. You can download this file from `https://www.packtpub.com/sites/default/files/down loads/GNULinuxRapidEmbeddedProgramming.pdf`.

Errata

Although we have taken every care to ensure the accuracy of our content, mistakes do happen. If you find a mistake in one of our books-maybe a mistake in the text or the code-we would be grateful if you could report this to us. By doing so, you can save other readers from frustration and help us improve subsequent versions of this book. If you find any errata, please report them by visiting `http://www.packtpub.com/submit-errata`, selecting your book, clicking on the **Errata Submission Form** link, and entering the details of your errata. Once your errata are verified, your submission will be accepted and the errata will be uploaded to our website or added to any list of existing errata under the Errata section of that title.

To view the previously submitted errata, go to `https://www.packtpub.com/books/content/support` and enter the name of the book in the search field. The required information will appear under the **Errata** section.

Piracy

Piracy of copyrighted material on the Internet is an ongoing problem across all media. At Packt, we take the protection of our copyright and licenses very seriously. If you come across any illegal copies of our works in any form on the Internet, please provide us with the location address or website name immediately so that we can pursue a remedy.

Please contact us at copyright@packtpub.com with a link to the suspected pirated material.

We appreciate your help in protecting our authors and our ability to bring you valuable content.

Questions

If you have a problem with any aspect of this book, you can contact us at questions@packtpub.com, and we will do our best to address the problem.

1
Installing the Developing System

In this chapter, we will present three of the most used development kits for industrial applications. Respect to the most famous Raspberry Pi, these boards are based on widely used CPUs on custom boards in an industrial environment. In fact, while Raspberry Pi's CPU is not easily available on the components market, the CPUs of the following boards are widely available with different professional board makers.

In the upcoming sections, after a brief introduction of each board, we'll see how we can set them up to run a complete GNU/Linux distribution and then get access to the system console. After that, we will install a complete developing system on each board in order to be able to add our own programs.

A little tutorial about how to set up the host system is also present, and you can use it to set up a GNU/Linux-based working machine or a dedicated virtual one.

This chapter can be skipped if you already have a running embedded system with the relative host PC. However, you should consider reading it anyway due the fact that we'll present an overview of the embedded devices we're going to use in this book. In this chapter, we'll fix some common terms used in this book, and you may learn a different way to install a running system on your boards. Also, last but not least, the system that is already running on your boards may be different from the ones presented here. This means that you may need to change some commands presented in this book accordingly in order to have functional examples.

Embedded world terms

Before putting our hands on our new boards, it is recommended that you acquaint yourselves with some terms that a user should know in order to avoid misunderstandings. People who have already worked with some GNU/Linux and/or embedded systems may skip this part. The developer kits shown here are tiny single-board computers that can be embedded into a device, so the user should be familiar with some terms used in the wonderful world of embedded programming:

Term	Description
Target	The target system is the embedded computer that we wish to manage. Usually, it is an ARM platform, but this is not a fixed rule. In fact, **PowerPC** and **MIPS** are other (less) common platforms. Even the x86 platform (a standard PC) can be an embedded computer.
Host	The host system is the computer we will use to manage the target system. Usually, it is a normal PC (x86 platform or MAC), but even other platforms can be used (for example, years ago, I used a PowerPC-based computer as a host PC). Normally, the host system is more powerful than the target one since it's usually used for heavy compiling tasks that the target cannot perform at all or for tasks that it takes a long time to perform.
Serial console	This is the most important communication port in an embedded system. Using the serial console, the user has complete control of the system. It's not only indispensable for debugging, but is also the last resort if, by chance, the operating system files are messed up and the board refuses to boot. Without the serial console, the user can still control the system (if correctly set up), but for the developer/debugger, it's a must-have!
Compiler (or native compiler)	The native compiler is just a compiler! This is the compiler running on a machine (host or target) that builds the code for the current machine (that is, the compiler running on a PC builds the code for the PC, like the one running on an ARM machine builds the code for ARM itself).
Cross-compiler	Strictly speaking, the cross-compiler is just a compiler that builds the code for a foreign platform (that is, a cross-compiler can run on a PC in order to generate binaries for an ARM platform). However, usually, by using this term, the embedded developers also mean the complete compilation suite, that is, the compiler, linker, binutils, libc, and so on.

Toolchain	A **toolchain** is a set of programming tools that is used to create a software product, that is, another computer program or a set of related programs. The term *toolchain* is due the fact that the tools forming a toolchain are executed consecutively as in a chain, so the output of each tool becomes the input for the next one. However, this is not a fixed rule. In fact, the tools in a toolchain are not necessarily executed consecutively. A simple software development toolchain may consist of a compiler, a linker (plus other binutils), one or more libraries (which provide interfaces to the operating system), and a debugger (used to debug programs).
Distribution	A distribution (or *Linux distribution*, often called *distro* for short) is an operating system made from a software collection based on Linux (the kernel) and several software packages (most from the GNU project or based on a Libre Software license) managed by a **package management system**. There are several distributions, and they are available for a wide variety of systems ranging from embedded devices (**OpenWrt** or **Yocto**) and personal computers to powerful supercomputers.
Root filesystem	The root filesystem (or *rootfs*) is the filesystem contained on the same partition on which the root directory is located. This is the most important filesystem in an UNIX system, and it's the first one to be mounted by the kernel. All the other filesystems are mounted on it.
System on chip	A system on chip (**SoC**) is an integrated circuit that integrates a CPU and different kinds of peripherals (SATA and SD/MMC controller, GPIOs, I²C/SPI/W1 controllers, ADC/DAC converters, audio/video signals, and Ethernet or UART ports) into a single chip. These chips are widely used in embedded systems where they found their typical application.
Microcontroller	A microcontroller (MCU) is a small computer on a single integrated circuit (like a SoC) that contains a processor core, memory, and programmable IO peripherals. So, the main difference between a SoC is that it has the flash memory (where the program is stored) as well as a small amount of RAM (to execute the program) included on its chip. Microcontrollers are designed for embedded applications where the tasks to be accomplished are not too complex. They are also used when we need have time constraints or just because they are cost effective.

Flash memory	Flash memory is an electronic non-volatile computer storage medium that can be electrically erased and reprogrammed.
	In contrast to a normal PC, this kind of memory is widely used on embedded applications as mass storage due the fact it has no moving parts and it has better resistance to a hostile environment.

Now that some important terms have been pointed out, we are ready to step into the next section and discover our developer kits!

Systems' overview

Here is a brief introduction of the developer kits we will use into this book.

The first kit is the **BeagleBone Black,** which is a low-cost, community-supported development platform for developers and hobbyists. It's able to boot Linux in under 10 seconds and get started on development in few minutes with just a single USB cable. This board is widely used on several prototypes on the Internet, so it's a board that every embedded programmer should know.

The second kit is **SAMA5D3 Xplained,** which is a fast prototyping and evaluation platform that comes with a rich set of ready-to-use connectivity, storage peripherals, and expansion headers for easy customization. A USB device connector can be used to power the board as well as for programming and debugging it. This board is very interesting due the fact it uses a very low power-consuming CPU with good performances and with a lot of industrial-oriented peripherals.

The last (but not least) kit is **Wandboard,** which is a complete computer with high-performance multimedia capabilities, a good peripheral equipment and, in contrast with the other boards, it's composed by a core module and an easy interface board to customize or modify. The board is very interesting because it can be equipped with a multicore CPU and because it comes as a CPU module connected to a carrier board, which allows embedded developers to have a highly hardware-customizable device.

The BeagleBone Black

In the following image, there is a picture of the BeagleBone Black, with a credit card, so that you can have an idea about the real dimensions of the whole system:

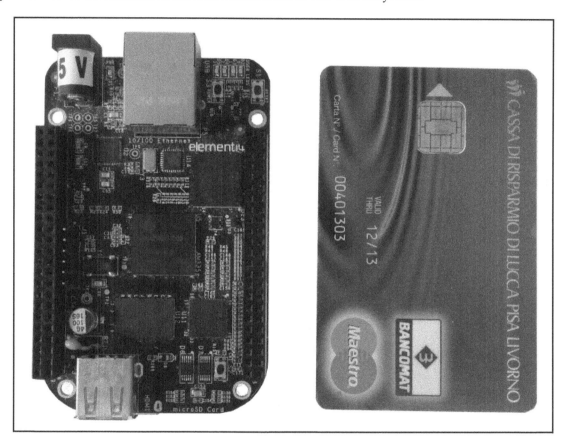

Here are some interesting URLs where you can read some useful information regarding BeagleBone Black:

- https://beagleboard.org/black
- http://beagleboard.org/static/beaglebone/latest/Docs/Hardware/BONE_SRM.pdf
- http://beagleboard.org/getting-started
- https://eewiki.net/display/linuxonarm/BeagleBone+Black

The main hardware key features of my BeagleBone Black (revision C) are reported in the following table:

Part	Specification
Main processor	ARM processor: Cortex-A8 @ 1Ghz
Graphic processor	PowerVR SGX
SDRAM memory	512MB DDR3
On-board flash	4GB, 8-bit eMMC
USB 2.0 ports	1 device 1 host
Serial port	UART0 via 6 pin 3.3 V TTL connector
Ethernet	1 port 10/100 via RJ45 connector
SD/MMC	1 slot microSD
Video/audio out	Micro HDMI
Buttons	1 for power 1 for reset 1 user controllable
LED indicators	1 for power 2 on Ethernet port 4 user controllable
On-board Wi-Fi/bluetooth	None
SATA	None
Expansion Connectors	Power 5V, 3.3V, VDD ADC (1.8V) GPIOs 3.3V SPI, I2C, LCD, GPMC, MMC0-1, CAN 7 ADC (1.8V max) 4 timers 4 serial ports 3 PWMs
J-TAG connector	20 pins J-TAG (not populated)

Then, the following image shows a top view of the BeagleBone Black, where we can see some interesting things:

- The connector *J1* used to access the serial console.
- The Ethernet connector.
- The power connector.
- The two expansion connectors *P8* and *P9*, where we can connect the dedicated extension boards and/or custom peripherals (these connectors will be explained in detail in the upcoming chapters).
- The microSD slot.
- The USB host port.
- The reset button does what it says while the power button can be used to turn on/off the board, and the user button, which is user controllable, can be used to do an alternate boot on the microSD card instead of the on-board eMMC.

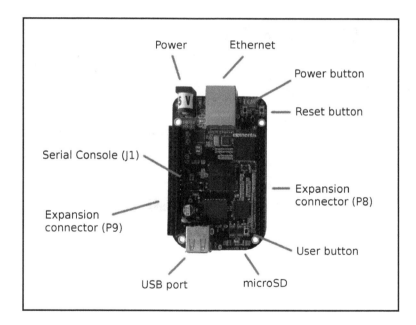

From the preceding image, we can see that the BeagleBone Black doesn't look like a PC, but it can act as a PC! The BeagleBone Black is a fully functional single-board computer and can be readily used as a PC if required by connecting a monitor to the HDMI port and attaching a USB keyboard and mouse through a USB hub. However, it is more suited to embedded applications, where it can act as more than a PC due its expansion connectors, and we can stack up to four expansion boards (named capes) that are useful for several purposes.

In this book, we'll see how we can manage (and reinstall) a complete Debian distribution that allows us to have a wide set of ready-to-run software packages, as a normal PC may have (in fact, the Debian ARM version is equivalent to the Debian x86 version). Then, we'll see how we can use the expansion connectors to connect to the board. Several peripherals are used to monitor/control the external environment.

The SAMA5D3 Xplained

In the following image, as done earlier, there is a picture of the SAMA5D3 Xplained, with a credit card, where we can easily notice that compared to the BeagleBone Black, this board is larger. This is due the fact that we have more connectors and ports mounted on the board. In particular, the expansion connector in the center of the board is **Arduino R3** compatible, so we can use its extension boards on it:

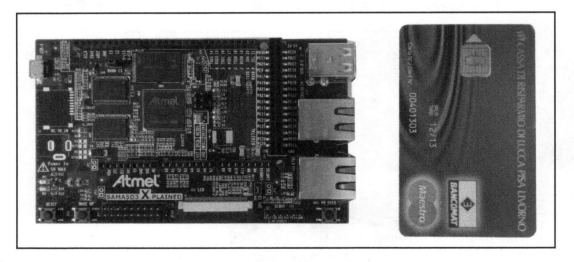

Here are some interesting URLs where you can read about SAMA5D3 Xplained:

- http://www.atmel.com/tools/ATSAMA5D3-XPLD.aspx
- http://www.atmel.com/images/atmel-11269-32-bit-cortex-a5-microcontroller-sama5d3-xplained_user-guide.pdf
- http://www.at91.com/linux4sam/bin/view/Linux4SAM/Sama5d3XplainedMainPage
- https://eewiki.net/display/linuxonarm/ATSAMA5D3+Xplained

Note that there are several versions of the SAMA5D3 Xplained board depending on the CPU version, so we can have SATSAMA5D31, SATSAMA5D33, SATSAMA5D34, SATSAMA5D35, and ATSAMA5D36. Each CPU has the same core, but a different peripheral set.

In this book, we will use ATSAMA5D36, and the main hardware key features of this version are reported in the following table:

Part	Specification
Main processor	ARM processor: Cortex-A5 @ 536Mhz
Graphic processor	LCD controller with graphics accelerator
SDRAM memory	256MB DDR2
On-board flash	256MB, NAND flash
USB 2.0 ports	1 device 2 host
Serial port	UART0 via 6 pin 3.3 V TTL connector
Ethernet	1 port 10/100/1000 via RJ45 connector 1 port 10/100 via RJ45 connector
SD/MMC	1 slot SD/MMCPlus 8-bit 1 slot microSD 4-bit (not soldered)
Video/audio out	Digital interface
Buttons	1 for reset 1 for wake up 1 user controllable
LED indicators	1 for power 2 on each Ethernet port 1 user controllable
On-board Wi-Fi/bluetooth	Optional WiFi via SDIO expansion
SATA	None

Expansion Connectors	GPIOs 3.3V SPI, I^{2}C0-1, CAN0-1, VBAT 12 ADC (3.3V max) 2 timers 6 serial ports 2 PWMs
J-TAG connector	20 pins J-TAG (populated)

The following image shows a top view of the SAMA5D3 Xplained, where we can see some interesting things:

- The connector *J23* can be used to access the serial console.
- The USB micro port can be used obviously as a USB device interface, but it is used also as a power supply port and as a SAM-BA USB device and USB CDC connection.
- The two Ethernet connectors.
- The LCD connector.
- The JTAG connector.
- The two USB host ports.
- The expansion connector (note that these connectors are Arduino R3 compatible).
- The reset button can be used to reset the board. The wake up button can be used to turn on/off the board.

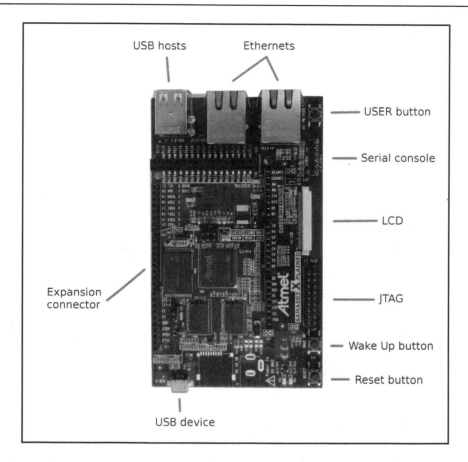

This board can also act as a PC, even if it is designed for typical industrial tasks. It can resist in very hostile environment. It has low power consumption and a lot of useful peripherals for professional applications. In contrast to the BeagleBone Black, it has no HDMI connector for external monitor, but it has a dedicated connector for an LCD with touch screen.

Even for this board, we'll install a complete Debian distribution and see how we can use the expansion connectors to connect to the board.

The Wandboard

In the following image, there is a picture of the Wandboard, with the same credit card shown earlier:

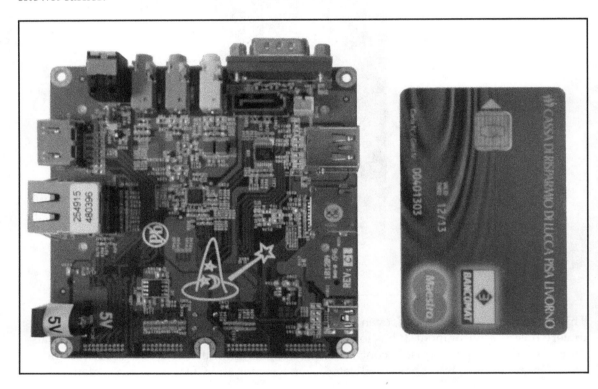

The board seems quite small, but it's actually composed of two parts: the core module is on top of the interface (or carrier) module (see the following image):

Here are some interesting URLs where you can gain some useful information regarding your Wandboard:

- http://www.wandboard.org/
- http://www.wandboard.org/images/downloads/wbquad-revb1-userguide.pdf
- http://wiki.wandboard.org/Main_Page
- https://eewiki.net/display/linuxonarm/Wandboard

Note that there are several versions of the Wandboard board depending on the CPU version, so we can have the Wandboard Solo, Wandboard Dual, and Wandboard Quad. Each version has a different CPU with the same core but a different peripheral set and core numbers. In fact, the Wandboard is available as a single-, dual-, and quad-core CPU!

In this book, we will use the Wandboard Quad (revision C1), and the main hardware key features of this version are reported in the following table:

Part	Specification
Main processor	ARM processor: Quad Cortex-A9 @ 1Ghz
Graphic processor	Vivante GC 2000 + Vivante GC 355 + Vivante GC 320
SDRAM memory	2GB DDR3
On-board flash	None
USB 2.0 ports	1 OTG 2 host
Serial port	UART0 via standard RS232 pin9 connector
Ethernet	1 port 10/100/1000 via RJ45 connector
SD/MMC	2 slot SD/MMCPlus 8-bit
Video/audio out	HDMI Analog audio plus optical S/P DIF Digital camera connector
Buttons	1 for reset
LED indicators	1 for power 2 on Ethernet port
On-board Wi-Fi/bluetooth	802.11n/4.0
SATA	1 connector
Expansion connectors	GPIOs 3.3V SPI, I2C0-1, CAN0-1, VBAT 12 ADC (3.3V max) 2 timers 6 serial ports 2 PWMs
J-TAG connector	8 pins J-TAG (not populated)

The following two images show the bottom and top views of the Wandboard, where we can see some interesting things. Here are the features of the bottom side of the board:

- The RS-232 9-pins connector *COM1* can be used to access the serial console
- The USB mini port used as USB OTG connector
- The USB host port
- The secondary microSD connector
- The power connector
- The Ethernet connector
- The audio ports
- The SATA connector
- The HDMI connector

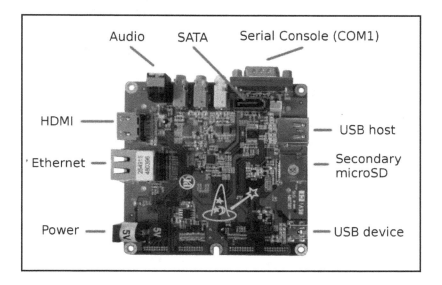

On the top side (we split the core module on the left and the interface board on the right) we have:

- The camera interface connector
- The primary microSD
- The Wi-Fi chip
- The four expansion connectors
- The reset button can be used to reset the board

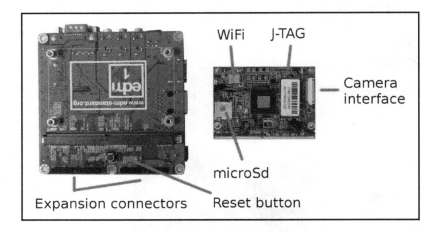

This board too can act as a PC, and that's why we will install a complete Debian distribution on it too. This board, as in the case of the BeagleBone Black, has a HDMI connector for external monitor.

Installing a development system

The target of this book is to explain how to get access to the several peripherals present on our boards and how to quickly write programs to manage their data. In order to do it, we need a good developing system. That's why, in this section, we will install a Debian OS on each board.

One of the main advantages of GNU/Linux-based boards is the fact that we can have the same developing environment regardless of the board we decide to use. In order to practically demonstrate this fact, we will install exactly the same OS on each board (even if a preloaded OS may be already present on some boards). To do this, we just need an SD (or microSD) card to store our developing OS and then follow the instructions in the upcoming sections.

However, before putting our hands on the embedded boards, we need to set up our host machine.

Setting up the host machine

As every good embedded developer knows, a host machine is absolutely necessary. Even if the embedded devices are getting more powerful nowadays, there are some resource-consuming tasks where a host machine can help.

The host machine we decide to use could be a normal PC or a virtualized one. The important thing is that it runs a GNU/Linux-based OS! In this book, we will use an Ubuntu 15.10 based system (since this is currently my laptop's configuration), you can decide to use the same (maybe in a virtual machine) or just to use an Ubuntu **Long Term Support** (**LTS**) release, such as 16.04 for instance, without any problem or major changes. However, we can also try to replicate some settings and installation commands that we will use during the course of the book into another Linux distribution with little effort.

Basic tools

If we did a clean installation or we have never used our machine as a developing one, then we have to install some useful developing tools before continuing. As the first step, we will install the aptitude tool, which is quite similar to the most famous apt-get command, but it's smarter (note that this is not required since we may still continue using apt-get without any problems). Here is the installing command:

```
$ sudo apt-get install aptitude
```

Then, we can install other useful basic tools using the aptitude command as shown here:

```
$ sudo aptitude install openssh-server tree git device-tree-compiler
                        lzma lzop libncurses5-dev:amd64 minicom
```

After all packages have been installed, we can go further and install the cross-compiler with the relative toolchain.

The cross-compiler

Every host machine needs a proper cross-compiler for the target board we wish to work on, so we have to install one. As we can see in the upcoming chapters, we mainly need a cross-compiler to build the bootloader and the kernel, since we can directly compile user-space applications on the target itself due the fact we're using Debian. However, we can use it for several other tasks, for instance, to compile specific drivers and/or to compile user-space applications even if, in this last case, we need to be careful to keep the cross toolchain in step with the target (having compatible library versions, header files, and so on). Otherwise, it would case subtle problems from time to time.

 Note that if we use an embedded distribution such as **Yocto** or **OpenWrt** (`Chapter 5`, *Setting Up an Embedded OS*), we must use the cross-compiler to compile user-space applications too, since we have no native compiler to execute on the boards.

There are several solutions to install a cross-compiler, starting from installing the one supplied by the used distribution to using a pre-built one. Ubuntu has its own cross-compiler, as shown here, using the following command:

```
$ apt-cache search gcc-[0-9.]*-arm
gcc-5-arm-linux-gnueabihf - GNU C compiler
gcc-5-arm-linux-gnueabihf-base - GCC, the GNU Compiler Collection (bas
e package)
gcc-4.7-arm-linux-gnueabi - GNU C compiler
gcc-4.7-arm-linux-gnueabi-base - GCC, the GNU Compiler Collection (bas
e package)
gcc-4.7-arm-linux-gnueabihf - GNU C compiler
gcc-4.7-arm-linux-gnueabihf-base - GCC, the GNU Compiler Collection (b
ase package)
gcc-4.8-arm-linux-gnueabihf - GNU C compiler
gcc-4.8-arm-linux-gnueabihf-base - GCC, the GNU Compiler Collection (b
ase package)
gcc-4.9-arm-linux-gnueabi - GNU C compiler
gcc-4.9-arm-linux-gnueabi-base - GCC, the GNU Compiler Collection (bas
e package)
gcc-4.9-arm-linux-gnueabihf - GNU C compiler
gcc-4.9-arm-linux-gnueabihf-base - GCC, the GNU Compiler Collection (b
ase package)
gcc-5-arm-linux-gnueabi - GNU C compiler
gcc-5-arm-linux-gnueabi-base - GCC, the GNU Compiler Collection (base
package)
```

Downloading the example code

Detailed steps to download the code bundle are mentioned in the Preface of this book.

The code bundle for the book is also hosted on GitHub at: `https://githu b.com/PacktPublishing/GNU-Linux-Rapid-Embedded-Programming/`. We also have other code bundles from our rich catalog of books and videos available at: `https://github.com/PacktPublishing/`. Check them out!

However in order to have a distro-independent installation, we decide to use a pre-built one. Looking at the available ones, we chose the toolchain from the **Linaro** project (`http://www.linaro.org/`), which is a de-facto standard. So, let's see how to install it.

First of all, we must download the archive using the following command:

```
$ wget -c https://releases.linaro.org/components/toolchain/binaries/5.
3-2016.02/arm-linux-gnueabihf/gcc-linaro-5.3-2016.02-x86_64_arm-linux-
gnueabihf.tar.xz
```

After the download, we need to extract the code using the following command:

```
$ tar xf gcc-linaro-5.3-2016.02-x86_64_arm-linux-gnueabihf.tar.xz
```

You can put your new toolchain whenever you wish inside the host's filesystem. We put it in the `/opt/linaro` directory.

Then, we have to set up our environment in order to be able to execute the cross-compiler and other components:

```
$ export PATH=/opt/linaro/gcc-linaro-5.3-2016.02-x86_64_arm-linux-gnue
abihf/bin/:$PATH
```

You should not forget to replace the installation directory `/opt/linaro` with your directory!

Now, we should get the following lines of code:

```
$ arm-linux-gnueabihf-gcc --version
arm-linux-gnueabihf-gcc (Linaro GCC 5.3-2016.02) 5.3.1 20160113
Copyright (C) 2015 Free Software Foundation, Inc.
This is free software; see the source for copying conditions. There is
NO warranty; not even for MERCHANTABILITY or FITNESS FOR A PARTICULAR
PURPOSE.
```

Each time we log in to our host machine, we have to execute the preceding export command. To avoid it, we can use the following two lines to the .bashrc file (if we use the Bash shell):

```
# Setup the cross-compiler
export PATH=/opt/linaro/gcc-linaro-5.3-2016.02-x86_
64_arm-linux-gnueabihf/bin/:$PATH
```

OK. Now, we're ready to set up our developer kits!

Setting up the BeagleBone Black

Let's start by putting our hands on the first developer kit: the BeagleBone Black. As we can see, it comes with a pre-loaded Debian system on the on-board eMMC. However, since we'd like to have the same OS on all developer kits, let's see how to install a fresh OS on a new microSD and then boot from it.

Serial console for the BeagleBone Black

As already stated (and as any real programmer of embedded devices knows), the serial console is a must-have during the low-level development stages! So, let's see how we can get access to it on our BeagleBone Black.

As shown in the following image, the connector J1 is exposed to the serial console pins. So, using a proper adapter, we can connect it to our host PC. However, since the pins have electrical signals at the TTL level, we need an adapter device to do the job, and we have several possibilities.

The first one is a standard **RS232-to-TTL** converter shown in the following image:

 The **RS232-to-TTL** converter can be purchased
at: http://www.cosino.io/product/rs-232-serial-adapter or by surfing
the Internet.

In this case, we need a PC equipped with a standard **RS232** port. Nowadays, it is not easy having one, but we can easily find a RS232-to-USB adapter to solve the problem, or as a second possibility, we can use a standard **USB-to-TTL** cable shown here:

The solution allows us to use a more common USB port to do the job.

However, a last solution exists, and it consists of still using an **USB-to-TTL** converter. However, in contrast with the solution mentioned earlier, this time, we have a micro USB port used in every smartphone. The converter is shown in the following image:

The devices can be purchased at:
`http://www.cosino.io/product/usb-to-serial-converter` or by surfing the Internet.
The datasheet of this device is available at:
`https://www.silabs.com/Support%20Documents/TechnicalDocs/cp2104.pdf`.

Whichever solution we decide to use, we have to connect the *J1* connector with the selected adapter in order to correctly capture the electrical signal. In particular, the relevant pins are reported in the following table. You have to connect the **GND (Ground)** signal with the adapter's GND pin and then swap **TxD (Transmitter)** and **RxD (Receiver)** to correctly establish the serial connection.

Connector J1	Function
Pin 1	GND
Pin 4	TxD
Pin 5	RxD

Here is the my setup:

If all connections are OK, we can execute any serial terminal emulator to see the data from the serial console. We will use the `minicom` tool, and the command to use it is shown here:

```
$ minicom -o -D /dev/ttyUSB0
```

You must now verify that the serial port to be used is `/dev/ttyUSB0`, and that its setup is `115200,8N1` without hardware and software flow control (in `minicom`, these settings can be checked using the *CTRL+A-O* key sequence and then selecting the serial port setup menu entry).

To correctly get access to the serial console, we may need proper privileges. In fact, we may try to execute the preceding `minicom` command, and we don't get an output! This is because the `minicom` command silently exits if we don't have enough privileges to get access to the port.
We can verify our access to privileges by simply using another command on it as shown here:

```
$ cat /dev/ttyUSB0
cat: /dev/ttyUSB0: Permission denied
```

In this case, the `cat` command perfectly tells us what's wrong. In this case, we can fix this issue using the `sudo` command or, even better, by properly adding our system's user to the right group as shown here:

$ ls -l /dev/ttyUSB0
crw-rw—- 1 root dialout 188, 0 Jan 12 23:06 /dev
/ttyUSB0
$ sudo adduser $LOGNAME dialout

oinThen, log out and log in again, and we can access the serial devices without any problem.

The BeagleBone Black should come with a pre-loaded system, so we should see the booting sequence in the `minicom` window as soon as we power up the system.

Now, we only need the software to start working with our BeagleBone Black board.

U-Boot (with MLO)

First of all, we have to download the sources and select a proper release to compile. To clone the U-Boot's repository, we can use the following command:

```
$ git clone https://github.com/u-boot/u-boot
```

However, instead of using the preceding command, let me suggest that you clone U-Boot's repository into a dedicated directory in the bare form (we use a directory named `common`) and then clone the BeagleBone Black's files into another subdirectory by referencing the local bare repository to the dedicated one (we use the directory `BBB`).

To download the bare repository, the commands are as follows:

```
$ cd common
$ git clone --bare https://github.com/u-boot/u-boot
```

Then, the new commands to get the BeagleBone Black's sources are as follows:

```
$ cd BBB
$ git clone --reference ~/Projects/common/u-boot.git
            https://github.com/u-boot/u-boot
```

In this manner, we can save a lot of disk space since we will use the same sources for all our developer kits.

Now, let's go into the newly created directory and check out a proper U-Boot release:

```
$ cd u-boot
$ git checkout v2016.03 -b v2016.03
```

Now, we need some patches to properly support the BeagleBone Black, and we can get and install them using the following commands:

```
$ wget -c https://rcn-ee.com/repos/git/u-boot-patches/v2016.03/0001-am
335x_evm-uEnv.txt-bootz-n-fixes.patch
$ patch -p1 < 0001-am335x_evm-uEnv.txt-bootz-n-fixes.patch
```

Now, we're ready to compile. Let's do it with the following commands:

```
$ make ARCH=arm CROSS_COMPILE=arm-linux-gnueabihf-
        am335x_evm_defconfig
$ make ARCH=arm CROSS_COMPILE=arm-linux-gnueabihf-
```

Now, it's time to install the bootloader into the microSD, and to do this, we have plug a new microSD into our host PC. Then, we have to erase the current partition table and install a new one.

Note that the microSD should be a *class 10* and at least of 4GB size.

However, we first have to discover the microSD associated device. There exist several ways to do it. We usually use the dmesg command after we have plugged in the microSD into my host machine so that we see the following kernel messages:

```
Attached scsi generic sg3 type 0
[sdd] 7774208 512-byte logical blocks: (3.98 GB/3.71 GiB)
[sdd] Write Protect is off
[sdd] Mode Sense: 0b 00 00 08
[sdd] No Caching mode page found
[sdd] Assuming drive cache: write through
 sdd: sdd1
[sdd] Attached SCSI removable disk
```

In this way, we know that on our system, the microSD is associated with the device `/dev/sdd`.

Note that our configuration may vary. In fact, you may discover that the right device to use is `/dev/sdb`, `/dev/sdc` or `/dev/sde` or even a device named `/dev/mmcblk0`! This last case means that the **host** PC is using an **MMC** device instead of a **USB adapter** to manage its **SD** or **microSD** slot. In this special situation, the kernel messages look like this:

```
mmc0: cannot verify signal voltage switch
mmc0: new ultra high speed SDR50 SDHC card at address
0007
mmcblk0: mmc0:0007 SD4GB 3.70 GiB
mmcblk0: p1
```

However, we can also use the `lsblk` command that nicely lists all the currently attached block devices into the system as show here:

```
$ lsblk
NAME      MAJ:MIN RM    SIZE RO TYPE MOUNTPOINT
sda       8:0      0 465.8G  0 disk
+-sda1    8:1      0  21.5G  0 part
+-sda2    8:2      0 116.4G  0 part
+-sda3    8:3      0     1K  0 part
\-sda5    8:5      0 327.9G  0 part /opt
sdb       8:16     0 931.5G  0 disk
\-sdb1    8:17     0 931.5G  0 part /home
sdc       8:32     0 223.6G  0 disk
\-sdc1    8:33     0 223.6G  0 part /
sdd       8:48     1   3.7G  0 disk
\-sdd1    8:49     1   3.7G  0 part
```

Now, we can clear the current partition table using the following command:

```
$ sudo dd if=/dev/zero of=/dev/sdX bs=1M count=10
```

This is a very important step!
The reader should not forget to replace device `/dev/sdX` with the device associated with the microSD plugged into their system and follow the next steps carefully or they may damage the host system!

Then, we can install the newly compiled bootloaders:

```
$ sudo dd if=MLO of=/dev/sdX count=1 seek=1 bs=128k
$ sudo dd if=u-boot.img of=/dev/sdX count=2 seek=1 bs=384k
```

Now, we can prepare the needed partition for the root filesystem, which will be installed in the upcoming sections. Here are the commands:

```
$ echo '1M,,L,*' | sudo sfdisk /dev/sdX
$ sudo mkfs.ext4 -L rootfs /dev/sdX1
```

Since in `mkfs.ext4` version 1.43, the options `metadata_csum` and `64bit` are enabled by default. However, we need to make sure that they are disabled; otherwise, U-Boot cannot boot from our `ext4` partitions. If this is our case, we need to replace the preceding command with the following one:

```
$ sudo mkfs.ext4 -L rootfs
          -O ^metadata_csum,^64bit /dev/sdX1
```

In order to get the current version of `mkfs.ext4`, we can use the command with the -V option argument.

Then, mount the newly created partition and copy the bootloaders in it (these will be used soon). Here are the commands:

```
$ sudo mkdir /media/rootfs
$ sudo mount /dev/sdX1 /media/rootfs/
$ sudo mkdir -p /media/rootfs/opt/backup/uboot/
$ sudo cp MLO /media/rootfs/opt/backup/uboot/
$ sudo cp u-boot.img /media/rootfs/opt/backup/uboot/
```

Now, we have just to add U-Boot's environment commands to properly load the kernel. We have to put all commands into a file called uEnv.txt in rootfs as follows:

```
$ sudo mkdir /media/rootfs/boot/
$ sudo cp uEnv.txt /media/rootfs/boot/
```

The content of the uEnv.txt file is reported here:

```
loadaddr=0x82000000
fdtaddr=0x88000000
rdaddr=0x88080000

initrd_high=0xffffffff
fdt_high=0xffffffff
```

```
mmcroot=/dev/mmcblk0p1

loadximage=load mmc 0:1 ${loadaddr} /boot/vmlinuz-${uname_r}
loadxfdt=load mmc 0:1 ${fdtaddr} /boot/dtbs/${uname_r}/${fdtfile}
loadxrd=load mmc 0:1 ${rdaddr} /boot/initrd.img-${uname_r}; setenv rds
ize ${filesize}
loaduEnvtxt=load mmc 0:1 ${loadaddr} /boot/uEnv.txt ; env import -t ${
loadaddr} ${filesize};
loadall=run loaduEnvtxt; run loadximage; run loadxfdt;
mmcargs=setenv bootargs console=tty0 console=${console} ${optargs} ${c
ape_disable} ${cape_enable} root=${mmcroot} rootfstype=${mmcrootfstype
} ${cmdline}

uenvcmd=run loadall; run mmcargs; bootz ${loadaddr} - ${fdtaddr};
```

The preceding text can be found in the `chapter_01/BBB-uEnv.txt` file in the book's example code repository.

Now, it's time to compile the kernel.

Linux kernel for the BeagleBone Black

The kernel sources can be downloaded from the several repositories, and we decided to use the ones from Robert C. Nelson archives instead of the standard Debian repositories because these repositories are really well done, easy to use, and well supported in terms of custom kernel sources for our embedded kits!

The command is here:

```
$ git clone https://github.com/RobertCNelson/bb-kernel
```

Then, we have to enter into the newly created directory and choose which version of the kernel we wish to use. There are several choices, and I decided to use the kernel version 4.4 (no specific reasons for that, it's just the release in the middle and you can choose whatever better fits your needs). So, we used the commands here:

```
$ cd  bb-kernel
$ git checkout origin/am33x-v4.4 -b am33x-v4.4
```

Now, before continuing, we can do something similar to what we did for U-Boot and then pre-download a Linux bare repository from the `linux-stable` tree into the `common` directory with the following command:

```
$ cd common
$ git clone --bare
        https://git.kernel.org/pub/scm/linux/kernel/git/stable/linux-
stable.git
```

Then, we have to do a little trick to transform the just downloaded data in a form suitable for the `build_kernel.sh` script we've to use here:

```
$ mkdir linux-stable
$ mv linux-stable.git/ linux-stable/.git
$ cd linux-stable
$ git config --local --bool core.bare false
```

In this manner, we converted a bare repository into a normal one, but without checking out any file and saving a lot of disk space!

Now, by properly setting the `LINUX_GIT` variable into the `system.sh` file, we can reference the just downloaded repository. The `system.sh` file can be easily obtained from `system.sh.sample` as follows:

```
$ cp system.sh.sample system.sh
```

Then, we need to properly set the `LINUX_GIT` and the `CC` variables (to specify the cross-compiler to be used) as reported in the following patch:

```
--- system.sh.sample  2016-04-15 18:04:18.178681406 +0200
+++ system.sh  2016-04-18 17:40:11.229958465 +0200
@@ -16,12 +16,14 @@
 #CC=<enter full path>/bin/arm-none-eabi-
 #CC=<enter full path>/bin/arm-linux-gnueabi-
 #CC=<enter full path>/bin/arm-linux-gnueabihf-
+CC=arm-linux-gnueabihf-
 ###OPTIONAL:
 ###OPTIONAL: LINUX_GIT: specify location of locally cloned git tree.
 #
 #LINUX_GIT=/home/user/linux-stable/
+LINUX_GIT=~/Projects/common/linux-stable
 ###OPTIONAL: MMC: (REQUIRED FOR RUNNING: tools/install_kernel.sh)
 #Note: This operates on raw disks, NOT PARTITIONS..
```

Now, we have to set up our identity into the new `git` repository with the following commands:

```
$ git config --global user.name "Rodolfo Giometti"
$ git config --global user.email "giometti@hce-engineering.com"
```

Then, we can start the compilation with the following command:

```
$ ./build_kernel.sh
```

 This step and the subsequent ones are time consuming and require patience, so you should take a cup of your preferred tea or coffee and just wait.

We should see that the correct cross-compiler is set and also the `linux-stable` repository is correctly referenced. Here is what I gets on my system:

```
$ ./build_kernel.sh
+ Detected build host [Ubuntu 15.10]
+ host: [x86_64]
+ git HEAD commit: [72cf1bea12eea59be6632c9e9582f59e7f63ab3d]
----------------------------
scripts/gcc: Using: arm-linux-gnueabihf-gcc (Linaro GCC 5.3-2016.02) 5
.3.1 20160113
Copyright (C) 2015 Free Software Foundation, Inc.
This is free software; see the source for copying conditions. There i
s NO warranty; not even for MERCHANTABILITY or FITNESS FOR A PARTICULA
R PURPOSE.
----------------------------
CROSS_COMPILE=arm-linux-gnueabihf-
----------------------------
scripts/git: Debug: LINUX_GIT is setup as: [/home/giometti/Projects/co
mmon/linux-stable].
scripts/git: [url=https://git.kernel.org/pub/scm/linux/kernel/git/stab
le/linux-stable.git]
From https://git.kernel.org/pub/scm/linux/kernel/git/stable/linux-stab
le
 * branch HEAD -> FETCH_HEAD
----------------------------
Cloning into '/home/giometti/Projects/BBB/bb-kernel/KERNEL'...
done.
...
```

After a while, the classic kernel configuration panel should appear. Just confirm the default settings by selecting the **< Exit >** menu option and then continue.

When finished, we should see several messages as shown here:

```
...
------------------------------
'arch/arm/boot/zImage' -> '/home/giometti/Projects/BBB/bb-kernel/deplo
y/4.4.7-bone9.zImage'
'.config' -> '/home/giometti/Projects/BBB/bb-kernel/deploy/config-4.4.
7-bone9'
-rwxrwxr-x 1 giometti giometti 7,1M apr 15 18:54 /home/giometti/Projec
ts/BBB/bb-kernel/deploy/4.4.7-bone9.zImage
------------------------------
Building modules archive...
Compressing 4.4.7-bone9-modules.tar.gz...
-rw-rw-r-- 1 giometti giometti 58M apr 15 18:55 /home/giometti/Project
s/BBB/bb-kernel/deploy/4.4.7-bone9-modules.tar.gz
------------------------------
Building firmware archive...
Compressing 4.4.7-bone9-firmware.tar.gz...
-rw-rw-r-- 1 giometti giometti 1,2M apr 15 18:55 /home/giometti/Projec
ts/BBB/bb-kernel/deploy/4.4.7-bone9-firmware.tar.gz
------------------------------
Building dtbs archive...
Compressing 4.4.7-bone9-dtbs.tar.gz...
-rw-rw-r-- 1 giometti giometti 328K apr 15 18:55 /home/giometti/Projec
ts/BBB/bb-kernel/deploy/4.4.7-bone9-dtbs.tar.gz
------------------------------
Script Complete
eewiki.net: [user@localhost:~$ export kernel_version=4.4.7-bone9]
------------------------------
```

The last line tell us which is the kernel version to be defined into the uEnv.txt file defined earlier when we installed the bootloaders. The command is shown here:

```
$ sudo sh -c 'echo "uname_r=4.4.7-bone9" >>
            /media/rootfs/boot/uEnv.txt'
```

The /media/rootfs directory has been already mounted in the previous section.

Now, we should install the kernel, but before doing it, we need the root filesystem, so let's move to the next subsection.

Debian 8 (jessie) for the BeagleBone Black

To install the `rootfs` directory containing our Debian OS, we can use a pre-built image, and again, we can download it into the `common` directory to save space. The commands are shown here:

```
$ cd common
$ wget wget -c https://rcn-ee.com/rootfs/eewiki/minfs/debian-8.4-minim
al-armhf-2016-04-02.tar.xz
```

Then, we can explore it by using the `tar` command:

```
$ tar xf debian-8.4-minimal-armhf-2016-04-02.tar.xz
```

 By the time you read this, new versions could be available or the current one could be missing. Then, we should verify the available versions in the case of errors while downloading the rootfs image used earlier.

When finished, a new directory named `debian-8.4-minimal-armhf-2016-04-02` should be available on the current working directory, and to copy it on the microSD, we can use this command:

```
$ cd debian-8.4-minimal-armhf-2016-04-02/
$ sudo tar xpf armhf-rootfs-debian-jessie.tar
        -C /media/rootfs/
```

 We have already mounted the microSD into `/media/rootfs`.

When finished, we can add the kernel image and its related files compiled earlier by switching back to the kernel repository and then using these commands:

```
$ cd BBB/bb-kernel
$ sudo cp deploy/4.4.7-bone9.zImage
        /media/rootfs/boot/vmlinuz-4.4.7-bone9
$ sudo mkdir -p /media/rootfs/boot/dtbs/4.4.7-bone9/
$ sudo tar xf deploy/4.4.7-bone9-dtbs.tar.gz
        -C /media/rootfs/boot/dtbs/4.4.7-bone9/
$ sudo tar xf deploy/4.4.7-bone9-modules.tar.gz
        -C /media/rootfs/
```

Now, to finish the job, we must set up the filesystem table using the following command:

```
$ sudo sh -c "echo '/dev/mmcblk0p1  /  auto  errors=remount-ro  0  1' >
        /media/rootfs/etc/fstab"
```

Do the networking configuration by executing the following commands:

```
$ sudo sh -c "echo 'allow-hotplug lo\niface lo inet loopback\n' >
        /media/rootfs/etc/network/interfaces"
$ sudo sh -c "echo 'allow-hotplug eth0\niface eth0 inet dhcp\n' >>
        /media/rootfs/etc/network/interfaces"
```

Now, we should be ready to boot our new system! Let's unmount the microSD from the host PC and plug it into the BeagleBone Black and power on the board. The umount command line is shown here:

```
$ sudo umount /media/rootfs/
```

If everything works well on the serial console, we should see something like this:

```
U-Boot SPL 2016.03-dirty (Apr 15 2016 - 13:44:25)
Trying to boot from MMC
bad magic
U-Boot 2016.03-dirty (Apr 15 2016 - 13:44:25 +0200)

 Watchdog enabled
I2C: ready
DRAM: 512 MiB
Reset Source: Power-on reset has occurred.
MMC: OMAP SD/MMC: 0, OMAP SD/MMC: 1
Using default environment

Net: <ethaddr> not set. Validating first E-fuse MAC
cpsw, usb_ether
Press SPACE to abort autoboot in 2 seconds
switch to partitions #0, OK
mmc0 is current device
Scanning mmc 0:1...
...
debug: [console=ttyO0,115200n8 root=/dev/mmcblk0p1 ro rootfstype=ext4
rootwait].
debug: [bootz 0x82000000 - 0x88000000] ...
Kernel image @ 0x82000000 [ 0x000000 - 0x710b38 ]
## Flattened Device Tree blob at 88000000
 Booting using the fdt blob at 0x88000000
 Using Device Tree in place at 88000000, end 88010a19

Starting kernel ...
```

```
[ 0.000000] Booting Linux on physical CPU 0x0...
[ 5.466604] random: systemd urandom read with 17 bits of entropy av
ailable
[ 5.484996] systemd[1]: systemd 215 running in system mode. (+PAM +
AUDIT +SE)
[ 5.498711] systemd[1]: Detected architecture 'arm'.

Welcome to Debian GNU/Linux 8 (jessie)!

[ 5.535458] systemd[1]: Set hostname to <arm>.
[ 5.861405] systemd[1]: Cannot add dependency job for unit display-
manager.s.
...
[ OK ] Started LSB: Apache2 web server.
[ 12.903747] random: nonblocking pool is initialized

Debian GNU/Linux 8 arm ttyS0

default username:password is [debian:temppwd]

arm login:
```

 In order to work, we may need to completely power the BeagleBone Black and then re-power it while keeping the user button pressed. Otherwise, the board will still continue booting from the on-board eMMC.

Great! Everything is working now. We can log in by entering the string root as both username and password.

Setting up the SAMA5D3 Xplained

Now, it's the turn of the SAMA5D3 Xplained. Even this board may have a pre-loaded distribution into its flash memory, but it is an embedded distribution that is not suitable for our purposes. So, as we did for the BeagleBone Black, we will install a fresh Debian OS on a microSD card (in reality, the SAMA5D3 Xplained comes with an SD slot, but we can still use a microSD plugged in an SD adapter).

Serial console for SAMA5D3 Xplained

As shown in the previous section, we have the *J23* connector where the serial console pins are exposed. So, again, using a proper adapter, we can connect our host PC with it.

The relevant pins are reported in the table, and you, exactly as you did earlier, have to connect the GND signal with the adapter's GND pin and then swap the TxD and RxD to correctly establish the serial connection.

Connector J1	Function
Pin 6	GND
Pin 2	TxD
Pin 3	RxD

The next image shows my setup:

If all connections are OK, we can execute the `minicom` tool again to see the data from the serial console.

If our SAMA5D3 Xplained comes with a pre-loaded system, we should see the booting sequence in the serial console window. Otherwise, we should simply see the **RomBOOT** message. In any case, the serial console should be functional.

You should not forget to verify the serial port to be used. You should also see that its setup is `115200, 8N1` without hardware and software flow control. See the BeagleBone Black settings earlier.

Now, let's install the software to start working with our SAMA5D3 Xplained board.

U-Boot (with boot.bin)

To obtain the bootloader's sources, we can use the same trick used for BeagleBone Black's sources. However, this time, the bare repository is already downloaded, so we just need to clone a new one with the following commands (to work with this board, we created the `A5D3` directory):

```
$ cd A5D3
$ git clone --reference ~/Projects/common/u-boot.git
          https://github.com/u-boot/u-boot
```

Now, let's go into the newly created directory and check out a proper U-Boot release to use. Here are the commands used:

```
$ cd u-boot
$ git checkout v2016.03 -b v2016.03
```

Now, just as before, we need some patches to properly support the SAMA5D3 Xplained. We can get them using the following commands:

```
$ wget -c https://rcn-ee.com/repos/git/u-boot-patches/v2016.03/0001-sa
ma5d3_xplained-uEnv.txt-bootz-n-fixes.patch
$ patch -p1 < 0001-sama5d3_xplained-uEnv.txt-bootz-n-fixes.patch
```

Now, we're ready to compile:

```
$ make ARCH=arm CROSS_COMPILE=arm-linux-gnueabihf-
        sama5d3_xplained_mmc_defconfig
$ make ARCH=arm CROSS_COMPILE=arm-linux-gnueabihf-
```

Now, let's install the bootloader into the microSD.

 As already done earlier, we have to discover the device associated with the microSD (see the the BeagleBone Black subsection).

We can clear the current partition table using the following command:

```
$ sudo dd if=/dev/zero of=/dev/sdX bs=1M count=50
```

 You should not forget to replace `device /dev/sdX` with the device associated with the microSD plugged into your system and follow the next steps carefully. Otherwise, it may damage the host system!

Now, we can prepare the needed partitions for the root filesystem, which will be installed in the upcoming sections. Here are the commands:

```
$ echo -e '1M,48M,0xE,*\n,,,-' | sudo sfdisk /dev/sdX
$ sudo mkfs.vfat -F 16 -n BOOT /dev/sdX1
$ sudo mkfs.ext4 -L rootfs /dev/sdX2
```

 As already stated for the BeagleBone Black, we must notice that since the `mkfs.ext4` version 1.43, the `metadata_csum` and `64bit` options are enabled by default. However, we need to make sure that they are disabled. Otherwise, U-Boot cannot boot from our `ext4` partitions. If this is our case, we need to replace the preceding command with the following one:

```
$ sudo mkfs.ext4 -L rootfs
            -O ^metadata_csum,^64bit /dev/sdX2
```

Now, we can mount the newly created `boot` and `rootfs` partitions in order to be ready to copy the bootloaders and the distro's file into them. Here are the commands:

```
$ sudo mkdir /media/boot
$ sudo mkdir /media/rootfs
$ sudo mount /dev/sdX1 /media/boot
$ sudo mount /dev/sdX2 /media/rootfs
```

Then, we can install the newly compiled bootloaders:

```
$ sudo cp boot.bin /media/boot/
$ sudo cp u-boot.img /media/boot/
```

 This time, we don't need any configuration file for U-Boot (file `uEnv.txt`).

Now, it's time to compile the kernel.

Linux kernel for SAMA5D3 Xplained

Again, the kernel sources can be downloaded from Robert C. Nelson archives. The command is shown here:

```
$ git clone https://github.com/RobertCNelson/armv7_devel
```

Then, we have to enter into the newly created directory and choose which version of the kernel we wish to use. Of course, we choose the same kernel release as we did earlier, and here are the commands:

```
$ cd armv7_devel/
$ git checkout origin/v4.4.x-sama5-armv7 -b v4.4.x-sama5-armv7
```

Now, we can redo the previous settings into the `system.sh` file, and then, we can start the compilation using the following command:

```
$ ./build_kernel.sh
```

 This step and the subsequent ones are time consuming and require patience, so you should take a cup of your preferred tea or coffee and just wait.

We should see that the correct cross-compiler is set and also see that the `linux-stable` repository is correctly referenced. Here is what I get on my system:

```
$ ./build_kernel.sh
+ Detected build host [Ubuntu 15.10]
+ host: [x86_64]
+ git HEAD commit: [cc996bf444c2fb5f3859c431fbc3b29fe9ba6877]
-------------------------------
scripts/gcc: Using: arm-linux-gnueabihf-gcc (Linaro GCC 5.3-2016.02) 5
.3.1 20160113
Copyright (C) 2015 Free Software Foundation, Inc.
This is free software; see the source for copying conditions. There i
s NO warranty; not even for MERCHANTABILITY or FITNESS FOR A PARTICULA
R PURPOSE.
-------------------------------
CROSS_COMPILE=arm-linux-gnueabihf-
-------------------------------
scripts/git: Debug: LINUX_GIT is setup as: [/home/giometti/Projects/co
mmon/linux-stable].
scripts/git: [url=https://git.kernel.org/pub/scm/linux/kernel/git/stab
le/linux-stable.git]
From https://git.kernel.org/pub/scm/linux/kernel/git/stable/linux-stab
le
```

```
 * branch HEAD -> FETCH_HEAD
------------------------------
Cloning into '/home/giometti/Projects/A5D3/armv7_devel/KERNEL'...
done.
...
```

After a while, the classic kernel configuration panel should appear, but this time, we should change the default configuration. In particular, we wish to change the **USB Gadget** settings as shown in the following screenshot:

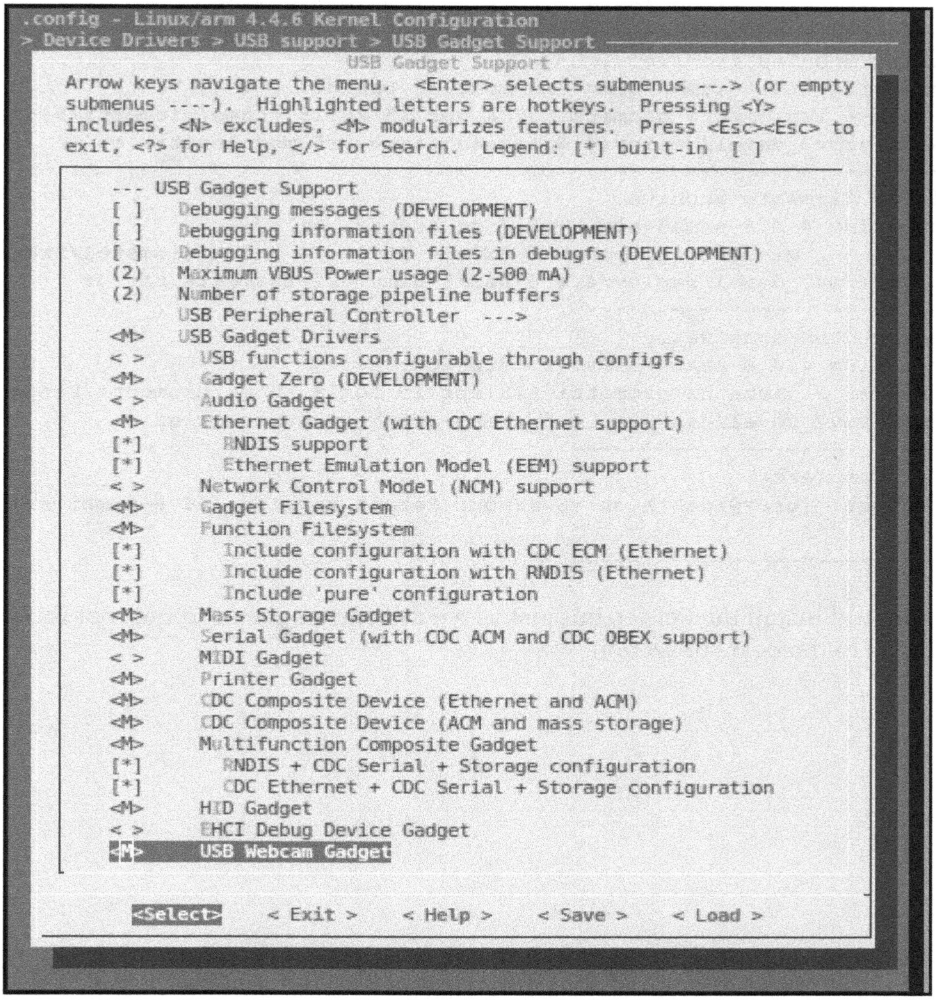

Then, save the configuration and continue. When finished, we should see several messages as shown here:

```
...
------------------------------
'arch/arm/boot/zImage' -> '/home/giometti/Projects/A5D3/armv7_devel/de
ploy/4.4.6-sama5-armv7-r5.zImage'
'.config' -> '/home/giometti/Projects/A5D3/armv7_devel/deploy/config-4
.4.6-sama5-armv7-r5'
-rwxrwxr-x 1 giometti giometti 3,7M apr 15 20:19 /home/giometti/Projec
ts/A5D3/armv7_devel/deploy/4.4.6-sama5-armv7-r5.zImage
------------------------------
Building modules archive...
Compressing 4.4.6-sama5-armv7-r5-modules.tar.gz...
-rw-rw-r-- 1 giometti giometti 328K apr 15 20:19 /home/giometti/Projec
ts/A5D3/armv7_devel/deploy/4.4.6-sama5-armv7-r5-modules.tar.gz
------------------------------
Building firmware archive...
Compressing 4.4.6-sama5-armv7-r5-firmware.tar.gz...
-rw-rw-r-- 1 giometti giometti 1,2M apr 15 20:19 /home/giometti/Projec
ts/A5D3/armv7_devel/deploy/4.4.6-sama5-armv7-r5-firmware.tar.gz
------------------------------
Building dtbs archive...
Compressing 4.4.6-sama5-armv7-r5-dtbs.tar.gz...
-rw-rw-r-- 1 giometti giometti 64K apr 15 20:19 /home/giometti/Project
s/A5D3/armv7_devel/deploy/4.4.6-sama5-armv7-r5-dtbs.tar.gz
------------------------------
Script Complete
eewiki.net: [user@localhost:~$ export kernel_version=4.4.6-sama5-armv7
-r5]
------------------------------
```

Now, we should install the kernel, but just as we did earlier, we need the root filesystem. So, let's move to the next subsection.

Debian 8 (jessie) for SAMA5D3 Xplained

Like rootfs we can use the one already downloaded for the BeagleBone Black, so let's copy it into the microSD:

```
$ cd common/debian-8.4-minimal-armhf-2016-04-02/
$ sudo tar xpf armhf-rootfs-debian-jessie.tar -C /media/rootfs/
```

 We have already mounted the microSD into /media/rootfs.

When finished, we can add the kernel image and the related files:

```
$ cd A5D3/armv7_devel
$ sudo cp deploy/4.4.6-sama5-armv7-r5.zImage /media/boot/zImage
$ sudo mkdir -p /media/boot/dtbs/
$ sudo tar xf deploy/4.4.6-sama5-armv7-r5-dtbs.tar.gz
        -C /media/boot/dtbs/
$ sudo tar xf deploy/4.4.6-sama5-armv7-r5-modules.tar.gz
        -C /media/rootfs/
```

Now, to finish the job, we must set up the filesystem table using the following commands:

```
$ sudo sh -c "echo '/dev/mmcblk0p2  /  auto  errors=remount-ro  0  1' >
        /media/rootfs/etc/fstab"
$ sudo sh -c "echo '/dev/mmcblk0p1 /boot/uboot  auto  defaults  0  2' >>
        /media/rootfs/etc/fstab"
```

Also set up the networking configuration by executing the following commands:

```
$ sudo sh -c "echo 'allow-hotplug lo\niface lo inet loopback\n' >
        /media/rootfs/etc/network/interfaces"
$ sudo sh -c "echo 'allow-hotplug eth0\niface eth0 inet dhcp\n' >>
        /media/rootfs/etc/network/interfaces"
$ sudo sh -c "echo 'allow-hotplug eth1\niface eth1 inet dhcp' >>
        /media/rootfs/etc/network/interfaces"
```

Now, we should be ready to boot our new system! Let's unmount the microSD from the host PC, plug it into the SAMA5D3 Xplained, and power on the board. The umount command lines are shown here:

```
$ sudo umount /media/boot/
$ sudo umount /media/rootfs/
```

If everything works well on the serial console, we should see something as shown here:

```
RomBOOT

U-Boot SPL 2016.03-dirty (Apr 15 2016 - 19:51:18)
Trying to boot from MMC
reading u-boot.img
reading u-boot.img


U-Boot 2016.03-dirty (Apr 15 2016 - 19:51:18 +0200)

CPU: SAMA5D36
Crystal frequency: 12 MHz
CPU clock : 528 MHz
Master clock : 132 MHz
DRAM: 256 MiB
NAND: 256 MiB
MMC: mci: 0
...
reading /dtbs/at91-sama5d3_xplained.dtb
34694 bytes read in 10 ms (3.3 MiB/s)
reading zImage
3832792 bytes read in 245 ms (14.9 MiB/s)
Kernel image @ 0x22000000 [ 0x000000 - 0x3a7bd8 ]
## Flattened Device Tree blob at 21000000
 Booting using the fdt blob at 0x21000000
 Loading Device Tree to 2fadc000, end 2fae7785 ... OK

Starting kernel ...

[ 0.000000] Booting Linux on physical CPU 0x0
...
[ 2.170000] random: systemd urandom read with 11 bits of entropy av
ailable
[ 2.180000] systemd[1]: systemd 215 running in system mode. (+PAM +
AUDIT +SELINUX +IMA +SYSVINIT +LIBCRYPTSETUP +GCRYPT +ACL +XZ -SECC
OMP -APPARMOR)
[ 2.190000] systemd[1]: Detected architecture 'arm'.

Welcome to Debian GNU/Linux 8 (jessie)!

[ 2.240000] systemd[1]: Set hostname to <arm>.
[ 2.790000] systemd[1]: Cannot add dependency job for unit display-
manager.se
...
 Starting Update UTMP about System Runlevel Changes...
[ OK ] Started Update UTMP about System Runlevel Changes.
```

```
Debian GNU/Linux 8 arm ttyS0

default username:password is [debian:temppwd]

arm login:
```

Great! Everything is working now. We can log in by entering the `root` string as both username and password.

Setting up the Wandboard

This has no pre-loaded distribution. So, as done for the previous boards, we will install a fresh Debian OS on a microSD card.

Serial console for the Wandboard

Like the other boards presented in this book, the Wandboard has the *COM1* connector where the serial console pins are exposed. However, in this case, the port is a a standard RS-232 port. So, we don't have the TTL level signal! What we can do now is just connect the *COM1* port to our host PC serial port through a null modem cable (a serial cable where the TxD and RxD signals are crossed) or use a **USB-to-RS232** adapter and then connect this device to the null modem cable.

The relevant pins are reported in the following table, and just as you did earlier, you have to connect the GND signal with the adapter's GND pin and then swap the TxD and RxD to correctly establish the serial connection.

COM1	Function
Pin 5	GND
Pin 2	TXD
Pin 3	RXD

In the next image, the pin out of a standard RS-232 9-pins connector is shown:

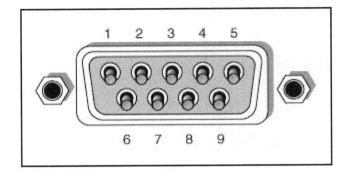

This image is my setup (where we used three adapters: two genders changers and one null modem):

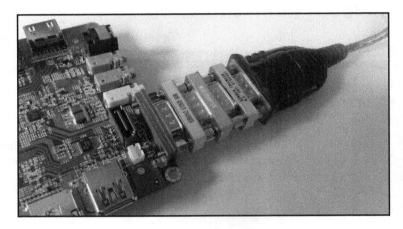

Now, let's install the software to start working with our WindBoard board.

U-Boot (with SPL)

To obtain the bootloader's sources, we can use the same trick used for the other boards, so we just need to clone a new one with the following command:

```
$ git clone --reference ~/Projects/common/u-boot.git
        https://github.com/u-boot/u-boot
```

Now, let's go into the newly created directory and check out a proper U-boot release to use. Here are the commands used:

```
$ cd u-boot
$ git checkout v2016.03 -b v2016.03
```

Here are the patches for the Wandboard:

```
$ wget -c https://rcn-ee.com/repos/git/u-boot-patches/v2016.03/0001-wa
ndboard-uEnv.txt-bootz-n-fixes.patch
$ patch -p1 < 0001-wandboard-uEnv.txt-bootz-n-fixes.patch
```

Now, we're ready to compile. Let's do it using the following commands:

```
$ make ARCH=arm CROSS_COMPILE=arm-linux-gnueabihf-
      wandboard_defconfig
$ make ARCH=arm CROSS_COMPILE=arm-linux-gnueabihf-
```

Now, let's install the bootloader into the microSD.

 As done earlier, we have to discover the device associated with the microSD (see the BeagleBone Black or SAMA5D3 Xplained subsections). On my system, the device is still /dev/sdd.
In this case, we used a 16 GB microSD since we're going to install a lot of software on this board!

Now, we can clear the current partition table using the following command:

```
$ sudo dd if=/dev/zero of=/dev/sdX bs=1M count=10
```

 You must not forget to replace device /dev/sdX with the device associated with the microSD plugged into your system and follow the next steps carefully. Otherwise, it may damage the host system!

Then, we can install the newly compiled bootloaders:

```
$ sudo dd if=SPL of=/dev/sdX seek=1 bs=1k
$ sudo dd if=u-boot.img of=/dev/sdX seek=69 bs=1k
```

Now, we can prepare the needed partition for the root filesystem, which will be installed in the upcoming sections. The commands are shown here:

```
$ echo '1M,,L,*' | sudo sfdisk /dev/sdX
$ sudo mkfs.ext4 -L rootfs /dev/sdX1
```

As already stated for the other boards, we must notice that since the `mkfs.ext4` version 1.43, the `metadata_csum` and `64bit` options are enabled by default. However, we need to make sure that they are disabled. Otherwise, U-Boot cannot boot from our ext4 partitions. If this is our case, we need to replace the preceding command with the following one:

```
$ sudo mkfs.ext4 -L rootfs
              -O ^metadata_csum,^64bit /dev/sdX1
```

Now, we can mount the newly created `boot` and `rootfs` partition as done earlier. Here are the commands:

```
$ sudo mkdir /media/rootfs
$ sudo mount /dev/sdX1 /media/rootfs
```

Then, as done for the SAMA5D3 Xplained, we don't define an environment file `uEnv.txt` right now, but we will define it later since, in contrast to SAMA5D3 Xplained, we need it.

Now, it's time to compile the kernel.

Linux kernel for the Wandboard

The kernel sources are still the ones from Robert C. Nelson archives. The command is shown here:

```
$ git clone https://github.com/RobertCNelson/armv7-multiplatform
```

Then, we have to enter into the newly created directory and choose which version of the kernel we wish to use. Of course, we choose the same kernel release as the one mentioned earlier, and the commands are shown here:

```
$ cd armv7-multiplatform/
$ git checkout origin/v4.4.x -b v4.4.x
```

Now, we can redo the previous settings into the `system.sh` file, and then, we can start the compilation using the following command:

```
$ ./build_kernel.sh
```

 This step and the subsequent ones are time consuming and require patience, so you should take a cup of your preferred tea or coffee and just wait.

We should see that the correct cross-compiler is set and also see that the `linux-stable` repository is correctly referenced. Here is what I get on my system:

```
$ ./build_kernel.sh
+ Detected build host [Ubuntu 15.10]
+ host: [x86_64]
+ git HEAD commit: [44cd32b5f0ff74d2705541225c0d7cbdfb59bf50]
---------------------------
scripts/gcc: Using: arm-linux-gnueabihf-gcc (Linaro GCC 5.3-2016.02) 5
.3.1 20160113
Copyright (C) 2015 Free Software Foundation, Inc.
This is free software; see the source for copying conditions. There i
s NO warranty; not even for MERCHANTABILITY or FITNESS FOR A PARTICULA
R PURPOSE.
---------------------------
CROSS_COMPILE=arm-linux-gnueabihf-
---------------------------
scripts/git: Debug: LINUX_GIT is setup as: [/home/giometti/Projects/co
mmon/linux-stable].
scripts/git: [url=https://git.kernel.org/pub/scm/linux/kernel/git/stab
le/linux-stable.git]
From https://git.kernel.org/pub/scm/linux/kernel/git/stable/linux-stab
le
  * branch HEAD -> FETCH_HEAD
---------------------------
Cloning into '/home/giometti/Projects/WB/armv7-multiplatform/KERNEL'..
.
done.
. . .
```

After a while, the classic kernel configuration panel should appear. Just confirm the default settings by selecting the **< Exit >** menu option and continue.

When finished, we should see several messages as shown here:

```
...
-------------------------------
'arch/arm/boot/zImage' -> '/home/giometti/Projects/WB/armv7-multiplatf
orm/deploy/4.4.7-armv7-x6.zImage'
'.config' -> '/home/giometti/Projects/WB/armv7-multiplatform/deploy/co
nfig-4.4.7-armv7-x6'
-rwxrwxr-x 1 giometti giometti 5,6M apr 17 18:46 /home/giometti/Projec
ts/WB/armv7-multiplatform/deploy/4.4.7-armv7-x6.zImage
-------------------------------
Building modules archive...
Compressing 4.4.7-armv7-x6-modules.tar.gz...
-rw-rw-r-- 1 giometti giometti 89M apr 17 18:47 /home/giometti/Project
s/WB/armv7-multiplatform/deploy/4.4.7-armv7-x6-modules.tar.gz
-------------------------------
Building firmware archive...
Compressing 4.4.7-armv7-x6-firmware.tar.gz...
-rw-rw-r-- 1 giometti giometti 1,2M apr 17 18:47 /home/giometti/Projec
ts/WB/armv7-multiplatform/deploy/4.4.7-armv7-x6-firmware.tar.gz
-------------------------------
Building dtbs archive...
Compressing 4.4.7-armv7-x6-dtbs.tar.gz...
-rw-rw-r-- 1 giometti giometti 3,1M apr 17 18:47 /home/giometti/Projec
ts/WB/armv7-multiplatform/deploy/4.4.7-armv7-x6-dtbs.tar.gz
-------------------------------
Script Complete
eewiki.net: [user@localhost:~$ export kernel_version=4.4.7-armv7-x6]
-------------------------------
```

The last line tells us which is the kernel version to be defined in the uEnv.txt file defined earlier when we installed the bootloaders. The command is shown here:

```
$ sudo sh -c 'echo "uname_r=4.4.7-armv7-x6" >>
            /media/rootfs/boot/uEnv.txt'
```

 The /media/rootfs directory has been already mounted in the previous section.

Now, we should install the kernel, but first, we need the root filesystem. So, let's move to the next subsection.

Debian 8 (jessie) for the Wandboard

Like rootfs we can use the one already downloaded for the BeagleBone Black, so let's copy it into the microSD:

```
$ cd common/debian-8.4-minimal-armhf-2016-04-02/
$ sudo tar xpf armhf-rootfs-debian-jessie.tar -C /media/rootfs/
```

 We have already mounted the microSD into /media/rootfs.

When finished, we can add the kernel image and the related files:

```
$ cd WB/armv7-multiplatform/
$ sudo cp deploy/4.4.7-armv7-x6.zImage
          /media/rootfs/boot/vmlinuz-4.4.7-armv7-x6
$ sudo mkdir -p /media/rootfs/boot/dtbs/4.4.7-armv7-x6/
$ sudo tar xf deploy/4.4.7-armv7-x6-dtbs.tar.gz
          -C /media/rootfs/boot/dtbs/4.4.7-armv7-x6/
$ sudo tar xf deploy/4.4.7-armv7-x6-modules.tar.gz
          -C /media/rootfs/
```

Now, to finish the job, we must set up the filesystem table using the following command:

```
$ sudo sh -c "echo '/dev/mmcblk0p1 / auto errors=remount-ro 0 1' >
          /media/rootfs/etc/fstab"
```

We also need to set up the networking configuration by executing the following commands:

```
$ sudo sh -c "echo 'allow-hotplug lo\niface lo inet loopback\n' >
          /media/rootfs/etc/network/interfaces"
$ sudo sh -c "echo 'allow-hotplug eth0\niface eth0 inet dhcp' >>
          /media/rootfs/etc/network/interfaces"
```

Now, we should be ready to boot our new system! Let's unmount the microSD from the host PC, plug it into the Wandboard, and power on the board. The umount command line is shown here:

```
$ sudo umount /media/rootfs/
```

If everything works well on the serial console, we should see something like this:

```
U-Boot SPL 2016.03-dirty (Apr 21 2016 - 10:41:24)
Trying to boot from MMC

U-Boot 2016.03-dirty (Apr 21 2016 - 10:41:24 +0200)

CPU: Freescale i.MX6Q rev1.5 at 792 MHz
Reset cause: POR
Board: Wandboard rev C1
I2C: ready
DRAM: 2 GiB
MMC: FSL_SDHC: 0, FSL_SDHC: 1
*** Warning - bad CRC, using default environment

No panel detected: default to HDMI
Display: HDMI (1024x768)
In: serial
Out: serial
Err: serial
Net: FEC [PRIME]
Press SPACE to abort autoboot in 2 seconds
switch to partitions #0, OK
mmc0 is current device
SD/MMC found on device 0
...
debug: [console=ttymxc0,115200 root=/dev/mmcblk0p1 ro rootfstype=ext4
rootwait] ...
debug: [bootz 0x12000000 - 0x18000000] ...
Kernel image @ 0x12000000 [ 0x000000 - 0x588ba0 ]
## Flattened Device Tree blob at 18000000
 Booting using the fdt blob at 0x18000000
 Using Device Tree in place at 18000000, end 1800f7f8

Starting kernel ...

[ 0.000000] Booting Linux on physical CPU 0x0
...
[ 5.569385] random: systemd urandom read with 10 bits of entropy av
ailable
[ 5.582907] systemd[1]: systemd 215 running in system mode. (+PAM +
AUDIT +SELINUX +IMA +SYSVINIT +LIBCRYPTSETUP +GCRYPT +ACL +XZ -SECC
OMP -APPARMOR)
[ 5.596522] systemd[1]: Detected architecture 'arm'.

Welcome to Debian GNU/Linux 8 (jessie)!

[ 5.637466] systemd[1]: Set hostname to <arm>.
```

```
. . .
[ OK ] Started LSB: Apache2 web server.

Debian GNU/Linux 8 arm ttymxc0

default username:password is [debian:temppwd]

arm login:
```

Great! Everything is working now. We can log in by entering the `root` string as both username and password.

Setting up the developing system

Before ending the chapter, let's review each board in order to verify that our newly created operating systems have whatever we need to proceed further in the book.

BeagleBone Black – USB, networking, and overlays

As soon as we log in to our new system, we see that the prompt looks like this:

```
root@arm:~#
```

Maybe, we can customize it a bit by changing the hostname from the generic string `arm` into a more appropriate `bbb` (which stands for *BeagleBone Black*). The commands to do the job are shown here:

```
root@arm:~# echo bbb > /etc/hostname
root@arm:~# sed -i -e's/\<arm\>/bbb/g' /etc/hosts
```

Now, we have to reboot the system using the classic `reboot` command, and at the next login, we should get a welcome message:

```
Debian GNU/Linux 8 bbb ttyS0
default username:password is [debian:temppwd]
bbb login:
```

After the login, we will get the new prompt:

```
root@bbb:~#
```

Then, we will update the distribution repositories and install the `aptitude` tool as done for the host machine:

```
root@bbb:~# apt-get update
root@bbb:~# apt-get install aptitude
```

OK, now it is time to add a useful feature, that is, the possibility to establish a virtual Ethernet connection between our BeagleBone Black and the host PC over the USB cable connected with BeagleBone Black's USB device port and the host. To do this, we have first to install the `udhcpd` package using the following command:

```
root@bbb:~# aptitude install udhcpd
```

Then, we must add the following lines to the `/etc/network/interfaces` file:

```
allow-hotplug usb0
iface usb0 inet static
        address 192.168.7.2
        netmask 255.255.255.252
        network 192.168.7.0
```

 Don't forget the tab character to indent the lines!

Then, restart the networking system as follows:

```
root@bbb:~# /etc/init.d/networking restart
```

IPv6: ADDRCONF(NETDEV_CHANGE): Black, we should see a message, as shown here, on the serial console:

```
g_ether gadget: high-speed config #1: CDC Ethernet (ECM)
IPv6: ADDRCONF(NETDEV_CHANGE): usb0: link becomes ready
```

A new Ethernet device should appear as reported here:

```
root@bbb:~# ifconfig usb0
usb0      Link encap:Ethernet  HWaddr 78:a5:04:ca:c9:f1
          inet addr:192.168.7.2  Bcast:192.168.7.3  Mask:255.255.255.252
          inet6 addr: fe80::7aa5:4ff:feca:c9f1/64 Scope:Link
          UP BROADCAST RUNNING MULTICAST  MTU:1500  Metric:1
          RX packets:46 errors:0 dropped:0 overruns:0 frame:0
          TX packets:32 errors:0 dropped:0 overruns:0 carrier:0
          collisions:0 txqueuelen:1000
          RX bytes:7542 (7.3 KiB)  TX bytes:5525 (5.3 KiB)
```

OK, now, we have to configure the new Ethernet device on the host and then we can try an `ssh` connection as shown here:

```
$ ssh root@192.168.7.2
```

On my host PC, which is Ubuntu based, before executing the `ssh` command, we had to properly configure the new Ethernet device by adding a new network connection in the entry **Edit Connections...** in the system settings menu.

```
The authenticity of host '192.168.7.2 (192.168.7.2)' can't be establis
hed.
ECDSA key fingerprint is SHA256:Iu23gb49VFKsFs+HMwjza1OzcpzRL/zxFxjFpF
EiDsg.
Are you sure you want to continue connecting (yes/no)? yes
Warning: Permanently added '192.168.7.2' (ECDSA) to the list of known
hosts.
root@192.168.7.2's password:
```

Now we have to enter the root's password that is `root` and the trick is done:

```
The programs included with the Debian GNU/Linux system are free
software; the exact distribution terms for each program are
described in the individual files in /usr/share/doc/*/copyright.

Debian GNU/Linux comes with ABSOLUTELY NO WARRANTY, to the
extent permitted by applicable law.
Last login: Sat Apr 2 18:28:44 2016
root@bbb:~#
```

We may need to modify the `ssh` daemon configuration if we cannot successfully log in to our system. In fact, the login by the root user may be disabled for security reasons. To enable the login, we have to modify the `/etc/ssh/sshd_config` file as follows:

```
--- /etc/ssh/sshd_config.orig 2016-04-02 18:40:31.
120000086 +0000
+++ /etc/ssh/sshd_config 2016-04-02 18:40:46.05000
0088 +0000
@@ -25,7 +25,7 @@

 # Authentication:
 LoginGraceTime 120
-PermitRootLogin without-password
+PermitRootLogin yes
 StrictModes yes
```

```
RSAAuthentication yes
```
Then, we have to restart the daemon using the following command:
```
root@bbb:~# /etc/init.d/ssh restart
Restarting ssh (via systemctl): ssh.service.
```

Now, we have to install the **overlay** system, that is, the mechanism that allow us to load at run time a part of a new device tree binaries and then change our kernel settings to get access to the board's peripherals (this mechanism will be used in the upcoming chapters, and it'll be more clear to you when we'll start using it).

To install the overlay mechanism, we must clone its repository into our BeagleBone Black as follows:

```
bbb@arm:~# git clone https://github.com/beagleboard/bb.org-overlays
```

Then, we must update the device tree compiler (the dtc command) with the following commands:

```
root@arm:~# cd bb.org-overlays/
root@arm:~/bb.org-overlays# ./dtc-overlay.sh
```

This command may take a while to complete. Be patient.

```
Installing: bison build-essential flex
Get:1 http://repos.rcn-ee.com jessie InRelease [4,347 B]
Get:2 http://repos.rcn-ee.com jessie/main armhf Packages [370 kB]
...
Installing into: /usr/local/bin/
        CHK version_gen.h
          INSTALL-BIN
          INSTALL-LIB
          INSTALL-INC
dtc: Version: DTC 1.4.1-g1e75ebc9
```

Then, we can install the dtbo files with the following command:

```
root@arm:~/bb.org-overlays# ./install.sh
   CLEAN    src/arm
   DTC      src/arm/BB-BONE-WTHR-01-00B0.dtbo
   DTC      src/arm/BB-BONE-LCD3-01-00A2.dtbo
   DTC      src/arm/BB-PWM2-00A0.dtbo
...
'src/arm/univ-hdmi-00A0.dtbo' -> '/lib/firmware/univ-hdmi-00A0.dtbo'
```

```
'src/arm/univ-nhdmi-00A0.dtbo' -> '/lib/firmware/univ-nhdmi-00A0.dtbo'
update-initramfs: Generating /boot/initrd.img-4.4.7-bone9
cape overlays have been built and added to /lib/firmware & /boot/initr
d.img-4.4.7-bone9, please reboot
```

OK, now, we can safely reboot the system to test it.

After reboot, to display the current overlay configuration, we can use the following `cat` command:

```
root@arm:~# cat /sys/devices/platform/bone_capemgr/slots
 0: PF----   -1
 1: PF----   -1
 2: PF----   -1
 3: PF----   -1
```

Then, we can try to enable the second SPI bus char device using the following command:

```
root@bbb:~# echo BB-SPIDEV1 > /sys/devices/platform/bone_capemgr/slots
bone_capemgr bone_capemgr: part_number 'BB-SPIDEV1', version 'N/A'
bone_capemgr bone_capemgr: slot #4: override
bone_capemgr bone_capemgr: Using override eeprom data at slot 4
bone_capemgr bone_capemgr: slot #4: 'Override Board Name,00A0,Override
 Manuf,BB-SPIDEV1'
bone_capemgr bone_capemgr: slot #4: dtbo 'BB-SPIDEV1-00A0.dtbo'
loaded; overlay id#0
```

Now, two new char devices should appear in the `/dev` directory:

```
root@bbb:~# ls -l /dev/spidev*
crw-rw---- 1 root spi 153, 0 Apr  2 19:27 /dev/spidev2.0
crw-rw---- 1 root spi 153, 1 Apr  2 19:27 /dev/spidev2.1
```

Also, the slots file in sysfs is updated accordingly:

```
root@bbb:~# cat /sys/devices/platform/bone_capemgr/slots
 0: PF----   -1
 1: PF----   -1
 2: PF----   -1
 3: PF----   -1
 4: P-O-L-    0 Override Board Name,00A0,Override Manuf,BB-SPIDEV1
```

Now, everything should be in place. However, as the last step, we can decide to copy our new system from the microSD card to eMMC in order to boot directly from the on-board eMMC device, thus avoiding pressing the user button each time we power up the board.

To do this, we have to install three new packages (`initramfs-tools`, `dosfstools`, and `rsync`) and then use a script form the Robert C. Nelson archive:

```
root@bbb:~# wget https://raw.githubusercontent.com/RobertCNelson/boot-
scripts/master/tools/eMMC/bbb-eMMC-flasher-eewiki-ext4.sh
```

Then, we just need to execute it using the following two commands, and the BeagleBone Black will start rewriting the eMMC contents:

```
root@bbb:~# chmod +x bbb-eMMC-flasher-eewiki-ext4.sh
root@bbb:~# /bin/bash ./bbb-eMMC-flasher-eewiki-ext4.sh
```

SAMA5D3 Xplained – USB and networking

Even for the SAMA5D3 Xplained, we can have a pretty prompt. So, let's change it as done for the BeagleBone Black:

```
root@arm:~# echo a5d3 > /etc/hostname
root@arm:~# sed -i -e's/\<arm\>/a5d3/g' /etc/hosts
```

Now, we can reboot, and we should get a new welcome message as shown here:

```
Debian GNU/Linux 8 a5d3 ttyS0
default username:password is [debian:temppwd]
a5d3 login:
```

Then, we will update the distribution repositories and install the `aptitude` tool as done for the host machine:

```
root@a5d3:~# apt-get update
root@a5d3:~# apt-get install aptitude
```

OK, now, we can try to replicate BeagleBone Black's configuration, allowing an `ssh` connection via the USB device port. However, this time, we'll do more. In fact, we will install two kinds of different virtual connections over the USB cable: an Ethernet and a serial connection.

 This configuration can be done on the BeagleBone Black too.

To do this, we need the **USB gadget** driver named **CDC Composite Device (Ethernet and ACM)** (see the kernel configuration settings done earlier for the SAMA5D3 Xplained):

```
root@a5d3:~# modprobe g_cdc host_addr=78:A5:04:CA:CB:01
```

The kernel messages we should see on the serial console are reported here, and they show that we have two new devices now:

```
using random self ethernet address
using random host ethernet address
using host ethernet address: 78:A5:04:CA:CB:01
usb0: HOST MAC 78:a5:04:ca:cb:01
usb0: MAC 22:6c:23:f0:10:62
g_cdc gadget: CDC Composite Gadget, version: King Kamehameha Day 2008
g_cdc gadget: g_cdc ready
g_cdc gadget: high-speed config #1: CDC Composite (ECM + ACM)
```

In fact, now. we should have a new Ethernet device named `usb0`:

```
root@a5d3:~# ifconfig usb0
usb0      Link encap:Ethernet  HWaddr da:a0:89:f9:a6:1d
          BROADCAST MULTICAST  MTU:1500  Metric:1
          RX packets:0 errors:0 dropped:0 overruns:0 frame:0
          TX packets:0 errors:0 dropped:0 overruns:0 carrier:0
          collisions:0 txqueuelen:1000
          RX bytes:0 (0.0 B)  TX bytes:0 (0.0 B)
```

And , we should have a new serial port:

```
root@a5d3:~# ls -l /dev/ttyGS0
crw-rw---- 1 root dialout 250, 0 Apr  2 18:28 /dev/ttyGS0
```

To force this new setting at every boot, we can add the kernel module name to the auto-loading module system:

```
root@a5d3:~# echo "g_cdc" >> /etc/modules-load.d/modules.conf
root@a5d3:~# echo "options g_cdc host_addr=78:A5:04:CA:CB:01" >>
               /etc/modprobe.d/modules.conf
```

The `host_addr` parameter is needed to allow the host PC to recognize our device and then correctly configure it by forcing a well-known MAC address each time we start the board.

Then, we can reboot the board, and the kernel module should be already present:

```
root@a5d3:~# lsmod
Module                    Size  Used by
```

```
usb_f_acm              3680  1
u_serial               6214  3 usb_f_acm
usb_f_ecm              4430  1
g_cdc                  2165  0
u_ether                6869  2 g_cdc,usb_f_ecm
libcomposite          26527  3 g_cdc,usb_f_acm,usb_f_ecm
```

Good! Now, we can start configuring them.

Regarding the Ethernet device, we can repeat what we did for the BeagleBone Black by adding the following lines to the `/etc/network/interfaces` file:

```
allow-hotplug usb0
iface usb0 inet static
        address 192.168.8.2
        netmask 255.255.255.252
        network 192.168.8.0
```

In order to avoid conflicts with the BeagleBone Black setting, we used the `192.168.8.X` subnetwork for this board instead of `192.168.7.X` used for the BeagleBone Black.

Then, we've to restart the networking system as follows:

```
root@a5d3:~# /etc/init.d/networking restart
```

As we did earlier, we may need to enable the root login via `ssh` by modifying the `PermitRootLogin` setting in the `/etc/ssh/sshd_config` file and then restarting the daemon.

Then, we have to install the `udhcpd` daemon as we did earlier and then replace its current configuration in the `/etc/udhcpd.conf` file with the following settings:

```
start       192.168.8.1
end         192.168.8.1
interface   usb0
max_leases  1
option subnet 255.255.255.252
```

We can save the daemon's old configuration with the following command:
```
root@a5d3:~# mv /etc/udhcpd.conf
                 /etc/udhcpd.conf.orig
```

Then, we must enable it by setting the DHCPD_ENABLED variable to yes in the /etc/default/udhcpd file. Then, restart the daemon:

```
root@a5d3:~# /etc/init.d/udhcpd restart
```

Now, regarding the serial connection, we can add the ability to do a serial login by adding a new getty service on it with the following commands:

```
root@a5d3:~# systemctl enable getty@ttyGS0.service
Created symlink from /etc/systemd/system/getty.target.wants/getty@ttyG
S0.service to /lib/systemd/system/getty@.service.
root@a5d3:~# systemctl start getty@ttyGS0.service
```

Now, we only need to add the following lines to the /etc/securetty file in order to allow the root user to login using this new communication channel:

```
# USB gadget
ttyGS0
```

OK, now, if we take a look at the host PC's kernel messages, we should see something as like this:

```
usb 1-1: new high-speed USB device number 3 using ehci-pci
usb 1-1: New USB device found, idVendor=0525, idProduct=a4aa
usb 1-1: New USB device strings: Mfr=1, Product=2, SerialNumber=0
usb 1-1: Product: CDC Composite Gadget
usb 1-1: Manufacturer: Linux 4.4.6-sama5-armv7-r5 with atmel_usba_udc
cdc_ether 1-1:1.0 eth0: register 'cdc_ether' at usb-0000:00:0b.0-1,
CDC Ethernet Device, 78:a5:04:ca:cb:01
cdc_acm 1-1:1.2: ttyACM0: USB ACM device
```

Then, we can test the networking connection with the ssh command with the following command line on the host PC:

```
$ ssh root@192.168.8.2
The authenticity of host '192.168.8.2 (192.168.8.2)' can't be establis
hed.
ECDSA key fingerprint is SHA256:OduXLAPIYgNR7Xxh8XbhSum+zOKHBbgv/tnbeD
j2030.
Are you sure you want to continue connecting (yes/no)? yes
Warning: Permanently added '192.168.8.2' (ECDSA) to the list of known
hosts.
root@192.168.8.2's password:
```

Now, enter the root's password that is the `root` string and the job is done:

```
The programs included with the Debian GNU/Linux system are free
software; the exact distribution terms for each program are
described in the individual files in /usr/share/doc/*/copyright.
Debian GNU/Linux comes with ABSOLUTELY NO WARRANTY, to the
extent permitted by applicable law.
Last login: Sat Apr  2 18:02:23 2016
root@a5d3:~#
```

Then, the serial connection can be tested using the `minicom` command as shown here:

```
$ sudo minicom  -o -D /dev/ttyACM0
Debian GNU/Linux 8 a5d3 ttyGS0
default username:password is [debian:temppwd]
a5d3 login:
```

Now, our SAMA5D3 Xplained is ready, and we can step next to the Wandboard.

Wandboard – USB and networking (wired and wireless)

Again, we like to have a pretty prompt. So, let's change it as we did for the BeagleBone Black:

```
root@arm:~# echo wb > /etc/hostname
root@arm:~# sed -i -e's/\<wb\>/a5d3/g' /etc/hosts
```

Now, we can reboot the system, and we should get a new welcome message as shown here:

```
Debian GNU/Linux 8 wb ttymxc0
default username:password is [debian:temppwd]
wb login:
```

Then, we will update the distribution repositories and install the `aptitude` tool as done for the host machine:

```
root@wb:~# apt-get update
root@wb:~# apt-get install aptitude
```

OK, now, we can try to replicate BeagleBone Black's configuration by allowing an `ssh` connection via the USB device port. So, let's install the `udhcpd` package using the usual `aptitude` command:

```
root@wb:~# aptitude install udhcpd
```

Then, add the following lines to the `/etc/network/interfaces` file:

```
allow-hotplug usb0
iface usb0 inet static
        address 192.168.9.2
        netmask 255.255.255.252
        network 192.168.9.0
```

> In order to avoid conflicts with the BeagleBone Black and SAMA5D3 Xplained settings, we used the subnetwork `192.168.9.X` for this board instead of `192.168.7.X` used for the BeagleBone Black or the `192.168.8.X` used for the SAMA5D3 Xplained.

Then, restart the networking system as follows:

```
root@wb:~# /etc/init.d/networking restart
```

> As we did earlier, we may need to enable the root login via `ssh` by modifying the `PermitRootLogin` setting in the `/etc/ssh/sshd_config` file and then restarting the daemon.

Then, we have to install the `udhcpd` daemon as we did earlier and then replace its current configuration in `/etc/udhcpd.conf` file with the following settings:

```
start       192.168.9.1
end         192.168.9.1
interface   usb0
max_leases  1
option subnet 255.255.255.252
```

> We can save the daemon's old configuration with the following command:
>
> ```
> root@wb:~# mv /etc/udhcpd.conf /etc/udhcpd.conf.orig
> ```

Then, we must enable it by setting the DHCPD_ENABLED variable to yes in the /etc/default/udhcpd file. Then, restart the daemon:

```
root@wb:~# /etc/init.d/udhcpd restart
```

Now, if we try to connect to the host PC with our Wandboard, we should see the following message on the serial console:

```
g_ether gadget: high-speed config #1: CDC Ethernet (ECM)
IPv6: ADDRCONF(NETDEV_CHANGE): usb0: link becomes ready
```

A new Ethernet device should appear as reported here:

```
root@wb:~# ifconfig usb0
usb0      Link encap:Ethernet  HWaddr 62:1e:f6:88:9b:42
          inet addr:192.168.9.2  Bcast:192.168.9.3  Mask:255.255.255.252
          inet6 addr: fe80::601e:f6ff:fe88:9b42/64 Scope:Link
          UP BROADCAST RUNNING MULTICAST  MTU:1500  Metric:1
          RX packets:0 errors:0 dropped:0 overruns:0 frame:0
          TX packets:30 errors:0 dropped:0 overruns:0 carrier:0
          collisions:0 txqueuelen:1000
          RX bytes:0 (0.0 B)  TX bytes:5912 (5.7 KiB)
```

OK, now, we have to configure the new Ethernet device on the host, and then, we can try an ssh connection as shown here:

```
$ ssh root@192.168.9.2
```

 On my host PC that is Ubuntu based, before executing the ssh command earlier, we had to properly configure the new Ethernet device by adding a new network connection in the entry **Edit Connections...** in the system settings menu.

```
The authenticity of host '192.168.9.2 (192.168.9.2)' can't be establis
hed.
ECDSA key fingerprint is SHA256:Xp2Bf+YOWLOkDSm00GxXw9CY5wH+ECnPzpOEHp
3+GM8.
Are you sure you want to continue connecting (yes/no)? yes
Warning: Permanently added '192.168.9.2' (ECDSA) to the list of known
hosts.
root@192.168.9.2's password:
```

Now, enter the root's password that is the root string and the job is done:

```
The programs included with the Debian GNU/Linux system are free
software; the exact distribution terms for each program are
described in the individual files in /usr/share/doc/*/copyright.
```

```
Debian GNU/Linux comes with ABSOLUTELY NO WARRANTY, to the
extent permitted by applicable law.
Last login: Sat Apr 2 17:45:31 2016
root@wb:~#
```

Ok now, as last step, we have to set up the on-board Wi-Fi chip. To do this, we need to download the firmware. Here are the commands:

```
root@wb:~# mkdir -p /lib/firmware/brcm/
root@wb:~# cd /lib/firmware/brcm/
root@wb:/lib/firmware/brcm# wget -c
        https://git.kernel.org/cgit/linux/kernel/git/firmware/linux-fi
rmware.git/plain/brcm/brcmfmac4329-sdio.bin
root@wb:/lib/firmware/brcm# wget -c
        https://git.kernel.org/cgit/linux/kernel/git/firmware/linux-fi
rmware.git/plain/brcm/brcmfmac4330-sdio.bin
root@wb:/lib/firmware/brcm# wget -c
        https://rcn-ee.com/repos/git/meta-fsl-arm-extra/recipes-bsp/br
oadcom-nvram-config/files/wandboard/brcmfmac4329-sdio.txt
root@wb:/lib/firmware/brcm# wget -c
        https://rcn-ee.com/repos/git/meta-fsl-arm-extra/recipes-bsp/br
oadcom-nvram-config/files/wandboard/brcmfmac4330-sdio.txt
```

Then, we have to reboot the system with the usual `reboot` command. After reboot, if everything works well, we should see a new interface named `wlan0` as shown here:

```
root@wb:~# ifconfig wlan0
wlan0     Link encap:Ethernet  HWaddr 44:39:c4:9a:96:24
          BROADCAST MULTICAST  MTU:1500  Metric:1
          RX packets:0 errors:0 dropped:0 overruns:0 frame:0
          TX packets:0 errors:0 dropped:0 overruns:0 carrier:0
          collisions:0 txqueuelen:1000
          RX bytes:0 (0.0 B)   TX bytes:0 (0.0 B)
```

Now, we have to verify that it works. So, as the first step, let's try a wireless network scan:

```
root@wb:~# ifconfig wlan0 0.0.0.0
root@wb:~# iwlist wlan0 scan | grep ESSID
                  ESSID:"EnneEnne"
```

Great, my home network has been recognized!

 We may need to connect the external antenna in order to correctly detect all wireless networks around. The external antenna connector is labeled as *ANT* near the Wi-Fi chip.

For the moment, we can stop the Wi-Fi setup here since it will be restarted later in this book in a proper chapter.

Common settings

Before ending this chapter, let me suggest that you install some basic and common tools we're going to use in this book. We can decide to install these tools now or, when needed, later during the reading of the book.

If we decide to perform this last step and then install these tools right now, we have to connect our boards to the Internet using, for example, an Ethernet cable, and then setting a suitable network configuration for it.

Let me remember that if our embedded kit doesn't automatically take a network configuration and we have a DHCP server in our LAN, we can force this behavior using the dhclient command:

```
# dhclient eth0
```

If we don't have a running DHCP service, we can manually set up a network configuration using the ifconfig and route commands as shown here:

```
# ifconfig eth0 <LOCAL-IP-ADDR>
# route add default gw <GATEWAY-IP-ADDR>
```

OK, now, to install our tools, we can use the aptitude command again and then wait for the complete installation:

```
# aptitude install autoconf git subversion make gcc libtool pkg-config
                   bison build-essential flex
                   strace php5-cli python-pip libpython-dev
```

Summary

In this chapter, we took a first look at our new embedded developer kits. You learned how to reinstall a fresh Debian OS from scratch on all systems and how to get access to their serial consoles.

In the next chapter, we will continue to experience the serial console in order to well understand how we can use it in every contest, from the early booting stages inside the bootloader to the normal system setup and management.

2
Managing the System Console

In the first chapter of this book, we saw how to set up our developer kits and (in part) the host PC. We already got a first login via the **serial console** by showing you how you can connect a serial (or **USB-to-Serial**) adapter to each kit; however, in this chapter, we're going to go further into exploring the serial console and the **shell** running in it.

In this section, you will learn some useful command-line tools to manipulate files and also learn how to manage the distribution's packages. These commands will be used into this book, and even if you may already know them, it's useful to briefly review them.

In the end, a special section will introduce the **bootloader** commands (**U-Boot** in our cases) so you may feel more confident in managing this important component of the system. In fact, the serial console is mostly used to set up the running system (that is, the running distribution), but it is used to set up the booting stages and (sometimes) the whole system update!

Again, experienced developers may safely skip this chapter. However, by reading it, you can find useful tips and tricks that can help you in the development stages.

Basic OS management

Now it's time to take a quick tour of some basic system management commands, which may be useful in the next sections.

You should notice that the following commands can be used indifferently into each developer kit presented in this book as is in the host PC as is in any other GNU/Linux-based OS! This is a really important feature of GNU/Linux systems that allows a developer to have the same command set into its working machine as the one in the embedded devices.

For the sake of simplicity, the following examples are executed into the host PC.

File manipulation and Co

One of the main principles of Unix systems is that *everything is a file*. This means that in a Unix system, (almost) everything can be accessed as a file! So we can use the same commands to read/write a file for every peripheral connected to the system (that is, disks, terminals, serial ports, and so on).

Since this book's main goal is to show you how to get access to the system's peripherals, it's quite obvious that these commands are very important to know. Moreover, in the next chapters, we are going to use several command-line tools to set up our developer kits and their attached peripherals, so in this section, we are going to do a little list of them.

 The following tutorial will not cover all possible file manipulation and tool commands nor all possible usages, so let me encourage those of you curious to get further information by surfing the Internet. A good starting point is at: http://en.wikipedia.org/wiki/List_of_Unix_commands.

For each presented command, you should take a look at the relative man pages, which we cannot entirely reproduce here due to spacing reasons because even an experienced developer may learn a lot of useful things by reading them from time to time.

To get the man pages of a generic command, we can try to use the following command line:

```
$ man <command>
```

Here, the <command> string is obviously the desired command to visit. If we have to use a different command to get this information, you will be informed accordingly.

echo and cat

Well, in order to manipulate the files, the first commands we can use are echo and cat; the former can be used to put some text into a file and the latter to read the file content:

```
$ echo 'Some text' > /tmp/foo
$ cat /tmp/foo
Some text
```

To append some text, instead of rewriting it, we can simply replace the > char with >> in the preceding command, as shown here:

```
$ echo 'Another line' >> /tmp/foo
$ cat /tmp/foo
Some text
Another line
```

In the `echo` command's man pages, we find that the command's description is **Echo the STRING(s) to standard output**; so, by using the Bash redirection behavior (with the > and >> characters), we can use it to write into a normal file due the fact that even the standard output is a file!

Again, as shown in the `cat` command in the relative man pages, we find that the description is **concatenate files and print on the standard output**. Again, what we already said about the `echo` command is still valid for `cat`, but looking at its description, we notice another interesting mode to use it, which is that it can be used to concatenate two or more files (the inverse operation of the `split` command). Let's consider the following commands:

```
$ ls -lh /bin/bash
-rwxr-xr-x 1 root root 664K Nov 12  2014 /bin/bash
$ split -b 100K /bin/bash bash_
$ ls -lh bash_*
-rw-r--r-- 1 root root 100K Apr  2 17:55 bash_aa
-rw-r--r-- 1 root root 100K Apr  2 17:55 bash_ab
-rw-r--r-- 1 root root 100K Apr  2 17:55 bash_ac
-rw-r--r-- 1 root root 100K Apr  2 17:55 bash_ad
-rw-r--r-- 1 root root 100K Apr  2 17:55 bash_ae
-rw-r--r-- 1 root root 100K Apr  2 17:55 bash_af
-rw-r--r-- 1 root root  64K Apr  2 17:55 bash_ag
```

We split the `/bin/bash` program (our shell) into six pieces of 100 KB plus a smaller one of about 64 KB. Then, we can rebuild the original file using `cat`, as shown here:

```
$ cat bash_* > bash_rebuilded
```

Then, we can check the `bash_rebuilded` file against the original one using the `md5sum` tool, as follows:

```
$ md5sum /bin/bash bash_rebuilded
4ad446acf57184b795fe5c1de5b810c4 /bin/bash
4ad446acf57184b795fe5c1de5b810c4 bash_rebuilded
```

They have the same hash and they have the same content!

> The `split` and `md5sum` commands are not covered in this book, but those of you curious may take a look at the relative man pages for further information on these tools:
> ```
> $ man split
> $ man md5sum
> ```

dd

The dd command is very powerful since it can be used for several different purposes. We already used it in Chapter 1, *Installing the Developing System, U-Boot (with MLO)* and others, where it were used in the following form:

```
$ sudo dd if=u-boot.img of=/dev/sdb count=2 seek=1 bs=384k
```

The if option argument defines the **input file** where you're reading data from, while the of option defines the **output file** where you're writing data to (note that while the input file is a normal file, the output file is a block device and for our command, they are absolutely interchangeable), and then the bs option defines a **block size** of 384 KB that shows how many bytes must be read and written at a time, so by specifying the option arguments, count=2 and seek=1, we ask dd to copy only two input blocks skipping one block at the start of the output. This operation is used to place a file at a specified offset into a block device. Take a look at the following figure for a graphical representation of this operation:

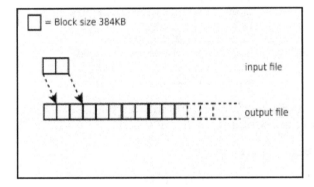

By looking at the command man pages, you should notice that as the seek option is used to skip *N* blocks of the output, the skip option can be used to do the same into the input file. Also it is useful to note that using the ibs and obs options, we can differentiate the input from the output block size.

Another usage of dd is the following:

```
$ dd if=/dev/sda of=/dev/sdb
```

In this case, both the input and output files are not common files but they are block devices; in particular, they are two hard disks, and by using the preceding command, we copy the entire content of the first **hard disk** to the second one!

Again, using the following command, we can create an image of the first hard disk in the sda_image file:

```
$ dd if=/dev/sda of=sda_image
```

On the other hand, we can wipe a disk by writing all zeros on it:

```
$ dd if=/dev/zero of=/dev/sda
```

Or, we can safely erase the hard disk content by writing random data into it:

```
$ dd if=/dev/urandom of=/dev/sda
```

The /dev/zero and /dev/urandom files are special files created by the kernel where we can read data from: in the former, we're going to read all zeros, while from the latter, we're going to read (pseudo) random data generated internally by the kernel.
For further information, you can take a look at the man pages of these files (yes, even files might have man pages) using the following commands:

```
$ man zero
$ man urandom
```

The last note on dd is about the possibility to transform the data read from the input file before writing it to the output file. In the next command, we read data from the standard input, we swap the byte in each word, and then we write the result to the standard output:

```
$ echo 1234 | dd conv=swab
2143
```

Or we can convert all characters in the input to the uppercase:

```
$ echo "test string" | dd conv=ucase
TEST STRING
```

There are only a few of the several converting options offered by dd. Refer to the man pages for a complete list.

grep and egrep

Another useful command is `grep` (and its variant `egrep`), which can be used to select some text from a file. If you remember, the file created earlier with the `echo` command can be executed as follows:

```
$ grep "Another" /tmp/foo
Another line
```

The output is just the line where the `Another` word is written.

If we spend some time to take a look at the `grep` command's man pages, we can see that there are tons of option arguments related to these commands; however, due to space reasons, we're going to report only the ones used in this book.

The first option argument is `-r`, which can be used to recursively read all files under a specified directory, for instance, the following command searches in which the file under the `/etc` directory of the Ubuntu release number of my host PC is stored:

```
$ rgrep -r '15\.10' /etc/ 2>/dev/null
/etc/issue.net:Ubuntu 15.10
/etc/os-release:VERSION="15.10 (Wily Werewolf)"
/etc/os-release:PRETTY_NAME="Ubuntu 15.10"
/etc/os-release:VERSION_ID="15.10"
/etc/apt/sources.list:#deb cdrom:[Ubuntu 15.10 _Wily Werewolf_ - Relea
se amd64 (20151021)]/ wily main restricted
/etc/lsb-release:DISTRIB_RELEASE=15.10
/etc/lsb-release:DISTRIB_DESCRIPTION="Ubuntu 15.10"
/etc/issue:Ubuntu 15.10 \n \l
```

Note that the `2>/dev/null` setting is used to drop all possible error messages due to invalid reading permissions into the `/dev/null` file. As for `/dev/zero` and `/dev/urandom`, you can take a look at the man pages of `/dev/null` using the following command:
```
$ man null
```

Another useful option argument is `-i`, which is used to ignore the case, so to search for the `Ubuntu 15.10` string in both lower case or uppercase (or mixed case), we can use the following command:

```
$ grep -r -i 'ubuntu 15\.10' /etc/ 2>/dev/null
/etc/issue.net:Ubuntu 15.10
/etc/os-release:PRETTY_NAME="Ubuntu 15.10"
/etc/apt/sources.list:#deb cdrom:[Ubuntu 15.10 _Wily Werewolf_ - Relea
se amd64 (20151021)]/ wily main restricted
```

```
/etc/lsb-release:DISTRIB_DESCRIPTION="Ubuntu 15.10"
/etc/issue:Ubuntu 15.10 \n \l
```

Note that in most distributions (as Ubuntu or Debian), the `grep -r` command as an alias named `rgrep` can be used in place, so the preceding command can be written as follows:

```
$ rgrep -i 'ubuntu 15\.10' /etc/ 2>/dev/null
```

You should take into account that all these commands are based on **regular expressions** that are not covered in this book, so you should use the man pages for further information on this powerful tool. Here's the command:

```
$ man 7 regex
```

tr and sed

If we need to modify a text file or a binary one (normally, we don't use these commands for binary files but we'll soon see that this can be done sometimes) in a quick and dirty manner, we can consider in using these commands.

The `tr` command can be used to translate or delete characters, and the simplest usage is as follows:

```
$ echo 'this is a testing string' | tr 'a-z' 'A-Z'
THIS IS A TESTING STRING
```

We've replaced all lowercases to the corresponding uppercase.

Note that a more cryptic but equivalent form of the preceding command is as follows:

```
$ echo 'this is a testing string' | \
        tr '[:lower:]' '[:upper:]'
```

Another interesting usage is its usefulness in removing a set of characters. For example, we can remove all non-printable characters from a binary file with the following command:

```
$ tr -d -c '[:print:]' < /bin/ls
```

The `-d` option argument tells `tr` to to delete the characters specified in the command, while the `-c` option negates the set. Since the set is defined by `'[:print:]'`, it means that `-c` transforms all printable characters into all the non-printable characters, and the desired result as shown as follows:

```
$ tr -d -c '[:print:]' < /bin/ls
ELF>I@@8@8@@@@@@88@8@@@ aah aaTT@T@DDPtdTTATAQtdRtdaa/lib64/ld-linux-x
86-64.so.2GNU GNUL7=K"q2rH?(rstvy{|~Pv2|qX|,cr<OBE9L>bA1 >[ju`=9)F^1=
+Um_{j}?p*$vD(NfKN- q<*6UH8< ]u=|nP |6ZZa<Aaj"@F@#@! aahae a`)A&na'Aa5
@a=(Aj!a#@(A0#aJ'A['A'@alibsel
```

We drop the command's output after a few lines since it's really quite long.

The last usage of `tr` we may need is the ability to replace binary data. In fact, using the \NNN form (where the NNN number is specified as octal), we can address every ASCII code. A useful aspect of this feature is when we need to fill a file (or a device) with a fixed value; when we talked about `dd`, we saw that we can wipe a hard disk by filling it with zeros with the following command:

```
$ dd if=/dev/zero of=/dev/sda
```

However, if we need to fill it with 255 (that is, 0xff in hexadecimal or 0377 in octal), we can use the following command:

```
$ dd if=/dev/zero | tr '\000' '\377' | dd of=/dev/sda
```

On the other hand, the `sed` command can be used when we need to modify a file holding normal text (for instance, a configuration file) using a single command instead of opening our preferred text editor. As an example, we can recall what we did in chapter 1, *Installing the Developing System, BeagleBone Black: USB, networking, and overlays* when we had to modify the settings into the /etc/ssh/sshd_config file by replacing the PermitRootLogin without-password line with PermitRootLogin yes. Most probably, we did it using a text editor but we could use the `sed` command, as follows:

```
$ sed -i -e 's/^PermitRootLogin without-password$/PermitRootLogin yes/'
/etc/ssh/sshd_config
```

The -i option tells `sed` to to edit the file in place, while using the -e option argument, we can specify the script to be executed.

Another useful form is the one we can use to comment out a string by adding a # character at the beginning of the line we want to comment out. For example, in the /etc/ssh/sshd_config file, if we want specify that we don't trust the ~/.ssh/known_hosts file for RhostsRSAAuthentication, we have to uncomment the following line:

```
#IgnoreUserKnownHosts yes
```

The command line to do it is as follows:

```
root@bbb:~# sed -i -e 's/^#IgnoreUserKnownHosts yes$/IgnoreUserKnownHo
sts yes/' /etc/ssh/sshd_config
root@bbb:~# grep IgnoreUserKnownHosts /etc/ssh/sshd_config
IgnoreUserKnownHosts yes
```

 This time, the command has been executed into BeagleBone Black instead of the host PC, but the result will be perfectly the same in both cases.

Another useful feature is the ability to replace eight consecutive spaces into a single tab character to perfectly indent a file holding our code. The sed command is the following:

```
$ sed -i -e 's/        /\t/g' code.c
```

head and tail

These commands can be used to display the beginning or the end of a file. Short examples are as follows:

```
$ echo -e '1\n2\n\3\n4\n5\n6\n7\n8\n9\n10' > /tmp/bar
$ head -2 /tmp/bar
1
2
$ tail -2 /tmp/bar
9
10
```

Here, we used the echo command to fill the /tmp/bar file with ten lines holding numbers 1 to 10, one per line, and then we used the head and tail commands to show, respectively, the first and the last two lines of the file.

These commands can be used in several other ways, but in this book, we're going to use mostly the tail command with the -f option arguments in order to display a file that can grow up. This class of files is usually log files and we can use the following command line to display the system's log messages as soon as they arrive:

```
$ tail -f /var/log/syslog
```

The command will start displaying the last ten lines (if available) and then it will display any other lines that will be appended to the /var/log/syslog log file.

od and hexdump

Other interesting commands are od and hexdump, which can be used to inspect file content one byte at a time (or in a more complex form). For instance, we can read the preceding /tmp/foo text file one byte at a time using a binary format:

```
$ od -Ax -tx1 < /tmp/foo
000000 53 6f 6d 65 20 74 65 78 74 0a 41 6e 6f 74 68 65
000010 72 20 6c 69 6e 65 65 0a
000017
```

The hexdump quasi equivalent command is as follows:

```
$ hexdump -C < /tmp/foo
00000000  53 6f 6d 65 20 74 65 78  74 0a 41 6e 74 68 65  |some text .A
nothe|
00000010  72 20 6c 69 6e 65 0a                            |r line.|
00000017
```

In the output of the second command, you can also easily note that each byte is the ASCII coding of each letter of the preceding strings.

file

The file command is used to detect a file type:

```
$ file /tmp/foo
/tmp/foo: ASCII text
$ file /dev/urandom
/dev/urandom: character special
$ file /usr/bin/file
/usr/bin/file: ELF 64-bit LSB executable, x86-64, version 1 (SYSV), dy
namically linked, interpreter /lib64/ld-linux-x86-64.so.2, for GNU/Lin
ux 2.6.32, BuildID[sha1]=ec8d8159accf4c85fde8985a784638f62e10b4e9, str
ipped
```

Looking at the preceding output, we discover that the /tmp/foo file we created in previous examples is just an ASCII text file; the /dev/urandom file is a special character file and the /usr/bin/file file (which is where the file command is stored) is an executable for the **x86-64** platform.

strings

The `strings` command is used to find strings in a binary file; for example, we can extract the usage string of the `file` command using this:

```
root@beaglebone:~# strings /usr/bin/file | grep Usage
Usage: %s [-bchikLlNnprsvz0] [--apple] [--mime-encoding] [--mime-type]
Usage: file [OPTION...] [FILE...]
```

strace

This is one of the most powerful debugging commands we can use in a GNU/Linux-based system. Using this command, we can trace all **system calls** a process does during its execution!

Even if this is not strictly related to *file manipulation*, we have to present it here due the fact that it can be used to easily debug a program and because we can use it to know which files are managed by a program without writing any extra code. In fact, the power of this command is that it can do its job even if the program is compiled with no debugging symbols at all. As an example, let's suppose we wish to know how the `cat` program works, which we can do as follows:

```
$ strace cat /tmp/foo
execve("/bin/cat", ["cat", "/tmp/foo"], [/* 29 vars */]) = 0
brk(0)                                  = 0x2409000
...
open("/tmp/foo", O_RDONLY)              = 3
fstat(3, {st_mode=S_IFREG|0664, st_size=23, ...}) = 0
fadvise64(3, 0, 0, POSIX_FADV_SEQUENTIAL) = 0
mmap(NULL, 139264, PROT_READ|PROT_WRITE,
MAP_PRIVATE|MAP_ANONYMOUS, -1, 0) = 0x7f80dc009000
read(3, "Some text\nAnother line\n", 131072) = 23
write(1, "Some text\nAnother line\n", 23Some text
Another line)                          = 23
read(3, "", 131072)                    = 0
munmap(0x7f80dc009000, 139264)         = 0
close(3)                               = 0
close(1)                               = 0
close(2)                               = 0
exit_group(0)                          = ?
+++ exited with 0 +++
```

In the preceding output, we can read that after a prologue (removed into this output due to spacing reasons), the program execute `open()` on the `/tmp/foo` file (which is the file we supplied to `cat`), which returns the file descriptor number 3, and then it executes `read()` on that file descriptor returning the file content and, in the end, it executes a `write()` system call on the file descriptor 1 (that is, the standard output), passing to it the just read buffer. When the program executes another `read()` and it returns 0 (that is, an End-of-File), the program exits, closing all opened files descriptors. In the end, `strace` returns the program's exit code as well.

Package management

In the first chapter, we already learned how install a package into our new **Debian** distribution; however, there are a few more things to add in order to manage the system's packages.

The following commands can be executed indifferently in the host PC or in one of our developer kits (for the next examples, as a developer kit, we used the BeagleBone Black).

Searching a software package

For example, we know that installing the **vim** (**Vi Improved**) package can be simply done using the following command:

```
root@bbb:~# aptitude install vim
```

In the preceding command, we're assuming that the package containing `vim` has the same name as that of the software tool. However, this is not always true! For instance, if we wish to install the PHP command-line interface (the tool used to execute PHP scripts from the command line), we may assume the package's name was `php-cli`, and then we can try to install the package using this command:

```
root@bbb:~# aptitude install php-cli
```

But, in this case, we will get the following error message:

```
Couldn't find package "php-cli". However, the following
packages contain "php-cli" in their name:
  php-google-api-php-client
No packages will be installed, upgraded, or removed.
0 packages upgraded, 0 newly installed, 0 to remove and 3 not upgraded
Need to get 0 B of archives. After unpacking 0 B will be used.
```

Doh! So, which is the correct package name? Here is where the `apt-cache` command comes in handy. Just type the following command on the console:

```
root@bbb:~# apt-cache search php cli
```

We will get a long list of packages related to the words `php` and `cli` (in fact, we can assume that both these words may be in both package names or descriptions). Now we can search which package suits our needs and we can try to filter the output using the `grep` command, as shown here:

```
root@bbb:~# apt-cache search php cli | grep '^php[^ ]*cli'
php-google-api-php-client - Google APIs client library for PHP
php-horde-cli - Horde Command Line Interface API
php-horde-imap-client - Horde IMAP Client
php-horde-socket-client - Horde Socket Client
php5-cli - command-line interpreter for the php5 scripting language
php-seclib - implementations of an arbitrary-precision integer arithme
tic library
```

The `^php[^ ]*cli` string is a regular expression, which asks `grep` to select only those lines whose hold at the beginning of the line is a string starting with `php` and ending with the `cli` chars without any space in the middle.

Now, as we can see, the output is now shorter and at a quick glance we can see that the desired package is named `php5-cli`.

Another useful command is the `apt-file`command, which can be used to find a package holding a specific file even if it is not installed on the system. It's unlikely that this command is installed into our developer kit's default distribution by default, so we must install it ourselves:

```
root@bbb:~# aptitude install apt-file
```

When the installation ends, we must update `apt-file` data through the following command:

```
root@bbb:~# apt-file update
```

Now, for example, if we get an error during a compilation where a file, say, `libcurses.so` is missing, we can obtain the package name holding that file using the `apt-file` command, as shown here:

```
root@bbb:~# apt-file search libncurses.so
libncurses-gst: /usr/lib/gnu-smalltalk/libncurses.so
libncurses5: /lib/arm-linux-gnueabihf/libncurses.so.5
```

```
libncurses5: /lib/arm-linux-gnueabihf/libncurses.so.5.9
libncurses5-dbg: /usr/lib/debug/lib/arm-linux-gnueabihf/libncurses.so.
5.9
libncurses5-dbg: /usr/lib/debug/libncurses.so.5
libncurses5-dbg: /usr/lib/debug/libncurses.so.5.9
libncurses5-dev: /usr/lib/arm-linux-gnueabihf/libncurses.so
```

The preceding message shows us that the desired package name is `libncurses5-dev`.

Installing a package

A brief note on some pitfalls in installing new packages must be added. We already told you how to install a package; we can use both `apt-get` and `aptitude` commands, as reported in the next two commands:

```
root@arm:~# apt-get install evtest
root@arm:~# aptitude install evtest
```

The commands can be used interchangeably even if, as reported in the next section, they have several differences. However, for both of them, we can get an error message as follows:

```
root@arm:~# aptitude install evtest
The following NEW packages will be installed:
  evtest libxml2{a} sgml-base{a} xml-core{a}
0 packages upgraded, 4 newly installed, 0 to remove and 29 not upgrade
d.
Need to get 846 kB of archives. After unpacking 1658 kB will be used.
Do you want to continue? [Y/n/?]
Err http://ftp.us.debian.org/debian/ wheezy/main libxml2 armhf 2.8.0+d
fsg1-7
   404  Not Found [IP: 64.50.233.100 80]
Err http://ftp.us.debian.org/debian/ wheezy/main sgml-base all 1.26+nm
u3
   404  Not Found [IP: 64.50.233.100 80]
...
```

In this case, the list of available packages is not updated to their latest version and they must be updated using one of the two commands here:

```
root@arm:~# apt-get update
root@arm:~# aptitude update
```

As in the `install` case, the preceding commands are perfectly equivalent. In fact we have:

```
root@arm:~# aptitude update
```

```
Ign http://ftp.us.debian.org wheezy InRelease
Get: 1 http://ftp.us.debian.org wheezy Release.gpg [2373 B]
Get: 2 http://ftp.us.debian.org wheezy Release [191 kB]
Get: 3 http://ftp.us.debian.org wheezy/main Sources [5984 kB]
...
```

Then the installation should go till the end without errors:

```
root@arm:~# aptitude install evtest
The following NEW packages will be installed:
  evtest libxml2{a} sgml-base{a} xml-core{a}
0 packages upgraded, 4 newly installed, 0 to remove and 111 not upgrad
ed.
Need to get 803 kB/848 kB of archives. After unpacking 1621 kB will be
 used.
Do you want to continue? [Y/n/?]
Get: 1 http://ftp.us.debian.org/debian/ wheezy/main libxml2 armhf 2.8.
0+dfsg1-7+wheezy5 [788 kB]
Get: 2 http://ftp.us.debian.org/debian/ wheezy/main sgml-base all 1.26
+nmu4 [14.6 kB]
...
```

As a final note, the next two commands can be used to upgrade all packages to their most recent version:

```
root@arm:~# apt-get dist-upgrade
root@arm:~# aptitude safe-upgrade
```

> There are other commands that can be used to upgrade all packages with different behaviors not reported in this book; however, you can take a look at the commands' man pages to get further information on them.

apt-get and friends versus aptitude

Since the first chapter, we suggested that you install the aptitude tool to manage the Ubuntu or Debian packages used in the host PC or our developer kits. We asserted that aptitude is smarter than apt-get; now it's time to explain a bit why.

Looking at the apt-get man pages, we see that this command is a command-line interface to handle packages and may be considered the backend for the other low-level tools of the package management system. In fact, using it, we can easily install or remove a package with its dependencies and/or update a single package or the whole system.

On the other hand, the `aptitude` command's man pages tells us similar things. In fact, this command is still a high-level interface for the package manager but, as already stated, it's smarter; we can use it for several useful tasks that we do with `apt-get` or `apt-cache` and other commands of the same family:

- **Easy package installation or removal at once**: We can install and remove packages using a single command. For instance, the following command will install `packageA`, remove `packageB`, and purge `packageC`:

  ```
  $ aptitude install  packageA packageB- packageC_
  ```

- We can put one or more packages in a hold status, that is, we inform the system to cancel any active installation, upgrade or remove, and prevent this package from being automatically upgraded in the future. The command is the same as earlier, but the package name is followed by the = sign. An example is `packageD=`.

- We can get very detailed information about one or more packages:

  ```
  $ aptitude show vim
  Package: vim
  State: installed
  Automatically installed: no
  Version: 2:7.4.1689-3ubuntu1
  Priority: optional
  Section: editors
  Maintainer: Ubuntu Developers
  <ubuntu-devel-discuss@lists.ubuntu.com>
  Architecture: amd64
  Uncompressed Size: 2377 k
  Depends: vim-common (= 2:7.4.1689-3ubuntu1),
          vim-runtime (= 2:7.4.1689-3ubuntu1),
          libacl1 (>= 2.2.51-8),libc6 (>= 2.15),
          libgpm2 (>= 1.20.4),
  libselinux1 (>= 1.32), libtinfo5 (>= 6)
  Suggests: ctags, vim-doc, vim-scripts
  Conflicts: vim:i386
  Provides: editor
  Provided by: vim-athena (2:7.4.1689-3ubuntu1), vim-athena-py2
          (2:7.4.1689-3ubuntu1),
              vim-gnome (2:7.4.16893ubuntu1),
  . . .
  Description: Vi IMproved - enhanced vi editor
   Vim is an almost compatible version of UNIX editor Vi.
   Many new features have been added: multi level undo,
   syntax highlighting,
   command-line history, online help, filename completion,
  ```

```
block operations,
folding, Unicode support, and so on.
This package contains a version of vim compiled with a
rather standard
set of features. This package does not provide a GUI version
of Vim.
Refer to the other  vim-* packages if you need more (or less).
Homepage: http://www.vim.org/
```

- We have a very powerful package searching engine! For example, using the following command, we can get a list of all installed packages that have the string editor in their description field:

```
$ aptitude search '~i?description(editor)'
i   dia                            - Diagram editor
i A dia-common                     - Diagram editor (common files)
i A dia-libs                       - Diagram editor (library files)
i A dia-shapes                     - Diagram editor
i A docbook-xml                    - standard XML documentation sys
                                     tem for soft
i   ed                             - classic UNIX line editor
i   emacs                          - GNU Emacs editor (metapackage)
...
i   nano                           - small,friendly text editor
                                     inspired by Pi
i   sed                            - The GNU sed stream editor
i   vim                            - Vi IMproved - enhanced vi
i   vim-common                     - Vi IMproved - Common files
i A vim-runtime                    - Vi IMproved - Runtime files
i   vim-tiny                       - Vi IMproved - enhanced vi
i A x11-apps                       - X applications
```

- Also, we can use boolean expressions; using the following command, we search all packages that have the firmware string in the name field and wireless in the description one:

```
$ aptitude search '?and(?name(firmware),?description(wireless))'
p   atmel-firmware             - Firmware for Atmel at76c50x
p   firmware-b43-installer     - firmware installer for the b43
p   firmware-b43legacy-installer  - firmware installer for the b431
```

- We can ask aptitude to explain the reason why a particular package should or cannot be installed on the system or to find a dependency chain leading to a conflict with the target package. If we try to execute this command selecting a package to install, we'll get all related information:

```
$ aptitude why xvile
```

```
i   vim              Suggests    vim-scripts
p   vim-scripts      Suggests    exuberant-ctags
p   exuberant-ctags Suggests    vim | nvi | vile | emacsen
p   vile             Depends     vile-common (= 9.8q-1build1)
p   vile-common      Recommends vile | xvile
```

- We can show all package names that are installed and that are not either *essential* or *automatically installed* by dependencies:

```
$ aptitude search '~i!(~E|~M)' -F '%p'
```

Refer to the following URL for a detailed guide: http://algebraicthunk. net/~dburrows/projects/aptitude/doc/en/ch02s03s05.html#tableSe archTermQuickGuide.

- Then, last but not least, aptitude has a text-based menu interface to manage all packages! In fact, if we execute it without any arguments, it starts in its visual interface, as shown in the following figure:

```
Actions  Undo  Package  Resolver  Search  Options  Views  Help
C-T: Menu  ?: Help  q: Quit  u: Update  g: Preview/Download/Install/Remove Pkgs
aptitude 0.7.4
--- New Packages (23459)
--- Installed Packages (2294)
--- Not Installed Packages (57315)
--- Obsolete and Locally Created Packages (79)
--- Virtual Packages (10950)
--- Tasks (53360)




These packages have been added to Ubuntu since the last time you cleared the
list of "new" packages (choose "Forget new packages" from the Actions menu to
empty this list).

This group contains 23459 packages.
```

The deb files

Another useful command to manage a package is dpkg. This is a very basic command to manage packages and it should be used by experienced users only since we can damage our system if improperly used!

However, we're going to use it when we have to install a package hold into a **deb** file using the following command line:

```
root@bbb:~# dpkg -i <package.deb>
```

Where `<package.deb>` is the package's file.

Managing the kernel messages

As already stated, the serial console is very helpful if we need to set up a system from scratch but it's also very useful if we wish to see kernel messages as soon as they are generated. However, using a silly trick, we can get these kernel messages on a terminal emulator through a normal SSH connection too by executing the `tail` command introduced earlier, as shown here:

```
root@bbb:~# tail -f /var/log/kern.log
```

In fact, the `tail` command executed with the option argument `-f` will open the target file and will display any new line appended to it. This can be very similar to what happens on a **serial console**, but you should consider the following:

1. If the system is not yet fully functional, we have no network devices to use for the **SSH** connection.
2. Using the `tail` command, we may miss important kernel messages, that is, an **Oops message**, due to the fact that the system can become unstable because of some kernel bugs! In this situation, we need to display the errors as soon as they arrive and the `tail` command cannot do it safely.

> An **Oops** is an error, a deviation from correct behavior of the kernel, that produces a **kernel panic** condition that may allow continued operation but with compromised reliability.
> The output produced by these errors is typically called **Oops messages**. They are special kernel debugging messages that may arrive, for instance, during an interrupt handler causing a system crash and, in this special situation, the `tail` command will not work as expected. Only the serial console can help the developer!

On the other hand, if we are connected to the serial console, we can capture these special messages since they are displayed on the serial console as soon as they arrive!

Note that this behavior can be disabled by default, and then the easier way to enable it again is using a special file in the **procfs** filesystem named `/proc/sys/kernel/printk`.

If we try to read its content, we get the following output:

```
root@bbb:~# cat /proc/sys/kernel/printk
4        4        1        7
```

These obscure numbers have a well-defined meaning; in particular, the first one represents the error message level that must be shown on the serial console.

Let me explain this a bit better. Kernel messages are defined in the `linux/include/linux/kern_levels.h` file.

The **procfs** (*proc filesystem*) is one of the most important filesystems we can find in a **Linux**-based system, so you may spend some time to study it. A good starting point can be found at
`http://en.wikipedia.org/wiki/Procfs`.
This file is present in the **Linux's** source tree, and in the next chapter, we'll learn how to obtain it.

The definitions are as follows:

```
#define KERN_EMERG    KERN_SOH "0" /* system is unusable */
#define KERN_ALERT    KERN_SOH "1" /* action must be taken immediat. */
#define KERN_CRIT     KERN_SOH "2" /* critical conditions */
#define KERN_ERR      KERN_SOH "3" /* error conditions */
#define KERN_WARNING  KERN_SOH "4" /* warning conditions */
#define KERN_NOTICE   KERN_SOH "5" /* normal but significant condit. */
#define KERN_INFO     KERN_SOH "6" /* informational */
#define KERN_DEBUG    KERN_SOH "7" /* debug-level messages */
```

Since the first number in the `/proc/sys/kernel/printk` file is 4, it means that the only displayed messages will be KERN_EMERG, KERN_ALERT, KERN_CRIT and KERN_ERR.

Now it's quite simple to guess that in order to enable all kernel messages, we must replace the first number 4 with 8 because there are no kernel messages with a lower priority than 7:

```
root@bbb:~# echo 8 > /proc/sys/kernel/printk
```

Kernel messages' priorities start from 0 (the highest) and go up till 7 (the lowest)!

On the other hand, we can disable all kernel messages using the number 0:

```
root@bbb:~# echo 0 > /proc/sys/kernel/printk
```

Note that the preceding commands just replace the first number; in fact, if we read the file content again, we get the following output:

```
root@bbb:~# cat /proc/sys/kernel/printk
0       4       1       7
```

A quick tour into the bootloader

As stated at the beginning of this chapter, using the serial console, we can get access to the bootloader.

Actually, all the developer kits presented in this book have two bootloaders: a **pre-bootloader** or **Secondary Program Loader** (**SPL**), named MLO for the BeagleBone Black, boot.bin for SAMA5D3 Xplained, and SPL for the Wandboard, which initializes the hardware components, such as the RAM and some mass storage devices, and bootloader named U-Boot for all boards, which is the real bootloader that initializes almost all the peripherals and has support for, among other things, booting over network and a scriptable shell through which basic commands can be given. Now the one million dollar question is: why should a developer be able to manage the bootloader too?

Well the answers are more than one; however, the most important ones are:

- By passing a well-formed command line to the kernel, we can change some functionalities in the running filesystem.
- From the bootloader, we can easily manage a *factory restore* method (it is usually made with a hidden button in a tiny hole on the system's box. By keeping that button pressed while powering up the system, the user can cause the whole system to reset to its *factory defaults*).
- Through the bootloader, we can decide which device to use to perform a boot. For instance, we can force a boot from a microSD or from a USB key.

So now let's see how we can get the U-Boot's prompt using one kit since they're running the same U-Boot version (the following messages are from SAMA5D3 Xplained).

Just after the power up, we will see some interesting messages on the serial console:

```
RomBOOT

U-Boot SPL 2016.03-dirty (Apr 15 2016 - 19:51:18)
Trying to boot from MMC
reading u-boot.img
```

```
U-Boot 2016.03-dirty (Apr 15 2016 - 19:51:18 +0200)

CPU: SAMA5D36
Crystal frequency: 12 MHz
CPU clock : 528 MHz
Master clock : 132 MHz
DRAM: 256 MiB
NAND: 256 MiB
MMC: mci: 0
reading uboot.env

** Unable to read "uboot.env" from mmc0:1 **
Using default environment

In: serial
Out: serial
Err: serial
Net: gmac0
Error: gmac0 address not set.
, macb0
Error: macb0 address not set.

Hit any key to stop autoboot: 1
```

At this time, we have less than 1 second to strike the Enter key to stop the countdown and get the U-Boot prompt shown as follows:

```
=>
```

Well, now we can get a list of the available commands using the `help` command:

```
=> help
?         - alias for 'help'
base      - print or set address offset
bdinfo    - print Board Info structure
boot      - boot default, i.e., run 'bootcmd'
bootd     - boot default, i.e., run 'bootcmd'
...
usb       - USB sub-system
usbboot   - boot from USB device
version   - print monitor, compiler and linker version
```

As you can see, the list is quite long; however, due to spacing reasons, we cannot report or explain all commands, so we'll take a look at the most important ones.

For further information regarding the U-Boot bootloader, you may take a look at the user manual at `http://www.denx.de/wiki/DULG/Manual`.

The `help` command can also be used to get more information about a command:

```
=> help help
help - print command description/usage
Usage:
help
        - print brief description of all commands
help command ...
- print detailed usage of 'command'
```

Note that most of the commands will display their helping message when executed without any arguments. Of course, this behavior is not respected by those commands that execute with no arguments.

The environment

Before starting to take a look at the commands, we should first see one of the most important features of U-Boot: the environment. We can store whatever we need to accomplish a safe system boot in the environment. We can store variables, commands, and even complete scripts in it!

To check the environment content, we can use the `print` command:

```
=> print
arch=arm
baudrate=115200
board=sama5d3_xplained
board_name=sama5d3_xplained
bootargs=console=ttyS0,115200 root=/dev/mmcblk0p2 ro rootwait
bootcmd=if test ! -n ${dtb_name}; then setenv dtb_name at91-${board_na
me}.dtb; fi; fatload mmc 0:1 0x21000000 /dtbs/${dtb_name}; fatload mmc
 0:1 0x22000000 zImage; bootz 0x22000000 - 0x21000000
bootdelay=1
cpu=armv7
ethact=gmac0
soc=at91
vendor=atmel
Environment size: 412/16380 bytes
```

If we need to inspect a specific variable, we can use the `print` command:

```
=> print baudrate
baudrate=115200
```

We can also inspect a complete script using the print command again:

```
=> print bootcmd
bootcmd=if test ! -n ${dtb_name}; then setenv dtb_name at91-${board_na
me}.dtb; fi; fatload mmc 0:1 0x21000000 /dtbs/${dtb_name}; fatload mmc
 0:1 0x22000000 zImage; bootz 0x22000000 - 0x21000000
```

The `bootcmd` command is the default boot command that is executed each time the system starts.

The command output is quite cryptic due the fact that the newline (\n) characters are missing (although U-Boot doesn't need them to correctly interpret a script); however, to make the output more readable, the preceding output has been rewritten here with the necessary newline characters:

```
if test ! -n ${dtb_name}; then
    setenv dtb_name at91-${board_name}.dtb;
fi;
fatload mmc 0:1 0x21000000 /dtbs/${dtb_name};
fatload mmc 0:1 0x22000000 zImage;
bootz 0x22000000 - 0x21000000
```

In this case, we cannot properly talk about man pages, but if we use the `help` command, we can take a kind of them.

Note that the `print` command is just a short form of the real command `printenv`.

To write/modify an environment variable, we can use the `setenv` command:

```
=> setenv myvar 12345
=> print myvar
myvar=12345
```

We can read the variable content by prefixing its name with the $ character:

```
=> echo "myvar is set to: $myvar"
myvar is set to: 12345
```

In a similar manner, to write a script, we can use this:

```
=> setenv myscript 'while sleep 1 ; do echo "1 second is passed away..
." ; done'
```

Note that we used the two ' characters to delimitate the script commands! This is to prevent U-Boot from doing some variable replacement before storing the script (it's something similar to what we do when we use the Bash shell's variable substitution).

Again, over here, we did not add the newlines; however, this time, the script is quite simple and readable. In fact, with the newline characters, the output should appear as follows:

```
while sleep 1 ; do
    echo "1 second is passed away..." ;
done
```

In the end, we can run a by using the `run` command, as follows:

```
=> run myscript
1 second is passed away...
1 second is passed away...
1 second is passed away...
...
```

We can stop the script by hitting *Ctr l+C*.
The environment is reset each time the system starts, but it can be altered by modifying the environment file in the microSD (refer to the next section).

In case we made some errors, don't panic! We can edit the variable with this command:

```
=> env edit myscript
edit: while sleep 1 ; do echo "1 second is passed away..." ; done
```

Now we can do all the required modifications to the script in an easy manner.

Managing the storage devices

The main goal of a bootloader is to load the kernel into the memory and then execute it; to do that, we must be able to get access to all the storage devices of the board where the kernel can be located. Our boards have several storage devices; however, in this book, we'll see only two of them: **MMC** (or **eMMC**) and **NAND flash**.

MMC

To show **MMC** (**Multi Media Card**) management in U-Boot, we are going to use the BeagleBone Black since it has both an **eMMC** and a microSD port on board. As already stated in the first chapter, we're able to choose our booting device simply using the user button, so it's very important to discover how we can manage these devices, so let's power on our BeagleBone Black and then stop the bootloader by pressing the spacebar within two seconds, as shown here:

```
U-Boot SPL 2016.03-dirty (Apr 15 2016 - 13:44:25)
Trying to boot from MMC
bad magic
U-Boot 2016.03-dirty (Apr 15 2016 - 13:44:25 +0200)
        Watchdog enabled
I2C:    ready
DRAM:   512 MiB
Reset Source: Global warm SW reset has occurred.
Reset Source: Power-on reset has occurred.
MMC:    OMAP SD/MMC: 0, OMAP SD/MMC: 1
Using default environment
Net:    <ethaddr> not set. Validating first E-fuse MAC
cpsw, usb_ether
Press SPACE to abort autoboot in 2 seconds
=>
```

Now, as already done earlier with SAMA5D3 Xplained, we can use the `help` command to see which are the MMC-related commands. We discover that the MMC support is implemented with the `mmcinfo` and `mmc` commands. The former can be used to get some useful information about the microSD/MMC present on the selected MMC slot, while the latter is used to effectively manage the microSD.

Let's look at some examples.

We know that our BeagleBone Black has an onboard eMMC on MMC slot 1, so to get some information about that device, we should first select the MMC slot to be examined using the following command:

```
=> mmc dev 1
switch to partitions #0, OK
mmc1(part 0) is current device
```

Then, we can ask for the MMC device information using the `mmcinfo` command:

```
=> mmcinfo
Device: OMAP SD/MMC
Manufacturer ID: 70
OEM: 100
Name: MMC04
Tran Speed: 52000000
Rd Block Len: 512
MMC version 4.5
High Capacity: Yes
Capacity: 3.6 GiB
Bus Width: 4-bit
Erase Group Size: 512 KiB
HC WP Group Size: 4 MiB
User Capacity: 3.6 GiB
Boot Capacity: 2 MiB ENH
RPMB Capacity: 128 KiB ENH
```

In the same manner, we can examine the alternate booting microSD we built in Chapter 1, *Installing the Developing System*, and that we used to boot the system. Here is the output that appears on my system:

```
=> mmc dev 0
switch to partitions #0, OK
mmc0 is current device
=> mmcinfo
Device: OMAP SD/MMC
Manufacturer ID: 41
OEM: 3432
Name: SD4GB
Tran Speed: 50000000
Rd Block Len: 512
SD version 3.0
High Capacity: Yes
Capacity: 3.7 GiB
Bus Width: 4-bit
Erase Group Size: 512 Bytes
```

Now we can examine the microSD partition table by using the following command:

```
=> mmc part
Partition Map for MMC device 0  --    Partition Type: DOS
  Part    Start Sector    Num Sectors    UUID          Type
    1     2048            7772160        5697a348-01   83 Boot
```

We get only one partition where our Debian filesystem is located.

Let's examine the / (root) directory using another command that's useful in listing the content of a EXT4 filesystem, which is the command etx4ls, as shown here:

```
=> ext4ls mmc 0:1
<DIR>         4096 .
<DIR>         4096 ..
<DIR>        16384 lost+found
<DIR>         4096 opt
<DIR>         4096 boot
<DIR>         4096 lib
<DIR>         4096 sys
<DIR>         4096 home
<DIR>         4096 mnt
<DIR>         4096 dev
. . .
<DIR>         4096 sbin
<DIR>         4096 proc
<DIR>         4096 tmp
```

We found the root directory of a Debian OS, and we can use the following command to read the contents of the /boot directory:

```
=> ext4ls mmc 0:1 /boot
<DIR>         4096 .
<DIR>         4096 ..
               726 uEnv.txt
           7408440 vmlinuz-4.4.7-bone9
<DIR>         4096 dtbs
<DIR>         4096 uboot
           9089599 initrd.img-4.4.7-bone9
```

Now, as an example, in order to import the uEnv.txt file content, we can use the load command:

```
=> load mmc 0:1 $loadaddr /boot/uEnv.txt
726 bytes read in 28 ms (24.4 KiB/s)
```

 Note that the value for the loadaddr variable is usually defined in the default environment (that is, the default built in the U-Boot image at the compilation stage) or using the uEnv.txt configuration file.

The command loads a file from the microSD into the RAM, and then we can parse it and store the data into the environment using the env command:

```
=> env import -t $loadaddr $filesize
```

In contrast with the earlier `loadaddr` variable, the `filesize` variable is dynamically set after each file manipulation command's execution, for instance, the just used `load` command.

To save a variable/command in the environment (in a way that the new value is reloaded at the next boot), we can use U-Boot itself, but the procedure is quite complex and, in my humble opinion, the quickest and simplest way to do it is by just putting the microSD on a host PC and then changing the file on it!

In any case, we can take a look at the read data using the md command, as follows:

```
=> md $loadaddr
82000000:  64616f6c  72646461  3878303d  30303032   loadaddr=0x82000
82000010:  0a303030  61746466  3d726464  38387830   000.fdtaddr=0x88
82000020:  30303030  720a3030  64646164  78303d72   000000.rdaddr=0x
82000030:  38303838  30303030  6e690a0a  64727269   88080000..initrd
82000040:  6769685f  78303d68  66666666  66666666   _high=0xffffffff
82000050:  7464660a  6769685f  78303d68  66666666   .fdt_high=0xffff
82000060:  66666666  636d6d0a  746f6f72  65642f3d   ffff.mmcroot=/de
82000070:  6d6d2f76  6b6c6263  0a317030  616f6c0a   v/mmcblk0p1..loa
82000080:  6d697864  3d656761  64616f6c  636d6d20   dximage=load mmc
82000090:  313a3020  6c7b2420  6164616f  7d726464    0:1 ${loadaddr}
820000a0:  6f622f20  762f746f  6e696c6d  242d7a75   /boot/vmlinuz-$
820000b0:  616e757b  725f656d  6f6c0a7d  66786461   {uname_r}.loadxf
820000c0:  6c3d7464  2064616f  20636d6d  20313a30   dt=load mmc 0:1
820000d0:  64667b24  64646174  2f207d72  746f6f62   ${fdtaddr} /boot
820000e0:  6274642f  7b242f73  6d616e75  7d725f65   /dtbs/${uname_r}
820000f0:  667b242f  69667464  0a7d656c  64616f6c   /${fdtfile}.load
```

In this manner, we do a memory dump at the address specified by the `loadaddr` variable, where we just loaded the `/boot/uEnv.txt` file content.

Managing the flash

The flash memories are very useful when we don't need relatively small storage devices and we want to keep the cost of a board very low.

In the past, they represented the only (and valid) solution for reliable mass memory devices for embedded systems due to the fact that they can work in very hostile environments (temperatures under 0° C or above 80° C and dusty air) and they have no moving parts that dramatically increase the life cycle of the system.

Nowadays, they are almost replaced by eMMC memories, but they are still present on really compact and low-power systems. In this book, the only boards where we can find them are SAMA5D3 Xplained, so let's switch to this board again.

In reality, eMMC or MMC (which is not a soldered version of an eMMC) is flash memory, but it takes a specific name because there is a flash controller inside the chip that actually manages the internal flash memory. So, using these devices, we can unload our embedded kits' CPUs of the duty to manage the flash.

The flash memory in our board is a NAND flash, which is a technology that uses floating gate transistors (just like the NOR flash) but is connected in a way that resembles a NAND gate.

For further information on these devices, a good starting point can be found at https://en.wikipedia.org/wiki/Flash_memory#NAND_flash.

To get some information on mounted chips, we can use the `nand info` command, as follows:

```
=> nand info
Device 0: nand0, sector size 128 KiB
  Page size       2048 b
  OOB size          64 b
  Erase size    131072 b
 ↖subpagesize     2048 b
  options       0x    200
  bbt options 0x   8000
```

In this case, we have just one NAND device, so we don't need to use the `nand device` command to select one, as we did earlier regarding the MMC devices on our BeagleBone Black.

The check for the bad blocks (that is, those parts of the chip that are broken), we can use the following command:

```
=> nand bad
Device 0 bad blocks:
   00c80000
   00ca0000
```

These blocks will never be used to store our data.

Now the last three useful commands to manage the flash content are nand erase, nand read, and nand write. The first command is split into two subcommands: nand erase.part, which erases an entire MTD partition, and nand erase.chip, which erases the entire chip.

> As you know for sure, a flash device needs the erase command because before writing a block, we must erase it! Refer to https://en.wikipedia.org/wiki/Flash_memory#Limitations for an explanation of the problem.

Then, the nand.read and nand.write commands are used as they are expected, that is, to read or write a flash block. At the moment, we are not going to add examples for these actions since we still have no valid data to store in the flash; however, we're going to show how these commands can be used in the *Managing a MTD device* section in Chapter 5, *Setting up an Embedded OS*.

Also note that in the NAND flash, we can store the current environment in a similar manner as earlier with the MMC/eMMC using the saveenv command; however, in order to work, this command must be correctly configured inside the U-Boot code by the developer.

> These topics are not covered in this book due to space issues and because they are almost accomplished by the board manufacturer, so we can consider them *already-fixed-up*. However, you can take a look at the configuration that defines CONFIG_ENV_OFFSET, CONFIG_ENV_SIZE and friends in U-Boot's repository for further information.

GPIO management

The **General Purpose Input Output** (**GPIO**) signals are input output pins with no special purpose defined; when a developer needs one of them working as an input pin or as an output pin (or another function), they can easily reconfigure the CPU in order to accommodate their needs (GPIOs will be widely presented in Chapter 6, *General Purposes Input Output signals – GPIO*).

Managing GPIO from early booting stages can be useful in selecting a specific mode of functioning: for instance, in a system that normally boots from the NAND flash, we can decide to completely erase it rewrite its contents from a file read by the MMC if a GPIO is set; otherwise, we do a normal boot.

The command to manage GPIO is `gpio`, and to try usage of this command, we can use the BeagleBone Black board where we can use this command to control the user LEDs. As for the other GPIO lines of the BeagleBone Black, they are mapped as follows:

Name	Label	GPIO #
USR0	D2	53
USR1	D3	54
USR2	D4	55
USR3	D5	56

So we can easily deduce that in order to toggle LED `USR0`, we can use the following commands:

```
=> gpio toggle 53
gpio: pin 53 (gpio 53) value is 1
=> gpio toggle 53
gpio: pin 53 (gpio 53) value is 0
```

Of course, we can turn the LED on and off simply using the `set` and `clear` options, respectively, while the `input` option can be used to read the input status of the related GPIO line.

You can take a look at what these LEDs are for at: `http://beagleboard.org/getting-started`.

Accessing an I2C device

Another useful device class to get access to in early booting stages is I^2C devices; in fact, these devices are commonly used to expand the CPU's peripheral set and they can be used for a large variety of purposes that, under some circumstances, must be read or set up during the boot (GPIO will be widely presented in Chapter 9, *Inter-Integrated Circuit – I2C*).

As for GPIO, I^2C devices are completely managed by the i2c command, and to test this command, we have to continue using the BeagleBone Black since it is the only one that has some onboard I^2C devices. The list of this devices can be obtained by some simple steps; first of all, let's display a list of all available I^2C buses:

```
=> i2c bus
Bus 0:   omap24_0
Bus 1:   omap24_1
Bus 2:   omap24_2
```

By taking a look at the board's schematics, we can discover that the bus where these devices are connected to is omap24_0, so let's set it as the current bus using the following command:

```
=> i2c dev 0
Setting bus to 0
```

Now we can ask the system to probe all connected devices for us with the following command:

```
=> i2c probe
Valid chip addresses: 24 34 50
```

Great! We found three devices; now we can try to read some data from them; in particular, we can try to read the onboard **EEPROM** content using the i2c md command at address 50 (which is the hexadecimal EEPROM's address):

```
=> i2c md 0x50 0x0.2 0x20
0000: aa 55 33 ee 41 33 33 35 42 4e 4c 54 30 30 43 30    .U3.A335BNLT00C0
0010: 33 32 31 34 42 42 42 4b 30 37 31 36 ff ff ff ff    3214BBBK0716....
```

With the preceding command, we asked to dump data from the device at address `0x50` starting from address `0x0` (expressed as a word thanks to the `.2` specifier) displaying `0x20` bytes as the output.

In this output, we can recognize the header (bytes `0xaa 0x55 0x33 0xee`) and then the board version.

> More information on the BeagleBone Black's EEPROM contents can be taken from the BeagleBone Black's user manual.

Loading files from the network

Another useful U-Boot feature is the ability to load a file from a network connection. This feature used during the developing stages helps the developer avoid having to continuously plug and unplug the microSD card from the system; in fact, as we saw in the first chapter, the system needs the bootloaders and kernel images to start up and, in case of errors during the development of these components, we will need to replace them frequently till they are OK. Well, supposing that at least the networking function works in our U-Boot release, we can use it to load a new image in the system memory.

Let's suppose that our kernel image is not functioning as well as we need it to be; we can set up U-Boot in order to load the kernel image from the network and then boot it to do all the required tests.

The command used to do this action is `tftp`. This command uses the **Trivial File Transfer Protocol** (TFTP) protocol to download a file from a remote server.

> You may get more information on the TFTP protocol
> at: `https://it.wikipedia.org/wiki/Trivial_File_Transfer_Protocol`.

The remote server, of course, is our host PC where we have to install a proper package with the following command:

```
$ sudo aptitude install tftpd
```

It may happen that during the installation, we get the following message:
Note: xinetd currently is not fully supported by update-inetd.
Please consult /usr/share/doc/xinetd/README.De bian and itox(8).

In this case, we have to add a file named tftp into the /etc/xinetd.d directory by hand. The file should hold the following code:

```
# default: yes
# description: The tftp server serves files using
#       the Trivial File Transfer
#       Protocol. The tftp protocol is often used to
#       boot diskless workstations, download
#       configuration files to network-aware
#       printers, and to start the installation
#       process for some operating systems.
service tftp
{
        disable     = no
        socket_type = dgram
        protocol    = udp
        wait        = yes
        user        = root
        server      = /usr/sbin/in.tftpd
        server_args = -s /srv/tftpboot
}
```

Then, we have to create the /srv/tftpboot directory, as follows:
```
$ sudo mkdir /srv/tftpboot
```
Then, restart the xinetd daemon with the usual command, as follows:
```
$ sudo /etc/init.d/xinetd restart
[ ok ] Restarting xinetd (via systemctl): xinetd.se
rvice.
```

When the installation is finished, we should have a new process listening on UDP port 69:

```
$ netstat -lnp | grep ':\<69\>'
(Not all processes could be identified, non-owned process info
 will not be shown, you would have to be root to see it all.)
udp        0        0 0.0.0.0:69              0.0.0.0:*
```

Also, the default `tftpd` root directory should be `/srv/tftpboot`, which is obviously empty:

```
$ ls -l /srv/tftpboot/
total 0
```

OK; let's copy our kernel image as we did in *Debian 8 (jessie) for Wandboard* section in `Chapter 1`, *Installing the Developing System*:

```
$ sudo cp deploy/4.4.7-armv7-x6.zImage /srv/tftpboot/vmlinuz-4.4.7-arm
v7-x6
```

Note that the `sudo` usage in the preceding command may not be needed in every system. I used it just because my host PC didn't properly install the daemon, as reported in earlier tip section.

Now in our Wandboard, we have to set up the `ipaddr` environment variable to be able to ping our host PC first. As an example, my host PC has the following network configuration:

```
$ ifconfig enp0s3
enp0s3    Link encap:Ethernet  HWaddr 08:00:27:22:d2:ed
          inet addr:192.168.32.43  Bcast:192.168.32.255  Mask:255.255.
255.0
          inet6 addr: fe80::a00:27ff:fe22:d2ed/64 Scope:Link
          UP BROADCAST RUNNING MULTICAST  MTU:1500  Metric:1
          RX packets:986 errors:0 dropped:0 overruns:0 frame:0
          TX packets:687 errors:0 dropped:0 overruns:0 carrier:0
          collisions:0 txqueuelen:1000
          RX bytes:226853 (226.8 KB)  TX bytes:100360 (100.3 KB)
```

Note that on your system, both the Ethernet card name and IP address settings may vary, so you have to change the settings in order to fit your LAN configuration.

Also, my **DHCP** server leaves the IP addresses from `192.168.32.10` to `192.168.32.40` available for my embedded boards, so we can do the following setting in Wandboard:

```
=> setenv ipaddr 192.168.32.25
```

Now, if everything works well, we should be able to ping my host PC:

```
=> ping 192.168.32.43
Using FEC device
host 192.168.32.43 is alive
```

Great! At this point, we can try to load a file from the host PC, so we have to assign the TFTP server's IP address to the `serverip` variable, as follows:

```
=> setenv serverip 192.168.32.43
```

Then, we can load our kernel image using the following command:

```
=> tftpboot ${loadaddr} vmlinuz-4.4.7-armv7-x6
Using FEC device
TFTP from server 192.168.32.43; our IP address is 192.168.32.25
Filename 'vmlinuz-4.4.7-armv7-x6'.
Load address: 0x12000000
Loading: #################################################################
         #################################################################
         . . .
         ###########################
         688.5 KiB/s
done
Bytes transferred = 5802912 (588ba0 hex)
```

Perfect, we did it! Now you can use the just download kernel image to continue your developing.

At the moment, this mode of operation is not explained here, but it will be explained in detail in the next chapter.

Before ending this chapter, let we address the fact that the Wandboard used only one Ethernet port, so it's quite obvious that whatever settings we do in U-Boot are referred to that device, but what happens if we have more that one device? For example, our SAMA5D3 Xplained has two Ethernet ports; how can we manage this setup if we wish to use the `tftp` command described earlier?

To answer this question, we have to switch the developer kit and power up SAMA5D3 Xplained. After the boot, we have to stop U-Boot and then we have to display the environment:

```
=> print
arch=arm
baudrate=115200
board=sama5d3_xplained
board_name=sama5d3_xplained
bootargs=console=ttyS0,115200 root=/dev/mmcblk0p2 ro rootwait
bootcmd=if test ! -n ${dtb_name}; then setenv dtb_name at91-${board_na
me}.dtb; fi; fatload mmc 0:1 0x21000000 /dtbs/${dtb_name}; fatload mmc
```

```
   0:1 0x22000000 zImage; bootz 0x22000000 - 0x21000000
bootdelay=1
cpu=armv7
ethact=gmac0
soc=at91
vendor=atmel

Environment size: 412/16380 bytes
```

Looking at the defined variables, we notice that one is named `ethact`; this is the variable that specifies the currently used Ethernet port. In the preceding output, we read that the system is set to `gmac0`, which is the gigabit Ethernet port (the port is labeled `ETH0/GETH` on the board).

So, if we repeat the preceding setup, we should be able to ping our host PC, as did earlier:

```
=> setenv ipaddr 192.168.32.25
=> ping 192.168.32.43
gmac0: PHY present at 7
gmac0: Starting autonegotiation...
gmac0: Autonegotiation complete
gmac0: link up, 100Mbps full-duplex (lpa: 0x45e1)
host 192.168.32.43 is alive
```

If we get the following error, it's because the Ethernet port has no default MAC address:

```
*** ERROR: `ethaddr' not set
ping failed; host 192.168.32.43 is not alive
```

In this case we, have to set a random one ourselves with the following command:

```
=> setenv ethaddr 3e:36:65:ba:6f:be
```

Then, we can repeat the `ping` command.

Now we can repeat the `ping` command through the other Ethernet port (the one labeled `ETH1` on the board) by changing the `ethact` variable, as follows:

```
=> setenv ethact macb0
```

The name we have to use is usually specified in the developer kit's documentation.

Now we can repeat the `ping` command:

```
=> ping 192.168.32.43
```

```
macb0: PHY present at 0
macb0: Starting autonegotiation...
macb0: Autonegotiation complete
macb0: link up, 100Mbps full-duplex (lpa: 0x45e1)
host 192.168.32.43 is alive
```

If we got an error regarding the missing definition of the `ethaddr` variable, we should get the following one, which is related to the `eth1addr` variable:

*** ERROR: `eth1addr' not set
ping failed; host 192.168.32.43 is not alive

This is in case we have to act in the same manner as earlier.

The last note is about the fact that usually, U-Boot will automatically switch the active port in case the autonegotiation fails. If our system has `ethact` set as `gmac0` but the cable is plugged into the `ETH1` port, we get the following output:

```
=> ping 192.168.32.25
gmac0: PHY present at 7
gmac0: Starting autonegotiation...
gmac0: Autonegotiation timed out (status=0x7949)
gmac0: link down (status: 0x7949)
macb0: PHY present at 0
macb0: Starting autonegotiation...
macb0: Autonegotiation complete
macb0: link up, 100Mbps full-duplex (lpa: 0x45e1)
host 192.168.32.43 is alive
```

We may experience some troubles regarding the networking support with the U-Boot version we're using in this book with SAMA5D3 Xplained. This is because this U-Boot release is not well aligned with the official one from Atmel. If so, don't worry, we can still use the official U-Boot release at: `http://www.at91.com/linux4sam/bin/view/Linux4SAM/Sama5d3Xplai nedMainPage#Build_U_Boot_from_sources`. That will work for sure!

The kernel command line

Before closing our tour of the bootloader, we should take a look at the way U-Boot uses to pass a command line to the kernel. This data is very important because it can be used to configure the kernel and pass some instruction to the user's programs on the root filesystem.

These arguments are stored in the `bootargs` variable and its setting depends on the board we are using. For example, if power on our Wandboard and, as done earlier, we stop its **bootloader**, as shown earlier, wecan see thatthis variable is not set at all:

```
=> print bootargs
## Error: "bootargs" not defined
```

This is because its content is set up by the booting scripts that are not executed if we stop the boot. On our system, by carefully reading the U-Boot environment, we can discover that sooner or later, the `run mmcargs` command is called.

 This is because U-Boot automatically executes the script held in the `bootcmd` variable.

This command is written as follows:

```
=> print mmcargs
mmcargs=setenv bootargs console=${console} ${optargs} root=${mmcroot}
rootfstype=${mmcrootfstype} ${cmdline}
```

This is where the **kernel command line** is built. As a useful exercise, you can now try to understand which are the values used for all the earlier variables; the only thing we wish to add is that we can add our custom settings using the `optargs` variable.

For instance, if we wish to set the `loglevel` kernel (that is the lower kernel message priority showed on the serial console, as shown in the *Managing the kernel messages* section), we can set `optargs` to this:

```
=> setenv optargs 'loglevel=8'
```

And then we ask to continue the boot:

```
=> boot
```

Once the system has been restarted, we can verify the new setting by looking into the booting messages of the kernel; we should see a line as shown here:

```
Kernel command line: console=ttymxc0,115200 loglevel=8 root=/dev/mmcbl
k0p1 ro rootfstype=ext4 rootwait
```

This can be checked by looking at the `procfs` file, which holds a copy of the kernel command line, that is, the `/proc/cmdline` file using the following command:

```
root@wb:~# cat /proc/cmdline
console=ttymxc0,115200 loglevel=8 root=/dev/mmcblk0p1 ro rootfstype=ext4 rootwait
```

> More information regarding the kernel command line and its parameters can be found in the kernel tree in the `Documentation/kernel-parameters.txt` file or online at: `https://www.kernel.org/doc/Documentation/admin-guide/kernel-parameters.txt`.

Summary

In this chapter, we took a first look at our newly embedded developer kits. We saw several useful command-line tools that will be used throughout this book, and then we took a long tour into the bootloader, discovering several useful commands to manage some hardware and/or onboard storage devices.

In the next chapter, we will look more closely look into the kernel, its mechanisms, and its recompilation with a deep look into the C compiler usage using both its native form as well as the cross-compiler one.

3
C Compiler, Device Drivers, and Useful Developing Techniques

In the previous chapter, we saw how to use the serial console to manage our developer kits and how it can be used to manage the bootloader too. Also, we introduced some device drivers to communicate with the host through a USB cable, and we installed a Debian OS, which is a collection of files in a filesystem, the main and the first filesystem that our embedded systems mount and boot.

In this chapter, we will focus our attention on the **C compiler** (with its counterpart, the **cross-compiler**). You will also learn when to use the native or cross-compilation and the differences between them.

Then, we'll see some kernel stuff used later in this book (configuration, recompilation, and the device tree). We'll also look a bit deeper at the **device drivers**, how they can be compiled, and how they can be put into a **kernel module** (that is kernel code that can be loaded at runtime). This is because starting from the next chapter, we'll present different kinds of computer peripherals, and for each of them, we'll try to explain how the corresponding device driver works, starting from the compilation stage through the configuration until the final usage. As an example, we'll try to implement a simple driver in order to give you some interesting points of view and some simple advice about kernel programming (which is not covered in this book!).

We will present the root filesystem's internals and spend some words about a particular root filesystem that can be very useful during the early developing stages – the network filesystem. As the final step, we'll propose the usage of an emulator in order to execute a complete target machine's Debian distribution on a host PC.

This chapter still is part of the introduction to this book. Experienced developers who already know these topics well may skip this chapter, but my suggestion is to read the chapter anyway in order to discover which developing tools will be used in the book and, maybe, some new technique to manage your programs.

The C compiler

The C compiler is a program that translates the C language into a binary format that the CPU can understand and execute. This is the basic way (and the most powerful one) to develop programs into a GNU/Linux system.

Despite this fact, most developers prefer using high-level languages other than C due the fact the C language has no garbage collection, no object-oriented programming and other issues, giving up part of the execution speed that a C program offers. However, if we have to recompile the kernel (the Linux kernel is written in C-plus few assemblers) to develop a device driver or to write high-performance applications, then the C language is a *must-have*.

As we already saw in the preceding chapters, we can have a compiler and a cross-compiler, and until now, we've already used the cross-compiler several times to recompile the kernel and the bootloaders. However, we can decide to use a native compiler too. In fact, using native compilation may be easier but, in most cases, very time consuming. That's why, it's really important to know the pros and cons.

Programs for embedded systems are traditionally written and compiled using a cross-compiler for that architecture on a host PC. In other words, we use a compiler that can generate code for a foreign machine architecture, which means a different CPU instruction set from the compiler host's one.

Native and foreign machine architecture

The developer kits shown in this book are ARM machines, while (most probably) our host machine is an **x86** (that is, a normal PC). So, if we try to compile a C program on our host machine, the generated code cannot be used on an ARM machine and vice versa.

Let's verify it! Here's the classic *Hello World* program:

```
#include <stdio.h>

int main()
{
    printf("Hello World\n");

    return 0;
}
```

Now, we will compile it on my host machine using the following command:

```
$ make CFLAGS="-Wall -O2" helloworld
cc -Wall -O2     helloworld.c    -o helloworld
```

 You should notice here that we've used the `make` command instead of the usual `cc` command. This is a perfectly equivalent way to execute the compiler due the fact that even without a Makefile, the `make` command already knows how to compile a C program.

We can verify that this file is for the x86 (that is the PC) platform using the `file` command:

```
$ file helloworld
helloworld: ELF 64-bit LSB  executable, x86-64, version 1 (SYSV), dyna
mically linked (uses shared libs), for GNU/Linux 2.6.24, BuildID[sha1]
=0f0db5e65e1cd09957ad06a7c1b7771d949dfc84, not stripped
```

 Note that the output may vary according to your host machine platform.

Now, we can just copy the program into one developer kit (for instance, the the BeagleBone Black) and try to execute it:

```
root@bbb:~# ./helloworld
-bash: ./helloworld: cannot execute binary file
```

As we expected, the system refuses to execute the code generated for a different architecture!

On the other hand, if we use a cross-compiler for this specific CPU architecture, the program will run as a charm! Let's verify this by recompiling the code, but paying attention to specify that we wish to use the cross-compiler instead. So, delete the previously generated x86 executable file (just in case) using the `rm helloworld` command and then recompile it using the cross-compiler:

```
$ make CC=arm-linux-gnueabihf-gcc CFLAGS="-Wall -O2" helloworld
arm-linux-gnueabihf-gcc -Wall -O2    helloworld.c   -o helloworld
```

Note that the cross-compiler's filename has a special meaning: the form is `<architecture>-<platform>-<binary-format>-<tool-name>`. So, the filename `arm-linux-gnueabihf-gcc` means ARM architecture, Linux platform, **GNU EABI Hard-Float (gnueabihf)** binary format, and **GNU C Compiler (gcc)** tool.

Now, we will use the `file` command again to see whether the code is indeed generated for the ARM architecture:

```
$ file helloworld
helloworld: ELF 32-bit LSB  executable, ARM, EABI5 version 1 (SYSV), d
ynamically linked (uses shared libs), for GNU/Linux 2.6.32, BuildID[sh
a1]=31251570b8a17803b0e0db01fb394a6394de8d2d, not stripped
```

If we transfer the file as before on the BeagleBone Black and try to execute it, we will get the following lines of code:

```
root@bbb:~# ./helloworld
Hello World!
```

Therefore, we will see that the cross-compiler ensures that the generated code is compatible with the architecture we are executing it on.

In reality, in order to have a perfectly functional binary image, we have to make sure that the library versions, header files (also the headers related to the kernel), and cross-compiler options match the target exactly or, at least, they are compatible. In fact, we cannot execute cross-compiled code against the `glibc` on a system having, for example, `musl libc` (or it can run in an unpredictable manner).

In this case, we have perfectly compatible libraries and compilers, but in general, the embedded developer should perfectly know what they are doing. A common trick to avoid compatibility problems is to use static compilation, but in this case, we get huge binary files.

Now, the question is, when should we use the compiler and when should we use the cross-compiler?

We should compile on an embedded system for the following reasons:

- There would be no compatibility issues as all the target libraries will be available. In cross-compilation, it becomes difficult when we need all the libraries (if the project uses any) in the ARM format on the host PC. So, we not only have to cross-compile the program but also its dependencies. If the same version dependencies are not installed on the embedded system's `rootfs`, then good luck with troubleshooting!
- It's easy and quick.

We should cross-compile for the following reasons:

- We are working on a large codebase, and we don't want to waste too much time compiling the program on the target, which may take from several minutes to several hours (or it may even be impossible). This reason might be strong enough to overpower the other reasons in favor of compiling on the embedded system itself.
- PCs nowadays have multiple cores, so the compiler can process more files simultaneously.
- We are building a full Linux system from scratch.

In any case, here, I will show you an example of both native compilation and cross-compilation of a software package so that you can understand the differences between them.

Compiling a C program

As the first step, let's see how we can compile a C program. To keep it simple, we'll start compiling a user-space program in the upcoming sections, and we will compile some kernel space code.

Knowing how to compile a C program can be useful because it may happen that a specific tool (most probably) written in C is missing in our distribution or it's present, but with an outdated version. In both cases, we need to recompile it!

To show the differences between a native compilation and a cross-compilation, we will explain both methods. However, a word of caution for you here is that this guide is not exhaustive at all! In fact, the cross-compilation steps may vary according to the software packages we will cross-compile.

The package we will use is the **PicoC** interpreter. Each real programmer (TM) knows the C compiler, which is normally used to translate a C program into the machine language, but (maybe) not all of them know that a C interpreter exists too!

Actually, there are many C interpreters, but we focus our attention on **PicoC** due its simplicity in cross-compiling it.

As we already know, an interpreter is a program that converts the source code into executable code on the fly and does not need to parse the complete file and generate code at once.

This is quite useful when we need a flexible way to write brief programs to resolve easy tasks. In fact, to fix bugs in the code and/or change the program behavior, we simply have to change the program source and then re-execute it without any compilation at all. We just need an editor to change our code!

For instance, if we wish to read some bytes from a file, we can do this using a standard C program, but for this easy task, we can write a script for an interpreter too. The choice of the interpreter is up to the developer, and since we are C programmers, the choice is quite obvious. That's why we have decided to use PicoC.

The PicoC tool is quite far from being able to interpret all C programs! In fact, this tool implements a fraction of the features of a standard C compiler. However, it can be used for several common and easy tasks. Consider PicoC as an education tool and avoid using it in a production environment!

The native compilation

Well, as the first step, we need to download the PicoC source code from its repository at: `git://github.com/zsaleeba/picoc.git` into our embedded system (the repository is browseable at: `https://github.com/zsaleeba/picoc`). This time, we decided to use the BeagleBone Black and the command is as follows:

```
root@bbb:~# git clone git://github.com/zsaleeba/picoc.git
```

A screenshot of the preceding repository can be found in the `chapter_03/picoc/picoc-git.tgz` file of the book's example code repository.

When finished, we can start compiling the PicoC source code using the following lines of code:

```
root@bbb:~# cd picoc/
root@bbb:~/picoc# make
```

If we get the following error, during the compilation we can safely ignore it:
```
/bin/sh: 1: svnversion: not found
```

However, during the compilation we get the following lines of code:

```
platform/platform_unix.c:5:31: fatal error: readline/readline.h: No su
ch file or directory
#include <readline/readline.h>
                              ^
compilation terminated.
<builtin>: recipe for target 'platform/platform_unix.o' failed
make: *** [platform/platform_unix.o] Error 1
```

Bad news is that we have got an error! This is because the **readline** library is missing. Hence, we need to install it to keep this going. Recalling what we said in *Searching a software package* section in Chapter 2, *Managing the System Console*, in order to discover which package's name holds a specific tool, we can use the following command to discover the package that holds the readline library:

```
root@bbb:~# apt-cache search readline
```

The command output is quite long, but if we carefully look at it, we can see the following lines:

```
libreadline5 - GNU readline and history libraries, run-time libraries
libreadline5-dbg - GNU readline and history libraries, debugging libra
ries
libreadline-dev - GNU readline and history libraries, development file
s
libreadline6 - GNU readline and history libraries, run-time libraries
libreadline6-dbg - GNU readline and history libraries, debugging libra
ries
libreadline6-dev - GNU readline and history libraries, development fil
es
```

This is exactly what we need to know! The required package is named **libreadline-dev**.

> In the Debian distribution, all libraries' packages are prefixed by the `lib` string, while the `-dev` postfix is used to mark the development version of a library package. Note also that we choose the libreadline-dev package, intentionally leaving the system to choose to install version 5 or 6 of the library.
>
> The development version of a library package holds all the needed files that allow the developer to compile their software to the library itself and/or some documentation about the library functions.
>
> For instance, into the development version of the **readline** library package (that is, into the libreadline6-dev package), we can find the header and the object files needed by the compiler. We can see these files using the following command:
>
> ```
> root@bbb:~# dpkg -L libreadline6-dev | \
>                     egrep '\.(so|h)'
> /usr/include/readline/rltypedefs.h
> /usr/include/readline/readline.h
> /usr/include/readline/history.h
> /usr/include/readline/keymaps.h
> /usr/include/readline/rlconf.h
> /usr/include/readline/tilde.h
> /usr/include/readline/rlstdc.h
> /usr/include/readline/chardefs.h
> /usr/lib/arm-linux-gnueabihf/libreadline.so
> /usr/lib/arm-linux-gnueabihf/libhistory.so
> ```

So, let's install it:

```
root@bbb:~# aptitude install libreadline-dev
```

When finished, we can relaunch the `make` command to definitely compile our new C interpreter:

```
root@bbb:~/picoc# make
gcc -Wall -pedantic -g -DUNIX_HOST -DVER="`svnversion -n`" -c -o clib
rary.o clibrary.c
...
gcc -Wall -pedantic -g -DUNIX_HOST -DVER="`svnversion -n`" -o picoc pi
coc.o  table.o lex.o parse.o  expression.o heap.o type.o variable.o cl
ibrary.o platform.o include.o debug.o platform/platform_unix.o platfor
m/library_unix.o cstdlib/stdio.o cstdlib/math.o cstdlib/string.o cstdl
ib/stdlib.o cstdlib/time.o cstdlib/errno.o cstdlib/ctype.o cstdlib/std
bool.o cstdlib/unistd.o -lm -lreadline
```

Well, now, the tool is successfully compiled as expected!

To test it, we can use the standard *Hello World* program again, but with a little modification. In fact, the `main()` function is not defined as before! This is due to the fact that PicoC returns an error if we use the typical function definition. Here is the code:

```
#include <stdio.h>

int main()
{
    printf("Hello World\n");

    return 0;
}
```

Now, we can directly execute it (that is, without compiling it) using our new C interpreter:

```
root@bbb:~/picoc# ./picoc helloworld.c
Hello World
```

An interesting feature of PicoC is that it can execute the C source file like a script. We don't need to specify a `main()` function as C requires and the instructions are executed one by one from the beginning of the file as a normal scripting language does.

Just to show it, we can use the following script that implements the *Hello World* program as a C-like script (note that the `main()` function is not defined):

```
printf("Hello World!\n");
return 0;
```

If we put the preceding code into the `helloworld.picoc` file, we can execute it using the following lines of code:

```
root@bbb:~/picoc# ./picoc -s helloworld.picoc
Hello World!
```

Note that this time, we add the `-s` option argument to the command line in order to instruct the PicoC interpreter that we wish to use its scripting behavior.

The cross-compilation

Now, let's try to cross-compile the PicoC interpreter on the host system. However, before continuing, we've to point out that this is just an example of a possible cross-compilation useful to expose a quick and dirty way to recompile a program when the native compilation is not possible. As already reported earlier, the cross-compilation works perfectly for the bootloader and the kernel, while for user-space application, we must ensure that all involved libraries (and header files) used by the cross-compiler are perfectly compatible with the ones present on the target machine. Otherwise, the program may not work at all! In our case, everything is perfectly compatible, so we can go further.

As we did earlier, we need to download the PicoC's source code using the same `git` command. Then, we have to enter the following command into the newly created `picoc` directory:

```
$ cd picoc/
$ make CC=arm-linux-gnueabihf-gcc
arm-linux-gnueabihf-gcc -Wall -pedantic -g -DUNIX_HOST -DVER="`svnvers
ion -n`"    -c -o picoc.o picoc.c
...
platform/platform_unix.c:5:31: fatal error: readline/readline.h: No su
ch file or directory
compilation terminated.
<builtin>: recipe for target 'platform/platform_unix.o' failed
make: *** [platform/platform_unix.o] Error 1
```

We specified the `CC=arm-linux-gnueabihf-gcc` command-line option to force the cross-compilation. However, as already stated, the cross-compilation commands may vary according to the compilation method used by the single software package.

The system returns a linking error due to the fact that the readline library is missing. However, this time, we cannot install it as before since we need the ARM version (specifically, the armhf version) of this library, and my host system is a normal PC!

Actually, a way to install a foreign package into a Debian/Ubuntu distribution exists, but it's not a simple task nor is it an argument of this book. A curious reader may take a look at the **Debian/Ubuntu Multiarch** at: https://help.ubuntu.com/community/MultiArch.

Now, we have to resolve this issue, and we have two possibilities:

- We can try to find a way to install the missing package.
- We can try to find a way to continue the compilation without it.

The former method is quite complex since the readline library has other dependencies, and we may take a lot of time trying to compile them all, so let's try to use the latter option.

Knowing that the readline library is just used to implement powerful interactive tools (such as recalling a previous command line to re-edit it) and since we are not interested in the interactive usage of this interpreter, we can hope to avoid using it. So, looking carefully at the code, we see that the USE_READLINE define exists. Changing the code as shown here should resolve the issue, allowing us to compile the tool without the readline support:

```
$ git diff
diff --git a/Makefile b/Makefile
index 6e01a17..c24d09d 100644
--- a/Makefile
+++ b/Makefile
@@ -1,6 +1,6 @@
 CC=gcc
 CFLAGS=-Wall -pedantic -g -DUNIX_HOST -DVER="`svnversion -n`"
-LIBS=-lm -lreadline
+LIBS=-lm
 TARGET = picoc
 SRCS   = picoc.c table.c lex.c parse.c expression.c heap.c type.c \
diff --git a/platform.h b/platform.h
index 2d7c8eb..c0b3a9a 100644
--- a/platform.h
+++ b/platform.h
@@ -49,7 +49,6 @@
 # ifndef NO_FP
 #   include <math.h>
 #   define PICOC_MATH_LIBRARY
-#   define USE_READLINE
 #   undef BIG_ENDIAN
 #   if defined(__powerpc__) || defined(__hppa__) || defined(__sparc__)
 #     define BIG_ENDIAN
```

> The preceding patch can be found in the chapter_03/picoc/picoc-drop-readline.patch file of the book's example code repository.

The preceding output is in the *unified context diff* format. So, the preceding code means that in the `Makefile` file, the `-lreadline` option must be removed from the `LIBS` variable and that in the `platform.h` file, the `USE_READLINE` define must be commented out.

After all the changes are in place, we can try to recompile the package with the same command as we did earlier:

```
$ make CC=arm-linux-gnueabihf-gcc
arm-linux-gnueabihf-gcc -Wall -pedantic -g -DUNIX_HOST -DVER="`svnvers
ion -n`"    -c -o table.o table.c
...
arm-linux-gnueabihf-gcc -Wall -pedantic -g -DUNIX_HOST -DVER="`svnvers
ion -n`" -o picoc picoc.o table.o lex.o parse.o expression.o heap.o ty
pe.o variable.o clibrary.o platform.o include.o debug.o platform/platf
orm_unix.o platform/library_unix.o cstdlib/stdio.o cstdlib/math.o cstd
lib/string.o cstdlib/stdlib.o cstdlib/time.o cstdlib/errno.o cstdlib/c
type.o cstdlib/stdbool.o cstdlib/unistd.o -lm
```

Great! We did it! Now, just to verify that everything is working correctly, we can simply copy the `picoc` file into our BeagleBone Black and test it as we did earlier.

Compiling a kernel module

As a special example of cross-compilation, we'll take a look at a very simple code that implements a dummy module for the Linux kernel (the code does nothing, but it prints some messages on the console), and we'll try to cross-compile it.

Let's consider this following kernel C code of the dummy module:

```
#include <linux/module.h>
#include <linux/init.h>

/* This is the function executed during the module loading */
static int dummy_module_init(void)
{
    printk("dummy_module loaded!\n");
    return 0;
}

/* This is the function executed during the module unloading */
static void dummy_module_exit(void)
{
    printk("dummy_module unloaded!\n");
    return;
}
```

```
module_init(dummy_module_init);
module_exit(dummy_module_exit);

MODULE_AUTHOR("Rodolfo Giometti <giometti@hce-engineering.com>");
MODULE_LICENSE("GPL");
MODULE_VERSION("1.0.0");
```

Apart from some defines relative to the kernel tree, the file holds two main functions, `dummy_module_init()` and `dummy_module_exit()`, and some special definitions, in particular, `module_init()` and `module_exit()`, that address the first two functions as the entry and exit the functions of the current module (that is, the functions that are called at module loading and unloading).

Then, consider the following `Makefile`:

```
ifndef KERNEL_DIR
$(error KERNEL_DIR must be set in the command line)
endif
PWD := $(shell pwd)
CROSS_COMPILE = arm-linux-gnueabihf-

# This specifies the kernel module to be compiled
obj-m += module.o

# The default action
all: modules

# The main tasks
modules clean:
    make -C $(KERNEL_DIR) ARCH=arm CROSS_COMPILE=arm-linux-gnueabihf- \
        SUBDIRS=$(PWD) $@
```

> The C code of the dummy module (`dummy.c`) and the `Makefile` can be found in the `chapter_03/module` directory of the book's example code repository.

OK, now, to cross-compile the dummy module on the host PC, we can use the following command:

```
$ make KERNEL_DIR=~/A5D3/armv7_devel/KERNEL/
make -C /home/giometti/A5D3/armv7_devel/KERNEL/ \
        SUBDIRS=/home/giometti/github/chapter_03/module modules
make[1]: Entering directory '/home/giometti/A5D3/armv7_devel/KERNEL'
  CC [M]  /home/giometti/github/chapter_03/module/dummy.o
  Building modules, stage 2.
  MODPOST 1 modules
  CC       /home/giometti/github/chapter_03/module/dummy.mod.o
  LD [M]  /home/giometti/github/chapter_03/module/dummy.ko
make[1]: Leaving directory '/home/giometti/A5D3/armv7_devel/KERNEL'
```

It's important to note that when a device driver is released as a separate package with a `Makefile` compatible with Linux's file, we can compile it natively too! However, even in this case, we need to install a kernel source tree on the target machine. Not only that, the sources must also be configured in the same manner of the running kernel. Otherwise, the resulting driver will not work at all! In fact, a kernel module will only load and run with the kernel it was compiled against.

The cross-compilation result is now stored in the dummy.ko file. , in fact we have:

```
$ file dummy.ko
dummy.ko: ELF 32-bit LSB relocatable, ARM, EABI5 version 1 (SYSV), Bui
ldID[sha1]=ecfcbb04aae1a5dbc66318479ab9a33fcc2b5dc4, not stripped
```

The kernel modules have been compiled for the SAMA5D3 Xplained, but of course, it can be cross-compiled for the other developer kits in a similar manner.

So, let's copy our new module to the SAMA5D3 Xplained using the `scp` command through the USB Ethernet connection:

```
$ scp dummy.ko root@192.168.8.2:
root@192.168.8.2's password:
dummy.ko                        100% 3228     3.2KB/s   00:00
```

Now, if we switch on the SAMA5D3 Xplained, we can use the `modinfo` command to get some information on the kernel module:

```
root@a5d3:~# modinfo dummy.ko
filename:          /root/dummy.ko
version:           1.0.0
license:           GPL
author:            Rodolfo Giometti <giometti@hce-engineering.com>
srcversion:        1B0D8DE7CF5182FAF437083
depends:
vermagic:          4.4.6-sama5-armv7-r5 mod_unload modversions
                   ARMv7 thumb2 p2v8
```

Then, to load and unload it to and from the kernel, we can use the `insmod` and `rmmod` commands:

```
root@a5d3:~# insmod dummy.ko
[ 3151.090000] dummy_module loaded!
root@a5d3:~# rmmod dummy.ko
[ 3153.780000] dummy_module unloaded!
```

As expected, the dummy's messages have been displayed on the serial console.

If we are using an SSH connection, we have to use the `dmesg` or `tail -f /var/log/kern.log` command to see the kernel's messages.
The `modinfo`, `insmod`, and `rmmod` commands are explained in detail in the following section.

The Kernel and DTS files

The main target of this book is to give several suggestions for rapid programming methods to be used on an embedded GNU/Linux system. However, the main target of every embedded developer is to realize programs to manage peripherals, to monitor or to control devices, and other similar tasks to interact with the real world. So, we mainly need to know the techniques useful to get access to the peripheral's data and settings.

That's why, we need to know how to recompile the kernel and how to configure it.

Recompiling the kernel

Our developer kits are well supported, and in this situation, it is quite rare that we need a complete kernel recompilation. However, knowing how to do this step is quite essential for every embedded developer (it may happen that we need to add some external peripherals or modify the default configuration).

Since we decided to use the Robert C. Nelson repositories, we can still continue using them. However, some words must be spent to clarify some basic commands useful to manage the kernel code even if we use a generic kernel repository.

Referring to the SAMA5D3 Xplained kernel compilation in *SAMA5D3 Xplained* section in `Chapter 1`, *Installing the Developing System*, we used the `build_kernel.sh` script to operate on the sources. However, this is not the standard way to manage the kernel code. In fact, Robert C. Nelson did a very good job, but we want to learn how to manage the kernel even without using his tools! So, let's take a look at what steps `build_kernel.sh` follows to do its job.

Like every good program, the main procedure is at the end of the file, and there, we will see the following code:

```
...
. "${DIR}/version.sh"
export LINUX_GIT

unset FULL_REBUILD
#FULL_REBUILD=1
if [ "${FULL_REBUILD}" ] ; then
    /bin/sh -e "${DIR}/scripts/git.sh" || { exit 1 ; }

    if [ "${RUN_BISECT}" ] ; then
        /bin/sh -e "${DIR}/scripts/bisect.sh" || { exit 1 ; }
    fi

    if [ ! -f "${DIR}/.yakbuild" ] ; then
        patch_kernel
    fi
    copy_defconfig
fi
if [ ! "${AUTO_BUILD}" ] ; then
    make_menuconfig
fi
if [ -f "${DIR}/.yakbuild" ] ; then
    BUILD=$(echo ${kernel_tag} | sed 's/[^-]*//'|| true)
fi
make_kernel
```

```
make_modules_pkg
make_firmware_pkg
if grep -q dtbs "${DIR}/KERNEL/arch/${KERNEL_ARCH}/Makefile"; then
    make_dtbs_pkg
fi
echo "----------------------------"
echo "Script Complete"
echo "${KERNEL_UTS}" > kernel_version
echo "eewiki.net: [user@host:~$ export kernel_version=${KERNEL_UTS}]"
echo "----------------------------"
```

So, the following steps are performed:

1. FULL_REBUILD : Where the sources are checkout out form the Git repositories and then pached

2. AUTO_BUILD: Where we configure the kernel

3. make_kernel: Where we effectively build up the kernel and its components (modules, firmware, and device trees)

4. make_modules_pkg, make_firmware_pkg, and make_dtbs_pkg: Where we create some packages holding the kernel's modules, the firmware binaries, and the device trees

The first step is not related to kernel compilation since it's needed to get the kernel's sources only.

At this point, we should notice that in order to avoid download the kernel sources each time we execute the script, we should disable this step by unsetting the FULL_REBUILD variable with the following patch:

```
--- a/build_kernel.sh
+++ b/build_kernel.sh
@@ -227,8 +227,7 @@ fi
 . "${DIR}/version.sh"
 export LINUX_GIT     -#unset FULL_REBUILD
-FULL_REBUILD=1
+unset FULL_REBUILD
 if [ "${FULL_REBUILD}" ] ; then
 /bin/sh -e "${DIR}/scripts/git.sh" || { exi
t 1 ; }
```

Again, the fourth step is just to pack the modules and other kernel's components, and it's not relevant to us. So, the second and third steps are the ones we have to look at carefully:

The `make_menuconfig` function is defined here:

```
make_menuconfig () {
    cd "${DIR}/KERNEL" || exit
    make ARCH=${KERNEL_ARCH} CROSS_COMPILE="${CC}" menuconfig
    if [ ! -f "${DIR}/.yakbuild" ] ; then
        cp -v .config "${DIR}/patches/defconfig"
    fi
    cd "${DIR}/" || exit
}
```

This tells to us that the command to execute the kernel configuration menu is as follows:

```
make ARCH=${KERNEL_ARCH} CROSS_COMPILE="${CC}" menuconfig
```

Of course, we have to specify the `KERNEL_ARCH` and `CROSS_COMPILE` variables, but considering what we did before, it's quite obvious that the command changes to this:

```
make ARCH=arm CROSS_COMPILE=arm-linux-gnueabihf- menuconfig
```

To test it, we can go into the directory where SAMA5D3 Xplained's kernel sources are placed (directory `A5D3/armv7_devel/KERNEL`) and then execute the `make` command:

```
$ cd A5D3/armv7_devel/KERNEL
$ make ARCH=arm CROSS_COMPILE=arm-linux-gnueabihf- menuconfig
```

Great, it works! This is the configuration kernel command to use in every situation. When we look at the `make_menuconfig` function, we see that the result of the kernel configuration is stored in the `.config` file. This is the file where every setting we do in the kernel configuration stage is placed.

The `make_kernel` function is a bit more complex, but the relevant code is shown here:

```
##uImage, if you really really want a uImage, zreladdr needs to be
##defined on the build line going forward...
##make sure to install your distro's version of mkimage
#image="uImage"
#address="LOADADDR=${ZRELADDR}"

cd "${DIR}/KERNEL" || exit
echo "-------------------------------"
echo "make -j${CORES} ARCH=${KERNEL_ARCH} LOCALVERSION=${BUILD} CROSS_
COMPILE="${CC}" ${address} ${image} modules"
echo "-------------------------------"
```

```
make -j${CORES} ARCH=${KERNEL_ARCH} LOCALVERSION=${BUILD} CROSS_COMPIL
E="${CC}" ${address} ${image} modules
echo "----------------------------"

if grep -q dtbs "${DIR}/KERNEL/arch/${KERNEL_ARCH}/Makefile"; then
    echo "make -j${CORES} ARCH=${KERNEL_ARCH} LOCALVERSION=${BUILD} CR
OSS_COMPILE="${CC}" dtbs"
    echo "----------------------------"
    make -j${CORES} ARCH=${KERNEL_ARCH} LOCALVERSION=${BUILD} CROSS_CO
MPILE="${CC}" dtbs
    echo "----------------------------"
fi
```

We can find the `make` commands again that do the job. They're reported here:

```
make -j${CORES} ARCH=${KERNEL_ARCH} LOCALVERSION=${BUILD} CROSS_COMPIL
E="${CC}" ${address} ${image} modules
make -j${CORES} ARCH=${KERNEL_ARCH} LOCALVERSION=${BUILD} CROSS_COMPIL
E="${CC}" dtbs
```

The former compiles the kernel and its modules, while the latter generates the device tree files (see the next section for further information on the device tree).

Again, we have to substitute the proper values to the variables mentioned earlier, but this is a tricky task. In fact, the CORES variable is just a number equal to the core number of our host PC. KERNEL_ARCH and CROSS_COMPILE must be obviously set to arm and arm-linux-gnueabihf-, while BUILD is just a descriptive string. So, we can choose whatever we wish. The last variables address and image need some more explanation. In fact, we can choose to compile the kernel in two main formats: **uImage** and **zImage**. For the former compilation, we need to specify a load address also (the LOADADDR variable), while for the latter, we don't. Since it's the form we used in our developer kits, the two commands mentioned earlier can be rewritten as follows:

```
make -j8 ARCH=arm LOCALVERSION="dummy" CROSS_COMPILE=arm-linux-gnueabi
hf- zImage modules dtbs
```

Then, to verify that everything is well configured, we just have to test the command:

```
$ make -j8 ARCH=arm LOCALVERSION="dummy"
        CROSS_COMPILE=arm-linux-gnueabihf- zImage modules dtbs
  CHK     include/config/kernel.release
  ...
  LD      kernel/built-in.o
  LINK    vmlinux
  LD      vmlinux.o
  MODPOST vmlinux.o
  GEN     .version
```

```
CHK     include/generated/compile.h
UPD     include/generated/compile.h
CC      init/version.o
LD      init/built-in.o
KSYM    .tmp_kallsyms1.o
KSYM    .tmp_kallsyms2.o
LD      vmlinux
SORTEX  vmlinux
SYSMAP  System.map
Building modules, stage 2.
OBJCOPY arch/arm/boot/Image
Kernel: arch/arm/boot/Image is ready
...
```

Yes, it works! Now, we're ready to recompile every kernel tree.

The device tree

The device tree is a data structure to describe hardware. That's all. Rather than hard coding every kernel setting into the code, it can be described in a well-defined data structure that is passed to the kernel at boot time.

The difference between the device tree and the kernel configuration file (the `.config` file) is that while the `.config` file tells us which components of the kernel are enabled and which are not, the device tree holds their configurations. So, if we wish to add a driver from the kernel's sources to our system, we have to specify it into the `.config` file. On the other hand, if we wish to specify the driver settings (memory addresses, special settings, and so on), we have to specify them in the device tree.

In all our developer kits, during the boot stage, we can see some messages from U-Boot's serial console as shown here:

```
...
reading /dtbs/at91-sama5d3_xplained.dtb
34918 bytes read in 11 ms (3 MiB/s)
reading zImage
3810568 bytes read in 244 ms (14.9 MiB/s)
Kernel image @ 0x22000000 [ 0x000000 - 0x3a2508 ]
## Flattened Device Tree blob at 21000000
   Booting using the fdt blob at 0x21000000
   Loading Device Tree to 2fadc000, end 2fae7865 ... OK
Starting kernel ...
...
```

Here, we can see that U-Boots loads a DTB file (the binary form of a device tree) and that it passes the file to the kernel.

So, it's time to take a look at how a **device tree source** (**DTS**) file is done and how we can generate a **device tree binary** (**DTB**) file from it in order to be used to our kernel. As a very simple example, let's see how the *LEDs driver* (will see this special driver in *LEDs and triggers section*, `Chapter 6`, *General Purposes Input Output signals – GPIO*) can be enabled and how it's defined into the default SAMA5D3 Xplained's DTS file.

To enable the LED driver compilation, we must open the **Kernel Configuration** menu and then navigate to **Device Drivers** | **LED Support** sub menu to enable the proper entries, as shown in the following screenshot:

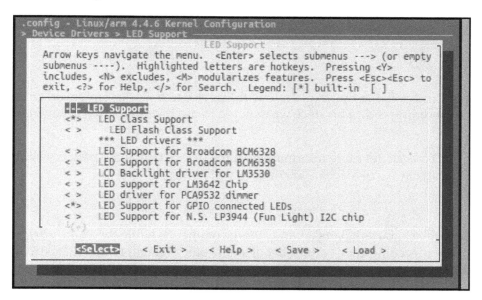

These settings result in the following output in the `.config` file:

```
$ grep '^CONFIG_LEDS_' .config
CONFIG_LEDS_CLASS=y
CONFIG_LEDS_GPIO=y
CONFIG_LEDS_PWM=y
CONFIG_LEDS_TRIGGERS=y
CONFIG_LEDS_TRIGGER_TIMER=y
CONFIG_LEDS_TRIGGER_HEARTBEAT=y
CONFIG_LEDS_TRIGGER_GPIO=y
```

This enabled the de-facto kernel compilation. However, to effectively define the LEDs present into the SAMA5D3 Xplained, we have to use the following code hold in the `arch/arm/boot/dts/at91-sama5d3_xplained.dts` file from the kernel's tree:

```
leds {
    compatible = "gpio-leds";

    d2 {
        label = "d2";
        gpios = <&pioE 23 GPIO_ACTIVE_LOW>;
        linux,default-trigger = "heartbeat";
    };

    d3 {
        label = "d3";
        gpios = <&pioE 24 GPIO_ACTIVE_HIGH>;
    };
};
```

The scope of this book does not explain how the device tree works. However, we must explain the preceding code a bit since we're going to use the device tree in several parts of this book.

You can get more information on the device tree at the project's home site at: `http://www.devicetree.org/`.

Text between the characters pairs /* and */ are comments, while the `leds` string on the first line of the preceding code is the label of a new block related to the LEDs driver. In fact, this is specified by the next line where the `compatible` property is. The `gpio-leds` string defines the *LEDs driver* as specified in the `drivers/leds/leds-gpio.c` file:

```
static const struct of_device_id of_gpio_leds_match[] = {
    { .compatible = "gpio-leds", },
    {},
};
```

Then, the sub-blocks labeled as `d2` and `d3` define two LEDs labeled with the same names. The `gpios` lines definition follows, that is, the specification of the GPIOs where the LEDs are physically connected.

As a final note, we see that in the d2 block definition, there is specified a special setting:

```
linux,default-trigger = "heartbeat";
```

This is to define the trigger to be used for the LED.

> For further information regarding the *LEDs driver* and its trigger, you can take a look at the `Documentation/leds/` directory in the Linux's code repository.

The preceding device tree code is very simple, and it cannot explain all the device tree's components. However, don't worry. Each time, we'll use a device tree settings, we're going to explain it as best as possible.

What is a device driver?

A device driver is a special code that interfaces a physical device into the system and exports it to the user-space processes using a well-defined API. In a UNIX-like OS, where *everything is a file,* the physical device is represented as a file. Then, the device driver implements all the system calls a process can do on a file.

> The difference between a normal C function and a system call is just the fact that the latter is mainly executed into the kernel while a function executes into the user space only. For example, `printf()` is a function while `write()` is a system call. The latter (except for the prologue and epilogue part of a C function) executes into the kernel space, while the former executes into the user space (even if it calls `write()` to actually write its data to the output stream).
> The system calls are used to communicate with the peripherals, with other processes, and to get access to the kernel's internal data. That's why a system call triggers a switch from user space to kernel space where important code is executed, and after execution, the code switched back to user space to execute normal code. For this reason, the code executed in the kernel space is considered a code that is executed in a *privileged mode*.

As an example, let's consider the GPIO subsystem we already saw in the previous chapter where we talked about U-Boot. In Linux, we can manage these devices easily using some files in sysfs (we'll discuss more in detail in the following paragraphs). For each GPIO lines, we got a directory called `/sys/class/gpio/gpioXX/` where we can find the `value` and `direction` files. Each `read()` system calls on the `value` file (for example, by issuing the `cat /sys/class/gpio/gpioXX/value` command) and is translated by the kernel in the `gpio_read()` kernel method that actually does the reading of the `gpioXX` status.

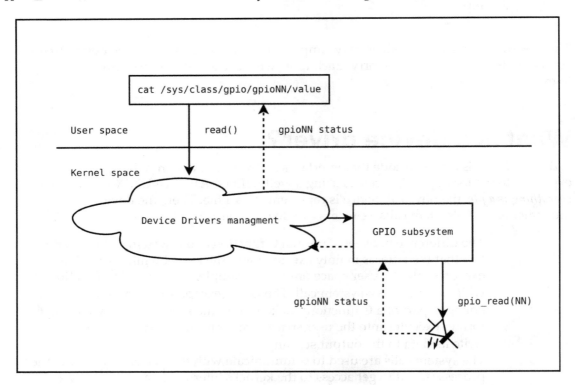

 At the moment, we cannot still try these commands, so the reader should believe that this is actually what happens! Otherwise, they can skip to `Chapter 6`, *General Purposes Input Output signals – GPIO*, where GPIOs management is shown.

When we do a `read()` system call on another file under the `/dev` directory, the kernel translates the `read()` system call into the corresponding device driver's method that actually executes the reading.

Note that the system call is always the same (`read()`), but inside the kernel, the right method is called each time! You should imagine that this mechanism works like an object programming language: `read()` is a method that operates in a different manner according to the object (device) passed to it.

> For further information on how this complex mechanism exactly works and for everything about the device drivers in Linux, you can take a look at the book *Linux Device Drivers, Third Edition* available at the bookshop and online at: `http://lwn.net/Kernel/LDD3/`.

Char, block, and net devices

In the Linux kernel, three major device types exist:

- **Char device** : This kind of device groups all the peripherals that can be accessed as a stream of bytes, such as a file (that is, serial ports, audio devices, and so on). A char driver is in charge of implementing this behavior usually by implementing at least the `open()`, `close()`, `read()`, and `write()` system calls. Char device drivers have the `ioctl()` system call that allows the developer to invent any interface necessary (it acts as a general purpose method).
- **Block device** : This kind of device groups all the peripherals that can host a filesystem, so it is accessed as a block of bytes (usually 512 or a larger power of two).
- **Net device** : This kind of device groups all the peripherals that can manage a network transaction. In a different manner from char and block devices, these special devices have no related filesystem nodes, such as `/dev/ttyACM0` or `/dev/sdb1`.

A driver interfacing, a char device is usually called **char driver**, while a driver for a block device is called **block driver**, and of course, the **net driver** is the driver for a net device.

Despite these three major groups, in recent kernel releases, we can find several subgroups (or classes) of device drivers that are still based on one of the major groups but that are specialized in managing a particular device type, for example, the **real-time clock** (**RTC**) devices that are represented by a dedicated device driver class defined under the `/drivers/rtc` directory in the Linux source tree. In the same manner, the *Pulse Per Second devices* (**PPS**) have a dedicated device driver class defined under the `/drivers/pps` directory, and the same is the case for the input devices (mice, keyboards, and so on) that are defined under the `/drivers/input` directory. All these specific device drivers are implemented using the char drivers.

Another way to interact with a device is to use the sysfs filesystem (see the relative section below in this chapter). Strictly speaking, this not regular a device driver, that is, it's not implemented as a char or block or net device, but it uses a different API. It uses an in-memory representation of the device's internals that permits to get access to it in a simple and clean way using the file abstraction (that is *everything is a file*).

Modules versus built-in devices

The Linux kernel holds by default a lot of device drivers, but it may happen that we need to install into the system a recent one not yet imported into the kernel tree for several reasons (that is, the driver is very new, or nobody asked for its insertion, or just because we write it ourselves!). In this case, we need to know some techniques about how a device driver can be compiled (advanced details about a device driver and how it can be used to exchange data with a peripheral will be explained in detail in the following chapters).

The device driver compilation steps may vary, and two major possibilities exist:

1. The driver's source code is a `patch` to be applied to the kernel tree.
2. The driver's source code has a standard `Makefile` compatible with Linux's file.

The first case is quite simple since after the device driver's patch has been applied, the developer just needs to recompile the kernel. In this case, the driver can be compiled as **kernel built-in** or as **kernel module**.

A kernel module is a special binary file that can be inserted in the kernel at runtime when a specific functionality is requested. This prevents us from having a very large kernel image. In fact, we can select which functionalities are required since the boot and which ones can be loaded later on a demand basis.

For example, when a new device is inserted into the system, the kernel may ask for loading a kernel module that holds the corresponding device driver. However, a module may also be built as a monolithic part of the kernel (kernel built-in).

The first case is just a normal kernel recompilation, while the latter case is a bit more complex, but all the complexity is managed by `Makefile`. The user has to properly configure it and then execute the `make` command only.

When a device driver code is not merged into the kernel sources, then the driver can be compiled as a kernel module only!

We just saw how to write a simple kernel module. Right now, we've to see the tools to effectively manage such modules.

The modutils

The basic command to load a module into the kernel is `insmod`. However, another command exists to load a module (and its dependencies), and its name is `modprobe`.

Actually, there is a group of commands to manage the kernel modules. They are called the **modutils**. On a Debian or Ubuntu system, the modutils are stored into a package named `kmod`:

```
$ apt-cache show kmod
Package: kmod
Priority: important
Section: admin
Installed-Size: 241
Maintainer: Ubuntu Developers <ubuntu-devel-discuss@lists.ubuntu.com>
Original-Maintainer: Marco d'Itri <md@linux.it>
Architecture: amd64
Version: 22-1ubuntu4
Depends: libc6 (>= 2.17), libkmod2 (= 22-1ubuntu4), lsb-base (>= 4.1+D
ebian11ubuntu7)
Breaks: oss-compat (= 4)
Filename: pool/main/k/kmod/kmod_22-1ubuntu4_amd64.deb
Size: 89122
MD5sum: bcfb58ca2dbc2f77137193b73c61590d
SHA1: 539d2410d0182f212b78a67b649135507c9fd9bb
SHA256: a65398f087ad47192e728ecbffe92e0363c03d229d72dc1d2f8b409880c9d0
ea
Description-en: tools for managing Linux kernel modules
 This package contains a set of programs for loading, inserting, and
 removing kernel modules for Linux.
 It replaces module-init-tools.
 . . .
```

The available commands in the preceding package can be listed here:

```
$ dpkg -L kmod | grep sbin\/
/sbin/insmod/sbin/depmod
/sbin/modprobe
/sbin/rmmod
/sbin/lsmod
/sbin/modinfo
```

Let's see a bit of these commands in detail:

- The `insmod` loads a module into the kernel.
- The `lsmod` command shows to the user all the current modules loaded into the kernel. By running it on my PC, I get a long listing. So, here are a few lines:

```
$ lsmod
Module                  Size  Used by
pci_stub               16384  1
vboxpci                24576  0
vboxnetadp             28672  0
vboxnetflt             28672  0
vboxdrv               454656  3 vboxnetadp,vboxnetflt,vboxpci
pl2303                 20480  0
ftdi_sio               53248  0
```

On the first column are reported all the modules currently loaded into my system. The second column is the module size in bytes, while the third column is the use count by other modules or user space accesses, which are listed in the fourth column.

- The `modprobe` command is more complex than `insmod`, because it can handle the dependencies of the module, that is, it can load all the modules needed by the user-requested one to run.
- The `depmod` command can be used to build a dependencies table suitable for the `modprobe` command.

Explaining in detail how this mechanism works is out of the scope of this book. You can take a look at the `depmod` command's man pages using the `man depmod` command.

- The `rmmod` command can be used to unload a module from the system releasing the RAM and other resources taken during its usage.

This can be done only if the module is not actually used by other modules in the system. This fact is true when the number in the `Used by` column in the preceding output of the `lsmod` command is equal to `0`.

Writing our own device driver

We can now try to implement GPIOs management code that allows us to count how many state transactions a single GPIO line does. Actually, what we are going to do is not write a *proper* device driver, but we're going to write a kernel code that manages a peripheral, which is very close to be a *real* device driver! Simply speaking, I can use the next example to show you how a kernel functionality can be abstracted as a file.

Let's suppose we need to count some pulses that arrive on our SAMA5D3 Xplained at a certain amount of time. In this case, we can use one GPIO for each pulse source.

 Note that this situation is quite common, and it can be found in some counters' devices! In fact, these devices, that simply count a quantity (water or oil litres, an energy power meter, and so on), return the counting as frequency modulated pulses.

In this situation, we can use a really simple kernel code to implement a new device class under sysfs that we can use to abstract these measurements to the user space. We use kernel code since the pulses can go fast. So, in order to have better responsiveness from our board, we must use interrupts. What we wish to do is install an **interrupt handler** that is called each time a specified GPIO line changes its status from low to high or from high to low or both. Then, we wish to have some dedicated files where we can read how many pulses have arrives since the last measurement.

As already stated, to simplify the implementation, we're not going to write a regular device driver (char, block or net device), but we're going to use a class instead. Even if this is not a proper driver, this solution allows us to see how a really simple kernel code works without going too deeply into device drivers programming (this topic is not covered by this book).

Using our new driver, you will see a new class named **pulse** and a new directory per device where you can read the actual counting.

Here is a simple example of the final result:

```
root@a5d3:~# tree -l -L 2 /sys/class/pulse/
/sys/class/pulse/
+-- oil -> ../../devices/soc0/pulses/pulse/oil
|   +-- counter
|   +-- counter_and_reset
|   +-- device -> ../../../pulses [recurs., not follow]
|   +-- power
|   +-- set_to
|   +-- subsystem -> ../../../../../class/pulse [recurs., not follow]
|   \-- uevent
\-- water -> ../../devices/soc0/pulses/pulse/water
```

```
        +-- counter
        +-- counter_and_reset
        +-- device -> ../../../pulses  [recurs., not follow]
        +-- power
        +-- set_to
        +-- subsystem -> ../../../../../class/pulse [recurs., not follow]
        \-- uevent
 8 directories, 8 files
```

In the preceding example, we have two **pulse** devices named oil and water, represented by the same name directories, and for each device, three attributes files are named: counter, counter_and_reset, and set_to (the other files named power and subsystem are not of interest to us).

You can now use the counter file to read the counting data, while by using the counter_and_reset file, you can do the same as with the counter file. However, after reading the data, the counter is automatically reset to the value 0. On the other side, using the set_to file, you can initialize the counter to a specific value different from 0.

Now, before continuing to describe the driver, a simple explanation of the code is needed. We have three files, and the first one is Makefile shown here:

```
ifndef KERNEL_DIR
$(error KERNEL_DIR must be set in the command line)
endif
PWD := $(shell pwd)
CROSS_COMPILE = arm-linux-gnueabihf-

obj-m = pulse.o
obj-m += pulse-gpio.o

all: modules

modules clean:
    $(MAKE) -C $(KERNEL_DIR) ARCH=arm CROSS_COMPILE=$(CROSS_COMPILE) \
        SUBDIRS=$(PWD) $@
```

The code is held in the chapter_03/pulse/Makefile file in the book's example code repository.

As we can see, it's quite similar to the one presented earlier. The only difference is in the `obj-m` variable. In fact, this time, it declares two object files: `pulse.o` and `pulse-gpio.o`.

The `pulse-gpio.o` file can obviously be obtained by compiling the `pulse-gpio.c` file that holds the definition of the pulse's GPIO sources, because we can suppose that not only the GPIOs can be possible pulse sources.

The relevant part of the `pulse-gpio.c` file is the `pulse_gpio_probe()` function, which is reported here:

```
static int pulse_gpio_probe(struct platform_device *pdev)
{
    struct device *dev = &pdev->dev;
    struct fwnode_handle *child;
    struct pulse_gpio_priv *priv;
    int count, ret;
    struct device_node *np;

    /* Get the number of defined pulse sources */
    count = device_get_child_node_count(dev);
    if (!count)
        return -ENODEV;

    /* Allocate private data */
    priv = devm_kzalloc(dev, sizeof_pulse_gpio_priv(count),
                        GFP_KERNEL);
    if (!priv)
        return -ENOMEM;

    device_for_each_child_node(dev, child) {
        int irq, flags;
        struct gpio_desc *gpiod;
        const char *label, *trigger;
        struct pulse_device *new_pulse;

        /* Get the GPIO descriptor */
        gpiod = devm_get_gpiod_from_child(dev, NULL, child);
        if (IS_ERR(gpiod)) {
            fwnode_handle_put(child);
            ret = PTR_ERR(gpiod);
            goto error;
        }
        gpiod_direction_input(gpiod);

        np = to_of_node(child);

        /* Get the GPIO's properties */
```

```
    if (fwnode_property_present(child, "label")) {
        fwnode_property_read_string(child, "label",
                    &label);
    } else {
        if (IS_ENABLED(CONFIG_OF) && !label && np)
            label = np->name;
        if (!label) {
            ret = -EINVAL;
            goto error;
        }
    }

    flags = 0;
    ret = fwnode_property_read_string(child, "trigger",
                    &trigger);
    if (ret == 0) {
        if (strcmp(trigger, "rising") == 0)
            flags |= IRQF_TRIGGER_RISING;
        else if (strcmp(trigger, "fallng") == 0)
            flags |= IRQF_TRIGGER_FALLING;
        else if (strcmp(trigger, "both") == 0)
            flags |= IRQF_TRIGGER_RISING | \
                        IRQF_TRIGGER_FALLING;
        else {
            ret = -EINVAL;
            goto error;
        }
     }

    /* Register the new pulse device */
    new_pulse = pulse_device_register(label, dev);
    if (!new_pulse) {
        fwnode_handle_put(child);
        ret = PTR_ERR(new_pulse);
        goto error;
    }

    /* Is GPIO in pin IRQ capable? */
    irq = gpiod_to_irq(gpiod);
    if (irq < 0) {
        ret = irq;
        goto error;
    }

    /* Ok, now we can request the IRQ */
    ret = request_irq(irq, (irq_handler_t) irq_handler,
                    flags, PULSE_GPIO_NAME, new_pulse);
    if (ret < 0)
```

```
                    goto error;

            priv->pulse[priv->num_pulses].dev = new_pulse;
            priv->pulse[priv->num_pulses].irq = irq;
            priv->num_pulses++;
    }

    platform_set_drvdata(pdev, priv);

    return 0;

error:
    /* Unregister everything in case of errors */
    for (count = priv->num_pulses - 1; count >= 0; count--) {
        if (priv->pulse[count].dev)
            pulse_device_unregister(priv->pulse[count].dev);
        if (priv->pulse[count].irq && priv->pulse[count].dev)
            free_irq(priv->pulse[count].irq, priv->pulse[count].dev);
    }

    return ret;
}
```

This function parses the device tree settings and then defines the new pulse devices according to these settings. As already stated earlier, the device tree is defined into a DTS file. In particular, for the SAMA5D3 Xplained, the file is `KERNEL/arch/arm/boot/dts/at91-sama5d3_xplained.dts` (see the kernel sources downloaded in *SAMA5D3 Xplained* section in `Chapter 1`, *Installing the Developing System*, in the `A5D3/armv7_devel` directory). So, if we modify it as shown here, we can define two pulse devices named `oil` and `water` connected to `gpio17` (*PA17*) and `gpio19` (*PA19*), respectively, both exported on the SAMA5D3 Xplained expansion connector:

```
--- a/arch/arm/boot/dts/at91-sama5d3_xplained.dts
+++ b/arch/arm/boot/dts/at91-sama5d3_xplained.dts
@@ -332,5 +332,22 @@
            label = "d3";
            gpios = <&pioE 24 GPIO_ACTIVE_HIGH>;
        };
+
+    };
+
+    pulses {
+        compatible = "gpio-pulses";
+
+        oil {
+            label = "oil";
+            gpios = <&pioA 17 GPIO_ACTIVE_HIGH>;
```

```
+                    trigger = "both";
+            };
+
+        water {
+            label = "water";
+            gpios = <&pioA 19 GPIO_ACTIVE_HIGH>;
+            trigger = "rising";
+        };
+    };
+  };
```

 The patch is held in the chapter_03/pulse/pulse-gpio_at91-sama5d3_xplained.dts.patch file in the book's example code repository.

You should also notice that while the water pulse device is triggered on the rising edge of the input transaction, the oil one is triggered on both edges.

Using the preceding code into our DTS file, we can expect that pulse_gpio_probe() executes two loops where it reads all the configuration data of each pulse source and then calls the pulse_device_register() function to define the new device into the kernel. After that, it calls the request_irq() function, which is used to declare an interrupt handler (the handler irq_handler() function) connected to the GPIO status where the effective counting takes place. In fact, the handler looks like this:

```
static irqreturn_t irq_handler(int i, void *ptr, struct pt_regs *regs)
{
    struct pulse_device *pulse = (struct pulse_device *) ptr;

    BUG_ON(!ptr);

    pulse_event(pulse);

    return IRQ_HANDLED;
}
```

At this point, we must point out three important things:

1. The kernel module does not use the classic module_init() and module_exit() functions used into our kernel module example shown earlier.

2. The `pulse_gpio_probe()` function and its opposite `pulse_gpio_remove()` calls the functions `pulse_device_register()` and `pulse_device_unregister()`, respectively to add and remove a pulse device from the kernel.

3. The interrupt handler `irq_handler()` calls the `pulse_event()` function to signal to the system that a particular pulse event has arrived.

Regarding the first point, we can observe that the missing functions are actually used by the `module_platform_driver()` statement, which is defined into the kernel file `include/linux/platform_device.h` as follows:

```
#define module_platform_driver(__platform_driver) \
    module_driver(__platform_driver, platform_driver_register, \
                  platform_driver_unregister)
```

Then, `module_driver()` is defined into the kernel file `include/linux/device.h` as shown here, where we can see that `module_init()` and `module_exit()` are called:

```
#define module_driver(__driver, __register, __unregister, ...) \
static int __init __driver##_init(void) \
{ \
    return __register(&(__driver) , ##__VA_ARGS__); \
} \
module_init(__driver##_init); \
static void __exit __driver##_exit(void) \
{ \
    __unregister(&(__driver) , ##__VA_ARGS__); \
} \
module_exit(__driver##_exit);
```

Regarding the second and third points, about the `pulse_device_register()`, `pulse_device_unregister()`, and `pulse_event()` functions, we observed that these functions are defined into the third file composing our driver, that is, the `pulse.c` file. Here is a snippet of such a file where the functions are defined:

```
void pulse_event(struct pulse_device *pulse)
{
    atomic_inc(&pulse->counter);
}
EXPORT_SYMBOL(pulse_event);

struct pulse_device *pulse_device_register(const char *name,
                                           struct device *parent)
{
    struct pulse_device *pulse;
```

```
        dev_t devt;
        int ret;

        /* First allocate a new pulse device */
        pulse = kmalloc(sizeof(struct pulse_device), GFP_KERNEL);
        if (unlikely(!pulse))
            return ERR_PTR(-ENOMEM);

    mutex_lock(&pulse_idr_lock);
    /*
     * Get new ID for the new pulse source.  After idr_alloc() calling
     * the new source will be freely available into the kernel.
     */
    ret = idr_alloc(&pulse_idr, pulse, 0, PULSE_MAX_SOURCES,
    GFP_KERNEL);
    if (ret < 0) {
        if (ret == -ENOSPC) {
            pr_err("%s: too many PPS sources in the system\n", name);
            ret = -EBUSY;
        }
        goto error_device_create;
    }
    pulse->id = ret;
    mutex_unlock(&pulse_idr_lock);

    devt = MKDEV(MAJOR(pulse_devt), pulse->id);

        /* Create the device and init the device's data */
        pulse->dev = device_create(pulse_class, parent, devt, pulse,
                                "%s", name);
        if (unlikely(IS_ERR(pulse->dev))) {
            dev_err(pulse->dev, "unable to create device %s\n", name);
            ret = PTR_ERR(pulse->dev);
            goto error_idr_remove;
        }
        dev_set_drvdata(pulse->dev, pulse);
        pulse->dev->release = pulse_device_destruct;

        /* Init the pulse data */
        strncpy(pulse->name, name, PULSE_NAME_LEN);
        atomic_set(&pulse->counter, 0);
        pulse->old_status = -1;

        dev_info(pulse->dev, "pulse %s added\n", pulse->name);

        return pulse;

    error_idr_remove:
```

```
    mutex_lock(&pulse_idr_lock);
    idr_remove(&pulse_idr, pulse->id);

error_device_create:
    mutex_unlock(&pulse_idr_lock);
    kfree(pulse);

    return ERR_PTR(ret);
}
EXPORT_SYMBOL(pulse_device_register);

void pulse_device_unregister(struct pulse_device *pulse)
{
    /* Drop all allocated resources */
    device_destroy(pulse_class, pulse->dev->devt);

    dev_info(pulse->dev, "pulse %s removed\n", pulse->name);
}
EXPORT_SYMBOL(pulse_device_unregister);
```

You can see all the steps done to create the driver data structures into the `register` function and the respective inverse steps done into the `unregister` one. Then, the `pulse_event()` function is just a counter increment.

Also, you should notice that all functions are declared as **exported symbols** by the code:

```
EXPORT_SYMBOL(pulse_event);
EXPORT_SYMBOL(pulse_device_register);
EXPORT_SYMBOL(pulse_device_unregister);
```

This says to the compiler that these functions are special because they can be used by other kernel modules.

At the module initialization (the `pulse_init()` function), we use `class_create()` to create our new `pulse` class and, as the opposite action, at the module exit (the `pulse_exit()` function), we destroyed it by calling `class_destroy()`.

You should now take attention to the `pulse_init()` function at line:

```
pulse_class->dev_groups = pulse_groups;
```

Using such an assignment, we will declare the three attribute files, `count`, `counter_and_reset`, and `set_to` that are all reported in `struct pulse_attrs`:

```
static struct attribute *pulse_attrs[] = {
    &dev_attr_counter.attr,
    &dev_attr_counter_and_reset.attr,
```

```
        &dev_attr_set_to.attr,
        NULL,
};
```

Each entry of the preceding structure is created by the `DEVICE_ATTR_XX()` function as outlined here:

```
static ssize_t counter_show(struct device *dev,
                    struct device_attribute *attr, char *buf)
{
    struct pulse_device *pulse = dev_get_drvdata(dev);

    return sprintf(buf, "%d\n", atomic_read(&pulse->counter));
}
static DEVICE_ATTR_RO(counter);
```

This code specifies the attributes of the `dev_attr_gpio.attr` entry by declaring the file attribute `counter` as read-only, and when the function body `counter_show()` is called each time from the user space, we do a `read()` system call on the file. In fact, as there are `read()` and `write()` system calls for files, there are `show()` and `store()` functions for sysfs attributes.

As a dual example, the following code declares the attributes of the `dev_attr_set_to.attr` entry by declaring the file attribute `set_to` as write-only, and when the `set_to_store()` function body is called each time from the user space, we do a `write()` system call on the file:

```
static ssize_t set_to_store(struct device *dev,
                        struct device_attribute *attr,
                        const char *buf, size_t count)
{
    struct pulse_device *pulse = dev_get_drvdata(dev);
    int status, ret;

    ret = sscanf(buf, "%d", &status);
    if (ret != 1)
        return -EINVAL;

    atomic_set(&pulse->counter, status);

    return count;
}
static DEVICE_ATTR_WO(set_to);
```

Note that the `sprintf()` and `sscanf()` functions, which are quite common functions for C programmers, are not the ones implemented into libc. Rather they are homonym functions written ad-hoc for the kernel space to simplify the kernel code development by representing to the developer well-known functions.

You should also notice that for the `show()` and `store()` functions we have that:

1. The attribute files are the ones that get/set the data from/to the user space by reading/writing the data into the buffer pointed by the `buf` pointer.
2. All these functions work on the `dev` pointer that represents the device that is currently accessed, that is, if the user gets access to the device `oil`, the `dev` pointer will point to a data structure representing such a device! This recalls the object-oriented programming model, and this magic allows the developer to write a clean and compact code!

At this time, the driver functioning should be clear. The `pulse.c` (the core of our driver) file defines the basic structures and functions, while the `pulse-gpio.c` file, by reading the device tree, defines the pulse sources based on GPIOs (note that this solution is quite generic, and it allows the developers to add other kinds of sources into `pulse.c` using the mechanisms).

Now, to test the code, we should compile it, so let's use the command:

```
$ make KERNEL_DIR=~/A5D3/armv7_devel/KERNEL/
```

If everything works well, we should get the two kernel modules `pulse.ko` and `pulse-gpio.ko` we defined in `Makefile`.

Note that `KERNEL_DIR` points to the directory where the kernel sources are downloaded into *SAMA5D3 Xplained* section in `Chapter 1`, *Installing the Developing System*, so you should set it according to your system configuration.

So, let's copy the two files into the SAMA5D3 Xplained using the `scp` command:

```
$ scp *.ko root@192.168.8.2:
```

Then, load the `pulse.ko` module with the following command:

```
root@a5d3:~# insmod pulse.ko
```

Looking at the kernel messages with `dmesg`, we should see the following message:

```
Pulse driver support v. 0.80.0 - (C) 2014-2016 Rodolfo Giometti
```

Great! The new device class is now defined into the kernel. In fact, looking into the sysfs directory `/sys/class/`, we see that the new class is up and running:

```
root@a5d3:~# ls -ld /sys/class/pulse/
drwxr-xr-x 2 root root 0 Apr  2 17:45 /sys/class/pulse/
```

Now, we should add the two devices `oil` and `water` defined into the device tree and enabled by the `pulse-gpio.ko` module as shown here:

```
root@a5d3:~# insmod pulse-gpio.ko
```

Again, using the `dmesg` command, we should see two new kernel messages:

```
pulse oil: pulse oil added
pulse water: pulse water added
```

This is what we expected! Now in the sysfs we now have:

```
root@a5d3:~# ls /sys/class/pulse/
oil   water
```

Perfect! The system is now ready to count the pulses on the programmed GPIOs, but how we can generate these pulses to test the new driver? Well, this is quite simple. We can use another GPIO as the pulse generator and the script in the `chapter_03/pulse_gen.sh` file of the book's example code repository to actually generate the pulses. If we connect `gpio16` (*PA16*) to `gpio17` (*PA17*), and in another terminal window, if we run the preceding script with the following command line, we would generate a 4Hz `pulse` signal from the first GPIO to the second one where the `oil` counter is connected:

```
root@a5d3:~# ./pulse_gen.sh a5d3 A16 4
```

So, if we try to read its data, we get the following line of code:

```
root@a5d3:~# cat /sys/class/pulse/oil/counter
48
```

If we try to read the `counter` file, we see that it increments (more or less) at the speed of 4 pulses per second. However, the functioning may be more clear if we use the following commands that reset the counter first (using the `set_to` file) and then use the `counter_and_reset` file to restart the counting after each reading:

```
root@a5d3:~# echo 0 > /sys/class/pulse/oil/set_to ; \
             while sleep 1 ; do \
```

```
        cat /sys/class/pulse/oil/counter_and_reset ; \
    done
7
8
8
8
```

Note that we get 8 instead of 4 because the pulse driver counts both *high-to-low* and *low-to-high* transactions (try to connect `gpio16` (*PA16*) to the `water` counter to see 4). Also, note that the 7 is due to the fact that there can be some delays in reading the counting data due to the fact we're using a Bash script to generate the waveform, which is certainly not the best solution (even if it's certainly the quickest).

The root filesystem (rootfs)

The *root filesystem* (**rootfs**) is the main filesystem for an UNIX-like operative system. It contains the very critical files needed for the whole system to work (for instance, the `init` process), so if the root filesystem gets corrupted, the system will not work at all!

The root filesystem is the first filesystem the kernel mounts at boot, and it is never unmounted.

A rootfs can be used on several different types of storage devices (disks, flashes, and so on). A filesystem can stay in the RAM or even over the network, and according to the storage device where it's placed on, it can have different formats. This is because it has to take into account some special feature of the underlying storage media. In a typical GNU/Linux system, a rootfs type can be (mostly) **EXT3/EXT4** or **JFFS2/UBIFS**. The first two formats are the standard Linux filesystems used into hard disks, USB storage devices, microSDs, and other block devices, while the JFFS2 and UBIFS are filesystems used on fla devices (nowadays, NAND flashes).

sh devices (nowadays, NAND flashes). You might be willing to know the differences between these filesystems so that you can start your studies from https://en.wikipedia.org/wiki/File_system#Unix_and_Unix-like_operating_systems.

Apart from the format we're using in our system, we can find the same files and directory set in a root filesystem. Here is the typical listing on both my host PC and one developer kit of this book (see the `uname` output to distinguish the architecture):

```
$ uname -a
Linux ubuntu1510 4.2.0-35-generic #40-Ubuntu SMP Tue Mar 15 22:15:45 U
TC 2016 x86_64 x86_64 x86_64 GNU/Linux
$ ls /
bin    dev   initrd.img      lib64      mnt    root   srv usr     vmlinuz.old
boot   etc   initrd.img.old  lost+found opt    run    sys var
cdrom  home  lib             media      proc   sbin   tmp vmlinuz
root@wb:~# uname -a
Linux wb 4.4.7-armv7-x6 #1 SMP Sun Apr 17 18:41:21 CEST 2016 armv7l GN
U/Linux
root@wb:~# ls /
bin    dev   home  lost+found  mnt   proc  run   srv   tmp   var
boot   etc   lib   media       opt   root  sbin  sys   usr
```

As we can see, they're almost the same (apart some files), and we can write the same directories. I can write a complete chapter on these directories and the files they hold, but this not the scope of this book. However, I can spend some paragraphs to explain the directories we're going to refer to in this book.

To get a complete listing of these directories and their contents and explanations, refer to
`https://en.wikipedia.org/wiki/Filesystem_Hierarchy_Standard`.

In particular, we'll see the following directories: `/dev` that is related to the system's devices or peripherals, `/proc` and `/sys` that are related to special virtual filesystem where we can get/set some system's settings, and `/run` and other directories related to the temporary filesystem.

The /dev directory

This is the directory where all devices (apart from the net devices) are mapped, that is, where the block or character special files (used to address all the relative peripherals into the system) are usually placed.

At very beginning of the UNIX era, this directory was simply a standard directory with several block and character files (one per possible device connected to the system). However, during the evolution of UNIX (and Linux), this solution become very inefficient (due the very large peripheral numbers). So, Linux developers implemented different solutions to address this problem until the current one that uses a special temporary filesystem named **devtmpfs**.

The devtmpfs filesystem is just like the temporary filesystem, but it lets the kernel create a **tmpfs** instance very early at kernel initialization, before any driver-core device is registered. This is because each device must be mapped here as soon as it is activated by its relative driver.

We can take a look at this using the `findmnt` command:

```
root@wb:~# findmnt /dev
TARGET SOURCE    FSTYPE    OPTIONS
/dev   devtmpfs devtmpfs  rw,relatime,size=1016472k,nr_inodes=186701,mo
de=7555
```

The files under `/dev` in the Wandboard are reported here:

```
root@wb:~# ls /dev/
apm_bios            mapper              stdin    tty29    tty51    uhid
ashmem              mem                 stdout   tty3     tty52    uinput
autofs              memory_bandwidth    tty      tty30    tty53    urandom
binder              mmcblk0             tty0     tty31    tty54    vcs
block               mmcblk0p1           tty1     tty32    tty55    vcs1
btrfs-control       mqueue              tty10    tty33    tty56    vcs2
bus                 net                 tty11    tty34    tty57    vcs3
char                network_latency     tty12    tty35    tty58    vcs4
console             network_throughput  tty13    tty36    tty59    vcs5
cpu_dma_latency     null                tty14    tty37    tty6     vcs6
cuse                port                tty15    tty38    tty60    vcsa
disk                ppp                 tty16    tty39    tty61    vcsa1
dri                 pps0                tty17    tty4     tty62    vcsa2
fb0                 psaux               tty18    tty40    tty63    vcsa3
fd                  ptmx                tty19    tty41    tty7     vcsa4
full                ptp0                tty2     tty42    tty8     vcsa5
fuse                pts                 tty20    tty43    tty9     vcsa6
i2c-0               random              tty21    tty44    ttymxc0  vga_arbiter
i2c-1               rfkill              tty22    tty45    ttymxc2  watchdog
initctl             rtc                 tty23    tty46    ttyS0    watchdog0
input               rtc0                tty24    tty47    ttyS1    xconsole
kmem                shm                 tty25    tty48    ttyS2    zero
kmsg                snapshot            tty26    tty49    ttyS3
log                 snd                 tty27    tty5     ttyS4
loop-control        stderr              tty28    tty50    ttyS5
```

We can recognize some known devices such as the serial ports (ttyS0, ttyS1, and so on), the I²C busses (i2c-0 and i2c-1), the real-time clock (rtc), and so on. Other devices are located into sub directories as disks:

```
root@wb:~# tree /dev/disk/
/dev/disk/
+-- by-id
|   +-- mmc-SL16G_0x28a39857 -> ../../mmcblk0
|   \-- mmc-SL16G_0x28a39857-part1 -> ../../mmcblk0p1
+-- by-label
|   \-- rootfs -> ../../mmcblk0p1
+-- by-path
|   +-- platform-2198000.usdhc -> ../../mmcblk0
|   +-- platform-2198000.usdhc-part1 -> ../../mmcblk0p1
\-- by-uuid
    \-- d38a7071-3fbf-4782-b406-ff64478c4266 -> ../../mmcblk0p1

4 directories, 6 files
```

Ot the sound devices:

```
root@wb:~# tree /dev/snd/
/dev/snd/
+-- by-path
|   +-- platform-120000.hdmi -> ../controlC0
|   +-- platform-sound -> ../controlC2
|   \-- platform-sound-spdif -> ../controlC1
+-- controlC0
+-- controlC1
+-- controlC2
+-- pcmC0D0p
+-- pcmC1D0p
+-- pcmC2D0c
+-- pcmC2D0p
+-- seq
\-- timer

1 directory, 12 files
```

You can use your host PC or embedded device to walk around the /dev directory and discover other block or character devices. You can see the device type just using the ls command with the -1 option arguments:

```
root@wb:~# ls -l /dev/mmcblk0*
brw-rw---- 1 root disk 179, 0 Jan 1 1970 /dev/mmc
blk0
brw-rw---- 1 root disk 179, 1 Jan 1 1970 /dev/mmc
blk0p1
root@wb:~# ls -l /dev/ttyS*
```

```
crw-rw---- 1 root dialout 4, 64 Jan 1 1970 /dev/t
tyS0
crw-rw---- 1 root dialout 4, 65 Jan 1 1970 /dev/t
tyS1
crw-rw---- 1 root dialout 4, 66 Jan 1 1970 /dev/t
tyS2
crw-rw---- 1 root dialout 4, 67 Jan 1 1970 /dev/t
tyS3
crw-rw---- 1 root dialout 4, 68 Jan 1 1970 /dev/t
tyS4
crw-rw---- 1 root dialout 4, 69 Jan 1 1970 /dev/t
tyS5
```

The block devices have a b character at the beginning of the first column of the ls output, while the character ones have a c. So, in the preceding output, we can see that /dev/mmcblk0xx are block devices while /dev/ttySx are character ones.

The tmpfs

The *temporary filesystem* (**tmpfs**) is a filesystem stored on top of volatile memory instead of a persistent storage device. Due to this fact, on reboot, everything in tmpfs will be lost.

Even if it may look really strange that a vanishing filesystem can be useful, it really is! In fact, it is used where the system needs quick read, write, and delete operations on several files that are to be recreated on every boot. These files are exactly the ones under the /run directory, that is, where (almost) every distribution stores temporary files related to its running services (daemons).

On the Wandboard, we have the following tmpfs filesystems:

```
root@wb:~# findmnt tmpfs
TARGET          SOURCE FSTYPE OPTIONS
/dev/shm        tmpfs  tmpfs  rw,nosuid,nodev
/run            tmpfs  tmpfs  rw,nosuid,nodev,mode=755
/run/lock       tmpfs  tmpfs  rw,nosuid,nodev,noexec,relatime,size=5120k
/sys/fs/cgroup  tmpfs  tmpfs  ro,nosuid,nodev,noexec,mode=755
```

You may notice that there are other places where tmpfs are used!

The procfs

The *proc filesystem* (**procfs**) is a virtual filesystem that holds information about the processes (and other system information) in a hierarchical file structure. This allows the user to find the necessary information quickly by looking at a well-defined point of the system where all information is pretty ordinated.

A virtual filesystem is a filesystem that contains virtual files (files stored nowhere filled with information created on the fly when they get accessed) used to export information about various kernel subsystems, hardware devices, and associated device drivers to user space. In addition to providing this information, these exported virtual files are also used for system configuration and device management.

The standard mount point of this filesystem is the /proc directory, as shown here:

```
root@wb:~# findmnt proc
TARGET SOURCE FSTYPE OPTIONS
/proc  proc   proc   rw,nosuid,nodev,noexec,relatime
```

Then, in this directory, we can find all process-related information. For instance, if we wish to have some information about the init process, the first process executed into the system (that is, the process with PID 1), we should have a look at the /proc/1 directory as shown here:

```
root@wb:~# ls /proc/1
attr              cpuset   limits      net             root       statm
autogroup         cwd      loginuid    ns              sched      status
auxv              environ  map_files   oom_adj         schedstat  syscall
cgroup            exe      maps        oom_score       sessionid  task
clear_refs        fd       mem         oom_score_adj   setgroups  timers
cmdline           fdinfo   mountinfo   pagemap         smaps      uid_map
comm              gid_map  mounts      personality     stack      wchan
coredump_filter   io       mountstats  projid_map      stat
```

Here is located all information regarding the init process. For example, we can find the environment:

```
root@wb:~# cat /proc/1/environ ; echo
HOME=/TERM=linux
```

The echo command has been used to force a newline (\n) character at the end of the preceding cat command's output.

We can retrieve the command line used to execute the process:

```
/sbin/initroot@wb:~# cat /proc/1/cmdline ; echo
/sbin/init
```

Or the `init`'s memory usage:

```
root@wb:~# cat /proc/1/maps
00010000-000cb000 r-xp 00000000 b3:01 655091       /lib/systemd/systemd
000db000-000eb000 r--p 000bb000 b3:01 655091       /lib/systemd/systemd
000eb000-000ec000 rw-p 000cb000 b3:01 655091       /lib/systemd/systemd
01da2000-01e67000 rw-p 00000000 00:00 0            [heap]
b6cc3000-b6d05000 rw-p 00000000 00:00 0
. . .
```

Here we discover that, in reality, the real `init` process is `systemd`. Visit https://en.wikipedia.org/wiki/Systemd for further information.

Or the file descriptors used:

```
root@wb:~# ls -l /proc/1/fd
total 0
lrwx------ 1 root root 64 Jan  1  1970 0 -> /dev/null
lrwx------ 1 root root 64 Jan  1  1970 1 -> /dev/null
lr-x------ 1 root root 64 Apr  2 19:04 10 -> /proc/swaps
lrwx------ 1 root root 64 Apr  2 19:04 11 -> socket:[13056]
lrwx------ 1 root root 64 Apr  2 19:04 12 -> socket:[13058]
lrwx------ 1 root root 64 Apr  2 19:04 13 -> anon_inode:[timerfd]
lr-x------ 1 root root 64 Apr  2 19:04 19 -> anon_inode:inotify
. . .
```

This information can be retrieved for every process running into the system. For instance, we can get the information regarding our Bash shell by discovering its PID first:

```
root@wb:~# pidof bash
588
```

My Wandboard is running just one instance of the Bash process, so I am sure that the preceding PID is referred to my shell.

Then, we can look at `/proc/588` directory:

```
root@wb:~# ls /proc/588/
attr               cpuset    limits       net             root        statm
autogroup          cwd       loginuid     ns              sched       status
auxv               environ   map_files    oom_adj         schedstat   syscall
cgroup             exe       maps         oom_score       sessionid   task
clear_refs         fd        mem          oom_score_adj   setgroups   timers
cmdline            fdinfo    mountinfo    pagemap         smaps       uid_map
comm               gid_map   mounts       personality     stack       wchan
coredump_filter    io        mountstats   projid_map      stat
```

Now, we can check out the shell's environment by looking at the `/proc/588/environ` file:

```
root@wb:~# cat /proc/588/environ ; echo
TERM=vt102LANG=en_US.UTF-8HOME=/rootSHELL=/bin/bashUSER=rootLOGNAME=ro
otPATH=/ulocal/sbin:/usr/local/bin:/usr/sbin:/usr/bin:/sbin:/binMAIL=/
var/mail/rootHUSHLON=FALSE
```

However, the procfs, as already shown in *Managing the kernel messages* section Chapter 2, *Managing the System Console,* where we used it to set the kernel console logging level, can be used to get/set other information regarding the system settings in general. For instance, we can get the listing of the currently loaded modules into the kernel by reading the file `/proc/modules`:

```
root@wb:~# cat /proc/modules
brcmfmac 254455 0 - Live 0xbf4d0000el
brcmutil 9092 1 brcmfmac, Live 0xbf4c2000
cfg80211 536448 1 brcmfmac, Live 0xbf3e0000
caam_jr 17297 0 - Live 0xbf34a000
snd_soc_fsl_ssi 15476 2 - Live 0xbf342000
...
```

Alternatively, we can read how many interrupts we have got per CPU since the boot from the `/proc/interrupts` file:

```
root@wb:~# cat /proc/interrupts
         CPU0    CPU1    CPU2    CPU3
  16:    1589    2441    3120    1370    GIC  29 Edge    twd
  17:       0       0       0       0    GPC  55 Level   i.MX Tk
  19:       0       0       0       0    GPC 115 Level   120000i
  20:       0       0       0       0    GPC   9 Level   130000u
  21:       0       0       0       0    GPC  10 Level   134000u
  24:       0       0       0       0    GPC  52 Level   200400f
  25:     661       0       0       0    GPC  26 Level   2020001
  26:       0       0       0       0    GPC  46 Level   202800i
  28:       0       0       0       0    GPC  12 Level   204000u
```

```
. . .
303:        0         0         0         0    IPU   23  Edge      imx_drm
304:        0         0         0         0    IPU   28  Edge      imx_drm
305:        0         0         0         0    IPU   23  Edge      imx_drm
306:        0         0         0         0    IPU   28  Edge      imx_drm
307:        0         0         0         0    GIC  137  Level     2101000
308:        0         0         0         0    GIC  138  Level     2102001
IPI0:       0         0         0         0  CPU wakeup interrupts
IPI1:       0         0         0         0  Timer broadcast interrupts
IPI2:    1370      4505      5119      9684  Rescheduling interrupts
IPI3:      92        69        55        96  Function call interrupts
IPI4:       0         2         2         0  Single function call interr.
IPI5:       0         0         0         0  CPU stop interrupts
IPI6:       0         0         0         0  IRQ work interrupts
IPI7:       0         0         0         0  completion interrupts
Err:        0
```

This file is really important when we work with the hardware since we can have an idea whether our device is generating interrupts or not. Also, we can have information regarding the correct interrupt handlers' configurations (we'll see these features in the upcoming chapters when we talk about the peripherals).

Also, we can get the actual device tree configuration by reading the contents of the /proc/device-tree directory as follows:

```
root@wb:~# ls /proc/device-tree
#address-cells  cpus                           memory     #size-cells
aliases         display-subsystem              model      soc
chosen          gpu-subsystem                  name       sound
clocks          interrupt-controller@00a01000  regulators sound-spdif
compatible      __local_fixups__               rfkill     __symbols__
```

Referring to our preceding sample driver, we can retrieve the pulse device's tree settings by reading into the /proc/device-tree/pulses/ directory as shown here (note that this time, we switch back to the SAMA5D3 Xplained):

```
root@a5d3:~# tree /proc/device-tree/pulses/
/proc/device-tree/pulses/
+-- compatible
+-- name
+-- oil
|    +-- gpios
|    +-- label
|    +-- name
|    \-- trigger
\-- water
     +-- gpios
```

```
        +-- label
        +-- name
        \-- trigger
2 directories, 10 files
```

Then, we can check the data by reading the several files. Here are the trigger settings:

```
root@a5d3:~# cat /proc/device-tree/pulses/oil/trigger ; echo
both
root@a5d3:~# cat /proc/device-tree/pulses/water/trigger ; echo
rising
```

Here are the GPIO settings (the GPIO number is the eighth byte):

```
root@a5d3:~# cat /proc/device-tree/pulses/oil/gpios | \
        hexdump -e '16/1 " %3i"' -e '"\n"'
    0   0   0 121   0   0   0  17   0   0   0   0

root@a5d3:~# cat /proc/device-tree/pulses/water/gpios | \
        hexdump -e '16/1 " %3i"' -e '"\n"'
    0   0   0 121   0   0   0  19   0   0   0   0
```

This is a nice feature to have in a system, but not all kernel developers agree that this information should be stored in the procfs because a proc filesystem should report processes' information only. That's why, the sysfs shown in the next paragraph was born (in reality, this is not the only reason).

 You may get further information by surfing the Internet or just reading the file `Documentation/filesystems/procfs.txt` from Linux's source tree.

The sysfs

The *system filesystem* (**sysfs**) is a virtual filesystem that exports information about all kernel subsystems, system's buses, and the hardware devices with their relative device drivers. This filesystem is deeply related to the device tree concept (as shown here) and the power system management, and it mainly resolves the problem to have a unified method of representing *driver-device* relationships and how to correctly put them in the power-saver mode.

From our point of view, the sysfs is really important since by using it, we can get/set most peripherals settings and we can get access to the peripherals data too.

The default mount point of this filesystem is the /sys directory as shown below:

```
root@wb:~# findmnt sysfs
TARGET SOURCE FSTYPE OPTIONS
/sys    sysfs   sysfs   rw,nosuid,nodev,noexec,relatime
```

Just by listing its contents, we can have an idea about its organization:

```
root@wb:~# ls /sys/
block  bus  class  dev  devices  firmware  fs  kernel  module  power
```

These directory names are quite self-explanatory. However, some words should be spent talking about the directories we're going to use into this book.

> You may get further information by surfing the Internet or just by reading the file Documentation/filesystems/sysfs.txt from Linux's source tree.

The first directory is /sys/class:

```
root@wb:~# ls /sys/class/
ata_device   drm          ieee80211  net           rtc           udc
ata_link     dvb          input      pci_bus       scsi_device   uio
ata_port     extcon       iommu      phy           scsi_disk     vc
backlight    firmware     leds       power_supply  scsi_host     video4linux
bdi          gpio         mbox       pps           sound         vtconsole
block        graphics     mdio_bus   ptp           spi_master    watchdog
bsg          hidraw       mem        pwm           switch
devcoredump  hwmon        misc       rc            thermal
devfreq      i2c-adapter  mmc_host   regulator     timed_output
dma          i2c-dev      mtd        rfkill        tty
```

It stores all devices' information grouped by the device class, that is, a logical set of devices that perform a common task in the system: graphics devices, sound devices, hardware monitor (**hwmon**) devices, and so on.

Referring to our preceding sample driver, we can retrieve the pulse class settings by reading into the /sys/class/pulse/ directory as shown here (note that we switch back to the SAMA5D3 Xplained again):

```
root@a5d3:~# tree -L 2 -l /sys/class/pulse/
/sys/class/pulse/
+-- oil -> ../../devices/soc0/pulses/pulse/oil
```

```
|    +-- counter
|    +-- counter_and_reset
|    +-- device -> ../../../pulses
|    +-- power
|    +-- set_to
|    +-- subsystem -> ../../../../../class/pulse  [recursive, not followed]
|    \-- uevent
\-- water -> ../../devices/soc0/pulses/pulse/water
     +-- counter
     +-- counter_and_reset
     +-- device -> ../../../pulses  [recursive, not followed]
     +-- power
     +-- set_to
     +-- subsystem -> ../../../../../class/pulse  [recursive, not followed]
     \-- uevent

8 directories, 8 files
```

For instance, we can get information regarding the **framebuffer** (these devices will not be presented in this book, however they refer to a graphic hardware-independent abstraction layer to show graphical data on a computer display) by taking a look at the `/sys/class/graphics/fb0/` directory:

```
root@wb:~# ls /sys/class/graphics/fb0/
bits_per_pixel  console  device  name   rotate  subsystem
blank           cursor   mode    pan    state   uevent
bl_curve        dev      modes   power  stride  virtual_size
```

Then, we can get the valid graphic modes using the command here:

```
root@wb:~# cat /sys/class/graphics/fb0/modes
U:1024x768p-0
```

Alternatively, we can get some information about a **hwmon** device (these devices will not be presented in this book, however they are used to monitoring some environment data, such as temperatures, and so on. of the system or external peripheral ones) on the Wandboard in the directory here:

```
root@wb:~# ls /sys/class/hwmon/hwmon0/
name  power  subsystem  temp1_crit  temp1_input  uevent
```

Then, by looking at the hwmon device, we can get the name, the critical temperature, and the current system's temperature using the command here:

```
root@wb:~# cat /sys/class/hwmon/hwmon0/{name,temp1_crit,temp1_input}
imx_thermal_zone
95000
28318
```

Returned data are in m°C, that is they are, respectively, 95°C and 28.318°C.

In the upcoming chapters, when we present the several devices a developer can find in its embedded board and how they can get access to them, we will use this filesystem often.

The Network FileSystem (NFS)

In `Chapter 2`, *Managing the System Console, Loading files from the network* section, we saw how to load a kernel image (with its DTB file) using an Ethernet connection, and we said that this feature is very useful during the kernel developing stages. Well, this feature is quite useless without the kernel's ability to use a filesystem located on another computer (usually the host PC) as a root filesystem, Simply speaking, instead of mounting a filesystem stored on a local disk or flash memory, the system mounts a remote filesystem using a network.

This allows the developer to test both the kernel, its drivers, and the whole root filesystem by downloading them from the network, avoiding the boring step to reprogram the mass memory devices (this actually saves a lot of the developer's time!).

Due to these reasons, this particular type of filesystem is called **Network FileSystem** (NFS).

Of course, we can use this feature over several different network connections, but only if our system has an Ethernet connection and its kernel has a running driver for it. However, if this is the case, this feature is very useful for several reasons:

- If our kernel still does not support its storage devices, we can use anyway a filesystem with a console where we can log in.
- Even if our system has a small storage device, we can use a complete distribution on it, with all debugging tools ready to be used. For instance, we can use a Debian OS, where we can easily install whatever we need to develop our application, even if our flash memory is very small (64 or 128MB).

- We can modify one or more files by simply modifying them directly on the host and then avoiding rebuilding the filesystem on the local flash or disk.

Well, to better fix these concepts, let's try to mount a remote filesystem on one of our developer kits. As already stated, we can choose whatever we wish, so for this test, we are going to use the Wandboard.

Exporting an NFS on the host

OK, an NFS is a remote filesystem, but it contains exactly all the files a usual filesystem has. So, we can use the filesystem used in Chapter 1, *Installing the Developing System*, in *Wandboard* section, to set up the microSD of our developer kits.

We can start by creating a new directory on the host PC and then by putting all files into it:

```
$ sudo mkdir /opt/armhf-rootfs-debian-jessie
$ cd common/debian-8.4-minimal-armhf-2016-04-02/
$ sudo tar xpf armhf-rootfs-debian-jessie.tar -C /opt/armhf-rootfs-deb
ian-jessie/
```

After that, the contents of our new NFS is ready in the /opt/armhf-rootfs-debian-jessie directory:

```
$ ls /opt/armhf-rootfs-debian-jessie/
bin    dev   home  media  opt   root  sbin  sys  usr
boot   etc   lib   mnt    proc  run   srv   tmp  var
```

However, this not enough since we have to teach our host PC in order to export this filesystem over the network. To do this, we can use the nfs-kernel-server package. Despite its name, this package holds all user space programs to manage an NFS, and it has the kernel word in its name because it uses the NFS kernel features to do its job.

Now, let's install the package with the usual aptitude command:

```
$ sudo aptitude install nfs-kernel-server
```

When the installation is completed, we have to set up the new service by editing the /etc/exports file. This file states which are the directories to be exported, and by taking a look at its contents we can get a brief idea of what we should do:

```
$ cat /etc/exports
# /etc/exports: the access control list for filesystems which may be
# exported to NFS clients.  See exports(5).
#
```

```
# Example for NFSv2 and NFSv3:
# /srv/homes          hostname1(rw,sync,no_subtree_check)
#                     hostname2(ro,sync,no_subtree_check)
#
# Example for NFSv4:
# /srv/nfs4           gss/krb5i(rw,sync,fsid=0,crossmnt,no_subtree_check)
# /srv/nfs4/homes     gss/krb5i(rw,sync,no_subtree_check)
#
```

So, since our files have been placed in /opt/armhf-rootfs-debian-jessie and we have used the IP address 192.168.32.25, that is, the IP of the host, for our developer kits, we can add the following line to the /etc/exports file:

```
/opt/armhf-rootfs-debian-jessie 192.168.32.25(rw,sync,no_subtree_check
,no_root_squash)
```

So, the new file contents should be as follows:

```
$ tail -3 /etc/exports
# /srv/nfs4/homes   gss/krb5i(rw,sync,no_subtree_check)
#
/opt/armhf-rootfs-debian-jessie 192.168.32.25(rw,sync,no_subtree_check
,no_root_squash)
```

> Note that the /etc/exports file supports several different configurations that the ones shown in the preceding lines. You can get further information by stating from the man exports pages:
> ```
> $ man exports
> ```

You will notice that we added no_root_squash option because as suggested by the exports man pages, this option is required for diskless clients (that is, systems that have no disks at all and they mount the root filesystem over the network). To finish the settings, we have to restart the NFS daemon:

```
$ sudo /etc/init.d/nfs-kernel-server restart
[ ok ] Restarting nfs-kernel-server (via systemctl): nfs-kernel-server
.service.
```

Now, to check if we did everything right, we can check all servers' exported directories using the showmount command:

```
$ showmount -e localhost
Export list for localhost:
/opt/armhf-rootfs-debian-jessie 192.168.32.25
```

OK, we can go ahead.

Setting up the kernel to mount an NFS

Now, we have to check whether the Wandboard kernel (or the developer kit's kernel) has all the necessary components to support the mount of an NFS.

First of all, we have to come back in the kernel directory and then recall `build_kernel.sh`:

```
$ cd WB/armv7-multiplatform/
$ ./build_kernel.sh
```

Once the kernel configuration menu is opened, we have to navigate to **Networking support | Networking options** and verify that the entry **IP: kernel level autoconfiguration** and its sub entries are checked as shown here:

```
.config - Linux/arm 4.4.7 Kernel Configuration
> Networking support > Networking options
                          Networking options
  Arrow keys navigate the menu.  <Enter> selects submenus ---> (or empty
  submenus ----).  Highlighted letters are hotkeys.  Pressing <Y>
  includes, <N> excludes, <M> modularizes features.  Press <Esc><Esc> to
  exit, <?> for Help, </> for Search.  Legend: [*] built-in  [ ]

        [*]      IP: equal cost multipath
        [*]      IP: verbose route monitoring
        [*]    IP: kernel level autoconfiguration
        [*]      IP: DHCP support
        [*]      IP: BOOTP support
        [*]      IP: RARP support
        <M>    IP: tunneling
        <M>    IP: GRE demultiplexer
        <M>    IP: GRE tunnels over IP
        [*]      IP: broadcast GRE over IP
        [*]    IP: multicast routing

            <Select>    < Exit >    < Help >    < Save >    < Load >
```

Then, we must go back to the first page and then enter into the **File systems** menu. Here, here we must check the **Network File Systems** entry, and then, enter into its menu and copy the configuration reported in the next screenshot:

```
.config - Linux/arm 4.4.7 Kernel Configuration
> File systems > Network File Systems
                        Network File Systems
  Arrow keys navigate the menu.  <Enter> selects submenus ---> (or empty
  submenus ----).  Highlighted letters are hotkeys.  Pressing <Y>
  includes, <N> excludes, <M> modularizes features.  Press <Esc><Esc> to
  exit, <?> for Help, </> for Search.  Legend: [*] built-in  [ ]

        --- Network File Systems
        <*>   NFS client support
        <*>     NFS client support for NFS version 2
        <*>     NFS client support for NFS version 3
        [*]       NFS client support for the NFSv3 ACL protocol extension
        <*>     NFS client support for NFS version 4
        [*]     Provide swap over NFS support
        [*]   NFS client support for NFSv4.1
        [*]   NFS client support for NFSv4.2
        (kernel.org) NFSv4.1 Implementation ID Domain
        [ ]     NFSv4.1 client support for migration

        <Select>    < Exit >    < Help >    < Save >    < Load >
```

In reality, we just need support for NFS version 3, but we can safely add other options too.

OK, after all settings are in place, we can exit the kernel configuration menu to start the kernel's compilation. When finished, we can recall what we did in Chapter 2, *Managing the System Console*, in *Loading files from the network* section, to load a kernel image over an Ethernet connection from U-Boot and copy the kernel image and the DTS into the TFTP root directory as shown here:

```
$ sudo cp deploy/4.4.7-armv7-x6.zImage /srv/tftpboot/vmlinuz-4.4.7-arm
v7-x6
$ sudo mkdir -p /srv/tftpboot/dtbs/4.4.7-armv7-x6/
$ sudo tar xf deploy/4.4.7-armv7-x6-dtbs.tar.gz \
        -C /srv/tftpboot/dtbs/4.4.7-armv7-x6/
```

Then. we can switch to U-Boot.

U-Boot and the kernel command line to use a NFS

After stopping U-Boot at the boot, we can set up a kernel command line to instruct the kernel to mount a filesystem as its root filesystem over the network.

The parameters we have to add to the kernel command line are as follows:

- `root`: This specifies the root filesystem device to be used at the first mount. Note that it's not a real device, but just a synonym to tell the kernel to use NFS instead of a real device.
- `nfsroot`: This specifies where the root filesystem's files are physically located. The syntax is as follows:

      nfsroot=[<server-ip>:]<root-dir>[,<nfs-options>]

  The `<server-ip>` parameter should point to our host PC (that is, `192.168.32.25`), `<root-dir>` must be replaced with the exported directory (we have `/opt/armhf-rootfs-debian-jessie`), and `<nfs-options>` can be used to specify version 3 of the protocol.

- `ip`: This specifies the networking settings of our embedded device. The syntax is as follows:

      ip=<client-ip>:<server-ip>:<gw-ip>:<netmask>:<hostname>:
         <device>:<autoconf>:<dns0-ip>:<dns1-ip>

  So, `<client-ip>` is the client's IP address (`192.168.32.25` for us), `<server-ip>` is the host PC (`192.168.32.43`), `<gw-ip>` is the LAN's gateway (my LAN has `192.168.32.8`), `<netmask>` is the network's netmask (my class C networks has `255.255.255.0`), `<hostname>` should be set to whatever describes your machine (we used `wb`), `<device>` is the Ethernet port (`eth0` in our case), and `<autoconf>` must be set to `off` in order to force static IP assignment. The other parameters can be left void.

For further information on these kernel parameters, a good starting point is the `Documentation/kernel-parameters.txt` file and the `Documentation/filesystems/nfs/nfsroot.txt` file in Linux's repository.

OK, now, we have to define these new settings into U-Boot in order to mount the NFS. There are several ways to do so. Most of them are very tricky. However, we'd like to show a classic way to resolve this issue, So, you can use it even on a different embedded device.

First of all, we have to do a standard boot to check the command line normally used, so let's use the boot command to continue and to see the command line used:

```
=> boot
switch to partitions #0, OK
mmc0 is current device
SD/MMC found on device 0
Checking for: /uEnv.txt ...
Checking for: /boot/uEnv.txt ...
23 bytes read in 127 ms (0 Bytes/s)
Loaded environment from /boot/uEnv.txt
Checking if uname_r is set in /boot/uEnv.txt...
Running uname_boot ...
loading /boot/vmlinuz-4.4.7-armv7-x6 ...
5802912 bytes read in 405 ms (13.7 MiB/s)
loading /boot/dtbs/4.4.7-armv7-x6/imx6q-wandboard.dtb ...
51193 bytes read in 552 ms (89.8 KiB/s)
debug: [console=ttymxc0,115200 root=/dev/mmcblk0p1 ro rootfstype=ext4
rootwait]
...
debug: [bootz 0x12000000 - 0x18000000] ...
Kernel image @ 0x12000000 [ 0x000000 - 0x588ba0 ]
## Flattened Device Tree blob at 18000000
 Booting using the fdt blob at 0x18000000
 Using Device Tree in place at 18000000, end 1800f7f8

Starting kernel ...


...
[ 0.000000] PERCPU: Embedded 13 pages/cpu @eed94000 s23936 r8192 d2
1120 u53248
[ 0.000000] Built 1 zonelists in Zone order, mobility grouping on.
 Total pages: 522560
[ 0.000000] Kernel command line: console=ttymxc0,115200 root=/dev/m
mcblk0p1 ro rootfstype=ext4 rootwait
...
```

Great! The command line is as follows:

```
console=ttymxc0,115200 root=/dev/mmcblk0p1 ro rootfstype=ext4 rootwait
```

So, we need to fix up the `root` with the `/dev/nfs` option to tell the kernel to use NFS instead of a real device. We also need to remove the `rootfstype` option and then rewrite the kernel command line with the `setenv` command as follows:

```
=> setenv bootargs 'console=ttymxc0,115200 root=/dev/nfs rw nfsroot=19
2.168.32.43:/opt/armhf-rootfs-debian-jessie,v3,tcp ip=192.168.32.25:19
2.168.32.43:192.168.32.8:255.255.255.0:wb:eth0:off:: rootwait'
```

Then, we can proceed to load the kernel and the DTS file:

```
=> setenv ipaddr 192.168.32.25
=> setenv serverip 192.168.32.43
=> tftpboot ${loadaddr} vmlinuz-4.4.7-armv7-x6
=> tftpboot ${ftd_addr} dtbs/4.4.7-armv7-x6/imx6q-wandboard.dtb
```

> It may happen that our U-Boot has a bug and it'll not correctly load the DTB file into proper memory area. If we execute the second `tftpboot` command, we see something like this:
>
> ```
> => tftpboot ${ftd_addr} dtbs/4.4.7-armv7-x6/imx6q-w
> andboard.dtb
> Using FEC device
> TFTP from server 192.168.32.43; our IP address is 1
> 92.168.32.25
> Filename 'dtbs/4.4.7-armv7-x6/imx6q-wandboard.dtb'.
> Load address: 0x12000000
> Loading: ##########
>     756.8 KiB/s
> done
> Bytes transferred = 51193 (c7f9 hex)
> ```
>
> The load address is `0x12000000` instead of `0x18000000`. We must re-execute the preceding two commands by replacing the `loadaddr` and `fdt_addr` variables with the respective memory address as follows:
>
> ```
> => tftpboot 0x12000000 vmlinuz-4.4.7-armv7-x6
> => tftpboot 0x18000000 dtbs/4.4.7-armv7-x6/imx6q-w
> andboard.dtb
> ```

Note that the file names have been deduced by the following lines of the preceding booting messages:

```
loading /boot/vmlinuz-4.4.7-armv7-x6 ...
5802912 bytes read in 405 ms (13.7 MiB/s)
loading /boot/dtbs/4.4.7-armv7-x6/imx6q-wandboard.dtb ...
51193 bytes read in 552 ms (89.8 KiB/s)
```

OK, now, we can do the boot using the following command:

```
=> bootz ${loadaddr} - ${fdt_addr}
Kernel image @ 0x12000000 [ 0x000000 - 0x588000 ]
## Flattened Device Tree blob at 18000000
   Booting using the fdt blob at 0x18000000
   Using Device Tree in place at 18000000, end 1800f7f8
Starting kernel ...
[    0.000000] Booting Linux on physical CPU 0x0
[    0.000000] Initializing cgroup subsys cpuset
...
[    0.000000] Kernel command line: console=ttymxc0,115200 root=/dev/n
fs rw nfsroot=192.168.32.43:/opt/armhf-rootfs-debian-jessie,v3,tcp ip=
192.168.32.25:192.168.32.43:192.168.32.8:255.255.255.0:wb:eth0:off:: r
ootwait
```

OK the kernel has started with the right command line! Let's see what happens then:

```
[    5.456756] fec 2188000.ethernet eth0: Freescale FEC PHY driver [Ge
neric PHY] (mii_bus:phy_addr=2188000.ethernet:01, irq=-1)
[    5.468079] IPv6: ADDRCONF(NETDEV_UP): eth0: link is not ready
[    8.456629] fec 2188000.ethernet eth0: Link is Up - 100Mbps/Full -
flow control rx/tx
[    8.466228] IPv6: ADDRCONF(NETDEV_CHANGE): eth0: link becomes ready
[    8.486384] IP-Config: Complete:
[    8.489623]      device=eth0, hwaddr=00:1f:7b:b4:1e:97, ipaddr=192.
168.32.25, mask=255.255.255.0, gw=192.168.32.8
[    8.499920]      host=wb, domain=, nis-domain=(none)
[    8.504888]      bootserver=192.168.32.43, rootserver=192.168.32.43
, rootpath=
[    8.526701] VFS: Mounted root (nfs filesystem) on device 0:17.
[    8.533312] devtmpfs: mounted
[    8.537150] Freeing unused kernel memory: 1032K (c1058000 - c115a00
0)
[    8.857337] random: systemd urandom read with 53 bits of entropy av
ailable
[    8.875848] systemd[1]: systemd 215 running in system mode. (+PAM +
AUDIT +SELINUX +IMA +SYSVINIT +LIBCRYPTSETUP +GCRYPT +ACL +XZ -SECCOMP
 -APPARMOR)
[    8.889511] systemd[1]: Detected architecture 'arm'.
Welcome to Debian GNU/Linux 8 (jessie)!
```

Yeah! The kernel has been able to mount our NFS and the Debian OS has started.

At the end, we can log in to our system as we did earlier:

```
Debian GNU/Linux 8 arm ttymxc0
default username:password is [debian:temppwd]
arm login: root
Password:
Linux arm 4.4.7-armv7-x6 #4 SMP Sat May 14 19:35:00 CEST 2016 armv7l
The programs included with the Debian GNU/Linux system are free
software; the exact distribution terms for each program are
described in the individual files in /usr/share/doc/*/copyright.
Debian GNU/Linux comes with ABSOLUTELY NO WARRANTY, to the extent
permitted by applicable law.
root@arm:~#
```

Developing into an NFS

Now the question is, *Why we should use an NFS during the development?*

The answer is because it improves the develop-test-develop stages dramatically! In fact, if we have to replace a wrong version of a program or a complete directory, we can simply do it on the host, without copying anything on the client.

Let's do a simple example by considering what we did with the *Hello World* program during the cross-compilation. We cross-compiled it on the host, and then, we have to copy it on the target. However, if we use an NFS we can avoid such a copy.

Here is the C program on the target:

```
root@arm:~# ls
helloworld.c
```

Here is the same program on the host:

```
# ls /opt/armhf-rootfs-debian-jessie/root/
helloworld.c
```

Note that the root's privileges are necessary due the fact that the /opt/armhf-rootfs-debian-jessie/root/ directory is forbidden to everyone but the root!

Then, we can cross-compile it on the host:

```
# cd /opt/armhf-rootfs-debian-jessie/root/
# make CC=arm-linux-gnueabihf-gcc CFLAGS="-Wall -O2" helloworld
arm-linux-gnueabihf-gcc -Wall -O2    helloworld.c    -o helloworld
```

Then, program is already on the client too and ready to be used:

```
root@arm:~# ls
helloworld  helloworld.c
root@arm:~# ./helloworld
Hello World
```

This simple example shows the benefits on a single file. Let's consider it with a more complex program with tons of files.

Using an emulator

We just saw how useful it can be to have all the developer kits' rootfs on the host, but what if we can execute all the programs directly on the host? Referring to the earlier example with the *Hello World* program, we mean the possibility to compile it on the host and then executing it on the host too.

It is quite obvious that the advantages in this case are minimum, but consider the case where we have a complex program to compile with tons of libraries. Of course, this approach has some disadvantages. First of all, the fact that our x86 CPU has no idea about how to execute the ARM code, so we need a program that emulates the ARM CPU over the x86 one. This emulation needs a lot of CPU resources, and most probably, the execution time is slower than the original one. However, in some circumstances, it may be preferred to emulate the ARM CPU. A very powerful embedded system may have two 4 GB RAMs whereas a real powerful host PC may have 32 GB, without considering the fact that the host's disk can be 10 times quicker than a microSD or flash memory.

Despite wishing that we use an emulator, let's see how we can use it.

The emulator we're going to use is **QEMU**, a generic machine emulator (and virtualizer). If we take a quick look at QEMU's wiki site at `http://wiki.qemu.org/Main_Page`, we read the first lines:

When used as a machine emulator, QEMU can run OSes and programs made for one machine (e.g. an ARM board) on a different machine (e.g. your own PC). By using dynamic translation, it achieves very good performance.

It's exactly what we need!

Executing a program

As the first (and simple) example, let's see how we can execute the *Hello World* program on the host. We already cross-compiled it, and we got an ARM executable:

```
# file helloworld
helloworld: ELF 32-bit LSB executable, ARM, EABI5 version 1 (SYSV), dy
namically linked, interpreter /lib/ld-linux-armhf.so.3, for GNU/Linux
2.6.32, BuildID[sha1]=9d36da7eb92d0d552bc04a7771f5ebbb14d04497, not st
ripped
```

OK, now, we need to install the QEMU program, which is split into several packages:

```
$ apt-cache search qemu | grep '^qemu'
qemu-block-extra - extra block backend modules for qemu-system and qem
u-utils
qemu-kvm - QEMU Full virtualization
qemu-slof - Slimline Open Firmware -- QEMU PowerPC version
qemu-system - QEMU full system emulation binaries
qemu-system-arm - QEMU full system emulation binaries (arm)
qemu-system-common - QEMU full system emulation binaries (common)
qemu-system-mips - QEMU full system emulation binaries (mips)
qemu-system-misc - QEMU full system emulation binaries (miscelaneous)
qemu-system-ppc - QEMU full system emulation binaries (ppc)
qemu-system-sparc - QEMU full system emulation binaries (sparc)
qemu-system-x86 - QEMU full system emulation binaries (x86)
qemu-utils - QEMU utilities
qemu-efi - UEFI firmware for virtual machines
qemu - fast processor emulator
qemu-guest-agent - Guest-side qemu-system agent
qemu-launcher - GTK+ front-end to QEMU computer emulator
qemu-user - QEMU user mode emulation binaries
qemu-user-binfmt - QEMU user mode binfmt registration for qemu-user
qemu-user-static - QEMU user mode emulation binaries (static version)
qemubuilder - pbuilder using QEMU as backend
qemuctl - controlling GUI for qemu
qemulator - transitional dummy package to virtualbriks
```

However, we just need the **qemu-user** and **libc6-armhf-cross** packages, one that stores the emulator itself and the **libc** libraries for ARM. So, let's install them:

```
$ sudo aptitude install qemu-user libc6-armhf-cross
```

When the installation is finished, we can go back where the `helloworld` program is placed and execute it with QEMU:

```
# cd /opt/armhf-rootfs-debian-jessie/root/
# qemu-arm -L /usr/arm-linux-gnueabihf/ helloworld
Hello World
```

The root's privileges are not required by QEMU. We need them just because the directory where the program is located is owned by root.

As we can see, this is nice, but if limited to this usage, it can be quite useless. However, this is just the beginning, since QEMU can do much more. In particular, it can emulate a complete embedded system, that is, emulating the whole hardware (CPU, memories, and peripherals), or it can act as a generic CPU that uses the host PC resources.

The differences between these two different approaches is that the former needs a more complete support by QEMU (since it must emulate not only the CPU but all the other peripherals too), while the latter just needs the CPU and system calls emulations. This is just how the `qemu-arm` programs works, but we want more. We want to avoid specifying special paths for external libraries and/or other kind of dependencies. We'd like to execute a program or, better, a whole root filesystem as an ARM CPU does.

Due to space reasons and since this is not the main target of this book, we'll show the latter operation mode only. You may wish to emulate a whole ARM system and can take a look at the QEMU documentation.

Entering into an ARM rootfs tree

If we take a look at the qemu-user packages, we get three kinds of them:

```
$ apt-cache search qemu-user
qemu-user - QEMU user mode emulation binaries
qemu-user-binfmt - QEMU user mode binfmt registration for qemu-user
qemu-user-static - QEMU user mode emulation binaries (static version)
```

What is really interesting for us is the last one, qemu-user-static. Here the package's description:

```
$ apt-cache show qemu-user-static
Package: qemu-user-static
Priority: optional
```

```
Section: universe/otherosfs
...
Description-en: QEMU user mode emulation binaries (static version)
 QEMU is a fast processor emulator: currently the package supports
 ARM, CRIS, i386, M68k (ColdFire), MicroBlaze, MIPS, PowerPC, SH4,
 SPARC and x86-64 emulation. By using dynamic translation it achieves
 reasonable speed while being easy to port on new host CPUs.
 .
 This package provides the user mode emulation binaries, built
 statically. In this mode QEMU can launch Linux processes compiled for
 one CPU on another CPU.
 .
 If binfmt-support package is installed, qemu-user-static package will
 register binary formats which the provided emulators can handle, so
 that it will be possible to run foreign binaries directly.
 ...
```

So, using this package, we can launch Linux processes compiled for one CPU on another CPU. We can also use this static version, and we don't need any external native (x86) libraries. So, we can suppose to use chroot in the ARM rootfs and then start working as we were on an ARM CPU!

For those that doesn't know what the chroot command does, let me suggest to take a look at its man pages.

OK, maybe these concepts are quite obscure for a newbie, so let's do a demonstration of this fantastic feature.

First of all, let's install the needed package:

```
$ sudo aptitude install qemu-user-static
```

Then, we have to copy the binary of the ARM rootfs. Here, we can check that the binary is compiled statically using the ldd program:

```
$ ldd /usr/bin/qemu-arm-static
        not a dynamic executable
$ sudo cp /usr/bin/qemu-arm-static
          /opt/armhf-rootfs-debian-jessie/usr/bin/
```

Then, we need to mount some special filesystems on the ARM filesystem before doing `chroot`. In particular, we need the `/dev`, `/proc` and `/sys` directories due to the fact that they are needed to most of the Linux's standard commands. To do this without mounting them twice, we can use the `bind` option of the mount command, so we can have the devfs, procfs, and sysfs in more than one place at time.

So, let's duplicate the needed filesystems in our ARM rootfs:

```
$ for fs in dev proc sys ; do \
        sudo mount -o bind /$fs \
                    /opt/armhf-rootfs-debian-jessie/$fs ; \
    done
```

Then, we have to add some tempfs too (this is Debian specific):

```
$ sudo mount -t tmpfs -o 'rw,nosuid,nodev,mode=755' tmpfs
                    /opt/armhf-rootfs-debian-jessie/run
$ sudo mkdir /opt/armhf-rootfs-debian-jessie/run/lock
$ sudo mount -t tmpfs -o 'rw,nosuid,nodev,noexec,relatime,size=5120k'
                    tmpfs /opt/armhf-rootfs-debian-jessie/run/lock
```

We should copy some networking settings:

```
$ sudo cp /etc/resolv.conf
            /opt/armhf-rootfs-debian-jessie/etc/resolv.conf
```

As the last step, we have to jump into the ARM rootfs! In the following commands, we used the `uname` command before and after the jump in order to show you that we effectively changed the running platform:

```
giometti@ubuntu1510:~$ uname -a
Linux ubuntu1510 4.2.0-35-generic #40-Ubuntu SMP Tue Mar 15 22:15:45 U
TC 2016 x86_64 x86_64 x86_64 GNU/Linux
giometti@ubuntu1510:~$ sudo chroot /opt/armhf-rootfs-debian-jessie/
root@ubuntu1510:/# uname -a
Linux ubuntu1510 4.2.0-35-generic #40-Ubuntu SMP Tue Mar 15 22:15:45 U
TC 2016 armv7l GNU/Linux
```

Great! We are running an ARM rootfs on an X86 PC!

Note that for better readability, we didn't remove the prompt as we did on every command executed into the host PC. So, you can notice that before `chroot`, the prompt is `giometti@ubuntu1510:~$` while it becomes `root@ubuntu1510:/#` later on.

We can verify that all filesystems we created for this target are in place:

```
root@ubuntu1510:/# mount
udev on /dev type devtmpfs (rw,nosuid,relatime,size=1005904k,nr_inodes
=251476,mode=755)
proc on /proc type proc (rw,nosuid,nodev,noexec,relatime)
sysfs on /sys type sysfs (rw,nosuid,nodev,noexec,relatime)
tmpfs on /run type tmpfs (rw,nosuid,nodev,relatime,mode=755)
tmpfs on /run/lock type tmpfs (rw,nosuid,nodev,noexec,relatime,size=51
20k)
```

We can now execute our `helloworld` program as we were on the Wandboard:

```
root@ubuntu1510:/# cd root/
root@ubuntu1510:/root# ls
helloworld  helloworld.c
root@ubuntu1510:/root# file helloworld
helloworld: ELF 32-bit LSB executable, ARM, EABI5 version 1 (SYSV), dy
namically linked, interpreter /lib/ld-linux-armhf.so.3,for GNU/Linux 2
.6.32, BuildID[sha1]=9d36da7eb92d0d552bc04a7771f5ebbb14d04497, not str
ipped
root@ubuntu1510:/root# ./helloworld
Hello World
```

If we correctly set up the networking support, we can proceed in installing new packages as on every ARM machine. So, we can update the current repositories:

```
root@ubuntu1510:/root# apt-get update
Get:1 http://security.debian.org jessie/updates InRelease [63.1 kB]
Ign http://httpredir.debian.org jessie InRelease
Get:2 http://repos.rcn-ee.com jessie InRelease [4350 B]
Get:3 http://httpredir.debian.org jessie-updates InRelease [142 kB]
Get:4 http://security.debian.org jessie/updates/main armhf Packages [2
92 kB]
Get:5 http://repos.rcn-ee.com jessie/main armhf Packages [375 kB]
Get:6 http://httpredir.debian.org jessie Release.gpg [2373 B]
Get:7 http://httpredir.debian.org jessie Release [148 kB]
Get:8 http://httpredir.debian.org jessie-updates/contrib armhf Package
s [20 B]
Get:9 http://httpredir.debian.org jessie-updates/main armhf Packages [
9276 B]
Get:10 http://security.debian.org jessie/updates/contrib armhf Package
s [994 B]
Get:11 http://security.debian.org jessie/updates/non-free armhf Packag
es [20 B]
Get:12 http://httpredir.debian.org jessie/main armhf Packages [8834 kB
]
Get:13 http://httpredir.debian.org jessie-updates/non-free armhf Packa
```

```
ges [450 B]
Get:14 http://httpredir.debian.org jessie/contrib armhf Packages [44.6
 kB]
Get:15 http://httpredir.debian.org jessie/non-free armhf Packages [74.
5 kB]
Fetched 9992 kB in 1min 2s (160 kB/s)
Reading package lists... Done
```

> Note that all downloaded repositories are based on the **armhf** platform instead of **x86**.

Then, we can install a native ARM compiler:

```
root@ubuntu1510:/root# apt-get install make gcc
```

Then, we can natively recompile our *Hello World* program:

```
root@ubuntu1510:/root# make helloworld
cc      helloworld.c   -o helloworld
root@ubuntu1510:/root# file helloworld
helloworld: ELF 32-bit LSB executable, ARM, EABI5 version 1 (SYSV), dy
namically linked, interpreter /lib/ld-linux-armhf.so.3, for GNU/Linux
2.6.32, BuildID[sha1]=e124a6c84b518908a8c6e25365169fc18890dfde, not st
ripped
root@ubuntu1510:/root# ./helloworld
Hello World
```

> Of course, this demonstration is just a brief introduction about what we can do with QEMU and how we can use this operation mode to develop a complex application. To present all QEMU's features and all modes of functioning, I need to write a dedicated book.

As a final note, we have to remark that when we wish to close this ARM root filesystem emulation, we can simply type the exit program as follows:

```
root@ubuntu1510:/root# exit
exit
giometti@ubuntu1510:~$
```

Then, we have to unmount all the previously mounted filesystems:

```
$ for fs in dev proc sys run/lock run ; do \
      sudo umount /opt/armhf-rootfs-debian-jessie/$fs ; \
  done
```

Summary

In this chapter, we did a long tour into three of the most important topics of the GNU/Linux embedded programming: the C compiler (and the cross-compiler), the kernel (and the device drivers with the device tree), and the root filesystem. Also, we presented the NFS in order to have a remote root filesystem over the network, and we introduced the emulator usage in order to execute foreign code on the host PC.

In the next chapter, we move our attention from the low-level tools and kernel internals to the very high-level tools and programming techniques. We'll see how we can implement very complex tasks using Bash, PHP, or Python programming or using a dedicated daemon such as Apache, MySQL, and so on.

4
Quick Programming with Scripts and System Daemons

In the previous chapter, we dealt with **native compilation** and **cross-compilation** and saw that the C language is actually a *must-know* for an embedded developer; however, sometimes, it's better to use a script or an already written daemon to quickly solve a problem.

In this chapter, we're going to take a look at some common and useful system tools we can use in an embedded system to constantly execute a controlling/monitoring procedure. These kinds of software are usually called **daemon**. In Unix terminology, a daemon is a computer program that runs as a background process rather than being under the direct control of an interactive user, so they are perfect to execute a controlling/monitoring procedure. In this scenario, we're going to take a look at some existing daemons *ready-to-use* and that we can use to implement some repetitive and common tasks.

Then, we will look at how to install and use some common scripting languages in our embedded developer kits and how to solve a simple but real problem by writing the solution in different languages (we'll present PHP, Python, and Bash) in order to show you the differences between them and using a system daemon when required.

As a last step, we're going to show how an embedded developer can write an their own daemon in C or using a scripting language such as PHP, Python, and Bash. As for previous introductory chapters, experienced developers may decide to skip this chapter, but right now, it's should be quite clear that in any case, reading it might be really useful!

Setting up the system

Before starting, we must set up our embedded board by installing all the going to use the BeagleBone Black to test the code; however, as already stated earlier, every command or program used here can be used indifferently on the other embedded boards too.

First of all, we have to install the command-line interpreter for the PHP scripting language and the related plugin for the Apache web server. We can do it using the usual `aptitude` command, as follows:

```
root@bbb:~# aptitude install php5-cli libapache2-mod-php5
```

Then, a package for the Python interpreter proves to be useful in creating daemons:

```
root@bbb:~# aptitude install python-daemon
```

Then, we have to install the following packages for `xinetd`:

```
root@bbb:~# aptitude install xinetd telnet
```

For MySQL, we need the following packages:

```
root@bbb:~# aptitude install mysql-client mysql-server
```

During the installation of the preceding MySQL packages, the system should ask for an administrative root user. This is not the system's root user, but it's the root user of the MySQL server, so we should put a different password from the system's root user (even if it's not required at all).

Then, we need some extra packages to add some libraries to talk with the MySQL daemon in C, PHP, and Python languages. Here is the command to install these packages:

```
root@bbb:~# aptitude install libmysqlclient-dev php5-mysqlnd
        python-mysqldb
```

System daemons

As already stated, a daemon is a computer program that runs as a background process; in particular, for a Unix system, the Unix bible *Advanced Programming in the UNIX Environment* by Richard Stevens says:

> *Daemons are processes that live for a long time. They are often started when the system is bootstrapped and terminate only when the system is shutdown. We say they run in background, because they don't have a controlling terminal.*

This behavior is so important that a special function has been implemented in the **glibc** library that permits the developer to easily create a daemon process. The function is (obviously) named `daemon()`.

Just to fix this concept, we report a possible implementation of the `daemon()` function in order to show you which steps a process should carry out in order to turn itself into a daemon:

```c
int daemon(void)
{
    int fd;

    /* Create the daemon grand-child process */
    switch (fork()) {
    case -1:
        return -1;        /* error! */
    case 0:
        break;            /* child continues... */
    default:
        exit(0);          /* parent goes... bye bye!! */
    }

    /* This code is now executed by the shell's grand-child */

    if (setsid() < 0)     /* become a session leader */
        return -1;

    if (chdir("/") < 0)   /* change working directory */
        return -1;

    umask(0);             /* clear file mode creation mask */

    /* In the end close all open file descriptors */
    for (fd = sysconf(_SC_OPEN_MAX); fd > 0; fd--)
        close(fd);
```

```
    return 0;
}
```

The first thing to do for a daemon candidate process is to call `fork()` and then the `exit()` system calls. This is because if the daemon is started as a simple shell command with the parent terminate makes, the shell thinks that the command is done and the prompt can be returned to the user. Then, the `setsid()` call is needed to run the new daemon candidate process in a new session and have no controlling terminal.

The `chdir()` system call is needed in order to avoid the daemon the candidate process is running on a mounted filesystem and then prevent it from be unmounted. In fact, the current working directory is inherited by the parent and changing it to the root (the slash character `"/"` in the preceding code) is a trick to prevent this problem. The `umask()` system call is then used to permit the newly created daemon from creating files with specific permissions without restrictions.

The last step closes all open file descriptors eventually inherited by the grandparent (the shell in this case). By closing all the process communication channels, the daemon cannot be managed by the user anymore; however, in order to make it possible to change some daemon functionalities, it may reopen a dedicated channel (usually a **Unix domain socket**) when receiving some configuration commands, or it can be designed in such a way that it rereads its configuration file when a special signal arrives.

 Details of how a daemon works or how it can be created are out of the scope of this book. You can take a look around the Internet starting with `http://en.wikipedia.org/wiki/Daemon_%28computing%29` or (better) by reading the Unix bible, *Advanced Programming in the UNIX Environment* by Richard Stevens.

Useful and ready-to-use daemons

In a GNU/Linux system (and a Unix system in general), there exist a lot of *ready-to-use* daemons that are used to do real common tasks. The most notable ones are as follows:

- **Apache, uhttpd, and lighttpd**: The **HTTP** server daemons.
- **atd and crond**: The task scheduler daemons.
- **ftpd and tftpd**: The file transfer daemons.
- **inetd and xinetd**: The Internet super server daemons.
- **named/bind and C**: The **DNS** server daemons.
- **nfsd, lockd, mountd, and statd**: The **NFS** daemon and support daemons.
- **ntpd**: The **NTP** service daemon.

- **portmap, rpcbind**: The **SunRPC** port mappers.
- **mysqld, postgresql, and C.**: Database server daemons.
- **sendmail, exim, postfix, and C.**: The mail transfer agent daemons.
- **snmpd**: The Simple Network Management Protocol (**SNMP**) daemon.
- **syslogd** and C.: The system logging daemons.
- **systemd**: The system management daemon.
- **telnetd** and **sshd/dropbear**: Telnet and **SSH** server daemons.
- **vsftpd and Co.**: The File Transfer Protocol (**FTP**) server daemons.

Some of these have already been introduced in previous chapters due to the fact that they have been used in some examples, so we're going to add a little list of other useful daemons the developer may use to simplify their job with a brief explanation on how to use and how to get access to them using one of our developer kits.

For the other daemons, we encourage you to surf the Internet in order to know more about them; they may discover interesting thing.

System daemons management

Each Linux distribution has its own way to manage system daemons; in our systems, we're using Debian, so the way we have to use to manage our daemons is by calling the relative management script (which is placed in the `/etc/init.d` directory) with proper option arguments. This way of operation is the legacy mode related to the `initd` daemon, which is present in all Debian releases; however, in our embedded kits, we've installed a recent release that uses the `systemd` daemon. This new daemon is backward-compatible with `initd`, but it also introduces a new service management behavior.

 We have no space available to go deeply into what `initd` and `systemd` are and in what way they differ from each other, so you should start from the next two URLs to get further information on these important daemons: `https://en.wikipedia.org/wiki/Systemd` and `https://en.wikipedia.org/wiki/Init`.

In this book, we're going to use the legacy mode for two main reasons: the new way is present on latest releases only, while the legacy one can be used everywhere and because I still prefer using it; however, a brief note on the new behavior is reported for sake of completeness. So, as an example, let's start by taking a look at the `/etc/init.d` directory in order to have a list of the available services:

```
root@bbb:~# ls /etc/init.d/
```

alsa-utils	hostapd	mysql	sendsigs
apache2	hostname.sh	netscript	single
avahi-daemon	hwclock.sh	networking	skeleton
bootlogs	killprocs	pppd-dns	ssh
bootmisc.sh	kmod	procps	sudo
checkfs.sh	loadcpufreq	rc	udev
checkroot-bootclean.sh	motd	rc.local	udhcpd
checkroot.sh	mountall-bootclean.sh	rcS	umountfs
cpufrequtils	mountall.sh	README	umountnfs.sh
cron	mountdevsubfs.sh	reboot	umountroot
dbus	mountkernfs.sh	rmnologin	urandom
halt	mountnfs-bootclean.sh	rsync	xinetd
hdparm	mountnfs.sh	rsyslog	

With the new behavior, we can use the following command:

```
root@bbb:~# service --status-all
 [ - ] alsa-utils
 [ + ] apache2
 [ + ] avahi-daemon
 [ - ] bootlogs
 [ - ] bootmisc.sh
 [ - ] checkfs.sh
 ...
```

As we can see, there are a lot of available services; however, let's consider the Apache service and try to get its status, and then we have to execute the /etc/init.d/apache2 program with the status option argument, as follows:

```
root@bbb:~# /etc/init.d/apache2 status
. apache2.service - LSB: Apache2 web server
   Loaded: loaded (/etc/init.d/apache2; generated; vendor preset: enab
led)
   Active: active (running) since Mon 2016-10-10 12:01:10 UTC; 1 day 1
0h ago
     Docs: man:systemd-sysv-generator(8)
  Process: 3315 ExecReload=/etc/init.d/apache2 reload (code=exited, st
atus=0/SUCCESS)
  Process: 1641 ExecStart=/etc/init.d/apache2 start (code=exited, stat
us=0/SUCCESS)
   CGroup: /system.slice/apache2.service
           +-1972 /usr/sbin/apache2 -k start
           +-3371 /usr/sbin/apache2 -k start
           +-3372 /usr/sbin/apache2 -k start
           +-3373 /usr/sbin/apache2 -k start
           +-3374 /usr/sbin/apache2 -k start
           \-3375 /usr/sbin/apache2 -k start
```

```
Oct 10 12:01:06 bbb systemd[1]: Starting LSB: Apache2 web server...
Oct 10 12:01:10 bbb apache2[1641]: Starting web server: apache2.
Oct 10 12:01:10 bbb systemd[1]: Started LSB: Apache2 web server.
Oct 11 06:25:07 bbb systemd[1]: Reloading LSB: Apache2 web server.
Oct 11 06:25:08 bbb apache2[3315]: Reloading web server: apache2.
Oct 11 06:25:08 bbb systemd[1]: Reloaded LSB: Apache2 web server.
```

With the new behavior, we can use the following command to get the same output as earlier:

```
root@bbb:~# service apache2 stop
```

The service is in the active status, and if we wish to stop it, we can use the same preceding command but by specifying the stop option argument:

```
root@bbb:~# /etc/init.d/apache2 stop
[ ok ] Stopping apache2 (via systemctl): apache2.service.
```

With the new behavior, we can use the following command to stop the daemon:

```
root@bbb:~# service apache2 stop
```

We get no output by executing this command.

We can verify that the service is stopped by executing the status command again. Now, if we wish to restart the daemon, we can use the following command:

```
root@bbb:~# /etc/init.d/apache2 start
[ ok ] Starting apache2 (via systemctl): apache2.service.
```

With the new behavior, we can use the following command to stop the daemon:

```
root@bbb:~# service apache2 start
```

Again, we get no output by executing this command.

A useful trick to stop and start a daemon again-for example, after we've changed its configuration files-is using the restart option argument as follows:

```
root@bbb:~# /etc/init.d/apache2 restart
[ ok ] Restarting apache2 (via systemctl): apache2.service.
```

With the new behavior, we can use the following command to stop the daemon:

```
root@bbb:~# service apache2 restart
```

There's still no output by executing this command.

These commands work in the same manner for all the system daemons we can find in our Debian OS, so we can use them to manage the following daemons too.

syslogd

When we talk about daemons, one of the most important ones is **syslogd**! The syslogd daemon is a widely used standard for message logging that permits the separation of the software that generates messages from the system that stores them and from the software that reports and analyzes them.

Due to the fact that a daemon has all the communication channels closed by default, this is the most efficient and easy method to report a daemon's activities to the system administrator/developer.

In the Debian system, we've installed into our developer kits at the beginning of this book; the syslogd service is implemented by the **rsyslog** package, which holds the `rsyslogd` daemon. However, the scope of this book does not include a detailed explanation on how it works but just how it can be used to efficiently log some messages in order to keep track of our applications or just to debug them. In the next sections, we're going to see how it can be accessed using different programming languages but before we can start seeing how we can configure it in order to log a remote system (which can be very useful when we we work with embedded systems).

If we wish to send log messages from our BeagleBone Black to the host, we have to modify the rsyslog package's `/etc/rsyslog.conf` configuration file in the host, as follows:

```
--- /etc/rsyslog.conf.orig    2017-01-14 22:24:59.800606283 +0100
+++ /etc/rsyslog.conf    2017-01-14 22:25:06.208600601 +0100
@@ -15,8 +15,8 @@
 #module(load="immark")  # provides --MARK-- message capability

 # provides UDP syslog reception
-#module(load="imudp")
-#input(type="imudp" port="514")
+module(load="imudp")
+input(type="imudp" port="514")

 # provides TCP syslog reception
 #module(load="imtcp")
```

This will enable the ability to receive log messages from a remote machine via UDP (we can use TCP too). Then, to enable the new configuration, we have to restart the daemon on the host using the next command, as explained earlier:

```
$ sudo /etc/init.d/rsyslog restart
[ ok ] Restarting rsyslog (via systemctl): rsyslog.service.
```

 We need the `sudo` command on the host since the system's daemons can be managed by the root user only.

Then, on the BeagleBone Black, we have to add the following line on the `/etc/rsyslog.conf` file (usually at the end of the file):

```
*.* @192.168.7.1:514
```

In this manner, we ask to `rsyslog` to send all log messages to the host at the IP address `192.168.7.1` on port `514` (where our host PC is listening). Again, in order to enable the new configuration, we have to restart the daemon with the same command used on the host, as the one shown here:

```
root@bbb:~# /etc/init.d/rsyslog restart
[ ok ] Restarting rsyslog (via systemctl): rsyslog.service.
```

If everything works well, when we take a look at log messages on the host, we should see the ones from the BeagleBone Black, as reported here:

```
Jan 14 22:29:01 hulk ntpd[23220]: Soliciting pool server 193.234.225.2
37
Jan 14 22:29:20 hulk ntpd[23220]: Soliciting pool server 2a00:dcc0:dea
d:b9ff:fede:feed:e39:73d7
Oct 11 22:55:05 bbb rsyslogd: [origin software="rsyslogd" swVersion="8
.4.2" x-pid="5540" x-info="http://www.rsyslog.com"] start
Oct 11 22:55:04 bbb systemd[1]: Stopping System Logging Service...
Oct 11 22:55:04 bbb systemd[1]: Stopped System Logging Service.
Oct 11 22:55:04 bbb systemd[1]: Starting System Logging Service...
Oct 11 22:55:05 bbb systemd[1]: Started System Logging Service.
Oct 11 22:55:14 bbb rsyslogd: [origin software="rsyslogd" swVersion="8
.4.2" x-pid="5540" x-info="http://www.rsyslog.com"] exiting on signal
15.
```

 After the system date (which is wrong for the BeagleBone Black), we can see the system's name that is set as `hulk` for the author's host PC and as `bbb` for the BeagleBone Black.

syslogd in Bash

From the Bash shell, we can use the `logger` command, as follows:

```
root@bbb:~# logger -t mydaemon logging message in bash
```

This command will generate the following message in the `/var/log/syslog` file:

```
root@bbb:~# tail -f /var/log/syslog | grep mydaemon
Apr  2 18:29:03 bbb mydaemon: logging message in bash
```

syslogd in C

The same message can be also generated in **C** language using the code in the `chapter_04/syslogd/logger.c` file in the book's example code repository. The code simply calls three functions to do its job and this is the code snippet:

```
openlog("mydaemon", LOG_NOWAIT, LOG_USER);
syslog(LOG_INFO, "logging message in C");
closelog();
```

Just compile and execute it using the following command lines:

```
root@bbb:~# make logger
cc -Wall -O2    logger.c    -o logger
root@bbb:~# ./logger
```

Then, in the `/var/log/syslog` file, we should get the following output:

```
Apr  2 18:33:11 bbb mydaemon: logging message in C
```

syslogd in PHP

In PHP, we can use the code in the `chapter_04/syslogd/logger.php` file in the book's example code repository. Again, we just need three functions to do the job, and this is the code snippet:

```
openlog("mydaemon", LOG_NOWAIT, LOG_USER);
syslog(LOG_INFO, "logging message in PHP");
closelog();
```

The example program can be executed with the following command:

```
root@bbb:~# php logger.php
```

Again, as earlier, we can see the generated message as follows:

```
Apr  2 18:43:52 bbb mydaemon: logging message in PHP
```

 The complete documentation for the syslog library routine is
at: http://php.net/manual/en/function.syslog.php.

syslogd in Python

The last example is in Python, and it's stored in the `chapter_04/syslogd/logger.py` file
in the book's example code repository. We use the same three functions again:

```
syslog.openlog("mydaemon", syslog.LOG_NOWAIT, syslog.LOG_USER)
syslog.syslog(syslog.LOG_INFO, "logging message in Python")
syslog.closelog()
```

Then, we can execute it with the following command:

```
root@bbb:~# python logger.py
```

And, as earlier, it will generate the following message:

```
Apr  2 18:45:08 bbb mydaemon: logging message in Python
```

 The complete documentation for the syslog library routines is
at: https://docs.python.org/3.4/library/syslog.html.

cron

This daemon is very useful to execute simple and repetitive tasks in the background; in fact,
it executes scheduled shell commands according to a timetable called **crontab**, which the
developer can use to program their tasks.

The crontab must be accessed and updated using the `crontab` command, and in order to
better explain how the **cron** daemon works, you should take a look at the current crontab of
the root user with the following command:

```
root@bbb:~# crontab -e
```

It may happen that we get the following message:

```
/usr/bin/select-editor: 1: /usr/bin/select-editor:
gettext: not found
 'select-editor'.
/usr/bin/select-editor: 1: /usr/bin/select-editor:
gettext: not found
 1. /bin/nano <----
 2. /usr/bin/vim.basic
 3. /usr/bin/vim.tiny

/usr/bin/select-editor: 32: /usr/bin/select-editor:
gettext: not found
 1-3 [1]:
```

This is because we haven't chosen a default editor yet; however, we just need to select one in the list and the message will disappear.

When the preceding command is used, the embedded kit will open a text file using the current text editor, where the content is shown as follows:

```
# Edit this file to introduce tasks to be run by cron.
#
# Each task to run has to be defined through a single line
# indicating with different fields when the task will be run
# and what command to run for the task
#
# To define the time you can provide concrete values for
# minute (m), hour (h), day of month (dom), month (mon),
# and day of week (dow) or use '*' in these fields (for 'any').#
# Notice that tasks will be started based on the cron's system
# daemon's notion of time and timezones.
#
# Output of the crontab jobs (including errors) is sent through
# email to the user the crontab file belongs to (unless redirected).
#
# For example, you can run a backup of all your user accounts
# at 5 a.m every week with:
# 0 5 * * 1 tar -zcf /var/backups/home.tgz /home/
#
# For more information see the manual pages of crontab(5) and cron(8)
#
# m h  dom mon dow    command
```

Note that the default editor can be changed by setting the EDITOR
environment variable as follows:

root@bbb:~# export EDITOR=nano

Then, the BeagleBone Black will use the `nano` command to show the file
holding crontab.

Just reading the comments into the crontab file, it's quite easy to understand how the
daemon works: we have one task per line and the first five fields of each line define at
which instant the command in the sixth field must be executed. For example, as reported in
the earlier comments, in order to run a backup of all BeagleBone Black's user accounts at 5
a.m. every week, the schedule line should be as follows:

```
0 5 * * 1 tar -zcf /var/backups/home.tgz /home/
```

The first five fields do the trick; in fact, the first field tells cron that the command must be
run at minute (m) 0, the second set the execution hour (h) at 5 (hours are from 0 to 23), the
third and the fourth fields, using the wildcard * character, say respectively that the
command must be executed each day of month (dom) and each month (mon), while the
fifth says that the command must be executed on the day of week (dow) 1, that is on
Monday (numbers 0 or 7 is for Sunday).

Another useful feature is that in the crontab file, the developer can also set some variables
to modify the default behavior-for example, the default value for the PATH variable is
"/usr/bin:/bin" and we can modify it to add the user's bin directory using the following
line:

```
PATH=~/bin:/usr/bin/:/bin
```

Note that the ~ character is correctly interpreted by the shell (which is set to
SHELL=/bin/bash by default), while the same is not valid for the environmental
substitutions or replacement of variables, thus lines such as the following will not work as
you might expect; that is, there will not be any substitution:

```
PATH = $HOME/bin:$PATH
```

You can get more information by reading the crontab file's man pages
using the `man` command:

root@bbb:~# man 5 crontab

xinetd

This tool is a network daemon program that specializes in adding networking features to programs that normally do not not have it (we already saw this daemon for the host in Chapter 2, *Managing the System Console*, in *Loading files from the network* section). This daemon is an enhanced version of the standard **inetd** daemon, but nowadays, it replaces inetd in most distributions.

The xinetd configuration file is /etc/xinetd.conf, which usually looks like the following:

```
# Simple configuration file for xinetd
#
# Some defaults, and include /etc/xinetd.d/

defaults
{

# Please note that you need a log_type line to be able to use
# log_on_success
# and log_on_failure. The default is the following :
# log_type = SYSLOG daemon info

}

includedir /etc/xinetd.d
```

So the real configuration settings are in the /etc/xinetd.d directory, which in turn holds one file per service. In our BeagleBone Black, we have the following listing:

```
root@bbb:~# ls /etc/xinetd.d/
chargen  daytime  discard  echo  time
```

Each configuration file tells the daemon what program needs to be run when an incoming network connection is received, but before doing it, it redirects the program's stdin, stdout, and stderr streams to the socket used to manage the connection. By doing this, every program that simply writes and reads data to and from the standard Unix streams can talk remotely over a network connection!

Let's look at a simple example and consider the following Bash script:

```
/bin/bash

while /bin/true; do
    read line
```

```
    line=$(echo $line | tr -d '\n\r')
    [ "$line" == "quit" ] && break;

    echo -e "$line\r"
done

exit 0
```

 The code is hold in the `chapter_04/xinetd/echo.sh` file in the book's example code repository.

If we try to run it, we get this:

```
root@bbb:~# ./echo.sh
```

Now if try to enter the `Testing request` string, the script will echo it on its `stdout` (that is, on the terminal window). Then, in order to exit the program, we must enter the `quit` string. Here's a simple usage:

```
root@bbb:~# ./echo.sh
Testing request
Testing request
quit
root@bbb:~#
```

Now if we add the following code held in the `chapter_04/xinetd/echo_sh` file in the book's example code repository in the `/etc/xinetd.d` directory, we can test the `xinetd` functionality:

```
service at-echo
{
    disable      = no
    socket_type  = stream
    protocol     = tcp
    wait         = no
    user         = root
    server       = /root/echo.sh
}
```

Using the preceding code, we define a new service named `at-echo` defined in the `/etc/services` file, as follows:

```
root@bbb:~# grep at-echo /etc/services
at-echo             204/tcp                     # AppleTalk echo
at-echo             204/udp
```

Then, we specify the TCP protocol and the program to execute when a new connection is established; in our case, we execute `/root/echo.sh` as the user root when a new TCP connection at port 204 is done. The `/root/echo.sh` program simply reads a line from `stdin` and then writes it back to the `stdout` stream.

Now we must restart the daemon to activate the new settings:

```
root@bbb:~# /etc/init.d/xinetd restart
[ ok ] Restarting xinetd (via systemctl): xinetd.service.
```

As a first step, we can verify that the daemon is really listening on port 204, as expected:

```
root@bbb:~# netstat -lpn | grep 204
tcp    0    0 0.0.0.0:204    0.0.0.0:*    LISTEN    2724/xinetd
```

We can check whether our settings are OK and even looking at the system's logging messages in the `/var/log/syslog` file, as follows:

```
root@bbb:~# tail -f /var/log/syslog
Apr 2 20:28:29 bbb xinetd[2655]: Starting internet superserver: xinet
d.
Apr 2 20:28:29 bbb systemd[1]: Started LSB: Starts or stops the xinet
d daemon..
Apr 2 20:28:30 bbb xinetd[2664]: Reading included configuration file:
 /etc/xinetd.d/chargen [file=/etc/xinetd.conf] [line=14]
...
Apr 2 20:28:30 bbb xinetd[2664]: Reading included configuration file:
 /etc/xinetd.d/echo_sh [file=/etc/xinetd.d/echo_sh] [line=26]
Apr 2 20:28:30 bbb xinetd[2664]: Reading included configuration file:
 /etc/xinetd.d/time [file=/etc/xinetd.d/time] [line=9]
Apr 2 20:28:30 bbb xinetd[2664]: removing chargen
Apr 2 20:28:30 bbb xinetd[2664]: removing chargen
...
Apr 2 20:28:30 bbb xinetd[2664]: removing time
Apr 2 20:28:30 bbb xinetd[2664]: removing time
Apr 2 20:28:30 bbb xinetd[2664]: xinetd Version 2.3.15 started with 1
ibwrap loadavg options compiled in.
Apr 2 20:28:30 bbb xinetd[2664]: Started working: 1 available service
```

All configuration files are parsed and then only not disabled services are kept so, in the end, only our new service is up and running!

Now we can test our new network service from the host PC using the telnet program, as follows:

```
$ telnet 192.168.7.2 204
Trying 192.168.7.2...
Connected to 192.168.7.2.
Escape character is '^]'.
Testing request
Testing request
quit
Connection closed by foreign host.
```

This time, we execute the `echo.sh` script again but using a remote TCP connection!

> The `telnet` program has been installed in the preceding section with the xinetd daemon.

sshd

This daemon implements the secure shell service that allows us to use a computer's terminal from a remote machine using an encrypted protocol. This daemon is widely used and is very famous, so it doesn't need any presentation or usage examples; however, in this book, we're going to use it in several different ways:

- To copy files to or from a remote machine
- To execute a remote command
- With the `X11Forwarding` ability

Copying files to or from a remote machine is simple, and the command to be used is `scp` in the following form:

```
root@bbb:~# scp local_file giometti@192.168.7.1:/tmp/
```

The command copies the local_file file to the remote machine's `/tmp` directory at the address `192.168.7.1`. For further `scp` usage forms, you should take a look at the relative man pages.

Executing a remote command is a useful behavior we can use to get on the local machine the output of a command executed on a remote one (actually, we can also manage the program's input). As a simple example, the following command executes the `ls` command on the BeagleBone Black from the host PC and then displays the result on the host's terminal:

```
$ ssh root@192.168.7.2 ls /etc/init.d
root@192.168.7.2's password:
alsa-utils
apache2
avahi-daemon
. . .
```

After entering the root's password, we get the BeagleBone Black's `/etc/init.d` directory content. Again, for further information, the man pages are your best friends.

The last usage we wish to present here (and that will be used in the following chapter) is the `X11Forwarding` ability, that is, the possibility to execute an `X11` application on a remote machine and then see its window on the local machine. Strictly speaking, this behavior can be considered an extended form of the remote commands execution we saw earlier.

 In this book, we cannot explain in detail what the `X11` protocol is; so, you should consider taking a look at the next URL for further information: `https://en.wikipedia.org/wiki/X_Window_System`.

As a simple example, let's try to execute the `xcalc` graphical application on the BeagleBone Black from the host PC and then display its window on the host's display. First of all, we have to install the `xcalc` application on the BeagleBone Black with the `xauth` utility:

```
root@bbb:~# apt-get install x11-apps xauth
```

Then, we have to execute the `xauth` utility in order to build up the required configuration files:

```
root@bbb:~# xauth
xauth:  file /root/.Xauthority does not exist
Using authority file /root/.Xauthority
xauth>
```

Then, we can use the `quit` command to close the program and proceed to enable the X11Forwarding ability for the `sshd` daemon. This can be done by setting the X11Forwarding option to `yes` in the `/etc/ssh/sshd_config` file, as shown here:

```
root@bbb:~# grep X11Forwarding /etc/ssh/sshd_config
X11Forwarding yes
```

In this case, the option is already enabled, but in case it is not, we have to enable it and then we must restart the daemon in the usual manner in order to enable the new configuration.

Now we're ready; on the host, we can use the following command to log in to the BeagleBone Black:

```
$ ssh -X root@192.168.7.2
```

In the preceding command, the `-X` option argument enables the X11Forwarding, as stated in the `ssh` man pages. Now we can safely ignore the `/usr/bin/xauth: file /root/.Xauthority does not exist` warning message and can execute the `xcalc` application normally:

```
root@bbb:~# xcalc
```

If everything works well, the `xcalc` main window will appear on the host display.

Apache

The **Apache HTTP server** is (maybe) the most famous and used web server software in the world. It's installed in (almost) every distribution by default, and it can be used for tons of different tasks related to the *World Wide Web*.

We cannot report all possible configuration settings available for the Apache server here since we'll need a whole book for that; however, we're going to report some settings we're going to use later on in this book.

First of all, we have to verify that the server is up and running in our embedded system, so let's open the web browser in the host PC and point it to the internal IP address `192.168.7.2`; if everything works well, we should get something similar to what's shown in the following figure:

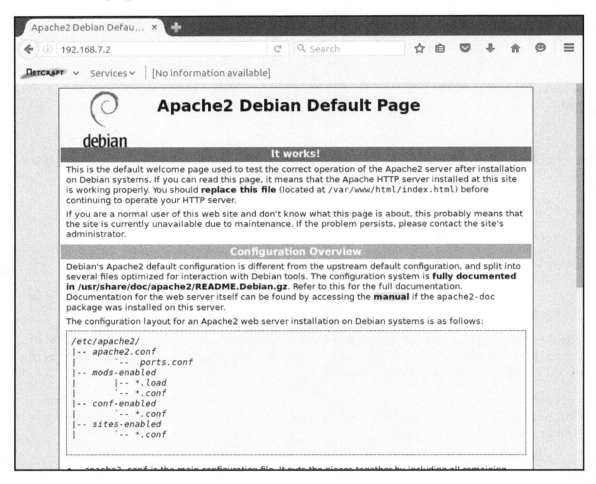

Now we need to check the PHP support, that is, the ability of the Apache server to execute PHP code. To do that, we have to create a `index.php` file, as follows, and then put it in the `/var/www/html` directory:

```php
<?php
    phpinfo();
?>
```

Then, if we point our web browser to the `http://192.168.7.2/index.php` URL, we should get the following output:.

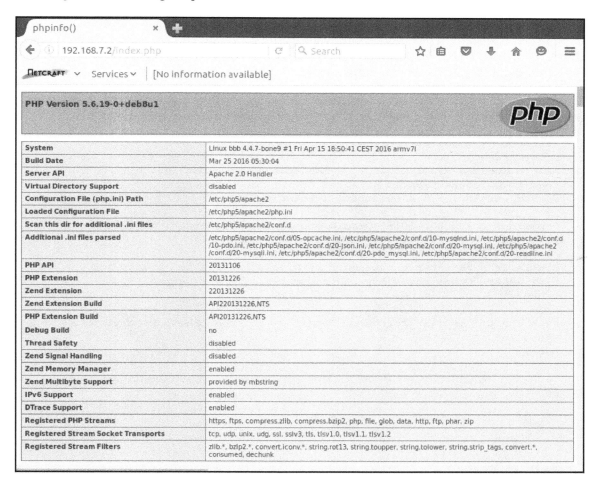

Note that the PHP support for Apache has been installed in the earlier section, where we've set up the system.

What we've done is just one of the several possibilities the Apache web server offers, and you can read more on *The Apache HTTP Server Project* at: `https://httpd.apache.org/`.

MySQL

Usually, we consider this daemon to be used on large servers, but it can be efficiently used in an embedded system too! For example, it can be used to implement a common configuration system or a status system where more processes can get/set the configuration data and/or status data. Or, it can be used efficiently to log several events and/or environment data collected from the sensors.

The daemon should already be set up and running, so now, we can see several ways to get access to its internals. From Bash, we can use the mysql command, as shown here:

```
root@bbb:~# mysql -u root -p
Enter password:
Welcome to the MySQL monitor. Commands end with ; or \g.
Your MySQL connection id is 47
Server version: 5.5.47-0+deb8u1 (Debian)

Copyright (c) 2000, 2015, Oracle and/or its affiliates. All rights
reserved.

Oracle is a registered trademark of Oracle Corporation and/or its
affiliates. Other names may be trademarks of their respective
owners.

Type 'help;' or '\h' for help. Type '\c' to clear the current input
statement.
mysql>
```

 When the BeagleBone Black asks for a password, we should just use the one we set up earlier during the daemon installation.

MySQL in Bash

To use MySQL efficiently, we should create a custom database and then use it to do our job. As an example, we can use the script in the chapter_04/mysql/my_init.sh file in the book's example code repository to generate a custom database called sproject.

The code is quite simple; after a warning message, we use the <<__EOF__ trick to pass a script from the command line to the mysql tool.

An example of the <<__EOF__ trick we refer to is reported as follows:

```
mysql -u root -p <<__EOF__
COMMAND 1
COMMAND 2
...
COMMAND n
__EOF__
```

This trick is often used when we need to supply one or more commands to a program directly in its standard input line (`stdin`). Using this syntax, we tell the Bash shell to send the lines between the command itself and the line holding the __EOF__ characters directly into the `stdin` of the executed command.

The script first recreates a new database (eventually deleting all the existing data) and then adds a new `status` table that we can use to store a system's status data. Here is the code snippet:

```
# Drop all existing data!!!
DROP DATABASE IF EXISTS sproject;

# Create new database
CREATE DATABASE sproject;

# Grant privileges
GRANT USAGE ON *.* TO user@localhost IDENTIFIED BY 'userpass';
GRANT ALL PRIVILEGES ON sproject.* TO user@localhost;
FLUSH PRIVILEGES;

# Select database
USE sproject;

# Create the statuses table
CREATE TABLE status (
    t DATETIME NOT NULL,
    n VARCHAR(64) NOT NULL,
    v VARCHAR(64) NOT NULL,
    PRIMARY KEY (n),
    INDEX (n)
) ENGINE=MEMORY;
```

Note that the table has been created using the MEMORY engine. This engine uses the system's memory to store the information instead of using the mass memory devices (that is, hard disks, microSD cards, and so on). This trick allows us to execute very quick queries to the database, but it can be used where the data is dynamically recreated each time our system restarts due to the fact that they vanish at the system reboot (also, we must consider that the maximum size of the database is limited by the amount of installed memory).

At this point, we can add some entries using the code in the chapter_04/mysql/my_set.sh file in the book's example code repository. We can use it with the following command line:

```
root@bbb:~# ./my_set.sh T1 23.5
```

The script uses the SQL REPLACE command to do the job. The code snippet is just a line of code:

```
REPLACE INTO status (t, n, v) VALUES(now(), '$name', '$value');
```

Now, to verify that the data is correctly collected in the database, we can do a simple dump of the status table created earlier using the my_init.sh file. Then, we use the following command to dump all data in the table:

```
root@bbb:~# ./my_dump.sh
t          n        v
2016-04-02 18:25:35      T1      23.5
```

In this case, all the job is done using the SQL SELECT command. Again, the code snippet is just a line of code:

```
SELECT * FROM status;
```

> A complete guide to the MySQL internals and SQL language can be found on the MySQL documentation site at: https://dev.mysql.com/doc/.

The real power of MySQL is that the preceding actions can be done in different languages, and just to give you some useful hints you can take to start developing your controlling/monitoring system with the BeagleBone Black, we're going to show you how to get access to the `sproject` database from the C, PHP, and Python languages.

 In the next example, we're not going to rewrite the `my_init.sh` script in different languages since it can be deduced from the other examples, and in any case, it is not a significant example indeed. It's just creating the database, and once used, it is not useful anymore.

MySQL in C

In C language, the `my_set` script can be implemented as reported in the `chapter_04/mysql/my_set.c` file in the book's example code repository. The code is quite similar to the Bash one even if it's a bit complex; however, the important parts are the tree calls to the `mysql_init()`, `mysql_real_connect()`, and `mysql_query()` functions. The first two just initiate the connection, while the third executes the query. Here is the code snippet:

```
/* Get connect to MySQL daemon */
c = mysql_init(NULL);
if (!c) {
    fprintf(stderr, "unable to init MySQL data struct\n");
    return -1;
}

if (!mysql_real_connect(c, "127.0.0.1", "user",
                        "userpass", "sproject", 0, NULL, 0)) {
    fprintf(stderr, "unable to connect to MySQL daemon\n");
    ret = -1;
    goto close_db;
}

/* Ok, do the job! */
ret = asprintf(&sql, query, name, value);
if (ret < 0) {
    fprintf(stderr, "unable to allocate memory for query\n");
    goto close_db;
}

ret = mysql_query(c, sql);
if (ret < 0)
    fprintf(stderr, "unable to access the database\n");
```

To complete our panoramic, we just have to show you how you can retrieve data from the MySQL daemon; to do that, we just need a simple implementation of my_dump as in the chapter_04/mysql/my_dump.c file in the book's example code repository. Note that in this case, the first three steps are quite similar to the my_set case, but now, we have to manage an answer from the MySQL daemon too! To do that, we use the mysql_store_result() function, which stores the received data in the q_res variable, and then, using the mysql_fetch_field(), mysql_num_fields(), and mysql_fetch_row() functions, we can extract the needed information. The code snippet for the relevant part is as follows:

```
/* Do the dump of the fields' names */
while ((field = mysql_fetch_field(q_res)))
    printf("%s\t", field->name);
printf("\n");

/* Do the dump one line at time */
n = mysql_num_fields(q_res);
while ((row = mysql_fetch_row(q_res))) {
    for (i = 0; i < n; i++)
        printf("%s\t", row[i] ? row[i] : NULL);
    printf("\n");
}

mysql_free_result(q_res);
```

Well, now we are ready to compile the preceding programs using make:

```
root@bbb:~# make
cc -Wall -O2 -D_GNU_SOURCE -I/usr/include/mysql  my_set.c  -lmysqlcli
ent -o my_set
cc -Wall -O2 -D_GNU_SOURCE -I/usr/include/mysql  my_dump.c  -lmysqlcl
ient -o my_dump
```

> By default, the libraries needed to compile this C program are not installed; however we did this in the earlier section, where we set up the system.

Now we can use them as we did earlier with Bash:

```
root@bbb:~# ./my_set T1 20
root@bbb:~# ./my_dump
t     n    v
2016-04-02 18:36:19    T1    20
```

 A complete guide to the *MySQL C API* can be found
at: http://dev.mysql.com/doc/refman/5.7/en/c-api.html.

MySQL in PHP

Now it's PHP's turn, and the my_set program is in the chapter_04/mysql/my_set.php
file in the book's example code repository. In this case, the code is more compact than in C,
but it looks like very similar: we still have a connection stage and then a query execution
stage. The involved functions are now mysql_connect(), mysql_select_db(), and
mysql_query(). The relevant code is reported in the following snippet:

```
# Get connect to MySQL daemon
$ret = mysql_connect("127.0.0.1", "user", "userpass");
if (!$ret)
    die("unable to connect with MySQL daemon");

$ret = mysql_select_db("sproject");
if (!$ret)
    die("unable to select database");

# Ok, do the job!
$query = "REPLACE INTO status (t, n, v) " .
        "VALUES(now(), '$name', '$value');";
$dbres = mysql_query($query);
if (!$dbres)
    die("unable to execute the query");
```

As in C, the PHP version of `my_dump` has to manage the answer from the MySQL daemon and the code is in the `chapter_04/mysql/my_dump.php` file in the book's example code repository. Even in this case, after the query, we get some data back, which we can extract using the `mysql_num_fields()`, `mysql_field_name()`, and `mysql_fetch_array()` functions. Here is the code snippet:

```
# Do the dump of the fields' names
$n = mysql_num_fields($dbres);
for ($i = 0; $i < $n; $i++)
    printf("%s\t", mysql_field_name($dbres, $i));
printf("\n");

# Do the dump one line at time
while ($row = mysql_fetch_array($dbres)) {
    for ($i = 0; $i < $n; $i++)
        printf("%s\t", $row[$i]);
    printf("\n");
}
```

 These functions are not supported by the basic PHP language and we need some external libraries that are not installed by default; we did this in the earlier section, where we set up the system.

These programs can now be used as the other programs, as follows:

```
root@bbb:~# ./my_set.php T1 19.5
root@bbb:~# ./my_dump.php
t    n    v
2016-04-02 18:42:29    T1    19.5
```

 A complete guide to the *MySQL PHP API* can be found at: `http://php.net/manual/it/book.mysql.php`.

MySQL in Python

In Python, the `my_set` program can be as in the `chapter_04/mysql/my_set.py` file in the book's example code repository. The program looks a bit different from the previous ones due the usage of the **cursor**; however, looking carefully at the code, we can see that there are very few differences. The `MySQLdb.connect()` method does the connection with the MySQL daemon, and the `execute()` method just executes the query. The following is the code snippet:

```
# Get connect to MySQL daemon
db = MySQLdb.connect(host = "localhost", user = "user",
                     passwd = "userpass", db = "sproject")

# Create the Cursor object to execute all queries
c = db.cursor()

# Ok, do the job!
query = "REPLACE INTO status (t, n, v) " \
        "VALUES(now(), '%s', '%s');" % (sys.argv[1], sys.argv[2])
c.execute(query)
```

Regarding `my_dump`, it can be as reported in the `chapter_04/mysql/my_dump.py` file in the book's example code repository. This time, to retrieve the query's data, we use the `fetchall()` method, and to get the headers, we use the `description` attribute. The relevant code is reported in the following snippet:

```
# Save the query result
data = c.fetchall()

# Do the dump of the fields' names
for field in c.description:
    print("%s\t" % (field[0])),
print

# Do the dump one line at time
n = len(c.description)
for row in data:
    for i in range(0, n):
        print("%s\t" % (row[i])),
    print
```

 The external library needed to execute these programs is not installed by default; however, we did this in the earlier section, where we set up the system.

In the end, we can test these programs using the following commands:

```
root@bbb:~# ./my_set.py T1 18
root@bbb:~# ./my_dump.py
t    n    v
2016-04-02 18:49:43    T1    18
```

 The complete *MySQLdb User's Guide* is reported
at: http://mysql-python.sourceforge.net/MySQLdb.html.

Scripting languages

No doubt, embedded developers must know the C language; however, there exist several tasks that can be resolved using a scripting language. In fact, a scripting language such as PHP or Python, or even the Bash language, can be used to implement a task to manage a computer peripheral. This is because these languages have several extensions to do it and because the kernel itself offers the possibility to manage its peripherals using common files (refer to the *everything-is-a-file* abstraction presented in Chapter 3, *C Compiler, Device Drivers, and Useful Developing Techniques*, in *What is a Device Driver?* section and the following sections).

In the next sections, we're going to show a simple example on how we can manage a peripheral using a scripting language exclusively. For the moment, we have to keep our example simple because we haven't presented any peripheral in detail yet; however, in the next chapters, we're going to discover several peripheral kinds in detail, and at that time, we're going to use more complex examples on this topic. Right now, we'll use a simple GPIO line, since even if not explained in detail yet, this is the only peripheral we know how to manage a bit.

For this demonstration, we'll use the BeagleBone Black and a simple LED connected to the expansion connector. The following is the schematic of the connections:

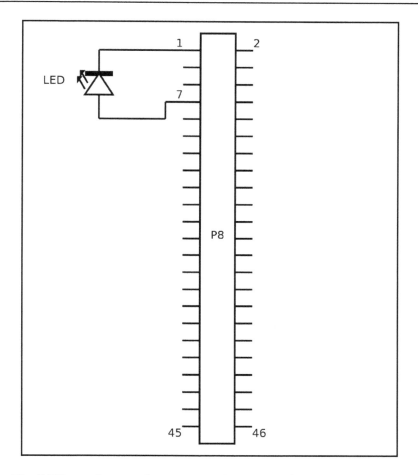

 The LED anode must be connected to pin 7 of connector *P8* (*P8.7*) and the cathode with the GND or ground (pin 1 or 2 of the same connector). Let's also remember that the flat spot on the LED is the cathode while the rounded one is the anode.

A careful reader with minimum electronic basics will notice that in the preceding schematic, we did not put any resistance in series with the LED to limit the output current from the GPIO pin. Even if it should be always done to avoid damages, it has been done to keep the connection very simple.

Then, to turn the LED on and off, we need to export the corresponding GPIO line, which is `gpio66`, so the commands are as follows:

```
root@bbb:~# echo 66 > /sys/class/gpio/export
root@bbb:~# echo out > /sys/class/gpio/gpio66/direction
```

Now to turn the LED on and off, we simply need to write 1 or 0 in the `/sys/class/gpio/gpio66/value` file, as follows:

```
root@bbb:~# echo 1 > /sys/class/gpio/gpio66/value
root@bbb:~# echo 0 > /sys/class/gpio/gpio66/value
```

OK, now supposing that the GPIO is already exported, let's start to see how we can implement the task to control an LED via the web browser using a scripting language only.

Managing a LED in PHP

Now it's time to learn how to manage our LED using the PHP language. There are two different possibilities to do that: the first one is to use the **LAMP** (**Linux** – **Apache** – **MySQL** – **PHP**) system, while the second one is to use the PHP built-in web server.

The LAMP solution

This is the easiest and the most classic way to implement a common web application; we just need a PHP script where we can implement our LED management. So let's start with writing some code!

As a first step, we must create a file in the `/var/www/html` directory of the BeagleBone Black named `turn.php` by copying the `chapter_04/webled/php/turn.php` file in the book's example code repository:

```php
<?php
    # 1st part - Global defines & functions
    define("value_f", "/sys/class/gpio/gpio66/value");

    function pr_str($val)
    {
        echo $val ? "on" : "off";
    }

    # 2nd part - Set the new led status as requested
    if (isset($_GET["led"])) {
        $led_new_status = $_GET["led"];
```

```
            file_put_contents(value_f, $led_new_status);
    }

    # 3rd part - Get the current led status
    $led_status = intval(file_get_contents(value_f));

    # 4th part - Logic to change the led status on the next call
    $led_new_status = 1 - $led_status;

    # 5th part - Render the led status by HTML code
?>
<html>
  <head>
    <title>Turning a led on/off using PHP</title>
  </head>

  <body>
    <h1>Turning a led on/off using PHP</h1>
    Current led status is: <? pr_str($led_status) ?>
    <p>

    Press the button to turn the led <? pr_str($led_new_status) ?>
    <p>

    <form method="get" action="/turn.php">
      <button type="submit" value="<? echo $led_new_status ?>"
        name="led">Turn <? pr_str($led_new_status) ?></button>
    </form>

  </body>
</html>
```

 This code does not export the gpio66 directory, so it must be exported as shown in the previous section before running the script!
All the next examples will assume that gpio66 is already exported.

The functioning is quite simple; the first part of the code reads the LED status and stores it in the led_status variable, while the second part is an HTML code with mixed PHP code required to simply report the LED status by echoing the led_status variable. Note that we use a dedicated function to convert a number into the on or off string to display the LED status, while in the second part, we use an HTML form to retrieve the user request, that is, whether we must turn the LED on or off and then execute it.

Note that the user request is done with an HTTP GET request in the `http://192.168.7.2/turn.php?led=1` form. The `led=1` string means that we ask to turn on the LED, so the code will get this value, and using the PHP `file_put_contents()` function, set the LED on by writing 1 in the `/sys/class/gpio/gpio66/value` file.

The third part reads the GPIO status by simply reading the content of the `/sys/class/gpio/gpio66/value` file (because *everything-is-a-file!*), while the fourth one just toggles the LED status from value 0 to 1 or vice versa. The fifth part is the HTML page that the server will return to the user with the current LED status and the needed button to toggle it. The next figure shows the resulting output in the browser:

It may happen that the code cannot change the LED status; in this case, we should check the `/var/log/apache2/error.log` file where the Apache web server logs possible errors.

If we see an error message, as reported here, the problem is due to a file permission issue:

```
[Sat Apr 02 19:25:07.556803 2016] [:error] [pid 825
] [client 192.168.7.1:59242] PHP Warning:
file_put_contents(/sys/class/gpio/gpio66/value): fa
iled to open stream: Permission denied in /var/www/
html/turn.php on line 13
```

So, let's check the file permission for the `/sys/class/gpio/gpio66/value` file:

```
root@bbb:~# ls -l /sys/class/gpio/gpio66/value
-rw-r--r-- 1 root root 4096 Apr 2 18:54 /sys/class
/gpio/gpio66/value
```

Only the root user has the right privileges to write in the file, so a possible workaround could be as follows:

```
root@bbb:~# chown :www-data /sys/class/gpio/gpio66/
value
root@bbb:~# chmod g+rw /sys/class/gpio/gpio66/value
root@bbb:~# ls -l /sys/class/gpio/gpio66/value
-rw-rw-r-- 1 root www-data 4096 Apr 2 18:54
/sys/class/gpio/gpio66/value
```

This is because the Apache web server runs with the same privileges of the www-data user and the www-data group, but after the preceding changes, our script should work as expected.

The built-in server solution

The PHP built-in web server can be executed with the following command line:

```
root@bbb:~# php -S 192.168.7.2:8080 -t /var/www/html/
PHP 5.6.19-0+deb8u1 Development Server started at Sat Apr 2
19:36:01 2016
Listening on http://192.168.7.2:8080
Document root is /var/www/html
Press Ctrl-C to quit.
```

You should notice that we used the 192.168.7.2:8080 listening address, so this time, the web address to be used is http://192.168.7.2:8080/turn.php; otherwise, we will get connected with the Apache server again!

If we wish to avoid specifying port 8080, we should stop the Apache web server as follows:

```
root@bbb:~# /etc/init.d/apache2 stop
[ ok ] Stopping apache2 (via systemctl): apache2.service.
```

And then, we re-run the PHP built-in web server with the following command:

```
root@bbb:~# php -S 192.168.7.2:80 -t /var/www/html/
PHP 5.6.19-0+deb8u1 Development Server started at Sat Apr 2
19:37:44 2016
Listening on http://192.168.7.2:80
Document root is /var/www/html
Press Ctrl-C to quit.
```

Now we can execute our script as earlier. Note that the server will log each browser request on the terminal where it's running:

```
[Sat Apr  2 19:38:17 2016] 192.168.7.1:59462 [200]: /turn.php
[Sat Apr  2 19:38:21 2016] 192.168.7.1:59464 [200]: /turn.php?led=0
[Sat Apr  2 19:38:21 2016] 192.168.7.1:59466 [200]: /turn.php?led=1
```

As reported in the PHP *built-in web server* manual at `http://php.net/manual/en/features.commandline.webserver.php`, this tool should be used for testing purposes or for application demonstrations that are run in controlled environments only!

Managing a LED in Python

Now let's try to manage our LED using a Python script. There are several possibilities to get a running web server with Python, but the easiest one is definitely the `BaseHTTPServer` library. A simple usage of the library is reported in the `chapter_04/webled/python/httpd_show_info.py` demo script in the book's example code repository, where we show how the server handler processes incoming requests by showing all the fields available at the disposal of the programmer.

In the first part, there is a definition of the server listening address, while the second part defines the GET requests handler, that is, the function to be called each time the browser performs an HTTP GET request.

The third and fourth parts are the most important ones since they implement the web data parsing. Here, we can see how the web requests are managed and how we can use them to do our job! The fourth part simply takes the answering message built by the third part and then sends it back to the browser. Here is a snippet of the relevant function:

```
def do_GET(self):
    parsed_path = urlparse.urlparse(self.path)

    # 3rd part - Build the answering message
    message_parts = [
        'CLIENT VALUES',
        'client_address -> %s (%s)' % (self.client_address,
                self.address_string()),
        'command -> %s' % self.command,
        'path -> %s' % self.path,
        'real path -> t%s' % parsed_path.path,
        'query -> %s' % parsed_path.query,
        'request_version -> %s' % self.request_version,
        '',
```

```
            'SERVER VALUES',
            'server_version -> %s' % self.server_version,
            'sys_version -> %s' % self.sys_version,
            'protocol_version -> %s' % self.protocol_version,
            '',
            'HEADERS RECEIVED',
        ]

        for name, value in sorted(self.headers.items()):
            message_parts.append('%s -> %s' % (name,
                    value.rstrip()))
        message_parts.append('')
        message = '\r\n'.join(message_parts)

        # 4th part - Send the answer
        self.send_response(200)
        self.end_headers()
        self.wfile.write(message)

        return
```

The last part is executed at the beginning and it sets up the server by creating a new server object by calling the `HTTPServer()` function and then runs it by calling the `serve_forever()` method.

To test the code, we can use the following command:

```
root@bbb:~# python httpd_show_info.py
Starting server at 192.168.7.2:8080, use <Ctrl-C> to stop
```

If everything works well, we'll see the server running by pointing the browser at the `http://192.168.7.2:8080/?led=1` address.

The output in the browser should be something similar to what's shown in the following figure:

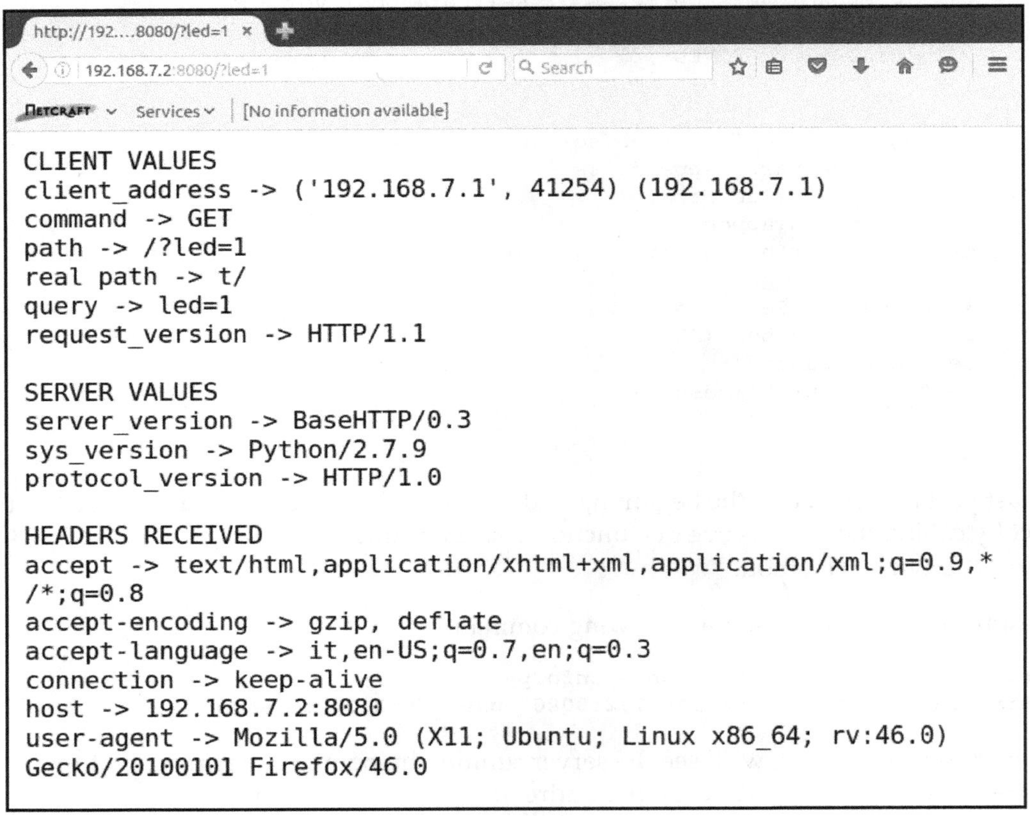

As we can see, there are tons of available data; however to manage our LED, we can just use the `query` variable, which is where the server stores the HTTP GET request data. So, a possible implementation of our LED management script in Python is reported in the `chapter_04/webled/python/httpd.py` file in the book's example code repository.

This time, the code is really more complex than earlier. First of all, we should note that in the first part of this new code, we've defined two functions, named `put_data()` and `get_data()`. These are used to put/get the `gpio66` status. Here is the snippet with these two functions:

```
def put_data(file, data):
    f = open(file, "w")
    f.write(data)
```

```
    f.close()

def get_data(file):
    f = open(file, "r")
    data = f.read()
    f.close()
    return data
```

The second part is not changed, while the third one has now been changed in order to retrieve the HTTP GET query and set up the new `gpio66` status accordingly. Parts four and five are very similar to the respective ones in PHP and the same is for the sixth one too, even if its layout is a bit different (it defines the HTML code to be returned to the browser). Part seven is the same as earlier, while part eight implements the server definition and initialization.

If we execute this new script as done before, we should get the same output as the one we got with the PHP version of this script.

 The documentation of the `BaseHTTPServer` library is at: `https://wiki.python.org/moin/BaseHttpServer`.

Managing a LED in Bash

Both Python and PHP are very powerful languages, and they can be used to solve a lot of complex problems; however, it may happen that the embedded system lacks both! In this case, we can use the C language, or if we like scripting, we can try to use Bash. In fact, even if the Bash scripting language is commonly used to solve system administrator tasks, it can also be used to resolve several issues with some tricks! So let's look at how we can use it in our web LED management problem.

By default, Bash has no networking features; however, as a workaround, we can use the `xinetd` daemon presented earlier in this chapter. The trick was in correctly setting up the `xinetd` configuration file in order to address our web LED management problem.

First of all, we should exactly know what the browser asks to a web server; to do that, we can use a modified version of our echo program, as reported here:

```
#!/bin/bash

# Read the browser request
read request
```

```
# Now read the message header
while /bin/true; do
    read header
    echo "$header"
    [ "$header" == $'\r' ] && break;
done

# And then produce an answer with a message dump
echo -e "HTTP/1.1 200 OK\r"
echo -e "Content-type: text/html\r"
echo -e "\r"

echo -e "request=$request\r"

exit 0
```

 The code is held in the `chapter_04/webled/bash/httpd_echo.sh` file in the book's example code repository.

This script is quite simple; it first reads the browser's request, and then it starts reading the message header, and when finished, it produces an answer with a message dump, so we can analyze it and understand what they say to each other.

Now we need a new xinetd configuration file to execute our Bash web server, as follows:

```
service http-alt
{
    disable        = no
    socket_type    = stream
    protocol       = tcp
    wait           = no
    user           = root
    server         = /root/httpd.sh
}
```

 The code is held in the `chapter_04/webled/bash/httpd_sh` file in the book's example code repository.
Note also that the `http-alt` service is defined as port 8080 in the `/etc/services` file:

```
root@bbb:~# grep 8080 /etc/services
http-alt 8080/tcp webcache # WWW caching service
http-alt 8080/udp
```

Then, we have to copy the file into the xinetd configuration directory, as follows:

```
root@bbb:~# cp httpd_sh /etc/xinetd.d/
```

Now we have to put the program into the `httpd_echo.sh` file in the `/root/httpd.sh` file, which is executed by xinetd when a new connection arrives on port `8080`:

```
root@bbb:~# cp httpd_echo.sh /root/httpd.sh
```

To start our new web server, we have to restart the xinetd daemon:

```
root@bbb:~# /etc/init.d/xinetd restart
Restarting xinetd (via systemctl): xinetd.service.
```

At this point, by pointing our web browser at the address `http://192.168.7.2:8080/index.html`, we will see a message like the following one:

```
Host: 192.168.7.2:8080
User-Agent: Mozilla/5.0 (X11; Ubuntu; Linux x86_64; rv:46.0) Gecko/201
00101 Firefox/46.0
Accept: text/html,application/xhtml+xml,application/xml;q=0.9,*/*;q=0.
8
Accept-Language: it,en-US;q=0.7,en;q=0.3
Accept-Encoding: gzip, deflate
Connection: keep-alive

HTTP/1.1 200 OK
Content-type: text/html

request=GET /index.html HTTP/1.1
```

The first seven lines are the message header, and then there are two lines with the server's answer, and in the end, there's the dump of the initial request. As we can see, the browser did a HTTP GET version 1.1 request asking for the `/index.html` file. So, our Bash web server should simply read the browser's request, then skip the header, and in the end, return the contents of the file specified in the request.

A possible implementation is reported as follows:

```
#!/bin/bash

# The server's root directory
base=/var/www/html

# Read the browser request
read request
```

```
# Now read the message header
while /bin/true; do
    read header
    [ "$header" == $'\r' ] && break;
done

# Parse the GET request
tmp="${request#GET }"
tmp="${tmp% HTTP/*}"

# Extract the code after the '?' char to capture a variable setting
var="${tmp#*\?}"
[ "$var" == "$tmp" ] && var=""

# Get the URL and replace it with "/index.html" in case it is set to "/"
url="${tmp%\?*}"
[ "$url" == "/" ] && url="/index.html"

# Extract the filename
filename="$base$url"
extension="${filename##*.}"

# Check for file exist
if [ -f "$filename" ]; then
    echo -e "HTTP/1.1 200 OK\r"
    echo -e "Contant-type: text/html\r"
    echo -e "\r"

    # If file's extension is "cgi" and it's executable the
    # execute it, otherwise just return its contents
    if [ "$extension" == "cgi" -a -x "$filename" ]; then
        $filename $var
    else
        cat "$filename"
    fi
    echo -e "\r"
else
    # If the file does not exist return an error
    echo -e "HTTP/1.1 404 Not Found\r"
    echo -e "Content-Type: text/html\r"
    echo -e "\r"
    echo -e "404 Not Found\r"
    echo -e "The requested resource was not found\r"
    echo -e "\r"
fi

exit 0
```

The code is held in the `chapter_04/webled/bash/httpd.sh` file in the book's example code repository.

So we only have to replace the `/root/httpd.sh` file with this file:

```
root@bbb:~# cp httpd.sh /root/httpd.sh
```

Now, after restarting the daemon, we can try our new web server written in the Bash language simply by pointing our web browser to the BeagleBone Black's IP address, as done earlier, and we'll get the same output we got earlier when we used the Apache web server. Nice, isn't it?

Something different exists, in fact, we don't have the Debian logo. This is because our script can't manage binary files as images. This is left to you as an exercise.

Before going on, let's spend some words on how the web server works. After reading the browser's request, we have to parse it in order to extract some useful information for the next steps; in fact, we have to check whether the request is a normal file or a CGI script; in this last case, we have to execute the file instead of reading it with the `cat` command. Here is the relevant code:

```
# If file's extension is "cgi" and it's executable the execute it,
# otherwise just return its contents
if [ "$extension" == "cgi" -a -x "$filename" ]; then
    $filename $var
else
    cat "$filename"
fi
echo -e "\r"
```

That is, instead of using the `cat` command to simply return the file content, we first verify that the file has the `cgi` extension and whether it's executable; in this case, we simply execute it. Note that before doing this, we need to extract the code after the ? character in order to get the variable settings when we use a URL in the `http://192.168.7.2:8080/?led=1` form. This task is done by the `var="${tmp#*\?}"` code.

OK, now the final version of the web server is ready, but to complete the server side actions, we need to add a CGI functionality. A possible GCI implementation is held in the `chapter_04/webled/bash/turn.cgi` file in the book's example code repository, and here is a snippet of the relevant functions where the LED status is managed:

```
# 2nd part - Set the new led status as requested
if [ -n "$1" ] ; then
    eval $1    ;# this evaluate the query 'led=0'
    led_new_status = $led
    echo $led_new_status > $value_f
fi

led_status=$(cat $value_f)

led_new_status=$((1 - $led_status))
```

Now everything is really in place! Let's copy the `turn.cgi` file into the `/var/www/html` directory and then point the browser as we did for the PHP and the Python version of our LED management code; we should get a function similar to the earlier one.

The Bash web server presented here is not a strictly compliant web server or a safe one! Even if it can work in most cases, it's just a simple demonstration program and it shouldn't be used in a production environment!
In these Bash examples, we used some special syntax that may be obscure for most of you (especially for beginners). Maybe looking at a Bash tutorial may help. A good starting point is at
`http://tldp.org/HOWTO/Bash-Prog-Intro-HOWTO.html`.

Writing a custom daemon

In this last section, we'll learn how to write our own daemon in several programming languages using a skeleton that can be used to quickly develop really complex daemons. Due to the lack of space, we cannot add all the possible features a daemon has, but the presented skeletons will have whatever you need to know about daemon creation.

All example code will implement a daemon with the following command line usage:

```
usage: mydaemon [-h] [-d] [-f] [-l]
    -h      - show this message
    -d      - enable debugging messages
    -f      - do not daemonize
    -l      - log on stderr
```

The −h option argument will show the help message, while −d will enable the debugging messages. The −f option argument will prevent the daemon from running in the background, and the −l option will print the logging messages to the standard error channel. Apart from the −h option argument, the other arguments are very useful during the debugging stages if used together in the form:

```
# ./mydaemon -d -f -l
```

The developer can run the daemon in the foreground with the debugging messages enabled and printed on the current terminal.

A daemon in C

In C language, a daemon skeleton can be written as in the chapter_04/mydaemon/my_daemon.c file in the book's example code repository. The most important steps here are from the openlog() function call and the daemon_body() one. In fact, the two signal() system calls are used to set up the signal handlers, while the whole job is done by the daemon() function call (refer to the beginning of this chapter). Here is the relevant code:

```
/* Open the communication with syslogd */
loglevel = LOG_PID;
if (logstderr)
    loglevel |= LOG_PERROR;
openlog(NAME, loglevel, LOG_USER);

/* Install the signals traps */
sig_h = signal(SIGTERM, sig_handler);
if (sig_h == SIG_ERR) {
    fprintf(stderr, "unable to catch SIGTERM");
    exit(-1);
}
sig_h = signal(SIGINT, sig_handler);
if (sig_h == SIG_ERR) {
    fprintf(stderr, "unable to catch SIGINT");
    exit(-1);
```

```
    }
    dbg("signals traps installed");

    /* Should run as a daemon? */
    if (daemonize) {
        ret = daemon(!daemonize, 1);
        if (ret) {
            fprintf(stderr, "unable to daemonize the process");
            exit(-1);
        }
    }

    daemon_body();
```

Now we can compile the code using `make` and then we can execute it using the following command line:

```
root@bbb:~# make
cc -Wall -O2 -D_GNU_SOURCE     mydaemon.c    -o mydaemon
root@bbb:~# ./mydaemon
root@bbb:~#
```

We notice that it seems that nothing happens since the prompt is returned! However, after looking at the system log files, we can see the daemon's activity:

```
root@bbb:~/mydaemon# tail -f /var/log/syslog
Apr  2 22:35:01 bbb mydaemon[3359]: I'm working hard!
Apr  2 22:35:02 bbb mydaemon[3359]: I'm working hard!
Apr  2 22:35:03 bbb mydaemon[3359]: I'm working hard!
```

The daemon can now be stopped using the `killall` command, as follows:

```
root@bbb:~# killall mydaemon
```

A daemon in PHP

In PHP, creating a daemon is a bit more complex due the fact that there is no dedicated function to daemonize a running process; however, the task is still quite simple, as shown in the `chapter_04/mydaemon/my_daemon.php` file in the book's example code repository. As for the C example, the important steps are all after the `openlog()` function call; the `pcntl_signal()` functions are used to install the signal handlers, while the daemon is created using the `pcntl_fork()`, `exit()`, `chdir()` and `fclose()` functions, as already explained at the beginning of this chapter. Here is the code snippet:

```
openlog(NAME, $loglevel, LOG_USER);
```

```
# Install the signals traps
pcntl_signal(SIGTERM, "sig_handler");
pcntl_signal(SIGINT,  "sig_handler");
dbg("signals traps installed");

# Start the daemon
if ($daemonize) {
    dbg("going in background...");
    $pid = pcntl_fork();
    if ($pid < 0) {
        die("unable to daemonize!");
    }
    if ($pid) {
        # The parent can exit...
        exit(0);
    }
    # ... while the children goes on!

    # Set the working directory to /
    chdir("/");

    # Close all of the standard file descriptors as we are running
    # as a daemon
    fclose(STDIN);
    fclose(STDOUT);
    fclose(STDERR);
}

daemon_body();
```

 The documentation of the `pcntl_fork()` function is online at: `http://php.net/manual/en/function.pcntl-fork.php`.

In this case, the daemon can be executed using the following command line, and we get the same output as the earlier one:

```
root@bbb:~# ./mydaemon.php
```

We can check it by using again the `tail` command:

```
root@bbb:~# tail -f /var/log/syslog
Apr  2 22:36:59 bbb mydaemon.php[3365]: I'm working hard!
Apr  2 22:37:00 bbb mydaemon.php[3365]: I'm working hard!
Apr  2 22:37:01 bbb mydaemon.php[3365]: I'm working hard!
```

Then, to stop it, we use the `killall` utility again:

```
root@bbb:~# killall mydaemon.php
```

A daemon in Python

In Python, the task is easier than in C due to the fact that we have a dedicated library to daemonize the running process.

The code is in the `chapter_04/mydaemon/my_daemon.py` file in the book's example code repository. As earlier, the relevant part is after the `syslog.openlog()` method call; we simply create a dedicated context with the `daemon.DaemonContext()` method, and then within that context, we execute our `daemon_body()` function. The relevant code is reported as follows:

```
# Open the communication with syslogd
loglevel = syslog.LOG_PID
if logstderr:
    loglevel |= syslog.LOG_PERROR
syslog.openlog(NAME, loglevel, syslog.LOG_USER)

# Define the daemon context and install the signals traps
context = daemon.DaemonContext(
    detach_process = daemonize,
)
context.signal_map = {
    signal.SIGTERM: sig_handler,
    signal.SIGINT: sig_handler,
}
dbg("signals traps installed")

# Start the daemon
with context:
    daemon_body()
```

 The documentation of the Python standard daemon process library is at: https://www.python.org/dev/peps/pep-3143/.

The daemon is launched as earlier with the following command line:

```
root@bbb:~# ./mydaemon.py
```

Again, we can check the functioning with `tail`:

```
root@bbb:~# tail -f /var/log/syslog
Apr  2 22:47:59 bbb mydaemon.py[4339]: I'm working hard!
Apr  2 22:48:00 bbb mydaemon.py[4339]: I'm working hard!
Apr  2 22:48:01 bbb mydaemon.py[4339]: I'm working hard!
```

Then, we use `killall` to stop the daemon:

```
root@bbb:~# killall mydaemon.py
```

A daemon in Bash

As a last example, we present the daemon implementation of a Bash script. This example is not as relevant as the previous ones since it is very rare to implement a daemon as a Bash script; however, it's interesting in order to show you how Bash scripting can be powerful.

The Bash demon code is reported in the `chapter_04/mydaemon/my_daemon.sh` file in the book's example code repository. In this case, the relevant code is after the `trap` command, which is used to install the signals handler, and it's all concentrated in the line with the `eval` command. The `daemon_body()` function is called in such a way that the `stdin` and `stdout` channels are redirected to the `/dev/null` file, while the `stderr` is redirected if no option is supplied, while the background or foreground execution mode is selected by the respective command-line option argument. The relevant code is as follows:

```
# Install the signals traps
trap sig_handler SIGTERM SIGINT
dbg "signals traps installed"

# Start the daemon
if [ -n "$daemonize" ] ; then
    dbg "going in background..."

    # Set the working directory to /
    cd /
fi
[ -z "$logstderr" ] && tmp="2>&1"
eval daemon_body </dev/null >/dev/null $tmp $daemonize
```

 To get more information on the background process execution, standard input/output redirection and other Bash-related stuff used in this example, you can take a look at Bash's man pages using the usual command:

```
$ man bash
```

In this case, we can run the daemon in the debugging mode and then look at its output directly on the terminal:

```
root@bbb:~# ./mydaemon.sh -d -f -1
mydaemon.sh: signals traps installed
mydaemon.sh: start main loop
mydaemon.sh: I'm working hard!
mydaemon.sh: I'm working hard!
mydaemon.sh: I'm working hard!
```

This time, we can stop the daemon by simply pressing the *CRTL + C* keys sequence, and this is the output:

```
^Cmydaemon.sh: signal trapped!
root@bbb:~#
```

Summary

In this chapter, we took a long tour into several tools that an embedded developer can use to simplify their job. We saw some system daemons with some practical usage modes, and we also talked about some famous scripting languages and how we can use them to implement some tasks involving the system's peripherals.

In the next chapter, we will completely switch our standard mode of operation by presenting two of the major embedded distributions we can use in order to reduce the rootfs memory footprint. In fact, a standard Debian distribution may need from 512MB to 1GB or more, while an embedded distribution needs from 4MB or 5MB to less then 100 MB even with several running services!

5
Setting Up an Embedded OS

Having a Debian OS or another major distribution running on an embedded computer is absolutely the best thing a developer can have. However, there are some situations that don't allow us to be so lucky! In fact, due to cost reasons, reduced sizes, or other minor issues, the available mass memory useful to store our rootfs (plus the bootloaders and the kernel) is very limited, and we cannot use our preferred distribution.

This is where an embedded OS comes in handy, allowing us to work with tiny mass memory's sizes, from 256 MB to 16 MB or less, by still having a reasonable set of ready-to-use programs and already made customization mechanisms.

In this chapter, we'll look at the flash memories (especially the NAND ones), and the software used to manage them and that allows the developer to see these storage devices more or less as a normal disk. So, we will present Linux's **Memory Technology Device (MTD)** and the two major filesystems that can run over them, that is, **JFFS2** and **UBIFS**.

Then, we'll present two of the most famous embedded distributions used in these days: **Yocto** and **OpenWrt**. We'll then show how you can download, compile, and then install them over the SAMA5D3 Xplained board, which is the only one that has a NAND flash onboard.

As the last step, for each embedded distribution, we will show you how an embedded developer can write their own application and how they can add it to Yocto and OpenWrt in order to extend them.

MTD versus block devices

There are several different kinds of embedded systems, especially today, since they're cheap. So, it's very important to know which device best fits our needs before starting the coding. As far as the name suggests, the embedded computers are embedded into the device they have to control or monitor. Often, these devices are placed into hostile environments: industrial plants (with dust and vibrations); open environment (extreme temperatures or rains); or aboard of trucks, cars, trains and other automotive systems.

In these scenarios, we have to carefully choose the hardware components that compose our embedded computer. Even if it's quite obvious, we cannot use a normal hard disk to store our data. More subtle is the fact that we cannot even choose a microSD! In fact, we can easily find these devices in every electronic store. However, they are not suitable for environments with vibrations (they are not soldered, and the contacts may get damaged) nor in places with very hot or cold temperatures (they usually are designed for standard, human-compatible environments). Also, they still have some problems regarding the device lifetime and possible corruption at power off. No way! We have to consider a different solution!

A possible (and relatively cheap) solution is to use **flash memories**. These special kinds of memories are obviously non-volatile, and they consist of one or more chips with very large temperature ranges that can be soldered on the board. The disadvantage in using these devices is that they cannot be accessed as a normal block device. That's why, in a Linux-based system, they are known as **MTD devices**.

What is an MTD device?

In Chapter 3, *C Compiler, Device Drivers, and Useful Developing Techniques*, in *Char, block, and net device* section, we introduced block devices, that is, devices accessed in blocks of data and that support a filesystem. The MTD devices are based on the flash memory technology (NOR or NAND and other variants) that can be get accessed as a block device, where we can mount on a special filesystem, but also as a character device because flash memories must be managed in a special way in order to function well. It seems complex but it's not. Let's explain these concepts a bit better, and everything will be clearer.

We already introduced flash memories into `Chapter 1`, *Installing the Developing System*, in *Embedded world terms* section, but what we omitted there is the fact that these devices need special management methods to work well. In fact, flash memories need the *bad block detection, error detection and recovery*, and a *wear leveling* system.

The bad block detection is a mechanism that informs the systems that a particular block of the flash is damaged and it cannot be used anymore. This is very important because for a flash device, this event is far from rare! In fact, repetitive erases and writes may damage a block, and in this scenario, when we write a new data block, we must discard it and then choose a new one. On the other hand, when we read a block, we need a way to recover the situation: this is where *error detection and recovery* comes in handy. The flash memory uses a supplement storage data to save some extra information that can be used later when an error occurs (in particular, NAND memories use the ECC data to do it).

See more information about flashes, *bad block detection, error detection and recovery*, NAND flashes, and their ECC data at: `https://en.wikipedia.org/wiki/Flash_memory`.

Detecting an error or a bad block is not enough to correctly manage these devices. In fact, they also need a good wear leveling system, that is, a mechanism that erases (and then writes) over the whole storage area to reduce possible errors. In fact, flash memories can get damaged each time our embedded system writes or yet reads (in the case of the NAND technology) data block on them, and this probability gets higher as far as the frequency of these operations increases. That's why, the wear leveling system avoids frequent writes or reads on the same area in order to increase the lifetime of these devices.

You can get more information on the wear leveling system at: `https://en.wikipedia.org/wiki/Wear_leveling`.

All these aspects are to present the fact that the MTD devices (which are on top of flash devices) must implement several mechanisms to work efficiently, and that's why, in the Linux kernel, we have a dedicated devices class into the `drivers/mtd` directory of the Linux repository.

In the kernel's configuration menu, we read the following:

Memory Technology Devices are flash, RAM and similar chips, often used for solid state filesystems on embedded devices.

So, MTD are used to support *solid state filesystems,* and they are referred by the files `/dev/mtd0`, `/dev/mtd1`, `/dev/mtdblock0`, `/dev/mtdblock1`, and so on and in a normal GNU/Linux filesystem (we'll see the differences between these two types of MTD devices soon). The MTD layer abstracts the different flash technologies to the user-level applications as shown in the following diagram:

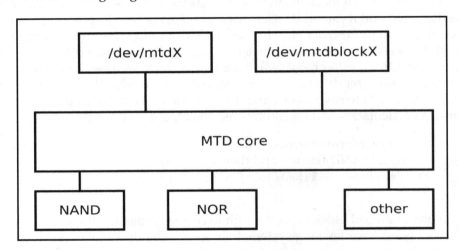

However, it is very important to point out that these *solid state* filesystems are not referred to USBkeys nor to microSDs and other similar devices. This is because even if they have flash memories inside them, they are abstracted to the system as normal block devices, thanks to a **Flash Translation Layer** (FTL) that implements in hardware the wear leveling system, and the bad block detection and the error detection and recovery systems. Usually, USBkeys, microSDs, and other similar devices are called managed flash devices.

More information on FTL can be retrieved
at: `https://en.wikipedia.org/wiki/Flash_file_system#FTL`.

Simply speaking, while the MTD devices need a FTL in software (in our case, implemented into the Linux kernel), the USBkeys, microSD, and so on don't need it at all since they have a FTL system inside them. These aspects are more important when we need a highly reliable system due the fact USBkeys, microSDs and so on may still have problems with wear leveling and possible corruptions at power off (the last two aspects are manufacture dependent).

A good explanation about the differences between the flash devices and the usual block devices (hard disks and so on) is reported at: http://www.linux-mtd.infradead.org/faq/general.html#L_mtd_vs_hdd, where we can read that a block device has the *read* and *write* operations only while a flash device has the erase one too. Also, for the block devices, sectors are devoid of the wear-out property, while for the flash devices, the erase block operations wear out and become bad and unusable after about 103 (for MLC NAND) and 105 (NOR, SLC NAND) erase cycles.

Managing an MTD device

At this point, we have to introduce the tools needed to manage an MTD device in order to be able to put a filesystem on top of it. For this purpose, we have no choices than using the SAMA5D3 Xplained board since it's the only one that has a flash memory onboard (actually, the BeagleBone Black also has a flash device onboard, but it's an eMMC, which is a managed flash device, and it's not useful for our purposes). However, what reported below can be used on every GNU/Linux system equipped with such devices (and with the proper drivers, of course).

During the boot of the SAMA5D3 Xplained, we can notice the following kernel messages:

```
atmel_nand 60000000.nand: Use On Flash BBT
atmel_nand 60000000.nand: Using dma0chan4 for DMA transfers.
nand: device found, Manufacturer ID: 0x2c, Chip ID: 0xda
nand: Micron MT29F2G08ABAEAWP
nand: 256 MiB, SLC, erase size: 128 KiB, page size: 2048, OOB si4
atmel_nand 60000000.nand: minimum ECC: 4 bits in 512 bytes
atmel_nand 60000000.nand: Initialize PMECC params, cap: 4, secto2
atmel_nand 60000000.nand: Using NFC Sram read
Bad block table found at page 131008, version 0x01
Bad block table found at page 130944, version 0x01
nand_read_bbt: bad block at 0x000000c80000
nand_read_bbt: bad block at 0x000000ca0000
6 ofpart partitions found on MTD device atmel_nand
Creating 6 MTD partitions on "atmel_nand":
0x000000000000-0x000000040000 : "at91bootstrap"
0x000000040000-0x0000000c0000 : "bootloader"
0x0000000c0000-0x000000180000 : "bootloader env"
0x000000180000-0x000000200000 : "device tree"
0x000000200000-0x000000800000 : "kernel"
0x000000800000-0x000010000000 : "rootfs"
```

These messages are all referred to the flash and MTD support. In particular, we need a driver for the flash controller and one for the particular flash chips (when we use the NAND flashes, the driver is named **Open NAND Flash Interface (ONFI)**).

After some description messages, we must note that the MTD partitions defined in the system is as follows:

MTD Device	Memory Offsets	Partition Name
mtd0	0x000000000000–0x000000040000	at91bootstrap
mtd1	0x000000040000–0x0000000c0000	bootloader
mtd2	0x0000000c0000–0x000000180000	bootloader
mtd3	0x000000180000–0x000000200000	device tree
mtd4	0x000000200000–0x000000800000	kernel
mtd5	0x000000800000–0x000010000000	rootfs

This data can be also extracted from the `/proc/mtd` file in the `procfs` filesystem:

```
root@a5d3:~# cat /proc/mtd
dev:    size    erasesize  name
mtd0: 00040000 00020000 "at91bootstrap"
mtd1: 00080000 00020000 "bootloader"
mtd2: 000c0000 00020000 "bootloader env"
mtd3: 00080000 00020000 "device tree"
mtd4: 00600000 00020000 "kernel"
mtd5: 0f800000 00020000 "rootfs"
```

Alternatively, we can take a look at the SAMA5D3 Xplained DTS file in the Linux source tree as reported in the following snippet of the `arch/arm/boot/dts/sama5d3xcm.dtsi` file:

```
nand0: nand@60000000 {
    nand-bus-width = <8>;
    nand-ecc-mode = "hw";
    atmel,has-pmecc;
    atmel,pmecc-cap = <4>;
    atmel,pmecc-sector-size = <512>;
    nand-on-flash-bbt;
    status = "okay";

    at91bootstrap@0 {
        label = "at91bootstrap";
```

```
            reg = <0x0  0x40000>;
    };

    bootloader@40000 {
        label = "bootloader";
        reg = <0x40000  0x80000>;
    };

    bootloaderenv@c0000 {
        label = "bootloader env";
        reg = <0xc0000  0xc0000>;
    };

    dtb@180000 {
        label = "device tree";
        reg = <0x180000  0x80000>;
    };

    kernel@200000 {
        label = "kernel";
        reg = <0x200000  0x600000>;
    };

    rootfs@800000 {
        label = "rootfs";
        reg = <0x800000  0x0f800000>;
    };
};
```

It's quite obvious that changing these settings can change SAMA5D3 Xplained's flash partitioning. This possibility is quite useful when we have to organize our mass memory due to the fact that we can divide a single chip into several logical partitions.

 For more information on all MTD-related concepts, you can take a look at the *Linux Memory Technology Devices* home page at: http://www.linux-mtd.infradead.org.

However, for our purposes, these settings are quite correct, in particular, regarding the partition labeled rootfs where our new embedded OS will be placed.

At this point, we have to introduce the **mtd-utils** package where all the needed tools are placed. On our Debian OS, everything is already installed (otherwise, the `aptitude` command is the solution), and using the following command, we can take a list of such tools:

```
root@a5d3:~# dpkg -L mtd-utils | grep bin/ | sort
/usr/sbin/docfdisk
/usr/sbin/doc_loadbios
/usr/sbin/flashcp
/usr/sbin/flash_erase
/usr/sbin/flash_eraseall
/usr/sbin/flash_lock
/usr/sbin/flash_otp_dump
/usr/sbin/flash_otp_info
/usr/sbin/flash_otp_lock
/usr/sbin/flash_otp_write
/usr/sbin/flash_unlock
/usr/sbin/ftl_check
/usr/sbin/ftl_format
/usr/sbin/jffs2dump
/usr/sbin/jffs2reader
/usr/sbin/mkfs.jffs2
/usr/sbin/mkfs.ubifs
/usr/sbin/mtd_debug
/usr/sbin/mtdinfo
/usr/sbin/nanddump
/usr/sbin/nandtest
/usr/sbin/nandwrite
/usr/sbin/nftldump
/usr/sbin/nftl_format
/usr/sbin/recv_image
/usr/sbin/rfddump
/usr/sbin/rfdformat
/usr/sbin/serve_image
/usr/sbin/sumtool
/usr/sbin/ubiattach
/usr/sbin/ubiblock
/usr/sbin/ubicrc32
/usr/sbin/ubidetach
/usr/sbin/ubiformat
/usr/sbin/ubimkvol
/usr/sbin/ubinfo
/usr/sbin/ubinize
/usr/sbin/ubirename
/usr/sbin/ubirmvol
/usr/sbin/ubirsvol
/usr/sbin/ubiupdatevol
```

These commands have different usage – the ones starting with the `flash` string are strictly related to the MTD device in general, the ones that start with the `ubi` string are **UBIFS** related, and the ones that start with `jffs2` are related to the **JFFS2** filesystem (see the next section).

 These tools are not documented well (they've no man pages too!). So, the curios reader has to surf the Internet to find useful information on their usage. However, in this chapter, we will present some commands that are useful enough to start.

As the first step, let's take a look at the commands to erase and then correctly write a MTD device (remember that each flash memory, in order to be written, must be erased before). So, to erase the `mtd0` device on the SAMA5D3 Xplained board, we have to use the following command:

```
root@a5d3:~# flash_erase /dev/mtd0 0 0
Erasing 128 Kibyte @ 20000 -- 100 % complete
```

Then, to write some data in the same device, we have a different way, depending on the flash technology the device is composed of. This is because these flash devices have different write modes.

On our SAMA5D3 Xplained board, we have a NAND device, so the command to use is `nandwrite`. So, to write data on the just erased `mtd0` device, we have to use this command:

```
root@a5d3:~# nandwrite -q -m -p /dev/mtd0 boot.bin
```

We will explain the command soon in the upcoming sections.

You can continue experiencing other commands using the `--help` option argument to take the command's documentation.

Filesystems for flash memories

In a GNU/Linux system, the two major filesystems developed to manage flash memory devices are the JFFS2 and UBIFS. They are quite different from each other, but they have the same goal: implementing a good Flash Transition Layer.

JFFS2 versus UBIFS

This book cannot explain in detail all the differences between the JFFS2 and UBIFS filesystems due to the fact that these aspects are really complicated. However, we can spend some words in trying to give an idea about what these filesystems offer to the embedded developer.

First of all, we have to notice that the UBIFS filesystem, in reality, doesn't talk directly with the MTD core, but it has another layer in the middle named **Unsorted Block Image (UBI)** as shown in the following diagram:

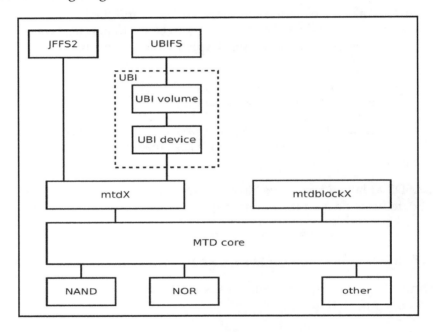

In the diagram, we can also notice that while JFFS2 uses the /dev/mtdX block devices, the UBIFS introduces the *UBI volume* concept. These UBI volumes are used to abstract the *Physical Erase Blocks* (known as PEB) of a MTD device into the *Logical Erase Blocks* (known as LEB) that allow a UBI volume to have the following major advantages:

- UBI volume has no bad LEBs due to the fact that the UBI layer transparency handles the bad PEBs.

- The LEBs do not wear out due to the fact that the UBI spreads the read/write/erase operations evenly across the whole flash device, implementing a transparency wear leveling system.
- UBI volumes are dynamic, and they can be created, deleted, and resized at run time.

For these reasons, using this layer, the **Unsorted Block Image File System** (**UBIFS**) can better manage the NAND flash bad blocks and provide wear leveling. However, the real advantage in using UBIFS rather than JFFS2 is that it supports the write caching and that it errs on the pessimistic side of free space calculation.

More information on UBIFS's write caching can be found at: `http://www.linux-mtd.infradead.org/doc/ubifs.html#L_writeback`, while information on free space calculation is located at: `http://www.linux-mtd.infradead.org/faq/ubifs.html#L_df_report`.

Besides these technical aspects, and simply speaking, the main advantage of UBIFS against JFFS2 is that the former scales better for larger flash memories. It also has a faster mounting, quicker access to large files, and improved write speeds. However, we still can find systems using the JFFS2 due its proven stability and a very wide usage (before the arriving of UBIFS). That's why, we present both it in this book anyway.

You can get more information on these aspects at: `http://www.linux-mtd.infradead.org/doc/general.html`, and especially at: `http://www.linux-mtd.infradead.org/doc/jffs2.html` for JFFS2 and at: `http://www.linux-mtd.infradead.org/doc/ubifs.html` and `http://www.linux-mtd.infradead.org/doc/ubi.html` for UBIFS and its UBI middle layer.

Building a JFFS2 filesystem

To build a JFFS2 filesystem, we have two main ways: the first one is by doing it directly on the target board while the second one is by doing it on the host PC. Of course, the latter is the most used one since we can generate a binary image that can be written directly into the flash with a **JTAG**.

The JTAGs usage is not covered into this book. However, it may be important due to the fact that using it, we can easily set up an embedded system without really running it and then simplifying large systems production. For more information on these topics and how to set up a JTAG system and then use it on an embedded system, a good starting point is `http://openocd.org`.

Let's start by verifying that our system supports JFFS2 filesystems by looking at `/proc/filesystems` as shown here:

```
root@a5d3:~# grep jffs2 /proc/filesystems
nodev    jffs2
```

If we get no output, it means that our system lacks the support for this filesystem and then we have to install it by recompiling the kernel as reported in Chapter 1, *Installing the Developing System*, in *Linux kernel for SAMA5D3 Xplained* section and modifying the kernel configuration by going to **File systems** | **Miscellaneous filesystems** | **Journalling Flash File System v2 (JFFS2) support**. We need just to enable it as built in, leaving the other parameters at their defaults.

Now, to create a JFFS2 filesystem on the SAMA5D3 Xplained, we have first of all to erase the flash partition with the `flash_erase` command. By taking a look at `flash_erase`'s help message, we notice that we can erase and then create a JFFS2 filesystem at the same time if we use the `--jffs2` option argument, so the actual command is shown here:

```
Erasing 128 Kibyte @ 0 -- 0 % complete flash_erase: Cleanmarker writ
ten at 0
Erasing 128 Kibyte @ 20000 -- 0 % complete flash_erase: Cleanmarker
written at 20000
Erasing 128 Kibyte @ 40000 -- 0 % complete flash_erase: Cleanmarker
written at 40000
Erasing 128 Kibyte @ 60000 -- 0 % complete flash_erase: Cleanmarker
written at 60000
...
flash_erase: Skipping bad block at 00480000
flash_erase: Skipping bad block at 004a0000
...
flash_erase: Skipping bad block at 0f780000
flash_erase: Skipping bad block at 0f7a0000
flash_erase: Skipping bad block at 0f7c0000
flash_erase: Skipping bad block at 0f7e0000
Erasing 128 Kibyte @ f7e0000 -- 100 % complete
```

During the execution, the command detects and signals every encountered bad blocks.

OK, that's all! Just mount the new JFFS2 partition with the usual `mount` command by specifying the partition's type using the `-t` option argument:

```
root@a5d3:~# mount -t jffs2 /dev/mtdblock5 /mnt/
```

To erase the partition, we used the `/dev/mtd5` character device, but to mount the partition, we used the `/dev/mtdblock5` block device! These devices, even if of different kinds, both refer to the same physical device area. However, the character device is needed during the erasing stage because for a block device, the erasing method does not make sense, while the `mount` command requires to work on a block device.

Now, in the `/mnt` directory, we can write some files, and they will be stored in our NAND flash where they will remain across a complete reboot:

```
root@a5d3:~# mount -t jffs2 /dev/mtdblock5 /mnt/
root@a5d3:~# echo "some text" > /mnt/just_a_file
root@a5d3:~# ls -l /mnt/
total 1
-rw-r--r-- 1 root root 10 Apr  2 17:44 just_a_file
root@a5d3:~# umount /mnt/
root@a5d3:~# mount -t jffs2 /dev/mtdblock5 /mnt/
root@a5d3:~# cat /mnt/just_a_file
some text
```

In the preceding example, we didn't reboot the system, but we just unmounted and then remounted the partition, which is (almost) the same.

Now, let's see how we can do the same on the host PC. This time, we need the **mtd-utils** package to be installed on the host PC too. So, let's install it with the usual `aptitude` command and then select the JFFS2-related commands:

```
$ dpkg -L mtd-utils | grep jffs2
/usr/share/man/man1/mkfs.jffs2.1.gz
/usr/sbin/jffs2dump
/usr/sbin/jffs2reader
```

OK, our command is obviously `mkfs.jffs2`. The command takes several options, but most of them are optional, while the only required ones (with two still optional but useful arguments within square brackets) are shown here:

```
mkfs.jffs2 --root=<root_filesystem> \
        --pagesize=<page_size> --eraseblock=<erase_block_size> \
        [--pad] [--little-endian] --output=<output_file>
```

By looking at the help message of `mkfs.jffs2`, we can discover what the preceding options are useful for, However, regarding the optional arguments, the `--pad` option can actually be omitted, but we keep it to remark that the output image must be padded until the end of the sector (this is because for a flash device, the sector must be completely rewritten and correctly filled with 0xFF). The `--little-endian` option is to remark the **endianness** of the output file since if both `--little-endian` and `--big-endian` are not specified, the system will create an output file of the same endianness of the host and, in some rare cases, this may create malfunctioning (especially if we work with hosts and clients with different endianness).

Now, to execute the `mkfs.jffs2` command in order to create our new JFFS2 filesystem, we need to know what is the page size and the erase block size to be put on the relative commands. We have two possible ways out: we can ask our hardware guys or we can get this information from the kernel itself. In fact, by looking at the kernel boot messages, we can get the information we need:

```
nand: 256 MiB, SLC, erase size: 128 KiB, page size: 2048, OOB si4
```

OK, now, we have just to create a dedicated directory and then create a file in it just for testing purposes:

```
$ mkdir mtd5_dir
$ echo "some text" > mtd5_dir/just_a_file
```

So, the command to create our filesystem is here:

```
$ mkfs.jffs2 --root=mtd5_dir --pagesize=2048 --eraseblock=128
        --pad --little-endian -output=mtd5.jffs2
```

Now, we have to move the file into our SAMA5D3 Xplained and then write it into the `/dev/mtd5` flash partition:

```
root@a5d3:~# flash_erase /dev/mtd5 0 0
Erasing 128 Kibyte @ 460000 -- 1 % complete flash_erase: Skipping bad
 block at 00480000
flash_erase: Skipping bad block at 004a0000
Erasing 128 Kibyte @ f760000 -- 99 % complete flash_erase: Skipping ba
d block at 0f780000
```

```
flash_erase: Skipping bad block at 0f7a0000
flash_erase: Skipping bad block at 0f7c0000
flash_erase: Skipping bad block at 0f7e0000
Erasing 128 Kibyte @ f7e0000 -- 100 % complete
root@a5d3:~# nandwrite /dev/mtd5 mtd5.jffs2
Writing data to block 0 at offset 0x0
```

First of all, don't forget to unmount the previous JFFS2 filesystem before erasing and then rewriting the data on the /dev/mtd5 partition! Then, note that this time, we didn't use the -j option argument for the flash_erase command as done before since now, the data we're going to write into the partition is already formatted as the JFFS2 filesystem. In the end, note also that the filesystem image is really small and it's not as large as the partition size where it is stored into. This is because the JFFS2 filesystem is capable of occupying the whole partition as soon as the system is running, and the reads/writes are performed on the flash device (this is a great feature for the system production since it dramatically reduces the setup time).

Now, we have to mount the partition and check whether the file we have created on the host PC is there:

```
root@a5d3:~# mount -t jffs2 /dev/mtdblock5 /mnt/
root@a5d3:~# cat /mnt/just_a_file
some text
```

OK, our job was correct.

Building a UBIFS filesystem

Now, let's try to redo what we did in the preceding section, but with the UBIFS this time. So, erase the mtd5 partition again (after unmounting the relative mtdblock5 device!), but this time, without any special argument options:

```
root@a5d3:~# flash_erase /dev/mtd5 0 0
```

After that, we have to do a more complicated procedure to do our job. In fact, we have to format the partition as we did with hard disks, but this time, the formatting command takes the character device instead of a block one (as the `fdisk` command does, for instance). The command to be used is `ubiformat`. The command takes several option arguments, but this time, we just need `--yes` to skip several questions where we have to answer yes in any case:

```
root@a5d3:~# ubiformat --yes /dev/mtd5
ubiformat: mtd5 (nand), size 260046848 bytes (248.0 MiB),
1984 eraseblocks of 1s
libscan: scanning eraseblock 1983 -- 100 % complete
ubiformat: 1978 eraseblocks are supposedly empty
ubiformat: 6 bad eraseblocks found, numbers: 36, 37, 1980, 1981, 1982,
1983
ubiformat: formatting eraseblock 1983 -- 100 % complete
```

OK, now, the partition has been formatted, and we are ready to attach the `mtd5` device to the UBI subsystem. This is the first real difference between UBIFS and JFFS2 (and other usual filesystems) since UBIFS requires that each partition is placed under the control of the UBI layer presented earlier. The command is `ubiattach`.

Our command is the one in the first example. However, we wish to keep the number 5 for the new UBI device for better readability since we're going to use the fifth MTD device. So, the command is as follows:

```
root@a5d3:~# ubiattach --dev-path=/dev/mtd5 --devn=5
ubi5: attaching mtd5
ubi5: scanning is finished
ubi5: attached mtd5 (name "rootfs", size 248 MiB)
ubi5: PEB size: 131072 bytes (128 KiB), LEB size: 126976 bytes
ubi5: min./max. I/O unit sizes: 2048/2048, sub-page size 2048
ubi5: VID header offset: 2048 (aligned 2048), data offset: 4096
ubi5: good PEBs: 1978, bad PEBs: 6, corrupted PEBs: 0
ubi5: user volume: 0, internal volumes: 1, max. volumes count: 18
ubi5: max/mean erase counter: 0/0, WL threshold: 4096, image seq4
ubi5: available PEBs: 1940, total reserved PEBs: 38, PEBs reserv4
ubi5: background thread "ubi_bgt5d" started, PID 2027
UBI device number 5, total 1978 LEBs (251158528 bytes, 239.5 MiB),
 available 19)
```

The output reported after the `ubiattach` command with the prefix `ubi5:` is not generated by the command itself. They're kernel messages, so they are not visible if we give the command outside the serial console. If this is the case, you can read these messages with the usual `dmesg` or `tail -f` command. That we can use the `--mtdn` option argument to specify the MTD device, just in case the character device is missing (this is useful in reduced systems where we have no automatic device nodes generation support at all as udev & Co.). In this case, the command is as follows:

```
root@a5d3:~# ubiattach --mtdn=5 --devn=5
```

We can now get the UBI status using the `ubinfo` command. The command usage is very simple, so using it with the `--all` option argument, we can get the information needed:

```
root@a5d3:~# ubinfo --all
UBI version: 1
Count of UBI devices: 1
UBI control device major/minor: 10:59
Present UBI devices: ubi5

ubi5
Volumes count: 0
Logical eraseblock size: 126976 bytes, 124.0 KiB
Total amount of logical eraseblocks: 1978 (251158528 bytes, 239.5
MiB)
Amount of available logical eraseblocks: 1940 (246333440 bytes, 234.9
MiB)
Maximum count of volumes 128
Count of bad physical eraseblocks: 6
Count of reserved physical eraseblocks: 34
Current maximum erase counter value: 0
Minimum input/output unit size: 2048 bytes
Character device major/minor: 249:0
```

Now, we need to take another step. We have to create the UBI volume related to our partition and the command to use is `ubimkvol`. So, the command to do our job is as follows:

```
root@a5d3:~# ubimkvol /dev/ubi5 --maxavsize -N rootfs
Set volume size to 246333440
Volume ID 0, size 1940 LEBs (246333440 bytes, 234.9 MiB), LEB size 126
976 bytes (124.0 KiB), dynamic, name "rootfs", alignment 1
```

Now, everything is in place. We just need to mount our new UBIFS partition with the usual `mount` command, but with proper arguments:

```
root@a5d3:~# mount -t ubifs ubi5:rootfs /mnt
UBIFS (ubi5:0): default file-system created
UBIFS (ubi5:0): background thread "ubifs_bgt5_0" started, PID 1738
UBIFS (ubi5:0): UBIFS: mounted UBI device 5, volume 0, name "rootfs"
UBIFS (ubi5:0): LEB size: 126976 bytes (124 KiB), min./max. I/O unit s
izes: 2048 bytes/2048 bytes
UBIFS (ubi5:0): FS size: 244682752 bytes (233 MiB, 1927 LEBs), journal
 size 12316672 bytes (11 MiB, 97 LEBs)
UBIFS (ubi5:0): reserved for root: 4952683 bytes (4836 KiB)
UBIFS (ubi5:0): media format: w4/r0 (latest is w4/r0), UUID 02B4EDD6-1
8CE-4FFF-88A4-4350C4126351, small LPT model
```

As shown in preceding code, the messages with prefix `UBIFS` came from the kernel. In the mount, we didn't specify a block device in the usual form `/dev/blockdev`, but we use the `volume` name instead.

OK, now, we can test the new UBIFS partition as we did earlier by creating a file in it and then verifying that it is still there across an unmount:

```
root@a5d3:~# echo "some text" > /mnt/just_a_file
root@a5d3:~# ls /mnt/
just_a_file
root@a5d3:~# umount /mnt/
UBIFS (ubi5:0): un-mount UBI device 5
UBIFS (ubi5:0): background thread "ubifs_bgt5_0" stops
root@a5d3:~# ls /mnt/
root@a5d3:~# mount -t ubifs ubi5:rootfs /mnt
UBIFS (ubi5:0): background thread "ubifs_bgt5_0" started, PID 1749
UBIFS (ubi5:0): UBIFS: mounted UBI device 5, volume 0, name "rootfs"
UBIFS (ubi5:0): LEB size: 126976 bytes (124 KiB), min./max. I/O unit s
izes: 2048 bytes/2048 bytes
UBIFS (ubi5:0): FS size: 244682752 bytes (233 MiB, 1927 LEBs), journal
 size 12316672 bytes (11 MiB, 97 LEBs)
UBIFS (ubi5:0): reserved for root: 4952683 bytes (4836 KiB)
UBIFS (ubi5:0): media format: w4/r0 (latest is w4/r0), UUID 02B4EDD6-1
8CE-4FFF-88A4-4350C4126351, small LPT model
root@a5d3:~# cat /mnt/just_a_file
some text
```

For completeness, we left all kernel messages with the UBIFS prefix for documentation purposes, but you should remember that they are not displayed if the commands are executed outside the serial console.

Well, now, as for JFFS2, we will create our UBIFS partition on the host PC. We can use the `mtd5_dir` directory created earlier and reshown here:

```
$ ls -l mtd5_dir/
total 4
-rw-rw-r-- 1 giometti giometti 10 giu 12 12:04 just_a_file
$ cat mtd5_dir/just_a_file
some text
```

This time, the command to be used is `mkfs.ubifs`. As for `mkfs.jffs2`, we have a lot of option arguments, but for our purposes the command to be used is quite similar:

```
$ mkfs.ubifs --root=mtd5_dir --min-io-size=2048 --leb-size=124KiB
       --max-leb-cnt=2048 --output=mtd5.ubifs
```

At this point, the real question is: how can we calculate the values for the option arguments `--min-io-size`, `--leb-size`, and `--max-leb-cnt`?

Well, the answer is not easy, since we have to know a bit more in depth how UBIFS works. However, the right thing to do is just creating the UBIFS filesystem on the target machine and then get these parameters directly from the UBIFS subsystem itself! In fact, if we take a look at the earlier `mount` command, we can see that the kernel tells us these values:

```
UBIFS (ubi5:0): background thread "ubifs_bgt5_0" started, PID 1749
UBIFS (ubi5:0): UBIFS: mounted UBI device 5, volume 0, name "rootfs"
UBIFS (ubi5:0): LEB size: 126976 bytes (124 KiB), min./max. I/O unit s
izes: 2048 bytes/2048 bytes
UBIFS (ubi5:0): FS size: 244682752 bytes (233 MiB, 1927 LEBs), journal
 size 12316672 bytes (11 MiB, 97 LEBs)
```

For `--min-io-size` and `--leb-size`, the values are exposed earlier, while for `--max-leb-cnt`, we have to consider that this option defines the maximum filesystem size (more strictly, the maximum UBI volume size). So, we must specify a value large enough to avoid to allocate too few LEBs for correctly mapping our `mtd5` device. The last line of the preceding messages tells us that we need 1927 LEBs for user data and 97 LEBs for journaling data, so we need at least 2024 LEBs and a safe value for `--max-leb-cnt` can be `2048`, which is the nearest power of 2 (for better performance).

Now, we have to create a UBI image suitable for the MTD layer where we put the UBIFS partition we just created and the command to be used is `ubinize`. Before executing the command, we have to create a proper INI file useful to describe our UBI image, so in our special case, the file looks like this:

```
[rootfs-volume]
mode=ubi
image=mtd5.ubifs
vol_id=5
vol_size=233MiB
vol_type=dynamic
vol_name=rootfs
vol_flags=autoresize
```

The `mode` parameter is currently fixed to `ubi`, while `image` must point to the UBIFS image created earlier. Then, the other parameters are quite obvious apart from `vol_size`, `vol_type` and `vol_flags`, so let's explain them a bit.

The `vol_type` and `vol_flags` specify that the UBI volume can be dynamically allocated, and it can grow in size if the available space is present. So, in `vol_size`, we can specify the minimum volume size and, when the system will attach the volume, it will increase dynamically until the maximum available size (we will verify this feature soon in this section).

OK, let's execute the `ubinize` command:

```
$ ubinize -v --min-io-size=2048 --peb-size=128KiB
         --sub-page-size=2048 --output=mtd5.ubi mtd5.ini
ubinize: LEB size:                    126976
ubinize: PEB size:                    131072
ubinize: min. I/O size:               2048
ubinize: sub-page size:               2048
ubinize: VID offset:                  2048
ubinize: data offset:                 4096
ubinize: UBI image sequence number: 949373716
ubinize: loaded the ini-file "mtd5.ini"
ubinize: count of sections: 1
ubinize: parsing section "jffs2-volume"
ubinize: mode=ubi, keep parsing
ubinize: volume type: dynamic
ubinize: volume ID: 5
ubinize: volume size: 251658240 bytes
ubinize: volume name: rootfs
ubinize: volume alignment: 1
ubinize: autoresize flags found
ubinize: adding volume 5
```

```
ubinize: writing volume 5
ubinize: image file: mtd5.ubifs
ubinize: writing layout volume
ubinize: done
```

Again, we have to spend some words on the several values we have used in the `ubinize` command line. The `-v` option argument is just for having a verbose output. The really important parameters are `--min-io-size`, which has the same meaning of the `mkfs.ubifs` command, `--peb-size`, which specifies the size of the physical erase blocks (note that with `mkfs.ubifs`, we have specified the LEB's size instead), and `--sub-page-size`, which depends on the NAND device used (but usually is equivalent to the minimum input/output unit size).

The UBIFS image is slightly bigger than the JFFS2 one even if they hold the same files:

```
$ ls -lh mtd5.{jffs2,ubi}
-rw-r--r-- 1 giometti giometti 128K giu 12 12:05 mt
d5.jffs2
 -rw-rw-r-- 1 giometti giometti 2,0M giu 14 16:14 mt
d5.ubi
```

Now, as we did for JFFS2, we have to move the UBIFS image on the SAMA5D3 Xplained and then put it on the `/dev/mtd5` partition. However, this time we cannot use the `nandwrite` utility to write UBI data due the fact it doesn't properly format the flash partition for UBIFS. To do it we have to use the ubiformat as reported below::

```
root@a5d3:~# flash_erase /dev/mtd5 0 0
root@a5d3:~# ubiformat /dev/mtd5 -s 2048 -O 2048 -f mtd5.ubi
```

OK, now, we have to attach our UBI volume as we did earlier:

```
root@a5d3:~# ubiattach --dev-path=/dev/mtd5 -devn=5
ubi5: attaching mtd5
ubi5: scanning is finished
gluebi (pid 1713): gluebi_resized: got update notification for unknown
 UBI device 5 volume 5
ubi5: volume 5 ("rootfs") re-sized from 1925 to 1940 LEBs
ubi5: attached mtd5 (name "rootfs", size 248 MiB)
ubi5: PEB size: 131072 bytes (128 KiB), LEB size: 126976 bytes
ubi5: min./max. I/O unit sizes: 2048/2048, sub-page size 2048
ubi5: VID header offset: 2048 (aligned 2048), data offset: 4096
ubi5: good PEBs: 1978, bad PEBs: 6, corrupted PEBs: 0
ubi5: user volume: 1, internal volumes: 1, max. volumes count: 128
ubi5: max/mean erase counter: 1/0, WL threshold: 4096, image sequence
number: 1394936512
```

```
ubi5: available PEBs: 0, total reserved PEBs: 1978, PEBs reserved for
bad PEB handling: 34
ubi5: background thread "ubi_bgt5d" started, PID 1717
UBI device number 5, total 1978 LEBs (251158528 bytes, 239.5 MiB), ava
ilable 0 LEBs (0 bytes), LEB size 126976 bytes (124.0 KiB)
```

As said earlier, at the attach time, the system discovers that it can enlarge the volume from 1925 to 1940 LEBs, that is, the maximum available space, and then, it proceeds to carry on the operation:

```
gluebi (pid 1713): gluebi_resized: got update notif
ication for unknown UBI device 5 volume 5
ubi5: volume 5 ("rootfs") re-sized from 1925 to 194
0 LEBs
ubi5: attached mtd5 (name "rootfs", size 248 MiB)
```

Note also that the messages with the ubi5: prefix are kernel messages.

Great! Now, the last step is to mount the partition and then verify that all data is in place:

```
root@a5d3:~# mount -t ubifs ubi5:rootfs /mnt
UBIFS (ubi5:5): background thread "ubifs_bgt5_5" started, PID 174
UBIFS (ubi5:5): UBIFS: mounted UBI device 5, volume 5, name "roo"
UBIFS (ubi5:5): LEB size: 126976 bytes (124 KiB), min./max. I/O s
UBIFS (ubi5:5): FS size: 244936704 bytes (233 MiB, 1929 LEBs), j)
UBIFS (ubi5:5): reserved for root: 0 bytes (0 KiB)
UBIFS (ubi5:5): media format: w4/r0 (latest is w4/r0), UUID 8A2B1
root@a5d3:~# ls /mnt/
just_a_file
root@a5d3:~# cat /mnt/just_a_file
some text
```

Note that the messages with the USBIFS prefix are kernel messages.

OK, everything is good.

OpenWrt

As stated at the OpenWrt home site:

OpenWrt is described as a Linux distribution for embedded devices.

Based on the Linux kernel, this distribution is primarily used on devices to route network traffic due to the fact that it is born because the **Linksys** released the source code of the firmware for their *WRT54G* series of wireless routers under the GNU/GPL license (that's why, the WRT into the name). Then, other chipsets, manufacturers, and device types have been included in turning the initial project into a valid and rock-solid software product.

OpenWrt's main components are the Linux kernel, the **uClibc** (or musl) C library, and **BusyBox**. All components have been optimized for size in order to fit into very small memory devices (bare but functional OpenWrt footprint is around 4 MB!). This distribution is known as the best distribution for embedded networking devices.

The distribution has its building system based on a (modified) **Buildroot** system that automates the building process, thanks to a set of makefiles and patches. The main tool used to manage the distribution is make.

 More information on the OpenWrt distribution can be retrieved from the project's home page at: https://openwrt.org.

In the upcoming sections, we will build a minimal image from scratch, and then, we'll show you how you can add some included packages and how to add a new (and simple) package in order to expand the distribution.

Using the default configuration

To install the base system for our SAMA5D3 Xplained board, we can use the OpenWrt default configuration we will show here. However, as the first step, we need to download the sources. This can be done with the git command as follows:

```
$ git clone git://git.openwrt.org/15.05/openwrt.git
```

Then move into the just created `openwrt` directory and execute the configuration menu as below:

```
$ cd openwrt
$ make menuconfig
```

It may happen that the command ends with an error:

```
Build dependency: Please install zlib. (Missing libz.so or zlib.h)
Build dependency: Please install the openssl library (with development
 headers)
Build dependency: Please install GNU 'awk'
Build dependency: Please install the Subversion client

/home/giometti/A5D3/openwrt/include/prereq.mk:12: recipe for target 'p
rereq' failed
Prerequisite check failed. Use FORCE=1 to override.
/home/giometti/A5D3/openwrt/include/toplevel.mk:140: recipe for target
 'staging_dir/host/.prereq-build' failed
make: *** [staging_dir/host/.prereq-build] Error 1
```

In this case, we have to manually add all missing dependencies to be able to compile our new OpenWrt distribution, so in the preceding error, our host PC tells us that several packages are missing. Then, we have to install them using the following command:

```
$ sudo aptitude install libz-dev libssl-dev gawk subversion
```

How we can deduce the missing packages' names from the output of the preceding configuration command is not a an act of magic, but we used the package management tools of the Ubuntu/Debian OS described at `Chapter 2`, *Managing the System Console*, in *Packages management* section.

Then, we can relaunch the command and, if all packages are in place, we should get a configuration menu similar to the one we got during the kernel configuration in `Chapter 1`, *Installing the Developing System*, in *SAMA5D3 Xplained* section. Now, we must select our SAMA5D3 Xplained board by setting **Atmel AT91** in the **Target System** entry, **SAMA5D3 (Cortex-A5)** for the **Subtarget** entry, and **Atmel AT91SAMA5D3XPLAINED** in **Target Profile**, as shown in the following screenshot:

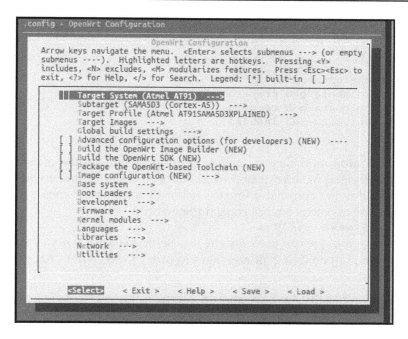

Before starting the compilation, we need to do a little patch at the OpenWrt sources. In fact, by default, the system will generate a single file for both the SAMA5D3 Xplained's kernel image and the DTB configuration file (the DTB file is actually appended to the kernel image), but since we want two separate files, in order to flash them into their matching MTD partitions, we must apply the following patch:

```
--- a/target/linux/at91/image/Makefile
+++ b/target/linux/at91/image/Makefile
@@ -50,7 +50,7 @@ Image/Build/Kernel/AT91SAM9G35EK=$(call MkuImageDtb,
9g35ek,at91sam9g35ek)
 Image/Build/Kernel/AT91SAM9M10G45EK=$(call MkuImageDtb,9m10g45ek,at91
sam9m10g45ek)
 Image/Build/Kernel/AT91SAM9X25EK=$(call MkuImageDtb,9x25ek,at91sam9x2
5ek)
 Image/Build/Kernel/AT91SAM9X35EK=$(call MkuImageDtb,9x35ek,at91sam9x3
5ek)
-Image/Build/Kernel/AT91SAMA5D3XPLAINED=$(call MkuImageDtb,sama5,at91-
sama5d3_xplained)
+Image/Build/Kernel/AT91SAMA5D3XPLAINED=$(call MkOftree,sama5,at91-sam
a5d3_xplained)
 # CalAmp
 Image/Build/Kernel/LMU5000=$(call MkuImageDtb,lmu5000,lmu5000)
 # Calao
```

Now, we are ready, so let's launch the compilation using the following `make` command:

```
$ make
 make[1] world
 make[2] toolchain/install
 make[3] -C toolchain/gdb prepare
 make[3] -C toolchain/gdb compile
 make[3] -C toolchain/gdb install
 . . .
```

 The compilation is very time consuming, so you should consider to take your time to have your preferred coffee! If we got some error, we can use the following command line to enable all compilation messages and force just one task to see what caused the error:

```
$ make -j1 V=s
```

In any case, we can use only the `V=s` settings to normally compile the system, but enabling all messages in order to see what's happening.

When the compilation has finished, we should get the following messages:

```
 . . .
 make[2] package/install
 make[3] package/preconfig
 make[2] target/install
 make[3] -C target/linux install
 make[2] package/index
$
```

Now, we can see the compilation results under the `bin/at91/` directory as shown here:

```
$ cd bin/at91/
$ ls
md5sums
openwrt-at91-sama5d3-AT91SAMA5D3XPLAINED-rootfs.tar.gz
openwrt-at91-sama5d3-root.ext4
openwrt-at91-sama5d3-root.jffs2-128k
openwrt-at91-sama5d3-root.jffs2-64k
openwrt-at91-sama5d3-root.ubi
openwrt-at91-sama5d3-root.ubifs
openwrt-at91-sama5d3-sama5-oftree.dtb
openwrt-at91-sama5d3-sama5-uImage
openwrt-at91-sama5d3-uImage
openwrt-at91-sama5d3-zImage
packages
sha256sums
```

The files we have to move to the SAMA5D3 Xplained are:

- file `openwrt-at91-sama5d3-zImage` – the kernel,
- file `openwrt-at91-sama5d3-sama5-oftree.dtb` – the DTB and
- file `openwrt-at91-sama5d3-root.ubi` – the rootfs.

The following command will copy all these files into a dedicated directory of our embedded board:

```
$ scp openwrt-at91-sama5d3-zImage
        openwrt-at91-sama5d3-sama5-oftree.dtb
        openwrt-at91-sama5d3-root.ubi root@192.168.8.2:nand/
```

 Note that the `nand` directory must be already present into the SAMA5D3 Xplained root user's home directory.

Now, we have to compile the bootloader. The OpenWrt has the possibility to do it for us, but this option seems disabled for our board! Then, keep calm and remember that we already compiled the SAMA5D3 Xplained's bootloader into `Chapter 1`, *Installing the Developing System*, in *SAMA5D3 Xplained* section. We can now redo the same steps, but this time, with two major differences:

- We have to use the `sama5d3_xplained_nandflash_defconfig` target in order to compile our U-Boot image for the NAND flash.
- We have to write the result image into the flash itself.

Let's see one step at time. First of all, we have to go into the directory we used to download the U-Boot's source code and reconfigure it for the NAND flash:

```
$ cd A5D3/u-boot
$ make ARCH=arm CROSS_COMPILE=arm-linux-gnueabihf-
      sama5d3_xplained_nandflash_defconfig
#
# configuration written to .config
#
```

Then, we have to re-compile it with the usual command:

```
$ make ARCH=arm CROSS_COMPILE=arm-linux-gnueabihf-
```

Again, the two bootloaders image files `boot.bin` and `u-boot.img` (the board has two bootloaders remember? See `Chapter 1`, *Installing the Developing System*, in *SAMA5D3 Xplained* section) are created, but this time, they are suitable to be used on the NAND instead of on the microSD. So, let's place them on the SAMA5D3 Xplained into the dedicated directory as we did earlier:

```
$ scp boot.bin u-boot.img root@192.168.8.2:nand/
```

Now, under the `/root/nand` directory on the SAMA5D3 Xplained, we should have all the needed files, and then, we have only to write them into the NAND flash to have a running OpenWrt system. However, before continuing, you should notice that we used the kernel and the rootfs from OpenWrt while the bootloaders have been generated outside OpenWrt! This fact can lead to some misconfigurations that can produce an unbootable system. The problem is about the flash partitioning. In fact, we must be sure that we write all data into the correct place. Let's see how.

Since we will use our Debian OS to set up the OpenWrt image files, we must check the current partitioning. This can be done with the following command:

```
root@a5d3:~# cat /proc/mtd
dev:    size     erasesize  name
mtd0: 00040000 00020000 "at91bootstrap"
mtd1: 00080000 00020000 "bootloader"
mtd2: 000c0000 00020000 "bootloader env"
mtd3: 00080000 00020000 "device tree"
mtd4: 00600000 00020000 "kernel"
mtd5: 0f800000 00020000 "rootfs"
```

The preceding output states a NAND partitioning as reported into the following table:

MTD Device	Label	Starting offset	Length
mtd0	at91bootstrap	0x00000000	0x00040000 (256 KB)
mtd1	bootloader	0x00040000	0x00080000 (512 KB)
mtd2	bootloader env	0x000c0000	0x000c0000 (768 KB)
mtd3	device tree	0x00180000	0x00080000 (512 KB)
mtd4	kernel	0x00200000	0x00600000 (6 MB)
mtd5	rootfs	0x00800000	0x0f800000 (248 MB)

In this scenario, we must be sure that:

- U-Boot will load the kernel and the DTB file at the right positions.
- the kernel has a compatible setting, that is, the rootfs must be placed into a partition from offset `0x00800000` and 248 MB length at maximum.

These settings must be done into the U-Boot, so we have to stop it the first time we try to execute our OpenWrt to check the current U-Boot's configuration. On the other hand, we are quite sure that `boot.bin` will safely load `u-boot.img` due to the fact that they derive from the same compilation and that the former has the correct settings to do it.

 You can verify it by looking at the `CONFIG_SYS_NAND_U_BOOT_OFFS` value in the `include/configs/sama5d3_xplained.h` file in the U-Boot's repository.

OK, let's start by flashing the bootloaders, erasing the `mtd2` partition, just to be sure to work with a void-saved environment:

```
root@a5d3:~# flash_erase -q /dev/mtd0 0 0
root@a5d3:~# flash_erase -q /dev/mtd1 0 0
root@a5d3:~# flash_erase -q /dev/mtd2 0 0
root@a5d3:~# nandwrite -q -m -p /dev/mtd0 nand/boot.bin
root@a5d3:~# nandwrite -q -m -p /dev/mtd1 nand/u-boot.img
```

Then, we can flash the DTB and the kernel images:

```
root@a5d3:~/nand# flash_erase -q /dev/mtd3 0 0
root@a5d3:~/nand# flash_erase -q /dev/mtd4 0 0
root@a5d3:~# nandwrite -q -m -p /dev/mtd3 nand/openwrt-at91-sama5d3-sa
ma5-oftree.dtb
root@a5d3:~# nandwrite -q -m -p /dev/mtd4 nand/openwrt-at91-sama5d3-zI
mage
```

And the last step is the rootfs image. However, this time, we cannot use the `nandwrite` utility due to the fact that it doesn't properly format the flash partition for UBIFS. To do this, we have to use the `ubiformat` as reported here:

```
root@a5d3:~# flash_erase -q /dev/mtd5 0 0
root@a5d3:~# ubiformat /dev/mtd5 -s 2048 -O 2048
                    -f nand/openwrt-at91-sama5d3-root.ubi
```

Now, we have to stop the system with the `halt` command, and then, we must remove the microSD and press the reset button (see `Chapter 1`, *Installing the Developing System*, in *SAMA5D3 Xplained* section). If everything works well, we should see the following messages on the serial console:

```
RomBOOT
U-Boot SPL 2016.03-dirty (Jun 15 2016 - 16:19:44)
Trying to boot from NAND
U-Boot 2016.03-dirty (Jun 15 2016 - 16:19:44 +0200)
CPU: SAMA5D36
Crystal frequency:        12 MHz
CPU clock        :        528 MHz
Master clock     :        132 MHz
DRAM:  256 MiB
NAND:  256 MiB
MMC:   mci: 0
*** Warning - bad CRC, using default environment
In:    serial
Out:   serial
Err:   serial
Net:   gmac0
Error: gmac0 address not set.
, macb0
Error: macb0 address not set.
Hit any key to stop autoboot:  1
```

We have to be quick and stop the autoboot by pressing a key, and then, we can show the U-Boot environment:

```
=> print
arch=arm
baudrate=115200
board=sama5d3_xplained
board_name=sama5d3_xplained
bootargs=console=ttyS0,115200 earlyprintk mtdparts=atmel_nand:256k(boo
tstrap)ro,512k(uboot)ro,256K(env),256k(env_redundent),256k(spare),512k
(dtb),6M(kernel)ro,-(rootfs) rootfstype=ubifs ubi.mtd=7 root=ubi0:root
fs
bootcmd=nand read 0x21000000 0x180000 0x80000;nand read 0x22000000 0x2
00000 0x600000;bootz 0x22000000 - 0x21000000
bootdelay=1
cpu=armv7
ethact=gmac0
soc=at91
vendor=atmel

Environment size: 484/131067 bytes
```

The relevant settings here are in the `bootcmd` and `bootargs` variables. The first variable defines the commands to load the kernel and the DTB file, and they are correct, while `bootargs` defines a slightly different settings regarding the UBIFS settings (`ubi.mtd`) and the flash partitioning for the kernel (`mtdparts`), so they must be fixed up. Recalling the preceding table, the correct values per the `mtdparts` and `ubi.mtd` settings are shown here:

```
mtdparts=atmel_nand:256k(at91bootstrap)ro,512k(bootloader)ro,768K(boot
loader env),512k(device tree),6M(kernel)ro,-(rootfs)
ubi.mtd=5
```

So, we can use the `setenv` command to do the job:

```
=> setenv bootargs 'console=ttyS0,115200 earlyprintk mtdparts=atmel_na
nd:256k(at91bootstrap)ro,512k(bootloader)ro,768K(bootloader env),512k(
device tree),6M(kernel)ro,-(rootfs) rootfstype=ubifs ubi.mtd=5 root=ub
i0:rootfs rw'
```

The usage of the ' character to delimit the variable content!

Then, we can save the new environment with the `saveenv` command:

```
=> saveenv
Saving Environment to NAND...
Erasing redundant NAND...
Erasing at 0x100000 -- 100% complete.
Writing to redundant NAND... OK
```

Now, everything is in place, and we can safely reset the system:

```
=> reset
resetting ...
RomBOOT

U-Boot SPL 2016.03-dirty (Jun 15 2016 - 16:19:44)
Trying to boot from NAND


U-Boot 2016.03-dirty (Jun 15 2016 - 16:19:44 +0200)

CPU: SAMA5D36
Crystal frequency: 12 MHz
CPU clock : 528 MHz
Master clock : 132 MHz
DRAM: 256 MiB
```

```
NAND: 256 MiB
MMC: mci: 0
In: serial
Out: serial
Err: serial
Net: gmac0
Error: gmac0 address not set.
, macb0
Error: macb0 address not set.

Hit any key to stop autoboot: 0

NAND read: device 0 offset 0x180000, size 0x80000
 524288 bytes read: OK

NAND read: device 0 offset 0x200000, size 0x600000
 6291456 bytes read: OK
Kernel image @ 0x22000000 [ 0x000000 - 0x155680 ]
## Flattened Device Tree blob at 21000000
 Booting using the fdt blob at 0x21000000
 Loading Device Tree to 2fadc000, end 2fae6abc ... OK

Starting kernel ...

Uncompressing Linux... done, booting the kernel.
[ 0.000000] Booting Linux on physical CPU 0x0
[ 0.000000] Linux version 3.18.29 (giometti@ubuntu1510) (gcc versio
n 4.8.3 (OpenWrt/Linaro GCC 4.8-2014.04 r49378) ) #2 Wed Jun 15 16:07:
48 CEST 2016
[ 0.000000] CPU: ARMv7 Processor [410fc051] revision 1 (ARMv7), cr=
10c53c7d
[ 0.000000] CPU: PIPT / VIPT nonaliasing data cache, VIPT aliasing
instruction cache
[ 0.000000] Machine model: SAMA5D3 Xplained
[ 0.000000] Memory policy: Data cache writeback
[ 0.000000] AT91: Detected soc type: sama5d3
[ 0.000000] AT91: Detected soc subtype: sama5d36
...
```

Great! The kernel has been correctly loaded, and now, we should wait until the rootfs is mounted:

```
...
[ 1.850000] UBIFS: mounted UBI device 0, volume 0, name "rootfs", R
/O mode
[ 1.850000] UBIFS: LEB size: 126976 bytes (124 KiB), min./max. I/O
unit sizes: 2048 bytes/2048 bytes
[ 1.860000] UBIFS: FS size: 244936704 bytes (233 MiB, 1929 LEBs), j
```

```
ournal size 9023488 bytes (8 MiB, 72 LEBs)
[ 1.870000] UBIFS: reserved for root: 0 bytes (0 KiB)
[ 1.880000] UBIFS: media format: w4/r0 (latest is w4/r0), UUID E598
066D-054B-44EB-BD77-EF8321F5F8A7, small LPT model
[ 1.920000] VFS: Mounted root (ubifs filesystem) readonly on device
 0:10.
[ 1.920000] Freeing unused kernel memory: 136K (c0396000 - c03b8000
)
[ 2.230000] init: Console is alive
...
```

OK! The rootfs has been correctly mounted, so it's time to wait for the console login message:

```
...
[    3.250000] init: - preinit -
/etc/preinit: .: line 1: can't open '/lib/at91.sh'
[    3.400000] procd: - early -
[    4.070000] procd: - ubus -
[    5.100000] procd: - init -
Please press Enter to activate this console.
```

We got it! Now, if we strike the *Enter* key, we get the following message:

```
BusyBox v1.23.2 (2016-06-15 13:48:20 CEST) built-in shell (ash)
```

```
CHAOS CALMER (Chaos Calmer, r49378)
-----------------------------------------------------------
  * 1 1/2 oz Gin            Shake with a glassful
  * 1/4 oz Triple Sec       of broken ice and pour
  * 3/4 oz Lime Juice       unstrained into a goblet.
  * 1 1/2 oz Orange Juice
  * 1 tsp. Grenadine Syrup
-----------------------------------------------------------
root@OpenWrt:/#
```

Before ending the paragraph, let me show you the actual flash memory occupation:

```
root@OpenWrt:/# df -h
Filesystem                Size      Used Available Use% Mounted on
rootfs                   215.4M     2.1M    213.3M   1% /
ubi0:rootfs              215.4M     2.1M    213.3M   1% /
tmpfs                    124.9M    56.0K    124.8M   0% /tmp
tmpfs                    512.0K        0    512.0K   0% /dev
```

Around 2MB, so cute!

Adding a (quasi) LAMP system

As you can easily verify using the just created OpenWrt distribution, its base system is very small and it's also quite useless. That's why we will show you how you can add a (quasi) LAMP system. In fact, we will install a **lighttpd** web server (that's why, the *quasi* word) with PHP support and a MySQL server.

To do our job, we should consider that the OpenWrt supports the *feeds*. They are external repositories based on **git** repositories useful to add additional packages without touching the main distribution. The feeds are managed by the `feeds` command placed in the `scripts` directory. So, first of all, we have to update all feeds' repositories with this command:

```
$ ./scripts/feeds update -a
```

Then, we can use the next command to search for the package holding the lighttpd web server:

```
$ ./scripts/feeds search lighttpd
Search results in feed 'packages':
lighttpd                    A flexible and lightweight web server
...
lighttpd-mod-cgi            CGI module
lighttpd-mod-cml            Cache Meta Language module
lighttpd-mod-compress       Compress output module
lighttpd-mod-evasive        Evasive module
lighttpd-mod-evhost         Exnhanced Virtual-Hosting module
lighttpd-mod-expire         Expire module
lighttpd-mod-extforward     Extract client module
lighttpd-mod-fastcgi        FastCGI module
...
```

Then, to install it (belong other useful modules, we can use the following command:

```
$ ./scripts/feeds install lighttpd lighttpd-mod-cgi lighttpd-mod-fastcgi
```

For the PHP language, we can do the same:

```
$ ./scripts/feeds search php5
Search results in feed 'packages':
php5                    PHP5 Hypertext preprocessor
php5-cgi                PHP5 Hypertext preprocessor (CGI & FastCGI)
php5-cli                PHP5 Hypertext preprocessor (CLI)
php5-fastcgi            FastCGI startup script
...
php5-mod-mysql          MySQL shared module
php5-mod-mysqli         MySQL Improved Extension shared module
php5-mod-opcache        OPcache shared module
php5-mod-openssl        OpenSSL shared module
php5-mod-pcntl          PCNTL shared module
php5-mod-pdo            PHP Data Objects shared module
php5-mod-pdo-mysql      PDO driver for MySQL shared module
php5-mod-pdo-pgsql      PDO driver for PostgreSQL shared module
php5-mod-pdo-sqlite     PDO driver for SQLite 3.x shared module
...
```

Then, the installation command can be as follows:

```
$ ./scripts/feeds install php5 php5-cgi php5-cli php5-fastcgi
              php5-mod-mysql php5-mod-mysqli php5-mod-pdo-mysql
```

Now, we know the trick, so for MySQL, the commands are as follows:

```
$ ./scripts/feeds search mysql
Search results in feed 'packages':
freeradius2-mod-sql-mysql  MySQL module
libdbd-mysql               MySQL database server driver for libdbi
libmysqlclient             MySQL client library
libmysqlclient-r           MySQL client library threadsafe
libzdb                     A thread-safe multi database connection poo
l library
lighttpd-mod-mysql_vhost   Mysql virtual hosting module
luasql-mysql               Lua SQL binding for MySQL
mysql-server               MySQL Server
php5-mod-mysql             MySQL shared module
php5-mod-mysqli            MySQL Improved Extension shared module
php5-mod-pdo-mysql         PDO driver for MySQL shared module
...
$ ./scripts/feeds install libmysqlclient libmysqlclient-r mysql-server
```

Now, we have to enable the compilation of these new packages, and in order to do it, we have to re-execute the `make menuconfig` command. Then, when the configuration menu appears, we have to choose the entry **Network** and then **Web Servers/Proxies** and then enable the **lighttpd** entry. Hit the *Enter* key on that entry to enter into the **lighttpd** menu where we have to select **lighttpd-mod-cgi** and **lighttpd-mod-fastcgi** as shown in the following screenshot:

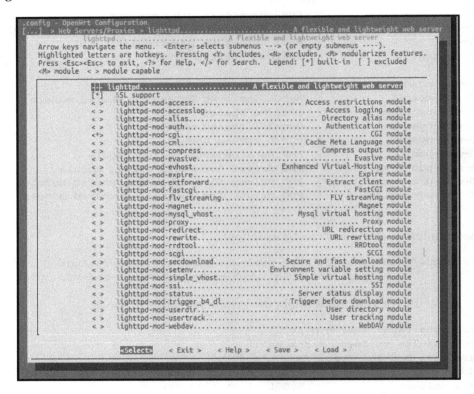

Note that instead of the Linux configuration menu you saw into `Chapter 1`, *Installing the Developing System*, Linux kernel for SAMA5D3 Xplained, this menu has a slightly different meaning for packages selection (even if they look like the same). In the Linux menu, a kernel component is selected as built-in with an * character, while we select it as module with an M. In this menu, using an M character, we select the program for compilation and packaging only. In other words, we get the program's package in the `bin/at91/packages` directory only, while using *, we select the program to be placed in the final rootfs image too.

Then, to enable the PHP support, we must go back to the main menu, then select the **Languages** entry, and then enter into the **PHP** entry. Then, we have to enable the PHP language support as built-in, and we must enable the PHP plugins for CGI and MySQL, as shown in the following screenshot:

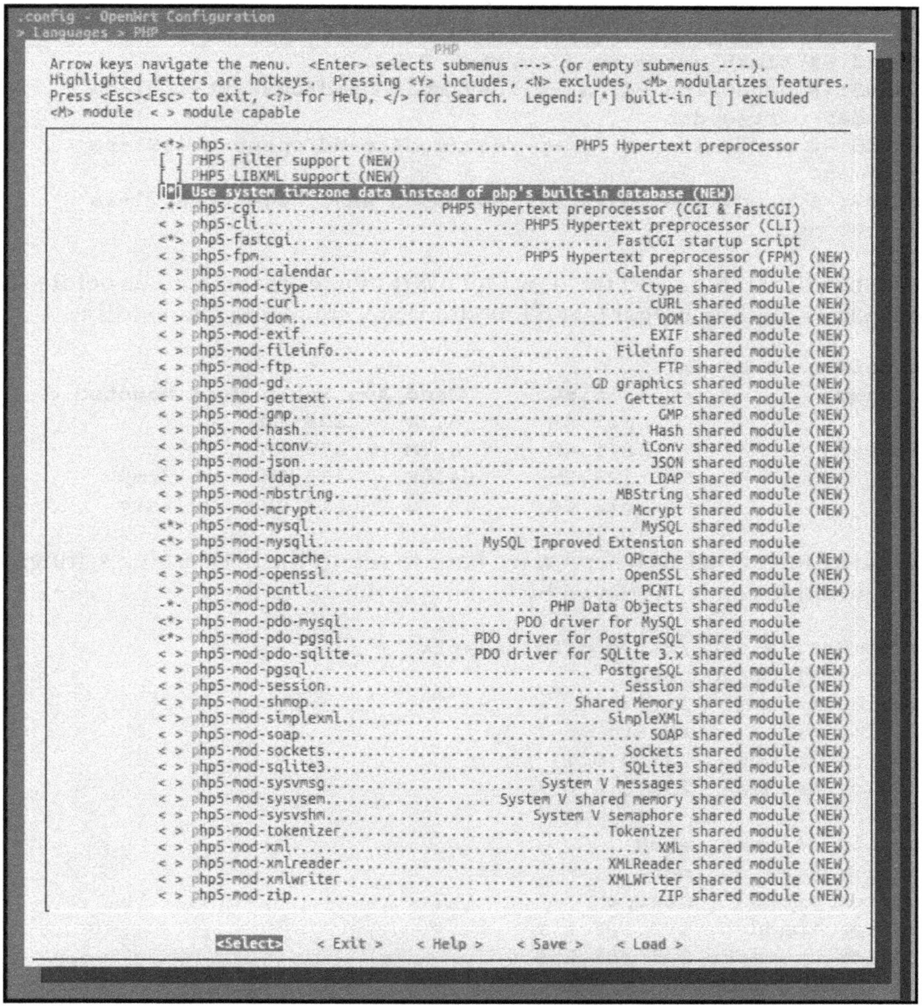

The last settings are for MySQL, so let's go back to the main menu and select the **Utilities** entry, then **database**, and just enable the **mysql-server** entry as built-in.

That's all! Now, we have to re-execute the `make` command and wait for the end of the compilation. When finished, we'll get a new kernel and a new image to be flashed as shown earlier. So, we have to restart our Debian on the SAMA5D3 Xplained, and then erase and flash the kernel and rootfs filesystem's partitions using the following commands:

```
root@a5d3:~# flash_erase -q /dev/mtd3 0 0
root@a5d3:~# flash_erase -q /dev/mtd4 0 0
root@a5d3:~# flash_erase -q /dev/mtd5 0 0
root@a5d3:~# nandwrite -q -m -p /dev/mtd3 nand/openwrt-at91-sa
ma5d3-sama5-oftree.dtb
root@a5d3:~# nandwrite -q -m -p /dev/mtd4 nand/openwrt-at91-sa
ma5d3-zImage
root@a5d3:~# nandwrite -q -m -p /dev/mtd5 nand/openwrt-at91-sa
ma5d3-root.ubi
```

Now, just restart the system, and the new OpenWrt image should start as before, This time, we can see that it's slightly bigger (even if is still really small, less than 9MB):

```
root@OpenWrt:/# df -h
Filesystem           Size      Used Available Use% Mounted on
rootfs               215.4M     8.7M    206.7M   4% /
ubi0:rootfs          215.4M     8.7M    206.7M   4% /
tmpfs                124.9M    64.0K    124.8M   0% /tmp
tmpfs                512.0K        0    512.0K   0% /dev
```

To get access to the internal web server, we have to set up the networking settings. The default configuration can be retrieved by looking at the `/etc/config/network` file:

```
root@OpenWrt:/# cat /etc/config/network
config interface loopback
    option ifname    lo
    option proto     static
    option ipaddr    127.0.0.1
    option netmask   255.0.0.0
config interface lan
    option ifname    eth0
    option type      none
    option proto     static
    option ipaddr    192.168.1.1
    option netmask   255.255.255.0
config interface debug
    option ifname    usb0
    option type      none
    option proto     static
    option ipaddr    172.18.0.18
    option netmask   255.255.255.0
```

We see that only one Ethernet device is configured and also the `usb0` device is present, but with a different configuration than our Debian. We can choose several solutions. However we decided to set up the `eth0` network device with DHCP, so the relative new settings are shown here:

```
config interface lan
    option ifname    eth0
    option type      none
    option proto     dhcp
```

When all our networking settings are in place, we have to restart the networking systems using the following command:

```
root@OpenWrt:/# /etc/init.d/network restart
[ 1225.880000] macb f0028000.ethernet eth0: link down
[ 1227.490000] IPv6: ADDRCONF(NETDEV_UP): eth0: link is not ready
[ 1227.880000] macb f0028000.ethernet eth0: link up (100/Full)
[ 1227.880000] IPv6: ADDRCONF(NETDEV_CHANGE): eth0: link becomes ready
```

Great, now, we can see our new IP address with the usual `ifconfig` command:

```
root@OpenWrt:/# ifconfig eth0
eth0      Link encap:Ethernet  HWaddr C6:4C:E4:F8:C4:11
          inet addr:192.168.32.51  Bcast:192.168.32.255 Mask:255.255.2
55.0
          inet6 addr: fe80::c44c:e4ff:fef8:c411/64 Scope:Link
          UP BROADCAST RUNNING MULTICAST  MTU:1500  Metric:1
          RX packets:4212 errors:0 dropped:0 overruns:0 frame:0
          TX packets:4137 errors:0 dropped:0 overruns:0 carrier:0
          collisions:0 txqueuelen:1000
          RX bytes:376053 (367.2 KiB)   TX bytes:424302 (414.3 KiB)
          Interrupt:49 Base address:0x8000
```

OK, now, let's check the lighttpd default configuration in the `/etc/lighttpd/lighttpd.conf` file as shown here:

```
root@OpenWrt:/# cat /etc/lighttpd/lighttpd.conf
server.modules = (
)
server.document-root       = "/www"
server.upload-dirs         = ( "/tmp" )
server.errorlog            = "/var/log/lighttpd/error.log"
server.pid-file            = "/var/run/lighttpd.pid"
server.username            = "http"
server.groupname           = "www-data"
index-file.names           = ( "index.php", "index.html",
                               "index.htm", "default.htm",
```

```
                                        "index.lighttpd.html" )
    static-file.exclude-extensions = ( ".php", ".pl", ".fcgi" )
    ...
```

Our web server seems OK. However, you should notice that the default root directory is
/www rather than /var/www as for Debian. Then, we have to verify the CGI support
configuration, which is placed in the /etc/lighttpd/conf.d/30-cgi.conf file:

```
root@OpenWrt:/# cat /etc/lighttpd/conf.d/30-cgi.conf
######################################################################
##
##  CGI modules
##  ---------------
##
## http://www.lighttpd.net/documentation/cgi.html
##
server.modules += ( "mod_cgi" )
##
## Plain old CGI handling
##
## For PHP don't forget to set cgi.fix_pathinfo = 1 in the php.ini.
##
cgi.assign                    = ( ".pl"  => "/usr/bin/perl",
                                  ".cgi" => "/usr/bin/perl",
                                  ".rb"  => "/usr/bin/ruby",
                                  ".erb" => "/usr/bin/eruby",
                                  ".py"  => "/usr/bin/python" )
    ...
```

Nope, this time, we need to apply the following patch since the .php extension is missing in
the cgi.assign array:

```
--- /etc/lighttpd/conf.d/30-cgi.conf.orig
2016-06-19 11:16:12.930534015 +0200
+++ /etc/lighttpd/conf.d/30-cgi.conf
2016-06-19 11:15:18.686718936 +0200
@@ -16,6 +16,7 @@
                                  ".cgi" => "/usr/bin/perl",
                                  ".rb"  => "/usr/bin/ruby",
                                  ".erb" => "/usr/bin/eruby",
+                                 ".php" => "/usr/bin/php-cgi",
                                  ".py"  => "/usr/bin/python" )
      ##
```

After the modifications are in place, let's restart the server:

```
root@OpenWrt:/# /etc/init.d/lighttpd restart
```

Then, we have to point our web browser at the IP address of our SAMA5D3 Xplained board, and we should see something similar to the following screenshot:

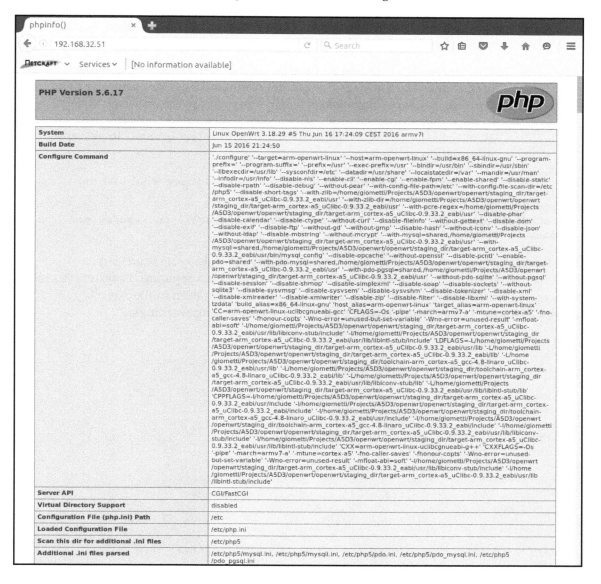

Now, it's time to verify the MySQL, and we can try the usual command line to log in as MySQL's root user:

```
root@OpenWrt:/# mysql -u root
ERROR 2002 (HY000): Can't connect to local MySQL server through socket
 '/var/run/mysqld.sock' (2)
```

The preceding command and the following ones are typical commands used to manage the MySQL from the command line. You can refer to Chapter 4, *Quick Programming with Scripts and System Daemons*, MySQL or to the online documentation of *The MySQL Command-Line Tool* at: http://dev.mysql.com/doc/refman/5.7/en/mysql.html to get more information on these commands.

The database is not running, so let's try to restart the daemon to see what's wrong:

```
root@OpenWrt:/# /etc/init.d/mysqld start
/etc/init.d/mysqld: Error: datadir '/mnt/data/mysql/' in /etc/my.cnf
doesn't exist
```

This is a typical error due the fact that, by default, MySQL takes as datadir the /mnt/data/mysql/ directory, which is usually mounted on a separate filesystem (usually, a microSD storage). No problem. We can change the configuration in the /etc/my.cnf file, so we can take a look at that file where we notice the following warnings:

```
[client]
port            = 3306
socket          = /var/run/mysqld.sock

[mysqld]
user            = root
socket          = /var/run/mysqld.sock
port            = 3306
basedir         = /usr

############ Don't put this on the NAND ############
# Figure out where I are going to put the databases
# And run mysql_install_db --force
datadir         = /mnt/data/mysql/

######### This should also not go on the NAND #######
tmpdir          = /mnt/data/tmp/
...
```

This is because the system heavily uses these directories for disk I/O activity, but since our system has nothing other than NAND, we have no choices (usually, these directories are pointing at an external filesystem on microSD or USB key. However, don't forget that also those devices are based on NAND flashes!). So, a reasonable solution for these directories' settings can be as follows:

```
datadir              = /var/data/mysql/
tmpdir               = /tmp/
```

Then, as suggested earlier, we have to execute `mysql_install_db` as shown here:

```
root@OpenWrt:/# mysql_install_db --force
Installing MySQL system tables...
OK
Filling help tables...
OK
To start mysqld at boot time you have to copy
support-files/mysql.server to the right place for your system
PLEASE REMEMBER TO SET A PASSWORD FOR THE MySQL root USER !
To do so, start the server, then issue the following commands:
/usr/bin/mysqladmin -u root password 'new-password'
/usr/bin/mysqladmin -u root -h OpenWrt password 'new-password'
Alternatively you can run:
/usr/bin/mysql_secure_installation
which will also give you the option of removing the test
databases and anonymous user created by default.  This is
strongly recommended for production servers.
See the manual for more instructions.
You can start the MySQL daemon with:
cd /usr ; /usr/bin/mysqld_safe &
You can test the MySQL daemon with mysql-test-run.pl
cd /usr/mysql-test ; perl mysql-test-run.pl
Please report any problems with the /usr/scripts/mysqlbug script!
```

Now, the starting command that failed before should now work without any errors:

```
root@OpenWrt:/# /etc/init.d/mysqld start
```

Then, we can retry the root login as we did earlier:

```
root@OpenWrt:/# mysql -u root
Welcome to the MySQL monitor.  Commands end with ; or g.
Your MySQL connection id is 1
Server version: 5.1.73 Source distribution
Copyright (c) 2000, 2013, Oracle and/or its affiliates.
All rights reserved.
Oracle is a registered trademark of Oracle Corporation and/or its
affiliates. Other names may be trademarks of their respective
```

```
owners.
Type 'help;' or 'h' for help. Type 'c' to clear the
current input statement.
mysql>
```

OK, everything is working, so let's try a little demo with our new (quasi) LAMP system. However, before starting, it is better to add a password for MySQL's root user. So, use the `quit` command to exit from the previous tools and execute the following command:

```
root@OpenWrt:/# mysqladmin -u root password 'myroot'
```

 In the preceding command, we used the `myroot` password, but of course, you can choose whatever you want in order to fit your needs.

Since now, to log in to MySQL from the command line, we must use the following command and then insert the new password when asked for:

```
root@OpenWrt:/# mysql -u root -p
```

Now, we have to copy the `chapter_05/phpdemo/demo_init.sh` and `chapter_05/phpdemo/demo_set.sh` files from the book's example code repository to the `/root` directory on our SAMA5D3 Xplained:

```
$ scp demo_init.sh demo_set.sh root@192.168.32.51:/root/
```

Then, still from the same repository, the `chapter_05/phpdemo/demo_dump.php` file in the `/www` directory:

```
$ scp demo_dump.php root@192.168.32.51:/www/
```

 It may happen that the `scp` command will not accept any root password and then refuse to copy the files. In this case, we have to reset the root's password using the `passwd` command:

```
root@OpenWrt:/# passwd
Changing password for root
Enter the new password (minimum of 5, maximum of 8
characters)
Please use a combination of upper and lower case le
tters and numbers.
New password:
Re-enter new password:
passwd: password changed.
```

Then, redo the command.

Then, we can set up the `demo` database using the `demo_init.sh` command:

```
root@OpenWrt:~# ./demo_init.sh
Warning, all data will be dropped!!! [CTRL-C to stop or ENTER to
continue]
Enter password:
```

Of course we have to enter here the MySQL root's password we set up before. Once the database has been set up we have only to add data to it and the command to do it is shown below:

```
root@OpenWrt:~# ./demo_set.sh temp 21.5
```

> These commands are quite similar to the ones used in `Chapter 4`, *Quick Programming with Scripts and System Daemons*, in *MySQL in Bash* section, so you can refer to those pages to know how the commands are functioning.

Now, to display the data, we have only to point our web browser to the `demo_dump.php` file at SAMA5D3 Xplained's IP address, and the result is reported in the next screenshot:

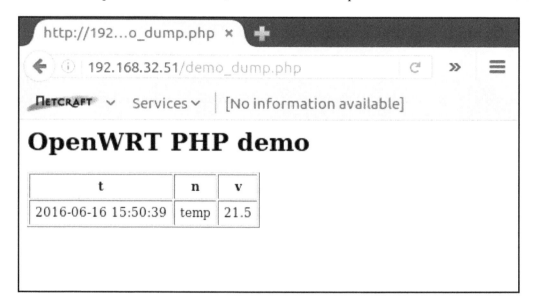

Of course, if we add new data and then reload the page, we'll get different results:

```
root@OpenWrt:~# ./demo_set.sh lamp on
```

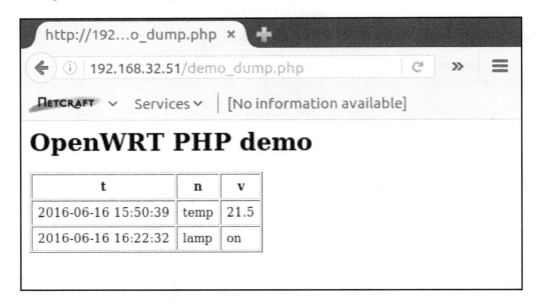

You should take a look at the `demo_dump.php` file since it's quite similar to the `my_dump.php` file presented in Chapter 4, *Quick Programming with Scripts and System Daemons*, in *MySQL in PHP* section, where we used the standard PHP's *mysql API*. However, in `demo_dump.php`, we used the newest *mysqli* API, which is going to supersede the old one in few releases.

Adding a custom package

As the last example on OpenWrt, let's see how we can add a new package to our new system. We'll use the famous *Hello World* example, and we'll see how we can add it into our current distribution and how we can install it on our running system.

The trick is to create a new feed named `applications` where we can put all our new programs. So, let's create a new directory named `helloworld` within `applications` as shown here:

```
$ cd A5D3/
$ mkdir -p applications/helloworld
$ cd applications/helloworld/
```

Then, we have to create `Makefile` where we will define our new applications to be added to OpenWrt:

```
include $(TOPDIR)/rules.mk

# Define package's name, version, release and the default package's
# build directory.
PKG_NAME:=helloworld
PKG_VERSION:=1.0.0
PKG_RELEASE:=1
PKG_BUILD_DIR:=$(BUILD_DIR)/$(PKG_NAME)-$(PKG_VERSION)

include $(INCLUDE_DIR)/package.mk

# Define package's section and category inside the OpenWRT system.
# These information are used to manage the package and to display
# it inside the comfiguration menu
define Package/$(PKG_NAME)
  SECTION:=apps
  CATEGORY:=Applications
  TITLE:=The Hello World program
  MAINTAINER:=Rodolfo Giometti <giometti@hce-engineering.com>
endef

# Define package's description (long version)
define Package/$(PKG_NAME)/description
  This package holds a program that display the "hello world" message
endef

# Set up the build directory in order to be use by the compilation
# stage.
# Our data are not downloaded from a remote site by we have them
# already into the "src" directory, so let's copy them accordingly
define Build/Prepare
  mkdir -p $(PKG_BUILD_DIR)
  $(CP) ./src/* $(PKG_BUILD_DIR)/
endef

# Define the package's installation steps after the compilation
# stage has done
define Package/$(PKG_NAME)/install
  $(INSTALL_DIR) $(1)/usr/bin
  $(CP) $(PKG_BUILD_DIR)/$(PKG_NAME) $(1)/usr/bin
endef

# The OpenWRT's main entry
$(eval $(call BuildPackage,$(PKG_NAME)))
```

The preceding code can be found in the
`chapter_05/openwrt-helloworld/Makefile` file in the book's
example code repository.

The content of the file is quite self-explicative. However, the reader should notice that everything is defined using several `make` macros. The OpenWrt system already has some default macros for the main building steps: downloading, compilation, installation, and so on. Our job is to integrate these default macros with our own ones in order to do the correct steps to build the new package inside the distribution.

 For further information on these topics, you can take a look
at: `https://wiki.openwrt.org/doc/devel/packages?s[]=define&s[]=pa`
`ckage`.

Then, we have to create a `src` directory where we can put our code:

```
$ mkdir src/
$ cd src/
$ ls
helloworld.c   Makefile
```

The two files `Makefile` and `helloworld.c` are obviously the makefile useful to compile the usual `helloworld.c` C program.

 The preceding files can be found in the `chapter_05/openwrt-`
`helloworld/src/` directory in the book's example code repository.

When finished, the tree layout of our new feed looks like this:

```
$ tree applications
applications
\-- helloworld
    +-- Makefile
    \-- src
        +-- helloworld.c
        \-- Makefile
2 directories, 3 files
```

OK, now, we can come back to the OpenWrt root directory and then modify the `feeds.conf` file as shown here:

```
--- a/feeds.conf.default
+++ b/feeds.conf.default
@@ -12,4 +12,4 @@ src-git management https://github.com/
openwrt-management/packages.git;for-15.05
#src-svn desktop svn://svn.openwrt.org/openwrt/feeds/desktop
#src-svn xfce svn://svn.openwrt.org/openwrt/feeds/xfce
#src-svn lxde svn://svn.openwrt.org/openwrt/feeds/lxde
-#src-link custom /usr/src/openwrt/custom-feed
+src-link applications /home/giometti/A5D3/applications
```

Note that `/home/giometti/A5D3/applications` is relative to my configuration, but you have to fix it up to suit your needs.

Now, we have to update our new repository by adding the new feed:

```
$ ./scripts/feeds update applications
Updating feed 'applications' from
'/home/giometti/Projects/A5D3/openwrt/applications' ...
Create index file './feeds/applications.index'
Collecting package info: done
Collecting target info: done
```

Then, we can verify that the new package is now available under the new feed:

```
$ ./scripts/feeds search hello
Search results in feed 'applications':
helloworld                    The Hello World program
```

Then, to install the new `helloworld` package, we can use the following command:

```
$ ./scripts/feeds install -f helloworld
Overriding package 'helloworld'
```

Note that the `-f` option argument can be necessary if a package with the same name is already present.

Now, if we execute the `make menuconfig` command again, a new entry labeled **Applications** should be present in the configuration menu. Just select it and then enable our new `helloworld` program as shown in the following screenshot:

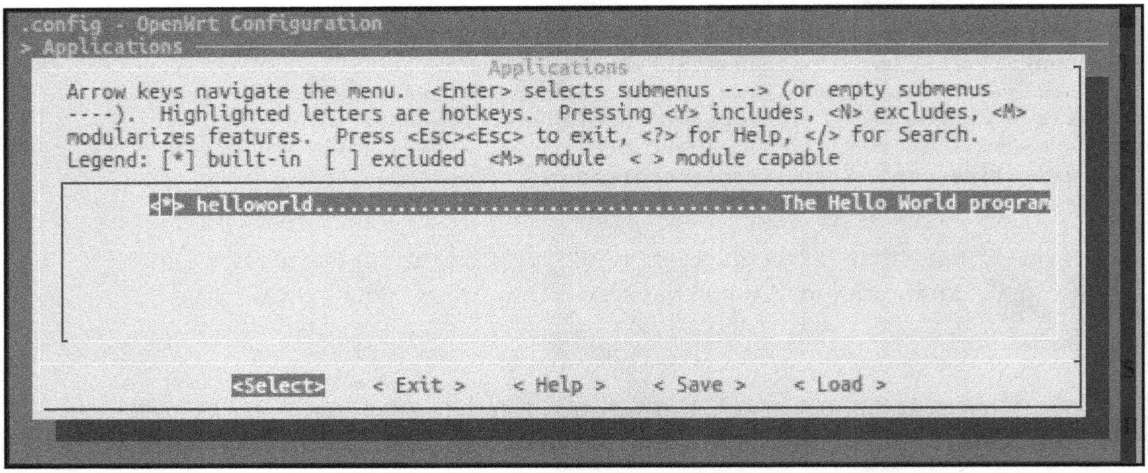

Great! Now, we can use the `make` command again to compile our new package or, just to avoid a long wait, we can use these commands to compile the program and then install it respectively:

```
$ make package/helloworld/compile
 make[1] package/helloworld/compile
 make[2] -C package/libs/toolchain compile
 make[2] -C /home/giometti/A5D3/applications/helloworld compile
$ make package/helloworld/install
 make[1] package/helloworld/install
 make[2] -C /home/giometti/A5D3/applications/helloworld install
```

We can now reflash the system, but we can just install the new package into our running system! In fact, we should find a new package file relative to our *Hello World* program in the `bin/at91/packages` directory as follows:

```
$ tree bin/at91/packages/applications
bin/at91/packages/applications
\-- helloworld_1.0.0-1_at91.ipk
0 directories, 1 file
```

So, let's move it into our SAMA5D3 Xplained with the usual `scp`:

```
$ scp bin/at91/packages/applications/helloworld_1.0.0-1_at91.ipk
      root@192.168.32.51:/root/
```

Then, we can install it with the `opkg` command (the OpenWrt equivalent packages management command of Debian ones):

```
root@OpenWrt:~# opkg install helloworld_1.0.0-1_at91.ipk
Installing helloworld (1.0.0-1) to root...
Configuring helloworld.
root@OpenWrt:~# helloworld
Hello World
```

Yocto

As stated on the Yocto home site:

> *The Yocto Project is an open source collaboration project that provides templates, tools and methods to help you create custom Linux-based systems for embedded products regardless of the hardware architecture.*

The Yocto Project is more than a distribution. It's intended to be a workgroup having the goal to produce tools and processes that will enable the creation of Linux distributions for embedded devices that are independent of the underlying architecture. The Yocto Project was announced by the Linux Foundation in 2010, and in the upcoming years, it aligned itself with OpenEmbedded, an existing framework with similar goals, with the result being The OpenEmbedded-Core Project.

Yocto's main components are the Linux kernel, the glibc C library, **BusyBox**, and **matchbox** (for the windowing system). This distribution is used as base distribution by the most important System-on-Chip manufactures. The distribution has its building system based on `bitbake` tool that automates the building process, thanks to a set of recipes and patches.

 More information on the Yocto Project can be retrieved from the project's homepage at: `https://www.yoctoproject.org`.

In the upcoming sections, we will build a minimal image from scratch, and then, we'll show you how you can add the **QT** graphic libraries and how to add a new (simple) package in order to expand the distribution.

Using the default recipe

To install the base system for our SAMA5D3 Xplained board, we can use the Yocto default recipe we're going to show here. However, as the first step, we need to download the sources. This can be done with the `git` command:

```
$ git clone git://git.yoctoproject.org/poky -b jethro
```

Then, we have to add the `meta-openembedded` git repository:

```
$ git clone git://git.openembedded.org/meta-openembedded -b jethro
```

Then, add the `meta-qt5` git repository to support the QT libraries (we're not using them in this first step, but we're going to use them soon, so let's do this step too):

```
$ git clone git://github.com/meta-qt5/meta-qt5.git -b jethro
```

And, as the last repository, we need `meta-atmel` to support our SAMA5D3 Xplained board:

```
$ git clone git://github.com/linux4sam/meta-atmel.git -b jethro
```

 For all repositories, we've selected the `jethro` branch but you can use the one which fits your needs.

OK, now, everything is in place, so let's move into the `poky` directory and initialize the Yocto build environment as shown here, where the `oe-init-build-env` file holds the environment settings needed to execute the compilation tools and `build-atmel` is the name of the directory where we wish to build our code:

```
$ cd poky
$ source oe-init-build-env build-atmel
You had no conf/local.conf file. This configuration file has therefore
been created for you with some default values. You may wish to edit it
to use a different MACHINE (target hardware) or enable parallel build
options to take advantage of multiple cores for example. See the file
for more information as common configuration options are commented.
You had no conf/bblayers.conf file. The configuration file has been
created for you with some default values. To add additional metadata
layers into your configuration please add entries to this file.

The Yocto Project has extensive documentation about OE including a
reference manual which can be found at:
    http://yoctoproject.org/documentation
```

```
For more information about OpenEmbedded see their website:
    http://www.openembedded.org/
### Shell environment set up for builds. ###
You can now run 'bitbake <target>'
Common targets are:
    core-image-minimal
    core-image-sato
    meta-toolchain
    adt-installer
    meta-ide-support
You can also run generated qemu images with a command like 'runqemu
qemux86'
```

As you can see, the system is telling us that we need two valid local configuration files, so we have to modify the existing `conf/local.conf` file as shown in the patch here:

```
--- ./conf/local.conf.orig  2016-06-15 14:27:11.081528459 +0200
+++ ./conf/local.conf  2016-06-15 14:27:56.653819242 +0200
@@ -34,7 +34,7 @@
 #MACHINE ?= "edgerouter"
 #
 # This sets the default machine to be qemux86 if no other machine is
 # selected:
-MACHINE ??= "qemux86"
+MACHINE ??= "sama5d3-xplained"
 #
 # Where to place downloads
@@ -47,7 +47,7 @@
 #
 # The default is a downloads directory under TOPDIR which is the
 # build directory.
-#DL_DIR ?= "${TOPDIR}/downloads"
+DL_DIR ?= "${TOPDIR}/downloads"

 # Where to place shared-state files
@@ -85,7 +85,7 @@
 # Ultimately when creating custom policy, people will likely end up
 # subclassing these defaults.
 #
-DISTRO ?= "poky"
+DISTRO ?= "poky-atmel"
 # As an example of a subclass there is a "bleeding" edge policy
 # configuration where many versions are set to the absolute latest
 # code from the upstream source control systems. This is just
 # mentioned here as an example, its not
@@ -104,7 +104,7 @@
 #  - 'package_rpm' for rpm style packages
 # E.g.: PACKAGE_CLASSES ?= "package_rpm package_deb package_ipk"
```

```
 # We default to rpm:
-PACKAGE_CLASSES ?= "package_rpm"
+PACKAGE_CLASSES ?= "package_ipk"
 #
 # SDK/ADT target architecture
@@ -137,7 +137,7 @@
 # There are other application targets that can be used here too, see
 # meta/classes/image.bbclass and meta/classes/core-image.bbclass for
 # more details. We default to enabling the debugging tweaks.
-EXTRA_IMAGE_FEATURES = "debug-tweaks"
+EXTRA_IMAGE_FEATURES = "debug-tweaks ssh-server-openssh package-manag
ement"
 #
 # Additional image features
```

In this manner, we set the SAMA5D3 Xplained board and other minor settings regarding:

- where to store the downloaded files with the DL_DIR define.
- which is the distribution version to use with the DISTRO define (in our example, it's set to poky-atmel, which is the official Atmel distribution based on Yocto).
- the software packages formats by setting the PACKAGE_CLASSES define to package_ipk in order to support the opkg format as OpenWrt.

Also note that we add the SSH server support and the IPK management system by adding the ssh-server-openssh and package-management settings to the EXTRA_IMAGE_FEATURES variable. Then, we have to replace (or modify) the conf/bblayers.conf file to add all the needed layers we downloaded earlier as shown here:

```
# LAYER_CONF_VERSION is increased each time build/conf/bblayers.conf
# changes incompatibly
LCONF_VERSION = "6"

BBPATH = "${TOPDIR}"
BBFILES ?= ""

BSPDIR := "${@os.path.abspath(os.path.dirname(d.getVar('FILE', True)) +
'/../../..')}"

BBLAYERS ?= "
  ${BSPDIR}/meta-atmel
  ${BSPDIR}/meta-qt5
  ${BSPDIR}/poky/meta
  ${BSPDIR}/poky/meta-yocto
  ${BSPDIR}/poky/meta-yocto-bsp
  ${BSPDIR}/meta-openembedded/meta-oe
```

```
${BSPDIR}/meta-openembedded/meta-networking
${BSPDIR}/meta-openembedded/meta-python
${BSPDIR}/meta-openembedded/meta-ruby
${BSPDIR}/meta-openembedded/meta-multimedia
"
BBLAYERS_NON_REMOVABLE ?= "
${BSPDIR}/poky/meta
${BSPDIR}/poky/meta-yocto
"
```

Apart from the first settings, the real important part here is BBLAYERS and BBLAYERS_NON_REMOVABLE that define the *layers* that the bitbake program should traverse in order to find the recipes to build the whole distribution. Each layer holds a specific part of the distribution, and it is usually based on other layers in such a way to have a well modular and stratified system.

> For further information on the layer concept and related information, you can take a look at the Yocto Project Development Manual at: http://www. yoctoproject.org/docs/2.1/dev-manual/dev-manual.html.

Now, if we re-execute the source command, we should get no errors:

```
$ source oe-init-build-env build-atmel
### Shell environment set up for builds. ###
You can now run 'bitbake <target>'
Common targets are:
    core-image-minimal
    core-image-sato
    meta-toolchain
    adt-installer
    meta-ide-support
You can also run generated qemu images with a command like 'runqemu
qemux86'
```

Great! Now, our first target is core-image-minimal, and to get it compiled, we have to execute the following command as suggested from the preceding message:

```
$ bitbake core-image-minimal
WARNING: Unable to get checksum for linux-at91 SRC_URI entry defconfig
: file could not be found
Parsing recipes:    3% |#                               | ETA:  00:04:52
```

It may happen that we get the following error:

```
$ bitbake core-image-minimal
ERROR: OE-core's config sanity checker detected a
potential misconfiguration.
 Either fix the cause of this error or at your o
wn risk disable the checker (see sanity.conf).
 Following is the list of potential problems / a
dvisories:

Please install the following missing utilities:
 makeinfo,chrpath
Summary: There was 1 ERROR message shown, returning
 a non-zero exit code.
```

In this case, as for OpenWrt, some dependency package is missing. In the preceding example, we can fix the error by installing the packages **texinfo** e **chrpath** using the usual `aptitude` or `apt-get` command.

If everything goes well, after the parsing stage, we should get something like this:

```
Parsing of 1924 .bb files complete (0 cached, 1924 parsed). 2470 targe
ts, 377 skipped, 0 masked, 0 errors.
NOTE: Resolving any missing task queue dependencies

Build Configuration:
BB_VERSION = "1.28.0"
BUILD_SYS = "x86_64-linux"
NATIVELSBSTRING = "Ubuntu-15.10"
TARGET_SYS = "arm-poky-linux-gnueabi"
MACHINE = "sama5d3-xplained"
DISTRO = "poky-atmel"
DISTRO_VERSION = "2.0.2"
TUNE_FEATURES = "arm armv7a vfp thumb callconvention-hard cortexa5
"
TARGET_FPU = "vfp"
meta-atmel = "jethro:4765d7064e4916784c15095347eda21cc10aabb4"
meta-qt5 = "jethro:ea37a0bc987aa9484937ad68f762b4657c198617"
meta
meta-yocto
meta-yocto-bsp = "jethro:ddbc13155f4db5d98976dc93b586c0be4fc740d1"
meta-oe
meta-networking
meta-python
meta-ruby
meta-multimedia = "jethro:cb7e68f2a39fa6f24add48fc7b8d38fb7291bb44"
```

Then, the compilation will start using one thread per available CPU:

```
NOTE: Preparing RunQueue
NOTE: Executing SetScene Tasks
NOTE: Executing RunQueue Tasks
Currently 2 running tasks (42 of 1634):
0: xz-native-5.2.1-r0 do_fetch (pid 19217)
1: m4-native-1.4.17-r0 do_configure (pid 19305)
...
```

 The compilation is very time consuming, so you should consider to take time to have your preferred coffee!

When the compilation is finished, we should get the compilation result in the `tmp/deploy/images/sama5d3-xplained/` directory as shown here:

```
$ ls tmp/deploy/images/sama5d3-xplained/
at91bootstrap.bin
at91bootstrap-sama5d3_xplained.bin
BOOT.BIN
core-image-minimal-sama5d3-xplained-20160618162845.rootfs.manifest
core-image-minimal-sama5d3-xplained-20160618162845.rootfs.tar.gz
core-image-minimal-sama5d3-xplained-20160618162845.rootfs.ubi
core-image-minimal-sama5d3-xplained-20160618162845.rootfs.ubifs
core-image-minimal-sama5d3-xplained.manifest
core-image-minimal-sama5d3-xplained.tar.gz
core-image-minimal-sama5d3-xplained.ubi
modules--4.1+git0+6546e3c770-r0-sama5d3-xplained-20160618162845.tgz
modules-sama5d3-xplained.tgz
README_-_DO_NOT_DELETE_FILES_IN_THIS_DIRECTORY.txt
sama5d3_xplained-nandflashboot-uboot-3.8.4.bin
ubinize.cfg
u-boot.bin
u-boot-sama5d3-xplained.bin
u-boot-sama5d3-xplained-v2015.01-at91-r0.bin
zImage
zImage--4.1+git0+6546e3c770-r0-at91-sama5d3_xplained-20160618162845.dt
b
zImage--4.1+git0+6546e3c770-r0-at91-sama5d3_xplained_pda4-201606181628
45.dtb
zImage--4.1+git0+6546e3c770-r0-at91-sama5d3_xplained_pda7-201606181628
45.dtb
zImage--4.1+git0+6546e3c770-r0-at91-sama5d3_xplained_pda7b-20160618162
845.dtb
zImage--4.1+git0+6546e3c770-r0-sama5d3-xplained-20160618162845.bin
```

```
zImage-at91-sama5d3_xplained.dtb
zImage-at91-sama5d3_xplained_pda4.dtb
zImage-at91-sama5d3_xplained_pda7b.dtb
zImage-at91-sama5d3_xplained_pda7.dtb
zImage-sama5d3-xplained.bin
```

They seem a lot of files, but in reality, most of them are just symbolic links to real image files that are only the following ones:

```
$ find . -type f
./zImage--4.1+git0+6546e3c770-r0-sama5d3-xplained-20160618162845.bin
./zImage--4.1+git0+6546e3c770-r0-at91-sama5d3_xplained-20160618162845.
dtb
./zImage--4.1+git0+6546e3c770-r0-at91-sama5d3_xplained_pda4-2016061816
2845.dtb
./ubinize.cfg
./zImage--4.1+git0+6546e3c770-r0-at91-sama5d3_xplained_pda7b-201606181
62845.dtb
./core-image-minimal-sama5d3-xplained-20160618162845.rootfs.ubifs
./modules--4.1+git0+6546e3c770-r0-sama5d3-xplained-20160618162845.tgz
./README_-_DO_NOT_DELETE_FILES_IN_THIS_DIRECTORY.txt
./zImage--4.1+git0+6546e3c770-r0-at91-sama5d3_xplained_pda7-2016061816
2845.dtb
./u-boot-sama5d3-xplained-v2015.01-at91-r0.bin
./core-image-minimal-sama5d3-xplained-20160618162845.rootfs.tar.gz
./sama5d3_xplained-nandflashboot-uboot-3.8.4.bin
./core-image-minimal-sama5d3-xplained-20160618162845.rootfs.ubi
./core-image-minimal-sama5d3-xplained-20160618162845.rootfs.manifest
```

For our purposes, the needed files are:

- `sama5d3_xplained-nandflashboot-uboot-3.8.4.bin` - that is the prebootloader, that is the `boot.bin` file we used into Chapter 1, *Installing the Developing System*, U-Boot (with `boot.bin`).
- `u-boot-sama5d3-xplained-v2015.01-at91-r0.bin` - that is the U-Boot image.
- `zImage-at91-sama5d3_xplained.dtb` - the DTB file.
- `zImage-sama5d3-xplained.bin` - the kernel image.
- `core-image-minimal-sama5d3-xplained.ubi` - that is the rootfs of our Yocto distribution (in the UBIFS format).

This time, the embedded distribution has compiled the bootloaders also.

OK, now, as done before for OpenWrt, we only have to move these files into our SAMA5D3 Xplained running the Debian OS (that is, we only have to reinsert the microSD and then restart the system) and then re-flash the NAND memory partitions again. So, let's start by copying the images on the SAMA5D3 Xplained board:

```
$ scp sama5d3_xplained-nandflashboot-uboot-3.8.4.bin
      u-boot-sama5d3-xplained-v2015.01-at91-r0.bin
      zImage-at91-sama5d3_xplained.dtb
      zImage-sama5d3-xplained.bin
      core-image-minimal-sama5d3-xplained.ubi
          root@192.168.8.2:nand/
```

Then, on the SAMA5D3 Xplained, we have to erase and then reprogram the flash as done earlier, but using the Yocto files:

```
root@a5d3:~# flash_erase -q /dev/mtd0 0 0
root@a5d3:~# flash_erase -q /dev/mtd1 0 0
root@a5d3:~# flash_erase -q /dev/mtd2 0 0
root@a5d3:~# flash_erase -q /dev/mtd3 0 0
root@a5d3:~# flash_erase -q /dev/mtd4 0 0
root@a5d3:~# flash_erase -q /dev/mtd5 0 0
root@a5d3:~# nandwrite -q -m -p /dev/mtd0 nand/sama5d3_xplained-nandfl
ashboot-uboot-3.8.4.bin
root@a5d3:~# nandwrite -q -m -p /dev/mtd1 nand/u-boot-sama5d3-xplained
-v2015.01-at91-r0.bin
root@a5d3:~# nandwrite -q -m -p /dev/mtd3 nand/zImage-at91-sama5d3_xpl
ained.dtb
root@a5d3:~# nandwrite -q -m -p /dev/mtd4 nand/zImage-sama5d3-xplained
.bin
root@a5d3:~# nandwrite -q -m -p /dev/mtd5 nand/core-image-minimal-sama
5d3-xplained.ubi
```

When finished, we have to redo the steps we did for OpwnWRT, that is, stopping the system and then resetting it and rebooting without the microSD.

> For some unknown reasons, it may happen that when we reboot the system, it will refuse to boot showing the usual RomBOOT message. In this case, the prebootloader image is corrupted, but we can recover it using the one we used for OpenWrt to successfully boot Yocto. We just need to re-erase the first partition and then put into it the OpenWrt's prebootloader image that should already be into the current nand directory:
>
> ```
> root@a5d3:~/nand# flash_erase -q /dev/mtd0 0 0
> root@a5d3:~/nand# nandwrite -q -m -p /dev/mtd0 boo
> t.bin
> ```

If everything works well after the reset, we should get the following output:

```
U-Boot SPL 2016.03-dirty (Jun 15 2016 - 16:19:44)
Trying to boot from NAND


U-Boot 2015.01-linux4sam_5.2-00004-g0bb0194 (Jun 18 2016 - 17:53:07)

CPU: SAMA5D36
Crystal frequency: 12 MHz
CPU clock : 528 MHz
Master clock : 132 MHz
I2C: ready
DRAM: 256 MiB
NAND: 256 MiB
MMC: mci: 0
*** Warning - bad CRC, using default environment

In: serial
Out: serial
Err: serial
Read from EEPROM @ 0x58 failed
Read from EEPROM @ 0x59 failed
Net: gmac0
Error: gmac0 address not set.
, macb0
Error: macb0 address not set.

Hit any key to stop autoboot: 0

NAND read: device 0 offset 0x180000, size 0x80000
 524288 bytes read: OK
```

```
NAND read: device 0 offset 0x200000, size 0x600000
  6291456 bytes read: OK
Kernel image @ 0x22000000 [ 0x000000 - 0x363c18 ]
## Flattened Device Tree blob at 21000000
  Booting using the fdt blob at 0x21000000
  Loading Device Tree to 2fb32000, end 2fb3d83f ... OK

Starting kernel ...

Booting Linux on physical CPU 0x0
Linux version 4.1.0-linux4sam_5.3-00050-g6546e3c (giometti@ubuntu1510)
  (gcc vers
ion 5.2.0 (GCC) ) #1 Sat Jun 18 18:40:31 CEST 2016
CPU: ARMv7 Processor [410fc051] revision 1 (ARMv7), cr=10c53c7d
CPU: PIPT / VIPT nonaliasing data cache, VIPT aliasing instruction cac
he
Machine model: SAMA5D3 Xplained
...
```

Great, as we can see Yocto has a kernel release 4.1 instead of the 3.18 of the OpenWrt.

Then we can verify that the flash has a compatible partitioning compared with the Debian's one:

```
...
8 cmdlinepart partitions found on MTD device atmel_nand
Creating 8 MTD partitions on "atmel_nand":
0x000000000000-0x000000040000 : "bootstrap"
0x000000040000-0x0000000c0000 : "uboot"
0x0000000c0000-0x000000100000 : "env"
0x000000100000-0x000000140000 : "env_redundent"
0x000000140000-0x000000180000 : "spare"
0x000000180000-0x000000200000 : "dtb"
0x000000200000-0x000000800000 : "kernel"
0x000000800000-0x000010000000 : "rootfs"
...
```

Yes, it's perfectly compatible since all the main partitions (kernel, DTB, and rootfs) are into their correct positions. In fact, here, we can see that the UBIFS is correctly mounted:

```
ubi0: attaching mtd7
ubi0: scanning is finished
gluebi (pid 1): gluebi_resized: got update notification for unknown UB
I device 0 volume 0
ubi0: volume 0 ("rootfs") re-sized from 38 to 1940 LEBs
ubi0: attached mtd7 (name "rootfs", size 248 MiB)
ubi0: PEB size: 131072 bytes (128 KiB), LEB size: 126976 bytes
ubi0: min./max. I/O unit sizes: 2048/2048, sub-page size 2048
```

```
ubi0: VID header offset: 2048 (aligned 2048), data offset: 4096
ubi0: good PEBs: 1978, bad PEBs: 6, corrupted PEBs: 0
ubi0: user volume: 1, internal volumes: 1, max. volumes count: 128
ubi0: max/mean erase counter: 1/0, WL threshold: 4096, image sequence
number: 607988663
ubi0: available PEBs: 0, total reserved PEBs: 1978, PEBs reserved for
bad PEB handling: 34
ubi0: background thread "ubi_bgt0d" started, PID 645
. . .
UBIFS (ubi0:0): UBIFS: mounted UBI device 0, volume 0, name "rootfs",
R/O mode
UBIFS (ubi0:0): LEB size: 126976 bytes (124 KiB), min./max. I/O unit s
izes: 2048 bytes/2048 bytes
UBIFS (ubi0:0): FS size: 244936704 bytes (233 MiB, 1929 LEBs), journal
 size 9023488 bytes (8 MiB, 72 LEBs)
UBIFS (ubi0:0): reserved for root: 0 bytes (0 KiB)
UBIFS (ubi0:0): media format: w4/r0 (latest is w4/r0), UUID 4F641563-5
796-4C7F-A57B-5D78E29FE530, small LPT model
VFS: Mounted root (ubifs filesystem) readonly on device 0:13.
devtmpfs: mounted
Freeing unused kernel memory: 188K (c068b000 - c06ba000)
random: nonblocking pool is initialized
INIT: version 2.88 booting
Starting udev
udevd[677]: starting version 182
. . .
```

Then, at the end of the boot stage, we finally get the login prompt:

```
. . .
INIT: Entering runlevel: 5
Configuring network interfaces... udhcpc (v1.23.2) started
Sending discover...
macb f0028000.ethernet eth0: link up (100/Full)
Sending discover...
Sending select for 192.168.32.57...
Lease of 192.168.32.57 obtained, lease time 268435455
/etc/udhcpc.d/50default: Adding DNS 192.168.32.8
done.
Starting OpenBSD Secure Shell server: sshd
  generating ssh RSA key...
  generating ssh ECDSA key...
  generating ssh DSA key...
  generating ssh ED25519 key...
done.
Starting syslogd/klogd: done
Poky (Yocto Project Reference Distro) 2.0.2 sama5d3-xplained /dev/ttyS0
sama5d3-xplained login:
```

Here, we just need to enter the `root` user, and we'll get the prompt without entering any password:

```
sama5d3-xplained login: root
root@sama5d3-xplained:~#
```

Now, we can take a look at the flash storage occupation as we did for OpenWrt:

```
root@sama5d3-xplained:~# df -h
Filesystem              Size    Used Available Use% Mounted on
ubi0:rootfs            215.4M   2.9M   212.5M   1% /
devtmpfs                91.2M     0     91.2M   0% /dev
tmpfs                  123.3M  96.0K   123.2M   0% /run
tmpfs                  123.3M  92.0K   123.2M   0% /var/volatile
```

Again, the footprint is very minimal, less than 3MB!

Now, before continuing, let's verify the networking support, so just plug an Ethernet cable and then execute the `ifconfig` command:

```
root@sama5d3-xplained:~# ifconfig
eth0      Link encap:Ethernet  HWaddr BA:A0:13:9E:7A:99
          inet addr:192.168.32.57  Bcast:192.168.32.255  Mask:255.255.
255.0
          UP BROADCAST RUNNING MULTICAST  MTU:1500  Metric:1
          RX packets:190 errors:0 dropped:0 overruns:0 frame:0
          TX packets:2 errors:0 dropped:0 overruns:0 carrier:0
          collisions:0 txqueuelen:1000
          RX bytes:46940 (45.8 KiB)  TX bytes:684 (684.0 B)
          Interrupt:51 Base address:0x8000
```

OK! The networking settings are set to DHCP. At this point, we can keep the current settings or we can modify them by modifying the /etc/network/interfaces file and the restarting the networking system with this command:

```
root@sama5d3-xplained:~# /etc/init.d/networking restart
```

Here is reported a snapped of the default version of the /etc/network/interfaces file where you can see the DHCP settings and the static IP ones:

```
# Wired or wireless interfaces
auto eth0
iface eth0 inet dhcp
iface eth1 inet dhcp

# Ethernet/RNDIS gadget (g_ether)
# ... or on host side, usbnet and random hwaddr
iface usb0 inet static
```

```
address 192.168.7.2
netmask 255.255.255.0
network 192.168.7.0
gateway 192.168.7.1
```

Adding the graphic support

One of the main advantages in using the Yocto distribution is that it natively supports the QT graphic library, and we can add a very impressive *Graphic User Interface* (GUI) in a quick and easy manner.

> For more information on the **QT** graphic library, you can go to the project homesite at: `https://www.qt.io`.

In this section, we will see how we can add this graphic support to our SAMA5D3 Xplained using the same Yocto code we just downloaded earlier. The only thing we have to do more is just add the following settings to the `conf/local.conf` file in order to avoid the compilation of non Software Libre into our image. It's quite obvious that we need an LCD to be connected to our board to run this demo, but you can buy it where they brought the SAMA5D3 Xplained.

OK, the modification for the `conf/local.conf` file is as follows:

```
--- conf/local.conf.orig  2016-06-05 19:04:17.788202448 +0200
+++ conf/local.conf  2016-06-19 10:36:50.574587468 +0200
@@ -237,3 +237,6 @@
 # track the version of this file when it was generated.
 # This can safely be ignored if this doesn't mean anything to you.
 CONF_VERSION = "1"
+
+LICENSE_FLAGS_WHITELIST += "commercial"
+SYSVINIT_ENABLED_GETTYS = ""
```

> Refer to Atmel in order to have more information on the licenses involved in this demo. I am programmer, not a lawyer!

Once the modification is in place, we just need to re-execute `bitbake` with the `atmel-qt5-demo-image` target in order to start the QT compilation:

```
$ bitbake atmel-qt5-demo-image
```

If the previous Yocto image compilation was time consuming, this one is even more time consuming! So, consider to have more coffees.

When finished, the results are still in the `tmp/deploy/images/sama5d3-xplained/` directory, but this time, the rootfs image files have been named with the `atmel-qt5-demo-image-sama5d3-xplained` prefix as shown here:

```
$ cd tmp/deploy/images/sama5d3-xplained/
$ ls atmel-qt5-demo-image-sama5d3-xplained*
atmel-qt5-demo-image-sama5d3-xplained-20160619195155.rootfs.manifest
atmel-qt5-demo-image-sama5d3-xplained-20160619195155.rootfs.tar.gz
atmel-qt5-demo-image-sama5d3-xplained-20160619195155.rootfs.ubi
atmel-qt5-demo-image-sama5d3-xplained-20160619195155.rootfs.ubifs
atmel-qt5-demo-image-sama5d3-xplained.manifest
atmel-qt5-demo-image-sama5d3-xplained.tar.gz
atmel-qt5-demo-image-sama5d3-xplained.ubi
```

Now, we have to flash a new DTB file, kernel image, and rootfs, so the `scp` command to transfer the new images on the SAMA5D3 Xplained is here:

```
$ scp zImage-at91-sama5d3_xplained_pda7.dtb
      zImage-sama5d3-xplained.bin
      atmel-qt5-demo-image-sama5d3-xplained.ubi
         root@192.168.8.2:nand/
```

We have several DTB files. You must select the right one in order to fit your LCD hardware.

Then, on the SAMA5D3 Xplained, we have to execute these commands:

```
root@a5d3:~# flash_erase -q /dev/mtd3 0 0
root@a5d3:~# flash_erase -q /dev/mtd4 0 0
root@a5d3:~# flash_erase -q /dev/mtd5 0 0
root@a5d3:~# nandwrite -q -m -p /dev/mtd3 nand/zImage-at91-sama5d3_xpl
ained_pda7.dtb
root@a5d3:~# nandwrite -q -m -p /dev/mtd4 nand/zImage-sama5d3-xplained
.bin
root@a5d3:~# nandwrite -q -m -p /dev/mtd5 nand/atmel-qt5-demo-image-sa
ma5d3-xplained.ubi
```

The last command is quite slow due to the fact that the new image is bigger than before. The graphic libraries take a lot of space.

If everything goes well, at the new reboot on the LCD, we should see something similar to the following image:

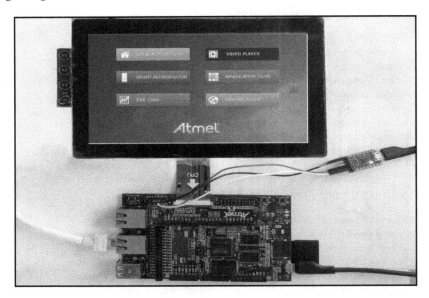

Just to show the differences between having or not having a graphical support below if the NAND usage on my system:

```
root@sama5d3-xplained:~# df -h
Filesystem      Size  Used Avail Use% Mounted on
ubi0:rootfs     216M  176M   40M  82% /
devtmpfs         92M     0   92M   0% /dev
tmpfs           124M  124K  124M   1% /run
tmpfs           124M  160K  124M   1% /var/volatile
```

As we can see, if we can largely stay below 16MB before, now, the NAND usage is more that 170MB!

 We can avoid compiling this demo and then get it already done to be flashed on the *Atmel Linux4SAM demo archives* page at `http://www.at91.com/linux4sam/bin/view/Linux4SAM/Sama5d3Xplained MainPage#Demo_archives`.Note also that at that link, we can find information regarding the LCDs available on the boards and the relative DTB files names.

Adding a custom recipe

Now, as the last step we'd like to add a custom program to our new Yocto distribution, so we can do the same as for OpenWrt by adding the classic *Hello World* example. However, this time, doing it is really easy since Yocto gives us a powerful tool to add a new layer that already holds the *Hello World* program!

As already stated earlier, Yocto has been composed of several layers, and in order to add our custom applications, it's preferred that we do it by creating a new layer. To do so, we can use the `yocto-layer` script that drastically simplifies the developer's job, so here is a snippet of the help message of its `create` command (the help message has been generated using the command line `./scripts/yocto-layer help create`).

OK, so let's go to the `poky` directory where we downloaded all Yocto's repositories and then execute the script as shown here:

```
$ cd ..
$ ./poky/scripts/yocto-layer create applications
Please enter the layer priority you'd like to use for the layer: [defa
ult: 6]
Would you like to have an example recipe created? (y/n) [default: n] y
Please enter the name you'd like to use for your example recipe: [defa
ult: example] helloworld
Would you like to have an example bbappend file created? (y/n) [defaul
t: n] y
Please enter the name you'd like to use for your bbappend file: [defau
lt: example] helloworld
Please enter the version number you'd like to use for your bbappend fi
le (this should match the recipe you're appending to): [default: 0.1]

New layer created in meta-applications.

Don't forget to add it to your BBLAYERS (for details see meta-applicat
ions\README).
```

In the preceding output, the highlighted text are the answers we gave to the command. Notice that we forced both the names of the example recipe and the bbappend file to helloworld.

Well, now, we have a new meta-applications directory where a new recipe tree has been created, as shown here:

```
$ ls
meta-applications/ meta-atmel/ meta-openembedded/ meta-qt5/ poky/
$ tree meta-applications/
meta-applications/
+-- conf
|   \-- layer.conf
+-- COPYING.MIT
+-- README
+-- recipes-example
|   +-- example
|       +-- helloworld-0.1
|       |   +-- example.patch
|       |   \-- helloworld.c
|       \-- helloworld_0.1.bb
\-- recipes-example-bbappend
    \-- example-bbappend
        +-- helloworld-0.1
        |   \-- example.patch
        \-- helloworld_0.1.bbappend
7 directories, 8 files
```

Now, we can take a look at the new files and, in particular, the helloworld_0.1.bb file, which holds the recipe that defines the new package's compilation steps, which are reported here:

```
#
# This file was derived from the 'Hello World!' example recipe in the
# Yocto Project Development Manual.
#

SUMMARY = "Simple helloworld application"
SECTION = "examples"
LICENSE = "MIT"
LIC_FILES_CHKSUM = "file://${COMMON_LICENSE_DIR}/MIT;md5=0835ade698e0b
cf8506ecda2f7b4f302"

SRC_URI = "file://helloworld.c"

S = "${WORKDIR}"
```

```
do_compile() {
    ${CC} helloworld.c -o helloworld
}

do_install() {
    install -d ${D}${bindir}
    install -m 0755 helloworld ${D}${bindir}
}
```

You should notice that even in this case, the recipe files have a similar structure like the OpenWrt's makefiles. We have several default actions (download, compile, install, and so on) that can be redefined according to our needs.

 For more information on how to write a new recipe (or whatever we wish to add), we can take a look
at: `http://www.yoctoproject.org/docs/2.1/dev-manual/dev-manual.ht ml#new-recipe-writing-a-new-recipe`.

Now, we only have to add our new meta directory to the `conf/bblayers.conf` file as shown here:

```
--- conf/bblayers.conf.orig  2016-06-19 19:13:52.380757585 +0200
+++ conf/bblayers.conf  2016-06-19 19:14:07.476705872 +0200
@@ -18,6 +18,7 @@
   ${BSPDIR}/meta-openembedded/meta-python
   ${BSPDIR}/meta-openembedded/meta-ruby
   ${BSPDIR}/meta-openembedded/meta-multimedia
+   ${BSPDIR}/meta-applications
   "
 BBLAYERS_NON_REMOVABLE ?= "
```

OK, everything is in place, and we can compile our new package by executing the `bitbake` command as follows:

```
$ bitbake helloworld
Loading cache: 100% |#########################################| ETA:
 00:00:00
Loaded 2464 entries from dependency cache.
Parsing recipes: 100% |######################################| Time
: 00:00:02
Parsing of 1925 .bb files complete (1917 cached, 8 parsed). 2471 targe
ts, 353 skipped, 0 masked, 0 errors.
NOTE: Resolving any missing task queue dependencies

Build Configuration:
BB_VERSION = "1.28.0"
BUILD_SYS = "x86_64-linux"
```

```
NATIVELSBSTRING = "Ubuntu-15.10"
TARGET_SYS = "arm-poky-linux-gnueabi"
MACHINE = "sama5d3-xplained"
DISTRO = "poky-atmel"
DISTRO_VERSION = "2.0.2"
TUNE_FEATURES = "arm armv7a vfp thumb callconvention-hard cortexa5
"
TARGET_FPU = "vfp"
meta-atmel = "jethro:4765d7064e4916784c15095347eda21cc10aabb4"
meta-qt5 = "jethro:ea37a0bc987aa9484937ad68f762b4657c198617"
meta
meta-yocto
meta-yocto-bsp = "<unknown>:<unknown>"
meta-oe
meta-networking
meta-python
meta-ruby
meta-multimedia = "jethro:cb7e68f2a39fa6f24add48fc7b8d38fb7291bb44"
meta-applications = "<unknown>:<unknown>"

NOTE: Preparing RunQueue
NOTE: Executing SetScene Tasks
NOTE: Executing RunQueue Tasks
NOTE: Tasks Summary: Attempted 378 tasks of which 365 didn't need to b
e rerun and all succeeded.
```

 Note that `bitbake` now sees our new layers!

When the compilation has been finished, the new package is ready to be installed in the `tmp/deploy/ipk/` directory:

```
$ ls tmp/deploy/ipk/cortexa5hf-vfp/helloworld*.ipk
tmp/deploy/ipk/cortexa5hf-vfp/helloworld_0.1-r0_cortexa5hf-vfp.ipk
tmp/deploy/ipk/cortexa5hf-vfp/helloworld-dbg_0.1-r0_cortexa5hf-vfp.ipk
tmp/deploy/ipk/cortexa5hf-vfp/helloworld-dev_0.1-r0_cortexa5hf-vfp.ipk
```

So, let's copy it into Yocto using the `scp` command:

```
$ scp tmp/deploy/ipk/cortexa5hf-vfp/helloworld_0.1-r0_cortexa5hf-vfp.i
pk root@192.168.32.57:/tmp/
```

Then, on the SAMA5D3 Xplained, we have to install the package with the usual `opkg` command, and then, we can execute it as shown here:

```
root@sama5d3-xplained:~# opkg install /tmp/helloworld_0.1-r0_cortexa5h
f-vfp.ipk
Installing helloworld (0.1-r0) on root.
Configuring helloworld.
root@sama5d3-xplained:~# helloworld
Hello World!
```

Summary

In this chapter, you saw how to manage flash devices using Linux's MTD devices, and the we discovered how to put JFFS2 and UBIFS filesystems over them. The filesystems were both created onboard and by using the host PC in such a way that we have different ways to do it.

Then, you learned how to download, compile, and then install an embedded distribution from scratch. In particular we saw OpenWrt and Yocto, that is, the currently most widely used embedded distributions on the Internet.

In the upcoming chapters, we'll start putting our hands on several kinds of computer peripherals, and we're going to see how we can get access to them using our embedded boards.

6
General Purposes Input Output signals – GPIO

From this chapter, we're going to look more deeply at all the computer peripherals that we can use on our embedded machines, and since the most important and used peripherals are GPIO lines, let's start from them.

The GPIO signals are used for tons of different usages; in fact, even in previous chapters, in order to introduce the basic concepts of embedded computer programming, we could not avoid using them! However, earlier we just used them superficially; now we're going to show their usage in more detail.

First of all, we'll introduce the GPIO lines with a short description, and then we'll see where they are physically located in our embedded machines. Then, we're going to see in detail how we can get access to these lines in a very simple (but efficient) manner and then in a smarter (but a bit more complex) way.

The last step will cover a rapid introduction of the GPIOs management inside the kernel, so we'll look at how we can request and manage these peripherals as simple GPIOs or as a more specific manner as LED devices. In the first part, we'll take a look at GPIOs-related IRQs management, while regarding the LED devices, we'll take a look at the concept of *trigger* in more detail.

What is a GPIO line?

A *General Purposes Input Output* (**GPIO**) line is a pin of a microcontroller or CPU or other integrated circuit whose behavior is controllable by the user at runtime. So, a GPIO pin has no predefined usage, but the developer has the ability to set it for input or output usage (for simpler implementations) or as an IRQ source or other functionalities.

In general, a GPIO line can:

- Be enabled/disabled.
- Be configured as input or output.
- Have readable/writable output values (typically, high is 1 and low is 0).
- Have readable input values (typically, high is 1 and low is 0).
- Have default pulled-up or pulled-down input values.
- Have input values to be used as IRQ source.

The GPIO lines are so generic that if adequately used in a dedicated program, they can be used to emulate another digital interface controller; in fact, inside the Linux kernel, we can find several kinds of peripheral controllers emulated via GPIO (the most famous and used are the keyboard, I²C and W1 controllers; in particular, the latter will be shown in this book in `Chapter 11`, *1-Wire – W1*, in *Using the GPIO interface* section).

 This technique is called *bit banging* and it's used to implement several Linux device drivers. The advantage in using it is the fact we can emulate pieces of hardware, but as is obvious, the downside is the amount of CPU cycles consumed, which in turn limits the maximum throughput of the interface.

Apart from this fact, the main usage for these lines is controlling signals (reset, power enable, suspend, card detect, and so on) and managing relays, LEDs, switches, buttons, and so on; that is, everywhere, we have to read or write two statuses: *high* or *low*, *open* or *close*, *0* or *1*.

GPIOs are also related with the **pinmux** functionality, which controls the CPU's physical I/O pins and allows the developer to alter the direction and input/drive characteristics as well as configure the pin peripheral multiplexer selection. In fact, our embedded kits are equipped with SoCs that have on-chip tons of peripherals and a limited (even if very high) number of available pins, so it's quite normal that most peripherals share some pins with the result that the developer cannot use these peripherals at the same time. In this scenario, the GPIOs subsystem is considered a normal peripheral that can share their pins with the other; that's why we have to deal with the pinmux functionality and its son: **pinctrl**.

We can get access to pinctrl under the `/sys/kernel/debug/pinctrl` directory, and as an example, on SAMA5D3 Xplained, we have the following:

```
root@a5d3:~# ls /sys/kernel/debug/pinctrl/
ahb:apb:pinctrl@fffff200   pinctrl-devices   pinctrl-handles
pinctrl-maps
```

Here, the relevant file is the `ahb:apb:pinctrl@fffff200` directory, which holds the status of the SAMA5D3 Xplained's pinmux system. Looking into it, we see the following files:

```
root@a5d3:~# cat /sys/kernel/debug/pinctrl/ahb\:apb\:pinctrl\@fffff200
/
gpio-ranges       pinconf-groups   pingroups        pinmux-pins
pinconf-config    pinconf-pins     pinmux-functions pins
```

In the `gpio-ranges` file, we can find all GPIOs defined in the system divided per **gpiochip**; in fact, SAMA5D3 Xplained has five gpiochips:

```
root@a5d3:~# cat /sys/kernel/debug/pinctrl/ahb\:apb\:pinctrl\@fffff200
/gpio-ranges
GPIO ranges handled:
0: fffff200.gpio GPIOS [0 - 31] PINS [0 - 31]
1: fffff400.gpio GPIOS [32 - 63] PINS [32 - 63]
2: fffff600.gpio GPIOS [64 - 95] PINS [64 - 95]
3: fffff800.gpio GPIOS [96 - 127] PINS [96 - 127]
4: fffffa00.gpio GPIOS [128 - 159] PINS [128 - 159]
```

In file pins, we have the complete list of all the defined pins with their identification number and name string:

```
root@a5d3:~# cat /sys/kernel/debug/pinctrl/ahb:apb:pinctrl@fffff200/pi
ns
registered pins: 160
pin 0 (pioA0)  ahb:apb:pinctrl@fffff200
pin 1 (pioA1)  ahb:apb:pinctrl@fffff200
pin 2 (pioA2)  ahb:apb:pinctrl@fffff200
pin 3 (pioA3)  ahb:apb:pinctrl@fffff200
...
```

Note that SAMA5D3 Xplained doesn't use the usual naming as `gpio0`, `gpio1`, `gpio2`, among others but `pioA0`, `pioA1`, and so on instead, where the `pioA` prefix is referred to the port name where the pin is attached to. SAMA5D3 Xplained has five ports named from A to E, so we also have `pioB0`, `pioB1`, ..., `pioC0`, `pioC1`, ..., `pioD0`, `pioD1`, ..., `PE0`, `pioE1`, ..., `pioE31`.

Each pin can be associated with a specific function, which can be listed by looking into the pingroups file. The following is reported part of the output we can get on SAMA5D3 Xplained, where we can see that pioB0 can be associated with two functions:

```
root@a5d3:~# cat /sys/kernel/debug/pinctrl/ahb\:apb\:pinctrl\@ffffff200
/pingroups
...
group: pwm0_pwmh0-1
pin 32 (pioB0)
...
group: macb0_data_rgmii
pin 32 (pioB0)
pin 33 (pioB1)
pin 34 (pioB2)
pin 35 (pioB3)
pin 36 (pioB4)
pin 37 (pioB5)
pin 38 (pioB6)
pin 39 (pioB7)
...
```

To learn how the current pinmux is set, we can take a look at the pinmux-pins file. On SAMA5D3 Xplained, we see the following (again, the output has been reduced for space reasons):

```
root@a5d3:~# cat /sys/kernel/debug/pinctrl/ahb\:apb\:pinctrl\@ffffff200
/pinmux-pins
Pinmux settings per pin
Format: pin (name): mux_owner gpio_owner hog?
pin 0 (pioA0): (MUX UNCLAIMED) (GPIO UNCLAIMED)
pin 1 (pioA1): (MUX UNCLAIMED) (GPIO UNCLAIMED)
...
pin 17 (pioA17): (MUX UNCLAIMED) (GPIO UNCLAIMED)
pin 18 (pioA18): f801c000.i2c (GPIO UNCLAIMED) function board group i2
c2_pu
pin 19 (pioA19): f801c000.i2c (GPIO UNCLAIMED) function board group i2
c2_pu
pin 20 (pioA20): f002c000.pwm (GPIO UNCLAIMED) function pwm0 group pwm
0_pwmh0-0
pin 21 (pioA21): (MUX UNCLAIMED) (GPIO UNCLAIMED)
pin 22 (pioA22): f002c000.pwm (GPIO UNCLAIMED) function pwm0 group pwm
0_pwmh1-0
...
```

Here, we can see which are unclaimed pins, which are claimed as GPIOs, and which ones are claimed for such peripherals.

> You can get further and more detailed information regarding pixmux and pinctrl at: `https://www.kernel.org/doc/Documentation/pinctrl.txt`.

GPIOs lines on the BeagleBone Black

As already mentioned in `Chapter 1`, *Installing the Developing System*, in *The BeagleBone Black* section, the BeagleBone Black has two expansion connectors where several signals are exposed and where we can find several GPIO pins, as reported in the following table:

GPIO pins on connector P8				GPIO pins on connector P9			
Pin	GPIO #	Pin	GPIO #	Pin	GPIO #	Pin	GPIO #
7	66	14	26	12	60	41	20
8	67	15	47	15	48		
9	69	16	46	23	49		
10	68	17	27	25	117		
11	45	18	65	27	115		
12	44	26	61	30	112		

In reality, almost all exported pins can be programmed for GPIO functionalities thanks to a **pinmux** (pin multiplexer) that can physically connect a CPU's pin to different internal peripherals. However, these settings are usually not needed and they are machine-dependent, so in this case, the developer has to know in detail how the CPU is composed and how it can be programmed in order to correctly set up pinmux.

> A complete BeagleBone Black's connector description and a quick introduction on the pins configuration for different usage is available at: `http://elinux.org/Beagleboard:Cape_Expansion_Headers`.

GPIOs on the SAMA5D3 Xplained

On SAMA5D3 Xplained, the GPIOs are exposed on the expansion connector, as already mentioned in chapter 1, in *Installing the Developing System*, in *The SAMA5D3 Xplained* section, and in this case, each pin is named *PA1, PA2, ..., PB1, ... PC1* and so on and can be used as a GPIO line.

 Even for SAMA5D3 Xplained, almost every pin can be reprogrammed for different usages by correctly setting up its pinmux.

The pin name and GPIO name association is reported in the following table:

Pin	GPIO #	Pin	GPIO #	Pin	GPIO #	Pin	GPIO #
PA16	16	PB15	47	PE9	137	PE17	145
PA17	17	PB25	57	PE10	138	PE20	148
PA18	18	PB26	58	PE11	139	PE24	152
PA19	19	PB27	59	PE12	140	PE25	153
PA20	20	PC16	80	PE13	141	PE26	154
PA21	21	PC17	81	PE14	142	PE29	157
PA22	22	PC26	90	PE15	143	PE31	159
PA23	23	PD30	126	PE16	144		

To quickly translate a pin name to GPIO number, let's consider the *L2V()* function as the one that associates the letter *A* as *0*, *B* as *1*, and so on. Then, the formula to convert the pin name into the corresponding GPIO number is as follows:

$$GPIO_{num} = L2V(PIN_{letter}) * 32 + PIN_{num}$$

For example, the *PE17* pin has $PIN_{letter}=E$ and $PIN_{num}=17$, so $L2V(E)=4$ and then this:

$$GPIO_{num} = 4 * 32 + 17 = 145$$

So, the pin named *PE17* corresponds to GPIO number 145.

Refer to the SAMA5D3 Xplained user manual
at: `http://www.atmel.com/Images/Atmel-11269-32-bit-Cortex-A5-Micr`
`ocontroller-SAMA5D3-Xplained_User-Guide.pdf` for further information.

GPIOs on the Wandboard

The Wandboard has ten GPIOs and only eight of them are routed on the expansion
connector *JP4*, and the pin name to GPIO number association is reported in the following
table:

Pin	GPIO #	Pin	GPIO #
4	75	12	200
6	91	14	90
8	191	16	72
10	24	18	100

A more detailed list of the Wandboard's GPIOs is reported on its Wiki
page at: `http://wiki.wandboard.org/index.php/External_gpios` and on
the Wandboard user guide at
`http://wandboard.org/images/downloads/wandboard-user-guide-20130`
`208.pdf`. Even for the Wandboard, almost every pin can be reprogrammed
for different usages by correctly setting up its pinmux.

GPIOs in Linux

In a Linux system, GPIO lines can be managed through the **sysfs** using simple Bash
commands; this is the easiest technique we can use to get access to these peripherals. In the
following examples, we are going to use the Wandboard but we can redo them on the other
systems too but using different GPIO lines, of course.

The sysfs interface to manage the GPIOs are under the `/sys/class/gpio/` directory, and
if we take a look at its content, we can see the following files:

```
root@wb:~# ls /sys/class/gpio/
export      gpiochip128  gpiochip192  gpiochip64  unexport
gpiochip0   gpiochip160  gpiochip32   gpiochip96
```

Files named `gpiochip0`, `gpiochip32`, and so on are related to the GPIO controller chips that are the entities that actually manage a GPIOs group. In our case, the Wandboard groups GPIOs by 32 and then each **gpiochip** takes its name according to the first managed GPIO number. So, `gpiochip0` manages GPIOs from 0 to 31, `gpiochip32` manages GPIOs from 32 to 63, and so on.

If we take a look at the `gpiochip64` directory, we get the following file list:

```
root@wb:~# ls /sys/class/gpio/gpiochip64/
base   device   label   ngpio   power   subsystem   uevent
```

The `ngpio` file holds the number of GPIOs managed, which is 32:

```
root@wb:~# cat /sys/class/gpio/gpiochip64/ngpio
32
```

In the base, we have the number of the first GPIO managed, which for `gpiochip64` is obviously `64`:

```
root@wb:~# cat /sys/class/gpio/gpiochip64/base
64
```

> A GPIO controller chip is the circuitry that controls the statuses of the GPIO lines physically connected to it. It's something similar to the relation between the I²C or SPI controllers and the devices connected to them.

However, for our purposes, the most important files here are `export` and `unexport`, which are used to ask the kernel to *export* or *unexport* control of a GPIO to user space by writing its number to this file.

For example, if we wish to control the `gpio91` of our Wandboard, we must use the following command:

```
root@wb:~# echo 91 > /sys/class/gpio/export
root@wb:~# ls /sys/class/gpio/
export    gpiochip0     gpiochip160   gpiochip32   gpiochip96
gpio91    gpiochip128   gpiochip192   gpiochip64   unexport
```

As we can see, the `gpio91` entry is now available in `/sys/class/gpio/`. On the other hand, if we don't need `gpio91` anymore, we can remove its entry using the inverse command:

```
root@wb:~# echo 91 > /sys/class/gpio/unexport
root@wb:~# ls /sys/class/gpio/
export      gpiochip128  gpiochip192  gpiochip64  unexport
gpiochip0   gpiochip160  gpiochip32   gpiochip96
```

You should note that in case a GPIO is reserved for other purposes and we try to export it, we'll get an error:

```
root@wb:~# echo 70 > /sys/class/gpio/export
-bash: echo: write error: Invalid argument
```

These errors can be related to the fact that a GPIO is already exported or because it's already requested by the kernel or because the GPIO is not available due a special pinmux configuration. You can look at the `/sys/kernel/debug/gpio` file, which shows which GPIOs are already used and which are not. On the Wandboard, we have the following:

```
root@wb:~# cat /sys/kernel/debug/gpio
GPIOs 0-31, platform/209c000.gpio, 209c000.gpio:
 gpio-2   (                    |cd              ) in  hi
 gpio-26  (                    |wl_reg_on       ) out hi
 gpio-29  (                    |wl_host_wake    ) in  hi
 gpio-30  (                    |wl_wake         ) out hi
GPIOs 32-63, platform/20a0000.gpio, 20a0000.gpio:
 gpio-62  (                    |spi_imx         ) out hi
GPIOs 64-95, platform/20a4000.gpio, 20a4000.gpio:
 gpio-73  (                    |cd              ) in  lo
 gpio-93  (                    |phy-reset       ) out hi
GPIOs 96-127, platform/20a8000.gpio, 20a8000.gpio:
GPIOs 128-159, platform/20ac000.gpio, 20ac000.gpio:
 gpio-148 (                    |bt_host_wake    ) in  hi
 gpio-149 (                    |bt_on           ) out hi
 gpio-158 (                    |bt_wake         ) out hi
 gpio-159 (                    |wl_ref_on       ) out hi
GPIOs 160-191, platform/20b0000.gpio, 20b0000.gpio:
 gpio-160 (                    |wl_rst_n        ) out hi
GPIOs 192-223, platform/20b4000.gpio, 20b4000.gpio:
```

OK, now let's export `gpio91` and then examine its control files; in fact, the newly created `gpio91` entry is a directory that holds several files:

```
root@wb:~# echo 91 > /sys/class/gpio/export
root@wb:~# ls /sys/class/gpio/gpio91/
active_low  device  direction  edge  power  subsystem  uevent  value
```

Here, the important files are `direction`, `value`, `edge`, and `active_low`, which in turn mean this:

- `direction`: This selects between the GPIO line directions `in` or `out`. If read, it returns either the strings `in` or `out` and if written as `out`, it defaults to initializing the value as `low` (strings `low` and `high` can be used to ensure glitch-free operations when we configure the GPIO at a desired status).
- `value`: If set as input, it returns the GPIO line input status, while if set as output, it forces the GPIO line status to either `0` (for low) or `1` (for high). Note that if the pin can be configured as the IRQ line and if it has been configured to generate interrupts (refer to the description of `edge`), we can use `poll()` on that file to know whenever the interrupt was triggered (refer to the following).
- `edge`: This reads as either `none`, `rising`, `falling`, or `both`. By writing these strings, we can select the signal edges that will make `poll()` on the `value` file return. This file is not present if the corresponding GPIO cannot generate interrupts.
- `active_low`: This returns as either `0` (false) or `1` (true), and by writing any nonzero value, we can invert the value attribute both for reading and writing.

Getting access to GPIOs

Now let's look at how we can get access to GPIOs using both the command line (using Bash) and then using the C language.

Bash

Now it's time for an example. A very simple usage is the following one, where we use the `gpio91` of the Wandboard to turn an LED on and off. The circuitry is reported in the following figure:

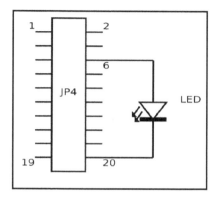

To control the LED, we must set the line as the output, so we should write `out` in the `/sys/class/gpio/gpio91/direction` file, but if we wish to set the LED to a precise state by default, it is better to write `low`, as show here:

```
root@wb:~# echo low > /sys/class/gpio/gpio91/direction
```

 You can now observe that the `low` value is the default for the `out` setting, but the preceding setting increases the code readability since it states the intention of the developer exactly.

OK, the LED is still off and we can turn it on and off by writing `1` and `0` in the file value, as shown in the following commands:

```
root@wb:~# echo 1 > /sys/class/gpio/gpio91/value
root@wb:~# echo 0 > /sys/class/gpio/gpio91/value
```

After the preceding command, the LED is off again, and if we take a look at `/sys/class/gpio/gpio91/active_low`, we get the following:

```
root@wb:~# cat /sys/class/gpio/gpio91/active_low
0
```

This means that the GPIO is not active low, but if we modify this behavior, everything will change:

```
root@wb:~# echo 1 > /sys/class/gpio/gpio91/active_low
```

Now the LED is still off, but the behavior of the value file has been changed in such a way that to turn the LED on and off, we must write 0 and 1 (inverse logic):

```
root@wb:~# echo 0 > /sys/class/gpio/gpio91/value
```

The LED is on and we can turn it off using the following command:

```
root@wb:~# echo 1 > /sys/class/gpio/gpio91/value
```

Now we can try to read the GPIO status when it's set from an external signal. To do that, we can connect a switch to gpio24, as shown in the next figure, in order to move the input status from 0 (GND) to 1 (Vcc).

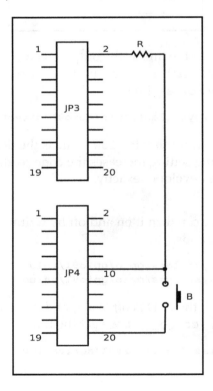

Note that Vcc pin must be connected to 3.3V (which is on the *JP3* connector) and not to 5V (which is present on the *JP4* connector)! Also consider the *R* resistor as a value of 10KΩ .

When the *B* button is not pressed, the GPIO input is set to Vcc, so to the logical 1, while when the *B* button is pressed, the GPIO input moves to GND, that is, the logical 0. Now let's export the GPIO as input and then read its status to verify the logical 1 when the button is not pressed:

```
root@wb:~# echo 24 > /sys/class/gpio/export
root@wb:~# echo in > /sys/class/gpio/gpio24/direction
root@wb:~# cat /sys/class/gpio/gpio24/value
1
```

OK, now let's press the button and then re-read the GPIO status:

```
root@wb:~# cat /sys/class/gpio/gpio24/value
0
```

Perfect! However, we wish to not have this inverse logic but have a direct logic instead. To do that, we can use the `active_low` file by setting it to `1`:

```
root@wb:~# echo 1 > /sys/class/gpio/gpio24/active_low
```

Now, if we re-read the GPIO when the button is not pressed, we get the following:

```
root@wb:~# cat /sys/class/gpio/gpio24/value
0
```

While when we press the button, the result is as follows:

```
root@wb:~# cat /sys/class/gpio/gpio24/value
1
```

Before ending this section, we must consider a little note regarding the SAMA5D3 Xplained GPIOs naming as stated at the beginning of this section. This is because the way the SAMA5D3 Xplained names the GPIOs after the export is a bit different than earlier. Just to show the difference, let's switch to that board and try to export `gpio22`, which is the GPIO line connected to pin *PA22*, and see the name of the new entry related to our GPIO:

```
root@a5d3:~# echo 22 > /sys/class/gpio/export
root@a5d3:~# ls /sys/class/gpio/
export       gpiochip128   gpiochip64   pioA22
gpiochip0    gpiochip32    gpiochip96   unexport
```

As we can see, this time, the new entry is not named `gpio22`, as is in the Wandboard, but the new directory is named `pioA22` in order to reflect the pin name. Apart from this little difference, whatever was said earlier for the files in the GPIO's control directory is still valid; in fact, we can find the same files as earlier in it:

```
root@a5d3:~# ls /sys/class/gpio/pioA22/
active_low  device  direction  edge  power  subsystem  uevent  value
```

C

Now it's time to go further, so let's look at an example on how to manage the GPIOs inside a C program in a way that we can use the `poll()` system call to know which is the GPIO that has changed its internal status. Using the C language, the developer can have a quicker responsiveness of the GPIO reads and writes with respect to the Bash scripting; however, for the best performance, we must switch to the kernel space (refer to the next section) but using the C programming, we can resolve a large variety of common tasks.

In this example, to change the GPIOs statuses, we can use several techniques, but the easiest and quickest one is the solution used earlier with the button. In fact, we can imagine replicating the preceding connections for two buttons and then using the code in the `chapter_05/gpio-poll/gpio-poll.c` file in the book's example code repository to capture the button pressing.

Before starting the test, let's spend some time on explaining the code. First of all, take a look at the following:

```
#define NAME            program_invocation_short_name
#define SYSFS_GPIO_DIR  "/sys/class/gpio"
#define POLL_TIMEOUT    (1 * 1000)          /* in ms */

/* Some useful GPIO defines */
#define GPIO_IN         0
#define GPIO_OUT        1
#define GPIO_NONE       "none"
#define GPIO_RISING     "rising"
#define GPIO_FALLING    "falling"
#define GPIO_BOTH       "both"
```

In the first group, we have generic definitions, where we should notice `SYSFS_GPIO_DIR`, which is used to address the usual sysfs directory for GPIOs management. Then, in the second group, we have some useful constants to be used with the Linux GPIO subsystem.

Then, we have the GPIO number for the GPIO name conversion function. This is needed in order to keep the Atmel nonstandard names we saw earlier in count:

```
#ifdef _ATMEL_GPIOS

char *lut[] = {
    [57] = "pioB25",
    [58] = "pioB26",
    [59] = "pioB27",
};

#else  /* ! _ATMEL_GPIOS */

char *lut[] = {
    [24] = "gpio24",
    [91] = "gpio91",
    [191] = "gpio191",
    [200] = "gpio200",
};

#endif /* _ATMEL_GPIOS */

char *gpio2name(int gpio)
{
    BUG_ON(gpio < 0);

    /* Check for gpio index out of range or if the corresponding entry
     * into the lut[] array is not defined
     */
    if (gpio >= ARRAY_SIZE(lut) || lut[gpio] == NULL) {
        err("unable to get GPIO%d name! "
            "Consider to fix up the lut[] array", gpio);
        BUG();
    }

    return lut[gpio];
}
```

The lut[] look-up-table is defined in a different manner according to the _ATMEL_GPIOS definition, which is automatically added (or not) to the compiler's CFLAGS by Makefile with the following code:

```
MACHINE = $(shell awk '/Hardware/ { print $$3 }' < /proc/cpuinfo)
ifeq ($(MACHINE),Atmel)
  CFLAGS += -D_ATMEL_GPIOS
endif
```

The preceding code is held in the `chapter_05/gpio-poll/Makefile` file in the book's example code repository.

The code is simple, since it takes the hardware manufacturer name from the `/proc/cpuinfo` file. In fact, on the Wandboard, at the end, it looks like this:

```
root@wb:~# cat /proc/cpuinfo | tail -3
Hardware    : Freescale i.MX6 Quad/DualLite (Device Tree)
Revision    : 0000
Serial      : 0000000000000000
```

On the SAMA5D3 Xplained, it looks like this instead:

```
root@a5d3:~# cat /proc/cpuinfo | tail -3
Hardware      : Atmel SAMA5
Revision      : 0000
Serial        : 0000000000000000
```

In this scenario, the `gpio2name()` function will take the correct look-up-table settings according to the underlying machine.

The look-up-table is probably not the perfect or most efficient solution, but it allow us the ability to restrict the set of possible usable GPIO lines that can be very useful in order to block undesired access to other GPIO lines; for this purpose, the function returns a `BUG()` condition if the `gpio` index is out of range or the corresponding entry in the `lut[]` array is NULL.

After the GPIOs conversion function, the GPIOs management functions follow, and as an example, we'll report some of them here with a little explanation. The `gpio_export()` function, which is used to export a GPIO line, is as follows:

```
int gpio_export(unsigned int gpio)
{
    int fd, len;
    char *buf;

    fd = open(SYSFS_GPIO_DIR "/export", O_WRONLY);
    if (fd < 0)
        return fd;

    len = asprintf(&buf, "%d", gpio);
    BUG_ON(len < 0);

    write(fd, buf, len);
```

```
        close(fd);

        free(buf);
        return 0;
}
```

As we can see, the function simply does what we did earlier using the `echo` command to write into the `/sys/class/gpio/export` file. Then following is reported in `gpio_set_dir()`, which is used to set the GPIO's direction:

```
int gpio_set_dir(unsigned int gpio, unsigned int out_flag)
{
        int fd, len;
        char *buf;

        len = asprintf(&buf, SYSFS_GPIO_DIR  "/%s/direction",
                        gpio2name(gpio));
        BUG_ON(len < 0);

        fd = open(buf, O_WRONLY);
        if (fd < 0) {
                free(buf);
                return fd;
        }

        if (out_flag)
                write(fd, "out", 4);
        else
                write(fd, "in", 3);

        free(buf);
                close(fd);

        return 0;
}
```

Again, the function does the same as we did earlier with the `/sys/class/gpio/gpioXX/direction` file. Then, as a last example, `gpio_get_value()` can be used to read the GPIO's status in the same manner as we did with the `/sys/class/gpio/gpioXX/value` file:

```
int gpio_get_value(unsigned int gpio, unsigned int *value)
{
        int fd, len, n;
        char *buf;
        char ch;
```

```
        len = asprintf(&buf, SYSFS_GPIO_DIR "/%s/value", gpio2name(gpio));
        BUG_ON(len < 0);

        fd = open(buf, O_RDONLY);
        if (fd < 0)
            return fd;

        n = read(fd, &ch, 1);

        *value = ch != '0' ? 1 : 0;

        free(buf);
        close(fd);

        return n;
    }
```

Now you should also note that an extra GPIO function is defined-that is, gpio_fd_open() which is used to open() a GPIO's value file and then get the corresponding file descriptor. This is needed later when we have to set up the poll() system call's data structures.

The usage() function just writes out the command's usage message and a list of the supported GPIOs we added in the lut[] array.

Then comes the main() function. First of all, we register all signal handlers and clean up the function needed to clean whatever we can get dirty (the clean up function and the SIGTERM and SIGINT handlers are used to restore the GPIOs settings under the /sys/class/gpio directory as earlier, so we simply un-export all previously exported GPIO lines), and then we check the command-line option arguments as usual:

```
    /* Register signal handlers in order to do some clean up stuff
     * at exit time...
     */
    atexit(cleanup);
    sig_h = signal(SIGTERM, sighand_exit);   /* clean up on SIGTERM */   if
    (sig_h == SIG_ERR) {
        err("unable to catch SIGTERM");
        exit(EXIT_FAILURE);
    }
    sig_h = signal(SIGINT, sighand_exit);
    if (sig_h == SIG_ERR) {
        err("unable to catch SIGINT");
        exit(EXIT_FAILURE);
    }
```

```
/* Check the command line */
while (1) {
    /* `getopt_long' stores the option index here. */
    int option_index = 0;

    c = getopt_long(argc, argv, "hd",
                    long_options, &option_index);

    /* Detect the end of the options. */
    if (c == -1)
        break;

    switch (c) {
    case 0:
        /* If this option set a flag, do nothing else now */
        BUG_ON(long_options[option_index].flag == NULL);

        break;

    case 'h':       /* --help */
        usage();

    case 'd':       /* --debug */
        enable_debug++;

        break;

    case ':':
        /* "getopt_long" already printed an error message */
        exit(EXIT_FAILURE);

    case '?':
        /* "getopt_long" already printed an error message */
        err("unrecognized option "%s"", argv[optind - 1]);
        exit(EXIT_FAILURE);

    default:
        BUG();
    }
}
dbg("debug is on (level=%d)", enable_debug);
```

However, after checking the command-line option arguments, we have to read the two numbers of the GPIOs line we wish to use for our test:

```
/*
 * Parse any remaining command line arguments (not options)
 */
```

```
argc -= optind;
argv += optind;
if (argc < 2)
    usage();

for (i = 0; i < 2; i++) {
    ret = sscanf(argv[i], "%d", &gpio[i]);
    if (ret != 1) {
        err("invalid entry "%s"", argv[i]);
        exit(EXIT_FAILURE);
    }
    info("got GPIO%d named as %s", gpio[i],
    gpio2name(gpio[i]));
}
```

Now in the `gpio[]` array, we have the numbers of the GPIOs to be used for our test and then we have to set up the relative settings in order to program them as input pins sensible to the falling edge of the input waveform. The following is the code:

```
for (i = 0; i < 2; i++) {
    ret = gpio_export(gpio[i]);
    if (ret < 0) {
        err("unable to export GPIO%d", gpio[i]);
        exit(EXIT_FAILURE);
    }

    ret = gpio_set_dir(gpio[i], GPIO_IN);
    if (ret < 0) {
        err("unable to set direction for GPIO%d", gpio[i]);
        exit(EXIT_FAILURE);
    }

    ret = gpio_set_edge(gpio[i], GPIO_FALLING);
    if (ret < 0) {
        err("unable to set edge for GPIO%d", gpio[i]);
        exit(EXIT_FAILURE);
    }

    ret = gpio_fd_open(gpio[i]);
    if (ret < 0) {
        err("unable to open GPIO%d", gpio[i]);
        exit(EXIT_FAILURE);
    }
    gpio_fd[i] = ret;
}
```

In the preceding code, we can recognize the same steps we did in the earlier example with the Bash commands plus the last call of the `gpio_fd_open()` function we need in order to get the two file descriptors of the relative `/sys/class/gpio/gpioXX/value` files to be used with `poll()`.

Now we can move on to analyzing the main loop:

```
while (1) {
    /* Set up the fdset data structs */
    memset((void*) fdset, 0, sizeof(fdset));
    for (i = 0; i < 2; i++) {
        fdset[i].fd = gpio_fd[i];
        fdset[i].events = POLLPRI;
    }

    /* Do the poll() with timeout */
    ret = poll(fdset, 2, POLL_TIMEOUT);
    BUG_ON(ret < 0);
    if (ret == 0) {
        /* No IRQs received!
         * If debug is enabled then print GPIOs statuses,
         * otherwise just print a dot "."
         */
        if (enable_debug) {
            for (i = 0; i < 2; i++) {
                ret = gpio_get_value(gpio[i], &val);
                BUG_ON(ret < 0);
                dbg("read() GPIO%d=%d", gpio[i], val);
            }
        } else {
            printf(".");
            fflush(stdout);
        }
    } else {
        /* IRQ received! Print out the new GPIO status */
        for (i = 0; i < 2; i++) {
            if (fdset[i].revents & (POLLPRI | POLLERR)) {
                ret = lseek(fdset[i].fd, SEEK_SET, 0);
                BUG_ON(ret < 0);
                ret = read(fdset[i].fd, &v, 1);
                BUG_ON(ret < 1);

                if (ret == 1) {
                    info("poll() GPIO%d=%c", gpio[i], v);
                }
            }
        }
    }
```

```
        }
    }
```

The code here is quite simple; first of all, we set up the poll() data structures, as requested in its man pages (a screenshot is reported here). Then, we call the poll() system call and examine its return value. In case of time-out, no interrupts are received; we simply print out a dot character (or some debugging information if enabled), but in case of interrupt, poll() will return the GPIO it has by printing the corresponding status. Note that in order to correctly read the status, we need to perform a lseek() before using the read() system call to read the data!

Now let's try the code. We have to compile it first with the usual make command directly on the Wandboard, and then we can start our test by calling the usage message:

```
root@wb:~/gpio-poll# ./gpio-poll -h
usage: gpio-poll [--help|-h] [--debug|-d] gpio1# gpio2#
    Supported GPIOs are:
        GPIO24 named as gpio24
        GPIO91 named as gpio91
        GPIO191 named as gpio191
        GPIO200 named as gpio200
```

If we try to compile and then execute the same program in the SAMA5D3 Xplained, we should get the following output instead:

```
root@a5d3:~/gpio-poll# ./gpio-poll -h
usage: gpio-poll [--help|-h] [--debug|-d] gpio1# gpio2#

    Supported GPIOs are:
        GPIO57 named as pioB25
        GPIO58 named as pioB26
        GPIO59 named as pioB27
```

Then supposing we connected our two buttons (using the preceding circuitry) to gpio91 and gpio24, we have to execute the following command:

```
root@wb:~/gpio-poll# ./gpio-poll 91 24
gpio-poll: got GPIO91 named as gpio91
gpio-poll: got GPIO24 named as gpio24
gpio-poll: poll() GPIO91=1
gpio-poll: poll() GPIO24=1
...
```

Then, the program will continue printing dot characters until we press a button, and in that case, we get the following:

```
......gpio-poll: poll() GPIO91=0
..gpio-poll: poll() GPIO24=0
```

The GPIOs statuses moved to 0, which means that the relative buttons have been pressed!

It's interesting to note that if we leave the program running and, using another terminal window, we take a look at the /sys/class/gpio directory, we can find that its content has been changed according to the GPIOs used:

```
root@wb:~# ls /sys/class/gpio/
export   gpio91      gpiochip128   gpiochip192   gpiochip64   unexport
gpio24   gpiochip0   gpiochip160   gpiochip32    gpiochip96
root@wb:~# cat /sys/class/gpio/gpio*/direction
in
in
root@wb:~# cat /sys/class/gpio/gpio*/value
1
1
```

However, when we stop the program by hitting the *Ctrl-C* keboard keys sequence, everything comes back to the initial status.

Using GPIOs with scripting languages

Having the possibility to manage the GPIO lines in a scripting language in an easy manner allows us to have a powerful tool to speed up simple tasks involving these peripherals. That's why in this section, we're going to see how the GPIO lines can be managed in both PHP and Python scripting languages in a manner similar to what we did in C.

However, in order to keep the code simple, we suppose that the GPIO lines gpio24 and gpio91 have been exported in some way already. For example, we can properly set them up with the following well-known commands:

```
root@wb:~# echo 24 > /sys/class/gpio/export
root@wb:~# echo in > /sys/class/gpio/gpio24/direction
root@wb:~# echo falling > /sys/class/gpio/gpio24/edge
root@wb:~# echo 91 > /sys/class/gpio/export
root@wb:~# echo in > /sys/class/gpio/gpio91/direction
root@wb:~# echo falling > /sys/class/gpio/gpio91/edge
```

Now the GPIO lines are ready to be used by the next two programs that are going to use their `poll()` equivalent functions to do their job. Both PHP and Python functions are based on the `select()` system call, which is equivalent to `poll()`. Even if related to the C language, but for sake of completeness and due to the fact the PHP and Python version are very similar.

PHP

Once the GPIO lines are set up as input and are sensible to the falling edge, the PHP code to manage them with the `select()` system call is as follows:

```php
#!/usr/bin/php
<?php
    define("gpio24", "/sys/class/gpio/gpio24/value");
    define("gpio91", "/sys/class/gpio/gpio91/value");

    # Get the GPIOs streams
    $stream24 = fopen(gpio24, 'r');
    $stream91 = fopen(gpio91, 'r');

    while (true) {
        # Set up stream sets for the select()
        $read = NULL;
        $write = NULL;
        $exept = array($stream24, $stream91);

        # Wait for IRQs (without timeout)...
        $ret = stream_select($read, $write, $exept, NULL);
        if ($ret < 0)
            die("stream_select: error");

        foreach ($exept as $input => $stream) {
            # Read the GPIO status
            fseek($stream, 0, SEEK_SET);
            $status = intval(fgets($stream));

            # Get the filename from "/sys/class/gpio/gpioXX/value"
            $meta_data = stream_get_meta_data($stream);
            $gpio = basename(dirname($meta_data["uri"]));

            printf("$gpio status=$statusn");
        }
    }
?>
```

The code is placed in the `chapter_05/gpio-poll.php` file in the book's example code repository

The code is still very simple; first, we get two streams related to the two GPIOs using the `fopen()` function, and then we simply call the `stream_select()` function, which internally uses `select()` to work (as we can see, this function is very similar to its counterpart in C). With `stream_select()`, we simply iterate on the `$exept` streams set in order to see which is the GPIO that generated the IRQ.

 We set the timeout parameter to `NULL` in order to disable it and keep the code as simple as possible.

If we try to test the code, we get the following:

```
root@wb:~# ./gpio-poll.php
gpio24 status=1
gpio91 status=1
```

Then, if we try to push the buttons, we get the following output:

```
gpio24 status=0
gpio91 status=0
```

 Note that even in this case, we can get multiple output lines even if we just press the button or an output, as follows, due to the signal bounce problem reported earlier:
```
gpio24 status=1
gpio91 status=1
```

Python

Regarding the Python language, the code to manage the GPIO lines with the `select()` system call is as follows:

```python
#!/usr/bin/python

from __future__ import print_function
import os
import sys
```

```
import select

gpio24  = "/sys/class/gpio/gpio24/value"
gpio91  = "/sys/class/gpio/gpio91/value"

# Get the GPIOs streams
stream24 = open(gpio24, 'r');
stream91 = open(gpio91, 'r');

while True :
    # Set up stream sets for the select()
    read = []
    write = []
    exept = [stream24, stream91]

    # Wait for IRQs (without timeout)...
    r, w, e = select.select(read, write, exept)
    for i, input in enumerate(e) :
        # Read the GPIO status
        input.seek(0, 0)
        status = input.read().rstrip("n")

        # Get the filename from "/sys/class/gpio/gpioXX/value"
        path = os.path.dirname(input.name)
        gpio = os.path.basename(path)
        print("%s status=%s" % (gpio, status))
```

The code is placed in the `chapter_05/gpio-poll.py` file in the book's example code repository.

Again, the code is simple. After getting the two streams as earlier using the `open()` function we pass to call the `select.select()` method in a similar manner as earlier. When a new IRQ is received by one or more `exept` streams, we iterate on them, showing the relative GPIO status.

In order to disable the timeout and keep the code as simple as possible, this time, we completely omit it.

As we can see, the Python `select.select()` function is very similar to its counterpart in C.

Now if we start the program, we should get the preceding output:

```
root@wb:~# ./gpio-poll.py
gpio24 status=1
gpio91 status=1
```

Then, as soon as we press a button, we get the following output:

```
gpio91 status=0
gpio24 status=0
```

 Even in this case, we can have the bouncing problems reported earlier.

Managing GPIO into the kernel

Having the ability to manage one or more GPIO lines from the user space is really important because it drastically simplifies the developer's job, but in some circumstances, that is not enough to solve a task. As you already saw in Chapter 3, *C Compiler, Device Drivers, and Useful Developing Techniques, Writing our own Device Driver*, where we introduced a kernel driver involving two GPIO lines, it was clear that if the pulse events go over a certain frequency, a user-space application is not suitable anymore and the management must be moved into the kernel.

However, the speed is not the only reason why we should move into the kernel space; another good reason is the abstraction level that the kernel offers to developers. In fact, we already saw that, for example, a simple GPIO line can be abstracted as an LED device with the ability to be managed by several triggers (refer to Chapter 3, *C Compiler, Device Drivers, and Useful Developing Techniques, The Device Tree*, for a simple example and then the next section for a more detailed explanation). Also, a GPIO line can be abstracted as an **input device** (that is, a keyboard) or as a more complicated device. For the input device, we're going to look at an example, while for the latter case, you can take a look at Chapter 11, *1-Wire – W1, Using the GPIO interface*, where we implemented a one-wire (W1) controller using a GPIO.

An input device using GPIOs

In this section, we're going to present a kernel code that emulates the behavior of the `gpio-poll.c` program in kernel space plus a special behavior: the generation of keyboard events. This is to demonstrate how easy it can be to capture a GPIO status event inside the kernel. In fact, in this environment, we don't need to use the `poll()` system call, nor do we need to implement a main loop at all; we just need to register an IRQ handler and the kernel will do the rest for us!

These events are generated and managed by the input devices, which are a device class dedicated to all peripherals that can generate events from keyboards, mouse, touchscreen, and other user input devices.

 You can take a look at: `https://www.kernel.org/doc/Documentation/input/input.txt` for further information.

The code used here is in the `chapter_06/gpio-irq/gpio-irq.c` file in the book's example code repository, and it can be compiled in the same manner as we did in Chapter 3, *C Compiler, Device Drivers, and Useful Developing Techniques, Writing our own Device Driver* for the *pulse* kernel module:

```
$ make KERNEL_DIR=~/WB/armv7-multiplatform/KERNEL/
```

If everything works well, we should get a new kernel module called `gpio-irq.ko`. However, before testing it, it is better to take a look at its code in order to understand how it works.

First of all, just note that this time, we didn't used a DTS file as in Chapter 3, *C Compiler, Device Drivers, and Useful Developing Techniques, Writing our own Device Driver*, but we preferred using a module parameter named `gpios` to declare the GPIO lines to be used. In the following code, we can learn how to declare the `gpio` parameter as a (maximum) two-cell array. Also, we can see the definition of an additional parameter (`debug`) to set up the debugging level. In this manner, we can declare the GPIOs to be used for our test from the command line, as we did with the user-space program earlier:

```
static int debug;
module_param(debug, int, S_IRUSR | S_IWUSR | S_IRGRP | S_IWGRP);
MODULE_PARM_DESC(int, "Set to 1 to enable debugging messages");

static int ngpios;
static int gpios[2] = { -1 , -1 };
module_param_array(gpios, int, &ngpios,
```

```
                        S_IRUSR | S_IWUSR | S_IRGRP | S_IWGRP);
MODULE_PARM_DESC(gpios, "Defines the GPIOs number to be used as a "
                        "list of numbers separated by commas.");
```

This code will generate the following output when we use the `modinfo` utility on the kernel module:

```
$ modinfo gpio-irq.ko
filename:        /home/giometti/github/chapter_06/gpio-irq/gpio-irq.ko
version:         0.0.1
license:         GPL
description:     GPIO IRQ module
author:          Rodolfo Giometti <giometti@hce-engineering.com>
srcversion:      F23DF96F9CCBAE41BEE6F59
depends:
vermagic:        4.4.7-armv7-x6 SMP mod_unload modversions ARMv7 p2v8
parm:            debug:int
parm:            int:Set to 1 to enable debugging messages
parm:            gpios:Defines the GPIOs number to be used as a list of
 numbers separated by commas. (array of int)
```

Then, we should skip all the code until the end (keep calm; we're going to go back soon), where we can find the basic `module_init()` and `module_exit()` functions of our module:

```
static int __init gpioirq_init(void)
{
    int i;
    int ret;

    /* Check the supplied GPIOs numbers */
    if (ngpios != 2) {
        usage();
        ret = -EINVAL;
        goto exit;
    }

    /* Request the GPIOs and then setting them up as needed */
    for (i = 0; i < 2; i++) {
        dbg("got GPIO%d", gpios[i]);

        /* Is the GPIO line free? */
        ret = gpio_request(gpios[i], NAME);
        if (ret) {
            err("unable to request GPIO%dn", gpios[i]);
            goto free_gpios;
        }
        keys[i].gpio = gpios[i];
```

```
    /* If so then setting it as input */
    gpio_direction_input(gpios[i]);

    /* Is GPIO in pin IRQ capable? */
    ret = gpio_to_irq(gpios[i]);
    if (ret < 0) {
        err("GPIO%d is not IRQ capablen", gpios[i]);
        ret = -EINVAL;
        goto free_gpios;
    }
    keys[i].irq = ret;

    /* Then request the IRQ */
    ret = request_irq(keys[i].irq, (irq_handler_t) irq_handler,
                    IRQF_TRIGGER_RISING | IRQF_TRIGGER_FALLING,
                    NAME, &keys[i]);
    if (ret < 0) {
        err("unable to request IRQ%d for GPIO%dn",
            keys[i].irq, keys[i].gpio);
        ret = -EINVAL;
        goto free_gpios;
    }
    dbg("GPIO%d (key="%s") mapped on IRQ %d",
                keys[i].gpio, keys[i].name, keys[i].irq);
}

/* Allocate the input device */
b_dev = input_allocate_device();
if (!b_dev) {
    err("cannot allocate memory");
    ret = -ENOMEM;
    goto free_gpios;
}
b_dev->evbit[0] = BIT_MASK(EV_KEY);
b_dev->name = NAME;
b_dev->dev.parent = NULL;
b_dev->id.bustype = BUS_HOST;
b_dev->id.vendor = 0x0001;
b_dev->id.product = 0x0001;
b_dev->id.version = 0x0001;

/* Define the keys mapping */
for (i = 0; i < 2; i++)
    set_bit(keys[i].btn, b_dev->keybit);

/* Register the input device */
ret = input_register_device(b_dev);
if (ret) {
```

```
            err("cannot register input device");
            goto free_dev;
    }

    info("input GPIO IRQ module loaded");

    return 0;

free_dev:
    input_free_device(b_dev);

free_gpios:
    for ( ; i >= 0; i--) {
        if (keys[i].irq >= 0)
            free_irq(keys[i].irq, &keys[i]);
            if (keys[i].gpio >= 0)
                gpio_free(keys[i].gpio);
    }

exit:
    return ret;
}

static void __exit gpioirq_exit(void)
{
    int i;

    input_unregister_device(b_dev);

    for (i = 0; i < 2; i++) {
        dbg("freeing IRQ %d for GPIO%d...", keys[i].irq,
            keys[i].gpio);
        free_irq(keys[i].irq, &keys[i]);
        gpio_free(keys[i].gpio);
    }

    info("input GPIO IRQ module released");
}

module_init(gpioirq_init);
module_exit(gpioirq_exit);
```

The `module_exit()` function just releases all kernel resources requested in the `module_init()` function and basically calls the `input_unregister_device()`, `free_irq()`, and `gpio_free()` functions, while the core of the code is in the `module_init()` function. In fact, after a little command-line parameter checking, it basically calls four main functions:

- `gpio_request()`: This requests a GPIO line inside the kernel to avoid someone usage.
- `gpio_direction_input()`: This sets the GPIO direction (as the input in our example).
- `request_irq()`: This requests a handler for the IRQ related to a GPIO (the function used to get the IRQ number from the corresponding GPIO line is `gpio_to_irq()`).
- `input_register_device()`: This registers the new input device into the system (note that we used `input_allocate_device()` just to allocate the required data structure).

You should notice that in the kernel code, it is very important to release whatever we request; otherwise, it will be lost until the next reboot! This problem doesn't occur in the user-space program, where all resources are released when the program exists.

Simply speaking, in the `module_init()` function, we have to request the GPIOs, setting the input direction and then requesting the IRQ handlers; after that, we have to allocate the new input device, setting its basic data (name, version, and so on) with the definition of its key mapping, and in the end, we have to register the input device in order to enable the code of our new keyboard.

After all settings, the other interesting part is, of course, the IRQ handler, where all the magic occurs and that looks like this:

```
static irqreturn_t irq_handler(int i, void *ptr, struct pt_regs *regs)
{
    struct keys_s *key = (struct keys_s *) ptr;
    int status;

    /* Get the gpio status */
    status = !!gpio_get_value(key->gpio);
    dbg("IRQ on GPIO%d status=%d", key->gpio, status);

    /* Report the button event */
    input_report_key(b_dev, key->btn, status);
    input_sync(b_dev);
```

```
        return IRQ_HANDLED;
    }
```

Note that during the IRQ registration, we passed a pointer to the `request_irq()` function to the specific cell of the `keys` array structure holding the GPIO data related to the IRQ currently requested, so at IRQ time, we can get back the GPIO number that is responsible for the IRQ event. The `struct keys_s` is defined as follows and opportunely filled, it can be used to get all the required information:

```
static struct keys_s keys[2] = {
    [0] = {
        .name = "0",
        .btn = KEY_0,
        .gpio = -1,
        .irq = -1,
    },

    [1] = {
        .name = "1",
        .btn = KEY_1,
        .gpio = -1,
        .irq = -1,
    },
};
```

It defines two keys named `0` and `1` that will generate events related to buttons `KEY_0` (keyboard button *0*) and `KEYS_1` (keyboard button *1*), so using them, we can notify the kernel, for instance, when key 0 has been pressed or released.

So, when we press a button, we generate an IRQ that is captured by the kernel that, in turn, executes the `irq_handler()` interrupt handler with the proper data, and especially with the correct pointer to one element of the preceding `keys` array. Then, we can get the GPIO line status by simply using the `gpio_get_value()` function, and then we can report the button press/release event to the upper layers using the `input_report_key()`/`input_sync()` functions.

OK, now we can perform our test; if we kept the same circuitry as earlier with the two buttons, we can load the kernel module using the following command:

```
root@wb:~# insmod gpio-irq.ko debug=1 gpios=91,24
gpio_irq: got GPIO91
gpio_irq: got GPIO24
gpio_irq: GPIO24 (key="1") mapped on IRQ 56
input: gpio_irq as /devices/virtual/input/input0
gpio_irq: input GPIO IRQ module loaded
```

> The preceding output can be seen only in the serial console! If we're executing the code in an SSH terminal, we must use the usual `dmesg` or `tail -f /var/log/kern.log` commands to see them.
>
> Also, even if in the serial console, it may happen that we get the last `input GPIO IRQ module loaded` message only. In this case, we have to increase the kernel logging level with the following command, as described in Chapter 2, *Managing the System Console,* in *Managing the kernel messages* section:
>
> `root@wb:~# echo 8 > /proc/sys/kernel/printk`

At this time, we can verify that our GPIOs have been really requested by our module, and we can do that by looking into file `/sys/kernel/debug/gpio` the, as follows:

```
root@wb:~# grep gpio_irq /sys/kernel/debug/gpio
 gpio-24  (                    |gpio_irq           ) in  hi
 gpio-91  (                    |gpio_irq           ) in  hi
```

Also, we can verify that the corresponding IRQ lines are also reserved by looking into `/proc/interrupts` file:

```
root@wb:~# grep gpio_irq /proc/interrupts
  56:    0       0       0        0  gpio-mxc  24 Edge   gpio_irq
 127:    0       0       0        0  gpio-mxc  27 Edge   gpio_irq
```

Then, we can verify that the new input device named `/sys/devices/virtual/input/input0` is present, so we can take a first look at the `/sys/class/input/` directory:

```
root@wb:~# ls /sys/class/input/
event0   input0   mice
root@wb:~# ls /sys/class/input/input0/
capabilities  id          name   power       subsystem  uniq
event0        modalias    phys   properties  uevent
```

OK, let's look at the name of the device to verify that it's really the one we just added:

```
root@wb:~# cat /sys/class/input/input0/name
gpio_irq
```

> Note that the event device connected to the input one is named `event0`, and the corresponding device file under the `/dev` directory has the same name:
>
> ```
> root@wb:~# ls /dev/input/
> event0 mice
> ```

Great! Our settings are OK. However, before starting to press the buttons to generate IRQs, it's interesting to note that nothing has changed in `/sys/class/gpio/`:

```
root@wb:~# ls /sys/class/gpio/
export      gpiochip128  gpiochip192  gpiochip64  unexport
gpiochip0   gpiochip160  gpiochip32   gpiochip96
```

However, if we try to export both GPIOs number 91 or 24 now, we get an error due to the fact that these resources have been reserved to our module:

```
root@wb:~# echo 91 > /sys/class/gpio/export
-bash: echo: write error: Device or resource busy
```

Now we can start pressing our buttons, and we should get something as what we got earlier in the kernel messages:

```
gpio_irq: IRQ on GPIO91 status=0
gpio_irq: IRQ on GPIO91 status=1
gpio_irq: IRQ on GPIO24 status=0
gpio_irq: IRQ on GPIO24 status=1
```

However, nothing happens and so, to see the generated keys from our new keyboard, we have to connect a display/LCD, or we can use the `evtest` utility to show the events generated by a generic input device; this is because input events on the embedded kit are not managed by an SSH terminal or the serial console since they are connected to the remote host.

Remembering that the event device related to our new keyboard is event0, we can use the following command:

```
root@wb:~# evtest /dev/input/event0
Input driver version is 1.0.1
Input device ID: bus 0x19 vendor 0x1 product 0x1 version 0x1
Input device name: "gpio_irq"
Supported events:
  Event type 0 (EV_SYN)
  Event type 1 (EV_KEY)
    Event code 2 (KEY_1)
    Event code 11 (KEY_0)
Properties:
Testing ... (interrupt to exit)
```

As we can see, here is all the information we set in our kernel module.

The evtest, if not present, can be installed using the usual package management tools, as follows:
```
root@wb:~# aptitude install evtest
```

Now, if we press our buttons again, we should see something like this:

```
gpio_irq: IRQ on GPIO91 status=0
gpio_irq: IRQ on GPIO91 status=1
Event: time 1459622898.213967, type 1 (EV_KEY), code 11 (KEY_0), value
 1
Event: time 1459622898.213967, -------------- EV_SYN -------------
gpio_irq: IRQ on GPIO24 status=0
gpio_irq: IRQ on GPIO24 status=1
Event: time 1459622900.972430, type 1 (EV_KEY), code 2 (KEY_1), value 1
Event: time 1459622900.972430, -------------- EV_SYN ------------
```

You should keep in mind that the lines starting with the gpio_irq: string come from the kernel messages, while the ones starting with the Event: string are generated by the evtest command.

When we press and release a button, we get the related key event as expected.

LEDs and triggers

As already shown in previous chapters, there are two different ways to manage an LED in a Linux-based system. The first one is using a GPIO, and the second one is also using a GPIO but defining it as an LED device. The GPIO solution can be implemented using whatever we just saw earlier, and it's the easiest and quickest way to do that. However, this is suitable for just turning the LED on and off; in fact, if we have to do more complicated management, this solution is not the best to use, and we have to switch to the second one, that is, we have to use an LED device.

These devices are obviously implemented using GPIOs, but it's the kernel that directly manages them according to the user settings. In fact, these can be simply turned on and off, but they can also be connected to a **trigger** that is able to manage them in several special ways.

To simplify the illustration of the LED subsystem, let's switch to the BeagleBone Black board and let's take a look at the /sys/class/leds/ directory, where all LEDs in the system are defined:

```
root@bbb:~# ls /sys/class/leds/
beaglebone:green:usr0   beaglebone:green:usr2
beaglebone:green:usr1   beaglebone:green:usr3
```

By default, here are the four user LEDs defined that the BeagleBone Black board has on board. Just to see which are the available triggers, we can read the trigger file under of one of the preceding directories (the entries under /sys/class/leds/ as directory as is the entries under the directory /sys/class/gpios/ seen earlier):

```
root@bbb:~# cat /sys/class/leds/beaglebone:green:usr0/trigger
none rc-feedback kbd-scrollock kbd-numlock kbd-capslock kbd-kanalock k
bd-shiftlock kbd-altgrlock kbd-ctrllock kbd-altlock kbd-shiftllock kbd
-shiftrlock kbd-ctrlllock kbd-ctrlrlock nand-disk usb-gadget usb-host
mmc0 mmc1 timer oneshot [heartbeat] backlight gpio cpu0 default-on
```

The active one is the trigger between the square brackets, so in the preceding output, the LED named beaglebone:green:usr0 is managed by the heartbeat trigger.

Before learning how to manage the LEDs and their triggers, let's look at a little description of the most used triggers defined in the kernel:

- `none`: This defines no trigger at all.
- `kbd*`: This signals specific keyboard key events.
- `usb-gadget` and `usb-host`: These signal the USB gadget or the host activity.
- `mmc*`: This signals the MMCs activity.
- `timer`: This turns the LEDs on and off with specified timing.
- `oneshot`: This signals that an event has happened.
- `heartbeat` : This does a heartbeat pulsing with a period length in dependency of the current (1 min) load.
- `backlight`: This signals the *blank* and *unblack* screen events.
- `gpio`: This signals a GPIO activity.
- `cpu*`: This signals CPU activity.
- `default-on`: This sets an LED in its on status by default.

For further information regarding the *LEDS driver* and its triggers, you can take a look at the `Documentation/leds/` directory in the Linux code repository.

To change the current trigger, we have to write the trigger name in the same `trigger` file as earlier, but instead of modifying the on-board BeagleBone Black's LEDs settings, let's define two new LEDs using the following DTS overlay. Using this technique, we can replace, or add, pieces of the current kernel configuration with another setting in such a way that we can have a dynamic kernel configuration that can change according to the current developer's needs:

```
fragment@1 {
    arget = <&ocp>;

    __overlay__ {
        c6_leds {
            compatible    = "gpio-leds";
            pinctrl-names = "default";
            pinctrl-0     = <&bb_led_pins>;

            yellow_led {
                label = "c6:yellow";
                gpios = <&gpio2 5 0>;
                linux,default-trigger = "none";
                default-state = "off";
```

```
        };

        red_led {
            label    = "c6:red";
            gpios    = <&gpio2 4 0>;
            linux,default-trigger = "none";
            default-state = "off";
        };
    };
  };
};
```

 The complete DTS file can be found in the `chapter_06/BB-LEDS-C6-00A0.dts` file in the book's example code repository.

In the preceding code, we define pins *P8.9* and *P8.10* as two LED devices that have the none trigger by default. Now, if we compile the DTS with the next command, we'll be able to enable the new settings:

```
root@bbb:~# dtc -O dtb -o /lib/firmware/BB-LEDS-C6-00A0.dtbo
              -b 0 -@ BB-LEDS-C6-00A0.dts
```

 Also note that if you want to try this on another board, you have to put the c6_leds DTS snippet in the proper DTS file of the board and recompile it in the kernel tree.

OK, let's enable the new overlay, and we should get the following output:

```
root@bbb:~# echo BB-LEDS-C6 > /sys/devices/platform/bone_capemgr/slots
bone_capemgr: part_number 'BB-LEDS-C6', version 'N/A'
bone_capemgr: slot #4: override
bone_capemgr: Using override eeprom data at slot 4
bone_capemgr: slot #4: 'Override Board Name,00A0,Override Manuf,BB-LED
S-C6'
bone_capemgr: slot #4: dtbo 'BB-LEDS-C6-00A0.dtbo' loaded; overlay id
#0
```

Now `/sys/class/leds/` should have changed as follows:

```
root@bbb:~# ls /sys/class/leds/
beaglebone:green:usr0   beaglebone:green:usr2   c6:red
beaglebone:green:usr1   beaglebone:green:usr3   c6:yellow
```

Now if we take a look at the default trigger, we can verify that it's the none one; as an instance, the c6:red directory looks like the following:

```
root@bbb:~# ls /sys/class/leds/c6:red/
brightness  device  max_brightness  power  subsystem  trigger  uevent
```

Now, in order to turn the LED on and off, we can write values 255 or 0 in the /sys/class/leds/c6:red/brightness file in a manner similar to what we do for GPIOs, but the interesting thing here is the ability to use a trigger! For instance, if we wish to blink at 1 Hz with the duty cycle at 50%, we can use the timer trigger, as follows:

```
root@bbb:~# echo timer > /sys/class/leds/c6:red/trigger
```

Now if we look at the directory, the files have been changed, as follows:

```
root@bbb:~# ls /sys/class/leds/c6:red/
brightness  delay_on   max_brightness  subsystem  uevent
delay_off   device     power           trigger
```

And now we have to set only the delay_on and delay_off files accordingly (the numbers are in milliseconds):

```
root@bbb:~# echo 500 > /sys/class/leds/c6:red/delay_on
root@bbb:~# echo 500 > /sys/class/leds/c6:red/delay_off
```

On the other side we can use the trigger cpu0 to see the CPU activity:

```
root@bbb:~# echo cpu0 > /sys/class/leds/c6:red/trigger
```

Now we should see the LED blinking poorly, but if we execute a task to load the CPU, the situation should drastically change. For example, let's try to execute the following command line:

```
root@bbb:~# while true ; do echo test ; done
```

Now the LEDs is always on!

Another interesting trigger is oneshot, which is very useful in signaling an event. For instance, we can imagine single blink of 200ms on and then staying off for 1s each time an event occurs. To do that, we have to enable the trigger and then program the relative delays:

```
root@bbb:~# echo oneshot > /sys/class/leds/c6:red/trigger
root@bbb:~# echo 200 > /sys/class/leds/c6:red/delay_on
root@bbb:~# echo 1000 > /sys/class/leds/c6:red/delay_off
```

Now, to signal the event, we see that in `/sys/class/leds/c6:red/`, a new file called `shot` is present:

```
root@bbb:~# ls /sys/class/leds/c6:red/
brightness   delay_on   invert                power   subsystem   uevent
delay_off    device     max_brightness   shot    trigger
```

So, if we write into that file, we signal that a new event has arrived:

```
root@bbb:~# echo 1 > /sys/class/leds/c6:red/shot
```

The LED should do a quick one-time blinking and then not do any blinking for more for 1 second even if we repeat the writing.

You can now try to repeat this command for the yellow LED and then combine the settings for both the LEDs in order to better understand the trigger usage.

Summary

The GPIO lines are really important and versatile computer peripherals, and their usage is quite essential for every embedded computer. In this chapter, we discovered several ways to manage these devices in both user and kernel-space, presenting different techniques to use them.

In the next chapter, we're going to discover another most important embedded computer peripheral, that is, the serial line! Until now, we simply used it to support the kernel (and bootloaders) serial console only, but it can be used in tons of different way; in fact, even in its age (these kinds of devices are practically the only ones still surviving until the beginning of the computer era), the serial lines (or serial ports) are still present, especially in devices for industrial applications.

Serial Ports and TTY Devices - TTY

7

In the previous chapter, we saw how to manage LED or generic GPIO lines within the kernel using the sysfs API. However, this was just a really simple example of kernel programming used to show to you how implementing a device driver can be simple. Unfortunately, this technique gets complex very quickly according to the peripheral complexity.

Starting from this chapter, we will see a bit in detail how several computers' peripherals can be connected to our embedded computers and how we can manage them in order to interact with the environment from the user space. That is, we will show you how you can get access to some peripherals by enabling and configuring the correct driver. In this case, we don't have to write a driver from scratch, but knowing how a driver works, we can try to correctly use an already written one.

In this chapter, we will present serial ports, one of the most important peripheral class a computer can have (at least a computer used in the control automation industry). After a brief description about what a serial port or serial device is, we'll see how we can manage them in a GNU/Linux system in order to use a real serial device. Then, we'll take a look at a kernel trick useful to communicate between two embedded systems using a serial line as they were connected by an Ethernet cable.

What are TTY, serial, and UART lines?

Early user terminals connected to computers through a serial line were electromechanical teleprinters or teletypewriters (*TeleTYpewriter*, **TTY**), and since then, TTY has continued to be used as the name for such text-only console and the relative serial port. In fact, in a GNU/Linux system, a serial port is usually referred to in the /dev directory with the /dev/ttyS0, /dev/ttyS1, /dev/ttyUSB0, or /dev/ttyUSB1 device for the USB emulated devices, as we already saw in the previous chapters.

So a serial port is not a peripheral, but it is just a *serial communication interface* through which information transfers in or out one bit at a time. This communication is implemented by modern computers via a **Universal Asynchronous Receiver/Transmitter (UART)** device, which has a side connected to the main CPU and the other side with a circuitry, that is, a physical interface (**Phy** in the following diagram) useful to translate the electronic signals in a suitable form for transmission:

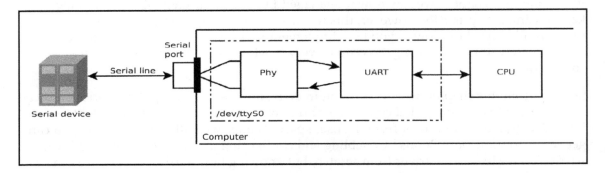

In this scenario, all the terms TTY, serial, and UART refer to the same interface, which is one of the most important communication ports we can have in an embedded device! In fact, since the first chapter, we have discovered that we can get the full control of our embedded system only by getting access to its serial console (which normally runs over a serial port even if, in our embedded kits, it has been emulated via a **USB device**).

In the industry market we can find tons of peripherals that use a serial port to communicate with the CPU. That's why, we must know how this communication interface works and how we can get access to its connected devices in order to exchange data with them.

A peripheral using a serial port to communicate with the CPU is normally called a serial peripheral or serial device.

The electrical lines

Serial port lines are reported in the following table:

Name	Description
TxD (Transmitted Data)	Carries data from DTE to DCE
RxD (Received Data)	Carries data from DCE to DTE
DTR (Data Terminal Ready)	Indicates the presence of DTE to DCE
DCD (Data Carrier Detect)	DCE is connected to the telephone line
DSR (Data Set Ready)	DCE is ready to receive commands or data
RI (Ring Indicator)	DCE has detected an incoming ring signal on the telephone line
RTS (Request To Send)	DTE requests the DCE to prepare to receive data
CTS (Clear To Send)	DCE is ready to accept data
GND	Common ground

Note that most of the preceding lines are control ones and are not strictly required for a simple communication channel, so they can be left unconnected (recall what we did in Chapter 1, *Installing the Developing System*, *Setting up the systems*, when we connected a serial adapter to the BeagleBone Black, to the SAMA5D3 Xplained, and to the Wandboard to get access to their serial consoles).

The required signals are TxD, RxD, and, of course, GND. So, in our upcoming examples, we will use these three signals only.

The **Data Terminal Equipment** (DTE) is the device with the male connector, that is, the PC, while the **Data Communication Equipment** (DCE) is the device with the female connector, that is, the controlled device.

You may get more information regarding these control lines on the Internet and a good starting point is http://en.wikipedia.org/wiki/Flow_control_%28data%29#Hardware_flow_control.

TTYs on the BeagleBone Black

As already mentioned in Chapter 1, *Installing the Developing System, The BeagleBone Black,* the BeagleBone Black has two expansion connectors where several signals are exposed and where we can find 4.5 serial UARTs as reported in the following table:

GPIO Pins on Connector P8				GPIO Pins on Connector P9			
Pin	Signal	Pin	Signal	Pin	Signal	Pin	Signal
31	UART5_CTS	32	UART5_RTS	11	UART4_RxD	20	UART1_CTS
33	UART4_RTS	34	UART3_RTS	13	UART4_TxD	22	UART2_RxD
35	UART4_CTS	36	UART3_CTS	19	UART1_RTS	24	UART1_TxD

The UART0 is reserved for the serial console, and as we already well know, it has a dedicated connector, while the 4.5 serial UARTs are due to the fact that UART3 has a single direction brought to the expansion header.

 A complete BeagleBone Black's connector's description and a quick introduction about the pin's configuration for different usage are available at: http://elinux.org/Beagleboard:Cape_Expansion_Headers.

Usually (and especially in older kernel releases), in the BeagleBone Black, the serial ports are named /dev/ttyO0, /dev/ttyO1 and so on, and by default, these serial lines (except UART0, that is, the /dev/ttyO0 device) are not enabled. So, in order to be used, they must be enabled before getting access to them. However, in our kernel, the situation is quite different since all serial ports' /dev/ttyO prefixes have been replaced with the more standard /dev/ttyS. So, from now on, we will name the serial ports with the devices /dev/ttyS0, /dev/ttyS1, and so on.

You should notice that during the boot, the following kernel message informs us about this name changing:

```
WARNING: Your 'console=ttyO0' has been replaced by
'ttyS0'
```

If we do log in to the system, we can list all serial devices using the following command:

```
root@bbb:~# ls -l /dev/ttyS*
crw------- 1 root tty      4, 64 Apr  2 17:53 /dev/ttyS0
crw-rw---- 1 root dialout 4, 65 Apr  2 17:42 /dev/ttyS1
crw-rw---- 1 root dialout 4, 66 Apr  2 17:42 /dev/ttyS2
crw-rw---- 1 root dialout 4, 67 Apr  2 17:42 /dev/ttyS3
crw-rw---- 1 root dialout 4, 68 Apr  2 17:42 /dev/ttyS4
crw-rw---- 1 root dialout 4, 69 Apr  2 17:42 /dev/ttyS5
```

It seems that all serial ports are enabled, but in reality, if we try to get access to one of them, apart from the first one, we would get the following error:

```
root@bbb:~# stty -F /dev/ttyS2
stty: /dev/ttyS2: Input/output error
```

In fact, we can verify that all devices, apart from the first one, are not defined and then disabled:

```
root@bbb:~# grep '0x' /sys/class/tty/ttyS*/iomem_base
/sys/class/tty/ttyS0/iomem_base:0x44E09000
/sys/class/tty/ttyS1/iomem_base:0x0
/sys/class/tty/ttyS2/iomem_base:0x0
/sys/class/tty/ttyS3/iomem_base:0x0
/sys/class/tty/ttyS4/iomem_base:0x0
/sys/class/tty/ttyS5/iomem_base:0x0
```

As expected, `/dev/ttyS0` is the only available serial port.

To enable the other serial ports, we need to modify the kernel settings in order to ask it to enable the serial port we wish to use. Which ports to enable depends on the pins we'd like to use to connect our device. Then, the following table may help us in choosing them:

Device	TxD	RxD	RTS	CTS	Name
ttyS1	P9.24	P9.26			UART1
ttyS2	P9.21	P9.22	P8.38	P8.37	UART2
ttyS4	P9.13	P9.11	P8.33	P8.35	UART4
ttyS5	P8.37	P8.38			UART5

The overlays related to serial ports are available in the /lib/firmware/ directory as shown here:

```
root@BeagleBone:~# ls /lib/firmware/BB-UART*.dtbo
/lib/firmware/BB-UART1-00A0.dtbo
/lib/firmware/BB-UART2-00A0.dtbo
/lib/firmware/BB-UART2-RTSCTS-00A0.dtbo
/lib/firmware/BB-UART4-00A0.dtbo
/lib/firmware/BB-UART4-RTSCTS-00A0.dtbo
/lib/firmware/BB-UART5-00A0.dtbo
```

All devices are usable for our scope, so we choose to use the /dev/ttyS2 device. In order to activate it, we can use this command:

```
root@bbb:~# echo BB-UART2 > /sys/devices/platform/bone_capemgr/slots
```

In the kernel messages, we should see the following activity:

```
bone_capemgr: part_number 'BB-UART2', version 'N/A'
bone_capemgr: slot #4: override
bone_capemgr: Using override eeprom data at slot 4
bone_capemgr: slot #4: 'Override Board Name,00A0,Override Manuf,BB-UAR
T2'
48024000.serial: ttyS2 at MMIO 0x48024000 (irq = 188, base_baud = 3000
000) is a 8250
bone_capemgr: slot #4: dtbo 'BB-UART2-00A0.dtbo' loaded; overlay id #0
```

Now, the /dev/ttyS2 device should be available, as shown here, by rechecking the iomem_base files:

```
root@bbb:~# grep '0x' /sys/class/tty/ttyS*/iomem_base
/sys/class/tty/ttyS0/iomem_base:0x44E09000
/sys/class/tty/ttyS1/iomem_base:0x0
/sys/class/tty/ttyS2/iomem_base:0x48024000
/sys/class/tty/ttyS3/iomem_base:0x0
/sys/class/tty/ttyS4/iomem_base:0x0
/sys/class/tty/ttyS5/iomem_base:0x0
```

Now, the serial port can get accessed without any error:

```
root@bbb:~# stty -F /dev/ttyS2
speed 9600 baud; line = 0;
-brkint -imaxbel
```

TTYs on the SAMA5D3 Xplained

On the SAMA5D3 Xplained, the TTYs are exposed on the expansion connector as already mentioned in `Chapter 1`, *Installing the Developing System*, *The SAMA5D3 Xplained* section. However, these signals are usually multiplexed with the standard GPIOs function. This behavior is named *alternate function*, and it must be considered each time we wish to use a pin for a different usage.

 These alternate functions can be found in almost all embedded systems such as the BeagleBone Black and the Wandboard.

The SAMA5D3 Xplained board has 3 UARTs (one is a debug port named BDGU and the other two are generic UARTs) and 4 USARTs (*Universal Synchronous/Asynchronous Receiver/Transmitter*). The pin name and UART signal name association is reported in this table:

Pin	Signal	Pin	Signal	Pin	Signal	Pin	Signal
PA30	UART1_RxD	PB30	DBGU_RxD	PD17	USART0_RxD	PE23	USART2_CTS
PA31	UART1_TxD	PB31	DBGU_TxD	PD18	USART0_TxD	PE24	USART2_RTS
PB26	USART1_CTS	PC29	UART0_RxD	PE16	USART3_CTS	PE25	USART2_RxD
PB27	USART1_RTS	PC30	UART0_TxD	PE17	USART3_RTS	PE26	USART2_TxD
PB28	USART1_RxD	PD15	USART0_CTS	PE18	USART3_RxD		
PB29	USART1_TxD	PD16	USART0_RTS	PE19	USART3_TxD		

 A **USART** controller is a type of a serial interface device that can be programmed to communicate asynchronously or synchronously. Visit https://en.wikipedia.org/wiki/Universal_Synchronous/Asynchronous _Receiver/Transmitter for further information.

On the SAMA5D3 Xplained, only one UART (apart from the one used to support the serial console) and two USARTs are enabled by default as reported in the next table:

Device	TxD	RxD	Name
`/dev/ttyS0`	J23.2	J23.3	**DBGU**
`/dev/ttyS1`	J20.5	J20.6	**USART0**
`/dev/ttyS2`	J20.3	J20.4	**USART1**
`/dev/ttyS5`	P18.7	P18.8	**UART0**

Look at the SAMA5D3 Xplained user manual
at: `http://www.atmel.com/Images/Atmel-11269-32-bit-Cortex-A5-Micr`
`ocontroller-SAMA5D3-Xplained_User-Guide.pdf` for further information.

If we wish to use the other peripheral, we have to do some software and hardware modifications.

TTYs on the Wandboard

The Wandboard has several TTYs, but all of them are reserved for special purposes and they cannot be used. Only one port is free (UART2), but unfortunately, it's not routed to any expansion connectors, and it can be accessed only by some **test points** (**TP**) on the board as reported in the next table:

Pin	Signal	Pin	Signal
TP63	UART2_CDC	TP121	UART2_CTS
TP65	UART2_DSR	TP123	UART2_TxD
TP66	UART2_DTR	TP125	UART2_RxD
TP68	UART2_RI	TP126	UART2_RTS

A more detailed list of the Wandboard's TTYs is reported on its user guide
at: `http://wandboard.org/images/downloads/wandboard-user-guide-20`
`130208.pdf`.

To use these signals, we need to physically solder some wires on these test points. Since this is not an easy task for unskilled people, we'll not use the built-in Wandboard's serial ports in this book.

Implementations of serial ports

While interfaces such as **Ethernet** or **USB** send data as a serial stream, the term serial port usually identifies hardware compliant to the **RS-232** or **RS-422/RS-485** standard.

In modern computers, serial ports have been replaced by **USB-to-serial** devices due to the fact that a **RS-232** port can be easily emulated by a dedicated USB device. However, standard serial ports hardware still exists in the embedded and industrial world. The reason is quite simple: serial ports are easy to use and easy to implement (they require little supporting software from the CPU). So, serial ports are still used in applications such as industrial automation systems and remote monitoring or in some scientific instruments. It's quite easy to find industrial devices (not only a normal peripheral, but just a complete system) that use one or more serial ports to communicate with other systems.

As already stated, the most used **serial port** implementations are RS-232, RS-422, and RS-485. RS-232 was so widely used that it has been used in every PC until the USB devices made it obsolete, but it's still quite common to find a standard RS-232 port on an embedded computer nowadays.

RS-422 and RS-485 are still serial interfaces just like RS-232, but with some electrical differences in order to allow long-distance communication, provide high-noise immunity, and have multi-slave communication support.

 Explaining all serial port devices is out of the scope of this book. However, you may take a first look at
http://en.wikipedia.org/wiki/Serial_port.
In this book, we'll consider the RS-232 implementation only.

As we already saw earlier, a special case of serial ports that can be found on an embedded computer is the **TTL UARTs** (*Universal Asynchronous Receiver/Transmitter*) or **USARTs** (*Universal Synchronous/Asynchronous Receiver/Transmitter*). These devices are integrated circuit designed for implementing the interface for serial ports on PCs and embedded computers, and they are often connected to the RS-232 (or 422/485) interface by proper hardware. However, they can be found also as raw connection with a TTL interface. Serial communication at a **Transistor-Transistor Logic** (TTL) level will always remain between the limits of GND and Vcc, which is often 5V or 3.3V. A logic high (typically referred to as *1*) is represented by Vcc, while a logic low (typically referred to as *0*) is GND.

This special case of serial port is usually used for in-board serial communications where the CPU communicates with a GPRS/GPS modem, several RFID readers, and so on, and in some cases, to exchange data with an external co-processor or DSP.

The serial ports in Linux

Despite all the preceding serial ports' names, in a GNU/Linux system, all these devices are seen in the same manner (actually some differences still remain, but they are special cases), that is, they are all represented by the the devices named /dev/ttyXXX, where the XXX string may vary according to the specific serial port implementations. For instance, the historical (and standard) names of PCs' UARTserial ports are /dev/ttyS0, /dev/ttyS1, but (as seen in the previous chapters) the USB-to-serial adapters can be named as /dev/ttyUSB0, /dev/ttyUSB1 or /dev/ttyACM0, /dev/ttyACM1.

As seen earlier, the tty prefix comes from the very old abbreviation of *teletypewriter* and was originally associated only with the physical connection to a UNIX system. Now that the name also represents any serial port style device as serial ports, USB-to-serial converters, tty virtual devices, and so on.

The Linux **tty driver** core (that is implemented using a **char driver**) is responsible for controlling both the flow of data across a **tty device** and the format of the data. This is obtained using a **LDISC (line discipline)**, which is a mid layer between the upper layer (the device seen from the user space) and the lower hardware driver (the code that communicates with the hardware) that specify how the data must be processed. For example, the standard line discipline processes the data it receives according to the requirements of a UNIX terminal. So, on input, it handles special characters such as the interrupt character (typically *Ctrl+C*) and the *erase* and *kill* characters (typically Backspace or Delete, and *Ctrl+U*, respectively), and on output, it replaces all the **LF** characters with a CR/LF sequence.

Due to this fact, we cannot simply open a tty device and then start reading and writing data to it. In fact, the sent or received data will be modified by the current line discipline, so we must configure the tty device properly in order to get the right data flow. Typically, we want a clean data flow, and this mode can be achieved by setting the port into the raw mode.

In our example, we'll show you how to manage this situation.

The communication parameters

Before starting to use a serial port in order to communicate with an external serial device, we must know the communication parameters it uses, that is, which are the specific configuration settings of the serial data we wish to transfer. So, we must know the **speed**, **data-bits**, **parity**, and **stop-bits** settings.

For the speed, only fixed values are typically allowed. In fact, we must choose from 75, 110, 300, 1200, 2400, 4800, 9600, 19200, 38400, 57600, and 115200 bit/s.

In reality, other speed settings can be used. You should carefully read the datasheet of the serial device to check the allowed baud rates.

Regarding data bits, the usual setting is 8 (that is, 8 bits are used to transfer the information) even if we can choose from 6 (rarely used), 7 (for ASCII), 8, or 9 (rarely used). In the upcoming examples, I'm going to use the value 8 for this setting.

The parity bits and stop bits are deeply related to the serial communication protocol that we have not exposed here. So, you should forgive us if we don't spend much words on them. In the next example, we're going to use the None value for parity bits and 1 for stop bit.

You may get more information on parity bits and stop bits on the Internet and a good starting point is
http://en.wikipedia.org/wiki/Serial_port#Parity.

A concise way to represent the serial communication settings is, for instance, 115200,8N1, which means *115200* bit/s, *8* data bits, *No* parity bit, and *1* stop bit.

Well, these communications settings are exactly the ones we will use in the upcoming examples.

Getting access to TTYs

There're several ways to get access to a serial port in a GNU/Linux system, starting from the minicom program we used to interact with the system's serial console from the host PC. However, since in a UNIX system, *everything is a file*, we can use generic tools such as echo and cat too! However, they are not enough due the fact that we have to set up several communication settings before starting the data transmission. To do this, we can use the stty command already introduced earlier, which allow us to set up all tty devices' parameters.

Its usage is not as tricky as we may think. However, after the first approach, everything should become easier. For instance, if we wish to display the current serial port settings, we can use the following command where we use the -F option argument to specify the device to operate on:

```
root@bbb:~# stty -F /dev/ttyS2
speed 9600 baud; line = 0;
-brkint -imaxbel
```

The long and complete form is the one we can get using the -a command-line option argument.

Then, we can change the communication speed using the following command:

```
root@bbb:~# stty -F /dev/ttyS2 115200
root@bbb:~# stty -F /dev/ttyS2
speed 115200 baud; line = 0;
-brkint -imaxbel
```

Also, we can force the raw mode using the next command line:

```
root@bbb:~# stty -F /dev/ttyS2 raw
root@bbb:~# stty -F /dev/ttyS2
speed 115200 baud; line = 0;
min = 1; time = 0;
-brkint -icrnl -imaxbel
-opost
-isig -icanon
```

For further information regarding the stty command usage, you can refer to the *Linux Network Administrators Guide* at: http://www.tldp.org/LDP/nag2/x-087-2-serial-configuration.html.

Distance sensor

OK, using the `stty` command, we can set up the communication parameters. However, now, it's time to see how we can do a very simple communication with a serial device using Bash's commands. To do so, let's start using the next device, which is a sonar range finder (or ultrasonic distance sensor), with the SAMA5D3 Xplained board:

The devices can be purchased
at: `http://www.cosino.io/product/ultrasonic-distance-sensor` or by surfing the Internet.
The datasheet of this device is available
at: `http://www.maxbotix.com/documents/XL-MaxSonar-EZ_Datasheet.pd f.`

This device is really interesting due to the fact that it has several output channels useful to retrieve the measured distance. In particular, it can give us the measurement via an analog voltage channel and via a serial port; the former communication channel is not of our interest at the moment while the latter definitely is.

Let's take a look at the datasheet section where the serial output capability of our sensor is described. In particular, we read:

> ... *the Pin 5 output delivers asynchronous serial with an RS232 format, except voltages are 0-Vcc. The output is an ASCII capital "R", followed by three ASCII character digits representing the range in centimeters up to a maximum of 765, followed by a carriage return (ASCII 13). The baud rate is 9600, 8 bits, no parity, with one stop bit. Although the voltage of 0-Vcc is outside the RS232 standard, most RS232 devices have sufficient margin to read 0-Vcc serial data. If standard voltage level RS232 is desired, invert, and connect an RS232 converter...*

So, the information can be sent over a RS-232 line if we use a circuitry to invert the TTL levels of the TX signal of the sensor. The connections with the SAMA5D3 Xplained board are reported in the next diagram:

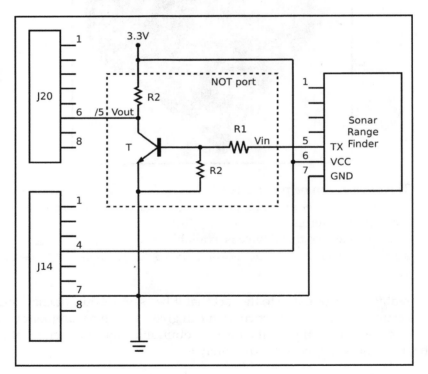

I used the resistor values R1-2,2KΩ , R$_2$=10KΩ and a BC546 transistor (T).

The functioning is quite simple; the inverting circuitry it's just a logical NOT port. When a logical *0* (a voltage near 0V) is applied to V$_{in}$, the transistor (T) is interdict. So, no current can pass through it. So, there is no voltage loss on resistor R2, and the V$_{out}$ is 3.3V (a logical *1*). On the other side, when a logical *1* (a voltage near 3.3V) is applied to V$_{in}$, the transistor (T) is turned on and a current can now flow through it and the V$_{out}$ drops down to a voltage near 0V (a logical *0*).

If we decide to use this setup for the distance sensor, from the software point of view, the job is simpler since no calibration is needed at all due to the fact that the sensor will return to us the distance in a digital format. In fact, we can get the distance simply by reading it from the serial port `/dev/ttyS1` once we set the right communication speed with the `stty` command reported here:

```
root@a5d3:~# stty -F /dev/ttyS1 9600
```

Then, the data can be displayed in real time with this command:

```
root@a5d3:~# cat /dev/ttyS1
R123
R123
. . .
```

You can stop reading using the *Ctrl-C* keys.

In this example, the measured distance is 123cm.

Even if getting access to a serial port (or to a serial device connected to it) from Bash is very useful, as we well know, for the best performance, we need to use the C language. As any other char device, we can set up the serial port using the ioctl() system call (see Chapter 3, *C Compiler, Device Drivers, and Useful Developing Techniques, Char, block and net device*). However, in order to simplify the developer's job, the libc provides us with some specific functions useful to manage the serial port configuration settings. The most used functions are tcgetattr(), cfsetispeed(), cfsetospeed(), and cfmakeraw(). The first one is used to get the current settings, the second and third ones are used to set up the communication speed, while the last one is used to set the current serial port into its raw mode in order to avoid data computation by the current line discipline (as discussed earlier).

In order to show how these functions work, let's consider the following code implementing the steps we did earlier using the stty and cat commands in order to receive the ASCII data from the distance sensor:

```
/* Open the serial device */
ret = open_serial(device);
if (ret < 0) {
    err("unable to open the serial device");
    exit(EXIT_FAILURE);
}
fd = ret;

/* Set up the serial device by setting the user defined baudrate
 * and the raw mode
 */
ret = set_serial(fd, baudrate);
if (ret < 0) {
    err("unable to setup the serial device");
    exit(EXIT_FAILURE);
}

/*
 * Do the job
 */

while (1) {
    /* Read the data from the serial port */
    ret = read(fd, buf, ARRAY_SIZE(buf));
    if (ret < 0) {
        err("error reading from the serial port");
        exit(EXIT_FAILURE);
    }
    n = ret;
```

```
    /* Check for End-Of-File condition */
    if (n == 0)
        break;

    /* Write the just read data to the stdout replacing the
     * non printable characters with a "."
     */
    for (i = 0; i < n; i++) {
        if (buf[i] == '\n' || buf[i] == '\r' ||
                isprint((int) buf[i]))
            ret = printf("%c", buf[i]);
        else
            ret = printf(".");
        if (ret < 0) {
            err("error reading from the serial port");
            exit(EXIT_FAILURE);
        }
    }

    /* Flush out the data */
    fflush(stdout);
}

close_serial(fd);
```

 The complete code is in the `chapter_07/scat/scat.c` file in the book's example code repository.

The code uses the `open_serial()` function to open the serial port requested by the user (it simply calls the `open()` system call), and then, it calls the `set_serial()` function that sets up the communication speed using the `cfsetispeed()`/`cfsetospeed()` functions and then sets the port in raw mode using the `cfmakeraw()` function. The code of the `set_serial()` function is reported here:

```
int set_serial(int fd, int rate)
{
    struct termios term;

    int ret;

    /* Sanity checks */
    switch (rate) {
    case 9600 :
        rate = B9600;
        break;
```

```
    case 19200 :
        rate = B19200;
        break;

    case 38400 :
        rate = B38400;
        break;

    case 57600 :
        rate = B57600;
        break;

    case 115200 :
        rate = B115200;
        break;

    default :           /* error */
        return -1;
    }

    ret = tcgetattr(fd, &term);
    if (ret < 0)
        return ret;

    ret = cfsetispeed(&term, rate);
    if (ret < 0)
        return ret;
    ret = cfsetospeed(&term, rate);
    if (ret < 0)
        return ret;

    cfmakeraw(&term);
    term.c_cc[VTIME] = 0;
    term.c_cc[VMIN] = 1;
    ret = tcsetattr(fd, TCSANOW, &term);

    return 0;
}
```

Then, the following steps are done using the usual `read()` and `write()` system calls as we are operating on a file.

Now, to test the code, we just need to compile it with the usual `make` command:

```
root@a5d3:~/scat# make
cc -Wall -O2 -D_GNU_SOURCE    scat.c    -o scat
```

Then, we can execute it using this command line:

```
root@a5d3:~/scat# ./scat -D /dev/ttyS1
R125
```

The distance data should now be visible in the output.

RFID LF reader

For the next example, we can use the following **RFID LF reader** that sends its data through a serial port at **TTL** 3.3V level with the BeagleBone Black board:

The device can be purchased
at: http://www.cosino.io/product/lf-rfid-low-voltage-reader or by
surfing the Internet.
The datasheet is available
at: http://www.id-innovations.com/httpdocs/ISO11785%20OEM%20modul
e%20serise%20ID2-12-20.pdf.

It can be directly connected to our BeagleBone Black at the following pins of the expansion connector *P9*, as shown in this diagram:

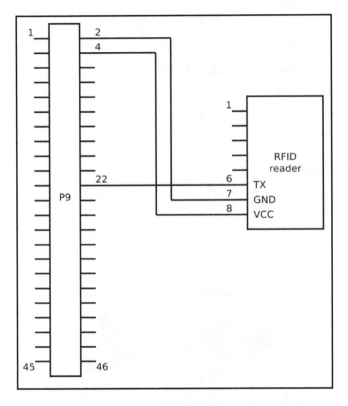

After all pins have been connected, the tags data will be available at the /dev/ttyS2 device, and in order to quickly verify it, we have to enable the serial port as we did earlier and then using the following commands to set up the communication parameters and to physically read the data:

```
root@bbb:~# stty -F /dev/ttyS2 9600 raw
root@bbb:~# cat /dev/ttyS2
```

Then, approaching a tag to the reader, we should hear a *beep* and the corresponding tag's ID should appear to the command line as follows:

```
root@bbb:~# cat /dev/ttyS2
.6F007F4E1E40
```

Looking at the datasheet, we can see that the output data sequence is done as follows:

STX (02h)	DATA (10 ASCII)	CHECK SUM (2 ASCII)	CR	LF	ETX (03h)

So, the `6F007F4E1E` string is the data, while the `40` string is the checksum.

> Even in this case, we can use the preceding `scat` program in order to read the RFID data. The command is shown here:
> ```
> root@bbb:~# ./scat -D /dev/ttyS2
> .6F007F4E1E40
> ```

The same steps can be now replied using the Python language and a possible implementation is in the `chapter_07/rfid_lf.py` file in the book's example code repository. To execute it, we have to use the following command line:

```
root@bbb:~# ./rfid_lf.py /dev/ttyS2
6F007F4E1E40
```

> It may happen that we get the following error:
> ```
> root@bbb:~# ./rfid_lf.py /dev/ttyS2
> Traceback (most recent call last):
>  File "./rfid_lf.py", line 8, in <module>
>  import serial
> ImportError: No module named serial
> ```
> In this case, we just need to install the Python serial support with the next command and then re-execute the `rfid_lf.py` program:
> ```
> root@bbb:~# aptitude install python-serial
> ```

The main function is `reader()`, which uses the `ser` object to read the data from the RFID reader:

```
def reader(ser):
    while True:
        line = ser.readline()
        line = filter(lambda x: x in string.printable, line)
        print(line.replace("\n", "")),
```

The function is really simple. In fact, `ser.realined()` gets the tag data. The `filter()` function just does some filtering actions to get human-readable characters, while the `print()` function displays the results.

The `ser` object is initialized into the main function as follows:

```
ser = serial.Serial(
    port            = dev,
    baudrate        = 9600,
    bytesize        = 8,
    parity          = 'N',
    stopbits        = 1,
    timeout         = None,
    xonxoff         = 0,
    rtscts          = 0
)
```

In the preceding code, we can find all the serial settings we did before with the `stty` command.

Managing TTY in the kernel with SLIP

We're not going to see any kernel code; let's see a nice kernel trick to use a serial communication line like it was an Ethernet cable! This can be done if we abstract the serial port as an Ethernet interface, that is, by defining a special Ethernet device that will use a serial cable to send and receive its data. This communication is done using the SLIP protocol.

The **Serial Line Internet Protocol (SLIP)** is an encapsulation of the Internet protocol designed to work over serial ports. Even if largely replaced by the **Point-to-Point Protocol (PPP)**, which is better engineered, SLIP is still the preferred way of encapsulating IP packets due to its very small overhead and simple implementation.

 Visit `https://en.wikipedia.org/wiki/Serial_Line_Internet_Protocol` for further information.

In order to do so, we need two embedded devices connected to each other through their serial ports. So, let's suppose we connect the BeagleBone Black with the SAMA5D3 Xplained using one of their UART ports as reported in the following diagram:

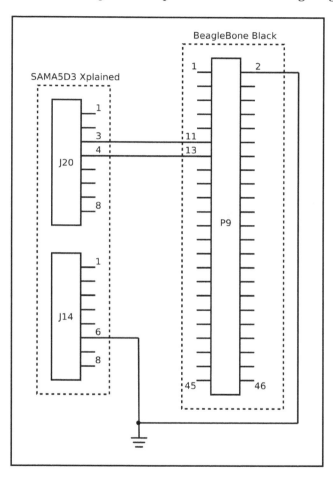

In this scenario, in the BeagleBone Black's serial communication port is /dev/ttyS4, while in the SAMA5D3 Xplained is the one named /dev/ttyS2.

Now, to test the connection, we can use the usual Bash commands, so first of all, let's enable the port on the BeagleBone Black:

```
root@bbb:~# echo BB-UART4 > /sys/devices/platform/bone_capemgr/slots
```

Then, we use the `stty` command to set the port to a reasonable communication speed and the raw mode:

```
root@bbb:~# stty -F /dev/ttyS4 115200 raw
```

Now, we have to set our two ports with the same communications settings. So, we have to copy the current configuration to the SAMA5D3 Xplained board as shown here. The first `stty` command on the BeagleBone Black gets all port settings in a format readable by the command itself to be used on the second board:

```
root@bbb:~# stty -g -F /dev/ttyS4
0:4:1cb2:8a38:3:1c:7f:15:4:0:1:0:11:13:1a:0:12:f:
17:16:0:0:0:0:0:0:0:0:0:0:0:0:0:0:0:0:0:0
```

Then, on the SAMA5D3 Xplained, we can use the following command to set the same configuration parameters:

```
root@a5d3:~# stty -F /dev/ttyS2
0:4:1cb2:8a38:3:1c:7f:15:4:0:1:0:11:13:1a:0:
12:f:17:16:0:0:0:0:0:0:0:0:0:0:0:0:0:0:0:0:0
```

Then, we can use the `cat` command on the BeagleBone Black to display the ASCII data we're going to receive from the SAMA5D3 Xplained. On the other side, we can use the usual `echo` command to send to the BeagleBone Black the data to exchange:

```
root@bbb:~# cat /dev/ttyS4
root@a5d3:~# echo TEST MESSAGE > /dev/ttyS2
```

On the BeagleBone Black, we should get the following lines of code:

```
root@bbb:~# cat /dev/ttyS4
TEST MESSAGE
```

Of course, this communication method can be used as is, but it's obviously not very useful. The real advantage would be in action if we're able to use an Ethernet communication over this serial channel, and the solution is using the SLIP protocol.

The Linux implementation of the SLIP protocol is under the `drivers/net/slip/` directory in Linux's source repository. If we take a look at the main `slip.c` file, we see that the module initialization function is `slip_init()`, which is reported here:

```
static int __init slip_init(void)
{
    int status;

    if (slip_maxdev < 4)
        slip_maxdev = 4; /* Sanity */
```

```
        printk(KERN_INFO "SLIP: version %s (dynamic channels, max=%d)"
#ifdef CONFIG_SLIP_MODE_SLIP6
                   " (6 bit encapsulation enabled)"
#endif
                   ".\n", SLIP_VERSION, slip_maxdev);
#if defined(SL_INCLUDE_CSLIP)
        printk(KERN_INFO "CSLIP: code copyright 1989 Regents
                of the University of California.\n");
#endif
#ifdef CONFIG_SLIP_SMART
        printk(KERN_INFO "SLIP linefill/keepalive option.\n");
#endif

        lip_devs =
        kzalloc(sizeof(struct net_device *)*slip_maxdev, GFP_KERNEL);
        if (!slip_devs)
            return -ENOMEM;

        /* Fill in our line protocol discipline, and register it */
        status = tty_register_ldisc(N_SLIP, &sl_ldisc);
        if (status != 0) {
            printk(KERN_ERR "SLIP: can't register line discipline
            (err = %d)\n", status);
            kfree(slip_devs);
        }
        return status;
}
```

As we can see, the function is very simple, and the main operation it does is calling the kernel function `tty_register_ldisc()`, which is used to register a new line discipline into the kernel. Once the new line discipline is successfully defined into the kernel, all the serial data passing through the designed serial port is managed by the line discipline, which, in turn, encapsulates the Ethernet traffic over the serial communication channel.

 For further information regarding the tty drivers, the line disciplines, and for everything about the serial drivers in Linux, you can take a look at the book *Linux Device Drivers, Third Edition* available at the bookshop and online at: `http://lwn.net/Kernel/LDD3/`.

Now that we know what the SLIP protocol is, we can try to establish our Ethernet communication using the serial one we tested earlier.

First of all, we have to verify and enable the SLIP support into the kernel. To do this, we must recall what we did in Chapter 1, *Installing the Developing System*, *Setting up the systems*, regarding the kernel reconfiguration, and we have to select the entries **Device Drivers**, **Network device support**, and **SLIP (serial line) support** on the kernel menu and enable the **CSLIP compressed headers**, **Keepalive and linefill**, and **Six bit SLIP encapsulation** sub options, as shown in the following screenshot:

```
.config - Linux/arm 4.4.6 Kernel Configuration
> Device Drivers > Network device support
                         Network device support
    Arrow keys navigate the menu.  <Enter> selects submenus ---> (or empty
    submenus ----).  Highlighted letters are hotkeys.  Pressing <Y>
    includes, <N> excludes, <M> modularizes features.  Press <Esc><Esc> to
    exit, <?> for Help, </> for Search.  Legend: [*] built-in  [ ]

         < >    PPP (point-to-point protocol) support
         <M>    SLIP (serial line) support
         [*]    CSLIP compressed headers
         [*]    Keepalive and linefill
         [*]    Six bit SLIP encapsulation
         <*>    USB Network Adapters   --->
         [*]    Wireless LAN   --->
                *** Enable WiMAX (Networking options) to see the WiMAX driv
         [ ]    Wan interfaces support  ----
         [ ]    ISDN support  ----

            <Select>    < Exit >    < Help >    < Save >    < Load >
```

Then, we have to save, recompile, and then reinstall the kernel. When the new kernel is up and running, we have to use the slattach command to change the default line discipline with the one implementing SLIP:

```
root@bbb:~# slattach -p slip -s 9600 /dev/ttyS4 &
[1] 1193
SLIP: version 0.8.4-NET3.019-NEWTTY (dynamic channel.
CSLIP: code copyright 1989 Regents of the University of Californ.
SLIP linefill/keepalive option.
```

The output reported after the `slattach` command with the prefix `SLIP` or `CSLIP` is not generated by the command itself, but they're kernel messages, so they are not visible if we give the command outside the serial console. If this is the case, you can read these messages with the usual `dmesg` or `tail -f` command useful to read the kernel messages.

Then, a new Ethernet interface named `sl0` should now be available:

```
root@bbb:~# ifconfig sl0
sl0       Link encap:Serial Line IP
          POINTOPOINT NOARP MULTICAST  MTU:296  Metric:1
          RX packets:0 errors:0 dropped:0 overruns:0 frame:0
          TX packets:0 errors:0 dropped:0 overruns:0 carrier:0
          collisions:0 txqueuelen:10
          RX bytes:0 (0.0 B)  TX bytes:0 (0.0 B)
```

At this point, we have to perform the same steps on the SAMA5D3 Xplained board:

```
root@a5d3:~# slattach -p slip -s 9600 /dev/ttyS2 &
[1] 1703
root@a5d3:~# ifconfig sl0
sl0       Link encap:Serial Line IP
          POINTOPOINT NOARP MULTICAST  MTU:296  Metric:1
          RX packets:0 errors:0 dropped:0 overruns:0 frame:0
          TX packets:0 errors:0 dropped:0 overruns:0 carrier:0
          collisions:0 txqueuelen:10
          RX bytes:0 (0.0 B)  TX bytes:0 (0.0 B)
```

Then, we have to configure two new interfaces in such a way they have the same subnet. On the BeagleBone Black, we do the following:

```
root@bbb:~# ifconfig sl0 192.168.100.1 pointopoint 192.168.100.2
```

On the SAMA5D3 Xplained, we do the same settings, but swap the IP addresses:

```
root@a5d3:~# ifconfig sl0 192.168.100.2 pointopoint 192.168.100.1
```

Now, the two boards should be connected, and we can test the new Ethernet-over-serial communication channel using the `ping` command:

```
root@a5d3:~# ping 192.168.100.2
PING 192.168.100.2 (192.168.100.2) 56(84) bytes of data.
64 bytes from 192.168.100.2: icmp_seq=1 ttl=64 time=0.244 ms
64 bytes from 192.168.100.2: icmp_seq=2 ttl=64 time=0.141 ms
64 bytes from 192.168.100.2: icmp_seq=3 ttl=64 time=0.140 ms
...
```

Great! It works. However, it is not finished here. Since the `s10` interfaces are generic Ethernet devices, we can log in from the SAMA5D3 Xplained to the BeagleBone Black using the `ssh` command as shown here:

```
root@a5d3:~# ssh root@192.168.100.2
The authenticity of host '192.168.100.2 (192.168.100.2)' can't be
 established.
ECDSA key fingerprint is
73:9a:d3:0b:ce:9c:f2:32:83:ab:a9:9a:11:47:82:68.
Are you sure you want to continue connecting (yes/no)? yes
Warning: Permanently added '192.168.100.2'
(ECDSA) to the list of known hosts.
root@192.168.100.2's password:
The programs included with the Debian GNU/Linux system are free
software; the exact distribution terms for each program are
described in the individual files in /usr/share/doc/*/copyright.
Debian GNU/Linux comes with ABSOLUTELY NO WARRANTY, to the extent
permitted by applicable law.
Last login: Sat Apr  2 17:42:28 2016 from 192.168.8.1
root@a5d3:~#
```

Now, the serial channel works like an Ethernet one (apart from the communication speed and the fact that it's limited to a point-to-point conversation).

Summary

Serial ports and serial devices are two of the most important concepts of an embedded computer, but tons of other peripherals exist. You should try to modify the example programs in this chapter in order to fit your needs, or you can go directly to the upcoming sections where we'll introduce new devices.

You've seen how to set up the communication parameters from the command line or using the C or Python language, and you saw how to manage the data flow from the serial devices. Also, we took a look at the SLIP line discipline in order to establish an Ethernet-over-serial port communication.

In the next chapter, we will take a look at the USB that allows people to connect several kinds of electronic devices to a computer through the same port, for instance, a hard disk, a keyboard, or a serial device, as just seen in this chapter.

8
Universal Serial Bus - USB

Now, it's time to take a look at the Universal Serial Bus, that is, a versatile bus widely used in modern PCs that allows people to connect an electronic device to a computer. For instance, a hard disk, a keyboard, or a serial device (as seen in the previous chapter) can be all connected to a computer through the same USB port.

After a brief introduction about what this bus is and how it works, we'll show you the different types of USB devices and how they are supported in the Linux kernel. We'll see how our embedded kits can act as USB hosts in order to manage a barcode reader and how we can use the BeagleBone Black as a USB device in order to exchange data with a host PC. In this case, we will show the multi gadget and the configfs one which allows the developer to switch between different functions dynamically.

What is the universal serial bus?

The **Universal Serial Bus** (**USB**) is a computer bus used by a CPU and its peripherals to communicate to each other. In every USB communication, at least one USB host and one USB device exists. The former is the one that effectively directs the traffic flow to devices, while the latter is the one that simply answers all the host's requests.

Practically, the USB host periodically queries all connected USB devices in order to discover if they want to send a message to it. So, the host is smart enough to understand which kind of peripheral the user has connected in, and it can reconfigure the system in order to correctly manage it. This magic happens each time a USB device is first connected to a USB host, thanks to the *enumeration process*.

The enumeration starts by sending a reset signal to the USB device (at this stage, the data rate of the USB device is automatically determined), and after the reset, all the information of the USB device is read by the host and then the peripheral device is unequivocally identified. At this stage, if the system has a proper device driver to manage the peripheral, it will load the driver and then the device is set to a *configured state*. If the USB host is restarted, the enumeration process is repeated for all connected devices.

 You can get further information on USB internals on the Internet where a good starting point would be: http://simple.wikipedia.org/wiki/Universal_Serial_Bus.

For instance, if we connect a USB keyboard to the Wandboard and we monitor the kernel messages, we should see something like this:

```
usb 1-1: new low-speed USB device number 2 using ci_hdrc
```

Here, the *enumeration process* ends when the device number 2 is assigned to the new device. Then, the system continues reading the information of the new device:

```
usb 1-1: New USB device found, idVendor=046d, idProduct=c312
usb 1-1: New USB device strings: Mfr=1, Product=2, SerialNumber=0
usb 1-1: Product: USB Multimedia Keyboard
usb 1-1: Manufacturer: LITEON Technology
```

At this point, the host has read all the information, and then, it sets the device configuration. In particular, we should notice the vendor ID (idVendor) and the product ID (idProduct) numbers; these are the ones that specify the device function into the kernel.

Now, the kernel has all that it needs to try to load a proper device driver, in fact, we see in the kernel messages:

```
input: LITEON Technology USB Multimedia Keyboard as
/devices/soc0/soc/2100000.aips-bus/2184200.usb/ci_hdrc.1/usb1/1-1/1-
1:1.0/0003:046D:C312.0001/input/input0
hid-generic 0003:046D:C312.0001: input,hidraw0: USB HID v1.10 Keyboard
[LITEON Technology USB Multimedia Keyboard] on usb-ci_hdrc.1-1/input0
```

OK, after this stage, the input driver input0 is loaded. It is the right one to manage a keyboard.

The electrical lines

USB port lines are reported in the following table:

Name	Description
D+	Data positive
D-	Data negative
Vcc	Power line at 5V
GND	Common ground

 Note that this table refers to **USB 1.1** and **USB 2.0** standards only, since starting from **USB 3.x**, more signals have been added.

As a special feature, the **USB** bus includes the **Vcc** signal too. This is because it can power the devices directly from the bus.

USB ports on the BeagleBone Black

The BeagleBone Black has two accessible ports: one USB host port and one USB device port we've already used in Chapter 1, *Installing the Developing System* The BeagleBone Black. Both ports are USB 2.0 compliant.

USB ports on the SAMA5D3 Xplained

On the SAMA5D3 Xplained, accessible ports are two USB host ports and one USB device port we've already used in Chapter 1, *Installing the Development System* USB ports on the Wandboard The SAMA5D3 Xplained. All ports are USB 2.0 compliant.

USB ports on the Wandboard

The Wandboard has a configuration similar to the BeagleBone Black, that is, it has two accessible ports: one USB host port and one USB device port we've already used in Chapter 1, *Installing the Development System* The Wandboard (in reality, this port can act as an OTG USB port, but this feature is not covered by this book).

Both ports are USB 2.0 compliant (even if the USB host connector is USB 3.0 compliant, we never plugged USB 3.0 devices to it).

The USB bus in Linux

As already stated, both USB host and USB device exist, and the same is valid for the Linux kernel where we can find dedicated device drivers for both types. The only difference is that in the kernel, USB devices are named USB gadgets to avoid misunderstanding with the typical meaning of the word *device*.

USB hosts are all those devices that act as a master in a USB communication. Typically, a PC or an embedded computer acts as a master, but an embedded computer can act as a USB gadget too! If you recall what we saw in `Chapter 1`, *Installing a Development System*, where we described how to set up our embedded devices, embedded kits were the USB gadgets while the host PC was the USB host.

The USB communication is very simple: there is a master that polls the various peripheral devices. This poll is done using several channels called **endpoints** that can carry data in one direction only, either from the host computer to the device (so, the endpoint is called **OUT endpoint**) or from the device to the host computer (so, the endpoint is called **IN endpoint**).

Along with the direction, a USB endpoint can be also classified by considering how the data is transmitted by it. So, there're four different endpoint types:

- **Control**: Control endpoints are commonly used to configure the device and/or retrieve information about the device. Every USB device must have a control endpoint called endpoint 0 which is used by the USB subsystem to configure the device as soon as it has inserted into the system.

  These endpoints are used for asynchronous data transfers.

- **Interrupt**: Interrupt endpoints are used to emulate the interrupt line we can find in every CPU. It can transfer small amounts of data at a fixed rate every time the USB host asks the device for data. Due to their specific task, these transfers are guaranteed by the USB protocol to always have enough reserved bandwidth to make it through.

  These endpoints are used for synchronous data transfers.

- **Bulk:** Bulk endpoints are used to transfer large amounts of data (a lot more than interrupt endpoints), and they are very common for devices that need to transfer any data that must get through with no data loss, but with no guarantee by the USB protocol to always make it through in a specific amount of time.

  These endpoints used for asynchronous data transfers are definitely not suitable for real-time data, such as audio and video devices, but they are used in printers, and storage and network devices.

- **Isochronous** endpoints exist to fill the gap left by the bulk endpoints, which is the ability to transfer large amounts of data in real time. The data loss may happen; only transfer time is guaranteed.

  These endpoints used for synchronous data transfers are common in audio and video devices.

Acting as a host

All our embedded machines have a USB host port, so of course, they can act as hosts. Nothing special to do here since the proper driver is already up and running in the default kernel configurations, and we can have several possibilities. We can use USB keys or external hard disks as storage devices, or we can use an USB to serial converter (as we saw in the first chapter), a USB keyboard or mouse as the input device, a USB Wi-Fi dongle, and so on (the list can be very long!).

As a real, simple, and educational example, we will see how to use a USB barcode reader with the Wandboard, but, of course, we can use another system we wish to use since the procedure is almost the same.

There are tons of device classes, and all of them work in the same manner. However, we have to choose one, so we will use this device:

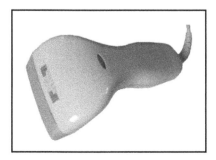

The device can be purchased at:
`http://www.cosino.io/product/usb-barcode-reader` or by surfing the Internet.

This device class simply acts as a normal USB keyboard. In fact, the result of using this device is that the string, corresponding to the just read the barcode ID, appears in the system as it was inserted through a keyboard. OK, it's simpler showing how it works than explaining it!

When we connect the reader to the Wandboard, we should see something like this in the kernel messages:

```
usb 1-1: new low-speed USB device number 2 using ci_hdrc
usb 1-1: New USB device found, idVendor=0d3d, idProduct=0001
usb 1-1: New USB device strings: Mfr=0, Product=2, SerialNumber=0
usb 1-1: Product: USBPS2
input: USBPS2 as /devices/soc0/soc/2100000.aips-
bus/2184200.usb/ci_hdrc.1/usb1/1-1/1-1:1.0/0003:0D3D:0001.0001
/input/input0
hid-generic 0003:0D3D:0001.0001: input,hidraw0: USB HID
v1.00 Keyboard [USBPS2] on usb-ci_hdrc.1-1/input0
input: USBPS2 as /devices/soc0/soc/2100000.aips-
bus/2184200.usb/ci_hdrc.1/usb1/1-1/1-1:1.1/0003:0D3D:0001.0002/
input/input1
hid-generic 0003:0D3D:0001.0002: input,hidraw1: USB HID v1.00
Mouse [USBPS2] on usb-ci_hdrc.1-1/input1
```

Note that the output may differ a bit even if we are using the same device. I'm showing in this example due to the fact that there are different versions of the same reader.

As we can see the system thinks a keyboard has been connected in and, as reported into the kernel messages, the new input device `input1` should appears in the `/sys/class/input` directory:

```
root@wb:~# ls /sys/class/input/input1/
capabilities    event1   modalias   name    power        subsystem   uniq
device          id       mouse0     phys    properties   uevent
```

Ok, the device is up and running! Now, to test it, we can use two ways: the first one is using the evtest tool already seen in Chapter 6, *General Purposes Input Output signals* GPIO An input device by using GPIOs, which is useful to test every input device. We can just run it, as shown here, and then choose the right device:

```
root@wb:~# evtest
No device specified, trying to scan all of /dev/input/event*
Available devices:
/dev/input/event0:       USBPS2
/dev/input/event1:       USBPS2
Select the device event number [0-1]:
```

Our device is /dev/input/event0, so let's enter 0 and we should get the following output:

```
Input driver version is 1.0.1
Input device ID: bus 0x3 vendor 0xd3d product 0x1 version 0x100
Input device name: "USBPS2"
Supported events:
  Event type 0 (EV_SYN)
  Event type 1 (EV_KEY)
    Event code 1 (KEY_ESC)
    Event code 2 (KEY_1)
. . .
    Event code 240 (KEY_UNKNOWN)
  Event type 4 (EV_MSC)
    Event code 4 (MSC_SCAN)
  Event type 17 (EV_LED)
    Event code 0 (LED_NUML)
    Event code 1 (LED_CAPSL)
    Event code 2 (LED_SCROLLL)
    Event code 3 (LED_COMPOSE)
    Event code 4 (LED_KANA)
 Key repeat handling:
  Repeat type 20 (EV_REP)
    Repeat code 0 (REP_DELAY)
      Value    250
    Repeat code 1 (REP_PERIOD)
      Value     33
Properties:
Testing ... (interrupt to exit)
```

Now, we can try to read whatever we wish. However, as an example, we can try to read this barcode:

In this case, we should get the following output:

```
Event: time 1468839598.795172, type 4 (EV_MSC), code 4 (MSC_SCAN),
value 700e1
Event: time 1468839598.795172, type 1 (EV_KEY), code 42
(KEY_LEFTSHIFT), value 1
Event: time 1468839598.795172, -------------- EV_SYN -------------
Event: time 1468839598.803175, type 4 (EV_MSC), code 4 (MSC_SCAN),
value 70017
Event: time 1468839598.803175, type 1 (EV_KEY), code 20 (KEY_T),
value 1
Event: time 1468839598.803175, -------------- EV_SYN -------------
Event: time 1468839598.811160, type 4 (EV_MSC), code 4 (MSC_SCAN),
value 70017
Event: time 1468839598.811160, type 1 (EV_KEY), code 20 (KEY_T),
value 0
...
Event: time 1468839599.003167, type 4 (EV_MSC), code 4 (MSC_SCAN),
value 70008
Event: time 1468839599.003167, type 1 (EV_KEY), code 18 (KEY_E),
value 1
Event: time 1468839599.003167, -------------- EV_SYN -------------
Event: time 1468839599.011159, type 4 (EV_MSC), code 4 (MSC_SCAN),
value 70008
Event: time 1468839599.011159, type 1 (EV_KEY), code 18 (KEY_E),
value 0
Event: time 1468839599.011159, -------------- EV_SYN -------------
Event: time 1468839599.019168, type 4 (EV_MSC), code 4 (MSC_SCAN),
value 70028
Event: time 1468839599.019168, type 1 (EV_KEY), code 28 (KEY_ENTER),
value 1
Event: time 1468839599.019168, -------------- EV_SYN -------------
Event: time 1468839599.027176, type 4 (EV_MSC), code 4 (MSC_SCAN),
```

```
value 70028
Event: time 1468839599.027176, type 1 (EV_KEY), code 28 (KEY_ENTER),
value 0
Event: time 1468839599.027176, -------------- EV_SYN ------------
```

If we try to read the keys sequence, we can recognize that the input device has received the `test barcode` input string followed by an *Enter* key. However, even if this a good way to test the device, it's definitely not the best way to use the device. So, we can use the second method, that is, using the code held in the `chapter_08/key_read.py` file in the book's example code repository. This program uses the Python `evdev` library that can be installed using the following command line:

root@wb:~# pip install evdev

The program is really simple, and the most interesting part is where we use the `evdev` library to read the data. A snippet of such code is reported here:

```python
# Now read data from the input device printing only letters and
numbers
# Try to open the input device
 try:
        dev = InputDevice(args[0])
 except:
        print("invalid input device", args[0], file=sys.stderr)
        sys.exit(1);

# Now read data from the input device printing only letters and
numbers
while True:
        r, w, x = select([dev], [], [])
        for event in dev.read():
                # Print key pressed events only
                if event.type == ecodes.EV_KEY and
                event.value==1:
                        print(keys[event.code], end = "")
                    sys.stdout.flush()        # needed by print()
```

Using the `InputDevice()` function, we get an input device handler of the device passed in by the user. Then, we wait for an input event (`EV_KEY`) with `select()`, and when it arrives, we read and decode it. In the end, we just print its data using the `keys` lookup table.

If we run the program using the following command and we retry to scan the preceding barcode, we should get the following output:

```
root@wb:~# ./key_read.py /dev/input/event0
.test..barcode.
```

 Note that we should press *CTRL+C* keys to kill the process.

Acting as a device

Acting as a host is, of course, very important due to the fact that we can easily expand our embedded platform in a reasonable and easy way. However, from the developer's point of view, an interesting functionality that a GNU/Linux embedded system can offer is the possibility to act as a USB device using the USB gadget subsystem. This permits us to use our embedded system as, for example, a USB key to store a complete filesystem or allow a serial/Ethernet communication between another PC over a normal USB cable.

In the first chapter for the SAMA5D3 Xplained and the Wandboard, we already used the USB serial communication in order to get connected with Linux's serial console. In these special cases, we used the serial port and the Ethernet port of the CDCgadget, that is, the `/dev/ttyACM0` serial device and the `usb0` Ethernet device. However, several other gadgets' devices can be used into our embedded board. In particular, we can use the old style (legacy) gadgets and the new style (function) gadgets. The former are available under the `/lib/modules/$(uname -r)/kernel/drivers/usb/gadget/legacy` directory, while the latter are under the `/lib/modules/$(uname - r)/kernel/drivers/usb/gadget/function` directory.

However, first of all, we have to verify and enable the USB gadget's support to the kernel. To do this, we must recall what we did in Chapter 1, *Installing the Developing System* Setting up the developing system regarding the kernel reconfiguration. We have to select the entries **Device Drivers**, **USB support**, and **USB Gadget Support** in the kernel menu and enable all the sub options, as shown in the following screenshot:

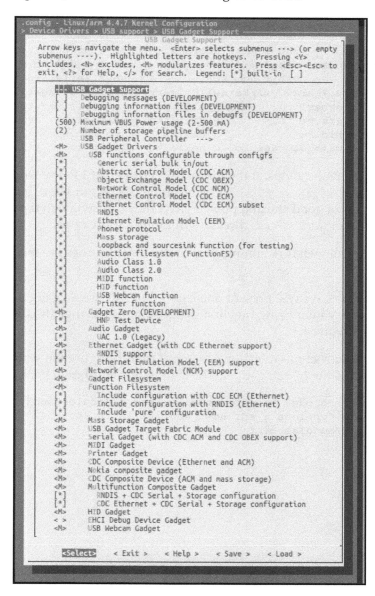

Then, we have to save, recompile, and then reinstall the kernel. When finished, these directories contain the result on the Wandboard:

```
root@wb:~# ls /lib/modules/$(uname
-r)/kernel/drivers/usb/gadget/{function,legacy}
/lib/modules/4.4.7-armv7-x6/kernel/drivers/usb/gadget/function:
u_ether.ko            usb_f_fs.ko            usb_f_obex.ko
usb_f_ss_lb.ko
usb_f_acm.ko          usb_f_hid.ko          usb_f_phonet.ko    usb_f_uac1.ko
usb_f_ecm.ko          usb_f_mass_storage.ko usb_f_printer.ko   usb_f_uac2.ko
usb_f_ecm_subset.ko   usb_f_midi.ko         usb_f_rndis.ko     usb_f_uvc.ko
usb_f_eem.ko          usb_f_ncm.ko          usb_f_serial.ko    u_serial.ko
/lib/modules/4.4.7-armv7-x6/kernel/drivers/usb/gadget/legacy:
g_acm_ms.ko   g_ether.ko          g_midi.ko    g_printer.ko   tcm_usb_gadget.ko
gadgetfs.ko   g_ffs.ko            g_multi.ko   g_serial.ko
g_audio.ko    g_hid.ko            g_ncm.ko     g_webcam.ko
g_cdc.ko      g_mass_storage.ko   g_nokia.ko   g_zero.ko
```

You can take a look at the Linux USB Gadget API Framework at `http://w
ww.linux-usb.org/gadget/` (the guide is a bit outdated, but it still
remains a good starting point). Then, they can switch to the
`Documentation/usb` directory in Linux's source tree.

Legacy gadgets are still well functioning, even if the function ones are recommended for the new applications.

In the next two sections, we will present one legacy but still usable gadget, the Multi gadget, and then a very interesting function gadget that can change its configuration dynamically at user request.

Note that after these kernel modifications, we need to reconfigure the system in order to ask the kernel to auto load the `g_cdc` gadget. The commands are shown here:

```
root@wb:~# echo "g_cdc" >> /etc/modules-load.d/modules.conf
root@wb:~# echo "options g_cdc host_addr=62:1e:f6:88:9b:42" >>
/etc/modprobe.d/modules.conf
```

The Multi gadget

The Multi gadget (and its subset, the CDC gadget) implement at once a USB storage, and a serial and an Ethernet communication channel.

Note that on some boards, this gadget cannot be used due to the limited available endpoints of the USB device controller of the running CPU. On our SAMA5D3 Xplained, we get the following lines of code:

```
root@a5d3:~# modprobe -r g_cdc
root@a5d3:~# modprobe g_multi
modprobe: ERROR: could not insert 'g_multi': Invalid
argument
```

With the corresponding kernel message given here:

```
g_multi 500000.gadget: failed to start g_multi: -22
```

First of all, we must unload the default gadget driver g_cdc that is loaded at boot. We can verify that g_cdc is running by using the lsmod command to list all the currently loaded modules:

```
root@wb:~# lsmod | grep g_cdc
g_cdc                   4151  0
u_ether                14413  2 g_cdc,usb_f_ecm
libcomposite           53784  3 g_cdc,usb_f_acm,usb_f_ecm
```

Now, to unload it, we can use the modprobe command with the -r option argument as shown here:

```
root@wb:~# modprobe -r g_cdc
```

OK, now, we can create a new file that will represent our USB storage. Using the following command line, we create a zero filled file of 64 MB size:

```
root@wb:~# dd if=/dev/zero of=/opt/mass_storage bs=1M count=64
64+0 records in
64+0 records out
67108864 bytes (67 MB) copied, 0.557685 s, 120 MB/s
```

Now, everything is in place. Just reload the `g_multi` driver with the following command line that specifies to the kernel that the storage file is now the one we just created and that specifies a device Ethernet address as the one we used with `g_cdc`:

```
root@wb:~# modprobe g_multi host_addr=62:1e:f6:88:9b:42
file=/opt/mass_storage ro=0
```

After executing the preceding command, we should see something like this on the kernel messages:

```
using random self ethernet address
using random host ethernet address
using host ethernet address: 62:1e:f6:88:9b:42
using random self ethernet address
using random host ethernet address
using host ethernet address: 62:1e:f6:88:9b:42
usb0: HOST MAC 62:1e:f6:88:9b:42
usb0: MAC 8e:b9:5e:db:9c:4b
Mass Storage Function, version: 2009/09/11
LUN: removable file: (no medium)
LUN: file: /opt/mass_storage
Number of LUNs=1
g_multi gadget: Multifunction Composite Gadget
g_multi gadget: userspace failed to provide iSerialNumber
g_multi gadget: g_multi ready
IPv6: ADDRCONF(NETDEV_UP): usb0: link is not ready
g_multi gadget: high-speed config #2: Multifunction with CDC ECM
IPv6: ADDRCONF(NETDEV_CHANGE): usb0: link becomes ready
```

On the host PC, we should see these kernel messages (if we have plugged in the USB cable):

```
usb 2-1.1: new high-speed USB device number 57 using ehci-pci
usb 2-1.1: New USB device found, idVendor=1d6b, idProduct=0104
usb 2-1.1: New USB device strings: Mfr=3, Product=4, SerialNumber=0
usb 2-1.1: Product: Multifunction Composite Gadget
usb 2-1.1: Manufacturer: Linux 4.4.7-armv7-x6 with 2184000.usb
```

Here, the new composite device has been detected and enumerated, while these are the kernel messages related to the new Ethernet device:

```
cdc_ether 2-1.1:2.0 usb0: register 'cdc_ether' at usb-0000:00:1d.0-1.1, CDC
Ethernet Device, 62:1e:f6:88:9b:42
cdc_acm 2-1.1:2.2: ttyACM0: USB ACM device
```

Then, a mass storage device is detected:

```
usb-storage 2-1.1:2.4: USB Mass Storage device detected
scsi host7: usb-storage 2-1.1:2.4
scsi 7:0:0:0: Direct-Access     Linux     File-Stor Gadget 0404 PQ:
0 ANSI: 2
sd 7:0:0:0: Attached scsi generic sg3 type 0
sd 7:0:0:0: [sdd] 131072 512-byte logical blocks: (67.1 MB/64.0 MiB)
sd 7:0:0:0: [sdd] Write Protect is off
sd 7:0:0:0: [sdd] Mode Sense: 0f 00 00 00
sd 7:0:0:0: [sdd] Write cache: enabled, read cache: enabled,
doesn't support DPO or FUA
sd 7:0:0:0: [sdd] Attached SCSI disk
```

As we can see preceding the host PC has found a 64 MB disk with an invalid partition table. This is quite obvious due the fact that the device is filled by zeros.

So, we just need to format the new disk by creating a FAT disk on the Wandboard:

```
# mkfs.vfat -i WB -I /dev/sdd
mkfs.fat 3.0.28 (2015-05-16)
```

Now, to test the new storage device, we can mount it and then write a test file on it:

```
# mount /dev/sdd /mnt/
# echo TEST_PC > /mnt/file_pc.txt
# ls /mnt/
file_pc.txt*
```

Now, we can unmount the disk and then mount it on the Wandboard filesystem in order to re-read the preceding file:

```
root@wb:~# mount -o loop /opt/mass_storage /mnt/
root@wb:~# ls /mnt/
file_pc.txt
root@wb:~# cat /mnt/file_pc.txt
TEST_PC
```

A dual action can now be done within the Wandboard by creating another file with the following command:

```
root@wb:~# echo TEST_WB > /mnt/file_wb.txt
```

Now, the disk can be unmounted and then remounted on the host PC in order to verify that the new file is present.

The configfs gadget

In early gadgets implementations, there was the **GadgetFS**, which is a monolithic kernel driver that provides an interface to implement user-space gadgets (this gadget is still present in the `legacy` directory). Then, a successive rewrite of GadgetFS, the **FunctionFS**, was released to support user-space gadget functions that can be combined into a USB-composite gadget. Then, the **gadget** configfs is the last version of this infrastructure. This is an interface that allows the definition of arbitrary functions and configurations to define an application specific USB composite device from the user space. The trick is quite interesting since this new filesystem allows user-space instantiation of kernel object.

Let's see how it works by replying to the multi gadget. First of all, we have to unload the `g_cdc` module loaded at boot and then mount the new filesystem into a proper directory. By default, this directory is `/sys/kernel/config`:

```
root@wb:~# mount -t configfs none /sys/kernel/config
```

 If we get the following error, it means that the filesystem is already mounted and we can safely skip the preceding command:
`mount: none is already mounted or /sys/kernel/config busy`

Then, we have to go into the `configfs` directory relative to the USB gadget devices:

```
root@wb:~# cd /sys/kernel/config/usb_gadget/
```

The trick now is the fact that we can create new gadget devices just by creating new directories! In fact, to build up our first gadget device, we can use the following command:

```
root@wb:/sys/kernel/config/usb_gadget# mkdir g1
```

Then, we have to enter our new directory or device to see its attributes:

```
root@wb:/sys/kernel/config/usb_gadget# cd g1
root@wb:/sys/kernel/config/usb_gadget/g1# ls
bcdDevice bDeviceClass  bDeviceSubClass   configs idProduct  os_desc   UDC
bcdUSB    bDeviceProtocol bMaxPacketSize0 functions idVendor   strings
```

As we can see here, we can find several files whose names recall the USB devices' attributes, so as the first step, we can set our vendor and product IDs as the ones of the Multi gadget:

```
root@wb:/sys/kernel/config/usb_gadget/g1# echo 0x1d6b > idVendor
root@wb:/sys/kernel/config/usb_gadget/g1# echo 0x0104 > idProduct
```

A gadget also needs its serial number, manufacturer, and product strings. In order to have a place to store them, a strings subdirectory must be created for each language. For example, the following command defines the English language strings (code `0x409`):

```
root@wb:/sys/kernel/config/usb_gadget/g1# mkdir strings/0x409
```

Then, we will set the strings values:

```
root@wb:/sys/kernel/config/usb_gadget/g1# echo "0" >
strings/0x409/serialnumber
root@wb:/sys/kernel/config/usb_gadget/g1# echo
"Linux 4.4.7-armv7-x6 with 2184000.usb" > strings/0x409/manufacturer
root@wb:/sys/kernel/config/usb_gadget/g1# echo
"Multifunction Composite Gadget" > strings/0x409/product
```

Now, we have to create a configuration for our gadget. Each gadget will consist of a number of configurations that correspond to directories to be created with their strings and attributes:

```
root@wb:/sys/kernel/config/usb_gadget/g1# mkdir
configs/multi.1
root@wb:/sys/kernel/config/usb_gadget/g1# mkdir
configs/multi.1/strings/0x409
root@wb:/sys/kernel/config/usb_gadget/g1# echo "USB Multi config" >
configs/multi.1/strings/0x409/configuration
root@wb:/sys/kernel/config/usb_gadget/g1# echo 120 >
configs/multi.1/MaxPower
```

The gadget will provide some functions, and for each function, its corresponding directory must be created in the same manner as done earlier. Also, we must consider that each function provides its specific set of attributes that must be properly set. In our case, to add the Ethernet over USB function, we have to use these commands:

```
root@wb:/sys/kernel/config/usb_gadget/g1# mkdir functions/ecm.usb0
root@wb:/sys/kernel/config/usb_gadget/g1# echo '62:1e:f6:88:9b:42' >
functions/ecm.usb0/host_addr
```

In the preceding command, we set the `host_addr` attribute as we did before for the `g_cdc` gadget. Then, it's the turn of the mass storage function:

```
root@wb:/sys/kernel/config/usb_gadget/g1# mkdir
functions/mass_storage.1
root@wb:/sys/kernel/config/usb_gadget/g1# echo /opt/mass_storage >
functions/mass_storage.1/lun.0/file
```

Again, the file attribute must be set to point the file we're going to use as storage memory (we used the same file earlier). Then, the last step is the turn of the serial channel where we did not set any attribute due to the fact that we leave the default settings:

```
root@wb:/sys/kernel/config/usb_gadget/g1# mkdir functions/acm.1
```

At this moment, our gadget is created. Also, we have a number of configurations specified and a number of functions available. What remains to do is specifying which function is available in which configuration (the same function can be used in multiple configurations) for each gadget. This is achieved by creating the symbolic links as shown here:

```
root@wb:/sys/kernel/config/usb_gadget/g1# ln -s
functions/ecm.usb0 configs/multi.1
root@wb:/sys/kernel/config/usb_gadget/g1# ln -s
functions/mass_storage.1 configs/multi.1
root@wb:/sys/kernel/config/usb_gadget/g1# ln -s
functions/acm.1 configs/multi.1
```

Now, our new gadget is really ready. We just need to activate it by bounding it to a **USB Device Controller (UDC)**. The list of available controllers is in the `/sys/class/udc/` directory:

```
root@wb:/sys/kernel/config/usb_gadget/g1# ls /sys/class/udc/
ci_hdrc.0
```

In the Wandboard, we have just one UDC, so the command to enable the gadget is shown here:

```
root@wb:/sys/kernel/config/usb_gadget/g1# cd ..
root@wb:/sys/kernel/config/usb_gadget# echo "ci_hdrc.0" > g1/UDC
```

If everything works well in the kernel of the Wandboard, we should see the following messages:

```
usb0: HOST MAC 62:1e:f6:88:9b:42
usb0: MAC 9e:4a:8e:06:94:81
IPv6: ADDRCONF(NETDEV_UP): usb0: link is not ready
configfs-gadget gadget: high-speed config #1: multi
IPv6: ADDRCONF(NETDEV_CHANGE): usb0: link becomes ready
```

Also, on the host PC, we should see the new USB device, which is a clone of `g_multi`:

```
$ lsusb -v -d 1d6b:0104
Bus 002 Device 013: ID 1d6b:0104 Linux Foundation Multifunction
Composite Gadget
Couldn't open device, some information will be missing
Device Descriptor:
  bLength                18
  bDescriptorType         1
  bcdUSB               2.00
  bDeviceClass            0 (Defined at Interface level)
  bDeviceSubClass         0
  bDeviceProtocol         0
  bMaxPacketSize0        64
  idVendor           0x1d6b Linux Foundation
  idProduct          0x0104 Multifunction Composite Gadget
  bcdDevice            4.04
  iManufacturer           1
  iProduct                2
  iSerial                 3
  bNumConfigurations      1
...
```

In the kernel messages of the host PC, we should see the next message where we can verify that all the three functions are active:

```
usb 2-1.1: new high-speed USB device number 13 using ehci-pci
usb 2-1.1: New USB device found, idVendor=1d6b, idProduct=0104
usb 2-1.1: New USB device strings: Mfr=1, Product=2, SerialNumber=3
usb 2-1.1: Product: Multifunction Composite Gadget
usb 2-1.1: Manufacturer: Linux 4.4.7-armv7-x6 with 2184000.usb
usb 2-1.1: SerialNumber: 0
cdc_ether 2-1.1:1.0 usb0: register 'cdc_ether' at
usb-0000:00:1d.0-1.1, CDC Ethernet Device, 62:1e:f6:88:9b:42
usb-storage 2-1.1:1.2: USB Mass Storage device detected
scsi host10: usb-storage 2-1.1:1.2
cdc_acm 2-1.1:1.3: ttyACM0: USB ACM device
cdc_ether 2-1.1:1.0 enp0s29u1u1: renamed from usb0
IPv6: ADDRCONF(NETDEV_UP): enp0s29u1u1: link is not ready
```

```
scsi 10:0:0:0: Direct-Access     Linux    File-Stor Gadget 0404
PQ: 0 ANSI: 2
sd 10:0:0:0: Attached scsi generic sg3 type 0
sd 10:0:0:0: [sdd] 131072 512-byte logical blocks: (67.1 MB/64.0 MiB)
sd 10:0:0:0: [sdd] Write Protect is off
sd 10:0:0:0: [sdd] Mode Sense: 0f 00 00 00
sd 10:0:0:0: [sdd] Write cache: enabled, read cache: enabled,
doesn't support DPO or FUA
sdd:
sd 10:0:0:0: [sdd] Attached SCSI removable disk
FAT-fs (sdd): Volume was not properly unmounted. Some data may
be corrupt. Please run fsck.
```

Now, we can verify that everything works like the multi gadget we tested earlier. When finished, we can disable the new device using this command here that unbounds the UDC to the gadget:

```
root@wb:/sys/kernel/config/usb_gadget# echo "" > g1/UDC
```

Here are the kernel activities on the Wandboard just after the execution of the command:

```
configfs-gadget gadget: unbind function 'cdc_ethernet'/ed055ac0
configfs-gadget gadget: unbind function 'Mass Storage Function'
/ed20e880
configfs-gadget gadget: unbind function 'acm'/ed0231c0
```

At this point, it is quite clear that this feature is very powerful, but the real power is about the ability to define multiple gadgets and the easy switch between them! As an example, let's define another gadget device that we will use in the next section and then see how we can switch between them. As a new device, we will define a clone of the gadget zero (g_zero, see the next section) but with a little difference, We will use the loopback function, that is, whatever we write into the OUT endpoint will be returned to us by the IN one.

First of all, let's create the new gadget and then set up its attributes:

```
root@wb:/sys/kernel/config/usb_gadget# mkdir g2
root@wb:/sys/kernel/config/usb_gadget# cd g2
root@wb:/sys/kernel/config/usb_gadget/g2# echo 0x1a0a > idVendor
root@wb:/sys/kernel/config/usb_gadget/g2# echo 0xbadd > idProduct
root@wb:/sys/kernel/config/usb_gadget/g2# mkdir strings/0x409
root@wb:/sys/kernel/config/usb_gadget/g2# echo "0" >
strings/0x409/serialnumber
root@wb:/sys/kernel/config/usb_gadget/g2# echo "Linux
4.4.7-armv7-x6 with 2184000.usb" > strings/0x409/manufacturer
root@wb:/sys/kernel/config/usb_gadget/g2# echo "Loopback Gadget" >
strings/0x409/product
```

Then, let's define the configuration:

```
root@wb:/sys/kernel/config/usb_gadget/g2# mkdir configs/zero.1
root@wb:/sys/kernel/config/usb_gadget/g2# mkdir configs/zero.1/
strings/0x409
root@wb:/sys/kernel/config/usb_gadget/g2# echo "USB g_zero
config" > configs/zero.1/strings/0x409/configuration
```

Then, let's add the loopback function and connect it to the gadget configuration:

```
root@wb:/sys/kernel/config/usb_gadget/g2# mkdir functions/Loopback.1
root@wb:/sys/kernel/config/usb_gadget/g2# ln -s functions/Loopback.1
configs/zero.1
```

OK, now, the new gadget is defined and we can enable it as we did earlier:

```
root@wb:/sys/kernel/config/usb_gadget/g2# cd ..
root@wb:/sys/kernel/config/usb_gadget# echo "ci_hdrc.0" > g2/UDC
```

If everything works well, here is the relative kernel message from the Wandboard:

```
configfs-gadget gadget: high-speed config #1: zero
```

On the host PC, we should see something like this:

```
$ lsusb -v -d 1a0a:badd
Bus 002 Device 034: ID 1a0a:badd USB-IF non-workshop USB
OTG Compliance test device
Couldn't open device, some information will be missing
Device Descriptor:
  bLength                18
  bDescriptorType         1
  bcdUSB               2.00
  bDeviceClass            0 (Defined at Interface level)
  bDeviceSubClass         0
  bDeviceProtocol         0
  bMaxPacketSize0        64
  idVendor           0x1a0a USB-IF non-workshop
  idProduct          0xbadd USB OTG Compliance test device
  bcdDevice            4.04
  iManufacturer           1
  iProduct                2
  iSerial                 3
  bNumConfigurations      1
  Configuration Descriptor:
    bLength                 9
    bDescriptorType         2
    wTotalLength           32
    bNumInterfaces          1
```

```
        bConfigurationValue      1
        iConfiguration           4
        bmAttributes            0x80
          (Bus Powered)
        MaxPower                500mA
        Interface Descriptor:
          bLength                9
          bDescriptorType        4
          bInterfaceNumber       0
          bAlternateSetting      0
          bNumEndpoints          2
          bInterfaceClass        255 Vendor Specific Class
          bInterfaceSubClass     0
          bInterfaceProtocol     0
          iInterface             5
          Endpoint Descriptor:
            bLength                7
            bDescriptorType        5
            bEndpointAddress      0x81  EP 1 IN
            bmAttributes           2
              Transfer Type             Bulk
              Synch Type                None
              Usage Type                Data
            wMaxPacketSize        0x0200  1x 512 bytes
            bInterval              0
          Endpoint Descriptor:
            bLength                7
            bDescriptorType        5
            bEndpointAddress      0x01  EP 1 OUT
            bmAttributes           2
              Transfer Type             Bulk
              Synch Type                None
              Usage Type                Data
            wMaxPacketSize        0x0200  1x 512 bytes
            bInterval              0
```

This time, we've reported the `lsusb` command-line output since we like to point out the gadget structure: it has one OUT endpoint and one IN endpoint as the gadget zero does.

Now, switching between the two gadgets is quite simple, and the command lines needed are shown here with the relative kernel messages in order to see each command's effect:

```
root@wb:/sys/kernel/config/usb_gadget# echo "" > g2/UDC
root@wb:/sys/kernel/config/usb_gadget# echo "ci_hdrc.0" > g1/UDC
configfs-gadget gadget: high-speed config #1: multi
root@wb:/sys/kernel/config/usb_gadget# echo "" > g1/UDC
configfs-gadget gadget: unbind function 'cdc_ethernet'/ed204dc0
configfs-gadget gadget: unbind function 'Mass Storage
```

```
Function'/ed689a00
configfs-gadget gadget: unbind function 'acm'/ed204e80
root@wb:/sys/kernel/config/usb_gadget# echo "ci_hdrc.0" > g2/UDC
configfs-gadget gadget: high-speed config #1: zero
```

The USB tools

USB devices connected to our system can be listed and inquired by some specific utilities in the usbutils package (the package should be already installed, in case we can done it in the usual ways).

If we can even use sysfs to inspect connected devices, using these tools, the developer can simplify their job. For example, to get a list of connected USB devices, we can use the following command line:

```
root@bbb:~# lsusb
Bus 001 Device 001: ID 1d6b:0002 Linux Foundation 2.0 root hub
```

In this example, on our BeagleBone Black, we get the root hub only (the root hub is a phony device and represents the USB bus itself into the system. It always has a device number of one on whatever bus it sits on and a fixed manufacturer, that is, *Linux Foundation*, with ID 0x1d6b). However, if we plug in a USB device into the host port (for example, a USB key), we get the following lines of code:

```
root@bbb:~# lsusb
Bus 001 Device 003: ID 058f:6387 Alcor Micro Corp. Flash Drive
Bus 001 Device 001: ID 1d6b:0002 Linux Foundation 2.0 root hub
```

Now, we can inquire a specific device by its vendor:product couple or the bus:devnum one as follows:

```
root@bbb:~# lsusb -d 058f:6387
Bus 001 Device 003: ID 058f:6387 Alcor Micro Corp. Flash Drive
root@bbb:~# lsusb -s 001:003
Bus 001 Device 003: ID 058f:6387 Alcor Micro Corp. Flash Drive
```

Then we can use the -v option argument to get a verbose output reporting a lot of information of the device:

```
root@bbb:~# lsusb -v -d 058f:6387
Bus 001 Device 003: ID 058f:6387 Alcor Micro Corp. Flash Drive
Device Descriptor:
  bLength                18
  bDescriptorType         1
  bcdUSB               2.00
```

```
   bDeviceClass              0 (Defined at Interface level)
   bDeviceSubClass           0
   bDeviceProtocol           0
   bMaxPacketSize0          64
   idVendor            0x058f Alcor Micro Corp.
   idProduct           0x6387 Flash Drive
   bcdDevice             1.03
   iManufacturer             1 Generic
   iProduct                  2 Miss Storage
   iSerial                   3 9B4B5BCC
   bNumConfigurations        1
   Configuration Descriptor:
     bLength                 9
     bDescriptorType         2
     wTotalLength           32
     bNumInterfaces          1
     bConfigurationValue     1
     iConfiguration          0
     bmAttributes         0x80
       (Bus Powered)
     MaxPower            100mA
     Interface Descriptor:
       bLength               9
       bDescriptorType       4
       bInterfaceNumber      0
       bAlternateSetting     0
       bNumEndpoints         2
       bInterfaceClass       8 Mass Storage
       bInterfaceSubClass    6 SCSI
       bInterfaceProtocol   80 Bulk-Only
       iInterface            0
       Endpoint Descriptor:
         bLength             7
         bDescriptorType     5
         bEndpointAddress 0x01 EP 1 OUT
         bmAttributes        2
           Transfer Type         Bulk
           Synch Type            None
           Usage Type            Data
         wMaxPacketSize   0x0200 1x 512 bytes
         bInterval           0
       Endpoint Descriptor:
         bLength             7
         bDescriptorType     5
         bEndpointAddress 0x82 EP 2 IN
         bmAttributes        2
           Transfer Type         Bulk
             Synch Type              None
```

```
          Usage Type                    Data
          wMaxPacketSize      0x0200  1x 512 bytes
          bInterval                 0
Device Qualifier (for other device speed):
   bLength                   10
   bDescriptorType            6
   bcdUSB                  2.00
   bDeviceClass               0 (Defined at Interface level)
   bDeviceSubClass            0
   bDeviceProtocol            0
   bMaxPacketSize0           64
   bNumConfigurations         1
Device Status:       0x0000
   (Bus Powered)
```

In the preceding output, we can discover that our device is compatible with USB 2.0 version. We can see its description data, its power consumption, and that is has two bulk endpoints.

A similar tool (even if less common in an embedded device) is `usb-devices`, which can be used to get a compact (even if quite detailed) list of connected devices as shown here:

```
root@bbb:~# usb-devices
T:  Bus=01 Lev=00 Prnt=00 Port=00 Cnt=00 Dev#=  1 Spd=480 MxCh= 1
D:  Ver= 2.00 Cls=09(hub  ) Sub=00 Prot=01 MxPS=64 #Cfgs=  1
P:  Vendor=1d6b ProdID=0002 Rev=04.04
S:  Manufacturer=Linux 4.4.7-bone9 musb-hcd
S:  Product=MUSB HDRC host driver
S:  SerialNumber=musb-hdrc.1.auto
C:  #Ifs= 1 Cfg#= 1 Atr=e0 MxPwr=0mA
I:  If#= 0 Alt= 0 #EPs= 1 Cls=09(hub  ) Sub=00 Prot=00 Driver=hub
T:  Bus=01 Lev=01 Prnt=01 Port=00 Cnt=01 Dev#=  3 Spd=480 MxCh= 0
D:  Ver= 2.00 Cls=00(>ifc ) Sub=00 Prot=00 MxPS=64 #Cfgs=  1
P:  Vendor=058f ProdID=6387 Rev=01.03
S:  Manufacturer=Generic
S:  Product=Miss Storage
S:  SerialNumber=9B4B5BCC
C:  #Ifs= 1 Cfg#= 1 Atr=80 MxPwr=100mA
I:  If#= 0 Alt= 0 #EPs= 2 Cls=08(stor.)
Sub=06 Prot=50 Driver=usb-storage
```

In this output, we find less information as the previous one, but just enough to understand how our devices are connected to the system and how they are working (or not).

The raw USB bus

In some circumstances, a USB device may lack a dedicated device driver. In this case, a GNU/Linux system simply enumerates it, and then, no driver is loaded at all. In this situation, the user cannot get access to the new USB device in any usual manner, except by using raw commands directly over the bus. Simply speaking, it consists of directly sending the USB messages to the new device and then managing the answers without using any dedicated driver at all.

You should note that if this new device has no available driver, then it cannot be seen from the system as any usual device (that is, a keyboard or a storage disk), so we have no /dev/event2 or /dev/sdb entries to use! However, even if this situation may appear quite strange and difficult, in reality, it's not so terrible. In fact, for very simple devices, we can implement a simple management code in user space using the libusb library on the host PC.

> We can use the libusb library on the BeagleBone Black too if we decide to use it as a USB host and attach a device to the BeagleBone Black and be able to control it.

Accessing as a host

As a simple demonstration about using this technique, let's look at the following example that runs on the host PC, acting as a USB host, and that uses the USB gadget driver g_zero (gadget Zero) on our Wandboard, acting as a USB gadget. This particular device has two bulk endpoints, one for input and one for output. They can receive and send special messages when requested, respectively.

Well, let's see how we can interact with this special gadget from the user space. To do this, we must unload the g_cdcdriver and then load the g_zero driver with the following command line:

```
root@wb:~# modprobe -r g_cdc
root@wb:~# modprobe g_zero
zero gadget: Gadget Zero, version: Cinco de Mayo 2008
zero gadget: zero ready
zero gadget: high-speed config #3: source/sink
```

On the host PC, all the USB devices managed by the `g_multi` driver should now disappear, and a new device should be on the scene. In fact, looking at host PC kernel messages, we should see the following lines of code:

```
usb 2-1.1: new high-speed USB device number 58 using ehci-pci
usb 2-1.1: New USB device found, idVendor=1a0a, idProduct=badd
usb 2-1.1: New USB device strings: Mfr=1, Product=2, SerialNumber=3
usb 2-1.1: Product: Gadget Zero
usb 2-1.1: Manufacturer: Linux 4.4.7-armv7-x6 with 2184000.usb
usb 2-1.1: SerialNumber: 0123456789.0123456789.0123456789
```

Also, using the `lsusb` command, we can read its attributes as shown here:

```
$ lsusb -v -d 1a0a:badd
Bus 002 Device 033: ID 1a0a:badd USB-IF non-workshop
USB OTG Compliance test device
Device Descriptor:
  bLength                 18
  bDescriptorType          1
  bcdUSB                2.00
  bDeviceClass           255 Vendor Specific Class
  bDeviceSubClass          0
  bDeviceProtocol          0
  bMaxPacketSize0         64
  idVendor            0x1a0a USB-IF non-workshop
  idProduct           0xbadd USB OTG Compliance test device
  bcdDevice             4.04
  iManufacturer            1
  iProduct                 2
  iSerial                  3
  bNumConfigurations       2
  Configuration Descriptor:
    bLength                9
    bDescriptorType        2
    wTotalLength          69
    bNumInterfaces         1
    bConfigurationValue    3
    iConfiguration         4
    bmAttributes        0xe0
      Self Powered
      Remote Wakeup
    MaxPower           500mA
    Interface Descriptor:
      bLength              9
      bDescriptorType      4
      bInterfaceNumber     0
      bAlternateSetting    0
      bNumEndpoints        2
```

```
bInterfaceClass            255 Vendor Specific Class
bInterfaceSubClass           0  udev
bInterfaceProtocol           0
iInterface                   0
Endpoint Descriptor:
  bLength                    7
  bDescriptorType            5
  bEndpointAddress        0x81  EP 1 IN
  bmAttributes               2
    Transfer Type              Bulk
    Synch Type                 None
    Usage Type                 Data
  wMaxPacketSize        0x0200  1x 512 bytes
  bInterval                  0
Endpoint Descriptor:
  bLength                    7
  bDescriptorType            5
  bEndpointAddress        0x01  EP 1 OUT
  bmAttributes               2
    Transfer Type              Bulk
    Synch Type                 None
    Usage Type                 Data
  wMaxPacketSize        0x0200  1x 512 bytes
  bInterval                  0
```

 Note that the output is longer than the one reported earlier, but the data that we need in this test is just the preceding output.

OK, the gadget is connected with the host PC, so let's move on it and get the testing code compiled into the `chapter_08/usb_sendrecv/usb_sendrecv.c` file in the book's example code repository. However, we need the `libusb` package on the host PC to compile it, so let's install the package with the following command:

```
$ sudo aptitude install libusb-1.0-0-dev
```

Now, we can compile the code using the usual `make` command as well.

If we take a look at the following code, we can see that after initializing the library with the `libusb_init()` function, we open the device using `libusb_open_device_with_vid_pid()` with the proper vendor (`VENDOR_ID`) and product IDs (`PRODUCT_ID`) for the gadget Zero. Then, after claiming the device's interface `0`, we start the data bulk transfers using the `libusb_bulk_transfer()` function:

```
/* Send an all-zeros message to endpoint 0x01 */
ret = libusb_bulk_transfer(handle, 0x01, buffer,
                           sizeof(buffer), &n, 100);
if (ret) {
    fprintf(stderr,
            "error sending message to device ret=%d\n", ret);
    exit(-1);
}
printf("%d bytes transmitted successfully\n", n);

/* Receive an all-zeros message from endpoint 0x81 */
ret = libusb_bulk_transfer(handle, 0x81, buffer,
                           sizeof(buffer), &n, 100);
if (ret) {
    fprintf(stderr,
            "error receiving message from device ret=%d\n", ret);
    exit(-1);
}
if (n != sizeof(buffer)) {
    fprintf(stderr,
            "error receiving %d bytes while expecting %d\n",
                   n, sizeof(buffer));
    exit(-1);
}
printf("%d bytes received successfully\n", n);
```

Note that the USB device interfaces are not covered in this book (see *USB specifications* for detailed info). However, you should know that using such interfaces ,we can create a composite device like the Wandboard, which exposes serial interface, mass storage device, and network interface all on the same device.

In the preceding code, we should notice that in the first call of `libusb_bulk_transfer()`, we send an all-zero message to the BeagleBone Black through the `0x01` endpoint, that is, the OUT endpoint. Then, with the same function, we receive an all-zeros message from the BeagleBone Black through the `0x81` endpoint, that is, the IN endpoint.

Now, we can test the communication with the `g_zero` driver from the user space by running the program as shown here:

```
$ sudo ./usb_sendrecv
usb_sendrecv: g_zero device found
usb_sendrecv: 4096 bytes transmitted successfully
usb_sendrecv: 4096 bytes received successfully
string=
```

 Note that we need the `sudo` command in order to run the program as a privileged user since, by default, the raw access to the bus is not allowed to a normal user. However, this behavior can be changed by writing a proper `udev` rule, but unfortunately, this topic is out of the scope of this book.

The same test can now be done with the clone device we defined earlier. In this case, we should see that whatever we send to the OUT endpoint will came back through the IN one. For this purpose, the preceding code prints the first characters of the buffer used to exchange the data. In fact, it's defined as follows:

```
uint8_t buffer[4096] = "TEST STRING\n";
```

When we used the gadget Zero, the returned string is of course all zeros, so the printed string is void, but with the loopback function used into the gadget Zero clone, the return should be different. In fact, if we remove the legacy gadget Zero and we enable the clone one on the Wandboard, we get the following lines of code:

```
root@wb:/sys/kernel/config/usb_gadget# modprobe -r g_zero
root@wb:/sys/kernel/config/usb_gadget# echo "ci_hdrc.0" > g2/UDC
configfs-gadget gadget: high-speed config #1: zero
```

On the host PC, we get the following results:

```
$ sudo ./usb_sendrecv
usb_sendrecv: g_zero device found
usb_sendrecv: 4096 bytes transmitted successfully
usb_sendrecv: 4096 bytes received successfully
string=TEST STRING
```

Now, the returning data holds TEST STRING as expected.

Summary

The USB has become the ubiquitous standard for peripheral connections, and the discoveries are endless. If you are interested, you can explore more about these possibilities. In this chapter, we started to discover the USB by giving you some interesting starting points by showing how the Wandboard (but the same considerations can be done for every GNU/Linux embedded system) can be used as a USB host in order to manage one or more devices, or as a USB device to emulate a USB peripheral. Also, we discovered how to manage a USB peripheral when a dedicated driver is not present by using a raw access to the bus and how to use two legacy gadget drivers or the new configfs mechanism.

In the upcoming chapters, we'll present some peripherals kinds that are not so common as serial ports and USB devices since they are not directly accessible on a normal PC. Only an embedded device permits us to really discover and manage them. In these chapters, we will take a look at the I^2C devices.

9

Inter-Integrated Circuits - I2C

In the previous chapter, we explored the serial ports and the USB bus (with the relative devices), that is, peripherals that are typically used to connect a computer to another computer or to a device that is *external* to the main computer. Starting from this chapter, we will present some communication buses that are typically used to connect *on-board* devices, that is, the main computer with devices that are all placed on the same board.

One of the most important device class is the *Inter-Integrated Circuit*, which is abbreviated with the acronym **I²C** (or **I2C**). Several devices use the I²C bus to communicate with the CPU, and in this chapter, we will give you a panoramic view of them: we'll see several kinds of different devices with different configurations in order to cover the combinations offered by this bus as much as possible. For all of them, we'll see how these devices can be connected to our embedded kits and the drivers we can use to get access to their data using different techniques. Then, we will see how we can directly get access to the I²C bus in order to manage a simple device from the user space.

What is the Inter-Integrated Circuit bus?

The *Inter-Integrated Circuit* (I²C) is a multi-master, multi-slave, serial computer bus invented in order to simplify the board schematics. Thanks to the fact that it needs two wires only (apart the GND) to do its job, it's widely used into embedded computers to connect on-board sensor/actuators chips to the main CPU.

Despite the fact that the **I²C bus** is multi-master, a typical configuration is a single master device (the CPU) connected to several slave devices (the sensors/actuators) where, as for the USB bus, the master directs all transfers. However just a main difference should be outlined: a **I²C device** can have a dedicated interrupt line to the CPU that can be used to signal that a message must be read by the master (in the USB bus the interrupt messages go over the bus too!). So, a simple I²C connections need two wires only while, in case of interrupt lines, they need three or more lines.

 For further reading on the working of I²C bus the reader can start from the URL:
`http://en.wikipedia.org/wiki/I%C2%B2C.`

The electrical lines

The I²C bus lines are reported in the table below:

Name	Description
SCL – *Serial Clock*	The bus clock signal
SDA – *Serial Data*	The bus data signal
GND	Common Ground

The (eventual) interrupt line has not be reported since, strictly speaking, it's not part of the **I²C protocol**. It is usually implemented as a dedicated interrupt line connected to a CPU's interrupt capable pin (GPIO lines). Also the GND line has been added just because it's needed for electrical reasons since the I²C protocol just talks about the SCL and SDA signals only.

In case of multiple devices connection the I²C devices can be connected in parallel as in the figure below:

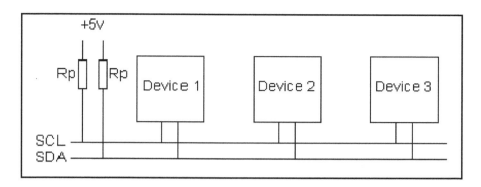

Figure 1: I²C ports on the BeagleBone Black

 The pull-up resistances *Rp* can be omitted in most cases because the **I²C controllers** often integrate them in the SoC and keep them activated by default.

The BeagleBone Black has three I²C buses (each managed by a dedicated **I²C master**), but one is not exported at all on the expansion connectors and one is already utilized for reading EEPROMs on cape add-on boards (so we can consider it as reserved, even if we can still use it being aware to not interfere with the capes manager). This situation is summarized in the table below:

Name	SDA	SCL	Memory address
I2c0	Not exported		0x44E0B000
I2c1	P9.18 or P9.26	P9.17 or P9.24	0x4802A000
I2c2	P9.20 or P9.22	P9.19 or P9.21	0x4819C000

 The BeagleBone Black's capes mechanism is not covered into this book but the curious reader can take a look on the Internet for further information maybe starting from this URL:
`http://elinux.org/Beagleboard:Cape_Expansion_Headers#Cape_EEPR OM_Contents`.

Note that under some BeagleBone Black's Linux releases these buses are named in the order they are enumerated, so their names may have nothing to do with the physical names. That's why in the above table the *Memory address* column has been added which reports the memory addresses where the I²C controllers are mapped too. Then by checking the mapping in /sys/bus/i2c/devices we can easily recognize the right name of each bus. For example, on our board running the kernel installed into the first chapter, that is Linux 4.4.7, the buses have correct names, that is *i2c0* bus is mapped to the file /dev/i2c-0 and *i2c2* is mapped to the file /dev/i2c-2 as shown below:

```
root@bbb:~# ls -l /sys/bus/i2c/devices/i2c-*
lrwxrwxrwx 1 root root 0 Apr  2 19:57 /sys/bus/i2c/devices/i2c-0 ->
../../../devices/platform/ocp/44e0b000.i2c/i2c-0
lrwxrwxrwx 1 root root 0 Apr  2 19:57 /sys/bus/i2c/devices/i2c-2 ->
../../../devices/platform/ocp/4819c000.i2c/i2c-2
```

So, on our system, we can see that both buses have a reasonable name but this cannot be a fixed rules, so keep attention at the I²C connections!

In our next example we will manage a real device using the raw access to the bus, so we need to use the free bus and, in order to do it, we have to enable it.

The magic to do it is by using something similar to what we saw for the serial ports of our BeagleBone Black in the *TTYs on the BeagleBone Black* section, in Chapter 7, *Serial Ports and TTY Devices – TTY* we can use the following command:

```
root@bbb:~# echo BB-I2C1 > /sys/devices/platform/bone_capemgr/slots
```

This should cause kernel messages activity reported below:

```
bone_capemgr: part_number 'BB-I2C1', version 'N/A'
bone_capemgr: slot #4: override
bone_capemgr: Using override eeprom data at slot 4
bone_capemgr: slot #4: 'Override Board Name,00A0,Override Manuf,BB-I2C1'
omap_i2c 4802a000.i2c: bus 1 rev0.11 at 100 kHz
bone_capemgr bone_capemgr: slot #4: dtbo 'BB-I2C1-00A0.dtbo' loaded;
overlay id #0
```

At this point the new bus should be present:

```
root@bbb:~# ls -l /sys/bus/i2c/devices/i2c-*
lrwxrwxrwx 1 root root 0 Apr  2 19:57 /sys/bus/i2c/devices/i2c-0 ->
../../../devices/platform/ocp/44e0b000.i2c/i2c-0
lrwxrwxrwx 1 root root 0 Apr  2 20:04 /sys/bus/i2c/devices/i2c-1 ->
../../../devices/platform/ocp/4802a000.i2c/i2c-1
lrwxrwxrwx 1 root root 0 Apr  2 19:57 /sys/bus/i2c/devices/i2c-2 ->
../../../devices/platform/ocp/4819c000.i2c/i2c-2
```

I2C ports on the SAMA5D3 Xplained

The **SAMA5D3 Xplained** has three I²C buses exported on different connectors. The interesting thing here is the fact that the manufacturer developed a modified (but compatible) version of the I²C bus for its boards named **Two-wire Serial Interface** (**TWI**). In fact, as reported into a dedicated application note we can read the following:

> *The TWI is compatible with Philips I²C protocol. The bus allows simple, robust, and cost effective communication between integrated circuits in electronics. The strengths of the TWI bus is that it is capable of addressing up to 128 devices using the same bus, arbitration, and the possibility to have multiple masters on the bus.*

This means that, whenever we read a document from the manufacturer of the SAMA5D3 Xplained about the I²C protocol we should keep in mind that when we read TWI we should think about I²C.

Available lines are reported in the table following:

Name	SDA	SCL
TW0	J15.9 – SDA0	J15.10 – SCL0
TW1	J20.7 – SDA	J15.8 – SCL
TW2	J15.9 – PA18	J15.9 – PA19

Also controllers listed into the sysfs are shown following:

```
root@a5d3:~# ls -l /sys/bus/i2c/devices/i2c-*
lrwxrwxrwx 1 root root 0 Jul 20 15:15 /sys/bus/i2c/devices/i2c-0 ->
../../../devices/soc0/ahb/ahb:apb/f0014000.i2c/i2c-0
lrwxrwxrwx 1 root root 0 Jul 20 15:15 /sys/bus/i2c/devices/i2c-1 ->
../../../devices/soc0/ahb/ahb:apb/f0018000.i2c/i2c-1
lrwxrwxrwx 1 root root 0 Jul 20 15:15 /sys/bus/i2c/devices/i2c-2 ->
../../../devices/soc0/ahb/ahb:apb/f801c000.i2c/i2c-2
```

I2C ports on the Wandboard

The **Wandboard** has, by default, two I^{2}C buses (even if on the user manual has been reported three – the third bus must be enabled via DTS file and it is not covered in this book) and relative connections are summarized in the table below:

Name	SDA	SCL
I2c-0	JP2.7 – I2C1_SDA	JP2.9 – I2C1_SCL
I2c-1	JP2.11 – I2C2_SDA	JP2.13 – I2C2_SCL

As for other two boards above controllers are reported into the sysfs as shown following:

```
root@wb:~# ls -l /sys/bus/i2c/devices/i2c-*
lrwxrwxrwx 1 root root 0 Jul 18 16:27 /sys/bus/i2c/devices/i2c-0 ->
../../../devices/soc0/soc/2100000.aips-bus/21a0000.i2c/i2c-0
lrwxrwxrwx 1 root root 0 Jul 18 16:27 /sys/bus/i2c/devices/i2c-1 ->
../../../devices/soc0/soc/2100000.aips-bus/21a4000.i2c/i2c-1
```

The I2C bus in Linux

Each I²C device has a well defined 7 bits address that the master must use in order to communicate with a device. This address is not assigned at runtime as for the USB devices, it's assigned by the board designer by setting some chip's pins.

 Typically the chip manufacturer set most significant 3 or 4 bits and the board designer can set remaining bits in order to suite his/her needs. I²C bus specifications are controlled by NXP (Philips) and they are the ones who allocate addresses to I²C devices.

Another thing to be outlined regarding the I²C bus is that for each message the master must specify if the message wants read or write data from the slave. This special action is done by adding a final bit (least significant bit) to the slave address, the master uses a 0 to write data and a 1 to read data from the slave.

As for the USB bus we still have two main actors: master and slave. So in the kernel we find both the device driver types.

Regarding I²C master device there is nothing special to do here since the proper driver is already up and running into our embedded kits' default kernel configurations, but regarding I²C devices to be connected with them we can have several possibilities: external memories, I/O extenders, sensors, converters, etc. (the list can be very long!).

 Note that on some embedded system the on-chip I²C controller can be programmed to work as a master or as a slave device (even if this functionality must be supported by the respective driver). Strictly speaking the developer can choose if his/her I²C controller can be used to master the communication with other I²C devices or to act as a I²C device instead and then working as a simple slave. However it's quite rare that an embedded system is used in the latter case, that's why in this book we don't talk about this possibility.

The I2C tools

This are stored into the package **i2c-tools** and they are a set of utility programs we can use to easily manipulate an I2C device in user-space. They rely on the I^2C */dev interface* driver stored into the file `drivers/i2c/i2c-dev.c` in the Linux's sources repository tree.

 See the file `Documentation/i2c/dev-interface` into the Kernel's repository for further information about this special driver.

If our device is not managed by the kernel, that is, if we have not defined any driver that actually control it we can use the above driver with the followings utilities to get access to its registers.

First of all we can use the `i2cdetect` command to get a list of all available I^2C buses. For instance on the Wandboard we get the following:

```
root@wb:~# i2cdetect -l
i2c-0    i2c          21a0000.i2c                    I2C adapter
i2c-1    i2c          21a4000.i2c                    I2C adapter
```

Then with the same command we can get a list of all connected device with a specified bus. Still working on the Wandboard we can get a list of all devices connected with its first bus `i2c-0` by using the command below:

```
root@wb:~# i2cdetect -y 0
     0  1  2  3  4  5  6  7  8  9  a  b  c  d  e  f
00:          -- -- -- -- -- -- -- -- -- -- -- -- --
10: -- -- -- -- -- -- -- -- -- -- -- -- -- -- -- --
20: -- -- -- -- -- -- -- -- -- -- -- -- -- -- -- --
30: -- -- -- -- -- -- -- -- -- -- -- -- -- -- -- --
40: -- -- -- -- -- -- -- -- -- -- -- -- -- -- -- --
50: -- -- -- -- -- -- -- -- -- -- 5a -- -- -- -- --
60: -- -- -- -- -- -- -- -- -- -- -- -- -- -- -- --
70: -- -- -- -- -- -- -- --
```

 Note that in this screenshot we have connected a device to our board, in fact if no I^2C devices are present we'll get the string `--` for every addresses.

Then we can use the command `i2get` or `i2cset` to read from or write data to a device into a specified register. For instance to read a word of data from the device above at location `0x07` we can do as below:

```
root@wb:~# i2cget -y 0 0x5a 0x07 wp
0x3b9e
```

The last useful tool is `i2cdump` which can dump at once all content of each device's registers. Following is an example by still using the same device at address `0x5a`:

```
root@wb:~# i2cdump -y 0 0x5a w
      0,8  1,9  2,a  3,b  4,c  5,d  6,e  7,f
00: 2e33 00b8 4328 1ad6 0015 bbe4 3b45 3b87
08: 0000 0000 0000 0000 053a 0000 432d 0000
10: 000e 1b58 040e 0008 000c 0002 0000 0000
18: 01ff 0000 0551 0005 01ba 013e 0546 01b3
20: 9993 62e3 0201 f71c ffff 9fb4 8d05 8ddd
28: 906f 95b2 a8b7 2200 8643 20a8 be5a 0000
30: 0000 7e0f 460b 800a 0000 1d2d 00d1 3517
38: 0000 0000 1a46 8011 540a 2185 408c b100
40: XXXX XXXX XXXX XXXX XXXX XXXX XXXX XXXX
48: XXXX XXXX XXXX XXXX XXXX XXXX XXXX XXXX
50: XXXX XXXX XXXX XXXX XXXX XXXX XXXX XXXX
58: XXXX XXXX XXXX XXXX XXXX XXXX XXXX XXXX
60: XXXX XXXX 445e XXXX XXXX 3c82 0000 45cd
68: XXXX XXXX XXXX XXXX XXXX XXXX XXXX XXXX
70: XXXX XXXX XXXX XXXX XXXX XXXX XXXX XXXX
...
d8: XXXX XXXX XXXX XXXX XXXX XXXX XXXX XXXX
e0: XXXX XXXX XXXX XXXX XXXX XXXX XXXX XXXX
e8: XXXX XXXX XXXX XXXX XXXX XXXX XXXX XXXX
f0: 0000 001f 0000 0039 00b3 001f 0000 008a
f8: 00ba 45d1 000f fa10 3b0a 001c 0000 XXXX
```

As we can see some registers gives no data and then, in this case, they are marked with the `XXXX` string.

Getting access to I2C devices

Now we are ready to manage real I²C devices. We can find tons of supported devices into the Linux kernel tree whose are usually grouped according to their specific operations so, for instance, all I²C real-time clock chips are under the directory `drivers/rtc/` while I²C EEPROMs are under directory `drivers/misc/eeprom/`, and so on of the Linux's source repository.

In the next section we're going to see several different kinds of devices all connected to the main CPU through the I^{2}C bus, also we're going to use different embedded kits to test them, but as said before, every commands can be easily repeated on every GNU/Linux based boards with a similar configuration.

EEPROM, ADC and IO Expander

As first example we're going to use the following development board carrying five I^{2}C devices:

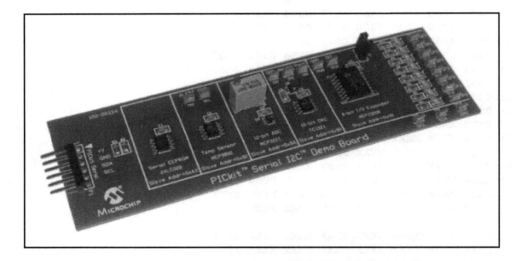

 The device can be purchased at the following link (or by surfing the Internet):
http://www.cosino.io/product/i2c-sensors-board

On this board we have an EEPROM, an ADC, a DAC, a temperature sensor and an I/O expander so it's perfect to show to the reader how the I^{2}C bus works and how above device classes can be accessed within our BeagleBone Black.

First of all we must do the electrical connections so, in the figure following, we reported the connection between the BeagleBone Black's pins and the I^2C developing board's pins.

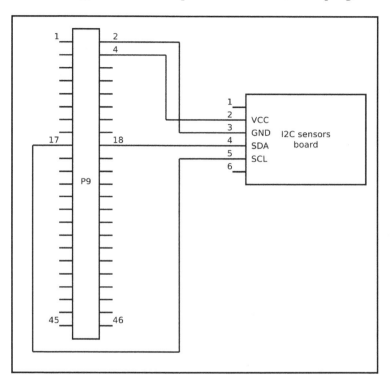

Now, if everything has been well connected, we have to enable the *i2c1* bus (if not already enabled) and then we can use the i2cdetect command to scan all the connected devices:

```
root@bbb:~# echo BB-I2C1 > /sys/devices/platform/bone_capemgr/slots
root@bbb:~# i2cdetect -y -r 1
     0  1  2  3  4  5  6  7  8  9  a  b  c  d  e  f
00:          -- -- -- -- -- -- -- -- -- -- -- -- --
10: -- -- -- -- -- -- -- -- -- -- -- -- -- -- -- --
20: 20 -- -- -- -- -- -- -- -- -- -- -- -- -- -- --
30: -- -- -- -- -- -- -- -- -- -- -- -- -- -- -- --
40: -- -- -- -- -- -- -- -- 48 49 -- -- -- 4d -- --
50: 50 51 52 53 54 55 56 57 -- -- -- -- -- -- -- --
60: -- -- -- -- -- -- -- -- -- -- -- -- -- -- -- --
70: -- -- -- -- -- -- -- --
```

If we take a closer look at the I²C board we can see that each device has reported its I²C address.

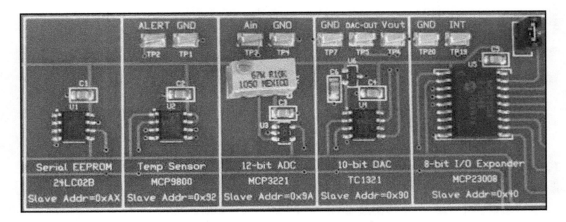

 Note that the EEPROM has up to 7 valid I²C address.

The table below reports the correspondences between 7 bits and 8 bits notations:

Device	I²C address as reported on the board	I²C address as reported by Linux
EEPROM	0xAx	0x5x
Temperature sensor	0x92	0x49
12-bit ADC	0x9A	0x4d
10-bit DAC	0x90	0x48
8-bit I/O Expander	0x40	0x20

 The 8-bit address is just the corresponding 7-bit one plus one zeroed bit as LSB.

So we can easily verify that all devices are now available. However we have not finished yet, in fact even if all the devices are detected not all of them are available as device files into the BeagleBone Black's /dev directory or in sysfs due the fact the system has not loaded the proper device drivers yet. To do so we must first load a proper driver and than write a suitable configuration file for the kernel in order to enable it. However, before seeing these steps by using some examples let's starting from the EEPROM which is not affect by this problem since it has an already up and running driver.

EEPROM

The EEPROM mounted on our I²C developer board is based on the chip family named AT24 so the corresponding driver is already statically compiled into the kernel due the fact the BeagleBone Black cape's management system uses an EEPROM based on that chip.

The user guide of this device is available at:
http://www.atmel.com/Images/doc5121.pdf.

We can verify it by listing the currently enabled AT24 devices on our BeagleBone Black with the following command:

```
root@bbb:~# ls /sys/bus/i2c/drivers/at24/
0-0050   2-0054   2-0055   2-0056   2-0057   bind   uevent   unbind
```

On the bus i2c-0 at address 0x50 there is a device, let's inspect it:

```
root@bbb:~# ls /sys/bus/i2c/drivers/at24/0-0050
0-00500   driver   eeprom   modalias   name   of_node   power   subsystem   uevent
root@bbb:~# cat /sys/bus/i2c/drivers/at24/0-0050/name
24c256
```

Yes! It's an EEPROM device based on the AT24 family. So the driver is already up and running but we've to enable it into the kernel by using a proper DTS file or by using an user-space command dedicated to this scope.

In reality there are several ways to declare an I²C device all reported into the file Documentation/i2c/instantiating-devices in the Linux's sources repository. However only above two methods will be discussed in this book due the fact other one are poor practical or old techniques.

Regarding the DTS method the reader can find into the file chapter_09/BB-EEPROM-A24-00A0.dts in the book's example code repository. In the snippet below is reported the main configuration settings:

```
/* Set the desired clock frequency */
clock-frequency = <400000>;

/* Define the EEPROM device as based on at24c256
 * and with I2C address 0x50
 */
eeprom: eeprom@50 {
    compatible = "at24,24c02";
    reg        = <0x50>;
};
```

This special syntax is suitable for the command dtc (*Device Tree Compiler*) and defines our I²C device according to the hardware settings. Now we should compile it by using the command following:

```
root@bbb:~# dtc -O dtb -o /lib/firmware/BB-EEPROM-A24-00A0.dtbo
              -b 0 -@ BB-EEPROM-A24-00A0.dts
```

After that we can enable our new EEPROM by using a command similar with the one used above to setup a new kernel configuration:

```
root@bbb:~# echo BB-EEPROM-A24 >
            /sys/devices/platform/bone_capemgr/slots
```

Now looking at BeagleBone Black's kernel messages we should see the following activity:

```
bone_capemgr: part_number 'BB-EEPROM-A24', version 'N/A'
bone_capemgr: slot #5: override
bone_capemgr: Using override eeprom data at slot 5
bone_capemgr: slot #5: 'Override Board Name,00A0,Override Manuf,BB-EEPROM-A24'
at24 1-0050: 256 byte 24c02 EEPROM, writable, 1 bytes/write
bone_capemgr: slot #5: dtbo 'BB-EEPROM-A24-00A0.dtbo' loaded; overlay id #1
```

Now our new EEPROM should now be enabled:

```
root@bbb:~# ls /sys/bus/i2c/drivers/at24/
0-0050  1-0050  2-0054  2-0055  2-0056  2-0057  bind  uevent  unbind
```

The new directory is `1-0050` which represent our EEPROM, in the file name we can read the device name as preceding:

```
root@bbb:~# cat /sys/bus/i2c/drivers/at24/1-0050/name
24c02
```

While we can use the file `eeprom` to read/write our desired data. For instance we can write a string and then we can reread it by using the commands following:

```
root@bbb:~# echo "Testing message" >
               /sys/bus/i2c/drivers/at24/1-0050/eeprom
root@bbb:~# strings /sys/bus/i2c/drivers/at24/1-0050/eeprom
Testing message
```

> The command `strings` has been used in order to discard all non ASCII characters due the fact the `cat` command will read all the EEPROM content and not only the string we wrote!

The second method to enable the EEPROM's driver is by using user-space method, that is by writing the device name and its I^{2}C address into the file `new_device` relative to the controller where the device is connected to. Let's do an example relative to this device by first removing the EEPROM device:

```
root@bbb:~# cat /sys/devices/platform/bone_capemgr/slots
 0: PF----   -1
 1: PF----   -1
 2: PF----   -1
 3: PF----   -1
 4: P-O-L-    0 Override Board Name,00A0,Override Manuf,BB-I2C1
 5: P-O-L-    1 Override Board Name,00A0,Override Manuf,BB-EEPROM-A24
root@bbb:~# echo -5 > /sys/devices/platform/bone_capemgr/slots
bone_capemgr: Removed slot #5
```

We can verify that the EEPROM is no longer available just re-looking at the content of the `/sys/bus/i2c/drivers/at24/` directory:

```
root@bbb:~# ls /sys/bus/i2c/drivers/at24/
0-0050  2-0054  2-0055  2-0056  2-0057  bind  uevent  unbind
```

Now we can use the file `new_device` which takes two parameters: the name of the I²C device and the address of the I²C device (a number, typically expressed in hexadecimal starting with `0x`, but can also be expressed in decimal). In our case we have the following:

```
root@bbb:~# echo 24c02 0x50 > /sys/bus/i2c/devices/i2c-1/new_device
at24 1-0050: 256 byte 24c02 EEPROM, writable, 1 bytes/write
i2c i2c-1: new_device: Instantiated device 24c02 at 0x50
```

Now the device `1-0050` is present again:

```
root@bbb:~# ls /sys/bus/i2c/drivers/at24/
0-0050   1-0050   2-0054   2-0055   2-0056   2-0057   bind   uevent   unbind
root@bbb:~# cat /sys/bus/i2c/drivers/at24/1-0050/name
24c02
```

Now, in order to verify that the device is just the same as before, we can read again into the `eeprom` file where we wrote out testing string:

```
root@bbb:~# strings /sys/bus/i2c/drivers/at24/1-0050/eeprom
Testing message
```

As expected the device holds the our string.

Now, to delete the device, we can use the file `delete_device` which takes a single parameter: the address of the I²C device:

```
root@bbb:~# echo 0x50 > /sys/bus/i2c/devices/i2c-1/delete_device
i2c i2c-1: delete_device: Deleting device 24c02 at 0x50
```

 Note that since no two devices can live at the same address on a given I²C address on the same bus, the address is sufficient to uniquely identify the device to be deleted.

ADC

Now we can take a look at the ADC chip which is based on a chip named **MCP3221** and managed by the driver `mcp3021.c`. This driver should be included into a standard kernel distribution, however the reader can verify this situation by looking into the following directory for the file name `mcp3021.ko` as reported following:

```
root@bbb:~# find /lib/modules/$(uname -r)/kernel/drivers
                -name mcp3021.ko
/lib/modules/4.4.7-bone9/kernel/drivers/hwmon/mcp3021.ko
```

The user guide of this device is available at:
`http://ww1.microchip.com/downloads/en/DeviceDoc/21732D.pdf`.

If we get no output from the find command we have to recompile the kernel as described into `Chapter 1`, *Installing the Development System,* to add the missing driver. In this case, to enable the driver compilation we must surf into the kernel configuration menu and enable the following setting: **Device Drivers | Hardware Monitoring support | Microchip MCP3021 and compatibles**. After the driver recompilation we have to reinstall the kernel as usual.

When the driver is in place we need the proper kernel configuration only. As done before we can use the `dtc` utility on the file `chapter_09/BB-ADC-MCP322-00A0.dts` in the book's example code repository. The file is very similar with the EEPROM's one presented above and it's self-explanatory, however a snippet is below in order to outline important lines:

```
/* Set the desired clock frequency */
clock-frequency = <400000>;

/* Define the ADC device as based on mcp3221
 * and with I2C address 0x4d
 */
adc: adc@4d {
    compatible = "mcp3221";
    reg        = <0x4d>;
};
```

Well, let's compile it as preceding:

```
root@bbb:~# dtc -O dtb -o /lib/firmware/BB-ADC-MCP322-00A0.dtbo
                -b 0 -@ BB-ADC-MCP322-00A0.dts
```

Then we can enable the ADC by using the following command:

```
root@bbb:~# echo BB-ADC-MCP322 >
                /sys/devices/platform/bone_capemgr/slots
```

The kernel activity in this case is reported following:

```
bone_capemgr: part_number 'BB-ADC-MCP322', version 'N/A'
bone_capemgr: slot #6: override
bone_capemgr: Using override eeprom data at slot 6
bone_capemgr: slot #6: 'Override Board Name,00A0,Override Manuf,BB-ADC-
MCP322'
bone_capemgr: slot #6: dtbo 'BB-ADC-MCP322-00A0.dtbo' loaded; overlay id #2
```

If everything works well the ADC data can now be accessed by using the following command:

```
root@bbb:~# cat /sys/bus/i2c/drivers/mcp3021/1-004d/in0_input
125
```

Data read above is just a random value due the fact the input pin is floating, if we wish to get well defined data we can try to connect the *Ain* pin to GND and then to Vcc, so we should get an output as following:

```
root@bbb:~# cat /sys/bus/i2c/drivers/mcp3021/1-004d/in0_input
0
root@bbb:~# cat /sys/bus/i2c/drivers/mcp3021/1-004d/in0_input
4095
```

We get exactly the expected values due the fact the GND corresponds to 0 and Vcc is the maximum allowed value and it corresponds to 4095 (that is $2^{12}-1$).

To convert between the raw data value and the input voltage present at *Ain* pin, the reader can use the formula:

Vout = Vcc * (raw_value / 4096)

Where *Vcc* is the maximum value in volt that the system can read, *raw_value* is the current read value and *Vout* is the converted voltage value.

IO Expander

Now we can take a look at the IO Expander chip which is based on a chip named **MCP23008** and managed by the driver `gpio-mcp23s08.c`. This driver should be included into a standard kernel distribution, however the reader can verify this situation by looking into the following directory for the file name `gpio-mcp23s08.ko` as reported following:

```
root@bbb:~# find /lib/modules/$(uname -r)/kernel/drivers
                -name gpio-mcp23s08.ko
/lib/modules/4.4.7-bone9/kernel/drivers/gpio/gpio-mcp23s08.ko
```

The user guide of this device is available at following URL:
http://ww1.microchip.com/downloads/en/DeviceDoc/21919e.pdf.

If we get no output from the find command we have to re-compile the kernel as described into Chapter 1, *Installing the Development System,* setting up the systems to add the missing driver. To enable the driver compilation we must surf into the kernel configuration menu and enable the following setting: **Device Drivers | GPIO Support | SPI or I2C GPIO expanders | Microchip MCP23xxx I/O expander**. After the driver recompilation we have to reinstall the kernel as usual.

When the driver is in place we need the proper kernel configuration only. As done before we can use the dtc utility on the file chapter_09/BB-IOEXP-MCP23-00A0.dts in the book's example code repository. Following is reported a snippet to outline the important lines:

```
/* Set the desired clock frequency */
clock-frequency   = <400000>;

/* Define the IO Expander device as based on mcp23xxx
 * and with I2C address 0x20
 */
gpio: gpio@20 {
    compatible   = "microchip,mcp23008";
    reg          = <0x20>;
    gpio-controller;
    #gpio-cells = <2>;
};
```

Even if very similar to the above DTS files, this time we should notice two entries with prefix gpio-, the gpio-controller string marks the device node as a GPIO controller while the #gpio-cells defines that it needs two cells to store its data: the first cell is the pin number while second cell is used to specify flags (even if currently unused).

Well, let's compile it as preceding:

```
root@bbb:~# dtc -O dtb -o /lib/firmware/BB-IOEXP-MCP23-00A0.dtbo
             -b 0 -@ BB-IOEXP-MCP23-00A0.dts
```

Then we can enable the IO Expander by using the following command:

```
root@bbb:~# echo BB-IOEXP-MCP23 >
             /sys/devices/platform/bone_capemgr/slots
```

The kernel activity in this case is reported following:

```
bone_capemgr: part_number 'BB-IOEXP-MCP23', version 'N/A'
bone_capemgr: slot #7: override
bone_capemgr: Using override eeprom data at slot 7
bone_capemgr: slot #7: 'Override Board Name,00A0,Override Manuf,BB-IOEXP-
MCP23'
bone_capemgr: slot #7: dtbo 'BB-IOEXP-MCP23-00A0.dtbo' loaded; overlay id
#3
```

If everything works well a new `gpiochip` device can now be accessed into the GPIO directory into the sysfs (see `Chapter 6`, *General Purposes Input Output Signals – GPIO*):

```
root@bbb:~# ls /sys/class/gpio/
export  gpiochip0  gpiochip32  gpiochip504  gpiochip64  gpiochip96
unexport
```

The `gpiochip504` directory holds the following:

```
root@bbb:~# cat /sys/class/gpio/gpiochip504/label
mcp23008
root@bbb:~# cat /sys/class/gpio/gpiochip504/base
504
root@bbb:~# cat /sys/class/gpio/gpiochip504/ngpio
8
```

Into the `label` file we find, as expected, the name of our chip while into the `base` and `ngpio` files we have respectively the base number and the count of our new GPIOs. So, for example, if we wish to read data from the *GP1* line of the **MCP23008** chip we have to use the commands below (note that 505 is `504` plus 1, that is the GPIOs' base number plus *GP1* line number):

```
root@bbb:~# echo 505 > /sys/class/gpio/export
root@bbb:~# echo in > /sys/class/gpio/gpio505/direction
root@bbb:~# cat /sys/class/gpio/gpio505/value
0
```

The careful reader can notice that this chip can act also as interrupt controller, in fact it can generate different IRQs according to its input statuses. However this is not covered into this book but the reader can take a look at file `Documentation/devicetree/bindings/gpio/gpio-mcp23s08.txt` into the kernel's sources tree for further information.

The temperature/humidity and pressure sensors

Now it's time so see other two interesting environment sensors useful, for example, to build up a weather station but also useful to show to the reader how we can connect more than one I^2C device at the same time. The first device is a combo temperature/humidity sensor while the second one is barometric sensor and they will be tested by using the SAMA5D3 Xplained board.

The temperature and humidity sensor is in the figure following and it's based on the **HTU21D** chip:

The devices can be purchased at the following link (or by surfing the Internet):
http://www.cosino.io/product/humidity-sensor.
The datasheet of this device is available at:
http://dlnmh9ip6v2uc.cloudfront.net/datasheets/BreakoutBoards/HTU21D.pdf.

While the barometric sensor, based on the **T5403** chip, is reported in the figure following:

The devices can be purchased at the following link (or by surfing the Internet):
http://www.cosino.io/product/barometric_sensor.
The datasheet of this device is available at:
http://www.epcos.com/inf/57/ds/T5400.pdf and an useful application note is at http://www.epcos.com/inf/57/ds/T5400.pdf.

These devices are very simple and the I^{2}C connections for both are reported following:

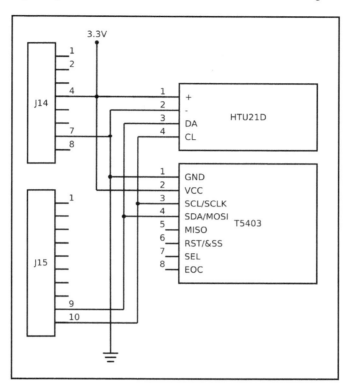

Now, to verify connections, we can use the `i2cdetect` command as follow:

```
root@a5d3:~# i2cdetect -y 0
     0  1  2  3  4  5  6  7  8  9  a  b  c  d  e  f
00:          -- -- -- -- -- -- -- -- -- -- -- -- --
10: -- -- -- -- -- -- -- -- -- -- -- -- -- -- -- --
20: -- -- -- -- -- -- -- -- -- -- -- -- -- -- -- --
30: -- -- -- -- -- -- -- -- -- -- -- -- -- -- -- --
40: 40 -- -- -- -- -- -- -- -- -- -- -- -- -- -- --
50: -- -- -- -- -- -- -- -- -- -- -- -- -- -- -- --
60: -- -- -- -- -- -- -- -- -- -- -- -- -- -- -- --
70: -- -- -- -- -- -- -- 77
```

Note that we may need to disable on-board pull-up resistors by clearing the soldered jumper on our sensor board. In fact all I²C controllers on our embedded kits have the internal pull-up required by the I²C bus specifications and under some circumstances the pull-up on the sensor board may interfere with it.

It may happen that we get the UU string in place of 40 or 77 but the device is connected anyway! However it may happen also that we have no 40 nor UU strings at all due some hardware issues regarding the first device, in this case we can use the command i2cget as follow in order to force an I²C activity on the device.

```
root@a5d3:~# i2cget -y 0 0x40 0xe7 b
0x02
```

OK, the device is connected, while if we get the following output we must recheck the connections.

```
root@a5d3:~# i2cget -y 0 0x40 0xe7 w
Error: Read failed
```

Now to enable devices we can use the user-space method presented above, however we're going to use a proper DTS settings since we wish to specify the bus clock also. A possible implementation can be found into the file chapter_09/A5D3-IIO-HTU21D+T5403-dts.patch in the book's example code repository while following is a snippet:

```
--- a/arch/arm/boot/dts/at91-sama5d3_xplained.dts
+++ b/arch/arm/boot/dts/at91-sama5d3_xplained.dts
@@ -68,6 +68,17 @@
            i2c0: i2c@f0014000 {
                pinctrl-0 = <&pinctrl_i2c0_pu>;
                status = "okay";
+               clock-frequency = <400000>;
+
+               htu21: htu21@40 {
+                   compatible = "htu21";
+                   reg = <0x40>;
+               };
+
+               t5403: t5403@77 {
+                   compatible = "t5403";
+                   reg = <0x77>;
+               };
            };
```

```
i2c1: i2c@f0018000 {
```

Note that we put two devices inside the i2c0 block but, of course, we can have more if we connect more devices.

Now we can take a look at drivers which should be included into a standard kernel distribution, however the reader can verify this situation by looking into the following directory for file names htu21.ko and t5403.ko as reported following:

```
root@a5d3:~# find /lib/modules/$(uname -r)/kernel/drivers
                -name htu21.ko -o -name t5403.ko
/lib/modules/4.4.6-sama5-armv7-r5/kernel/drivers/iio/pressure/t5403.ko
/lib/modules/4.4.6-sama5-armv7-r5/kernel/drivers/iio/humidity/htu21.ko
```

If we get no output from the find command we have to recompile the kernel as described into Chapter 1, *Installing the Development System*, to add the missing drivers. To enable the drivers compilation we must surf into the kernel configuration menu and enable the following setting: **Device Drivers | Industrial I/O support** and then, for the first device the entries **Humidity sensors | Measurement Specialties HTU21 humidity & temperature sensor** while, for the second device the entries **Pressure sensors | EPCOS T5403 digital barometric pressure sensor driver**. After the driver recompilation we have to reinstall the kernel as usual.

Industrial I/O (IIO) devices are the defacto Linux's sensor devices whose allow developers in having a standard and common interface for different types of embedded sensors. These devices are not covered into this book due space reasons (even if they are used in some examples) so curious reader can get further information at URL:
https://wiki.analog.com/software/linux/docs/iio/iio.

After the reboot we should see that both devices at addresses 0x40 and 0x77 on the first I²C bus has been added:

```
root@a5d3:~# ls /sys/bus/i2c/devices/
0-0040  0-0077  i2c-0  i2c-1  i2c-2
```

Then inside the `0-0040` directory we should find the following:

```
root@a5d3:~# ls /sys/bus/i2c/devices/0-0040/
driver  iio:device2  modalias  name  of_node  power  subsystem  uevent
```

It may happen that the device is not detected at boot time so, in the above listing, the entry `iio:device2` is missing which means that the no driver has been loaded. In this case we can force the module loading by using the `modprobe` command as following:

```
root@a5d3:~# modprobe htu21
[  239.920000] htu21 0-0040: Serial number : 48540017999f3211
```

 Then we can force the module loading at boot time by adding the module name to the file `/etc/modules-load.d/modules.conf` as we did into Chapter 1, *Installing the Development System*.

And a similar result should be for the directory `0-0077`:

```
root@a5d3:~# ls /sys/bus/i2c/devices/0-0077/
driver  iio:device1  modalias  name  of_node  power  subsystem  uevent
```

Now we have two new IIO devices that can be read to get the environment data.

 The reader should carefully note here that the new devices are named `iio:device1` and `iio:device2`; in fact the `iio:device0` is a voltage regulator already defined into the standard DTS file of the SAMA5D3 Xplained.

As example below are the commands we can use to read the temperature, humidity and pressure data:

```
root@a5d3:~# cat /sys/bus/iio/devices/iio\:device2/in_temp_input
30638
root@a5d3:~# cat /sys/bus/iio/devices/iio\:device2/in_humidityrelative
_input
58250
root@a5d3:~# cat /sys/bus/iio/devices/iio\:device1/in_pressure_input
101.459000
```

Just for completeness the temperature is given in thousandths of celsius degrees (m° C), the humidity is given as of relative humidity percentage (m%RH) while the pressure is given in kilopascal (kPa).

Serial port

Now let's see how we can easily add another serial port to our system by using the device below based on chip **SC16IS750**, also this device is useful to show how we can use an IRQ line with a I2C device:

The device can be purchased at the following link (or by surfing the Internet):

http://www.cosino.io/product/i2c-uart-io-expander-board.

The user guide of this device is available at

http://www.nxp.com/documents/data_sheet/SC16IS740_750_760.pdf.

First of all we must do the electrical connections so, in the figure following, we reported the connection between **SAMA5D3** Xplained's pins and I²C board's pins.

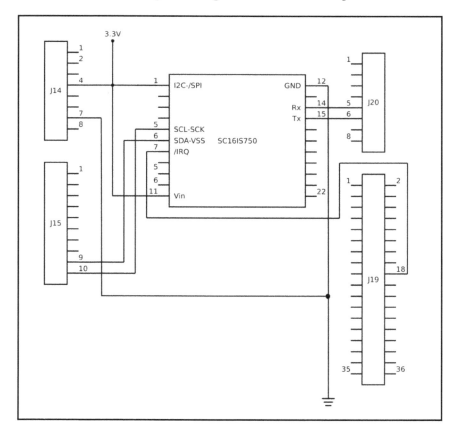

We can verify that all connects are OK with the following command:

```
root@a5d3:~# i2cdetect -y 0
     0  1  2  3  4  5  6  7  8  9  a  b  c  d  e  f
00:          -- -- -- -- -- -- -- -- -- -- -- -- --
10: -- -- -- -- -- -- -- -- -- -- -- -- -- -- -- --
20: -- -- -- -- -- -- -- -- -- -- -- -- -- -- -- --
30: -- -- -- -- -- -- -- -- -- -- -- -- -- -- -- --
40: -- -- -- -- -- -- -- -- -- -- -- -- -- 4d -- --
50: -- -- -- -- -- -- -- -- -- -- -- -- -- -- -- --
60: -- -- -- -- -- -- -- -- -- -- -- -- -- -- -- --
70: -- -- -- -- -- -- -- --
```

However to verify all connections, that is not only the I²C related ones such as the IRQ line, we need to fully enable the driver and to do so we need a proper DTS file. A possible implementation can be found into the file chapter_09/A5D3-TTY-SC16IS7-dts.patch in the book's example code repository while following is reported a snippet:

```
--- a/arch/arm/boot/dts/at91-sama5d3_xplained.dts
+++ b/arch/arm/boot/dts/at91-sama5d3_xplained.dts
@@ -29,6 +29,12 @@
        main_xtal {
            clock-frequency = <12000000>;
        };
+
+       sc16is7xx_ck: sc16is7xx_ck {
+           compatible = "fixed-clock";
+           #clock-cells = <0>;
+           clock-frequency = <14745600>;
+       };
    };
    ahb {
@@ -68,6 +74,14 @@
        i2c0: i2c@f0014000 {
            pinctrl-0 = <&pinctrl_i2c0_pu>;
            status = "okay";
+
+           sc16is750: sc16is750@4d {
+               compatible = "nxp,sc16is750";
+               reg = <0x4d>;
+
+               clocks = <&sc16is7xx_ck>;
+               interrupts-extended = <&pioA 22 IRQ_TYPE_EDGE_FALLING>;
+           };
        };
        i2c1: i2c@f0018000 {
```

Note that we have to define `clocks` and `interrupts-extended` entries to define base clock settings and the GPIO line we choose as IRQ source.

Now we can take a look at driver which should be included into a standard kernel distribution, however the reader can verify this situation by looking into the following directory for the file name `sc16is7xx.ko` as reported following:

```
root@a5d3:~# find /lib/modules/$(uname -r)/kernel/drivers
              -name sc16is7xx.ko
/lib/modules/4.4.6-sama5-armv7-r5/kernel/drivers/tty/serial/sc16is7xx.
ko
```

If we get no output from the find command we have to re-compile the kernel as described into `Chapter 1`, *Installing the Development System*, to add the missing driver. To enable the driver compilation we must surf into the kernel configuration menu and enable the following setting: **Device Drivers | Character devices | Serial drivers | SC16IS7xx serial support** and enable the I^{2}C interface version as a module.

 Note that even if the driver `sc16is7xx.ko` is present it may be configured to support the SPI bus only! In this case the recompilation is a must.

After the driver recompilation we have to reinstall the kernel as usual. Note that with this step we're going to install the DTS with our modifications also but, if the running kernel already has the driver, we must install the DTS and then reboot the system.

After the reboot we should see that the device at address `0x4d` on the first I^{2}C bus has been added:

```
root@a5d3:~# ls /sys/bus/i2c/devices/
0-004d   i2c-0   i2c-1   i2c-2
```

Then inside the `0-004d` directory we should find the following:

```
root@a5d3:~# ls /sys/bus/i2c/devices/0-004d/
driver   gpio   modalias   name   of_node   power   subsystem   tty   uevent
```

Into the file `name` we should find the name of the chip we're using:

```
root@a5d3:~# cat /sys/bus/i2c/devices/0-004d/name
sc16is750
```

While the directory `tty` tells to us that a new tty device is now present into the system. In fact by looking into it we get the output following:

```
root@a5d3:~# ls /sys/bus/i2c/devices/0-004d/tty/
ttySC0
```

Great! This means that the new `tty` device should now be accessible at the file `/dev/ttySC0`.

 A careful reader should notice also that inside the `/sys/bus/i2c/devices/0-004d` directory is present also an entry named `gpio`. This because our chip is also a GPIO extender (see the same device kind above) and the driver also supports it.

```
root@a5d3:~# ls /sys/bus/i2c/devices/0-004d/gpio/
gpiochip504
```

The fact that the device is an I²C one is now perfectly masked by the kernel and for the user-space process we have a new serial port and we can do whatever we did into Chapter 7, *Serial Ports and TTY Devices – TTY*:

```
root@a5d3:~# stty -F /dev/ttySC0
speed 9600 baud; line = 0;
-brkint -imaxbel
```

Looking at the connections above we saw that the new serial port is connected to the serial port `/dev/ttyS1` (see Chapter 7, *Serial Ports and TTY Devices – TTY*, on the SAMA5D3 Xplained) and then we can test the new device by simply exchanging some data these two ports (see Chapter 7, *Serial Ports and TTY Devices – TTY*, getting access to TTYs and following):

```
root@a5d3:~# stty -F /dev/ttyS1 115200 raw
root@a5d3:~# stty -F /dev/ttySC0 115200 raw
root@a5d3:~# cat /dev/ttyS1 &
[1] 2085
root@a5d3:~# echo TEST STRING > /dev/ttySC0
TEST STRING
```

The above example is very basic: firstly we set the same configuration for both two ports and then on the first one we put the `cat` process in sleeping mode waiting for incoming data, then on the second port we write a message, by using the `echo` command, which is then displayed on the terminal. Note that the `TEST STRING` is the output of the background `cat` process!

The Raw I2C Bus

Now, as done for USB bus we should take a look at how we can get direct access to the I²C bus. In the same manner as for USB devices when one of them hasn't a dedicated driver it can be managed directly from the user space. The only problem may arise if the I²C device can generate interrupts, in this case we cannot manage these signals from the user-space and a kernel driver must be used. However this is a rare case and the presented technique can be used in most cases.

Writing data in C

As first example we're going to write some data to the DAC chip named **TC1321** which is mounted on the development board we used above connected to the BeagleBone Black board.

 The datasheet is available at the URL:
`http://ww1.microchip.com/downloads/en/DeviceDoc/21387C.pdf`

By looking at the chip's datasheet we see that its functioning is very simple: it has one 16-bit register at offset `0x00` where we can write digital data to be converted. In fact the register has the format reported below:

Data register = first byte									Data register = second byte						
D9	D8	D7	D6	D5	D4	D3	D2	D1	D0	-	-	-	-	-	-
MSB	X	X	X	X	X	X	X	X	LSB	-	-	-	-	-	-

So, for example, is we wish to write the hexadecimal value `0x41` into the DAC we must build the 16-bit hexadecimal value `0x0140` (that is `0x41` shifted by six positions to the left).

Recalling what we did at the beginning of this chapter we have to create the I²C bus device we should use in order to get access to the bus. We can do it by using the command:

```
root@bbb:~# echo BB-I2C1 > /sys/devices/platform/bone_capemgr/slots
```

Now the device `/dev/i2c-1` is ready and we can run on it the program into the file `chapter_09/i2c_dac/i2c_dac.c` in the book's example code repository. The program can be compiled directly on the BeagleBone Black by using the command `make` as usual.

Two functions below named `reg2value()` and `value2reg()` are used to convert the data exchanged with the chip, while the following function `main()` is the core part of the program:

```
static void reg2value(unsigned char b1, unsigned char b2, int *val)
{
    *val = (b1 << 2) | (b2 >> 6);
}

static void value2reg(int val, unsigned char *b1, unsigned char *b2)
{
    *b1 = val >> 2;
    *b2 = val << 6;
}
```

The code snipped below shows the main part of the `main()` function's body where we can see that, after opening the device `/dev/i2c-2`, whose corresponds to our I²C bus, we set the I²C address of the device we wish to talk to by using the `ioctl()` system call:

```
/* Select the I2C bus to talk with */
ret = ioctl(fd, I2C_SLAVE, I2C_SLAVE_ADDR);
if (ret < 0) {
    fprintf(stderr, "%s: cannot acquire access to address 0x%x\n",
        NAME, I2C_SLAVE_ADDR);
    exit(1);
}
```

After that the code has two different behaviors according to the command line used. If the user uses the command line following:

```
root@bbb:~# ./i2c_dac 100
```

The program will write the value `100` to the DAC's register by using the code following:

```
/* Convert the user's value into a suitable form for the DAC */
value2reg(val, &wbuf[1], &wbuf[2]);

/* Write the data to the device */
ret = write(fd, wbuf, sizeof(wbuf));
if (ret != sizeof(wbuf)) {
    fprintf(stderr, "%s: failed to write: %m\n", NAME);
    exit(1);
}
```

On the other case we can use the command following:

```
root@bbb:~# ./i2c_dac
100
```

Then the program will read the DAC's register by using the following code:

```
ret = read(fd, rbuf, sizeof(rbuf));
if (ret != sizeof(rbuf)) {
    fprintf(stderr, "%s: failed to read: %m\n", NAME);
    exit(1);
}

/* Convert the just read data to a readable form */
reg2value(rbuf[0], rbuf[1], &val);
```

Now, to do a simple check to verify if the above code is really working, we can shortcut the pin labeled *Ain* of the ADC to the pin labeled *Vout* of the DAC (see the picture of the I^{2}C board above). In this situation we can write an analog voltage on the DAC and then read it back by using the ADC:

```
root@bbb:~# ./i2c_dac 100
root@bbb:~# cat /sys/bus/i2c/drivers/mcp3021/1-004d/in0_input
296
root@bbb:~# ./i2c_dac 500
root@bbb:~# cat /sys/bus/i2c/drivers/mcp3021/1-004d/in0_input
1472
```

Note that digital values read from the ADC and written into the DAC do not perfectly correspond due electrical reasons and due the fact they have different resolutions, however we can notice that, more or less, `1472` if five times `296` as `500` is respect to the value `100`.

Before closing this section we should put some words about the `ioctl()` interface of I²C devices. In fact, as described into Linux's documentation into file `Documentation/i2c/dev-interface`, we can use several `ioctl()` arguments and, in particular, the `I2C_RDWR` looks really interesting. By using it we can combine read and write transactions without any stop bit in between and this functionality is fundamental due the fact some chips refuses to work if that bit is present. This mode of operation is often used to address internal registers of an I²C chip, in fact to get access a register we have first of all to do a dummy write by writing zero bytes at the register's address to select it and then we do a read to get register's content.

To better explain it and as simple example lets consider the procedure below to read a generic register:

```
int get_i2c_register(int fd,
        unsigned char addr, unsigned char reg,
        unsigned char *val)
{
    unsigned char inbuf, outbuf;
    struct i2c_rdwr_ioctl_data pkt;
    struct i2c_msg msg[2];

    /* Setup the first message as a write */
    outbuf = reg;
    msg[0].addr  = addr;
    msg[0].flags = 0;
    msg[0].len   = sizeof(outbuf);
    msg[0].buf   = &outbuf;

    /* Setup the second message as a read.
     * Data will get returned here
     */
    msg[1].addr  = addr;
    msg[1].flags = I2C_M_RD/* | I2C_M_NOSTART*/;
    msg[1].len   = sizeof(inbuf);
    msg[1].buf   = &inbuf;

    /* Send the request to the system and get the result back */
    pkt.msgs      = msg;
    pkt.nmsgs     = 2;
    ret = ioctl(fd, I2C_RDWR, &pkt);
    if (ret < 0) {
        perror("Unable to send data");
        return ret;
    }
    *val = inbuf;
```

```
        return 0;
    }
```

In this procedure we use a two cells array of `struct i2c_msg` where we set up the write and read transactions and the we send them to the `ioctl()` by using the `struct i2c_msg`. Note that if the I²C device supports more complex transactions we can manage them by adding more cells to the array configured as necessary.

Reading data in Python

As second example we're going to read some data from the infrared temperature sensor below base chip named **MLX90614**.

 The device can be purchased at the following link (or by surfing the Internet):
`http://www.cosino.io/product/contactless-temperature-sensor`.
The user guide of this device is available at
`https://www.sparkfun.com/datasheets/Sensors/Temperature/SEN-0957`
`0-datasheet-3901090614M005.pdf`.

This device is really interesting since it's capable to measure the temperature of an object without touching it! In fact it is an infrared thermometer with a 17 bits resolution in wide temperature ranges: -40° C to 85° C for the ambient temperature and -70° C to 382.2° C for the object temperature.

The measured value is the average temperature of all objects in the *field-of-view* of the sensor so it's quite obvious that we can use it to measure the environment temperature as for as the human body temperature, we simply need to approach the sensor to our body and the trick is done.

Another important feature of this sensor is the fact it is a digital device, that is data can be retrieved by using a digital connection which is immune to disturbs from the environment even on a (relative) long distances, so we can consider to put it on a hand piece for a more practical usage.

The needed connections are reported in the table below and they are referred to the Wandboard.

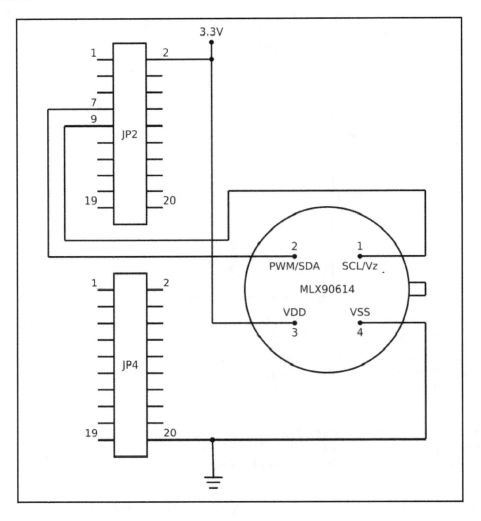

Now, if everything has been well connected, by using the `i2cdetect` command, we should get something as following:

```
root@wb:~# i2cdetect -y 0
     0  1  2  3  4  5  6  7  8  9  a  b  c  d  e  f
00:          -- -- -- -- -- -- -- -- -- -- -- -- --
10: -- -- -- -- -- -- -- -- -- -- -- -- -- -- -- --
20: -- -- -- -- -- -- -- -- -- -- -- -- -- -- -- --
30: -- -- -- -- -- -- -- -- -- -- -- -- -- -- -- --
40: -- -- -- -- -- -- -- -- -- -- -- -- -- -- -- --
50: -- -- -- -- -- -- -- -- -- -- 5a -- -- -- -- --
60: -- -- -- -- -- -- -- -- -- -- -- -- -- -- -- --
70: -- -- -- -- -- -- -- --
```

Where we can see that a device at address `0x5a` has answered.

 Note that we may got different address due the fact some devices uses different addresses, in this case all following commands must be modified accordingly.

By looking at the datasheet we discover that the temperature can be retrieved by reading at the device location `0x07`, so by using the `i2cget` command we can do:

```
root@wb:~# i2cget -y 0 0x5a 0x07 wp
0x3b9e
```

The output value, which is a hexadecimal number in Kelvin degrees(° K), can be converted in Celsius degrees (° C) by the following formula after converting it in a decimal value:

*celsius_degree = raw_value$_{10}$ * 0.02 − 273.15*

Where *raw_value$_{10}$* is the register content base 10. So we can use the following command:

```
# echo "$(printf "ibase=16; %X\n" $(i2cget -y 0 0x5a 0x07 wp) | bc) * 0.02
- 273.15" | bc
32.19
```

The `bc` command may be not installed into the default distribution so, in case, it can be installed by using the usual packages management commands as following:

```
# aptitude install bc
```

 The reader can also get further information regarding this command and its usage by surfing the Internet or, more quickly, by using the `man` command in order to display the `bc`'s man pages.

Now to do same steps very quickly by using a scripting language as Python. First of all we need the `python-smbus` package which can be installed in the usual way by using `aptitude` or `apt-get` commands, then we have to consider the code into file `chapter_09/i2c_temp.py` in the book's example code repository which is also reported following:

```python
#!/usr/bin/python

from __future__ import print_function
import os
import sys
import smbus

# Defines
BUS = 0
ADDRESS = 0x5a
REG = 0x07

# Open the I2C bus /dev/i2c-X
bus = smbus.SMBus(BUS)

# Read a single register
raw_value = bus.read_word_data(ADDRESS, REG)

# Convert the data in C degrees and then display it
degrees = raw_value * .02 - 273.15
print("%0.2f" % degrees)
```

The code is very simple and we can easily see how it works: the call `smbus.SMBus()` is used to generate a new object related to the first I²C bus of the Wandboard while the method `read_word_data()` is used to read the desired data as we did above with the `i2cget` command.

The **System Management Bus** (**SMBus**) is subset of I²C that defines the protocol use more strictly and, sometimes they are used interchangeably even if they are not the same thing. The reader can get more information by starting from the URL:
https://en.wikipedia.org/wiki/System_Management_Bus.

If we execute the command we get the temperature as shown below:

```
root@wb:~# ./i2c_temp.py
30.79
```

Summary

In this chapter we learnt about the I²C bus and how we can use specific Linux device drivers to access I²C devices of different kinds. We discovered how to enable them by using a proper DTS file or directly form the user-space. We also explored how we could write our own I²C driver as a user-space application in both C or Python languages.

However, even if the I²C bus is widely used in every embedded computer and a large variety of I²C peripherals exist, another on-board bus can be found on most systems, that is the SPI bus and its devices, so it's time to go to the next chapter.

10
Serial Peripheral Interface - SPI

As we have already seen in the previous chapter, the I²C bus is widely used to connect on-board devices with the main CPU, but another bus with similar features exists: the (**SPI**Serial Peripheral Interface (SPI). However, and opposed to the I²C bus, this bus can transfer data at higher rates than I²C, and since it's full-duplex, data transfer can take place bidirectionally at the same time. Due to these features, the SPI bus is normally used to implement an efficient data stream for multimedia applications (LCDs/video) or digital signal processing and/or telecommunications devices (Ethernet, WLAN, CAN, Serial Ports, and so on) and SD cards. However, despite this fact, it can be used to communicate with standard sensors, ADC/DAC converters, GPIOs controllers, and other similar devices.

In order to demonstrate the versatility of the SPI bus, in this chapter, we will present several different kinds of devices connected to the main CPU by this bus.

What is the Serial Peripheral Interface bus?

The SPI bus is a full-duplex, single-master, multi-slave, synchronous serial data bus and, as the I²C bus, it's used for on-board connection of sensor chips with the main CPU. This bus require at least (apart the GND signal) three wires plus one chip select signal per slave, this line is typically called **Slave Select** (**SS**) or **Chip Select** (**CS**) and usually it's active low (that is the master must set it to 0 to enable the desired slave chip).

Some terms need to be explained here:

- **Full-duplex**: It means transmitting and receiving are at the same time on the bus.
- **Synchronous**: It means that the clock is sent along with the data (in this case, it is the master that provides the clock).
- **Single-master and multi-slave**: It mean that on the bus, there is one master only that directs the communication, while more than one slave can be connected on the bus.
- **Serial data**: It means data is transmitted one bit at a time over the bus.

The communication starts when the bus master configures the clock using a frequency supported by connected slave devices. Then, the master selects a slave using the proper select line. For each SPI clock cycle, the master sends a bit on the MOSI line and the slave reads it (the MOSI line represents the output line of the master), while the slave sends a bit on the MISO line and the master reads it (the MOSI line represents the input line of the master). Note that this sequence is maintained even in the case of one-directional data transfers. The most important thing is that each slave on the bus that is not activated for data transmission must drop both the input clock and MOSI signals, and must not drive MISO at all in order to not interfere with the selected slave output. It's quite obvious that in an SPI communication, the master must select one slave at a time only.

Here is quite clear that respecting to I²C, whereas the bus is request/reply sharing a single line apart the clock, the SPI bus has two communications happening in parallel: the slave writes while the master is writing at the same time. That's why, we have separate MOSI/MISO lines.

Typically, SPI communications are 8-bit wide, even if other sizes are also common: 16-bit words for touchscreen controllers or audio codecs, or 12-bit words for many **digital-to-analog (DAC)** or **analog-to-digital (ADC)** converters.

The intricate details of how the SPI bus works is out of the scope of this book. If interested, you can visit `http://en.wikipedia.org/wiki/Serial_Peripheral_Interface_Bus` for further information.

The electrical lines

The SPI bus lines are reported in the following table:

Name	Description
SCLK (Serial clock)	The bus clock signal
MOSI (Master Out Slave In)	The bus data signal (*Master Output Slave Input*)
MISO (Master In Slave Out)	The bus data signal (*Master Input Slave Output*)
SS (Slave Select)	Chip or slave select signal (one per slave)
GND	Common ground

 It's quite common that an SPI controller has few SS lines (usually two or three). So, when more SPI devices are needed at once, a trick must be used. The solution is to generate the necessary SS signals using common GPIO lines managed by the driver instead of by the controller hardware itself. Despite the fact that this behavior can permit a very large number of devices to be connected to a single master, it slows down the whole bus' performance because signals are driven in software rather than in hardware. Also, note that this feature must be supported by the SPI master controller's device driver!

Multiple devices must be connected in parallel, but SS signals must be routed to one slave at time.

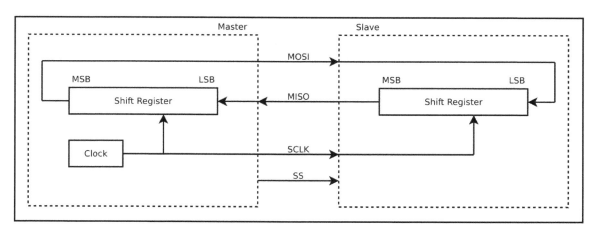

SPI ports on the BeagleBone Black

The BeagleBone Black has two SPI buses, and they are summarized in this table:

Name	MISO	MOSI	SCLK	SS0	SS1
spi0	P9.21	P9.18	P9.22	P9.17	Not available
spi1	P9.29	P9.30	P9.31	P9.20 or P9.28	P9.19 or P9.42

To enable these buses, we can use similar commands as we did in the previous chapters, so the following command enables the `spi0` bus:

```
root@bbb:~# echo BB-SPIDEV0 > /sys/devices/platform/bone_capemgr/slots
bone_capemgr bone_capemgr: part_number 'BB-SPIDEV0', version 'N/A'
bone_capemgr bone_capemgr: slot #4: override
bone_capemgr bone_capemgr: Using override eeprom data at slot 4
bone_capemgr bone_capemgr: slot #4: 'Override Board Name,00A0, Overrid
e Manuf,BB-SPIDEV0'
bone_capemgr bone_capemgr: slot #4: dtbo 'BB-SPIDEV0-00A0.dtbo' loaded
; overlay id #0
```

Relative kernel messages have been reported just after the command line. The next one (with relative kernel messages) enables the `spi1` bus:

```
root@bbb:~# echo BB-SPIDEV1 > /sys/devices/platform/bone_capemgr/slots
bone_capemgr bone_capemgr: part_number 'BB-SPIDEV1', version 'N/A'
bone_capemgr bone_capemgr: slot #5: override
bone_capemgr bone_capemgr: Using override eeprom data at slot 5
bone_capemgr bone_capemgr: slot #5:
'Override Board Name,00A0,Override Manuf,BB-SPIDEV1'
bone_capemgr bone_capemgr: slot #5:
dtbo 'BB-SPIDEV1-00A0.dtbo' loaded; overlay id #1
```

Note that our BeagleBone Black's default configuration reserves the `spi1` bus to the **HDMI** support. So, if we try to enable it with the preceding command, we may get the following error:

```
root@bbb:~# echo BB-SPIDEV1 > /sys/devices/platform/bone_capemgr/slots
-bash: echo:   write error: File exists
```

Then, in the kernel messages, we can read the following reasons:

```
bone_capemgr bone_capemgr: slot #5: BB-SPIDEV1 conflict P9.31 (#3:BB-B
ONELT-HDMI) bone_capemgr
bone_capemgr: slot #5: Failed verification
```

The solution to this situation is to disable the HDMI support by editing the **U-Boot** settings in the /boot/uEnv.txt file and then enabling the following line by uncommenting it:

```
optargs=capemgr.disable_partno=BB-BONELT-HDMI,BB-BONELT-HDMIN
```

If we have no capemgr.disable_partno entry to disable the HDMI support, we can obtain the same result by forcing the loading of the device tree file named am335x-boneblack-overlay.dtb by adding the next line to the U-Boot configuration file:

```
fdtfile=am335x-boneblack-overlay.dtb
```

Then, we only have to reboot the system. Note that in the latter case, at boot time, we should see the following U-Boot message, telling us that the right DTB file is being loaded:

loading /boot/dtbs/4.4.7-bone9/am335x-boneblack-overlay.dtb ...

Once we have fixed this issue we can check if no errors are reported, then SPI devices are now available:

```
root@bbb:~# ls -l /sys/bus/spi/devices/
total 0
lrwxrwxrwx 1 root root 0 Apr  2 20:40 spi1.0 ->
../../../devices/platform/ocp/48030000.spi/spi_master/spi1/spi1.0
lrwxrwxrwx 1 root root 0 Apr  2 20:40 spi1.1 ->
../../../devices/platform/ocp/48030000.spi/spi_master/spi1/spi1.1
lrwxrwxrwx 1 root root 0 Apr  2 20:40 spi2.0 ->
../../../devices/platform/ocp/481a0000.spi/spi_master/spi2/spi2.0
lrwxrwxrwx 1 root root 0 Apr  2 20:40 spi2.1 ->
../../../devices/platform/ocp/481a0000.spi/spi_master/spi2/spi2.1
```

The effective bus numbering is shifted by one, so bus number 0 is named spi1.X and number 1 is named spi2.X.

Then, relative char devices are now present in the /dev directory as usual:

```
root@bbb:~# ls -l /dev/spidev*
crw-rw---- 1 root spi 153, 0 Apr  2 20:35 /dev/spidev1.0
crw-rw---- 1 root spi 153, 1 Apr  2 20:35 /dev/spidev1.1
crw-rw---- 1 root spi 153, 2 Apr  2 20:36 /dev/spidev2.0
crw-rw---- 1 root spi 153, 3 Apr  2 20:36 /dev/spidev2.1
```

While writing this chapter, the author discovered that the SPI overlay is buggy in the kernel release used in this book to test the SPI devices presented. Due this reason, no SPI pins are correctly configured during the execution of the preceding `echo BB-SPIDEV0` and `echo BB-SPIDEV0` commands.

This malfunctioning can be recognized by taking a look at the `/sys/kernel/debug/pinctrl/44e10800.pinmux/pinmux-pins` file where the actual configuration of the BeagleBone Black's pins is reported. After `echo` commands, we can execute the `grep` command to verify that everything is working. If so, the following output should appear:

```
root@bbb:~# echo BB-SPIDEV0 > /sys/devices/platform
/bone_capemgr/slots
root@bbb:~# grep spi0 /sys/kernel/debug/pinctrl/44e
10800.pinmux/pinmux-pins
pin 84 (44e10950.0): 48030000.spi (GPIO UNCLAIMED)
function pinmux_bb_spi0_pins group pinmux_bb_spi0_p
ins
pin 85 (44e10954.0): 48030000.spi (GPIO UNCLAIMED)
function pinmux_bb_spi0_pins group pinmux_bb_spi0_p
ins
pin 86 (44e10958.0): 48030000.spi (GPIO UNCLAIMED)
function pinmux_bb_spi0_pins group pinmux_bb_spi0_p
ins
pin 87 (44e1095c.0): 48030000.spi (GPIO UNCLAIMED)
function pinmux_bb_spi0_pins group pinmux_bb_spi0_p
ins
```

However, if `grep` returns no output, then the running kernel is buggy, and the only way to enable the SPI bus (as a workaround) is by forcing the loading of the overlay file at boot time by adding the following line to the u-boot configuration file `/boot/uEnv.txt`:

cape_enable=bone_capemgr.enable_partno=BB-SPIDEV0

You should now pay attention to the fact that the SPI device `/dev/spidev1.0` is not referred to the whole bus like for the I²C bus. Rather it points to the SPI device connected to the first chip select line, while the `/dev/spidev1.1` device points to the SPI device connected to the second chip select line!

Also, note that this setting, which allows the user to have a raw access to the bus, is quite generic and will be used in the next section where we'll describe how to manage a simple SPI device using this raw access mode.

SPI ports on the SAMA5D3 Xplained

The SAMA5D3 Xplained has two SPI buses exposed on expansion connectors. However, the spi0 bus is reserved to get access to an optional NOR flash. So, if we wish to use this bus, we have to reprogram the CPU internal pins multiplexer to reroute SPI signals (for space reasons, this operation is not reported in this book, but it consists of changing the pinctrl-0 attribute for the spi0 entry).

Available lines are reported in this table:

Name	MISO	MOSI	SCLK	SS0
spi1	J15.12 – SPI1_MISO	J15.11 – SPI1_MOSI	J15.13 – SPI1_SPCK	J15.10 – NPCS0

Note that even if we have one **chip select** (**CS**) signal only by default, we can add more than just one device by modifying and then recompiling the SAMA5D3 Xplanied's DTS file arch/arm/boot/dts/at91-sama5d3_xplained.dts into the Linux tree. We have to modify the following section by adding up to four GPIO pins to act as four chip select lines. The default settings are shown here:

```
spi1: spi@f8008000 {
    cs-gpios = <&pioC 25 0>;
    status = "okay";
};
```

So, for example, we can add the pin *A22* as a third chip select line by modifying the settings:

```
spi1: spi@f8008000 {
    cs-gpios = <&pioC 25 0>, <0>, <&pioA 22 0>;
    status = "okay";
};
```

Also, if we wish to have the spidev device as we did for the BeagleBone Black, we have to modify the spi1 section as follows:

```
spi1: spi@f8008000 {
    cs-gpios = <&pioC 25 0>, <0>, <&pioA 22 0>;
    status = "okay";

    spi@0 {
        compatible = "spidev";
        reg = <0>;
        spi-max-frequency = <1000000>;
    };
```

```
spi@2 {
    compatible = "spidev";
    reg = <2>;
    spi-max-frequency = <1000000>;
};
};
```

After the new DTS has been converted into the relative DTB and the board has been rebooted, we should get our new SPI controllers listed into the sysfs, as shown here:

```
root@a5d3:~# ls -l /sys/bus/spi/devices/
total 0
lrwxrwxrwx 1 root root 0 Jan  1  2007 spi32765.0 -> ../../../devices/s
oc0/ahb/ahb:apb/f8008000.spi/spi_master/spi32765/spi32765.0
lrwxrwxrwx 1 root root 0 Jan  1  2007 spi32765.2 -> ../../../devices/s
oc0/ahb/ahb:apb/f8008000.spi/spi_master/spi32765/spi32765.2
```

You should now notice that for the SAMA5D3 Xplained, specifically adding the spidev device into the DTS file in latest kernel releases will cause kernel warning messages as follows:

```
spidev spi32765.0: buggy DT: spidev listed directly in DT
------------[ cut here ]------------
WARNING: CPU: 0 PID: 1 at drivers/spi/
spidev.c:719 spidev_probe+0x141/0x154()
Modules linked in:
CPU: 0 PID: 1 Comm: swapper Not tainted 4.4.6-sama5-armv7-r5 #12
Hardware name: Atmel SAMA5
[<c00122bd>] (unwind_backtrace) from [<c0010393>] (show_stack+0xb/0xc)
[<c0010393>] (show_stack) from [<c0018ac7>] (warn_slowpath_common
...
```

This is done intentionally by the kernel developers as reported into the comment of the commit that introduced this behavior:

```
spi: spidev: Warn loudly if instantiated from DT as "spidev"

    Since spidev is a detail of how Linux controls a device rather
    than a description of the hardware in the system we should never
    have a node described as "spidev" in DT, any SPI device could be a
    spidev so this is just not a useful description.
    In order to help prevent users from writing such device trees
    generate a warning if spidev is instantiated as a DT node without
    an ID in the match table.
    Signed-off-by: Mark Brown <broonie@kernel.org>
```

Like the `i2c` char device discussed in `Chapter 9`, *Inter-Integrated Circuits – I2C*, the `spidev` one doesn't talk directly to any hardware. So, kernel developers are encouraging people to work around this behavior by adding their specific devices to the list of compatible strings (however, this technique is not be discussed in this book for space reasons and because it's a minor issue).

SPI ports on the Wandboard

The Wandboard has exported only one SPI bus (even if the CPU has four), and relative connections are summarized in the following table:

Name	MISO	MOSI	SCLK	SS0	SS1
spi1	JP4.9 – CSPI1_MISO	JP4.7 – CSPI1_MOSI	J4.11 – CSPI1_SPCK	J4.13 – CSPI1_CS0	J4.15 – CSPI1_CS1

However, by default, this bus is not enabled. To enable it, we have to modify the Wandboard's `arch/arm/boot/dts/imx6qdl-wandboard.dtsi` DTS file into the Linux tree by adding a proper section as follows, and then recompiling and reinstalling it:

```
&ecspi1 {
    fsl,spi-num-chipselects = <2>;
    cs-gpios = <&gpio2 30 0>, <&gpio4 10 0>;
    pinctrl-names = "default";
    pinctrl-0 = <&pinctrl_ecspi1_1>;
    status = "okay";

    spidev@0 {
        compatible = "spidev";
        reg = <0>;
        spi-max-frequency = <16000000>;
    };

    spidev@1 {
        compatible = "spidev";
        reg = <1>;
        spi-max-frequency = <16000000>;
    };
};
```

Also, note that the pins multiplexer settings named `pinctrl_ecspi1_1` must be defined into the Wandboard's DTS file. The full patch is reported in `chapter_10/imx6qdl-wandboard-spidev.dtsi.patch` in the book's example code repository.

As for the other two boards, if everything works well, after the reboot, our new SPI controllers are reported into the sysfs, as shown here:

```
root@wb:~# ls -l /sys/bus/spi/devices/
total 0
lrwxrwxrwx 1 root root 0 Jul 22 13:23 spi0.0 -> ../../../devices/soc0/
soc/20000aips-bus/2000000.spba-bus/2008000.ecspi/spi_master/spi0/spi0.
0
lrwxrwxrwx 1 root root 0 Jul 22 13:23 spi0.1 -> ../../../devices/soc0/
soc/2000000.aips-bus/2000000.spba-bus/2008000.ecspi/spi_master/spi0/sp
i0.1
```

The SPI bus in Linux

As in the I^{2}C case, the SPI bus has the concept of master and slave device too. Again, regarding the SPI master device, there is nothing special to do here since the proper driver is already up and running in our embedded kits' default kernel configurations (as seen earlier). However, to be connected with SPI devices, we can have several possibilities: external memories, I/O extenders, sensors, serial ports, and so on (the list can be very long!).

As seen earlier, we can also have a generic `spidev` driver to get access to the raw bus functionalities, but this time, we have no prebuild tools to manage it! The only things we can do is write our own program, maybe take some basic tools provided into the kernel's tree (see the next section for an example) as examples to manage our device through the `spidev` driver.

For further information on the API in Linux for SPI, we can take a look at the `Documentation/spi/spidev` file in Linux's sources repository.

The SPI tools

In complete analogy to the I²C case, even for SPI, we have some basic tools to manage it. However, as stated earlier, this time, these tools are not into a dedicated Debian package, but they are stored directly in the `Documentation/spi/` directory of Linux's sources repository. Honestly, these SPI tools offer a poor support against the I²C counterpart. However, they can be used for basic functionalities and taken as examples to build our own programs.

As shown here, the available programs are just two:

```
$ ls Documentation/spi/*.c
Documentation/spi/spidev_fdx.c
Documentation/spi/spidev_test.c
```

Both of them can be compiled on the host PC (or directly on our embedded kits) using the following command:

```
$ make CC=arm-linux-gnueabihf-gcc
       CFLAGS="-Wall -O2" spidev_fdx spidev_test
arm-linux-gnueabihf-gcc -Wall -O2 spidev_fdx.c   -o spidev_fdx
arm-linux-gnueabihf-gcc -Wall -O2 spidev_test.c   -o spidev_test
```

> Of course, if we decide to compile them natively, the `CC=arm-linux-gnueabihf-gcc` setting must be omitted.

The `spidev` prefix suggests that they must be used with the `spidev` device, and once placed into our embedded kit, they can be executed with the following command lines. The first one is the command line of `spidev_fdx`:

```
root@bbb:~# ./spidev_fdx -h
usage: ./spidev_fdx [-h] [-m N] [-r N] /dev/spidevB.D
```

Then comes the command line of `spidev_test`:

```
root@bbb:~# ./spidev_test -h
./spidev_test: invalid option -- 'h'
Usage: ./spidev_test [-DsbdlHOLC3]
    -D --device    device to use (default /dev/spidev1.1)
    -s --speed     max speed (Hz)
    -d --delay     delay (usec)
    -b --bpw       bits per word
    -l --loop      loopback
    -H --cpha      clock phase
```

```
-O --cpol       clock polarity
-L --lsb        least significant bit first
-C --cs-high    chip select active high
-3 --3wire      SI/SO signals shared
-v --verbose    Verbose (show tx buffer)
-p              Send data (e.g. "1234\xde\xad")
-N --no-cs      no chip select
-R --ready      slave pulls low to pause
-2 --dual       dual transfer
-4 --quad       quad transfer
```

The `spidev_fdx` can be used to send and receive simple messages from the SPI device, while `spidev_test` can be used to do several functional tests on our SPI bus, in particular, we can use it to verify that our SPI controller is well configured. As a practical example, considering what we saw earlier about the possible buggy `spidev` support for BeagleBone Black's kernel 4.4 release, we can do a specific test to verify that our system has the correct SPI settings.

Let's suppose we want to test the `spidev1` device. Then, we have to connect relative MOSI and MISO pins together (that is, pins *P9.29* and *P9.30*) and then execute the `spidev_test` command as follows:

```
root@bbb:~# ./spidev_test --device /dev/spidev2.0
spi mode: 0x0
bits per word: 8
max speed: 500000 Hz (500 KHz)
RX | FF FF FF FF FF FF 40 00 00 00 00 95 FF FF FF
FF FF FF FF FF FF FF FF FF FF FF FF FF FF
FF F0 0D  | ......@....+................+.
```

The command's output tells us that in this case, the data transfer is correct. Otherwise, if we get the following output, it means something went wrong:

```
root@bbb:~# ./spidev_test --device /dev/spidev2.0
spi mode: 0x0
bits per word: 8
max speed: 500000 Hz (500 KHz)
RX | 00 00 00 00 00 00 00 00 00 00 00 00 00 00 00 00 00 00
00 00 00 00 00 00 00 00 00 00 00 00
00 00  | ...............................
```

Getting access to SPI devices

Now, we are ready to manage real SPI devices. We can find tons of supported devices in Linux's tree that are usually grouped according to their specific operations in complete analogy to the I²C case.

In the next section, we will see several different kinds of devices all connected to the main CPU through the SPI bus. Also, we will use different embedded kits to test them, but as said earlier, every command can be easily repeated on every GNU-/Linux-based boards with a similar configuration.

LCD display

As the first example, we will use the following tiny LCD display, which can be used in simple applications because it's cheap and well supported by BeagleBone Black's kernel:

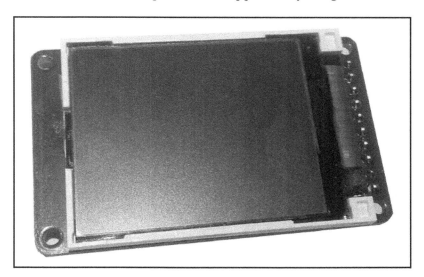

The device can be purchased at
http://www.cosino.io/product/color-tft-lcd-1-8-160×128 or by surfing the Internet.
The LCD is based on the chip ST7735R, which has its datasheet at: https://www.adafruit.com/datasheets/ST7735R_V0.2.pdf.

First of all, we must do the following electrical connections:

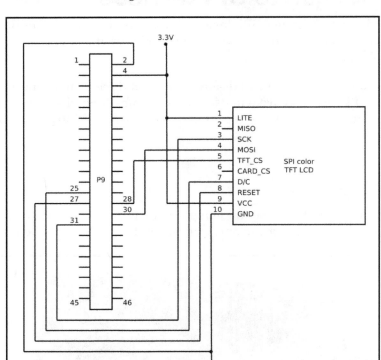

You can note that we used SPI-dedicated pins, plus some GPIOs lines. This configuration is quite typical in SPI connections, since it's more efficient using additional lines to specify special data, which means using proper SPI messages to manage the device. In our LCD, we use the **D/C** (**Data/Command**) line to specify which data is simple graphical data and which data is special commands for the LCD instead. The meaning of the *RESET* line is obvious, while the *LITE* line is used to manage the backlight intensity (note that this line should not be a simple GPIO, but it should be a **PWM** line in order to be able to control the backlight intensity; in fact, if used as a normal GPIO, the intensity will stay at a maximum level all the time, or it can be completely turned off).

The PWM lines are special lines that can generate a *Pulse Width Modulated* signal (see `Chapter 18`, *Pulse-Width Modulation – PWM*).

Now, we should verify that the correct driver is available in our system. We can do this by using the following command:

```
root@bbb:~# zcat /proc/config.gz | grep -i st7735
CONFIG_FB_TFT_ST7735R=m
```

In our kernel configuration, the driver is present as a module, but it's OK having it statically linked into the kernel too. In this case, the output should be something like this:

```
CONFIG_FB_TFT_ST7735R=y
```

If we get no output, then we must enable the driver into the kernel configuration menu: **Device Drivers | Staging drivers | Support for small TFT LCD display modules | FB driver for the ST7735R LCD Controller**. We then need to recompile the kernel (in `Chapter 1`, *Installing the Development System*).

You should notice that the driver we're using is under the *Staging drivers* section, which holds standalone drivers (and other kernel stuff) that are not ready to be merged into the main portion of the Linux kernel tree for various technical reasons. They can be used, but at complete risk of the developer/user! For further information regarding staging drivers, go to `https://lwn.net/Articles/324279/`.

Now, we have to enable the `spidev1` device using the usual `echo` command as follows:

```
root@bbb:~# echo BB-SPIDEV1 > /sys/devices/platform/bone_capemgr/slots
```

If the kernel has the bug reported earlier, the only way we have to correctly enable the SPI bus is by adding the next line to the `/boot/uEnv.txt` file:

cape_enable=bone_capemgr.enable_partno=BB-SPIDEV1

In any case, the HDMI support must be disabled to be able to use the `spidev1` device!

Now, if everything was done correctly, we should be able to execute the preceding command without errors:

```
root@bbb:~# modprobe fbtft_device busnum=2 name=adafruit18
gpios=dc:117,reset:115
```

Kernel messages should be as follows:

```
fbtft: module is from the staging directory, the quality is unknown, y
ou have been warned.
fbtft_device: module is from the staging directory, the quality is unk
nown, you have been warned.
```

Here, we have two warnings related to the fact that we've just loaded two staging drivers. Then, we should see the following code snippet:

```
spidev spi2.1: spidev spi2.1 16000kHz 8 bits mode=0x00
spidev spi2.0: spidev spi2.0 16000kHz 8 bits mode=0x01
spidev spi2.0: Deleting spi2.0
```

We saw have the selection of the `spidev1` device (remember the numbering shift). Here is the selection of the GPIOs we need to control our LCD:

```
fbtft_device: GPIOS used by 'adafruit18':
fbtft_device: 'dc' = GPIO117
fbtft_device: 'reset' = GPIO115
```

Then, the last messages are as follows:

```
spidev spi2.1: spidev spi2.1 16000kHz 8 bits mode=0x00
spi spi2.0: fb_st7735r spi2.0 32000kHz 8 bits mode=0x00
fb_st7735r: module is from the staging directory, the quality is unkno
wn, you have been warned.
Console: switching to colour frame buffer device 16x20
graphics fb0: fb_st7735r frame buffer, 128x160, 40 KiB video memory, 4
 KiB DMA buffer memory, fps=20, spi2.0 at 32 MHz
```

At this point, the device is finally activated, and now, we see that the BeagleBone Black has a new color framebuffer device of 128×160 pixels, represented in the user space by the `/dev/fb0` device.

Framebuffer devices are not covered by this book, so if you need more information regarding them, you can start reading the `Documentation/fb/framebuffer.txt` file in the kernel's repository.

Also, the `Console: switching to colour frame buffer device 16x20` message tells us that we have a console 16 x 20 characters wide! In fact, the LCD displays a normal login message, as shown in the following image:

Serial port

Now, let's see how we can easily add another serial port to our system using the same device used in Chapter 9, *Inter-Integrated Circuits – I2C*, that is, the chip **SC16IS750**, which implements a serial port controller. The electrical connections between SAMA5D3 Xplained's pins and board's pins are reported here:

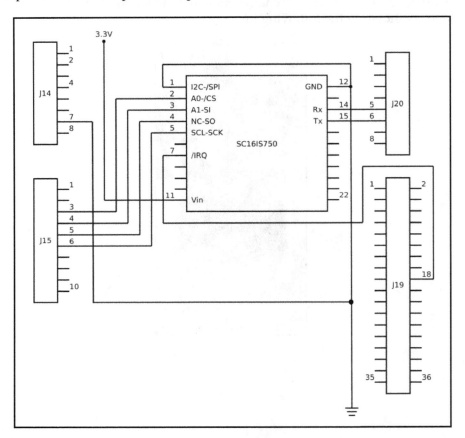

This time, the only way we have to test connections is by just loading the driver. So, we need a proper DTS file, and a possible implementation can be found in the chapter_10/A5D3-TTY-SC16IS7-dts.patch file in the book's example code repository. However, a snippet is also reported here:

```
main_xtal {
    clock-frequency = <12000000>;
};
```
+

```
+        sc16is7xx_ck: sc16is7xx_ck {
+            compatible = "fixed-clock";
+            #clock-cells = <0>;
+            clock-frequency = <14745600>;
+        };
    };
    ahb {
@@ -159,6 +165,15 @@
        spi1: spi@f8008000 {
            cs-gpios = <&pioC 25 0>;
            status = "okay";
+
+            sc16is750: sc16is750@0 {
+                compatible = "nxp,sc16is750";
+                reg = <0>;
+                spi-max-frequency = <15000000>;
+
+                clocks = <&sc16is7xx_ck>;
+                interrupts-extended = <&pioA 22 IRQ_TYPE_EDGE_FALLING>;
+            };
        };
        adc0: adc@f8018000 {
```

Note that as in the case of I²C, we have to define `clocks` and `interrupts-extended` entries to define base clock settings and the GPIO line we choose as IRQ source.

Now, we can take a look at the driver that should be included in a standard kernel distribution. However, you can verify this situation by looking into the following directory for the file name `sc16is7xx.ko` as reported here:

```
root@a5d3:~# find /lib/modules/$(uname -r)/kernel/drivers
                -name sc16is7xx.ko
/lib/modules/4.4.6-sama5-armv7-r5/kernel/drivers/tty/serial/sc16is7xx.
ko
```

If we get no output from the find command, we have to recompile the kernel as described into Chapter 1, *Installing the Developing System*, Setting up the systems to add the missing driver. To enable the driver compilation, we must navigate to the kernel configuration menu and enable the following settings: **Device Drivers | Character devices | Serial drivers | SC16IS7xx serial support**. Then, we need to enable the SPI interface version as a module.

Even if the `sc16is7xx.ko` driver is present, it may be configured to support the I²C bus only! In this case, the recompilation is necessary.

After the driver recompilation, we have to reinstall the kernel as usual with the DTS holding our modifications. However, if the running kernel already has the driver, we just need to install the DTS and then reboot the system. If we did everything correctly, we should see that a new SPI device has been added:

```
root@a5d3:~# ls /sys/bus/spi/devices/
spi32765.0
```

Then, inside the spi32765.0 directory, we should find the following files:

```
root@a5d3:~# ls /sys/bus/spi/devices/spi32765.0
driver     gpio  modalias  of_node  power  statistics
subsystem  tty   uevent
```

The tty directory suggests that a new TTY device is now present into the system. In fact, by looking into it, we will get the following output:

```
root@a5d3:~# ls /sys/bus/spi/devices/spi32765.0/tty/
ttySC0
```

Great! This means that the new TTY device should now be accessible in the /dev/ttySC0 file.

You can note that as far as the analogous I²C example in Chapter 9, *Inter-Integrated Circuits – I2C*, into the /sys/bus/spi/devices/spi32765.0 directory is present also an entry named gpio due the GPIO extender functionalities the chip has and that the driver also supports:

```
root@a5d3:~# ls /sys/bus/spi/devices/spi32765.0/gpio/
gpiochip504
```

The fact that the device is an SPI one is now perfectly masked by the kernel, and for the user-space process, we have a new serial port and we can do whatever we did in Chapter 7, *Serial Ports and TTY Devices – TTY*:

```
root@a5d3:~# stty -F /dev/ttySC0
speed 9600 baud; line = 0;
-brkint -imaxbel
```

As in the previous chapter, the new serial port is connected to the serial port /dev/ttyS1 (see Chapter 7, *Serial Ports and TTY Devices – TTY*), and then, we can test the new device, as done earlier by simply exchanging some data between these two ports (see Chapter 7, *Serial Ports and TTY Devices – TTY*):

```
root@a5d3:~# stty -F /dev/ttyS1 115200 raw
root@a5d3:~# stty -F /dev/ttySC0 115200 raw
```

```
root@a5d3:~# cat /dev/ttyS1 &
[1] 1714
root@a5d3:~# echo TEST STRING > /dev/ttySC0
TEST STRING
```

The raw SPI bus

As for USB and I^{2}C buses the SPI bus supports the raw access in order to directly send and receive messages from the SPI slaves, so it's time to show a little example about how we can do it on our Wandboard.

As for other raw accesses, the only problem is that it interrupts management. In this case, we cannot manage these signals from the user space. A kernel driver must be used.

Exchanging data in C

To show how we can manage the raw SPI bus, we are going to manage a really simple device using the Wandboard, that is, the thermocouple to digital converter based on the **MAX31855** chip:

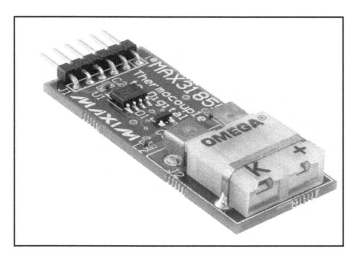

The device can be purchased
at: `http://www.cosino.io/product/thermocouple-max31855` or by surfing
the Internet.
The datasheet of the MAX31855 is available at:
`https://datasheets.maximintegrated.com/en/ds/MAX31855.pdf`.

Electrical connections are reported in this image:

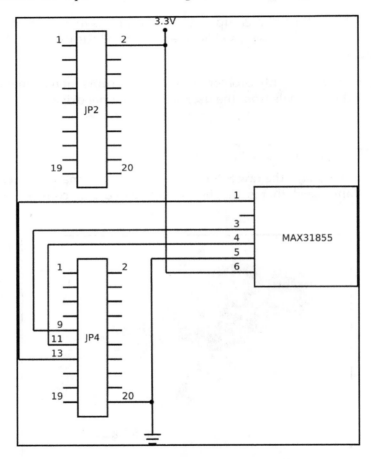

By looking at the chip's datasheet, we see that its functioning is very simple: it has one 32-bit register where we can read the temperature information. The register has the format reported here:

14-bit Thermocouple Data				Res	Fault	12-bit Internal Temperature				Res	SCV	SCG	OC
D31	D30	..	D18	D17	D16	D15	D14	...	D4	D3	D2	D1	D0
Sign	MSB	X	LSB	-	X	X	MSB	X	LSB	-	X	X	X

So, to read the temperature data, we have to read the preceding register and extract the data from bits **D30–D18**. Note that we should check bit **D16** also in order to know if the peripheral is into a faulting state or not.

 Note that D30 corresponds to value 2^{10}, while D18 to 2^{-2}, so the data into bits D30-D18 must be divided by 4 to get the real temperature data. You can notice that this chip can give us more information, but we decide to keep our example as simple as possible for better readability. But of course, you can improve it to fully retrieve all the necessary information.

The SPI device to be used is spidev0.0 we enabled earlier in the Wandboard section. Then, the code to read thermocouple data is reported in chapter_10/spi_thermo/spi_thermo.c in the book's example code repository. A screenshot of this program is reported here where it's easy to see that we simply open the SPI device file /dev/spidev0.0 and then we do a read. The remaining code is just for decoding the data read:

```
/* Open the SPI bus device connected to the thermocouple chip */
fd = open(SPI_DEV, O_RDWR);
if (fd < 0) {
    fprintf(stderr, "%s: cannot get access to SPI bus\n", NAME);
    exit(1);
}

/* Read the 32-bit data */
ret = read(fd, &data, 4);
if (ret < 0) {
    fprintf(stderr, "%s: cannot read data from SPI device\n", NAME);
    exit(1);
}
if (ret != 4) {
    fprintf(stderr, "%s: short read\n", NAME);
    exit(1);
}
```

Now, we can compile the code using the make command as usual. If everything works well, we can read the environment temperature using the following command:

```
root@wb:~# ./spi_thermo
25.50
```

Exchanging data in Python

To show another possibility about how to manage the raw SPI bus, we can use the board reported in the following figure, which is based on two SPI chips: the **CLT01-38SQ7**, which provides an 8-line protected input termination, and the **VNI8200XP** chip, which provides an 8-line monolithic output driver. The board has been designed to be plugged onto any CPU board having the **Arduino UNO R3** connectors, and it can be used to build basic PLC (*Programmable Logic Controller*) applications, where the feature of managing eight analog inputs and eight outputs through the SPI bus is needed.

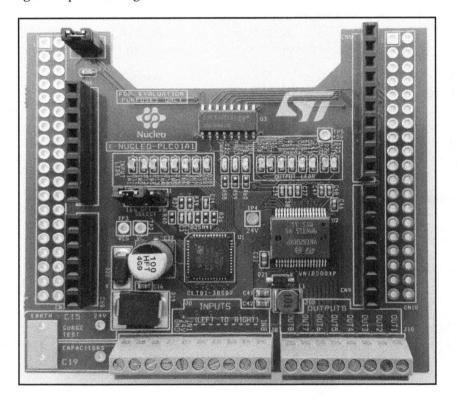

The device is by STMicroelectronics and can be purchased on several e-commerce sites on the Internet. The datasheet of the whole board is at: htt p://www.st.com/content/ccc/resource/technical/document/user_ma nual/group0/9c/25/64/62/4f/bc/4d/9f/DM00213568/files/DM

---

[480]

`00213568.pdf/jcr:content/translations/en.DM00213568.pdf.`

The datasheet of the single chips are available at: `http://www.st.com/con tent/ccc/resource/technical/document/datasheet/5f/67/d9/9c/7a /e2/4a/55/DM00218826.pdf/files/DM00218826.pdf/jcr:content/trans lations/en.DM00218826.pdf`and `http://www.st.com/content/ccc/resource/technical/document/user_m anual/group0/9c/25/64/62/4f/bc/4d/9f/DM00213568/files/DM00213568 .pdf/jcr:content/translations/en.DM00213568.pdf.`

To manage the board, we're going to use the SAMA5D3 Xplained board that has the Arduino UNO R3 connectors. However, since some pins conflict with the Ethernet port's ones, we're going to use some wires to connect the board instead of disabling the Ethernet port.

The connections needed to talk with on-board SPI chips are shown here:

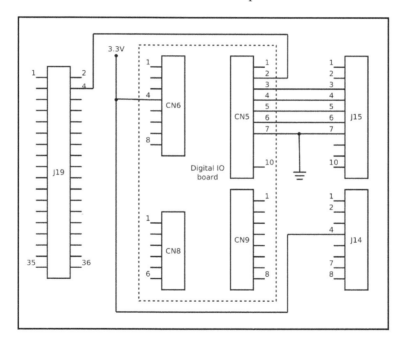

Before starting to write the code, we need to take a look at chips' datasheets in order to know how these work and then which data should be sent over the SPI channels we're going to use. Note that one chip is for the digital input, while the other one is for the digital output. However, in any case, we have to write and read data through both chips.

The important information regarding how to talk with these chips is that messages are 16 bits long, and they are arranged in this table. For the CLT01-38SQ7 we have:

Bit 0 LSB	Bit 1	Bit 2	Bit 3	Bit 4	Bit 5	Bit 6	Bit 7	Bit 8	Bit 9	Bit 10	Bit 11	Bit 12	Bit 13	Bit 14	Bit 15 MSB
1	0	PC4	PC3	PC2	PC1	/OTA	/UV A	IN1	IN2	IN3	IN4	IN5	IN6	IN7	IN8

Here, IN1 to IN8 bits are our digital line's statuses, and the other bits are control statuses (see the datasheet for further information). Then, for the VNI8200XP we have:

Bit 0 LSB	Bit 1	Bit 2	Bit 3	Bit 4	Bit 5	Bit 6	Bit 7	Bit 8	Bit 9	Bit 10	Bit 11	Bit 12	Bit 13	Bit 14	Bit 15 MSB
nP0	P0	P1	P2					IN0	IN1	IN2	IN3	IN4	IN5	IN6	IN7

Again, IN0 to IN7 bits are our digital lines statuses, and the other bits are control statuses (see the datasheet for further information).

Note that in both cases, both chips will send us an answer to each data transfer where we can extract useful information regarding the success of the last operation and the chips' status (again, we cannot explain these aspects in detail, and the datasheet is the only reference for you).

DTS modifications to enable the communication between the CPU and these chips are reported in the patch snippet here, and it's more or less the one we already saw earlier regarding the `spidev1` bus:

```
        };

    spi1: spi@f8008000 {
            cs-gpios = <&pioC 25 0>;
-
+           cs-gpios = <&pioC 25 0>, <&pioC 16 0>;
            status = "okay";
+
```

```
+                    vni8200xp@0 {
+                        compatible = "spidev";
+                        reg = <0>;
+                        spi-max-frequency = <1000000>;
+                    };
+
+                    clt01_38sq7@1 {
+                        compatible = "spidev";
+                        reg = <1>;
+                        spi-max-frequency = <1000000>;
+                    };
+                };

        adc0: adc@f8018000 {
```

The complete patch can be found in the `chapter_10/A5D3-digital-IO-spi.patch` file in the book's example code repository.

Now, we need to install a new Python library to manage our `spidev` device. Then, we can ask the `pip` command for help, as shown here:

```
root@a5d3:~# pip search spidev
max7219                  - A library to drive a MAX7219 LED
                           serializer using hardware spidev
SPIlib                   - A small library to use the SPIdev
                           linux interface
spidev                   - Python bindings for Linux SPI access
                           through spidev
Adafruit-PureIO          - Pure python (i.e. no native extensions)
                           access to Linux IO including I2C and SPI.
                           Drop in replacement for smbus and spidev
                           modules.
spi                      - Pure Python SPI Interface using spidev
RPimax7219               - A small library to drive a MAX7219 LED
                           serializer using hardware spidev
```

In order to execute the `pip` command and then install a new Python package through it, we must first install the **python-pip** and **libpython-dev** packages as usual.

OK, the library is **spidev**, and using the next command line, we can install it into our SAMA5D3 Xplained board:

```
root@a5d3:~# pip install spidev
```

 The home site of the **spidev** Python library is at: https://pypi.python.org/pypi/spidev.

Now, a possible implementation of the code to read and write data to our devices is reported here:

```python
def do_write(data):
    spi = spidev.SpiDev()
    spi.open(32765, 0)          # the SPI device for output

    # Do some SPI settings
    spi.max_speed_hz = 1000000
    spi.bits_per_word = 16

    # Compute the checksum
    p0      = data ^ (data >> 1)
    p0      = p0 ^ (p0 >> 2)
    p0      = p0 ^ (p0 >> 4)
    p0      = p0 & 1;
    p1      = data ^ (data >> 2)
    p1      = p1 ^ (p1 >> 4)
    p2      = p1 & 1
    p1      = p1 & 2
    p1      = p1 >> 1
    np0     = not p0
    tmp = (p2 << 3) | (p1 << 2) | (p0 << 1) | np0
    tmp = 0x01
    dbg("p2.p1.p0.np0=0x%01x" % (tmp))

    # Do the write
    dbg("write=0x%04x" % ((data << 8) | tmp))
    data = spi.xfer2([tmp, data])

    # Decode answer
    faults  = data[1]
    ok      = 1 if data[0] & 0b10000000 else 0
    twarn   = 0 if data[0] & 0b01000000 else 1
    pc      = 1 if data[0] & 0b00100000 else 0
    pg      = 0 if data[0] & 0b00010000 else 1
    p       = data[0] & 0b00001111
```

```
        dbg("faults=0x%02x ok=%d twarn=%d pc=%d
        pg=%d p2.p1.p0.np0=0x%01x" %
                    (faults, ok, twarn, pc, pg, p))

        spi.close()

def do_read():
        spi = spidev.SpiDev()
        spi.open(32765, 1)        # the SPI device for input

        # Do some SPI settings
        spi.max_speed_hz = 1000000
        spi.bits_per_word = 16

        data = spi.xfer2([0, 0])
        dbg("read=0x%04x" % ((data[1] << 8) | data[0]))

        spi.close()

        # Compute the checksum and extract alarms
        uva       = 1 if data[0] & 0b10000000 else 0
        ota       = 1 if data[0] & 0b01000000 else 0
        pc        = (data[0] >> 2) & 0b00001111
        ok        = 1 if (data[0] & 0b00000011) == 1 else 0

        dbg("inputs=0x%02x uva=%d ota=%d pc=0x%x ok=%d" %
                    (data[1], uva, ota, pc, ok))

        return data[1]
```

 The complete code is reported in `chapter_10/digital.py` in the book's example code repository.

The `do_write()` and `do_read()` functions basically call the `spidev.SpiDev()` method to create the object representing our SPI bus. Then, we use the `open()` and `close()` methods as usual, while the `xfer2()` method is used to both send and receive data through the SPI channel. Simply speaking, the command sequence for both functions is (more or less) like this:

```
spi = spidev.SpiDev()             # create the object
spi.open(AA, BB)                  # open the /dev/spidevAA.BB
spi.xxxxxxxx = xxxxxxxx           # do some SPI settings
data_in = spi.xfer2(data_out)     # do data transfer
spi.close()                       # close the device
```

In particular, note that during the reading we simply used some dummy values ([0, 0]) since each time we call the xfer2() method, we do a full duplex transfer (both MOSI and MISO channels are active at the same time). Then, we write and read data simultaneously.

At this point, to read the input's status, we can use the following command:

```
root@a5d3:~# ./digital.py -d r
digital.py :   read=0x00fd
digital.py :   inputs=0x00 uva=1 ota=1 pc=0xf ok=1
0x00
```

To write the output, we can use the following lines of code:

```
root@a5d3:~# ./digital.py -d w 0x80
digital.py :   p2.p1.p0.np0=0x1
digital.py :   write=0x8001
digital.py :   faults=0x00 ok=1 twarn=1 pc=0
                   pg=1 p2.p1.p0.np0=0x5
```

Both commands have been executed with the debugging messages turned on (using the -d option argument). So, you can see each single parameter we must take into account when we manage these devices.

For space reasons, we cannot explain in detail how these devices work, but you can easily get them by reading chips' datasheets.
To completely enable digital outputs, we have to properly manage an extra control line; otherwise, outputs are stuck at low level. A trick we can use is to connect the OUT_EN watchdog signal of the **VNI8200XP** chip to the chip select of **CLT01-38SQ7**. Then, we can refresh it using the following lines of code:

```
# while sleep .04 ; do \
        ./spidev_fdx -r 4 /dev/spidev32765.1 > \
                            /dev/null; \
    done
```

Here, the /dev/spidev32765.1 device corresponds to the CLT01-38SQ7 chip.

Summary

As you can see, the SPI bus is quite powerful, since while it implements an efficient data stream, it can also be easily managed with a large variety of different slave devices.

In the next chapter, we'll see another available bus for our embedded kits that allows us to communicate with some sensors using only one wire! It's time to move on to the next chapter and discover the **1-Wire** bus.

11

1-Wire - W1

After looking at the most frequently used buses that a developer can find on an embedded computer (USB, I²C, and SPI), it's time to present a less famous, but not less important communication bus: the 1-Wire bus (pronounced as *one-wire* and usually abbreviated with *W1* or *OW*).

Even if this bus is quite slow compared to other buses, it's interesting because it permits to communicate with a remote device using only one wire! This allows to simplify connections between the CPU and its peripherals, giving the designer the possibility to have the most economical and simply way to add electronic devices for identification, authentication, and delivery of calibration data or manufacturing information to a computer board.

What is the 1-Wire Bus?

The **one-wire** (**1-Wire**) bus is a half-duplex, single-master, multi-slave, asynchronous serial data bus designed to work with one wire only. In reality, for electrical reasons, the wires are at least two: one wire that carries a low-speed data signal with the power supply (data/power line) and the other one that is the ground (GND). However, despite this feature, most devices have three wires: the data signal, the GND, and the power supply (Vcc).

You should remember that *half-duplex* communication is when transmitting and receiving are not at the same time on the bus (the data can flow in one direction only), while *asynchronous* means that no clock is sent along with the data.

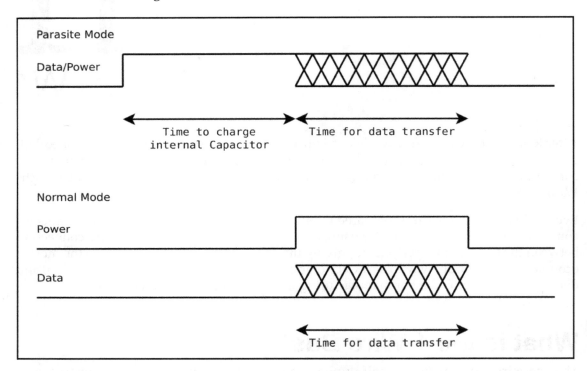

When a device has two wires only, it must include an in-built energy-storage mechanism (usually a capacitor) to store charge to power itself during periods when data is really exchanged. The device takes its power from the data pin instead of the regular power pin, and due to this reason, this functioning method is called *parasite mode*. The drawback of this feature is that the communication with this kind of device is slower. In fact, as shown in the figure below, in parasite mode, the data line must be pulled high prior to the beginning of the data transfer for at least an amount of time sufficient to charge the internal capacitor on the device. When the capacitor is charged, it can power the device to permit the data exchange.

On a 1-Wire bus, there is always one master, which typically is a microcontroller, and several slaves. The master initiates each communication activity on the bus, so the slaves can only act when addressed. Each slave has a unique 64-bit serial number that the master uses to address a well-defined device over the bus.

Since the slaves' addresses are not known by the master, the master uses an enumeration protocol (a particular broadcast message) to discover all connected devices called **singulation**. Once all devices are detected, the master can send a selection command with the address of a particular device, so the next command is executed only by the addressed device.

What is interesting about this bus is that every single slave can be disconnected and then reconnected without any problems for both the slave and the master. In fact, the master can detect a new slave and also discover when a slave has been removed. On the other hand, a slave can store its configuration into a non-volatile memory and start to work again as soon as it is reconnected to the bus.

 The details of how the **1-Wire** bus works is out of the scope of this book. If interested, you visit `http://en.wikipedia.org/wiki/1-Wire` for further information.

The electrical lines

1-Wire bus lines are reported in the following table:

Name	Description
data – *Data (and power when no Vcc)*	The bus data signal
GND	Common ground
Vcc (optional)	Optional power supply

Multiple devices must be connected in parallel as shown in the following diagram:

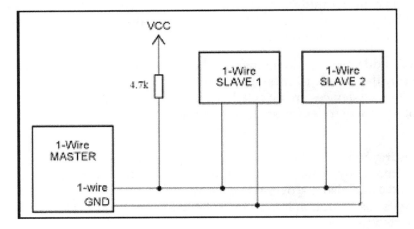

 The pull-up resistor is required to maintain logic 1 when the bus is not driven because 1-Wire devices have open-drain outputs (the reason for using open-drain outputs is to allow multiple devices on the same bus). The value of 4.7KΩ is most likely chosen to ensure a sufficiently small rise time with common cable lengths (the real parameter that governs the maximum allowed resistor value is the rise time of the signal determined by bus resistance and capacitance, and it should be carefully determinate for better performances).

1-Wire ports on the BeagleBone Black

The BeagleBone Black does not have 1-Wire controllers available. However, we can use a normal GPIO pin as an emulated 1-Wire controller. This is because the communication is quite slow for a normal CPU, and Linux can emulate the protocol very well.

For example, using the following DTS overlay settings, we can add an emulated 1-Wire controller on GPIO *P8.11*:

```
fragment@0 {
    target = <&am33xx_pinmux>;

    __overlay__ {
        bb_w1_pins: pinmux_bb_w1_pins {
            pinctrl-single,pins = <0x34 0x37>;
        };
    };
```

```
};

fragment@1 {
    target = <&ocp>;

    __overlay__ {
        #address-cells  = <1>;
        #size-cell      = <0>;
        status      = "okay";

        /* Setup the pins */
        pinctrl-names   = "default";
        pinctrl-0   = <&bb_w1_pins>;

        /* Define the new one-wire master as based on w1-gpio
         * and using GPIO1_13
         */
        onewire@0 {
            compatible   = "w1-gpio";
            gpios        = <&gpio1 13 0>;
        };
    };
};
```

 The complete DTS settings can be retrieved from the `chapter_11/BB-W1-GPIO-00A0.dts` file in the book's example code repository.

The first fragment defines GPIO settings, while the second one initializes the **w1-gpio** driver, which is the one needed to create our emulated 1-Wire controller.

The DTS file can be now compiled and installed with the following command lines:

```
root@bbb:~# dtc -O dtb -o /lib/firmware/BB-W1-GPIO-00A0.dtbo
                 -b 0 -@ BB-W1-GPIO-00A0.dts
root@bbb:~# echo BB-W1-GPIO > /sys/devices/platform/bone_capemgr/slots
bone_capemgr bone_capemgr: part_number 'BB-W1-GPIO', version 'N/A'
bone_capemgr bone_capemgr: slot #5: override
bone_capemgr bone_capemgr: Using override eeprom data at slot 5
bone_capemgr bone_capemgr: slot #5: 'Override Board Name,00A0, Overrid
e Manuf,BB-W1-GPIO'
bone_capemgr bone_capemgr: slot #5: dtbo 'BB-W1-GPIO-00A0.dtbo' loaded
; overlay id #1
```

In the preceding output, we've reported related kernel messages too.

Now, our new 1-Wire controller should be presented into the kernel, and it should be listed in the `/sys/bus/w1/devices/` directory, as shown here:

```
root@bbb:~# ls -l /sys/bus/w1/devices/
total 0
lrwxrwxrwx 1 root root 0 Oct 10 12:08 w1_bus_master1 -> ../../../devic
es/w1_bus_master1
```

1-Wire ports on the SAMA5D3 Xplained

The SAMA5D3 Xplained does not have 1-Wire controllers, but we can add an emulated one as we did earlier.

1-Wire ports on the Wandboard

The Wandboard does not have 1-Wire controllers, but we can add an emulated one as we did earlier.

The 1-Wire bus in Linux

These devices have a strange support in Linux, that is, they are fully managed by the sysfs interface and no special files are present in the `/dev` directory as usual.

In reality, there is another communication method between the 1-Wire core and the user space, which is not covered in this book. You can get further information by reading the `Documentation/w1/w1.netlink` file in the kernel's repository.

For each master, there exists a dedicated directory (as seen earlier) where several files are located, and this directory can be used to set up our controller. Here is an example from the controller emulated earlier:

```
root@bbb:~# ls /sys/bus/w1/devices/w1_bus_master1/
00-800000000000  w1_master_attempts           w1_master_search
driver           w1_master_max_slave_count  w1_master_slave_count
power            w1_master_name               w1_master_slaves
subsystem        w1_master_pointer            w1_master_timeout
uevent           w1_master_pullup             w1_master_timeout_us
w1_master_add    w1_master_remove
```

Each file has a well-defined functionality, and the most important ones are reported in the short list here:

- w1_master_search: Sets the number of searches left to do.
- w1_master_add: Manually registers a slave device.
- w1_master_remove: Manually removes a slave device.
- w1_master_timeout: The delay in seconds between searches.
- w1_master_timeout_us: The delay in microseconds between searches.
- w1_master_slave_count: The number of slaves found.
- w1_master_slaves: The names of slaves, one per line.

If we have a 1-Wire bus that never changes (that is, we don't add or remove devices), we can set w1_master_search to 0 (that is, searching is disabled) and then manually add serial numbers of each slave device using the w1_master_add device file (of course, the usage of both w1_master_add and w1_master_remove device files generally only makes sense when searching is disabled).

In the case of an unchangeable bus, another smart trick can also be setting w1_master_search to a small positive number in such a way as to do an initially small number of bus searches in order to detect all slaves and then stop new searches. This allows the system to automatically detect all slaves so that you don't lose time in unneeded searches.

Using files `w1_master_timeout` and `w1_master_timeout_us`, we can specify the interval at which bus searches occur (either of which may be 0) for as long as `w1_master_search` remains greater than 0 or is -1.

> The value of -1 for `w1_master_search` means continual searching.

Each search attempt decrements `w1_master_search` by 1 until it reaches 0 and then stops.

> See the `Documentation/w1/w1.generic` file in the kernel's repository for more information on the 1-Wire's device files usage.

Getting access to 1-Wire devices

In the next section, we will manage a 1-Wire device using both an emulated 1-Wire controller and a real one connected by I²C to the main CPU.

Using the GPIO interface

To show you how the 1-Wire bus works, we can use a really simple chip: the temperature sensor **DS18B20**. There are two possible ways or modes by which the chip can be powered: a *parasite version* (that is, the one that works in the *parasite mode*) with two wires only and a *normal version* with a dedicated power pin, which uses three wires instead. In our example, we will use the three wires and a waterproof version of this chip. There is a special packaging of the chip so that it can be used in hostile environments (look at the following image to see the packaging version of the two chips):

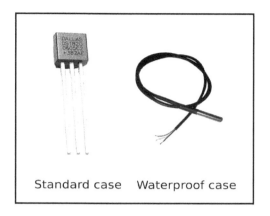

Standard case   Waterproof case

 The device can be purchased at
`http://www.cosino.io/product/waterproof-temperature-sensor` or by
surfing the Internet.
The datasheet is available at
`http://datasheets.maximintegrated.com/en/ds/DS18B20.pdf`.

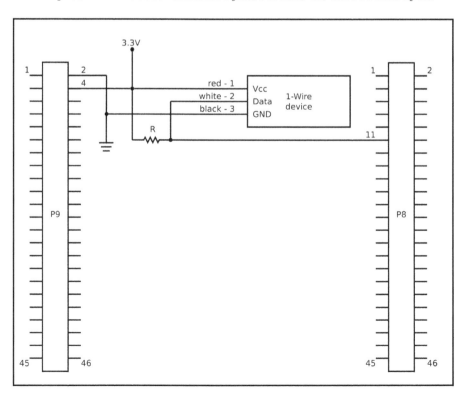

First of all, we have to set up electrical connections. The preceding diagram shows the correspondence between BeagleBone Black's pins and sensor's cables (*R=4.7KΩ*).

Now, we can take a look at the driver, which should be included in a standard kernel distribution. However, you can verify this situation by looking into the following directory for the file name `w1_therm.ko`:

```
root@bbb:~# find /lib/modules/$(uname -r)/kernel/drivers
                    -name w1_therm.ko
/lib/modules/4.4.7-bone9/kernel/drivers/w1/slaves/w1_therm.ko
```

If we get no output from the find command, we have to recompile the kernel as described in `Chapter 1`, *Installing the Development System*, to add the missing driver. To enable the driver compilation, we must surf the kernel configuration menu and enable the following settings: **Device Drivers | Dallas's 1-wire support | 1-wire Slaves | Thermal family implementation**. We then need to enable the driver compilation as a module.

Once connected, the sensor is automatically detected, and it should be listed in the `/sys/bus/w1/devices/` directory, as shown here:

```
root@bbb:~# ls -l /sys/bus/w1/devices/
total 0
lrwxrwxrwx 1 root root 0 Oct 10 12:18 28-000004b541e9 -> ../../../devi
ces/w1_bus_master1/28-000004b541e9
lrwxrwxrwx 1 root root 0 Oct 10 12:08 w1_bus_master1 -> ../../../devic
es/w1_bus_master1
```

In the preceding output, we see that our sensor has the 1-Wire ID set to `28-000004b541e9`. Note that in the case of multiple 1-Wire buses, we can discover where they are connected by looking at each controller's directory as displayed here:

```
root@bbb:~# ls -l /sys/bus/w1/devices/w1_bus_master1/
total 0
drwxr-xr-x 3 root root    0 Oct 10 12:18 28-000004b541e9
lrwxrwxrwx 1 root root    0 Oct 10 12:22 driver -> ../../bus/w1/driver
s/w1_master_driver
drwxr-xr-x 2 root root    0 Oct 10 12:22 power
lrwxrwxrwx 1 root root    0 Oct 10 12:08 subsystem -> ../../bus/w1
-rw-r--r-- 1 root root 4096 Oct 10 12:08 uevent
-rw-rw-r-- 1 root root 4096 Oct 10 12:22 w1_master_add
-r--r--r-- 1 root root 4096 Oct 10 12:22 w1_master_attempts
-rw-rw-r-- 1 root root 4096 Oct 10 12:22 w1_master_max_slave_count
-r--r--r-- 1 root root 4096 Oct 10 12:22 w1_master_name
-r--r--r-- 1 root root 4096 Oct 10 12:22 w1_master_pointer
-rw-rw-r-- 1 root root 4096 Oct 10 12:22 w1_master_pullup
-rw-rw-r-- 1 root root 4096 Oct 10 12:22 w1_master_remove
```

```
-rw-rw-r-- 1 root root 4096 Oct 10 12:12 w1_master_search
-r--r--r-- 1 root root 4096 Oct 10 12:22 w1_master_slave_count
-r--r--r-- 1 root root 4096 Oct 10 12:22 w1_master_slaves
-r--r--r-- 1 root root 4096 Oct 10 12:22 w1_master_timeout
-r--r--r-- 1 root root 4096 Oct 10 12:22 w1_master_timeout_us
```

Obviously, our controller's name is `w1_bus_master1`, and the files in the same directory are all related to it, for instance, files `w1_master_slave_count` and `w1_master_slaves`. As mentioned earlier, we can find how many slaves have been detected by the controller and the corresponding slaves list using these files, respectively:

```
root@bbb:~# cat /sys/bus/w1/devices/w1_bus_master1/w1_master_slave_cou
nt
1
root@bbb:~# cat /sys/bus/w1/devices/w1_bus_master1/w1_master_slaves
28-000004b541e9
```

OK, now, let's come back to our temperature sensor. In order to get the temperature's environment, we can take a look at the slave's directory:

```
root@bbb:~# ls -l /sys/bus/w1/devices/28-000004b541e9/
total 0
lrwxrwxrwx 1 root root     0 Oct 10 12:23 driver -> ../../../bus/w1/dri
vers/w1_slave_driver
-r--r--r-- 1 root root 4096 Oct 10 12:23 id
-r--r--r-- 1 root root 4096 Oct 10 12:23 name
drwxr-xr-x 2 root root     0 Oct 10 12:23 power
lrwxrwxrwx 1 root root     0 Oct 10 12:23 subsystem -> ../../../bus/w1
-rw-r--r-- 1 root root 4096 Oct 10 12:18 uevent
-r--r--r-- 1 root root 4096 Oct 10 12:23 w1_slave
```

In the `id` file, we can read the device's ID in a raw binary format:

```
root@bbb:~# od -tx1 /sys/bus/w1/devices/28-000004b541e9/id
0000000 28 e9 41 b5 04 00 00 0b
0000010
```

In the `name` file, we can read the device's ID as string:

```
root@bbb:~# cat /sys/bus/w1/devices/28-000004b541e9/name
28-000004b541e9
```

However, the file where we can find the temperature we wish to get is `w1_slave`. In fact, if we read it, we get the following code snippet:

```
root@bbb:~# cat /sys/bus/w1/devices/
28-000004b541e9/w1_slave
80 01 00 04 1f ff 10 10 b1 : crc=b1 YES
80 01 00 04 1f ff 10 10 b1 t=24500
```

The desired temperature is then `24500`, which is in m° C, that is, 24.5° C.

Using an external controller

Now, let's see how we can manage the preceding device using a real 1-Wire controller connected to the main CPU using the I²C bus (Chapter 9, *Inter-integrated Circuits – I2C*). This can be useful when we need to unload the CPU in emulating the controller via a GPIO pin.

The controller we're going to use is shown here:

Note that the device has been mounted on a special adapter useful to simplify the wired connections. This is because the case is very small, and we cannot use simple wires to connect the device to the Wandboard as usual.
The datasheet is available at
`https://datasheets.maximintegrated.com/en/ds/DS2482-100.pdf`.

Connections for both the temperature sensor and the controller to the Wandboard are reported in the following diagram (R=4.7KΩ):

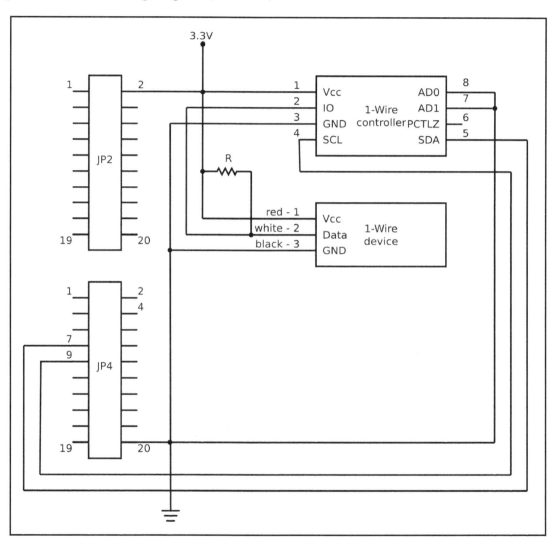

If everything works well, we should see the controller device on the first I²C bus as shown here:

```
root@wb:~# i2cdetect -y 0
     0  1  2  3  4  5  6  7  8  9  a  b  c  d  e  f
00:          -- -- -- -- -- -- -- -- -- -- -- --
10: -- -- -- -- -- -- -- -- 18 -- -- -- -- -- -- --
20: -- -- -- -- -- -- -- -- -- -- -- -- -- -- -- --
30: -- -- -- -- -- -- -- -- -- -- -- -- -- -- -- --
40: -- -- -- -- -- -- -- -- -- -- -- -- -- -- -- --
50: -- -- -- -- -- -- -- -- -- -- -- -- -- -- -- --
60: -- -- -- -- -- -- -- -- -- -- -- -- -- -- -- --
70: -- -- -- -- -- -- -- --
```

The driver to manage the controller should be included in a standard kernel distribution. However, you can verify this situation by looking into the following directory for the file name `ds2482.ko`:

```
root@wb:~# find /lib/modules/$(uname -r)/kernel/drivers
               -name ds2482.ko
/lib/modules/4.4.7-armv7-x6/kernel/drivers/w1/masters/ds2482.ko
```

If we get no output from the find command, we have to recompile the kernel as described in Chapter 1, *Installing the Development System*, to add the missing driver. To enable the driver compilation, we must surf the kernel configuration menu and enable the following settings: **Device Drivers | Dallas's 1-wire support | 1-wire Bus Masters | Maxim DS2482 I2C to 1-Wire bridge**. Then, we need to enable the driver compilation as a module.

OK, if the driver is already present, we can easily enable it using this command line:

```
root@wb:~# echo ds2482 0x18 > /sys/bus/i2c/devices/i2c-0/new_device
i2c i2c-0: new_device: Instantiated device ds2482 at 0x18
```

Note that the driver can also be enabled by adding a proper definition into the DTS file as explained in Chapter 9, *Inter-integrated Circuits – I2C*.

If everything works well, we should see the 1-Wire device:

```
root@wb:~# ls -l /sys/bus/w1/devices/
total 0
lrwxrwxrwx 1 root root 0 Jul 22 19:29 28-000004b541e9 -> ../../../devi
ces/w1_bus_master1/28-000004b541e9
lrwxrwxrwx 1 root root 0 Jul 22 19:29 w1_bus_master1 -> ../../../devic
es/w1_bus_master1
```

Now, the 1-Wire device can be accessed:

```
root@wb:~# cat /sys/bus/w1/devices/28-000004b541e9/w1_slave
30 01 00 04 1f ff 10 10 df : crc=df YES
30 01 00 04 1f ff 10 10 df t=19000
```

Summary

In this chapter, we discovered the 1-Wire bus and how it can be used in order to get data from a simple temperature sensor device. We used a 1-Wire controller emulated by the GPIO interface and a more complex I^2C device, which implements a complete 1-Wire controller. In both cases, we discovered that device management is almost the same and it's very simple.

In the next chapter, we're going to see another kind of bus that allows us to exchange data with several remote computers and that is at the base of almost every local computer network: Ethernet devices.

12
Ethernet Network Device - ETH

An embedded computer can do several things, but having the possibility to communicate with other devices (even over long distances) is a powerful feature we have to deal with, and Ethernet devices offer an easy and powerful way to do it. The GNU/Linux-based systems offer a really good support for Ethernet devices and their relative networking protocols. That's why, most of networking devices around the world are based on this technology.

In this chapter, we will briefly look at the very basics of Ethernet devices in the Linux kernel and, of course, into our embedded kits. Then, we'll see a simple TCP/IP client/server implementation and how to interact with these programs using *ready-to-use* tools.

In the end, we'll briefly expose an example about how to set up a bridge on a multi-Ethernet equipped board.

What is an Ethernet network device?

A computer network (or more simply, a *network*) is a telecommunications equipment that allows computers to exchange data with each other. In a computer network, several computers exchange data with each other using a data link, which can be made of cable media or wireless media. More specifically, the Ethernet network is a family of wired computer-networking technologies commonly used in **Local Area Network** (**LAN**) where every device communicating over it divides a stream of data into shorter pieces called **frames** that contain a lot of information useful for data communication as the source and destination addresses, error-checking data, and so on. Then, obviously, there is also the data link layer (as per the OSI model) where the information are stored.

In a GNU/Linux system, an *Ethernet device* is a computer peripheral that is used to get access to an Ethernet network and then to exchange data with other Ethernet-equipped computers. In a GNU/Linux system, these devices are usually called `eth0`, `eth1`, and so on, even if some exceptions may exist (some of these special cases will be presented in this chapter). In any case, these devices are not present in the `/dev` directory as usual; that's why, they are so special.

Another feature that made Ethernet devices special is the fact that they can receive messages even if they never requested them! For example, let's consider a ping message. The receiving host never waits for an incoming ping message; it simply arrives.

Thanks to these aspects (and others not mentioned here), the Ethernet devices (and more generally, all networking devices) have a special device class in the Linux kernel named **net device** (see `Chapter 5`, *Setting Up an Embedded OS*, in *Char, block and net device* section).

 For further details on Ethernet networks and how they work, you can visit `https://en.wikipedia.org/wiki/Ethernet`.

Electrical lines

The Ethernet bus lines are not presented in this book as per other devices because they are not relevant to connect an Ethernet-equipped computer to a network. In fact, an Ethernet port is usually pre-mounted on a computer, and we just need to plug in a cable. Note also that due to very high communication frequencies involved in Ethernet communications, a handmade connection may result in no communications at all! So, you should avoid doing experimentation if you do not really they know what to do.

However, for the sake of completeness, a typical Ethernet port is shown in the following image. In this book, we will assume that all connections are made using this port with an Ethernet cable and, if needed, an Ethernet switch in the middle:

Ethernet port on the BeagleBone Black

The BeagleBone Black has one Ethernet port, which is a standard 100 Mb/s port. Here are the related kernel messages at boot:

```
net eth0: initializing cpsw version 1.12 (0)
net eth0: phy found : id is : 0x7c0f1
IPv6: ADDRCONF(NETDEV_UP): eth0: link is not ready
```

Ethernet ports on the SAMA5D3 Xplained

The SAMA5D3 Xplained has two Ethernet ports. One port is a standard 100 Mb/s port, while the other one is a 1000 MB/s (gigabit). Here are the related kernel messages at boot:

```
macb f0028000.ethernet: invalid hw address, using random
libphy: MACB_mii_bus: probed
macb f0028000.ethernet eth0: Cadence GEM rev 0x00020119 at 0xf0028000
irq 50 (6e:65:bc:82:d1:b3)
macb f0028000.ethernet eth0: attached PHY driver [Micrel KSZ9031 Gigab
it PHY] (mii_bus:phy_addr=f0028000.etherne:07, irq=-1)
macb f802c000.ethernet: invalid hw address, using random
libphy: MACB_mii_bus: probed
macb f802c000.ethernet eth1: Cadence MACB rev 0x0001010c at 0xf802c000
 irq 51 (36:da:fb:48:48:81)
macb f802c000.ethernet eth1: attached PHY driver [Micrel KSZ8081 or KS
Z8091] (mii_bus:phy_addr=f802c000.etherne:01, irq=-1)
IPv6: ADDRCONF(NETDEV_UP): eth0: link is not ready
IPv6: ADDRCONF(NETDEV_UP): eth1: link is not ready
```

Ethernet port on the Wandboard

The Wandboard has one Ethernet port, which is a 1000 MB/s (gigabit) port. Here are the related kernel messages at boot:

```
libphy: fec_enet_mii_bus: probed
fec 2188000.ethernet eth0: registered PHC device 0
fec 2188000.ethernet eth0: Freescale FEC PHY driver [Generic PHY] (mii
_bus:phy_addr=2188000.ethernet:01, irq=-1)
IPv6: ADDRCONF(NETDEV_UP): eth0: link is not ready
```

The Ethernet devices in Linux

As already stated earlier, in a GNU/Linux system, Ethernet devices are usually called eth0, eth1, and so on, even if some exceptions may exist. In fact, as we already saw in Chapter 1, *Installing the Developing System*, a virtual Ethernet connection (that is, an Ethernet port emulated over a USB connection) is called usb0, usb1, and so on. Also, in Chapter 7, *Serial Ports and TTY Devices – TTY*, Managing TTY into the Kernel with SLIP, we found that SLIP devices are called sl0, sl1, and so on.

Other examples can be found in *The Linux Documentation Project* at: `http://www.tldp.org/LDP/nag2/x-087-2-hwconfig.tour.html`.

Another example of special naming can be the ones created by USB Ethernet adapters like the one shown here:

If we try to connect one of these devices to our host PC, we should get something similar to the following kernel messages:

```
New USB device found, idVendor=0b95, idProduct=7720
New USB device strings: Mfr=1, Product=2, SerialNumber=3
Product: AX88772
Manufacturer: ASIX Elec. Corp.
SerialNumber: 000415
asix 2-1.2:1.0 eth1: register 'asix' at usb-0000:00:1d.0-1.2, ASIX AX8
8772 USB 2.0 Ethernet, 00:0e:c6:87:73:9f
asix 2-1.2:1.0 enx000ec687739f: renamed from eth1
IPv6: ADDRCONF(NETDEV_UP): enx000ec687739f: link is not ready
asix 2-1.2:1.0 enx000ec687739f: link down
IPv6: ADDRCONF(NETDEV_UP): enx000ec687739f: link is not ready
```

Then, the new Ethernet device is now named `enx000ec687739f`, as shown by the `ifconfig` command:

```
$ ifconfig enx000ec687739f
enx000ec687739f Link encap:Ethernet  HWaddr 00:0e:c6:87:73:9f
          UP BROADCAST MULTICAST  MTU:1500  Metric:1
          RX packets:0 errors:0 dropped:0 overruns:0 frame:0
          TX packets:0 errors:0 dropped:0 overruns:0 carrier:0
          collisions:0 txqueuelen:1000
          RX bytes:0 (0.0 B)  TX bytes:0 (0.0 B)
```

The `ifconfig` command is now deprecated even if it's still available on all systems (especially on embedded distributions). It should be replaced by the `ip` command (see next section), and the equivalent command of the above one is reported here:

```
$ ip link show enx000ec687739f
4: enx000ec687739f: <NO-CARRIER,BROADCAST,MULTICAST
,UP> mtu 1500 qdisc pfifo_fast state DOWN mode DEFA
ULT group default qlen 1000
 link/ether 00:0e:c6:87:73:9f brd ff:ff:ff:ff:ff
:ff
```

However, whatever the name is, the common thing is that these devices are not reported under the `/dev` directory. They cannot be accessed with the usual `open()` or `close()` system call, and they must be managed using special system calls and by dedicated networking tools (see the *client/server* example that follows).

The net tools

These tools are stored in the **net-tools** package, and they are a set of utility programs we can use to easily manipulate Ethernet devices. Inside this package, there are several programs, and few of them are specifically for Ethernet devices.

One of the most important Ethernet-related networking tool is `ifconfig`, which is used to configure a network interface. We already used it several times in this book to discover the available network interfaces on our system or just to set up our IP address.

Even if the `ifconfig` command can solve quite all the network settings, it's now deprecated, and a more powerful tool exists to replace it: the `ip` command (which is in the **iproute2** package). This command can be used for every task we can do with `ifconfig` and much more! Just as a simple example, here is a command to show the list of active network addresses in the SAMA5D3 Xplained using the `ip` command:

```
root@a5d3:~# ip address list
1: lo: <LOOPBACK,UP,LOWER_UP> mtu 65536 qdisc noqueue state UNKNOWN gr
oup default qlen 1
 link/loopback 00:00:00:00:00:00 brd 00:00:00:00:00:00
 inet 127.0.0.1/8 scope host lo
 valid_lft forever preferred_lft forever
 inet6 ::1/128 scope host
 valid_lft forever preferred_lft forever
2: can0: <NOARP,ECHO> mtu 16 qdisc noop state DOWN group default qlen
10
 link/can
3: eth0: <NO-CARRIER,BROADCAST,MULTICAST,UP> mtu 1500 qdisc pfifo_fast
 state DOWN group default qlen 1000
 link/ether 6e:65:bc:82:d1:b3 brd ff:ff:ff:ff:ff:ff
 inet6 fe80::6c65:bcff:fe82:d1b3/64 scope link
 valid_lft forever preferred_lft forever
4: eth1: <NO-CARRIER,BROADCAST,MULTICAST,UP> mtu 1500 qdisc pfifo_fast
 state DOWN group default qlen 1000
 link/ether 36:da:fb:48:48:81 brd ff:ff:ff:ff:ff:ff
5: sit0@NONE: <NOARP> mtu 1480 qdisc noop state DOWN group default qle
n 1
 link/sit 0.0.0.0 brd 0.0.0.0
6: usb0: <BROADCAST,MULTICAST,UP,LOWER_UP> mtu 1500 qdisc pfifo_fast s
tate UP group default qlen 1000
 link/ether ba:f7:1b:43:ae:9c brd ff:ff:ff:ff:ff:ff
 inet 192.168.8.2/30 brd 192.168.8.3 scope global usb0
 valid_lft forever preferred_lft forever
 inet6 fe80::b8f7:1bff:fe43:ae9c/64 scope link
 valid_lft forever preferred_lft forever
```

For further information on the iproute2 tools, a good starting point is https://wiki.linuxfoundation.org/networking/iproute2.

Another useful tool is the `mii-tool` command that can be used to check the Ethernet interface status, especially the status of a network interface's **Media Independent Interface (MII)** unit, which most Ethernet adapters use to auto-negotiate the link speed and duplex mode setting. Using this tool, we can easily check whether the cable is plugged in or not and the current connection speed:

```
root@a5d3:~# mii-tool
eth0: negotiated 1000baseT-HD flow-control, link ok
eth1: no link
```

 Another tool similar to `mii-tool` and that can be used to manage Ethernet devices is the `ethtool` command, which is held in the same package.

Communicating with a remote device

Since the scope of this book is not to provide details on networking programming, we're not going to spend too much time in showing the several available communication protocols or in explaining the details of the following example codes. However, we're going to show you how you can use an Ethernet port to quickly establish a networking communication.

A simple TCP client/server application

Just as a simple example of network communication, we can use two simple Python programs that implement a TCP/IP client and server examples. These examples are not so useful to show you how you can write a server or a client (there are tons of these examples on the Internet). However, they are useful to show you how you can easily interact with several *ready-to-use* tools (presented in the next section) that can speed up the development stage of every networking task.

The first program is named `tcp_srv.py`, and it implements a TCP/IP server. Here is its relevant code:

```
# Check the user input
try:
    port = int(args[0])
except ValueError, err:
    error("invalid number for <port>:", args[0])
    sys.exit(1)
if port < 0 or port > 65535:
    error("invalid number for port, must be [0, 65535]:", args[0])
```

```
      sys.exit(1)

# Create a TCP/IP socket object
s = socket.socket(socket.AF_INET, socket.SOCK_STREAM)
s.setsockopt(socket.SOL_SOCKET,
        socket.SO_REUSEADDR, 1) # avoid error: Address already in use
server_address = (host, port)
s.bind(server_address)
info("starting up on %s port %s" % s.getsockname())

# Now we can listen for an incoming client connection
s.listen(5)

# The main loop
while True:
    info("waiting for new connection...")

    # Establish connection with the client
    c, addr = s.accept()
    info("got connection from ", addr)

    # Send back an hello message
    c.send("Thank you for connecting!\n")

    # Close the connection
    c.close()
    info("connection closed!")
```

As we can see, after a brief check of the user input, we used the `socket.socket()` method to create the s TCP/IP socket, and then, we used the `setsockopt()`, `bind()`, and `listen()` methods to properly set up a TCP/IP server listening on the desired port.

To execute the program now, we can use the following command line, which is referred to a host PC (but on every embedded kit, it's just the same):

```
$ ./tcp_srv.py 12345
tcp_srv.py :  starting up on 0.0.0.0 port 12345
tcp_srv.py :  waiting for new connection...
```

The server is now running and waiting for a new connection.

The second program is named `tcp_cli.py` and implements a TCP/IP client. Here is its relevant code:

```
# Check the user inputs
host = args[0]
try:
```

```
        port = int(args[1])
except ValueError, err:
    error("invalid number for <port>:", args[1])
    sys.exit(1)
if port < 0 or port > 65535:
    error("invalid number for port, must be [0, 65535]:", args[0])
    sys.exit(1)

# Create a TCP/IP socket object
s = socket.socket(socket.AF_INET, socket.SOCK_STREAM)

# Connect with the server
info("starting new connection...")
s.connect((host, port))

# Print the server's hello message
info("server says:", s.recv(1024))

# Close the connection
s.close()
info("connection closed!")
```

 The full code of both programs can be found in the
`chapter_12/tcp_srv.py` and `chapter_12/tcp_cli.py` files in the
book's example code repository.

This time, the code is simpler since we just need to use the `socket.socket()` method again to create the s socket, but now, we will use the `connect()` method to establish the connection with the server.

At this time, the code flow is simple. We will use the `send()` and `recv()` methods to send and receive the data to the other peers, and when finished, we will close the connection with the `close()` method.

If we try to contact the server using our new client, we would get the following lines of code:

```
$ ./tcp_cli.py localhost 12345
tcp_cli.py :  starting new connection...
tcp_cli.py :  server says: Thank you for connecting!
tcp_cli.py :  connection closed!
```

On the other hand, on the server, we will see the following output:

```
tcp_srv.py :   starting up on 0.0.0.0 port 12345
tcp_srv.py :   waiting for new connection...
tcp_srv.py :   got connection from  ('127.0.0.1', 46938)
tcp_srv.py :   connection closed!
tcp_srv.py :   waiting for new connection...
```

Using ready-to-use networking tools

When we need to test a networking connection, we need some tools to quickly and safely do this job. In most cases, we can avoid writing new code or we can drastically reduce this task just using some dedicated tools. As an example, we can use the simple TCP/IP server tcp_srv.py as the client and the telnet program in such a way as to establish a connection:

```
$ telnet localhost 12345
Trying 127.0.0.1...
Connected to localhost.
Escape character is '^]'.
Thank you for connecting!
Connection closed by foreign host.
```

Since the telnet program is (more or less) a TCP/IP client, we get a behavior similar to using the tcp_cli.py client.

Another useful tool to test our server is **netcat**, which is universally known as the *hacker's Swiss army knife for network applications*. The power of netcat is the fact that it supports several networking protocols, and it can act as a client or a server! To use it as a client to interact with our server, we can use the following command line, where nc is the netcat program itself:

```
$ nc localhost 12345
Thank you for connecting!
```

If we wish to use it as tcp_srv.py replacement, we can use the following command line:

```
$ while true ; do \
        echo 'Thank you for connecting!' | nc -p 12345 -l ; \
   done
```

Then, on the other side, we can reuse our new client `tcp_cli.py` as follows:

```
$ ./tcp_cli.py localhost 12345
tcp_cli.py :  starting new connection...
tcp_cli.py :  server says: Thank you for connecting!
tcp_cli.py :  connection closed!
```

As we can see, the functioning is just the same!

Finally, we should remember the **xinetd** daemon we saw in Chapter 4, *Quick Programming with Scripts and System Daemons, Useful and Ready-to-Use Daemons – xinetd*. This daemon opens a TCP/IP connection as our server does, and then, it can be accessed in a similar way as we did here using the `telnet` or `nc` program for our client `tcp_cli.py` (you can try and verify it!).

The raw Ethernet bus

Like the USB and other communication buses presented in this book, even the Ethernet bus can be accessed in a raw mode. However, this method is not reported in this book because it's complex and it may need a dedicated book to be correctly explained! However, you can start your studies of the raw Ethernet programming by visiting `https://en.wikipedia.org/wiki/Raw_socket`.

A simple example of raw sockets will be presented in Chapter 14, *Controller Area Network – CAN*, The raw CAN bus when we'll implement a simple CAN communication between two devices.

Simple Ethernet bridging

Since our SAMA5D3 Xplained board has two Ethernet ports on board, it's quite interesting presenting a brief example of how we can set up a networking bridge on it in such a way as to connect two separate LANs into a single one. The idea is to set up our board in such a way that it can work as if it was (more or less) an Ethernet switch so that two separate LANs are physically merged into a bigger one in a transparent manner (that is, no special settings should be done on the networked devices on both LANs).

 For further information regarding what a bridge is, you should start by visiting `https://en.wikipedia.org/wiki/Bridging_(networking)`.

First of all, we need the package named **bridge-utils**, which holds the needed commands to enable the bridging functionality. The package holds the `brctl` command, which is used to set up our bridge (if it is missing, we can install the package using the usual installation commands).

Creating the bridge is quite simple. First of all, we have to create a bridge interface, that is, a virtual network device that the kernel recognizes as a bridge:

```
root@a5d3:~# brctl addbr br0
```

You should notice here that `br0` is just another name for the network interface device class.

If we get the following error, the bridging support is missing in our kernel. So, we have to recompile it by enabling the item **Networking support** | **Networking options** | **802.1d Ethernet Bridging** and then rebooting the system:

```
root@a5d3:~# brctl addbr br0
add bridge failed: Package not installed
```

To show bridges defined in our system, we will use the `brctl` command again:

```
root@a5d3:~# brctl show
bridge name     bridge id          STP enabled     interfaces
br0         8000.000000000000    no
```

Now, we simply have to add Ethernet devices that we wish to add to part of our new bridge:

```
root@a5d3:~# brctl addif br0 eth0
root@a5d3:~# brctl addif br0 eth1
```

Done! The bridge is now fully functional:

```
root@a5d3:~# brctl show
bridge name     bridge id          STP enabled     interfaces
br0         8000.9e3a4f189100    no      eth0    eth1
```

Now, we just have to plug in Ethernet cables, and our LANs will be merged into a big one!

It's still possible to get access to our embedded kit using the `br0` interface. We just need to assign to it an IP address in the usual manner (`ifconfig`, `ip`, and so on) and then use it as a normal Ethernet device.

Note that in this case, the two Ethernet interfaces should have no IP addresses or any services running on them (as DHCP or similar servers) because the only functional interface is now br0.

You should also note that we can create a bridge using the ip command too. The commands are shown here:

```
root@a5d3:~# ip link add name br0 type bridge
root@a5d3:~# ip link set dev br0 up
root@a5d3:~# ip link set dev eth0 master br0
root@a5d3:~# ip link set dev eth1 master br0
```

Summary

Ethernet devices offer tons of different possibilities to connect local and remote devices to each other, and embedded developers can use them for tons of different usages. In fact, the GNU/Linux-based systems offer full and complete support for these devices in both hardware and software. So, developers have to focus their attention on the final target only without losing their time in developing low-level communication protocols.

In the next chapter, we'll see another important networking device class similar to Ethernet devices: wireless networking devices that are commonly known as Wi-Fi.

13
Wireless Network Device - WLAN

The Ethernet connection discussed in the previous chapter allows several devices to talk each other. However, we need a wired connection to do that job. In this chapter, we will take a look at the wireless network devices that allow communication between several computers, but doing it without using wires. What is really interesting in using these networking interfaces is that a large part of communication protocols used on Ethernet interfaces can be used with these devices too!

We'll take a brief look at the basics of wireless devices in the Linux kernel and, of course, in our embedded kits. Then, we'll see an example of how we can do an encrypted connection with a normal access point using a wireless device attached to our embedded kits or how we can use our embedded kits to implement an access point.

What is a wireless network device?

A **Wireless Local Area Network (WLAN)**, or wireless network device, more simply, **Wi-Fi**, is a computer network that links more devices using a wireless connection method within a limited area (usually a home, office, school, and so on). These kinds of connections allow people to move around the radio coverage and still be connected to the network. Under this point of view, they are an evolution of the Ethernet network seen in the previous chapter, since even in this case, every device communicating over it divides a stream of data into shorter pieces called *frames* that contain several pieces of information useful for data communication.

As for the Ethernet, a wireless network device is a computer peripheral that is used to get access to a wireless network and then to exchange data with other wireless network equipped computers. In a GNU/Linux system, these devices are usually called `wlan0`, `wlan1` and so on even if some exceptions may exist (in some circumstances, it may happen that they are even called `eth0`, `eth1` and so on just to point out how these two device kinds are very similar from the user's point of view). Also, these device are not present in the `/dev` directory due to the fact that they are **net devices** (see `Chapter 5`, *Setting Up an Embedded OS, Char, block and net device* section).

The most relevant difference between these devices and Ethernet ones (even some minor differences are in place) are how they must be managed in the system in order to get connected into the wireless network and to properly exchange data with the other networked computer (this topic will be explained soon in the upcoming sections).

 For further details of WLANs and how they work, you can visit `https://en.wikipedia.org/wiki/Wireless_LAN`.

The electrical lines

As for the Ethernet, WLAN's bus lines are not presented in this book for the same reasons discussed in the previous chapter. However, here is an image of the wireless chip mounted on the Wandboard in order to show you how a wireless network device can appear on an embedded computer board:

 To be able see the chip as in the figure, we must remove the screwed heatsink on Wandboard's CPU module.

WLAN device on the BeagleBone Black

The BeagleBone Black has no premounted wireless LAN devices, so they must be added using an available bus such as USB, SDIO, SPI, and so on.

WLAN device on the SAMA5D3 Xplained

Like the BeagleBone Black, the SAMA5D3 Xplained has no wireless LAN devices premounted. However, it has a dedicated extended board to be inserted into the MMC slot, providing a wireless device (look at the following section).

WLAN device on the Wandboard

As already stated earlier, the Wandboard has one wireless LAN device, which is a 802.11n capable port. Here are the related kernel messages at boot:

```
brcmfmac: brcmf_c_preinit_dcmds: Firmware version = wl0: Oct 25 2011 1
9:34:12 version 5.90.125.104
brcmfmac: brcmf_cfg80211_reg_notifier: not a ISO3166 code
```

 We already encountered and set up Wandboard's wireless device in `Chapter 1`, *Installing the Developing System,*Wireless support & Co. on the Wandboard.

WLAN devices in Linux

WLAN devices (or Wi-Fi) are usually identified in the GNU/Linux system with `wlan0`, `wlan1`, and so on, and they can be added to an existing system in several ways. The Wandboard comes with its own Wi-Fi chip but it's quite common (especially for cost reasons) that an embedded computer has no Wi-Fi at all. So, in this case, we can provide a wireless connection to our embedded kit using an available CPU's communication bus, such as the USB bus and (sometimes) the SDIO or SPI bus.

Pluggable external WLAN devices

As a simple example, in the following image, there is a picture of a USB WLAN device that can be connected with every computer that has a USB host port:

The device can be purchased
at: http://www.cosino.io/product/usb-realtek-wifi-adapter or by
surfing the Internet.

If we try to connect one of these devices to our host PC, we should get following kernel
messages:

```
usb 2-1.1: new high-speed USB device number 13 using ehci-pci
usb 2-1.1: New USB device found, idVendor=7392, idProduct=7811
usb 2-1.1: New USB device strings: Mfr=1, Product=2, SerialNumber=3
usb 2-1.1: Product: 802.11n WLAN Adapter
usb 2-1.1: Manufacturer: Realtek
usb 2-1.1: SerialNumber: 00e04c000001
rtl8192cu: Chip version 0x10
rtl8192cu: MAC address: 80:1f:02:8f:75:8d
rtl8192cu: Board Type 0
rtl_usb: rx_max_size 15360, rx_urb_num 8, in_ep 1
rtl8192cu: Loading firmware rtlwifi/rtl8192cufw_TMSC.bin
ieee80211 phy1: Selected rate control algorithm 'rtl_rc'
usbcore: registered new interface driver rtl8192cu
usbcore: registered new interface driver rtl8xxxu
rtl8192cu 2-1.1:1.0 wlx801f028f758d: renamed from wlan1
IPv6: ADDRCONF(NETDEV_UP): wlx801f028f758d: link is not ready
rtl8192cu: MAC auto ON okay!
rtl8192cu: Tx queue select: 0x05
IPv6: ADDRCONF(NETDEV_UP): wlx801f028f758d: link is not ready
```

The new wireless device is now named wlx801f028f758d as shown by the iwconfig
command:

```
$ iwconfig wlx801f028f758d
wlx801f028f758d  IEEE 802.11bgn  ESSID:off/any
          Mode:Managed  Access Point: Not-Associated   Tx-Power=20 dBm
          Retry short limit:7   RTS thr=2347 B   Fragment thr:off
          Power Management:off
```

Another example of a WLAN device is the one shown in the following image:

 The image presents the same device in both its top and bottom views in order to show the Wi-Fi chip (in the bottom-right corner) and its SDIO bus connections (in the top-left corner).

This is a Wi-Fi device that uses the SDIO bus to communicate with the host CPU, and it's designed for the SAMA5D3 Xplained (and MMC slot compatible boards). Since it uses the SDIO bus, we cannot use our Debian stored into the microSD to test it because it uses the same bus. So, we have to use an embedded distribution like the one we presented in Chapter 5, *Setting Up an Embedded OS,OpenWrt* or Chapter 5, *Setting Up an Embedded OS, Yocto*, where we must install the proper drivers (the latest Yocto releases support this device by default).

The Wi-Fi operation modes

Once the WLAN device is connected to our main CPU and it's up and running, we have to manage it in order to get connected to the wireless network. We already know that we can have several wireless connection kinds. However, the major two are the **station (STA)** mode and the **Access Point (AP)** mode . The first mode is also known as the *client mode* and it's the usual mode of functioning (that is, every wireless LAN chip supports this mode of functioning). When our device uses this mode, our computer acts as a station. On the other side, the second mode of functioning allows several stations to get connected to each other in a common wireless network by accepting them according to certain credentials. In this mode, a computer uses its wireless device as a common access point where the other devices can be accredited and then get connected in a common network (possibly protected with some encryption way from the other ones).

In the usual way of speaking, a station asks for a new connection to an access point, which, in turn, allows it to speak with other already connected stations.

For more examples and details about the WLAN modes of connections, you can start reading
at: https://en.wikipedia.org/wiki/Wireless_access_point.

In a GNU/Linux-based system, the STA and AP modes are managed by specific programs. We're going to show you how the STA mode works using the Wandboard (however, the same steps can be performed on the other embedded kit once we have installed a wireless device on them) in a dedicated section that follows.

The wireless tools

These tools are a collection of user-space utilities written to support the configuration of the WLAN devices and some related aspects of networking using the *Linux Wireless Extension*.

The *Linux Wireless Extension* is a generic API that allows a driver to expose to the user-space configuration and statistics specific to common WLAN devices. Further information on this topic can be accessed
at: http://www.labs.hpe.com/personal/Jean_Tourrilhes/Linux/Tools.html.

They are held in the **wireless-tools** package, and they should be already installed in the Wandboard (otherwise, we can install them as usual).

One of the most important tools of this collection is `iwconfig`, which is used to manipulate the basic wireless parameters. As reported in the command's description, the `iwconfig` command is very similar to `ifconfig`. In fact, it can be used in a similar manner to get basic information of our WLAN, as shown here:

```
root@wb:~# iwconfig wlan0
wlan0     IEEE 802.11abgn  ESSID:off/any
          Mode:Managed  Access Point: Not-Associated
          Retry short limit:7   RTS thr:off   Fragment thr:off
          Encryption key:off
          Power Management:on
```

Using it, we can get or set several basic information of our WLAN, and for instance, we can get connected to an open wireless network (that is without any authentication method) named `open_wireless_ESSID` just using the following command:

```
root@wb:~# iwconfig wlan0 essid <OPEN_WIRELESS_ESSID>
```

However, we can do it because we know the network's name (remember that the wireless network's name is usually called **Extended Service Set Identification (ESSID)**), but in case we don't know it, which are the available networks to be connected to? Well, in this case, the `iwlist` wireless tool comes to help us. In fact, we can use it to do a scan of available networks in the air using the next command:

```
root@wb:~# iwlist wlan0 scan
```

If we get the following output, it means that we have to bring up the network device from before:
```
wlan0       Interface doesn't support scanning : Netw
ork is down
```
The command to set up the device is shown here (note that `wlan0` is a network device after all):
```
root@wb:~# ifconfig wlan0 up
```

If some wireless network is in the air around us, we should get the following output:

```
wlan0     Scan completed :
          Cell 01 - Address: 64:D1:A3:40:C3:B5
                    Channel:2
                    Frequency:2.417 GHz (Channel 2)
                    Quality=31/70  Signal level=-79 dBm
                    Encryption key:on
                    ESSID:"EnneEnne2"
                    Bit Rates:1 Mb/s; 2 Mb/s; 5.5 Mb/s; 11 Mb/s; 9 Mb/s
                              18 Mb/s; 36 Mb/s; 54 Mb/s
                    Bit Rates:6 Mb/s; 12 Mb/s; 24 Mb/s; 48 Mb/s
```

```
Mode:Master
Extra:tsf=0000000000000000
Extra: Last beacon: 40ms ago
IE: Unknown: 0009456E6E65456E6E6532
IE: Unknown: 010882848B961224486C
IE: Unknown: 030102
IE: Unknown: 2A0104
IE: Unknown: 32040C183060
IE: Unknown: 2D1A0E1017FFFF00000
               10000000000000000000000000C0
IE: Unknown: 3D16020506000000000000000000
               0000000000000000000
IE: IEEE 802.11i/WPA2 Version 1
    Group Cipher : CCMP
     Pairwise Ciphers (1) : CCMP
     Authentication Suites (1) : PSK
IE: Unknown: DD180050F2020101000003A40000
               27A4000042435E00620
IE: Unknown: 0B05040020127A
IE: Unknown: 4A0E14000A002C01C800140005001900
IE: Unknown: DD07000C4304000000
IE: Unknown: 0706434E20010D10
IE: Unknown: DDB90050F204104A0001101044000102
               103B00010310470
```

The command's output can be much longer than the one shown earlier due to the presence of more detected networks. However, the output format for each of them is similar to the preceding format.

The `iwlist` then gives us more information than `iwconfig` as well explained by its man pages.

Even if the `iwconfig` command (and other wireless tools) can solve quite all the network settings, in complete analogy as the Ethernet devices, a more powerful tool exists. This tool is the `iw` command (which is held in the package of the same name and that can be installed as usual), and it can be used for every task we can perform with `iwconfig` and much more!

Just as a simple example, here is a command to show the list of available wireless network devices in the Wandboard:

```
root@wb:~# iw dev
phy#0
      Interface wlan0
            ifindex 4
            wdev 0x1
            addr 44:39:c4:9a:96:24
            type managed
```

Another useful usage of iw is the following command line that shows all capabilities of our wireless device:

```
root@wb:~# iw phy phy0 info
Wiphy phy0
      max # scan SSIDs: 10
      max scan IEs length: 2048 bytes
      Retry short limit: 7
      Retry long limit: 4
      Coverage class: 0 (up to 0m)
      Device supports roaming.
      Supported Ciphers:
            * WEP40 (00-0f-ac:1)
            * WEP104 (00-0f-ac:5)
            * TKIP (00-0f-ac:2)
            * CCMP (00-0f-ac:4)
            * CMAC (00-0f-ac:6)
      Available Antennas: TX 0 RX 0
      Supported interface modes:
            * IBSS
            * managed
            * AP
            * P2P-client
            * P2P-GO
            * P2P-device
      Band 1:
            Capabilities: 0x1020
                  HT20
                  Static SM Power Save
                  RX HT20 SGI
                  No RX STBC
                  Max AMSDU length: 3839 bytes
                  DSSS/CCK HT40
            Maximum RX AMPDU length 65535 bytes (exponent: 0x003)
            Minimum RX AMPDU time spacing: 16 usec (0x07)
            HT TX/RX MCS rate indexes supported: 0-7
            Bitrates (non-HT):
```

```
* 1.0 Mbps
* 2.0 Mbps (short preamble supported)
* 5.5 Mbps (short preamble supported)
* 11.0 Mbps (short preamble supported)
* 6.0 Mbps
* 9.0 Mbps
* 12.0 Mbps
* 18.0 Mbps
* 24.0 Mbps
* 36.0 Mbps
* 48.0 Mbps
* 54.0 Mbps
Frequencies:
        * 2412 MHz [1] (20.0 dBm)
        * 2417 MHz [2] (20.0 dBm)
        * 2422 MHz [3] (20.0 dBm)
        * 2427 MHz [4] (20.0 dBm)
        * 2432 MHz [5] (20.0 dBm)
        * 2437 MHz [6] (20.0 dBm)
        * 2442 MHz [7] (20.0 dBm)
        * 2447 MHz [8] (20.0 dBm)
        * 2452 MHz [9] (20.0 dBm)
        * 2457 MHz [10] (20.0 dBm)
        * 2462 MHz [11] (20.0 dBm)
        . . .
```

The command's output has been broken for space reasons, but it continues for several lines!

Also, note Supported interface modes reported by the preceding command. It tells us that our wireless device can act as a station, access point, and others modes such as P2P, which is also known as *WiFi Direct*

mode (https://en.wikipedia.org/wiki/Wi-Fi_Direct):

```
* IBSS
* managed
* AP
* P2P-client
* P2P-GO
* P2P-device
```

The WPA supplicant

Wireless tools are very useful for simple settings. However, for normal usage, they are not enough. In fact, in a normal wireless connection, we have to use some sort of encryption in order to protect our data that flows through the air! To do it, we need special tools for each mode of functioning discussed earlier. As an example, we will show how we can set up a station on our Wandboard using the WPA as an encryption method.

When acting as a station, that is, as a computer that wishes to get connected to a wireless network having an authentication protocol, we need a **wireless supplicant**. A *supplicant* is a program that is responsible for making login requests to a wireless network by passing the login and encryption credentials to the authentication server (that is, the access point). A good wireless supplicant for GNU/Linux-based systems is the tool named **WPA-Supplicant**, which can be easily installed in our Debian by getting the **wpasupplicant** package.

 WPA stands for *Wi-Fi Protected Access* and it means that the program was written in order to support this authentication method. However, WPA-Supplicant supports the latest **WPA2** as far as several older wireless authentication methods are concerned. They are explained at: https://en.wikipedia.org/wiki/Wpa_supplicant.

After the package installation, we get two main programs: the `wpa_supplicant` command and `wpa_cli`. The former is our supplicant, while the latter is its controlling tool.

OK, now, it's time to try a connection. After the program installation, we need to supply a very basic configuration file by adding the following lines to the `/etc/wpa_supplicant.conf` file:

```
ctrl_interface=/var/run/wpa_supplicant
update_config=1
```

Then, we have to execute the supplicant using this command line:

```
root@wb:~# wpa_supplicant -B -Dnl80211 -iwlan0
                         -c/etc/wpa_supplicant.conf
```

At this point, we can control `wpa_supplicant` using the `wpa_cli` command, so let's start by asking WPA-Supplicant to do a wireless network scan in order to discover possible available networks to get connected to:

```
root@wb:~# wpa_cli scan
Selected interface 'wlan0'
OK
```

Then, let's retrieve the scan's results with this command:

```
root@wb:~# wpa_cli scan_results
Selected interface 'wlan0'
bssid / frequency / signal level / flags / ssid
64:d1:a3:40:c3:b5      2417     -82      [WPA2-PSK-CCMP][WPS][ESS]
EnneEnne2
```

Each time we execute a command, the supplicant shows us the `Selected interface 'wlan0'` message. This is because we never selected a default interface. We can do it using the `-i` option argument as done in the following commands.

Well, at this point, we can get connected to the `EnneEnne2` network using the following commands:

```
root@wb:~# wpa_cli -iwlan0 add_network
0
root@wb:~# wpa_cli -iwlan0 set_network 0 ssid '"EnneEnne2"'
OK
root@wb:~# wpa_cli -iwlan0 set_network 0 psk '"EnneEnne password"'
OK
root@wb:~# wpa_cli -iwlan0 select_network 0
OK
```

The ' and " characters that delimit our network's credentials strings. Also, note that in the preceding command, we selected the network 0 because this is the number that WPA-Supplicant assigned to our network when we used the `add_network` command.

If everything works well, we should see the following kernel message notifying us that the wireless network is up and running:

```
IPv6: ADDRCONF(NETDEV_CHANGE): wlan0: link becomes ready
```

Then, we can ask our supplicant about the interface connection status with this command:

```
root@wb:~# wpa_cli -iwlan0 status
bssid=64:d1:a3:40:c3:b5
freq=2417
ssid=EnneEnne2
id=0
mode=station
pairwise_cipher=CCMP
group_cipher=CCMP
key_mgmt=WPA2-PSK
wpa_state=COMPLETED
p2p_device_address=44:39:c4:9a:96:24
address=44:39:c4:9a:96:24
uuid=9ccc6c2b-a494-52df-9676-fb423dc39728
```

At this point the connection is done and we have to configure network's parameters only as we do with any other network device. Then to do it, if we know our LAN's parameters, we can use the `ifconfig` command (and related ones) or we can use the DHCP service (if available) as follow:

```
root@wb:~# dhclient wlan0
```

Now the interface should be configured:

```
root@wb:~# ifconfig wlan0
wlan0     Link encap:Ethernet  HWaddr 44:39:c4:9a:96:24
          inet addr:192.168.32.52  Bcast:192.168.32.255  Mask:255.255
.255.0
          inet6 addr: fe80::4639:c4ff:fe9a:9624/64 Scope:Link
          UP BROADCAST RUNNING MULTICAST  MTU:1500  Metric:1
          RX packets:175 errors:0 dropped:59 overruns:0 frame:0
          TX packets:30 errors:0 dropped:0 overruns:0 carrier:0
          collisions:0 txqueuelen:1000
          RX bytes:26451 (25.8 KiB)  TX bytes:4927 (4.8 KiB)
```

The Hostapd daemon

As already stated earlier, acting as a station is one of the possible way of operation of a common wireless device, but another important one is the access point mode. This mode of functioning can be enabled using the **hostapd** daemon implemented by the `hostapd` program.

The hostapd daemon (held in the package of the same name, **hostapd**) is a special daemon for wireless access point and authentication servers. It can be used to create a wireless hot spot on a GNU/Linux-based computer using compatible wireless interfaces that support the kernel's **mac80211** subsystem (and other specific and old drivers such as Host AP, MadWifi, Prism54, and so on).

For further information regarding `hostapd` and the mac80211 subsystem, you can visit
`https://wireless.wiki.kernel.org/en/users/documentation/hostapd`.

To show you how to use the hostapd daemon, we can use the BeagleBone Black with the USB pluggable external wireless LAN device shown earlier. We can reproduce a simple access point device to allow Wi-Fi devices to get connected with it and then surf the Internet. The trick is to use hostapd to accept connections from wireless clients, use the Ethernet port to get access to the Internet, and then use the Linux's bridging functionality (already presented in *Chapter 12, Ethernet Network Device – ETH, Simple Ethernet bridging*) to exchange network packets from the wireless port to the Ethernet one and vice versa.

First of all, we have to install the needed software, that is, the **hostapd**, **bridge-utils**, and **iw** packages using usual manners (the `apt-get` or `aptitude` command). Then, let's start by verifying that our USB wireless LAN device supports the AP mode using the `iw` command as done earlier:

```
root@bbb:~# iw dev
phy#0
        Interface wlx801f028f758d
                ifindex 4
                wdev 0x1
                addr 80:1f:02:8f:75:8d
                type managed
```

OK, the BeagleBone Black supports the wireless device, and then, we can get its information:

```
root@bbb:~# iw phy phy0 info
Wiphy phy0
    max # scan SSIDs: 4
    max scan IEs length: 2257 bytes
    RTS threshold: 2347
    Retry short limit: 7
    Retry long limit: 4
    Coverage class: 0 (up to 0m)
    Device supports RSN-IBSS.
    Supported Ciphers:
```

```
          * WEP40 (00-0f-ac:1)
          * WEP104 (00-0f-ac:5)
          * TKIP (00-0f-ac:2)
          * CCMP (00-0f-ac:4)
          * 00-0f-ac:10
          * GCMP (00-0f-ac:8)
          * 00-0f-ac:9
          * CMAC (00-0f-ac:6)
          * 00-0f-ac:13
          * 00-0f-ac:11
          * 00-0f-ac:12
   Available Antennas: TX 0 RX 0
   Supported interface modes:
          * IBSS
          * managed
          * AP
          * AP/VLAN
          * monitor
          * mesh point
          * P2P-client
          * P2P-GO
          . . .
```

Great, one of the supported interface modes is AP, so we can go further and configure the hostapd daemon.

 The driver used for this wireless device is held in the `rtl8192cu.ko` module, and it can be enabled in Linux's configuration menu by navigating to **Device Drivers** | **Network device support** | **Wireless LAN** | **RTL8723AU/RTL8188[CR]U/RTL819[12]CU (mac80211) support**.

The `hostapd.conf` configuration file should be placed in the `/etc/hostapd/` directory with the following content:

```
ssid=BBBAccessPoint
wpa_passphrase=BBBpassphrase

ctrl_interface=/var/run/hostapd
interface=wlx801f028f758d
bridge=br0
driver=nl80211
hw_mode=g
channel=6
wpa=2

beacon_int=100
hw_mode=g
```

```
ieee80211n=1
wme_enabled=1
ht_capab=[SHORT-GI-20][SHORT-GI-40][HT40+]
wpa_key_mgmt=WPA-PSK
wpa_pairwise=CCMP
max_num_sta=8
wpa_group_rekey=86400
```

 The file can be retrieved from the `chapter_13/hostapd.conf` file in the book's example code repository.

In the preceding listing, we should notice the following relevant settings:

- `interface` is set equal to the `wlx801f028f758d` value, which is the name of the wireless device we wish to use as access point.
- `ssid` is the public name of our new wireless network. When everything will be up and running, we should see this name on our smartphone's wireless selection panel.
- `wpa_passphrase` is the passphrase we have to insert to get connected to the new wireless network.
- `wpa` sets (and force) the WPA encryption protocol.
- `driver` selects the **cfg80211** (and **mac80211**) based drivers.

The last note is for the bridge setting that specifies that once the hostapd daemon is up and running, it should automatically add the wireless interface to a bridge named `br0`.

Now, to start the daemon, we should use the next command line:

```
root@bbb:~# hostapd /etc/hostapd/hostapd.conf &
[1] 2427
root@bbb:~# Configuration file: /etc/hostapd/hostapd.conf
[ 755.090539] rtl8192cu: MAC auto ON okay!
[ 755.129917] rtl8192cu: Tx queue select: 0x05
[ 755.689681] IPv6: ADDRCONF(NETDEV_UP): wlx801f028f758d: link is not
 ready
[ 755.721302] device wlx801f028f758d entered promiscuous mode
wlx801f028f758d: interface state UNINITIALIZED->HT_SCAN
20/40 MHz operation not permitted on channel pri=6 sec=10 based on ove
rlapping BSSes
Using interface wlx801f028f758d with hwaddr 80:1f:02:8f:75:8d and ssid
 "BBBAccessPoint"
[ 757.557555] IPv6: ADDRCONF(NETDEV_CHANGE): wlx801f028f758d: link be
comes ready
```

```
wlx801f028f758d: interface state HT_SCAN->ENABLED
wlx801f028f758d: AP-ENABLED
```

This is the command's output where we should see that the AP is now enabled.

> We execute the daemon in the background using the Bash & option just to be able to show you the daemon's messages. In fact, the best way to execute the daemon is using the -B option argument, which automatically starts the daemon in the background mode.

Once we execute the preceding command, if everything works well, we should have our new bridge with the wireless device already attached, as reported here (see `Chapter 12`, *Ethernet Network Device – ETH*, Simple Ethernet bridging for further information regarding the `brctl` commands):

```
root@bbb:~# brctl show br0
bridge name bridge id        STP enabled interfaces
br0         8000.801f028f758d no          wlx801f028f758d
```

Now, in order to allow packet flow from the smartphone to the Internet through the wireless AP and the Ethernet port, we have just to add the `eth0` interface. The command is as follows:

```
root@bbb:~# brctl addif br0 eth0
```

If we re-execute the `show` command, we should get the correct (and final) bridge's configuration:

```
root@bbb:~# brctl show br0
bridge name     bridge id        STP enabled     interfaces
br0             8000.78a504cac9fe    no          eth0
                                                 wlx801f028f758d
```

> The user should remember to not execute these commands from an SSH connection involving the `eth0` interface; Otherwise, the connection will be lost!

If we wish to get access to the BeagleBone Black from the network, we can now assign an IP address to the bridge as follows:

```
root@bbb:~# ifconfig br0 192.168.32.25
br0: port 2(eth0) entered forwarding state
br0: port 2(eth0) entered forwarding state
br0: port 1(wlx801f028f758d) entered forwarding state
br0: port 1(wlx801f028f758d) entered forwarding state
br0: port 2(eth0) entered forwarding state
br0: port 1(wlx801f028f758d) entered forwarding state
```

The preceding kernel messages displayed after the ifconfig command line show that the bridge is up and running.

Now, to allow a normal smartphone to be able to use our new AP to surf the Internet, we have to set up a DHCP server to pass to it valid networking settings such as an IP address, some name servers, a gateway and so on. To do so, we can use the already installed DHCP daemon named udhcpd, which we used in Chapter 1, *Installing the Developing System, Setting up the developing system*. Since this daemon supports just one interface at a time, we have to use a custom configuration file and then execute another instance of the daemon using the following command line:

```
root@bbb:~# udhcpd -f udhcpd.conf.br0
```

The content of the udhcpd.conf.br0 file can be retrieved from the chapter_13/udhcpd.conf.br0 file in the book's example code repository. However, for completeness, it is reported here as well:

```
# udhcpd configuration file for bridging

start           192.168.32.100
end             192.168.32.200

interface       br0
max_leases      10

option    dns      8.8.8.8 8.8.4.4
option    subnet   255.255.255.0
option    router   192.168.32.41
option    lease    864000          # 10 days of seconds
```

You should notice that both the start and end options can be used to define a range of available IP addresses for wireless clients, while the interface setting can be used to address the bridge interface where we can send DHCP replies.

OK, now, everything should be in place, and we can try to use our new access point to surf the Internet with a smartphone. So, let's select the BBBAccessPoint wireless network and enter the BBBpassphrase passphrase to get connected with the Beaglebone Black. Then, we should see these logging messages:

```
hostapd: wlx801f028f758d: STA c4:9a:02:46:5a:3f
IEEE 802.11: authenticated
hostapd: wlx801f028f758d: STA c4:9a:02:46:5a:3f
IEEE 802.11: associated (aid 1)
hostapd: wlx801f028f758d: STA c4:9a:02:46:5a:3f
RADIUS: starting accounting session 7428D613-00000000
hostapd: wlx801f028f758d: STA c4:9a:02:46:5a:3f WPA:
pairwise key handshake completed (RSN)
```

Also, if we take a look at the udhcpd file's output, as reported here, we should see that the daemon has supplied an IP address to our smartphone as expected:

```
Sending OFFER of 192.168.32.129
Sending ACK to 192.168.32.129
```

Summary

WLAN devices are versatile network devices that allow several computers to communicate with each other without using wires and then allow them to move around without obstacles. Despite this fact, their management is more complex then Ethernet ports, and additional tools must be used to manage them, especially when protected connections are needed. However, GNU/Linux-based systems have a dedicated tool for every need!

In the next chapter, we'll see another important networking device class heavily used in the automotive industry, the CAN bus. It is another kind of networking mechanism that uses a simple protocol that can be used to exchange data between a complex computer and a simple microcontroller.

14
Controller Area Network - CAN

After looking at the most frequently used buses to exchange data with a remote device (or a remote computer), we should take a look at another communication bus that is widely used in the automotive industry (but is also used in many other contexts), that is, the CAN bus.

Originally implemented for multiplex electrical wiring within automobiles, this bus has been specifically designed to allow microcontrollers, computers, and devices to communicate with each other in applications without a host computer by having a message-based protocol. This bus is not as *famous* as the Ethernet or Wi-Fi. However, in the embedded world, it is used, and it is not rare to find SoCs that support it by default. That's why, we have dedicated a complete chapter to this bus.

What is the CAN bus?

The **Controller Area Network (CAN)** bus is a half-duplex, multi-master, multi-slave, asynchronous serial data bus designed for connecting **Electronic Control Units** (**ECU**), also known as *nodes*, using two wires bus. From the electrical point of view, data is sent on these wires in a differential mode (as the USB bus does), so we can send the information across long distances with a large quantities of connected devices.

Each node is able to send and receive messages, but not simultaneously, and a message (or frame) consists primarily of the identifier (or ID, which represents the priority of the message) and up to 8 (or 64, in the case of extended messages) data bytes followed by some acknowledge and other control data.

To do its job, each node requires:

- A CPU (microprocessor or host processor), which decides what received messages mean and which messages want to transmit.
- A CAN controller, which is often an integral part of the CPU (but it can be added as an external peripheral too).
- A transceiver, which converts the data stream from CAN bus levels (differential levels) to levels that the CAN controller uses (usually, the normal TXD and RXD couple). The transceiver also has protective circuitry to protect the CAN controller.

 Details on how the CAN bus works are out of the scope of this book. If you are interested, you can visit `https://en.wikipedia.org/wiki/CAN_bus` for further information.

The electrical lines

The CAN bus lines are reported in the table here:

Name	Description
CAN-Hi	The positive data level
CAN-Low	The negative data level

In the case of multiple devices connection, they must be connected in parallel, as shown in the diagram here:

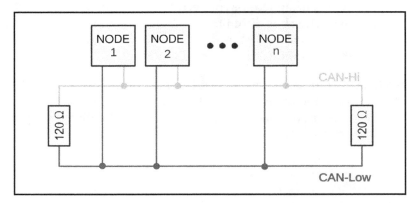

The two resistors at the two ends of the bus are just terminators, and they are required depending on how long the bus wires are (specific reasons are due to the transmission line theory).

Differential signals we saw in the preceding diagram (**CAN-Hi** and **CAN-Low**) allow us to have really long wires. However, in this book, we'll see a special CAN communication layout that doesn't use the transceiver and that can be used for short communication ranges ($\ll 1m$). To achieve this, we need to know a little about what the transceiver does. It can output a high or a low level to the bus (representing 1 and 0 symbols), but 0 dominates 1, so if two transceivers try to speak at the same time, and one is saying 1 and the other is saying 0, then 0 wins.

We can recreate the same situation simply using some diodes, as shown in the following diagram:

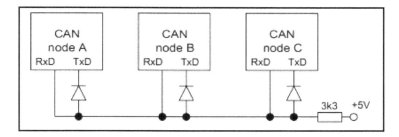

The resistor value depends on the value of supply voltage (**Vcc**) and some internals of the used controllers. So, the preceding diagram should be taken as an example of functioning only.

In this case, electrical lines are the ones reported in the following table:

Name	Description
RxD	The data receiver line
TxD	The data transmitter line
GND	Common ground

You can get further information on these connections in the document at `http://www.mikrocontroller.net/attachment/28831/siemens_AP2921.pdf`.

CAN ports on the BeagleBone Black

The BeagleBone Black has two CAN controllers available (without transceivers), `can0` and `can1`. However, `can0` cannot be used without breaking the Cape management. That's why, we're not going to use it. The available bus is summarized in this table:

Name	RxD	TxD
can1	P9.24	P9.26

The main DTS settings to enable the `can1` signals are reported in the following code. The first fragment defines pins settings, while the second one enables the CAN controller:

```
/* Define the pins usage */
exclusive-use =
    /* the pin header P9 uses */
    "P9.24",
    "P9.26",
    /* Hardware IP cores in use */
    "uart1";

fragment@0 {
    target = <&am33xx_pinmux>;

    __overlay__ {
        dcan1_pins_s0: dcan1_pins_s0 {
            pinctrl-single,pins = <
                0x180 0x12  /* d_can1_tx, SLEWCTRL_FAST |
                              INPUT_PULLUP | MODE2 */
                0x184 0x32  /* d_can1_rx, SLEWCTRL_FAST |
                              RECV_ENABLE | INPUT_PULLUP
                              | MODE2 */
            >;
        };
    };
};

fragment@1 {
    target = <&dcan1>;

    __overlay__ {
        #address-cells = <1>;
        #size-cells = <0>;

        status = "okay";
```

```
pinctrl-names = "default";
pinctrl-0 = <&dcan1_pins_s0>;
};
};
```

The complete DTS settings can be retrieved from the `chapter_14/BB-DCAN1-00A0.dts` file in the book's example code repository.

The DTS file can be now compiled and installed with the following command lines:

```
root@bbb:~# dtc -O dtb -o /lib/firmware/BB-DCAN1-00A0.dtbo
                -b 0 -@ BB-DCAN1-00A0.dts
root@bbb:~# echo BB-DCAN1 > /sys/devices/platform/bone_capemgr/slots
bone_capemgr bone_capemgr: part_number 'BB-DCAN1', version 'N/A'
bone_capemgr bone_capemgr: slot #5: override
bone_capemgr bone_capemgr: Using override eeprom data at slot 5
bone_capemgr bone_capemgr: slot #5: 'Override Board Name,00A0, Overrid
e Manuf,BB-DCAN1'
bone_capemgr bone_capemgr: slot #5: dtbo 'BB-DCAN1-00A0.dtbo' loaded;
overlay id #1
CAN device driver interface
c_can_platform 481d0000.can: c_can_platform device registered (regs=fa
1d0000, irq=186)
```

In the preceding output, we've reported the related kernel messages too.

Now, a new network device should be present:

```
root@bbb:~# ifconfig can0
can0      Link encap:UNSPEC HWaddr 00-00-00-00-00-00-00-00-00-00-00-00
          NOARP  MTU:16  Metric:1
          RX packets:0 errors:0 dropped:0 overruns:0 frame:0
          TX packets:0 errors:0 dropped:0 overruns:0 carrier:0
          collisions:0 txqueuelen:10
          RX bytes:0 (0.0 B) TX bytes:0 (0.0 B)
          Interrupt:186
```

CAN ports on the SAMA5D3 Xplained

The SAMA5D3 Xplained has two CAN controllers available (without transceivers), `can0` and `can1`. However, `can0` is the only one enabled by default, while the other can be enabled by properly modifying the DTS file (however, this is not shown in this book since we're not going to use it). The available bus is summarized in this table:

Name	RxD	TxD
can0	J21.8 – CANRX0	J21.8 – CANTX0

At boot time, we can read the following information in kernel messages:

```
at91_can f000c000.can: device registered (reg_base=d0982000, irq=50)
```

Then, we can see that the `can0` interface is already present:

```
root@a5d3:~# ifconfig can0
can0      Link encap:UNSPEC  HWaddr 00-00-00-00-00-00-00-00-00-00-00
          NOARP  MTU:16  Metric:1
          RX packets:0 errors:0 dropped:0 overruns:0 frame:0
          TX packets:0 errors:0 dropped:0 overruns:0 carrier:0
          collisions:0 txqueuelen:10
          RX bytes:0 (0.0 B)  TX bytes:0 (0.0 B)
          Interrupt:50
```

CAN ports on the Wandboard

The Wandboard has no CAN bus controllers available.

The CAN bus in Linux

As seen earlier, every CAN controller is represented in the system as a network device, and it can be listed as any other Ethernet or Wi-Fi device using the `ifconfig` command (or equivalent). The reason is that a CAN bus is just a network of several machines that are able to talk to each other into a LAN.

So, as we already saw earlier, we can use all networking commands on these devices. Here are two examples using both `ifconfig` and `ip` commands:

```
root@a5d3:~# ifconfig can0
can0       Link encap:UNSPEC  HWaddr 00-00-00-00-00-00-00-00-00-00-00
           NOARP  MTU:16  Metric:1
           RX packets:0 errors:0 dropped:0 overruns:0 frame:0
           TX packets:0 errors:0 dropped:0 overruns:0 carrier:0
           collisions:0 txqueuelen:10
           RX bytes:0 (0.0 B)  TX bytes:0 (0.0 B)
           Interrupt:50
root@a5d3:~# ip link show can0
2: can0: <NOARP,ECHO> mtu 16 qdisc noop state DOWN mode
DEFAULT group default qlen 10
    link/can
```

In particular, using the `ip` command, we can add a special type of CAN interface, the virtual one:

```
root@a5d3:~# ip link add dev vcan0 type vcan
```

Notice that the preceding command may return the following error:

```
RTNETLINK answers: Operation not supported
```

This is because the kernel misses the virtual CAN device's support. In this case, we can try to load the corresponding kernel module using the next command:

```
root@a5d3:~# modprobe vcan
```

However, if we still get an error message, we have to enable the compilation of this support by surfing in the kernel configuration menu and enabling the following settings: **Networking support | CAN bus subsystem support | CAN Device Drivers | Virtual Local CAN Interface (vcan)**. Then, after the boot, we have to redo the `modprobe` command.

Now, we have a new CAN device:

```
root@a5d3:~# ip link show vcan0
7: vcan0: <NOARP> mtu 16 qdisc noop state DOWN mode
DEFAULT group default qlen 1
    link/can
```

However, this is a virtual CAN device (or vcan device), and it can be used to send CAN frames around in memory. These devices are useful for simulation and testing. In fact, we can use them as a normal CAN device as shown in the upcoming sections.

> These devices are similar to the loopback Ethernet device; in fact, they are allocated into the system memory only.

The can-utils package

Using the C language to read or write data to a CAN device is, of course, the best way to do it. However, there is a quicker way, that is, using the **can-utils** package. It can be installed as usual, and it holds lots of useful programs we can use to manage our CAN devices.

> The package's repository is at
> https://gitorious.org/linux-can/can-utils.

The main two utilities for a basic CAN bus usage are cansend and candump. The first one is used to send a single CAN frame through a CAN device, and its syntax is reported here:

```
# cansend --help
Usage: cansend <device> <can_frame>.
```

> Unluckily, the CAN tools have no man pages, and all the related documentation must be retrieved from the Internet or using the internal help messages.

Here is a usage example where we send a message on the can0 interface with 0x5AA as identifier and 0xde, 0xad, 0xbe, and 0xef as data bytes (note that this tool always assumes that the values are given in hexadecimal):

```
# cansend can0 5AA#deadbeef
```

We can also use the extended form where the data is 0xde, 0xad, 0xbe, 0xef, 0x11, 0x22, 0x33, and 0x22:

```
# cansend can0 5AA#deadbeef11223344
```

On the other side, to listen to traffic on the bus, we can use candump, where, to display all traffic in real time on the can0 device, we can use the next command:

```
# candump can0
```

This time, the command's help message is a bit more clean and tells us what we can do with this command. So, here is the code block:

```
Usage: candump [options] <CAN interface>+
  (use CTRL-C to terminate candump)
Options: -t <type>    (timestamp: (a)bsolute/(d)elta/(z)ero/(A)bsolute w
date)
         -c           (increment color mode level)
         -i           (binary output - may exceed 80 chars/line)
         -a           (enable additional ASCII output)
         -S           (swap byte order in printed CAN data[]
                       - marked with '`' )
         -s <level>   (silent mode - 0: off 1: animation 2: silent)
         -b <can>     (bridge mode - send received frames to <can>)
         -B <can>     (bridge mode - like '-b' with disabled loopback)
         -u <usecs>   (delay bridge forwarding by <usecs> microseconds)
         -l           (log CAN-frames into file.Sets '-s 2' by default)
         -L           (use log file format on stdout)
         -n <count>   (terminate after receipt. of <count> CAN frames)
         -r <size>    (set socket receive buffer to <size>)
         -d           (monitor dropped CAN frames)
         -e           (dump CAN error frames in human-readable format)
         -x           (print extra message infos, rx/tx brs esi)
         -T <msecs>   (terminate after <msecs> without any reception)
Up to 16 CAN interfaces with optional filter sets can be specified
on the commandline in the form: <ifname>[,filter]*
Comma separated filters can be specified for each given CAN interface:
 <can_id>:<can_mask> (matches when <can_id> & mask == can_id & mask)
 <can_id>~<can_mask> (matches when <can_id> & mask != can_id & mask)
 #<error_mask>       (error filter, see include/linux/can/error.h)
CAN IDs, masks and data content are given and expected in hexadecimal
values.
When can_id and can_mask are both 8 digits, they are assumed to be 29
bit EFF.
Without any given filter all data frames are received ('0:0' default
filter).
Use interface name 'any' to receive from all CAN interfaces.
```

The interesting things here are that the comma-separated filters can be specified for each given CAN interface. In fact, using them, we can select useful messages transmitted over the CAN bus. For instance, to show only messages with the `0x123` identifier, we will use the following command:

```
# candump can0,0x123:0x7FF
```

To show messages with the `0x123` or `0x456` identifier, we can use the following command:

```
# candump can0,0x123:0x7FF,0x456:0x7FF
```

The `candump` command can take also more than one CAN device:

```
# candump can0,0x123:0x7FF,0x456:0x7FF can2,0x5AA:0x7FF can3 can8
```

In the preceding command, we ask to dump messages from CAN devices `can0`, `can2`, `can3`, and `can8` with several filters.

Note the usage of `can_mask` and `error_mask`. In fact, using these parameters, we can select several identifiers doing the selection bit per bit and per message type! For instance, using the next command, we can dump only error frames but no data frames:

```
# candump any,0~0,#FFFFFFFF
```

On the other hand, using the next one, we can dump error frames and also all data frames:

```
# candump any,0:0,#FFFFFFF
```

The raw CAN bus

In a Linux-based system, we can use the **SocketCAN** implementation to manage these devices and then exchange data between them. It uses the Berkeley socket API and the Linux network stack (and raw sockets) to implement CAN device drivers as network interfaces to allow programmers familiar with network programming to easily learn how to use CAN sockets.

See the `Documentation/networking/can.txt` file in the kernel's repository for more information.

Here is a simplified example in C language regarding how to open a SocketCAN socket:

```c
int s;
char *ifname;
struct sockaddr_can addr;
struct can_frame frame;
struct ifreq ifr;
int ret;

/* Open the PF_CAN socket */
s = socket(PF_CAN, SOCK_RAW, CAN_RAW);
if (s < 0) {
    perror("Error while opening socket");
    exit(-1);
}

/* Find the CAN device */
strcpy(ifr.ifr_name, ifname);
ret = ioctl(s, SIOCGIFINDEX, &ifr);
if (ret < 0) {
    perror("ioctl");
    exit(-1);
}
printf("%s: %s at index %d\n", NAME, ifname, ifr.ifr_ifindex);

/* Bind the socket */
addr.can_family = AF_CAN;
addr.can_ifindex = ifr.ifr_ifindex;
ret = bind(s, (struct sockaddr *)&addr, sizeof(addr));
if (ret < 0) {
    perror("bind");
    exit(-1);
}
```

A socket can also be bound to all CAN interfaces, and (in this case, the interface index must be 0) then, the socket receives CAN frames from every enabled CAN interface. In this special condition, in order to detect the originating CAN interface, the `recvfrom()` system call may be used instead of the `read()` one. On the other hand, to send the `sendto()` system call on such a socket, you need to specify the outgoing interface.

At this point, we can send and receive CAN frames, which are defined by `struct can_frame`:

```
struct can_frame {
    canid_t can_id;  /* 32 bit CAN_ID + EFF/RTR/ERR flags */
    __u8    can_dlc; /* frame payload length in byte (0 .. 8) */
    __u8    __pad;   /* padding */
    __u8    __res0;  /* reserved / padding */
    __u8    __res1;  /* reserved / padding */
    __u8    data[8] __attribute__((aligned(8)));
};
```

In our program, we do the following:

```
/* Fill the frame data */
frame.can_id  = 0x123;
frame.can_dlc = 2;
frame.data[0] = 0x11;
frame.data[1] = 0x22;
```

Then, the `write()` sequence is shown here:

```
/* Send the frame */
n = write(s, &frame, sizeof(struct can_frame));
if (ret < 0) {
    perror("write");
    exit(-1);
}
printf("%s: wrote %d bytes\n", NAME, n);
```

 The complete code can be retrieved from the `chapter_14/socketcan/socketcan_send.c` file in the book's example code repository, and it can be compiled as usual on the target machine using the provided `Makefile`.

To test the code, we can execute the following commands in a terminal in order to enable the virtual CAN interface created earlier and then, wait for new messages:

```
root@a5d3:~# sudo ip link set up vcan0
root@a5d3:~# candump vcan0
```

Then, on another terminal, we can execute our program in the `vcan0` interface as shown here:

```
root@a5d3:~# ./socketcan_send vcan0
socketcan_send: vcan0 at index 7
socketcan_send: wrote 16 bytes
```

As we can see, the commands found the `vcan0` interface, and then wrote 16 bytes into it. On the other terminal, the output of `candump` should appear as shown here:

```
root@a5d3:~# candump vcan0
  vcan0   123   [2]   11 22
```

Exchanging data via the CAN bus

In this section, we will see how we can use the CAN bus on our embedded kits using the transceiver-less connection only (in fact, using a transceiver is trivial; we just have to add one without any other software modifications). We'll see how to use both on-chip controllers on an external one connected via SPI to the main CPU.

Using the on-board controller

To do a transceiver-less communication with the on-board controller, we have to use the BeagleBone Black and the SAMA5D3 Xplained boards connected as shown in the following diagram. The circuitry has been realized considering what we said regarding the transceiver-less issues:

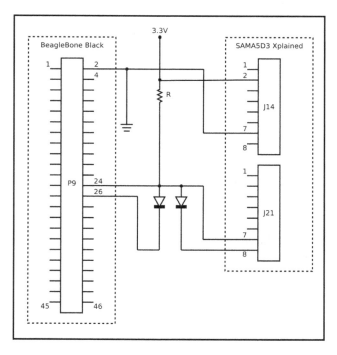

The resistor is set as *R=100KΩ*.

At this point, we have to enable our CAN interfaces as described earlier for both the BeagleBone Black and the SAMA5D3 Xplained. For the first board ,we can set up the interface as shown here:

```
root@bbb:~# ip link set can0 up type can bitrate 50000
                         loopback off triple-sampling on
```

Note that in order to be able to do the setting, the device must be disabled. If not, we can use the next command to do it:
```
root@bbb:~# ifconfig can0 down
```

Then, we can inspect the new status:

```
root@bbb:~# ip -details -statistics link show can0
4: can0: <NOARP,UP,LOWER_UP,ECHO> mtu 16 qdisc pfifo_fast state
UNKNOWN mode DEFAULT group default qlen 10
    link/can  promiscuity 0
    can <TRIPLE-SAMPLING> state ERROR-ACTIVE
    (berr-counter tx 0 rx 0) restart-ms 0
        bitrate 50000 sample-point 0.875
        tq 1250 prop-seg 6 phase-seg1 7 phase-seg2 2 sjw 1
        c_can: tseg1 2..16 tseg2 1..8 sjw 1..4 brp 1..1024 brp-inc 1
        clock 24000000
        re-started bus-errors arbit-lost error-warn error-pass bus-off
        0             0           0           0           0           0
    RX: bytes  packets  errors  dropped overrun mcast
    0          0        0       0       0       0
    TX: bytes  packets  errors  dropped carrier collsns
    0          0        0       0       0       0
```

OK, now, we can enable the CAN device:

```
root@bbb:~# ifconfig can0 up
```

Now, on the other board, we have to perform similar steps, that is, we must set up the network device as follows:

```
root@a5d3:~# ip link set can0 up type can bitrate 50000
                         triple-sampling on
```

Again, in order to be able to do the setting, the device must be disabled. Note that this time, the command is a bit different from the earlier one due to the fact that SAMA5D3 Xplained's controller doesn't support the `loopback off` option argument.

Again, we can take a look at our device settings:

```
root@a5d3:~# ip -details -statistics link show can0
2: can0: <NOARP,UP,LOWER_UP,ECHO> mtu 16 qdisc pfifo_fast
state UNKNOWN mode DEFAULT group default qlen 10
    link/can  promiscuity 0
    can <TRIPLE-SAMPLING> state ERROR-ACTIVE
    (berr-counter tx 0 rx 0) restart-ms 0
        bitrate 50000 sample-point 0.866
        tq 1333 prop-seg 6 phase-seg1 6 phase-seg2 2 sjw 1
        at91_can: tseg1 4..16 tseg2 2..8 sjw 1..4 brp 2..128 brp-inc 1
        clock 66000000
        re-started bus-errors arbit-lost error-warn error-pass bus-off
        0            0            0            0            0            0
    RX: bytes   packets   errors   dropped overrun mcast
    0           0         0        0       0       0
    TX: bytes   packets   errors   dropped carrier collsns
    0           0         0        0       0       0
```

Then, we have to enable the device as usual:

```
root@a5d3:~# ifconfig can0 up
```

Well, if everything is set up correctly, we should be able to send some data back and through both boards as shown here. On the BeagleBone Black, we start the receiving the command on interface `can0` and filtering the data having the identifier `0x5AA`:

```
root@bbb:~# candump can0,5AA:7FF
```

Then, on the SAMA5D3 Xplained, we use the sending command using the correct identifier and some random data (in the next example, the hexadecimal number `0xdeadbeef`):

```
root@a5d3:~# cansend can0 5AA#deadbeef
```

Then, on the first device, we get the following lines of code:

```
root@bbb:~# candump can0,5AA:7FF
  can0  5AA   [4]   DE AD BE EF
```

Using an external controller

In systems that don't have any CAN controller at all, we can add one using an external chip connected with a dedicated bus to the CPU. As an example, let's see how we can install and use the **MCP2515** chip as an external CAN controller connected to the Wandboard by the SPI bus (`Chapter 10`, *Serial Peripheral Interface – SPI*).

The **MCP2515** chip is reported in the image here:

 Note that the device has different package kinds, and in order to simplify their circuitry, you should get the 18-lead PDIP/SOIC package (the one in the figure), which is easily pluggable into a breadboard.
The datasheet is available at
`http://ww1.microchip.com/downloads/en/DeviceDoc/21801G.pdf`.

We're going to use this chip in order to try to establish a transitive-less CAN communication channel between the Wandboard and the BeagleBone Black. The needed connections between the MCP2515 and the Wandboard are reported in this diagram, and you can refer to the previous chapter in order to see how to connect the RxD and TxD signals to the CAN bus, as we did for the SAMA5D3 Xplained.

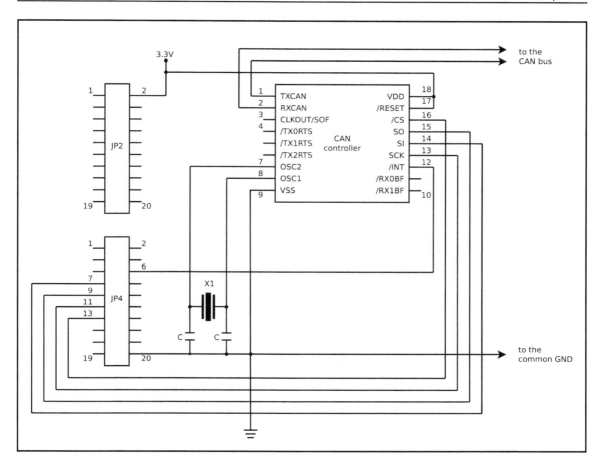

 The capacitor is set as $C=27pF$, and crystal **X1** has the frequency $F=4MHz$. Note that the ground (common GND) must be connected to BeagleBone Black's one.

In the preceding circuitry, we used a crystal to generate the needed clock for the MCP2515. However, using this solution may be difficult on a breadboard. That's why, we can use a little trick to override this problem. In fact, we can use one of BeagleBone Black's PWM generators in place of the external oscillators as reported in the following diagram (see the *PWMs on the BeagleBone Black* section, in Chapter 18, *Pulse-Width Modulation – PWM* for further information regarding these devices):

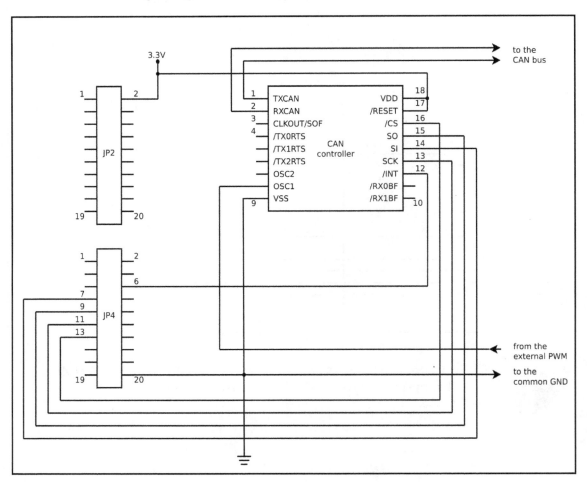

In the preceding circuitry, the signal labeled as *from the external PWM* is the PWM signal generated by BeagleBone Black's pin *P9.22* and goes directly to the *OSC1* pin of the MCP2515 chip. Now, to enable the PWM signal at 4MHz from the BeagleBone Black for the CAN controller, we have to use the following command sequence on the BeagleBone Black:

```
root@bbb:~# echo BB-PWM0 > /sys/devices/platform/bone_capemgr/slots
root@bbb:~# echo 0 > /sys/class/pwm/pwmchip0/export
root@bbb:~# echo 250 > /sys/class/pwm/pwmchip0/pwm0/period
root@bbb:~# echo 125 > /sys/class/pwm/pwmchip0/pwm0/duty_cycle
root@bbb:~# echo 1 > /sys/class/pwm/pwmchip0/pwm0/enable
```

As BeagleBone Black's PWMs are not really precise, we have to verify that the generated signal has the desired frequency. Otherwise, we would get a non-functional system. For instance, using an oscilloscope, we can discover that we have to use value 240 for `period` in order to get a precise 4MHz PWM signal! So, you should verify the actual value of your generated signal and then modify the value to be written in `period` accordingly.

Now, to enable the controller's driver, we have to set up the corresponding driver and then properly modify the kernel configuration in Wandboard's DTS file. The driver to manage the controller should be included in a standard kernel distribution. However, you can verify this situation by looking into the following directory for the file name `mcp251x.ko`:

```
root@wb:~# find /lib/modules/$(uname -r)/kernel/drivers
            -name mcp251x.ko
/lib/modules/4.4.7-armv7-x6/kernel/drivers/net/can/spi/mcp251x.ko
```

If we get no output from the find command, we have to recompile the kernel as described in the *Setting up the developing systems* section, in `Chapter 1`, *Installing the Developing System*, to add the missing driver (if not statically linked, of course). To enable the driver compilation, we must surf the kernel configuration menu and then enable the following setting: **Networking support | CAN bus subsystem support | CAN Device Drivers | CAN SPI interfaces | Microchip MCP251x SPI CAN controllers**.

Regarding the DTS settings, we have to do the following modifications to the SPI section:

```
&ecspi1 {
    fsl,spi-num-chipselects = <1>;
    cs-gpios = <&gpio2 30 0>;
    pinctrl-names = "default";
    pinctrl-0 = <&pinctrl_ecspi1_1>, <&pinctrl_can_int>;
    status = "okay";

    can@0 {
```

```
        compatible = "microchip,mcp2515";
        reg = <0>;
        spi-max-frequency = <1000000>;

        clocks = <&clk_4MHz>;

        interrupt-parent = <&gpio3>;
        interrupts = <27 IRQ_TYPE_EDGE_FALLING>;
    };
};
```

Note that now, we're using just one chip select, and the pinctrl-0 settings should appear as follows, where we've added the IRQ line labeled pinctrl_can_int:

```
pinctrl_ecspi1_1: ecspi1grp-1 {
    fsl,pins = <
        MX6QDL_PAD_EIM_D17__ECSPI1_MISO        0x100b1
        MX6QDL_PAD_EIM_D18__ECSPI1_MOSI        0x100b1
        MX6QDL_PAD_EIM_D16__ECSPI1_SCLK        0x100b1
        MX6QDL_PAD_EIM_EB2__GPIO2_IO30         0x000f0b0
    >;
};

pinctrl_can_int: cangrp-1 {
    fsl,pins = <
        MX6QDL_PAD_EIM_D27__GPIO3_IO27         0x80000000
    >;
};
```

 The patch for the DTS settings can be retrieved from the chapter_14/imx6qdl-wandboard-mcp2515.dtsi.patch file in the book's example code repository.

OK, if the driver is correctly configured (and we supplied the proper clock – see the note above), we should see a new can0 device in our Wandboard:

```
root@wb:~# ifconfig can0
can0        Link encap:UNSPEC  HWaddr 00-00-00-00-00-00-00-00-00-00-00
            NOARP  MTU:16  Metric:1
            RX packets:0 errors:0 dropped:0 overruns:0 frame:0
            TX packets:0 errors:0 dropped:0 overruns:0 carrier:0
            collisions:0 txqueuelen:10
            RX bytes:0 (0.0 B)  TX bytes:0 (0.0 B)
```

At this point, we can configure it as we did in the previous section and then try to exchange data with the BeagleBone Black. Here are the commands that you can use:

```
root@wb:~# ip link set can0 up type can bitrate 50000 loopback off
                            triple-sampling on
root@wb:~# ifconfig can0 up
root@wb:~# candump can0,5AA:7FF
   can0   5AA   [4]   DE AD BE EF
```

Summary

In this chapter, we discovered the CAN bus and how we can connect our embedded kits together in order to exchange data between them. We presented the CAN utilities we can use to quickly get access to the CAN bus, and we discussed a bit regarding the possibility to do a transceiver-less connection for a short-range communication.

In the next chapter, we will look at a group of devices that was rarely used in the past on an embedded computer. However, since the past few days, these devices are becoming one of the most important peripherals an embedded system must have. They are the multimedia devices.

15
Sound Devices - SND

Computers had the ability to manage audio since the beginning because sound is a good communication media, starting from human conversation to a more sophisticated mechanism to give feedback for an action to the user, playing an alarm, or even doing voice recognition in order to input commands. Also, don't forget gaming purposes, which form a huge market!

Embedded computers follow all innovations regarding this technology like a normal computer. For some implementations, the audio quality is even better than standard PCs. In fact, some embedded devices are used as Hi-Fi sound systems.

In this chapter, we will present sound devices in embedded kits and some possible usages of these devices to show you how you can use them to implement a simple and low-cost oscilloscope.

What is a sound device?

A sound (or audio) device is a computer peripheral that provides input and output of audio signals to and from a computer under the control of specific programs. Typical uses of sound cards include providing the audio component for multimedia applications, such as music, but they can also be used as input devices (by voice recognition) or sophisticated audio broadcasting for large plants, voice-recognition systems for control automation, music/audio processing, surveillance systems, and, with some limitations, even as a sophisticated ADC/DAC system useful to elaborate electrical signals (as an oscilloscope can do; look at Chapter 17, *Analog-to-Digital Converters – ADC* for more information regarding DACs).

Data sent to a device for output or data collected from the sound device are stored in a file in several formats (as WAV, MP3, or other audio format) or sent over the network as an audio stream (music or radio streaming).

Even if it may appear as an easy task, managing audio signals is not so simple because usually, the user requires a high-quality level of the audio reproduced (or captured) by a computer. That's why, even if a normal DAC/ADC couple is needed to manage audio signals, we prefer using a dedicated peripheral. It's also quite common to have this audio signal processing as an external peripheral rather than an internal one. Then, we usually have a CPU with an engine capable of only sending to or receiving data from an external device in some standard format (usually, the PCM). In fact, the audio playing or capturing process involves several processing steps:

- Applying some audio filters to reduce noise or increase the audio quality (let's think of equalization, for instance).
- Mixing of multiple audio sources (this is quite common during playback).
- Using accurate DAC/ADC timings in order to correctly sample the signals (human ears are able to detect weak audio).

These steps are performed by an external device called **audio codec**, which is physically connected to the microphone or loudspeakers. So, the audio data comes back and forth to the user space through the CPU's audio interface.

Just to give an idea about how these devices can be implemented, here is a simple blocks schematic:

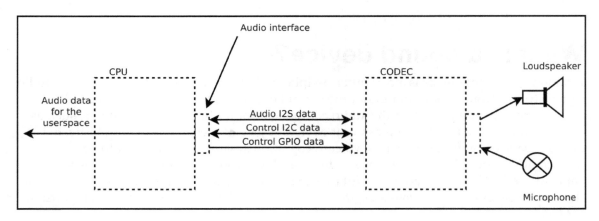

In order to have an idea regarding what we can find inside an audio codec, let's take a look at the datasheet of the Maxim Integrated **MAX98090** chip, a complete audio codec we can connect to an embedded CPU. In the following screenshot, there is a blocks diagram taken from that document, explaining whatever we can find in it:

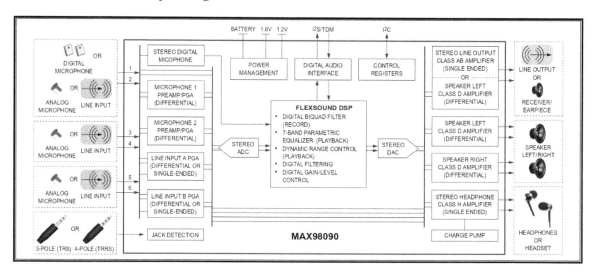

 The datasheet is available at
https://datasheets.maximintegrated.com/en/ds/MAX98090.pdf.

The CPU sends and receives from the codec the audio data through a special audio bus, usually a serial bus called **Inter-IC Sound (I^2S)**, while to control the audio codec, the CPU uses an I^2C bus with some GPIOs (see the following diagram for more details). A *simplified* internal representation of an audio codec with the data and control paths still taken from the MAX98090's datasheet is reported here (really, it's not a joke! It's really a simplified version):

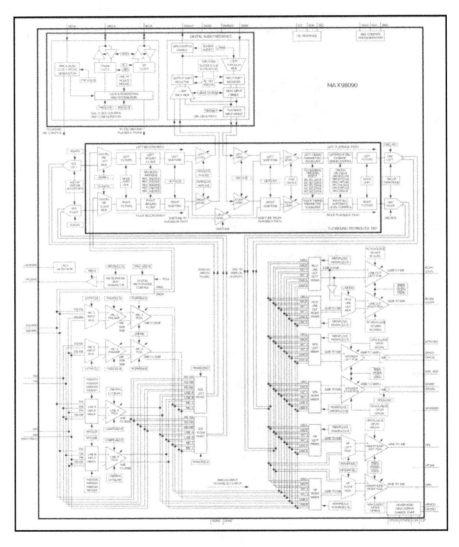

As we can see, inside an audio codec, there is more than one ADC/DAC couple, because for humans, the audio quality is very important, especially if our application is designed for Hi-Fi applications. So, apart from the sample rate and the quantization bits number, we have to control a lot of other settings!

The electrical lines

As shown earlier, connecting an audio codec with the audio port of a CPU means using several different lines depending mainly on how the CPU's audio port is built. However, a very common configuration is made by some GPIOs: an I²C bus and an **I²S** bus. The first two buses are well described in Chapter 6, *General Purposes Input Output signals – GPIO* and Chapter 9, *Inter-Integrated Circuits – I2C*, while the I²S bus is briefly explained here.

The I²S bus is a serial bus used for connecting digital audio devices together, where the clock and serial data are separated and they consist of (usually) three plus one lines:

- There is a bit clock line, officially called continuous **serial clock** (**SCK**) but usually called **bit clock** (**BCLK**). It pulses once for each discrete bit of data on data lines. It is the product of the audio sample rate, the number of bits per channels, and, of course, the number of channels. So, for instance, for a stereo audio sampled at 44.1KHz at 16 bits, the BCLK frequency is given by the following formula:
  Bit Clock frequency = 44100 * 16 * 2 = 1412200Hz = 1.4122MHz

- There is a word clock line, officially called **Word Select** (**WS**) but usually called **Left-Right Clock** (**LRCLK**). It is used to select which channel (left or right) is currently involved in the communication.

- There is a data line officially called **Data Line** (**DATA SD**). This line is sometime spitted into two separate lines, usually called DAC Line (DACL) or ADC Line (ADCL), that are used to send or receive audio data.

- Even if not defined by the protocol, a usual I²S implementation may also include another line called **master clock** (**MCLK**) that is commonly included for synchronizing the internal operation of ADC/DAC converters.

 You can get more information regarding the I²S bus by looking at its specifications
at http://www.semiconductors.philips.com/acrobat_download/various/I2SBUS.pdf.

For the sake of simplicity, in the next listing, we're going to report only I^{2}S lines for each audio port defined in our embedded kits.

Sound on the BeagleBone Black

The BeagleBone Black has one I^{2}S port available on expansion connectors, and the pins' layout is reported in the following table:

Name	Pin
MCLK	P9.25
LRCK	P9.29
BCLK	P9.31
DATA	P9.28

Sound on the SAMA5D3 Xplained

The SAMA5D3 Xplained has one I^{2}S port available on expansion connectors, and the pins' layout is reported in the following table:

Name	Pin
TF0/WS	J19.5
TK0/SCK	J19.4
TD0/DATA	J17.1
RF0	J21.1
RK0	J21.3
RD0	J21.2

You should notice that we've presented six lines instead of the usual four discussed earlier. This is because in reality, on SAMA5D3 Xplained's CPU, the I^{2}S bus is emulated by a device called **Synchronous Serial Controller** (**SSC**), which can emulate many other serial protocols generally used in audio and telecommunication applications. However, in the preceding table, we reported the typical I^{2}S signal names in order to show the correspondence between relevant signals.

More information on the SSC device can be retrieved directly from the SAMA5D3 datasheet at `http://www.atmel.com/Images/Atmel-11121-32-bit-Cortex-A5-Microco ntroller-SAMA5D3_Datasheet.pdf`.

Sound on the Wandboard

The Wandboard comes by default with a ready-to-use audio codec mounted on its baseboard. The codec used is the **SGTL5000** connected to the main CPU via its I^{2}C and I^{2}S buses, plus some clock sources as reported by the Wandboard schematic available at `http://www.wandboard.org/images/downloads/wand-rev-c1.pdf`.

For completeness, here is a simplified schematic about the codec internals taken from the chip's datasheet available at `http://www.nxp.com/assets/documents/data/en/data-sheets/SGTL5000.pdf`:

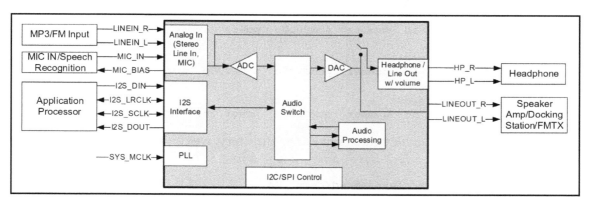

 We're not going to report the electrical lines list in this book because we cannot directly access them in order to test different codecs.

To see some information regarding the Wandboard's sound card, we can use the following command where we discover that the SGTL5000 audio codec is not the unique sound device available on board. In fact, using the following command, we can get a list of them:

```
root@wb:~# cat /proc/asound/cards
 0 [DWHDMI         ]: dw-hdmi-ahb-aud - DW-HDMI
                      DW-HDMI rev 0x0a, irq 19
 1 [imx6wandboardsg]: imx6-wandboard- - imx6-wandboard-sgtl5000
                      imx6-wandboard-sgtl5000
```

```
   2 [imxspdif       ]: imx-spdif - imx-spdif
                        imx-spdif
```

As we can see, we have two other sound devices than the one implemented by the SGTL5000 chip. The first one named DWHDMI is related to the **HDMI** interface (not covered in this book), the second one named imx6wandboardsg is the one based on the chip SGTL5000, while the last one named imxspdif is related to the **S/PDIF** interface (not covered into this book).

 For further information regarding the HDMI interface, you can start reading from https://en.wikipedia.org/wiki/HDMI, while a useful URL for the S/PDIF is https://en.wikipedia.org/wiki/S/PDIF.

The sound cards list can also be taken from the sysfs as well as using the following command:

```
root@wb:~# ls /sys/class/sound/card*
/sys/class/sound/card0:
controlC0  device  id  number  pcmC0D0p  power  subsystem  uevent

/sys/class/sound/card1:
controlC1  device  id  number  pcmC1D0c  pcmC1D0p  power  subsystem
uevent
/sys/class/sound/card2:
controlC2  device  id  number  pcmC2D0p  power  subsystem  uevent
```

Then, reading into each id files, into each cardN directory, we can find again all names of each card as shown here:

```
root@wb:~# cat /sys/class/sound/card*/id
DWHDMI
imx6wandboardsg
imxspdif
```

Sound in Linux

The sound support in Linux bears with the **Open Sound System** (**OSS**), which is also available for several UNIX-like systems. However, around 1998, this system lacked some important functionalities for a *good* sound system, such as MIDI hardware support, multiple audio channel mixing, and full duplex operations. That's why, a new API was born trying to solve these issues: the **Advanced Linux Sound Architecture** (**ALSA**).

Starting from kernel release 2.6, the ALSA replaced the OSS architecture even if, during that time, several improvements were into the OSS implemented too.

The ALSA architecture has hardware MIDI support, multiple audio channel mixing, and full duplex operations, and it's designed to work well on multiprocessor systems since it's thread safe. The ALSA's API is really complex (especially compared with the OSS one), but it allows developers to do incredible things with it, especially using the related user-space library named **alsa-lib** and ALSA plugins (a simple example will be presented in this chapter).

Even if ALSA has completely replaced the OSS, it has an optional emulation layer for OSS in such a way that every program written for it can be used as is on ALSA. This layer can be used with a special tool named `aoss` available in the **alsa-oss** package (see the end of this chapter for a practical example on how to use this tool).

In the ALSA system, there're several *cards* (usually up to eight), numbered starting at 0. Each of them is a physical (or logical) kernel device capable of input/output audio data. They are mapped one-to-one with the hardware. These devices can be addressed by their index number or by their IDs (a normal string). Then, each card has one or more *devices* (numbered starting at 0), which are capable of specific actions such as *audio playback, audio capture, control, timer, mixer,* or *sequencer*. Also, each device may have *sub devices* (numbered starting at 0) that represent some relevant sound endpoint, such as a speaker pair or microphone.

The *audio playback* and *audio capture* functionalities are quite self-explanatory, while for the others, we can add that a *control* is used to configure the sound card, for example, setting sampling rate, reading status and querying available settings, and so on. A *timer* provides access to timing hardware on the sound card. A *mixer* selects the input and output sources on the sound card and volumes (it's a higher level control interface), while a *sequencer* is related to the MIDI layer.

You can see a simple example of this identification method using the Wandboard and the `aplay`/`arecord` commands (see how to install and use them). They can be used as shown here to list the playback and capture devices defined into the system:

```
root@wb:~# aplay -l
**** List of PLAYBACK Hardware Devices ****
card 0: DWHDMI [DW-HDMI], device 0: DW HDMI [dw-hdmi-ahb-audio]
  Subdevices: 1/1
  Subdevice #0: subdevice #0
card 1: imx6wandboardsg [imx6-wandboard-sgtl5000], device 0: HiFi sgtl
5000-0 []
  Subdevices: 1/1
  Subdevice #0: subdevice #0
```

```
card 2: imxspdif [imx-spdif], device 0: S/PDIF PCM snd-soc-dummy-dai-0
[]
  Subdevices: 1/1
  Subdevice #0: subdevice #0
root@wb:~# arecord -l
**** List of CAPTURE Hardware Devices ****
card 1: imx6wandboardsg [imx6-wandboard-sgtl5000], device 0: HiFi sgtl
5000-0 []
  Subdevices: 1/1
  Subdevice #0: subdevice #0
```

An application typically describes sound output by combining these specifications together in the following forms (which are case-sensitive):

- `<interface>:<card>,<device>,<subdevice>`
- `<interface>:CARD=X,DEV=Y,SUBDEV=Z`

Here, the names CARD, DEV, and SUBDEV are the concepts just explained earlier, while an *interface* is a description of an ALSA protocol for accessing the sound card; They are also known with the name of *plugin*, and other possible names are hw, plughw, dmix, and so on. The name hw is used to have a direct access to the kernel device, without software mixing or stream adaptation support. The name plughw is used when mixing or channel duplication is required or for sample value conversion and, when necessary, resampling.

The dmix plugin (with several other plugins) is used to allow mixing of audio data, and it is usually enabled when we need a quick and easy manner to mix up two audio streams into the same device. As a simple example, let's see how we can use it on a system having one sound card and where we wish to play two audio files at the same time (look at the upcoming paragraphs for further information regarding how the following commands work). For simplicity, we're going to play the same audio file twice at the same time. However, this test works perfectly with two different files. If we execute the two commands one after the other (with the first one executed in the background by adding the & option), we get the busy error as follows:

```
root@bbb:~# aplay tone-sine-1000hz.wav &
[1] 1216
Playing WAVE 'tone-sine-1000hz.wav' : Signed 16 bit Little Endian, Rat
e 44100 Hz, Stereo
root@bbb:~# aplay tone-saplay tone-sine-1000hz.wav
aplay: main:722: audio open error: Device or resource busy
```

The first instance of the `aplay` command locks the default device. So, when the second one asks for it again, we get the error. This is because the audio device cannot be accessed by more than one device at a time. However, if we add a `dmix` plugin on top of it, we can resolve the problem. To do it, we have to modify an ALSA configuration file, placed in the `.asoundrc` file in the user's home directory, as shown here:

```
pcm.!default {
    type plug
    slave.pcm "dmixer"
}

pcm.dmixer   {
    type dmix
    ipc_key 1024
    slave {
        pcm "hw:1,0"
        period_time 0
        period_size 1024
        buffer_size 4096
        rate 44100
    }
    bindings {
        0 0
        1 1
    }
}

ctl.dmixer {
    type hw
    card 1
}
```

These settings add the `dmix` plugin and redefine the default audio card to `dmixer` on top of it.

For the sake of completeness, the original `.asoundrc` contents are shown here:

```
pcm.!default {
        type hw
        card 1
}

ctl.!default {
        type hw
        card 1
}
```

These settings are used to define `card 1` as the default device instead of the usual `card 0`.

You can get further information regarding the `.asoundrc` file (note the dot at the beginning) and its usage on the ALSA Project site at `http://www.alsa-project.org/main/index.php/Asoundrc`.

Now, if we re-execute the preceding two commands, we get the desired output without errors:

```
root@bbb:~# aplay tone-sine-1000hz.wav &
[1] 1231
Playing WAVE 'tone-sine-1000hz.wav' : Signed 16 bit Little Endian, Rat
e 44100 Hz, Stereo
root@bbb:~# aplay tone-sine-1000hz.wav
Playing WAVE 'tone-sine-1000hz.wav' : Signed 16 bit Little Endian, Rat
e 44100 Hz, Stereo
```

Other ALSA plugins exist and many more topics should be presented regarding the ALSA world. However, they cannot be presented here because this is not in the scope of this book. You can learn them or get further information on the ALSA architecture on ALSA's project site at `http://www.alsa-project.org`.

The audio tools

Just to remark that audio support in Linux is a big chunk of code. Let's see a brief list of the most famous tools dedicated to audio management and manipulation we can find in almost every GNU/Linux-based system.

The ALSA utils

The first toolset we can use to manage audio devices (the ones based on the ALSA specifications) is **alsa-utils**, which is held in the package of the same name and can be installed as usual into our embedded kits. This toolset is composed of several programs, but two of the most important ones are `aplay` and `arecord` (we mentioned earlier). So, let's see a bit more in detail how they work.

How we can imagine by looking at their names basic usages for of these programs is to play and record an audio file. However, they can also be used to detect available ALSA sound cards in the system, especially the playback and capture devices.

We already saw that if we execute the `aplay` program on the Wandboard, we get the following list:

```
root@wb:~# aplay -l
**** List of PLAYBACK Hardware Devices ****
card 0: DWHDMI [DW-HDMI], device 0: DW HDMI [dw-hdmi-ahb-audio]
  Subdevices: 1/1
  Subdevice #0: subdevice #0
card 1: imxspdif [imx-spdif], device 0: S/PDIF PCM snd-soc-dummy-dai-0
[]
  Subdevices: 1/1
  Subdevice #0: subdevice #0
card 2: imx6wandboardsg [imx6-wandboard-sgt15000], device 0:HiFi sgt15
000-0 []
  Subdevices: 1/1
  Subdevice #0: subdevice #0
```

We get the three sound cards we know the Wandboard is equipped with, but we also get the information we need to precisely address the card we wish to work with in all the `alsa-utils` programs. As an example, using the next `arecord` command, we can ask for a list of the captured hardware settings for the last card device, that is, the sound card device identified by the `HiFi sgt15000-0` label:

```
root@wb:~# arecord -D hw:2 --dump-hw-params
Recording WAVE 'stdin' : Unsigned 8 bit, Rate 8000 Hz, Mono HW Params
of device "hw:2":
```

```
--------------------
ACCESS:  MMAP_INTERLEAVED RW_INTERLEAVED
FORMAT:  S16_LE S24_LE S20_3LE
SUBFORMAT:  STD
SAMPLE_BITS: [16 32]
FRAME_BITS: [16 64]
CHANNELS: [1 2]
RATE: [8000 96000]
PERIOD_TIME: (166 2048000]
PERIOD_SIZE: [16 16384]
PERIOD_BYTES: [128 65535]
PERIODS: [2 255]
BUFFER_TIME: (333 4096000]
BUFFER_SIZE: [32 32768]
BUFFER_BYTES: [128 65536]
TICK_TIME: ALL
--------------------
arecord: set_params:1233: Sample format non available
Available formats:
- S16_LE
- S24_LE
- S20_3LE
```

Alternatively, if we wish to display the audio mixer of this last card, we can use the following command:

```
root@wb:~# alsamixer -c imx6wandboardsg
```

In particular, with the `alsamixer` command, which is useful to get access to the sound card's internal mixer, we can use the following two forms to correctly address the card:

```
root@wb:~# alsamixer -c 2
root@wb:~# alsamixer -D hw:2
```

It's important for you to notice that the -c option argument is usually used to address a *card* number (or identification), while the -D option argument is usually used to address a *device* identification. We can omit these option arguments with a simple trick in order to redefine the default audio device. In fact, all commands, when not specified, open the default device, and redefining it will do the trick. To do it, we can again use the .asoundrc file (or its system wide version, which is the /etc/asound.conf file) with the following settings:

```
pcm.!default {
    type hw
    card 2
}

ctl.!default {
```

```
    type hw
    card 2
}
```

Starting from now, every command we're going to use without the -c or -D option argument will address card number 2 by default. As an example, the following command will now play the audio to the second device:

```
root@wb:~# aplay tone-sine-1000hz.wav
```

Now, you should take a look at `alsamixer`'s man pages, especially at the MIXER VIEWS section (reported here). In fact, this section describes very well how a mixer is rendered on a standard terminal and how we can manage it:

```
MIXER VIEWS
        The top-left corner of alsamixer is the are to show some basic
        information: the card name, the mixer chip name, the current
        view mode and the currently selected mixer item. When the mixer
        item is switched off, [Off] is displayed in its name.
        Volume bars are located below the basic information area.
        You can scroll left/right when all controls can't be put in a
        single screen. The name of each control is shown in the bottom
        below the volume bars. The currently selected item is drawn in
        red and/of emphasized.

        Each mixer control with volume capability shows a box and the
        current volume filled in that box. The volume percentages are
        displayed below the volume bar for left and right channels. For
        a mono control, only one value is shown there.

        When a mixer control is turned off, M (mute) appears below the
        volume bar. When it's turned on, O in green appears instead.
        You can toggle the switch via m key.
        When a mixer control has capture capability, the capture flag
        appears below the volume bar, too. When the capture is turned
        off, ------- is shown. CAPTURE in red appears when the capture
        switch is turned on. In addition, L and R letters appear in
        left and right side to indicate that left and the right
        channels are turned on.
        Some controls have the enumeration list, and don't show boxes
        but only texts which indicate the currently active item. You
        can change the item via up/down keys.
```

In the next screenshot, you can see (a part of) the sound card device `HiFi sgtl5000-0` we get when we execute the `alsamixer` command:

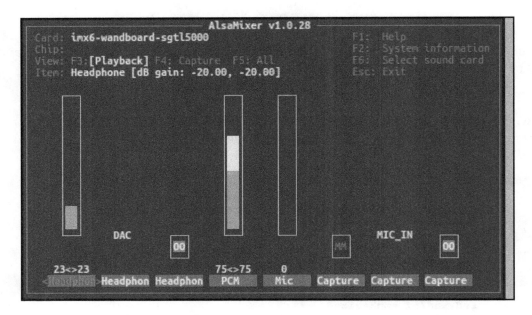

The `alsamixer` tool is very useful if we have to directly manage sound card's mixing controls. However, a more flexible mixer tool exists that allow us to modify mixing controls within a script. This tool is `amixer`. It has been specifically designed for the command-line usage as reported into its man pages too:

```
DESCRIPTION
        amixer allows command-line control of the mixer for the ALSA
        soundcard driver. amixer supports multiple soundcards.

        amixer with no arguments will display the current mixer
        settings for the default soundcard and device. This is a good
        way to see a list of the simple mixer controls you can use.
```

If we execute the `amixer` command into the Wandboard on the same sound card as we did earlier, asking for the list of the card's (simple) controls, we should get something similar to the following output:

```
root@wb:~# amixer -c 2 scontrols
Simple mixer control 'Headphone',0
Simple mixer control 'Headphone Mux',0
Simple mixer control 'Headphone Playback ZC',0
Simple mixer control 'PCM',0
Simple mixer control 'Mic',0
Simple mixer control 'Capture',0
Simple mixer control 'Capture Attenuate Switch (-6dB)',0
Simple mixer control 'Capture Mux',0
Simple mixer control 'Capture ZC',0
```

Then, we can get and modify the current settings of the control named PCM using the following commands:

```
root@wb:~# amixer -c 2 sget 'PCM'
Simple mixer control 'PCM',0
  Capabilities: pvolume
  Playback channels: Front Left - Front Right
  Limits: Playback 0 - 192
  Mono:
  Front Left: Playback 144 [75%]
  Front Right: Playback 144 [75%]
root@wb:~# amixer -c 2 sset 'PCM' 25,25
Simple mixer control 'PCM',0
  Capabilities: pvolume
  Playback channels: Front Left - Front Right
  Limits: Playback 0 - 192
  Mono:
  Front Left: Playback 25 [13%]
  Front Right: Playback 25 [13%]
```

Note that by specifying the 25,25 couple, we can set both left and right channels at once.

Another useful tool is `speaker-test` that can be used to test a sound card by generating testing signals such as pink noise, sine waves, or even human voice. As a simple example, we can test our device `HiFi sgt15000-0` by playing a sine waveform at 1KHz with this command:

```
root@wb:~# speaker-test -D hw:2 --test sine --frequency 1000
                                --nloops 1 --channels 2
speaker-test 1.0.28
Playback device is hw:2
Stream parameters are 48000Hz, S16_LE, 2 channels
Sine wave rate is 1000.0000Hz
Rate set to 48000Hz (requested 48000Hz)
Buffer size range from 64 to 16384
Period size range from 32 to 8192
Using max buffer size 16384
Periods = 4
was set period_size = 4096
was set buffer_size = 16384
 0 - Front Left
 1 - Front Right
Time per period = 5.647299
```

Moving back to the beginning, we told that using `aplay`, we can play an audio file. In fact, we can play a **WAV** file as follows:

```
root@wb:~# aplay -D hw:2 tone-sine-1000hz.wav
Playing WAVE 'tone-sine-1000hz.wav' : Signed 16 bit Little Endian, Rat
e 44100 Hz, Stereo
```

The file can be found in the `chapter_15/tone-sine-1000hz.wav` file in the book's example code repository.

On the other side, we can record a sound file using the next command until we press the *Ctrl + C* keys sequence:

```
root@wb:~# arecord -D hw:2 --rate=44100 --format S16_LE mic.wav
Recording WAVE 'mic.wav' : Signed 16 bit Little Endian, Rate 44100 Hz,
Mono
```

Otherwise, we can use the `-d` option argument to specify a recording duration time.

Note that in order to record something from the *MIC* input, the mixer settings should be set as follows before executing the command:

```
root@wb:~# amixer -c 2 sget 'Mic'
Simple mixer control 'Mic',0
  Capabilities: volume volume-joined
  Playback channels: Mono
  Capture channels: Mono
  Limits: 0 - 3
  Mono: 3 [100%] [40.00dB]
root@wb:~# amixer -c 2 sget 'Capture'
Simple mixer control 'Capture',0
  Capabilities: cvolume
  Capture channels: Front Left - Front Right
  Limits: Capture 0 - 15
  Front Left: Capture 12 [80%]
  Front Right: Capture 12 [80%]
root@wb:~# amixer -c 2 sget 'Capture Mux'
Simple mixer control 'Capture Mux',0
  Capabilities: enum
  Items: 'MIC_IN' 'LINE_IN'
  Item0: 'MIC_IN'
root@wb:~# amixer -c 2 sget 'Mic' 'Capture Mux'
Simple mixer control 'Mic',0
  Capabilities: volume volume-joined
  Playback channels: Mono
  Capture channels: Mono
  Limits: 0 - 3
  Mono: 3 [100%] [40.00dB]
```

Before ending this section, it is useful to notice that an interesting usage of these commands is also reported here, where we can use both at the same time in order to directly hear what we're currently recording:

```
root@wb:~# arecord -D hw:2 --rate=44100 --format S16_LE
                        --channels=2 | \
        aplay -D hw:2 --rate=44100 --format S16_LE
Recording WAVE 'stdin' : Signed 16 bit Little Endian, Rate 44100 Hz, Stereo
Playing WAVE 'stdin' : Signed 16 bit Little Endian, Rate 44100 Hz, Stereo
```

You should notice that we used --channels=2 in order to convert the mono input into two channels. Otherwise, we'll hear the sound in the headphone from one channel only.

Madplay

Both the `aplay` and `arecord` programs support hardware-related (and basic) sound formats only. As an example, if we try to play an MP3 file, we get the following error:

```
root@wb:~# aplay -D hw:2 tone-sine-1000hz.mp3
Playing raw data 'tone-sine-1000hz.mp3' : Unsigned 8 bit, Rate 8000
Hz, Mono
aplay: set_params:1233: Sample format non available
Available formats:
- S16_LE
- S24_LE
- S20_3LE
```

 The file can be found in the `chapter_15/tone-sine-1000hz.mp3` file in the book's example code repository.

The `aplay` command simply doesn't recognize the MP3 format! To solve this issue, we can use another useful tool named `madplay`, which is held in the package of the same name. Using **madplay**, we are now able to play an MP3 file too. However, this is not so easy. In fact, if we use the following command, most probably, we hear nothing from the speakers:

```
root@wb:~# madplay tone-sine-1000hz.mp3
```

This is because the `madplay` utility doesn't allow the user to specify which sound card should be used for playback. It always uses the default sound card defined into the system. To solve this issue, we can use the following command line where we ask `madplay` to send its output to the `stdout` pipe (instead of a sound device) and then we can use `aplay` to effectively send the audio stream to the correct audio device:

```
root@wb:~# madplay tone-sine-1000hz.mp3 -o wave:- | aplay -D hw:2
MPEG Audio Decoder 0.15.2 (beta) - Copyright (C) 2000-2004 Robert
Leslie et al.
Playing WAVE 'stdin' : Signed 16 bit Little Endian, Rate 44100 Hz, Stereo
```

Note that with `madplay`, the trick used earlier with the `/etc/asound.conf` file will not work because `madplay` doesn't use it.

 The **madplay** command's main site is
`http://www.underbit.com/products/mad/`.

Mplayer

Another very useful tool we can use to play almost every audio (and video) file format is
`mplayer`. The program is held in the **mplayer2** package and it can be installed as usual.

Once installed, we can take a look at its man pages (a very long document) in order to see
how it works. However, as a simple example, to play an M4A file on our Wandboard, we
can use the following command line:

```
root@wb:~# mplayer --ao=alsa:device=hw=2 tone-sine-1000hz.m4a
```

 The file can be found in the `chapter_15/tone-sine-1000hz.m4a` file in
the book's example code repository.

Here is reported a snippet of the man pages of `mplayer` where we can see tons of different
commands lines and possibilities it offers to the developers:

```
mplayer [options] [file|URL|playlist|-]
mplayer [options] file1 [specific options] [file2] [specific options]
mplayer [options] {group of files/options} [group-specific options]
mplayer [br]://[title][/device] [options]
mplayer [dvd|dvdnav]://[title|[start_title]-end_title][/device][opts]
mplayer vcd://track[/device]
mplayer tv://[channel][/input_id] [options]
mplayer radio://[channel|frequency][/capture] [options]
mplayer pvr:// [options]
mplayer dvb://[card_number@]channel [options]
mplayer mf://[filemask|@listfile] [-mf options] [options]
mplayer [cdda|cddb]://track[-endtrack][:speed][/device] [options]
mplayer cue://file[:track] [options]
mplayer [file|mms[t]|http|http_proxy|rt[s]p|ftp|udp|unsv|icyx|noicyx|s
mb]:// [user:pass@]URL[:port] [options]
mplayer sdp://file [options]
mplayer mpst://host[:port]/URL [options]
mplayer tivo://host/[list|llist|fsid] [options]
```

In the end, we should notice that mplayer is sensible to the ALSA configuration file
`/etc/asound.conf`. So, if you have defined this file as shown earlier, the command should
work correctly even if executed without the option argument `--ao`.

 The main site of mplayer is at `http://www.mplayerhq.hu`.

Sox

The last tool we're going to present here is **sox**, the *Swiss Army knife of audio manipulation*, which is held in the package of the same name. Once installed, we can take a look at its man pages, where it is made clear that it can not only play an audio file, but it can also manipulate it! Here are the lines of code:

```
SoX reads and writes audio files in most popular formats and
can optionally apply effects to them. It can combine multiple
input sources, synthesise audio, and, on many systems, act as
a general purpose audio player or a multi-track audio recorder.
It also has limited ability to split the input into multiple
output files.
All SoX functionality is available using just the sox command.
To simplify playing and recording audio, if SoX is invoked as
play, the output file is automatically set to be the default
sound device, and if invoked as rec, the default sound device
is used as an input source.
Additionally, the soxi(1) command provides a convenient way to
just query audio file header information.
The heart of SoX is a library called libSoX. Those interested
in extending SoX or using it in other programs should refer to
the libSoX manual page: libsox(3).
SoX is a command-line audio processing tool, particularly
suited to making quick, simple edits and to batch processing.
If you need an interactive, graphical audio editor, use
audacity(1).
```

As we can see in the preceding description, sox can be used for tons of different usages in manipulating audio files. As simple examples, let's see some typical usages.

First of all, we can play a supported audio file format simply using these command lines:

```
root@wb:~# sox tone-sine-1000hz.wav -t alsa hw:2
tone-sine-1000hz.wav:
 File Size: 1.76M      Bit Rate: 1.41M
  Encoding: Signed PCM
  Channels: 2 @ 16-bit
  Samplerate: 44100Hz
  Replaygain: off
  Duration: 00:00:10.00
In:78.9% 00:00:07.89 [00:00:02.11] Out:348k  [====|====] Hd:2.4 Clip:0
```

Using the /etc/asound.conf settings as done earlier to define the default audio device, we can omit the hw:2 specification or directly use the -d option argument, which is a placeholder for *the default device*.

Note that in building the command line, ordering of options is important! In fact, apart from optional arguments, the command syntax is as follows:

```
sox infile1 [[infile2] ...] outfile
```

So, in the preceding command, the `infile1` argument is `tone-sine-1000hz.wav`, while `outfile` is `-t alsa hw:2`, that is, the sound device. In fact, if we specify a normal file, then sox will simply proceed in converting the audio input file into a different one according to the output file extension. As an example, the following command will convert a WAV file into a **Sun/NeXT** audio data file:

```
root@wb:~# sox tone-sine-1000hz.wav tone-sine-1000hz.au
root@wb:~# file tone-sine-1000hz.au
tone-sine-1000hz.au: Sun/NeXT audio data: 16-bit linear PCM, stereo,
44100 Hz
```

> If involved files have no extensions at all, we can force the audio files using the `-t` option argument as follows:
>
> ```
> root@wb:~# sox tone-sine-1000hz.wav -t au tone-sine
> -1000hz
> root@wb:~# file tone-sine-1000hz
> tone-sine-1000hz: Sun/NeXT audio data: 16-bit linea
> r PCM, stereo, 44100 Hz
> ```

Another usage of sox is to generate specific audio files. As an example, here is a command line to generate a 5.5 second audio file sampled at 8KHz, signed 16 bits, containing a sine wave swept from 100 to 1000Hz:

```
root@wb:~# sox -r 8000 -e unsigned -b 16
                -n output.wav synth 00:00:05.5 sine 100-1000
root@wb:~# file output.wav
output.wav: RIFF (little-endian) data, WAVE audio, Microsoft PCM, 16
bit, mono 8000 Hz
```

Then, the file can be heard with the following command:

```
root@wb:~# sox output.wav -t alsa hw:2
output.wav:
 File Size: 88.0k     Bit Rate: 128k
  Encoding: Signed PCM
  Channels: 1 @ 16-bit
  Samplerate: 8000Hz
  Replaygain: off
  Duration: 00:00:05.50
In:100%  00:00:05.50 [00:00:00.00] Out:44.0k [        |       ]
Hd:0.0 Clip:0
```

`Done.`

The file can also be displayed with a spectrogram using this command line:

```
root@wb:~# sox output.wav -n spectrogram
```

The output graph is shown here:

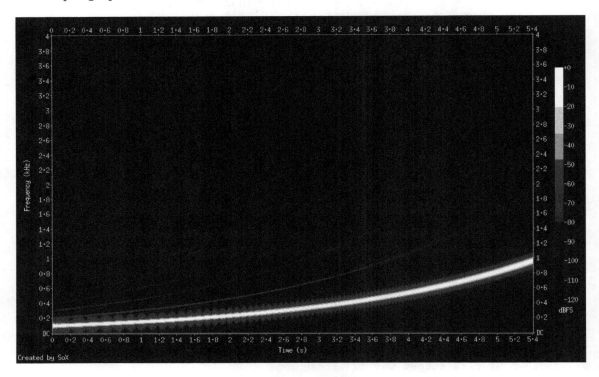

With sox, audio files can be mixed too. If we generate another file as we did earlier, but holding frequencies from 500 to 2KHz and then we mix them together using the following commands, we get the spectrogram in the next figure:

```
root@wb:~# sox -r 8000 -e unsigned -b 16
            -n output2.wav synth 00:00:05.5 sine 500-2000
root@wb:~# sox --combine mix output.wav output2.wav output-mix.wav
root@wb:~# sox output-mix.wav -n spectrogram
```

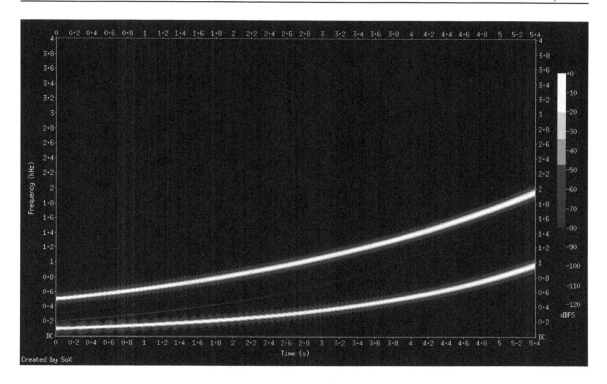

At this point, if we hear the resulting audio file, we can notice that the original ones have been actually mixed. However, the audio is mono… no problem!. With sox, we can turn it into stereo with the following command:

```
root@wb:~# sox output-mix.wav -c 2 output-mix-stereo.wav
```

Then, we can hear the file or generate a new spectrogram:

```
root@wb:~# sox output-mix-stereo.wav -n spectrogram
```

Here is the resulting figure:

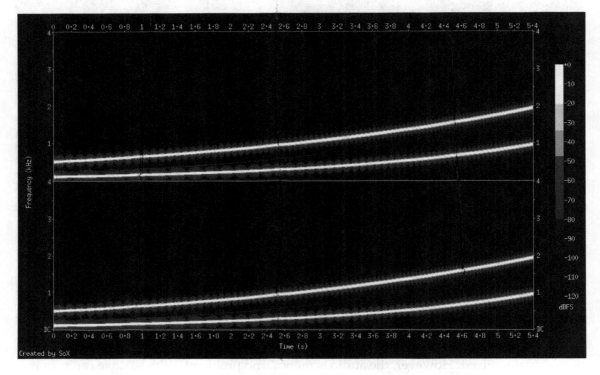

On the other hand, we can combine the two original files, one per channel, instead of mixing them using the following command:

```
root@wb:~# sox --combine merge output.wav output2.wav output-mer.wav
```

Then, we will get the relative spectrogram:

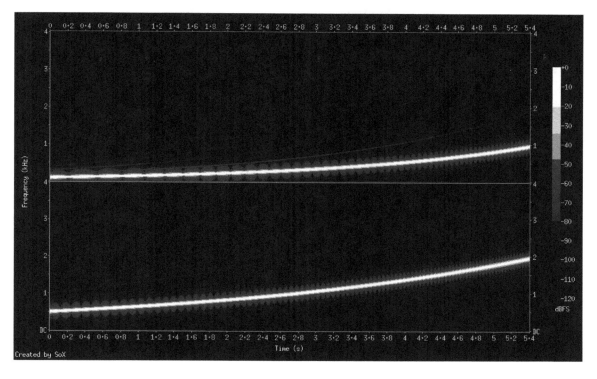

The inverse operation, that is, converting from stereo to mono, can be done in several ways:

- By averaging both channels:

```
root@wb:~# sox output-mer.wav output-mono.wav remix 1-2
```

- Just using one channel a at time:

```
root@wb:~# sox output-mer.wav output-mono.wav remix 1
root@wb:~# sox output-mer.wav output-mono.wav remix 2
```

The spectrograms of the last files are not displayed because they're replicas of the preceding figures.

Regarding the ability to record an audio signal, we can use this command:

```
root@wb:~# sox --rate=44100 --channels=1
                -t alsa hw:2 mic.wav trim 0 10
Input File     : 'hw:2' (alsa)
Channels       : 1
Sample Rate    : 44100
Precision      : 16-bit
Sample Encoding: 16-bit Signed Integer PCM
In:0.00% 00:00:10.03 [00:00:00.00] Out:441k  [ ===|=== ] Hd:4.6 Clip:0
Done.
```

The `trim 0 10` effect at the end of the command is used as a trick to record for 10 seconds; otherwise, we have to hit the *Ctrl* + *C* key sequence.

Then, we can do some interesting things on the just recorded file. First of all, we can increase or decrease the volume if we notice a wrong audio level using the –v option argument. For example, with the next command, we will play the file, decreasing the volume:

```
root@wb:~# sox -v 0.1 mic.wav -t alsa hw:2
```

Alternatively, we can change the sample rate:

```
root@wb:~# sox mic.wav --rate=8000 mic-8000.wav
sox WARN rate: rate clipped 36398 samples; decrease volume?
sox WARN dither: dither clipped 31940 samples; decrease volume?
root@wb:~# file mic-8000.wav
mic-8000.wav: RIFF (little-endian) data, WAVE audio, Microsoft PCM, 16
bit, mono 8000 Hz
```

Warnings are due to the new re-sampling rate, which implies some clipping.

Then, we can speed up the playback or play backward:

```
root@wb:~# sox mic.wav -t alsa hw:2 speed 2.0
```

```
root@wb:~# sox mic.wav -t alsa hw:2 reverse
```

We can continue for a long time in applying these alterations!

The main site of sox is at `http://sox.sourceforge.net`.

The USB audio device class

A special audio device class is represented by the *USB audio device class,* which describes devices capable of streaming audio. This class is really important due to the fact that it allows a single driver to work with various USB sound devices and interfaces on the market (however, many USB sound cards do not conform to the standard and require proprietary drivers from the manufacturer). The Linux kernel has a support for this device class and the driver. If not enabled into the running kernel, it can be enabled into the kernel configuration menu using the path **Device Drivers | Sound card support | Advanced Linux Sound Architecture | USB sound devices | USB Audio/MIDI driver**.

As an example, let's try to connect one of these devices to our BeagleBone Black. They can be found almost everywhere over the Internet, and here is an image of the one used in the upcoming examples:

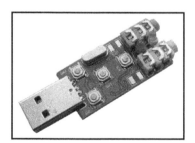

Once the device is connected to our embedded kit, we should see the following kernel messages:

```
usb 1-1: new full-speed USB device number 2 using musb-hdrc
usb 1-1: New USB device found, idVendor=0d8c, idProduct=013c
usb 1-1: New USB device strings: Mfr=1, Product=2, SerialNumber=0
usb 1-1: Product: USB PnP Sound Device
input: USB PnP Sound Device as /devices/platform/ocp/47400000.usb/ 474
01c00.usb/musb-hdrc.1.auto/usb1/1-1/1-1:1.3/0003:0D8C:013C.0001/input/
input1
hid-generic 0003:0D8C:013C.0001: input,hidraw0: USB HID v1.00 Device [
```

```
USB PnP Sound Device] on usb-musb-hdrc.1.auto-1/input3
usbcore: registered new interface driver snd-usb-audio
```

 The device presented here is quite complete since it implements, with the audio device, an input device as well. These companion devices are usually used to support additional functionalities as special action buttons to change the volume or to mute the speakers.

Now, we can use the `aplay` command shown earlier to show the new sound device:

```
root@bbb:~# aplay -l
**** List of PLAYBACK Hardware Devices ****
card 1: Device [USB PnP Sound Device], device 0: USB Audio [USB Audio]
  Subdevices: 1/1
  Subdevice #0: subdevice #0
```

Then, using the `alsamixer` tool, we can show the mixer settings as shown here:

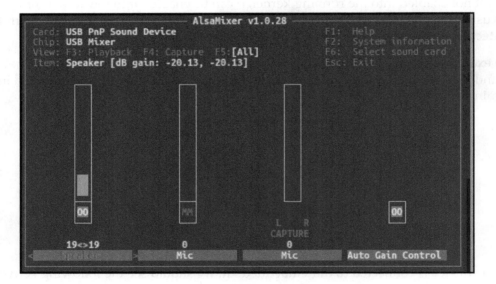

 Notice that the `alsamixer` tool has been executed with the command line here:

root@bbb:~# alsamixer -c 1

This is because the kernel numbered our device as `Card 1`, and since the default device is always `Card 0`, if we do not use the `-c` option argument, we'll get the following error:

```
root@bbb:~# alsamixer
cannot open mixer: No such file or directory
```

However, we can use the `.asoundrc` file to solve the issue.

As you can verify, the mixing controls displayed earlier are the only ones available for this device because this device class is really simple. Another way to verify it is using the `amixer` tool as shown here:

```
root@bbb:~# amixer -c 1 scontrols
Simple mixer control 'Speaker',0
Simple mixer control 'Mic',0
Simple mixer control 'Auto Gain Control',0
```

Managing sound devices

Now, it's time to see how we can practically manage a sound device and how we can add an addition audio codec to the system using the CPU's audio interface directly.

Adding an audio codec

In order to show how we can connect a codec to an embedded kit, we can use the development board reported in the following image, which is based on the chip WM8731:

The devices can be purchased at
`http://www.cosino.io/product/audio-codec-i2si2c` or by surfing the
Internet.

Here is the URL where we can get the datasheet of the board:
`http://download.mikroe.com/documents/add-on-boards/other/audio-a`
`nd-voice/audio-codec-proto/audio-codec-proto-manual-v100.pdf`.

While the datasheet of the codec chip WM8731 is found
here: `https://www.cirrus.com/jp/pubs/proDatasheet/WM8731_v4.9.pdf`.

To do this test, we will use the SAMA5D3 Xplained board, and here is the circuitry needed
to connect the board:

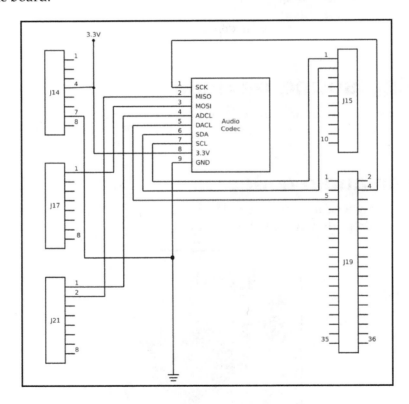

Then, we need to do the next modifications to the SAMA5D3 Xplained's DTS file:

```
--- a/arch/arm/boot/dts/at91-sama5d3_xplained.dts
+++ b/arch/arm/boot/dts/at91-sama5d3_xplained.dts
```

```
@@ -61,6 +61,12 @@
            status = "okay";
        };
+                    ssc0: ssc@f0008000 {
+                        pinctrl-0 = <&pinctrl_ssc0_tx &pinctrl_ssc0_rx>;
+                        status = "okay";
+                    };
+
+
                    can0: can@f000c000 {
                        status = "okay";
                    };
@@ -68,6 +74,11 @@
            i2c0: i2c@f0014000 {
                pinctrl-0 = <&pinctrl_i2c0_pu>;
                status = "okay";
+
+                wm8731: wm8731@1a {
+                    compatible = "wm8731";
+                    reg = <0x1a>;
+                };
            };
            i2c1: i2c@f0018000 {
@@ -333,4 +344,17 @@
                gpios = <&pioE 24 GPIO_ACTIVE_HIGH>;
            };
    };
+
+   sound {
+       compatible = "atmel,sam9x5-wm8731-audio";
+       atmel,model = "wm8731 @ SAMA5D3 Xplained";
+       atmel,audio-routing =
+           "Headphone Jack", "RHPOUT",
+           "Headphone Jack", "LHPOUT",
+           "LLINEIN", "Line In Jack",
+           "RLINEIN", "Line In Jack";
+
+       atmel,ssc-controller = <&ssc0>;
+       atmel,audio-codec = <&wm8731>;
+   };
 };
```

 The patch can also be found in the `chapter_15/audio-codec-wm8731.patch` file in the book's example code repository.

With this patch, we enabled the `ssc0` device, which is the audio interface used by the CPU to exchange the audio data. We defined a new chip at address `0x1a` in the I^2C bus `i2c0` (this connection is used to control the mixer settings and other configuration controls), and then, as the last step, we defined the sound section where `scc0` and `WM8731` are glued. This last section is then read by a special kernel code, which is the one that actually defines the new audio device into the kernel.

This *glue* code is device specific, that is, we need a specific file for each codec we wish to use in the system. It is needed to correctly set up the sound driver by connecting the driver of the CPU's audio interface, in this case, the driver of the SSC, which is in the `sound/soc/atmel/atmel_ssc_dai.c` file, and the driver of the codec, in this case, the `sound/soc/codecs/wm8731.c` file. In this case, we're lucky since this special code is already available in the kernel's tree, and it is the `sound/soc/atmel/sam9x5_wm8731.c` file. Here is a snippet of the relevant code of the `sam9x5_wm8731_driver_probe()` function:

```
card->dev = &pdev->dev;
card->owner = THIS_MODULE;
card->dai_link = dai;
card->num_links = 1;
card->dapm_widgets = sam9x5_dapm_widgets;
card->num_dapm_widgets = ARRAY_SIZE(sam9x5_dapm_widgets);
dai->name = "WM8731";
dai->stream_name = "WM8731 PCM";
dai->codec_dai_name = "wm8731-hifi";
dai->init = sam9x5_wm8731_init;
dai->dai_fmt = SND_SOC_DAIFMT_DSP_A | SND_SOC_DAIFMT_NB_NF
               | SND_SOC_DAIFMT_CBM_CFM;

ret = snd_soc_of_parse_card_name(card, "atmel,model");
if (ret) {
    dev_err(&pdev->dev, "atmel,model node missing\n");
    goto out;
}

ret = snd_soc_of_parse_audio_routing(card, "atmel,audio-routing");
if (ret) {
    dev_err(&pdev->dev, "atmel,audio-routing node missing\n");
    goto out;
}

codec_np = of_parse_phandle(np, "atmel,audio-codec", 0);
if (!codec_np) {
    dev_err(&pdev->dev, "atmel,audio-codec node missing\n");
    ret = -EINVAL;
    goto out;
```

```
    }

    dai->codec_of_node = codec_np;

    cpu_np = of_parse_phandle(np, "atmel,ssc-controller", 0);
    if (!cpu_np) {
        dev_err(&pdev->dev, "atmel,ssc-controller node missing\n");
        ret = -EINVAL;
        goto out;
    }
    dai->cpu_of_node = cpu_np;
    dai->platform_of_node = cpu_np;

    priv->ssc_id = of_alias_get_id(cpu_np, "ssc");

    ret = atmel_ssc_set_audio(priv->ssc_id);
    if (ret != 0) {
        dev_err(&pdev->dev,
                "ASoC: Failed to set SSC %d for audio: %d\n",
                ret, priv->ssc_id);
        goto out;
    }

    of_node_put(codec_np);
    of_node_put(cpu_np);

    ret = snd_soc_register_card(card);
    if (ret) {
        dev_err(&pdev->dev,
                "ASoC: Platform device allocation failed\n");
        goto out_put_audio;
    }

    dev_dbg(&pdev->dev, "ASoC: %s ok\n", __func__);

    return ret;
```

As we can see, the probing code first defines some basic settings as the names of the driver, stream and the **Digital Audio Interface** (**DAI**), the digital interface format and so on. Then, it parses the DTS settings we defined into the sound section shown earlier using the `snd_soc_of_parse_card_name()`, `snd_soc_of_parse_audio_routing()`, and `of_parse_phandle()` functions. In the end, it calls the `snd_soc_register_card()` function in order to register a new sound card into the system.

OK, now, we have to recompile the kernel, install it, and then reboot. If everything works well, we should see the following kernel messages during the boot:

```
sam9x5-snd-wm8731 sound: wm8731-hifi <-> f0008000.ssc mapping ok
...
ALSA device list:
  #0: wm8731 @ SAMA5D3 Xplained
```

It may be possible that we get the following error:

```
ssc f0008000.ssc: Missing dma channel for stream: 0
ssc f0008000.ssc: ASoC: pcm constructor failed: -22
sam9x5-snd-wm8731 sound: ASoC: can't create pcm WM8
731 PCM :-22
sam9x5-snd-wm8731 sound: ASoC: failed to instantiat
e card -22
sam9x5-snd-wm8731 sound: ASoC: Platform device allo
cation failed
sam9x5-snd-wm8731: probe of sound failed with error
-22
```

If so, we can solve the issue by disabling some DMA channels in order to reserve at least two for the sound interface. This is because the audio cannot work without DMA channels as the SPI controller does. The patch is shown here:

```
--- a/arch/arm/boot/dts/at91-sama5d3_xplained.dts
+++ b/arch/arm/boot/dts/at91-sama5d3_xplained.dts
@@ -58,6 +58,7 @@

spi0: spi@f0004000 {
        cs-gpios = <&pioD 13 0>, <0>, <0>, <&pioD 1
        6 0>;
+       dmas = <0>, <0>; /* disable audio DMAs */
        status = "okay";
};
```

Now, we should list the new sound device as follows:

```
root@a5d3:~# aplay -l
**** List of PLAYBACK Hardware Devices ****
card 0: Xplained [wm8731 @ SAMA5D3 Xplained], device 0: WM8731 PCM
wm8731-hifi-0
  []
  Subdevices: 1/1
  Subdevice #0: subdevice #0
```

Now, to enable the headphone output, we have to execute the following `amixer` command:

```
root@a5d3:~# amixer sset 'Output Mixer HiFi' on
```

```
Simple mixer control 'Output Mixer HiFi',0
  Capabilities: pswitch pswitch-joined
  Playback channels: Mono
  Mono: Playback [on]
```

At this point, we're ready to play our audio file as shown here:

```
root@a5d3:~# aplay tone-sine-1000hz.wav
Playing WAVE 'tone-sine-1000hz.wav' : Signed 16 bit Little Endian, Rat
e 44100 Hz, Stereo
```

It may be possible that the tone is a bit higher than usual. In this case, we should verify that everything is OK using the `time` command:

```
Playing WAVE 'tone-sine-1000hz.wav' : Signed 16 bit
Little Endian, Rate 44100 Hz, Stereo

real    0m7.755s
user    0m0.220s
sys     0m0.040s
```

Since the audio file `tone-sine-1000hz.wav` is 10 seconds long, if it is played in 7.755 s, as shown earlier, it means that obviously something is wrong. This is because most probably, the audio board used for the test has an on-board crystal at 16.9344MHz instead of the right one at 12.288MHz. So, in this case, we can fix the issue by modifying the `MCLK_RATE` define as follows:

```
--- a/sound/soc/atmel/sam9x5_wm8731.c
+++ b/sound/soc/atmel/sam9x5_wm8731.c
@@ -32,7 +32,7 @@
 #include "atmel_ssc_dai.h"

-#define MCLK_RATE 12288000
+#define MCLK_RATE 16934400

 #define DRV_NAME "sam9x5-snd-wm8731"
```

A simple oscilloscope

Now, let's see a fantastic way to use a sound card! Since this is fundamentally a DAC, we can imagine to use it to sample an electronic signal and then to display it as a normal oscilloscope can do. Of course, we cannot emulate a real oscilloscope due to the fact that sound cards have specific circuitry designed for signals audible by humans and suitable for a limited frequency range, but we can get an interesting application in any case.

To implement our oscilloscope, we can use our Wandboard and a special program called **xoscope**, which is held in the same package. Also, we need another tool that will be used as a wrapper to masquerade Wandboard's ALSA `imx6wandboardsg` device as on OSS device. This is because the `xoscope` program is a bit old, and it doesn't support ALSA API by default. The tool is `aoss`, and it is held in the **alsa-oss** package, so we can use the next command to install the necessary programs:

```
root@wb:~# aptitude install alsa-oss xoscope
```

When installation ends, we can take a look at the man page of `aoss` in order to know how we can use this tool (here is the relevant snippet):

```
aoss is a simple wrapper script which facilitates the use of the ALSA
OSS compatibility library. It just sets the appropriate LD_PRELOAD
path and then runs the command.

This is useful in cases where routing settings (which can be made in
your .asoundrc file) need to be applied to commands that use the OSS
API.

Examples of asoundrc configuration:

pcm.dsp0 { type plug slave.pcm "hw:0,0" }

or

pcm.dsp0 { type plug slave.pcm "dmix" }

In the above configuration examples, the pcm.dsp0 definition is used
to wrap calls do /dev/dsp0. You can also wrap usage of /dev/dsp1,
/dev/dsp2, etc. by defining pcm.dsp1, pcm.dsp2, etc..

The PCM name to open can be given explicitly via ALSA_OSS_PCM_DEVICE
environment variable, too. This overrides the default dsp0, etc.

Note on mmap: aoss mmap support might be buggy. Your results may vary
when trying to use an application that uses mmap'ing to access the OSS
device files.
```

As we can see, to use the tool, we just need to use proper settings in the well-known `.asoundrc` file. So, for the Wandboard, we have to use the next command to set up the file:

```
root@wb:~# echo 'pcm.dsp0 { type plug slave.pcm "hw:2,0" }'
            > ~/.asoundrc
```

Then, we have to connect a signal source to our Wandboard. We can use a microphone as we did earlier or, better, we can use another kit to generate a well-known waveform. For instance, we can use the BeagleBone Black equipped with the USB sound device and then connect its headphone output to the *MIC* input of the Wandboard. At this point, using the `sox` tool as shown here, we can generate a sine waveform at 100Hz:

```
root@bbb:~# sox -r 44100 -e signed -b 16 -n
                -t alsa hw:1 synth 01:00:00.0 sin 100
  Encoding: Signed PCM
  Channels: 1 @ 16-bit
  Samplerate: 44100Hz
  Replaygain: off
  Duration: unknown

In:0.00% 00:00:18.02 [00:00:00.00] Out:791k [!=====|=====!] Hd:0.0 Clip:291
```

Note that we specified a duration of 1 hour, which should be sufficient to do all our tests.

Now, everything is in place, and we can execute our `xoscope` program as follows:

```
root@wb:~# aoss xoscope
```

This tool uses the X-Window protocol to plot its user interface, so we have to execute it into a graphical environment. However, since we never used any graphical outputs in this book, we need a way to render the GUI of xoscope. We can use an SSH tunnel to forward the X-Window protocol over the network from the Wandboard to our host PC simply by doing a login with the `-X` option argument as shown here (see `Chapter 4`, *Quick Programming with Scripts and System Daemons*):

```
$ ssh -X root@192.168.9.2
```

this manner, every tool that needs a graphical X-Window compatible display can be executed on the Wandboard, but rendered on the host PC.

If everything works well, we should see something similar to the following screenshot:

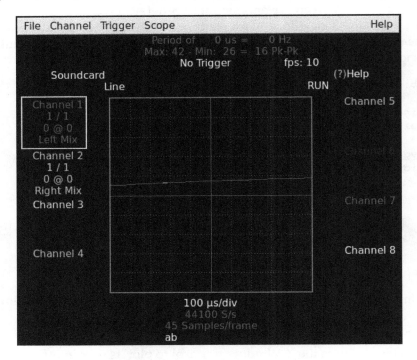

To fix the sine wave into the display, as in every normal oscilloscope, we have to regulate the time base using a trigger. So, let's use the menu entry **Scope | Slower Time Base** until we reach **5ms/div** and the **Trigger | Rising** to enable the trigger.

Then, the sine wave should be fixed and well displayed as shown here:

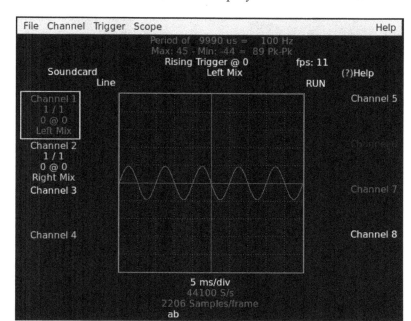

Now, we can play a bit with our oscilloscope by modifying its settings or trying to display other signals. For instance, if we stop the preceding command in the BeagleBone Black and execute the next one, we should see a square waveform:

```
root@bbb:~# sox -r 44100 -e signed -b 16 -n
                -t alsa hw:1 synth 01:00:00.0 square 100
```

Then, the display should change as in the next screenshot.

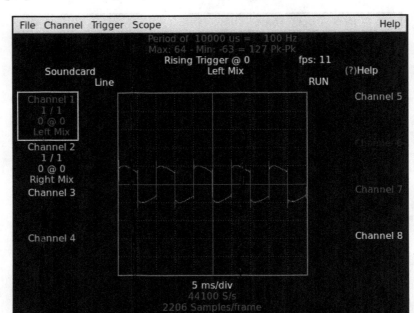

 You should now understand that the square waveform displayed is not perfect because both the Wandboard and BeagleBone Black's sound cards are designed to human-audible signals and they cannot allow all the necessary frequencies for a square wave to pass.

Summary

Audio devices may appear to be simple devices, but as shown in this chapter, they are very complex, and embedded devices can use them for several different tasks. Also, we presented a complete class of audio tools useful to do a lot of different signal manipulation. We also saw that using the ALSA drivers, we can use these tools in the same manner even on different audio devices.

In the next chapter, we'll see another important devices class. This is a class of devices that allows developers to manage images. This is the class of video devices.

16
Video devices - V4L

Even if not widely diffused, capturing video images or recording videos can be integrated into an embedded device to accomplish several different tasks, such as remote monitoring, video surveillance, image processing, and so on.

In this chapter, after a brief explanation about how these devices are defined in a GNU/Linux system, we're going to see a simple usage of common video-acquisition devices and how we can turn our embedded kit into a surveillance camera or a remote image recorder.

What is a video device?

A video-capture device is a device that is able to convert an analog video signal (such as that produced by a video camera, analog TV tuners, or other analog sources) to digital video. Then, the resulting digital data can be stored in a file (as AVI, MJPEG, or other image formats), sent over the network as a video stream (as **MJPEG** or **H264**, for instance), or simply displayed on local display.

> However, as we'll see in the upcoming sections, for Linux, video devices are those devices that are capable of generating a video image (as digital TV tuners), regardless of whether they are digital or analog devices.

An embedded device can be equipped with a video device for several reasons. However, the main one is usually for video surveillance purposes or video monitoring. The basic usage can be simply sending the images to a remote user, but more often, in these last days, it's not rare that the embedded system can do some analysis on the video stream in order to detect motion or other relevant events.

Special electronic circuitry is required to capture video from analog video sources, and in an embedded system, this circuitry is usually inside the CPU (more rarely, it may be external too). However, in any case, what we really have is a video engine capable only of the last steps of video acquisition, that is, the collection of the video data in some standard color space format (**RGB** or **YCbCr**) and its eventual conversion into some high-level video format (MJPEG or H264). In fact, the video-capture process involves several processing steps:

1. Digitalization of the analog signal, usually from a **charge-coupled device** (**CCD**) image sensor, by an analog-to-digital converter to produce a raw digital data stream.
2. Separation of the luminance and chrominance, and its demodulation to produce color difference video data.
3. Adjustment of brightness, contrast, saturation, and hue.
4. Standard color space transformation as RGB and YCbCr.

These steps are done by an external device called video codec, which is physically connected to the CCD image sensor. Then, the video data is passed to the CPU's video interface, which, in turn, makes it available at user space. In the case of a simple video interface, such as the **Image Sensor Interface** (**ISI**) controller of SAMA5D3 Xplained's CPU, the video data is passed to the user space as is (with minor processing steps) or to the LCD controller in order to be shown to the user. On the other hand, in the case of a more complex video interface, such as the **Image Processing Unit** (**IPU**) of Wandboard's CPU (*CAMERA1* interface), the video data can also be resampled via some hardware engine and converted into MJPEG or H264 for video streaming over the network (this operation can also be done via software, but, of course, in this case, the main CPU is more loaded).

Just to give an idea about how these devices can be implemented, the following diagram shows a simple blocks schematic:

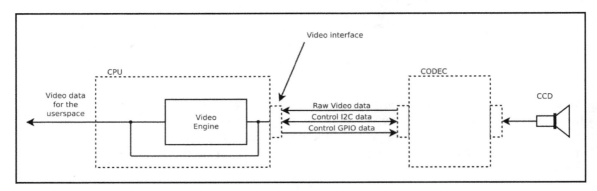

The CPU directly controls the video codec, which, in turn, controls the video CCD image sensor. Signals the CPU usually need to control the video codec are a video data bus, an I²C bus, and some GPIOs.

In order to have an idea regarding what we can find inside a video codec, let's take a look at a product brief document of the Omnivision **OV7740** chip, a good video codec we can connect to an embedded CPU. Here is a blocks diagram taken from that document explaining whatever we can find in it:

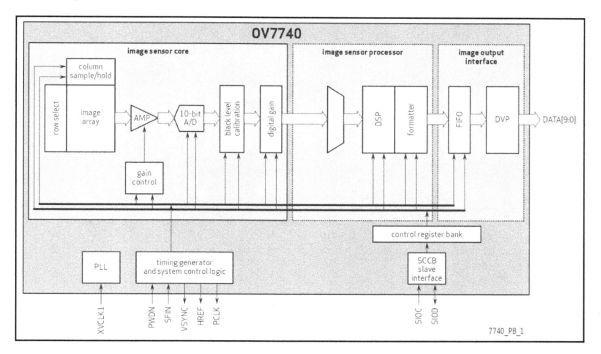

The document is available at http://www.ovt.com/download/sensorpdf /83/OmniVision_OV7740.pdf.

The diagram explains how the codec works. The CPU receives from the codec the raw video data through a parallel bus (*DATA[9:0]*), while it controls the codec using some control signals as we described earlier (the SCCB slave interface is the I²C interface).

Other interesting figures to see are the block diagrams of the internals of the two video engines mentioned earlier. The first one in the following diagram is the simplified schematic of the IPU of Wandboard's CPU taken from its datasheet:

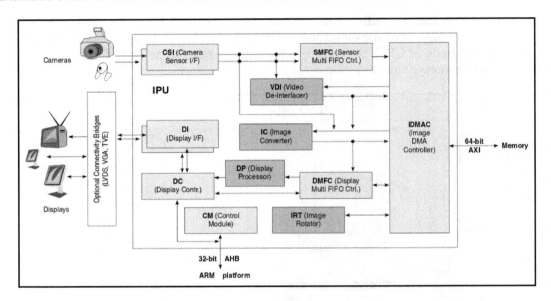

 The datasheet is available at
http://www.nxp.com/assets/documents/data/en/reference-manuals/IM X6DQRM.pdf.

In the diagram, we can see how a camera (or video) interface is connected with several blocks implementing the video engine functionalities. Also, it is evident how the video interface is related to the display interface (which controls the computer's displays) because the images we capture are not only for storage or remote viewing, but they can also be displayed on the computer local screen after some manipulations (as color adjustments, resizing, cropping, and so on).

Then, the next diagram is the simplified schematic of the ISI of SAMA5D3 Xplaioned's CPU taken from its datasheet:

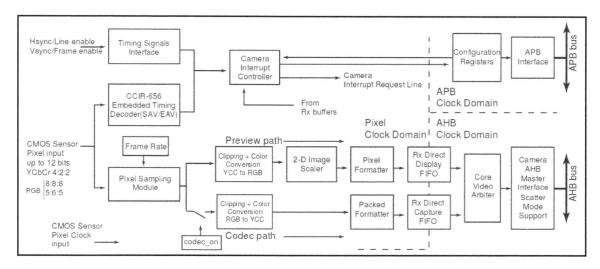

Here, we see that the CMOS sensor (the CCD) sends the raw video data to the video engine, which, in turn, does some minor computations (clipping plus color conversion), and then, the data is available in the user space. In this case, the video interface is simpler than before, even if it is suitable for (more limited) video streaming, storage, and so on.

It should be now clear to you that these functionalities are very specific to the CPU we decide to use, so the best thing to do, in order to understand how they work into our system, is to just start reading the datasheet of the system we're going to use.

The electrical lines

Video lines are not presented in this book as per other devices due to three main reasons; the first two are the usual ones we reported in other chapters:

- Due to very high communication frequencies involved, we can get a non-functional system if we try to connect a CCD by wires.
- They are not useful or relevant to understand how a video device works.

While the third one (the last but not least) is that every system (or each SoC) has its own electrical lines! In fact, even if manufacturers are moving forward towards a common solution, there still exist a lot of differences (and not only in hardware).

That's why, in order to keep the discussion simple, we're not going to present the specific solution implemented in the CPUs of our embedded kits, but we're going to present a quite *standard* solution using a USB camera device. In fact, this is the only video device that works the same on all systems.

Video on the BeagleBone Black

The BeagleBone Black has no video inputs.

Video on the SAMA5D3 Xplained

The SAMA5D3 Xplained has an input video called ISI available on the expansion connectors, and the relative pins are summarized in the table:

Name	Pin	Name	Pin
D0	J19.12	D8	J18.1
D1	J19.5	D9	J18.5
D2	J19.14	D10	J20.1
D3	J19.11	D11	J20.2
D4	J19.16	Hsync	J15.10
D5	J19.13	Vsync	J15.9
D6	J19.18	PCK	J15.2
D7	J19.15		

 Some signals can be mapped on different pins (see the *SAMA5D3 Xplained User Guide* for further information).

Pins D0-D11 are the image data, while **Hsync** (horizontal sync), **Vsync** (vertical sync), and **PCK** (pixel clock) are control signals.

To enable the ISI support, we have to enable the corresponding driver in **Device Drivers | Multimedia support | V4L platform devices | ATMEL Image Sensor Interface (ISI) support**, and if everything works well, we should get a new video device mapped in the /dev/video0 file.

Video on the Wandboard

The Wandboard has a dedicated input video connector (*camera interface* or *camera header*) named *CAMERA1* (see figure in the *The Wandboard* section, `Chapter 1`, *Installing the Developing System*). The connector has a complex pinout as shown here:

Name	Pin	Name	Pin
CSI_CLK0P	1	DSI_D1P	16
CSI_CLK0M	2	DSI_D1M	17
CSI_D0P	4	DSI_D0P	19
CSI_D0M	5	DSI_D0M	20
CSI_D1P	7	DSI_CLK0P	22
CSI_D1M	8	DSI_CLK0M	23
CSI_D2P	10	I2C2_SCL	25
CSI_D2P	11	I2C2_SDA	26
CSI_D3P	13	GPIO_3_CLK02	29
CSI_D3M	14	GPIO6	30

Note that in the preceding table, there are video signals only. Missing pins are just powering pins.

As we can see, signals are quite different from the ones of SAMA5D3 Xplained. However, thanks to the kernel's hardware abstraction, once we connect a camera board and enable the corresponding driver, we still should get a new video device mapped in the `/dev/video0` file.

You should notice that on the connector, there are other signals such as GPIOs and the I^2C signals. This is because, as we saw earlier, a video device is normally a video data bus and a controlling bus, which is usually composed by GPIOs (to enable/disable or reset the video system) and I^2c signals for the video settings (video size, format, and other settings).

Video in Linux

In a GNU/Linux-based system, all video devices are managed by a standard API called **Video4Linux** (*Video for Linux*), which is a collection of device drivers to support real-time video capture. It supports many USB webcams, TV tuners, and similar devices in such a way that they have a common interface so that users can get access to to the underlying hardware in the same manner independently and programmers can easily add video support to their applications. The **Video4Linux (V4L2)** API is currently in its second version, which can be referred as Video4Linux2. Using the name Video4Linux only is not erroneous since the first release of the API was dropped several years ago from the kernel main line.

In a GNU/Linux-based system, each Video4Linux device appears in the system as a `/dev/video0`, `/dev/video1` file. For example, to our BeagleBone Black, we have connected a webcam, and the video file we get is as follows:

```
root@bbb:~# ls -l /dev/video*
crw-rw---- 1 root video 81, 0 Oct 10 12:03 /dev/video0
```

A simple list of available video devices can be obtained from the sysfs as show here:

```
root@bbb:~# ls /sys/class/video4linux/
video0
```

Into each `videoX` directory, we can get some information about the corresponding device:

```
root@bbb:~# cat /sys/class/video4linux/video0/name
Microsoft LifeCam VX-800
```

The video tools

Even if using the sysfs interface to manage video devices in a more efficient manner, we can use a dedicated tool set named **v4l-utils** in the package by the same name, which can be installed as usual into the system if it is missing.

The main program in the package is `v4l2-ctl` that can be used to get a lot of information regarding a video device. Just to show the power of this command, let's try to explore all capabilities of a video device assuming we know about nothing of it. First of all, we can detect connected video devices using the `--list-devices` option argument as shown here:

```
root@bbb:~# v4l2-ctl --list-devices
USB 2.0 Camera (usb-musb-hdrc.1.auto-1):
```

```
/dev/video0
/dev/video1
```

Then, we have discovered that our device has been composed of two video devices mapped into the system with the /dev/video0 and /dev/video1 files. Then, we can get some information regarding the device driver we're currently using to manage this device. This can be done using the --info option argument as shown here:

```
root@bbb:~# v4l2-ctl -d /dev/video0 --info
Driver Info (not using libv4l2):
        Driver name    : uvcvideo
        Card type      : USB 2.0 Camera
        Bus info       : usb-musb-hdrc.1.auto-1
        Driver version: 4.4.7
        Capabilities   : 0x84200001
                Video Capture
                Streaming
                Extended Pix Format
                Device Capabilities
        Device Caps    : 0x04200001
                Video Capture
                Streaming
                Extended Pix Format
```

Note that the preceding output is the same if we use the /dev/video0 or /dev/video1 device since they are relying on the same hardware.

Here, some video capabilities are exposed, but to get more verbose and complete listing, we have to use the --all option argument:

```
root@bbb:~# v4l2-ctl -d /dev/video0 --all
Driver Info (not using libv4l2):
        Driver name    : uvcvideo
        Card type      : USB 2.0 Camera
        Bus info       : usb-musb-hdrc.1.auto-1
        Driver version: 4.4.7
        Capabilities   : 0x84200001
                Video Capture
                Streaming
                Extended Pix Format
                Device Capabilities
        Device Caps    : 0x04200001
                Video Capture
                Streaming
                Extended Pix Format
```

```
Priority: 2
Video input : 0 (Camera 1: ok)
Format Video Capture:
        Width/Height  : 1920/1080
        Pixel Format  : 'MJPG'
        Field         : None
        Bytes per Line: 0
        Size Image    : 4147789
        Colorspace    : Unknown (00000000)
        Flags         :
Crop Capability Video Capture:
        Bounds      : Left 0, Top 0, Width 1920, Height 1080
        Default     : Left 0, Top 0, Width 1920, Height 1080
        Pixel Aspect: 1/1
Selection: crop_default, Left 0, Top 0, Width 1920, Height 1080
Selection: crop_bounds, Left 0, Top 0, Width 1920, Height 1080
Streaming Parameters Video Capture:
        Capabilities      : timeperframe
        Frames per second: 25.000 (25/1)
        Read buffers      : 0
                      brightness (int)    : min=-64 max=64 step=1
                                            default=0 value=0
                        contrast (int)    : min=0 max=64 step=1
                                            default=32 value=32
                      saturation (int)    : min=0 max=128 step=1
                                            default=60 value=60
                             hue (int)    : min=-40 max=40 step=1
                                            default=0 value=0
   white_balance_temperature_auto (bool)  : default=1 value=1
                           gamma (int)    : min=72 max=500
                                            step=1 default=100
                                            value=100
                            gain (int)    : min=0 max=100 step=1
                                            default=0 value=0
            power_line_frequency (menu)   : min=0 max=2 default=1
                                            value=1
       white_balance_temperature (int)    : min=2800 max=6500 step=1
                                            default=4600 value=4600
                                            flags=inactive
                       sharpness (int)    : min=0 max=6 step=1
                                            default=3 value=3
           backlight_compensation (int)   : min=0 max=2 step=1
                                            default=1 value=1
                    exposure_auto (menu)  : min=0 max=3 default=3
                                            value=3
                exposure_absolute (int)   : min=1 max=5000 step=1
                                            default=156 value=156
                                            flags=inactive
```

```
      exposure_auto_priority (bool)     : default=0 value=0
                  brightness (int)      : min=-64 max=64 step=1
                                          default=0 value=0
                    contrast (int)      : min=0 max=64 step=1
                                          default=32 value=32
                  saturation (int)      : min=0 max=128 step=1
                                          default=60 value=60
                         hue (int)      : min=-40 max=40 step=1
                                          default=0 value=0
 white_balance_temperature_auto (bool)  : default=1 value=1
                       gamma (int)      : min=72 max=500 step=1
                                          default=100 value=100
                        gain (int)      : min=0 max=100 step=1
                                          default=0 value=0
        power_line_frequency (menu)     : min=0 max=2 default=1
                                          value=1
   white_balance_temperature (int)      : min=2800 max=6500 step=1
                                          default=4600
                                          value=4600 flags=inactive
                   sharpness (int)      : min=0 max=6 step=1
                                          default=3
                                          value=3
       backlight_compensation (int)     : min=0 max=2 step=1
                                          default=1
                                          value=1
```

The same command can be used on the second device, but with a different output. In fact, if we use the preceding command on the /dev/video1 device, we would get some differences:

```
...
Format Video Capture:
        Width/Height  : 1920/1080
        Pixel Format  : 'H264'
        Field         : None
        Bytes per Line: 3840
        Size Image    : 0
        Colorspace    : SRGB
        Flags         :
...
```

This tells to us that the video device /dev/video0 is capable of generating MJPEG pixel format, while for /dev/video1, the pixel format is H264.

However, the use of `v412-ctl` is not only to get information, but also to do some settings in a video device. For instance, to modify the brightness of the `/dev/video0` device, which is currently set to `0`, we can use the following commands:

```
root@bbb:~# v412-ctl -d /dev/video0 --get-ctrl=brightness
brightness: 0
root@bbb:~# v412-ctl -d /dev/video0 --set-ctrl=brightness=10
root@bbb:~# v412-ctl -d /dev/video0 --get-ctrl=brightness
brightness: 10
```

The USB video class device

A special video class device is represented by the **USB video class** (**UVC**) device , which is a USB device class that describes devices capable of streaming videos, such as webcams, digital camcorders, and so on. They are so important and widely used that they deserve a special section in this chapter to present them.

As said earlier, the CPUs used in most embedded systems usually have an internal video interface, but in some circumstances, these interfaces cannot be used. Examples would be when we need not overload the CPU to video related duties or when the CCD sensor is too distance from where the CPU is located and the data communication is difficult because of the parallel bus used. Well, in these cases, we can use a webcam that supports this standard.

The Linux kernel supports this device class in both kernel side (the `uvcvideo` device driver) and in user space with the `uvcdynctrl` utility. The driver, if not enabled into the running kernel, can be enabled into the kernel configuration menu, and enable the following setting: **Device Drivers | Multimedia support | Media USB Adapters | USB Video Class (UVC)**.

The `uvcdynctrl` utility it can be installed as usual from the package by the same name.

To show some usage of this tool with an UVC device, we can use a normal webcam based on these specifications (it can be found almost everywhere over the Internet). Once it is connected to our BeagleBone Black device through the USB host port, we should get some kernel messages:

```
usb 1-1: new high-speed USB device number 2 using musb-hdrc
usb 1-1: New USB device found, idVendor=05a3, idProduct=9422
usb 1-1: New USB device strings: Mfr=2, Product=1, SerialNumber=3
usb 1-1: Product: USB 2.0 Camera
usb 1-1: Manufacturer: Sonix Technology Co., Ltd.
usb 1-1: SerialNumber: SN0001
uvcvideo: Found UVC 1.00 device USB 2.0 Camera (05a3:9422)
input: USB 2.0 Camera as /devices/platform/ocp/47400000.usb/47401c00.u
```

```
sb/musb-hdrc.1.auto/usb1/1-1/1-1:1.0/input/input1
usbcore: registered new interface driver uvcvideo USB Video Class driv
er (1.1.1)
usbcore: registered new interface driver snd-usb-audio
```

The device presented here is quite complete since it implements, with the video device, an input device and a sound one as well. These companion devices are usually used to support additional functionalities such as special action buttons and environmental sound recording.

It may happen that the your device does not have these companion devices. However, the important thing is that it defines, at least, the USB video device. So, `uvcvideo` will print the `Found UVC 1.00 device USB 2.0 Camera (XXXX:YYYY)` message as done earlier.

Now, since a UVC device is a video device anyway, we can use `v4l2-ctl` to detect it:

```
root@bbb:~# v4l2-ctl --list-devices
USB 2.0 Camera (usb-musb-hdrc.1.auto-1):
        /dev/video0
        /dev/video1
```

Then, we can used all the commands we saw earlier, but, of course, it's now time for the `uvcdynctrl` utility. So, let's use it to detect our UVC webcam, as shown here:

```
root@bbb:~# uvcdynctrl --list
Listing available devices:
 video1 USB 2.0 Camera
 Media controller device /dev/media1 doesn't exist
ERROR: Unable to list device entities: Invalid device or device cannot
 be opened. (Code: 5)
 video0 USB 2.0 Camera
 Media controller device: /dev/media0
 Entity 1: USB 2.0 Camera. Type: 65537, Revision: 0, Flags: 1, Grou
p-id: 0, Pads: 1, Links: 0
 Device node
 Entity: 1, Pad 0, Flags: 1
 Entity 2: USB 2.0 Camera. Type: 65537, Revision: 0, Flags: 0, Grou
p-id: 0, Pads: 1, Links: 0
 Device node
 Entity: 2, Pad 0, Flags: 1
 Entity 3: Extension 4. Type: 131072, Revision: 0, Flags: 0, Group-
id: 0, Pads: 2, Links: 2
 Subdevice: Entity: 3, Pad 0, Flags: 1
 Entity: 3, Pad 1, Flags: 2
 Out link: Source pad { Entity: 3, Index: 1, Flags: 2 } => Sink p
```

```
ad { Entity: 1, Index: 0, Flags: 1 }
 Out link: Source pad { Entity: 3, Index: 1, Flags: 2 } => Sink p
ad { Entity: 2, Index: 0, Flags: 1 }
 Entity 4: Extension 3. Type: 131072, Revision: 0, Flags: 0, Group-
id: 0, Pads: 2, Links: 1
 Subdevice: Entity: 4, Pad 0, Flags: 1
 Entity: 4, Pad 1, Flags: 2
 Out link: Source pad { Entity: 4, Index: 1, Flags: 2 } => Sink p
ad { Entity: 3, Index: 0, Flags: 1 }
 Entity 5: Processing 2. Type: 131072, Revision: 0, Flags: 0, Group
-id: 0, Pads: 2, Links: 1
 Subdevice: Entity: 5, Pad 0, Flags: 1
 Entity: 5, Pad 1, Flags: 2
 Out link: Source pad { Entity: 5, Index: 1, Flags: 2 } => Sink p
ad { Entity: 4, Index: 0, Flags: 1 }
 Entity 6: Camera 1. Type: 131072, Revision: 0, Flags: 0, Group-id:
 0, Pads: 1, Links: 1
 Subdevice: Entity: 6, Pad 0, Flags: 2
 Out link: Source pad { Entity: 6, Index: 0, Flags: 2 } => Sink p
ad { Entity: 5, Index: 0, Flags: 1 }
```

In this listing, we get a lot of information regarding our webcam. In particular, we can see that with the two video devices /dev/video0 and /dev/video1, the tool is looking for the other two devices named /dev/media0 and /dev/media1, which are *media controller devices*. File /dev/media1 is not found because both video devices /dev/video0 and /dev/video1 rely on the same hardware device, and using /dev/media0, we can manage both.

Due to space reasons, we're not going to present the *Media controller device* in this book. However, a little explanation is given here, redirecting you to the *Linux Media Subsystem Documentation* at https://linuxtv.org/downloads/v4l-dvb-apis/index.html for further information.

Media devices are strictly related to video devices, and they have been introduced to resolve the problem of introducing a relationship between the several subparts a video device may have. In fact, since UVC cameras nowadays include microphones, video capture hardware, and so on and SoC camera interfaces also perform memory-to-memory operations similar to video codecs, the current approach of modeling each sub device as a separate device (as ALSA, input, and so on) will not scale, and these devices aim to solve this problem. Again, the *Linux Media Subsystem Documentation* will explain this problem at https://linuxtv.org/downloads/v4l-dvb-apis/uapi/mediactl/media-controller-intro.html.

These devices can be easily managed with the `media-ctl` utility of v4l2-ctl (see the previous section). So, for instance, the preceding device can be better explored using the next command:

```
root@bbb:~# media-ctl -d /dev/media0 --print-topology
Media controller API version 0.1.0
Media device information
------------------------
driver          uvcvideo
model           USB 2.0 Camera
serial          SN0001
bus info        1
hw revision     0x100
driver version  4.4.7
Device topology
- entity 1: USB 2.0 Camera (1 pad, 1 link)
            type Node subtype V4L flags 1
            device node name /dev/video0
        pad0: Sink
            <- "Extension 4":1 [ENABLED,IMMUTABLE]

- entity 2: USB 2.0 Camera (1 pad, 1 link)
            type Node subtype V4L flags 0
            device node name /dev/video1
        pad0: Sink
            <- "Extension 4":1 [ENABLED,IMMUTABLE]
- entity 3: Extension 4 (2 pads, 3 links)
            type V4L2 subdev subtype Unknown flags 0
        pad0: Sink
            <- "Extension 3":1 [ENABLED,IMMUTABLE]
        pad1: Source
            -> "USB 2.0 Camera":0 [ENABLED,IMMUTABLE]
            -> "USB 2.0 Camera":0 [ENABLED,IMMUTABLE]

- entity 4: Extension 3 (2 pads, 2 links)
            type V4L2 subdev subtype Unknown flags 0
        pad0: Sink
            <- "Processing 2":1 [ENABLED,IMMUTABLE]
        pad1: Source
            -> "Extension 4":0 [ENABLED,IMMUTABLE]

- entity 5: Processing 2 (2 pads, 2 links)
            type V4L2 subdev subtype Unknown flags 0
        pad0: Sink
            <- "Camera 1":0 [ENABLED,IMMUTABLE]
        pad1: Source
            -> "Extension 3":0 [ENABLED,IMMUTABLE]
- entity 6: Camera 1 (1 pad, 1 link)
```

```
            type V4L2 subdev subtype Unknown flags 0
    pad0: Source
        -> "Processing 2":0 [ENABLED,IMMUTABLE]
```

OK, now, to get a list of the available controls for the /dev/video0 device, we can use the uvcdynctrl command as follows:

```
root@bbb:~# uvcdynctrl -d /dev/video0 --clist
Listing available controls for device /dev/video0:
  Brightness
  Contrast
  Saturation
  Hue
  White Balance Temperature, Auto
  Gamma
  Gain
  Power Line Frequency
  White Balance Temperature
  Sharpness
  Backlight Compensation
  Exposure, Auto
  Exposure (Absolute)
  Exposure, Auto Priority
```

While with the next command, we can get the available video formats:

```
root@bbb:~# uvcdynctrl -d /dev/video0 --formats
Listing available frame formats for device /dev/video0:
Pixel format: MJPG (Motion-JPEG; MIME type: image/jpeg)
  Frame size: 1920x1080
    Frame rates: 30, 25, 20, 15, 10, 5
  Frame size: 1280x720
    Frame rates: 30, 25, 20, 15, 10, 5
  Frame size: 640x480
    Frame rates: 30, 25, 20, 15, 10, 5
  Frame size: 640x360
    Frame rates: 30, 25, 20, 15, 10, 5
  Frame size: 320x240
    Frame rates: 30, 25, 20, 15, 10, 5
  Frame size: 320x180
    Frame rates: 30, 25, 20, 15, 10, 5
  Frame size: 1920x1080
    Frame rates: 30, 25, 20, 15, 10, 5
Pixel format: YUYV (YUYV 4:2:2; MIME type: video/x-raw-yuv)
  Frame size: 1920x1080
    Frame rates: 5
  Frame size: 1280x720
    Frame rates: 10, 5
```

```
Frame size: 640x480
  Frame rates: 30, 25, 20, 15, 10, 5
Frame size: 640x360
  Frame rates: 30, 25, 20, 15, 10, 5
Frame size: 320x240
  Frame rates: 30, 25, 20, 15, 10, 5
Frame size: 320x180
  Frame rates: 30, 25, 20, 15, 10, 5
Frame size: 1920x1080
  Frame rates: 5
```

Like the `v412-ctl` command, this utility allows us to modify the current device settings. In fact, as shown earlier, we can set the brightness using the following commands:

```
root@bbb:~# uvcdynctrl -d /dev/video0 --get=Brightness
0
root@bbb:~# uvcdynctrl -d /dev/video0 --set=Brightness 10
root@bbb:~# uvcdynctrl -d /dev/video0 --get=Brightness
10
```

Managing video devices

Now, it's time to show some possible usages of video devices using two interesting software tools with normal USB cameras because our embedded kits have no premounted CCD sensors.

Streaming video over the Web

In this section, we're going to show you how we can stream video data over the network using the BeagleBone Black with an UVC camera. The necessary software is a tool named `mjpg-streamer`, which must be compiled into our embedded kit. Let' install the sources with this command:

```
root@bbb:~# svn checkout svn://svn.code.sf.net/p/
mjpg-streamer/code/ mjpg-streamer-code
```

 The `svn` tools (subversion) is held in the package named **subversion**, which can be installed as usual.

Once downloaded, we have to install some packages to get a successful compilation of the tool:

```
root@bbb:~# apt-get install libjpeg-dev imagemagick libv41-dev
```

Then, we simply have to enter the newly created directory and then use the make tool with a specific command line:

```
root@bbb:~# cd mjpg-streamer-code/mjpg-streamer/
root@bbb:~/mjpg-streamer-code/mjpg-streamer# make USE_LIBV4L2=true
```

Once the compilation has finished, to install the tool, we can use the following command:

```
root@bbb:~/mjpg-streamer-code/mjpg-streamer# make install
                                            DESTDIR=/usr/
```

OK, now, the tool is successfully installed, and then, we can take a look at its command line:

```
root@bbb:~# mjpg_streamer -h
-----------------------------------------------------------------
Usage: mjpg_streamer
  -i | --input "<input-plugin.so> [parameters]"
  -o | --output "<output-plugin.so> [parameters]"
 [-h | --help ]........: display this help
 [-v | --version ].....: display version information
 [-b | --background]...: fork to the background, daemon mode
-----------------------------------------------------------------
Example #1:
 To open an UVC webcam "/dev/video1" and stream it via HTTP:
  mjpg_streamer -i "input_uvc.so -d /dev/video1" -o "output_http.so"
-----------------------------------------------------------------
Example #2:
 To open an UVC webcam and stream via HTTP port 8090:
  mjpg_streamer -i "input_uvc.so" -o "output_http.so -p 8090"
-----------------------------------------------------------------
Example #3:
 To get help for a certain input plugin:
 mjpg_streamer -i "input_uvc.so --help"
-----------------------------------------------------------------
In case the modules (=plugins) can not be found:
 * Set the default search path for the modules with:
   export LD_LIBRARY_PATH=/path/to/plugins,
 * or put the plugins into the "/lib/" or "/usr/lib" folder,
 * or instead of just providing the plugin file name, use a complete
   path and filename:
   mjpg_streamer -i "/path/to/modules/input_uvc.so"
-----------------------------------------------------------------
```

We can now verify that it's perfect for us because this utility supports UVC devices! And a possible command line can be the next one:

```
root@bbb:~# mjpg_streamer -i "input_uvc.so -d /dev/video0
                                -n -f 30 -r VGA"
                                -o "output_http.so -p 80 -w /usr/www/"
MJPG Streamer Version: svn rev: 3:172
 i: Using V4L2 device.: /dev/video0
 i: Desired Resolution: 640 x 480
 i: Frames Per Second.: 30
 i: Format...........: MJPEG
 o: www-folder-path...: /usr/www/
 o: HTTP TCP port.....: 80
 o: username:password.: disabled
 o: commands.........: enabled
```

It may be possible that we get the following error:

bind: Address already in use In this case, it means that the TCP
port 80 we've selected in the preceding command is already in use by
another program (most probably, the default web server). To verify it, we
can use these lines of code:

```
root@bbb:~# netstat -lnp | grep '\<80\>'
tcp6      0      0 :::80     :::*    LISTEN 789/apache2
```

In our example, the apache2 program is holding the port 80. We can now
simply disable it as shown in Chapter 4, *Quick Programming with Scripts
and System Daemons*, System daemons management, or we can choose
another free port to be specified with option argument -p.

Before continuing, we should spend some time to explain the preceding command line.
With the option argument -i , we specified the input plugin, while with -o, we specified
the output plugin. As input plugin, we specified input_uvc.so, which must be used on
UVC devices, with some option arguments where their meaning can be displayed with the
next command:

```
root@bbb:~# mjpg_streamer -i "input_uvc.so --help"
MJPG Streamer Version: svn rev: 3:172
------------------------------------------------------------
Help for input plugin..: UVC webcam grabber
------------------------------------------------------------
The following parameters can be passed to this plugin:

[-d | --device ].......: video device to open (your camera)
[-r | --resolution ]...: the resolution of the video device,
                         can be one of the following strings:
                         QSIF QCIF CGA QVGA CIF VGA
                         SVGA XGA SXGA
                         or a custom value like the following
                         example: 640x480
[-f | --fps ]..........: frames per second
```

```
[-y | --yuv ]..........: enable YUYV format and disable MJPEG mode
[-q | --quality ]......: JPEG compression quality in percent
                         (activates YUYV format, disables MJPEG)
[-m | --minimum_size ].: drop frames smaller then this limit, useful
                         if the webcam produces small-sized garbage
                         frames may happen under low light conditions
[-n | --no_dynctrl ]...: not initalize dynctrls of Linux-UVC driver
[-l | --led ]..........: switch the LED "on", "off", let it "blink"
                         or leave it up to the driver using the value
                         "auto"
```

Now, almost all option arguments used for the input_uvc.so plugin are clear, apart from -n, which has been used to suppress the unnecessary commands, which may return error messages as the one shown here:

```
Adding control for Pan (relative)
UVCIOC_CTRL_ADD - Error: Inappropriate ioctl for device
```

Regarding the output plugin, which is output_http.so, we can do in a similar manner as above in order to get its option arguments' meanings:

```
root@bbb:~# mjpg_streamer -o "output_http.so --help"
MJPG Streamer Version: svn rev: 3:172
-------------------------------------------------------------
Help for output plugin..: HTTP output plugin
-------------------------------------------------------------
The following parameters can be passed to this plugin:

[-w | --www ]..........: folder that contains webpages in
                         flat hierarchy (no subfolders)
[-p | --port ].........: TCP port for this HTTP server
[-c | --credentials ]..: ask for "username:password" on connect
[-n | --nocommands ]...: disable execution of commands
-------------------------------------------------------------
```

OK, now that the command line is clear, we simply have to point our web browser on BeagleBone Black's IP address to get an output as shown in the following screenshot:

Note that latest versions of mjpg_streamer are buggy because they display no images at all. If this is your case, the solution is to apply the patch reported in the chapter_16/input_uvc.patch file in the book's example code repository:

```
root@bbb:~/mjpg-streamer-code/mjpg-streamer# \
             patch -p0 < input_uvc.patch
```

Then, we have to recompile and reinstall the tool:

```
root@bbb:~/mjpg-streamer-code/mjpg-streamer# \
            make clean &&
            make USE_LIBV4L2=true &&
            make install DESTDIR=/usr/
```

The homepage shows us how `mjpg_streamer` is powerful. In fact, just using an HTML page, we can put in it a static picture grabbed by the webcam. We just need to reload the page to update the view. This action of requesting one single picture from the image input, as reported in the preceding screenshot, is done using an HTTP request containing the GET parameter `action=snapshot`.

However, we want a video stream, so we have to click on the Stream item on the top-left main menu. Here is the output:

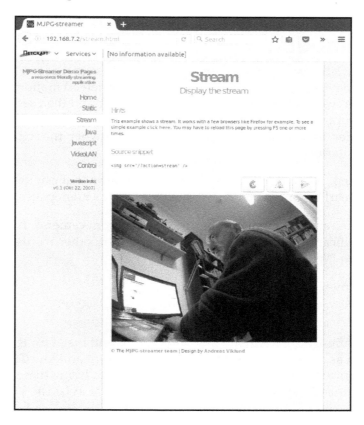

Again, we have another HTML page describing what we have to do in order to get a video streaming. We just need to add the code:

```
<img src="/?action=stream" />
```

Note that we can get a stream or a snapshot without using any HTML page at all by simply using these two URLs:

- `http://192.168.7.2/?action=snapshot` for a snapshot.
- `http://192.168.7.2/?action=stream` for a video streaming.

Note that the IP address used earlier is the one we can use with the USB Ethernet connection. If you are using a different connection with your embedded kit, you have to fix it accordingly.

Capturing motion

In this section, we wish to suggest another video device's usage that can be implemented into an embedded device, that is, the ability to capture (or detect) motion. If we use a video camera (or simply a webcam) in a room we wish to monitor and then send the captured video to a remote supervisor, we can also imagine doing some computation on the captured video frames in order, for example, to automatically detect when the scene changes and then to activate an alarm.

To do this special task, a good program we can use is **motion** that can use webcams as the ones we presented earlier. In fact, as reported at the project's homepage:

Motion is a program that monitors the video signal from cameras. It is able to detect if a significant part of the picture has changed; in other words, it can detect motion [Motion WebHome]

The project homepage is at
`http://www.lavrsen.dk/foswiki/bin/view/Motion/WebHome`.

The program is a command-line-driven tool written in C and made for the Video4Linux interface. It can run as a daemon with a rather small footprint and low CPU usage, and it can call user configurable *triggers* when certain events occur. Using these triggers, it can generate either pictures (**jpeg** or **netpbm**) or videos (**mpeg** or **avi**). The `motion` program is operated mainly via configuration files, but the end video streams can be viewed from a web browser.

This tool is held in the package by the same name, and then, it can be installed in the usual way into our Wandboard:

```
root@wb:~# aptitude install motion
```

Once installed, let's take a look at the system's log messages where we should see something like this:

```
wb motion[869]: Not starting motion daemon, disabled
via /etc/default/motion ... (warning).
```

The daemon is disabled by default because it must be correctly configured before enabling it. So, to configure it, we have to modify at least the /etc/motion/motion.conf file and, in case of multiple video devices, the per video device configuration files named /etc/motion/thread1.conf, /etc/motion/thread2.conf, and so on. In fact, the daemon creates one thread per input video device used, and all special settings referring to it must be done inside the corresponding file.

Since we're using just one webcam, we can verify that the tool detects it by running the daemon in the debugging mode with the following command line:

```
[0] [NTC] [ALL] conf_load: Processing thread 0 - config file /etc/moti
on/motion.conf
[0] [ALR] [ALL] conf_cmdparse: Unknown config option "sdl_threadnr"
[0] [NTC] [ALL] motion_startup: Motion 3.2.12+git20140228 Started
[0] [NTC] [ALL] motion_startup: Logging to syslog
[0] [NTC] [ALL] motion_startup: Using log type (ALL) log level (NTC)
[0] [NTC] [ENC] ffmpeg_init: ffmpeg LIBAVCODEC_BUILD 3670272 LIBAVFORM
AT_BUILD 3670272
[0] [NTC] [ALL] main: Motion running in setup mode.
[0] [NTC] [ALL] main: Thread 1 is from /etc/motion/motion.conf
[0] [NTC] [ALL] main: Thread 1 is device: /dev/video0 input -1
[0] [NTC] [ALL] main: Stream port 8081
[0] [NTC] [ALL] main: Waiting for threads to finish, pid: 911
[1] [NTC] [ALL] motion_init: Thread 1 started , motion detection Enabl
ed
[1] [NTC] [VID] vid_v4lx_start: Using videodevice /dev/video0 and inpu
t -1
[0] [NTC] [STR] httpd_run: motion-httpd testing : IPV4 addr: 127.0.0.1
 port: 8080
[0] [NTC] [STR] httpd_run: motion-httpd Bound : IPV4 addr: 127.0.0.1 p
ort: 8080
[0] [NTC] [STR] httpd_run: motion-httpd/3.2.12+git20140228 running, ac
cepting connections
[0] [NTC] [STR] httpd_run: motion-httpd: waiting for data on 127.0.0.1
 port TCP 8080
[1] [NTC] [VID] v4l2_get_capability:
```

```
------------------------
cap.driver: "uvcvideo"
cap.card: "Microsoft LifeCam VX-800"
cap.bus_info: "usb-ci_hdrc.1-1"
cap.capabilities=0x84200001
------------------------
[1] [NTC] [VID] v4l2_get_capability: - VIDEO_CAPTURE
[1] [NTC] [VID] v4l2_get_capability: - STREAMING
[1] [NTC] [VID] v4l2_select_input: name = "Camera 1", type 0x00000002,
 status 00000000
[1] [NTC] [VID] v4l2_select_input: - CAMERA
[1] [WRN] [VID] v4l2_select_input: Device doesn't support VIDIOC_G_STD
[1] [NTC] [VID] v4l2_set_pix_format: Config palette index 17 (YU12) do
esn't work.
[1] [NTC] [VID] v4l2_set_pix_format: Supported palettes:
[1] [NTC] [VID] v4l2_set_pix_format: (0) YUYV (YUYV 4:2:2)
[1] [NTC] [VID] v4l2_set_pix_format: 0 - YUYV 4:2:2 (compressed : 0) (
0x56595559)
[1] [NTC] [VID] v4l2_set_pix_format Selected palette YUYV
[1] [NTC] [VID] v4l2_do_set_pix_format: Testing palette YUYV (320x240)
[1] [NTC] [VID] v4l2_do_set_pix_format: Using palette YUYV (320x240) b
ytesperlines 640 sizeimage 153600 colorspace 00000000
[1] [NTC] [VID] v4l2_scan_controls: found control 0x00980900, "Brightn
ess", range -10,10
[1] [NTC] [VID] v4l2_scan_controls: "Brightness", default 2, curre
nt 2
[1] [NTC] [VID] v4l2_scan_controls: found control 0x00980901, "Contras
t", range 0,20
[1] [NTC] [VID] v4l2_scan_controls: "Contrast", default 10, curren
t 10
[1] [NTC] [VID] v4l2_scan_controls: found control 0x00980902, "Saturat
ion", range 0,10
[1] [NTC] [VID] v4l2_scan_controls: "Saturation", default 4, curre
nt 4
[1] [NTC] [VID] v4l2_scan_controls: found control 0x00980903, "Hue", r
ange -5,5
[1] [NTC] [VID] v4l2_scan_controls: "Hue", default 0, current 0
[1] [NTC] [VID] v4l2_scan_controls: found control 0x00980910, "Gamma",
 range 100,200
[1] [NTC] [VID] v4l2_scan_controls: "Gamma", default 130, current
130
[1] [NTC] [VID] v4l2_scan_controls: found control 0x00980913, "Gain",
range 32,48
[1] [NTC] [VID] v4l2_scan_controls: "Gain", default 34, current 34
[1] [NTC] [VID] vid_v4lx_start: Using V4L2
[1] [NTC] [ALL] image_ring_resize: Resizing pre_capture buffer to 1 it
ems
[1] [NTC] [STR] http_bindsock: motion-stream testing : IPV4 addr: 127.
```

```
0.0.1 port: 8081
[1] [NTC] [STR] http_bindsock: motion-stream Bound : IPV4 addr: 127.0.
0.1 port: 8081
[1] [NTC] [ALL] motion_init: Started motion-stream server in port 8081
 auth Disabled
```

As we can see from the preceding output, we can get a lot of useful information about the daemon status. First of all, we notice that each line begins with a number into square brackets that address per thread's output. The number 0 is for the motion main thread, while number 1 is for the first thread connected with the webcam (the /dev/video0 device) and so on if more input video devices are used.

Then, we see the daemon specifically says regarding our webcam:

```
[1] [NTC] [VID] v4l2_get_capability:
------------------------
cap.driver: "uvcvideo"
cap.card: "Microsoft LifeCam VX-800"
cap.bus_info: "usb-ci_hdrc.1-1"
cap.capabilities=0x84200001
------------------------
[1] [NTC] [VID] v4l2_get_capability: - VIDEO_CAPTURE
[1] [NTC] [VID] v4l2_get_capability: - STREAMING
[1] [NTC] [VID] v4l2_select_input: name = "Camera 1", type 0x00000002,
 status 00000000
[1] [NTC] [VID] v4l2_select_input: - CAMERA
[1] [WRN] [VID] v4l2_select_input: Device doesn't support VIDIOC_G_STD
[1] [NTC] [VID] v4l2_set_pix_format: Config palette index 17 (YU12) do
esn't work.
[1] [NTC] [VID] v4l2_set_pix_format: Supported palettes:
[1] [NTC] [VID] v4l2_set_pix_format: (0) YUYV (YUYV 4:2:2)
[1] [NTC] [VID] v4l2_set_pix_format: 0 - YUYV 4:2:2 (compressed : 0) (
0x56595559)
[1] [NTC] [VID] v4l2_set_pix_format Selected palette YUYV
[1] [NTC] [VID] v4l2_do_set_pix_format: Testing palette YUYV (320x240)
[1] [NTC] [VID] v4l2_do_set_pix_format: Using palette YUYV (320x240) b
ytesperlines 640 sizeimage 153600 colorspace 00000000
```

The current palette setting (**YU12**) is not valid for our webcam, and the system says that it is going to use **YUYV**. This is not an error. However, we wish to correctly set up the correct video palette in order to remove that warning. To do so, we notice that in the /etc/motion/motion.conf file, we see the following settings (the text is just a snippet of the whole file, which is really long!):

```
# Videodevice to be used for capturing  (default /dev/video0)
# for FreeBSD default is /dev/bktr0
videodevice /dev/video0
```

```
# v4l2_palette allows to choose preferable palette to be use by motion
# to capture from those supported by your videodevice. (default: 17)
# E.g. if your videodevice supports both V4L2_PIX_FMT_SBGGR8 and
# V4L2_PIX_FMT_MJPEG then motion will by default use
# V4L2_PIX_FMT_MJPEG.
# Setting v4l2_palette to 2 forces motion to use V4L2_PIX_FMT_SBGGR8
# instead.
#
# Values :
# V4L2_PIX_FMT_SN9C10X : 0   'S910'
# V4L2_PIX_FMT_SBGGR16 : 1   'BYR2'
# V4L2_PIX_FMT_SBGGR8  : 2   'BA81'
# V4L2_PIX_FMT_SPCA561 : 3   'S561'
# V4L2_PIX_FMT_SGBRG8  : 4   'GBRG'
# V4L2_PIX_FMT_SGRBG8  : 5   'GRBG'
# V4L2_PIX_FMT_PAC207  : 6   'P207'
# V4L2_PIX_FMT_PJPG    : 7   'PJPG'
# V4L2_PIX_FMT_MJPEG   : 8   'MJPEG'
# V4L2_PIX_FMT_JPEG    : 9   'JPEG'
# V4L2_PIX_FMT_RGB24   : 10  'RGB3'
# V4L2_PIX_FMT_SPCA501 : 11  'S501'
# V4L2_PIX_FMT_SPCA505 : 12  'S505'
# V4L2_PIX_FMT_SPCA508 : 13  'S508'
# V4L2_PIX_FMT_UYVY    : 14  'UYVY'
# V4L2_PIX_FMT_YUYV    : 15  'YUYV'
# V4L2_PIX_FMT_YUV422P : 16  '422P'
# V4L2_PIX_FMT_YUV420  : 17  'YU12'
#
v4l2_palette 17

# Tuner device to be used for capturing using tuner as source (default
# /dev/tuner0)
# This is ONLY used for FreeBSD. Leave it commented out for Linux
; tunerdevice /dev/tuner0

# The video input to be used (default: -1)
# Should normally be set to 0 or 1 for video/TV cards, and -1 for USB
# cameras
input -1
```

The videodevice and input settings are correct, but v4l2_palette is not, and to fix it, we must replace value 17 with the more appropriate 15. Now, if we rerun the daemon as we did earlier, the configuration error disappears.

Now, we can verify the video captured by the webcam by directly seeing a video stream. To do it `motion` set up several web servers to be used to monitor the main thread (numbered with 0) and the per camera threads (numbered from 1 to N). Since we're using just one webcam, we have to check the main configuration file only where we can find the following settings regarding thread 0:

```
########################################################
# HTTP Based Control
########################################################

# TCP/IP port for the http server to listen on (default: 0 = disabled)
webcontrol_port 8080

# Restrict control connections to localhost only (default: on)
webcontrol_localhost on

# Output for http server, select off to choose raw text plain
# (default: on)
webcontrol_html_output on

# Authentication for the http based control. Syntax username:password
# Default: not defined (Disabled)
; webcontrol_authentication username:password
```

So, to enable an HTTP access with the daemon, we have to modify `webcontrol_localhost` to `off` in order to allow a remote control connection. Also, for thread 1 (and next ones), we have the following settings:

```
########################################################
# Live Stream Server
########################################################

# The mini-http server listens to this port for requests
# (default: 0 = disabled)
stream_port 8081

# Quality of the jpeg (in percent) images produced (default: 50)
stream_quality 50

# Output frames at 1 fps when no motion is detected and increase to
# the rate given by stream_maxrate when motion is detected (default:
# off)
stream_motion off

# Maximum framerate for stream streams (default: 1)
stream_maxrate 1
```

```
# Restrict stream connections to localhost only (default: on)
stream_localhost on

# Limits the number of images per connection (default: 0 = unlimited)
# Number can be defined by multiplying actual stream rate by desired
# number of seconds
# Actual stream rate is the smallest of the numbers framerate
# and stream_maxrate
 stream_limit 0

# Set the authentication method (default: 0)
# 0 = disabled
# 1 = Basic authentication
# 2 = MD5 digest (the safer authentication)
stream_auth_method 0

# Authentication for the stream. Syntax username:password
# Default: not defined (Disabled)
; stream_authentication username:password
```

Again, to enable local HTTP access we have to modify setting stream_localhost to off. Now if we rerun the daemon we can verify that two motion web servers are running at ports 8080 and 8081 by using the command line below into a different terminal:

```
root@wb:~# netstat -pnl | grep motion
tcp     0    0 0.0.0.0:8080    0.0.0.0:*     LISTEN    1037/motion
tcp     0    0 0.0.0.0:8081    0.0.0.0:*     LISTEN    1037/motion
```

Note that port number 8081 has been used by default as far as if we had a second camera that will use port 8082 and so on. However, this numbering can be altered using per-camera configuration files.

Now, we can use a normal browser to connect with the main thread (thread number 0), but most important for us is to check the video stream from the webcam at URL `http://192.168.9.2:8081`, as shown in the following screenshot:

Note that in this last test, we executed the daemon without the `-s` switch in order to disable the setup mode, that is, using the following command line:

```
root@wb:~# motion -n
```

This is because we noticed that in the setup mode, the webcams work with a very bad video output (it is unknown whether this is a bug or a feature).

On the other side, the control thread can be controlled via the web browser at `http://192.168.9.2:8080`. In the following screenshot, there is the main page:

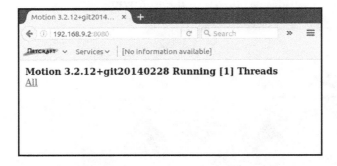

Then, if we click on the **All** | **Config** | **list** menu entries, we reach `http://192.168.9.2:8080/0/config/list`, where we can get a page with all configuration settings of the main thread, as in the following screenshot:

Note that we are able to change each setting just by clicking on the relative link and then entering the new value. However, we're not going to use these interfaces to set up the system in this book.

Now, our motion-detection system is ready. In fact, if we point the webcam into a room and then move in front of it, we can notice that the daemon will generate several events with the relative images as shown here:

```
[1] [NTC] [EVT] event_newfile: File of type 8 saved to: /var/lib/motio
n/01-20161024204255.avi
[1] [NTC] [ALL] motion_detected: Motion detected - starting event 1
[1] [NTC] [EVT] event_newfile: File of type 1 saved to: /var/lib/motio
n/01-20161024204255-00.jpg
[1] [NTC] [EVT] event_newfile: File of type 1 saved to: /var/lib/motio
n/01-20161024204255-01.jpg
[1] [NTC] [EVT] event_newfile: File of type 1 saved to: /var/lib/motio
n/01-20161024204256-00.jpg
[1] [NTC] [EVT] event_newfile: File of type 1 saved to: /var/lib/motio
n/01-20161024204256-01.jpg
[1] [NTC] [ALL] motion_loop: End of event 1
```

Now, the main settings have been done, but some fine settings are still to be done in order, for instance, to send an e-mail message with an attached picture whenever a motion event occurs. However, these are left to you in order to best fit their needs.

Summary

Video devices are complex devices to manage video streams that can be used in several control and surveillance applications as far as automation systems useful for industry and/or home automations. We've seen how they are defined in a GNU/Linux-based system and how we can easily add one of these devices to an embedded computer even if its CPU has no dedicated video interfaces.

In the next chapter, we'll see another important (even if very simple) device class that every control automation device that interacts with the environment should have: the ADC.

17
Analog-to-Digital Converters - ADC

In this chapter, we will present a specific peripheral type that can be used to get analogical signals from the environment. Our embedded kits are digital devices, but to interact with the environment, we need the ability to convert information from our world (the analogical one) to the digital world.

In particular, we will see the ADC class, which belongs to the **Industrial I/O** (**IIO**) devices and its specific sysfs interface. We'll see how we can use special software and hardware triggers in order to start conversions at a specific time or when some events occur.

What is an analog-to-digital converter device?

An **analog-to-digital** converter (**ADC**) is a device that can convert an analog signal into a digital one. The conversion involves quantization of the input, and instead of continuously performing the conversion, an ADC does the conversion periodically by sampling the input at specific *moments*. The result is a sequence of digital values (having a well-defined resolution, that is, the number of bits used to represent the converted digital value) that have been converted from a continuous time and continuous amplitude analog signal to a discrete time and discrete amplitude digital signal.

As a simple example, in the following graph, there is an 8-level ADC coding scheme where the input signal **Vin** is referred to with the **Vref** signal (the maximum allowed input value) and then encoded into a binary number:

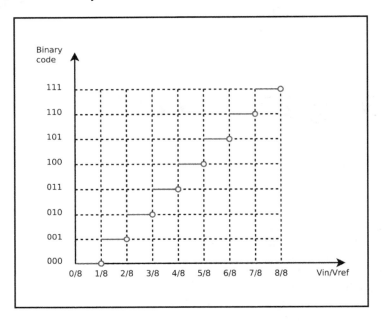

The small circles mean that the analog values at 1/8, 2/8, and so on are mapped using the bigger value. For example, if *Vin/Vref = 1/8*, the corresponding binary code is set to 001 instead of 000.

Note also that in this coding scheme, the input value *Vin/Vref = 1* is not allowed.

In this example, the resolution *res* is 3 bits, and it's quite obvious to say that the binary representation code *N* (in base 10) of the input signal is given by the following formula, where the *Integer()* function returns the integer part of its argument:

N = Integer(Vin/Vref * 2res)

These formulas are simplifications of the real transfer function of ADC devices, so it cannot be taken as is for a production environment. In this case, you should refer to the real converter device's datasheet.

These conversions are also characterized by another important parameter: the sampling rate (or sampling frequency). In fact, a continuously varying (band-limited signal) can be sampled at intervals of T seconds, the sampling time (the inverse of the sampling frequency), and then, the original signal can be *exactly* reproduced from the discrete time values by an interpolation formula. In order to exactly specify this sampling time, we can use two modes:

- By software (*software-triggered*), where the program executes the ADC conversions by itself at a specified timing.
- By hardware (*hardware-triggered)*, where the program sets the ADC converter in such a way that it can auto-generate a sampling frequency.

This last sampling mode can be divided into two more functions:

- Internal triggered, where the ADC conversions are triggered according to an internal clock.
- External triggered, where the ADC conversions are triggered according to an external signal. It's quite easy to find a dedicated input pin in an embedded device where we can connect a fixed timed signal (such as a PWM signal – see `Chapter 18`, *Pulse-Width Modulation – PWM*) that can be used to trigger the ADC convention events.

 You can find details on ADCs at `https://en.wikipedia.org/wiki/Analog-to-digital_converter`.

The electrical lines

ADC converter's lines are reported in the table:

Name	Description
ADC input	The ADC input signal
ADC trigger	The ADC trigger signal (optional)
GND	Common ground

ADCs on the BeagleBone Black

The BeagleBone Black has seven ADCs available on the expansion connectors, and the relative pins are summarized in the table here:

Name	ADC output
ain0	P9.39
ain1	P9.40
ain2	P9.37
ain3	P9.38
ain4	P9.33
ain5	P9.36
ain6	P9.35

To enable the ADCs, we can use the following command line:

```
root@bbb:~# echo BB-ADC > /sys/devices/platform/bone_capemgr/slots
bone_capemgr: part_number 'BB-ADC', version 'N/A'
bone_capemgr: slot #5: override
bone_capemgr: Using override eeprom data at slot 5
bone_capemgr: slot #5: 'Override Board Name,00A0,Override Manuf,BB-ADC
bone_capemgr: slot #5: dtbo 'BB-ADC-00A0.dtbo' loaded; overlay id #1
```

Related kernel messages are also reported for completeness.

If everything works well, a new directory named iio:device0 should appear in the /sys/bus/iio/devices/ directory as show here:

```
root@bbb:~# ls /sys/bus/iio/devices/
iio:device0
```

One important notice regarding BeagleBone Black's ADCs is about the maximum voltage we can apply to each input pin. In fact, it *must* be between 0 and 1.8V reference voltage; otherwise, serious damages may occur to the CPU!

ADCs on the SAMA5D3 Xplained

The SAMA5D3 Xplained has 10 ADCs available on the expansion connectors, and the relative pins are summarized in the table here (TRG is the trigger pin):

Name	ADC output	Name	ADC output
TRG	J21.6	ain5	J17.6
ain0	J17.1 [*]	ain6	J17.7
ain1	J17.2	ain7	J17.8
ain2	J17.3	ain8	J21.1 [*]
ain3	J17.4	ain9	J21.2 [*]
ain4	J17.5		

Note that the pins marked with [*] are only available on the expansion connectors after a hardware modification of the board (a resistor must be moved-refer to the *SAMA5D3 Xplained's User Guide* for further information).

Also, note that the SAMA5D3 Xplained can use part of these ADCs to manage a resistive touchscreen device, and in this case, the maximum available number of ADCs is lower (again, see the *SAMA5D3 Xplained's User Guide* for further information).

The ADCs should be already enabled by default, and the directory named iio:device0 should be present in the /sys/bus/iio/devices/ directory as shown here:

```
root@a5d3:~# ls /sys/bus/iio/devices/
iio:device0  trigger0  trigger1  trigger2  trigger3
```

The other files named trigger0, trigger1, and so on are related to the trigger we can use with our ADCs in order to start data capturing (see the upcoming sections for further information on how to use them).

ADCs on the Wandboard

The Wandboard has no ADCs available on its expansion connectors.

ADCs in Linux

To explain the functioning of ADCs in a GNU/Linux-based system, let's use the SAMA5D3 Xplained board since its ADC support is more complete than the BeagleBone Black's (however, during the explanation, each difference with the BeagleBone Black will be pointed out).

If we take a look at the `iio:device0` directory's content in the SAMA5D3 Xplained, we will find the listing shown here:

```
root@a5d3:~# ls /sys/bus/iio/devices/iio\:device0/
buffer             in_voltage1_raw in_voltage6_raw   name           trigger
dev                in_voltage2_raw in_voltage7_raw   of_node        uevent
in_voltage0_raw    in_voltage3_raw in_voltage8_raw   power
in_voltage10_raw   in_voltage4_raw in_voltage9_raw   scan_elements
in_voltage11_raw   in_voltage5_raw in_voltage_scale  subsystem
```

Files in the `in_voltageX_raw` form can be used to read a single ADC input from a particular channel. This interface can be used, as shown here:

```
root@a5d3:~# cat /sys/bus/iio/devices/iio\:device0/in_voltage0_raw
1662
```

> It may be possible that you get the following error while trying to read from each ADC channel:
> ```
> root@a5d3:~# cat /sys/bus/iio/devices/iio\:device0/
> in_voltage0_raw
> cat: /sys/bus/iio/devices/iio:device0/in_voltage0_r
> aw: Connection timed out
> ```
> This is because the currently used board has a buggy initialization of the analog-to-digital power section of the CPU (named **VDDANA**), which is not correctly powered by the default PMIC configuration. To solve the problem, you will have to send a couple of I²C commands to the PMIC to set its *output5* pin to 3.3V:
> ```
> root@a5d3:~# i2cset -y 1 0x5b 0x54 0x39 &&
>              i2cset -y 1 0x5b 0x55 0xc1
> ```
> See *The I2C tools* in `Chapter 9`, *Inter-Integrated Circuits – I2C*, regarding `i2cset` command usage.

The returned number represents the raw value of the actual read voltage. To get the value in volt, we can use the content of the `in_voltage_scale` file that holds the scale factor to be applied to the `in_voltageX_raw` after the addition of `in_voltageX_offset` (if present; otherwise, we consider it as 0) in order to obtain the microvolts.

The formula for the generic `in_voltageX` input is shown here:

$$in\_voltageX = in\_voltage\_scale * in\_voltageX\_raw + in\_voltageX\_offset$$

The BeagleBone Black has none of these files, so the formula to get the ADCs' data in microvolts is shown here, where R is just the read raw value:
$V = 3300 * R/4095$

This mode of reading data from the ADCs is named *one-shot* mode (or *software-triggered*). However, a more interesting mode to get data from the ADCs is the *continuous mode* (or *hardware-triggered*). Regarding this usage, the important files are held in the `buffer` and `scan_elements` directories; in `buffer`, we find the files here:

```
root@a5d3:~# ls /sys/bus/iio/devices/iio\:device0/buffer/
enable   length   watermark
```

Using these files, we can manage the buffer where our samples are stored during the *continuous mode* of the ADC. In fact, in `length`, we can store the number of scans contained by the buffer, while with `enable`, we actually start the buffer capture up. With `watermark`, we can specify the maximum number (positive integer) of scan elements to wait for, so when we do a blocking `read()` to get sampled data, it will wait until the minimum between the requested read amount and the low water mark value is available.

In the `scan_elements` directory, we find these files:

```
root@a5d3:~# ls /sys/bus/iio/devices/iio\:device0/scan_elements/
in_timestamp_en       in_voltage1_index    in_voltage5_type
in_timestamp_index    in_voltage1_type     in_voltage6_en
in_timestamp_type     in_voltage2_en       in_voltage6_index
in_voltage0_en        in_voltage2_index    in_voltage7_en
in_voltage0_index     in_voltage2_type     in_voltage7_index
in_voltage0_type      in_voltage3_en       in_voltage7_type
in_voltage10_en       in_voltage3_type     in_voltage8_en
in_voltage10_index    in_voltage4_en       in_voltage8_index
in_voltage10_type     in_voltage4_index    in_voltage8_type
in_voltage11_index    in_voltage4_type     in_voltage9_en
in_voltage11_type     in_voltage5_en       in_voltage9_index
in_voltage1_en        in_voltage5_index    in_voltage9_type
```

Here, each ADC has its own tern of files:

- `in_voltageX_en`: which defines whether channel `X` is enabled or not.
- `in_voltageX_index`: which defines the index of channel `X` in the buffer's

chunks.

- `in_voltageX_type` : which states how the ADC stores its data in buffer for channel X.

By reading this last file, it returns a string like this:

```
root@a5d3:~# cat /sys/bus/iio/devices/iio\:device0/scan_elements/in_vo
ltage0_type
le:u12/16>>0
```

Here, string `le` represents the datum endianness (here, little endian), character `u` is the sign of the value returned (it could be either `u` for unsigned or `s` for signed), number `12` is the number of relevant bits of information, and `16` is the actual number of bits used to store the datum. In the end, `0` is the number of right shifts needed to correctly get the datum within the buffer.

See the `Documentation/ABI/testing/sysfs-bus-iio` file in Linux's tree repository for further information regarding the ADC interface into the IIO devices.

You must have noticed that another tern is present, that is, the `in_timestamp_en`, `in_timestamp_index` and `in_timestamp_type` files. These are related to the ability to have a timestamp to each captured data. The files' content is similar to the voltage files earlier; however, the resolution is a bit different:

```
root@a5d3:~# cat /sys/bus/iio/devices/iio\:device0/scan_elements/in_ti
mestamp_type
le:s64/64>>0
```

As a simple example, let's try to continuously read data (that is, using a hardware trigger) from three ADCs with timestamping. So, we need to enable buffer and the channels to be used:

```
root@a5d3:~# echo 1 >
    /sys/bus/iio/devices/iio\:device0/scan_elements/in_timestamp_en
root@a5d3:~# echo 1 >
    /sys/bus/iio/devices/iio\:device0/scan_elements/in_voltage0_en
root@a5d3:~# echo 1 >
    /sys/bus/iio/devices/iio\:device0/scan_elements/in_voltage2_en
root@a5d3:~# echo 1 >
    /sys/bus/iio/devices/iio\:device0/scan_elements/in_voltage4_en
```

Then, we will set up the buffer length to `100` and a watermark to half buffer:

```
root@a5d3:~# echo 100 >
    /sys/bus/iio/devices/iio\:device0/buffer/length
root@a5d3:~# echo 50 >
    /sys/bus/iio/devices/iio\:device0/buffer/watermark
```

Now, we can simply enable the capture by writing 1 in the `enable` file in the `buffer` directory. Then, all captures are exposed in the `/dev/iio:device0` character device. To stop the capture, we have to write 0 in the same file.

To do quick tests on the buffer from the command line, we can use the tool present in the `tools/iio/` directory within the Linux's sources repository. Just copy the directory's content in the SAMA5D3 Xplained board and use the `make` command:

```
root@a5d3:~# cd iio/
root@a5d3:~/iio# make
```

If we get the following error during compilation, it means we missed the needed include files:

```
iio_event_monitor.c:28:30: fatal error: linux/iio/e
vents.h: No such file or directory
 #include <linux/iio/events.h>
                              ^
compilation terminated.
```

To solve the issue, we can manually install them by creating `/usr/include/linux/iio` and then copying the necessary files from the host PC using, as an example, the `scp` command:

```
root@a5d3:~# mkdir /usr/include/linux/iio
root@a5d3:~# scp giometti@192.168.32.54:BBB/bb-kern
el/KERNEL/include/uapi/linux/iio/{events,types}.h /
usr/include/linux/iio/
```

If everything works well, we should have two new programs, and the first one is `lsiio`, which can be used to get a list of IIO devices currently defined in the system:

```
root@a5d3:~/iio# ./lsiio
Device 000: f8018000.adc
Trigger 000: f8018000.adc-dev0-external-risin"
Trigger 001: f8018000.adc-dev0-external-falli"
Trigger 002: f8018000.adc-dev0-external-any
Trigger 003: f8018000.adc-dev0-continuous
```

The second one is `generic_buffer`, which is the tool we can use to test our ADCs in the continuous mode. Here is the code block showing its help message.

```
root@a5d3:~/iio# ./generic_buffer
Device name not set
Usage: generic_buffer [options]...
Capture, convert and output data from IIO device buffer
  -c <n>       Do n conversions
  -e           Disable wait for event (new data)
  -g           Use trigger-less mode
  -l <n>       Set buffer length to n samples
  -n <name>    Set device name (mandatory)
  -t <name>    Set trigger name
  -w <n>       Set delay between reads in us (event-less mode)
```

Then, the command line to get 10 samples once from `iio:device0` (our ADCs) using the continuous trigger (the `Trigger 003` above) is shown here with its output:

```
root@a5d3:~/iio# ./generic_buffer -n f8018000.adc
                             -t f8018000.adc-dev0-continuous
                             -l 10 -c 1
iio device number being used is 0
iio trigger number being used is 3
/sys/bus/iio/devices/iio:device0 f8018000.adc-dev0-continuous
1178.466797 279.052734 103.271484 1478100858118937669
270.996094 279.052734 103.271484 1478100858118993305
270.996094 159.667969 103.271484 1478100858119010638
270.996094 159.667969 94.482422 1478100858119032638
225.585938 159.667969 94.482422 1478100858119052214
225.585938 156.005859 94.482422 1478100858119074820
225.585938 156.005859 93.017578 1478100858119096032
222.656250 156.005859 93.017578 1478100858119115790
222.656250 156.005859 93.017578 1478100858119136699
222.656250 156.005859 94.482422 1478100858119157729
```

The analogous command line for the BeagleBone Black is as follows:
```
root@bbb:~/iio# ./generic_buffer -n TI-am335x-adc
                          -g -l 10 -c 1
```
Note that, in this case, we have to use the `-g` option argument because the BeagleBone Black has no available triggers.

By taking a look at the timestamp column (the last one) of the preceding output, we notice that the period is (more or less) 20 milliseconds, and it cannot be directly modified. In fact, the new read starts when the previous one ends. In this case, the sampling is not much useful (apart from for debugging purposes), However, an elegant solution to this problem exists: we can use a PWM signal routed to the trigger pin and then select, for example, the external falling trigger (`Trigger 001`). Then, using this trick, we can simply set the sampling period by setting the PWM period (see the example in the next section).

Before moving to the new section, it is interesting to take a look at the relevant code of the preceding program in order to understand how it works to collect data. Here is the main loop with some initialization functions:

```c
/* Setup ring buffer parameters */
ret = write_sysfs_int("length", buf_dir_name, buf_len);
if (ret < 0)
    goto error;

/* Enable the buffer */
ret = write_sysfs_int("enable", buf_dir_name, 1);
if (ret < 0) {
    fprintf(stderr, "Failed to enable buffer: %s\n", strerror(-ret));
    goto error;
}

scan_size = size_from_channelarray(channels, num_channels);
data = malloc(scan_size * buf_len);
if (!data) {
    ret = -ENOMEM;
    goto error;
}

ret = asprintf(&buffer_access, "/dev/iio:device%d", dev_num);
if (ret < 0) {
    ret = -ENOMEM;
    goto error;
}

/* Attempt to open non blocking the access dev */
fp = open(buffer_access, O_RDONLY | O_NONBLOCK);
if (fp == -1) { /* TODO: If it isn't there make the node */
    ret = -errno;
    fprintf(stderr, "Failed to open %s\n", buffer_access);
    goto error;
}

for (j = 0; j < num_loops; j++) {
    if (!noevents) {
        struct pollfd pfd = {
            .fd = fp,
            .events = POLLIN,
        };

        ret = poll(&pfd, 1, -1);
        if (ret < 0) {
            ret = -errno;
            goto error;
```

```
        } else if (ret == 0) {
            continue;
        }

        toread = buf_len;
    } else {
        usleep(timedelay);
        toread = 64;
    }

    read_size = read(fp, data, toread * scan_size);
    if (read_size < 0) {
        if (errno == EAGAIN) {
            fprintf(stderr, "nothing available\n");
            continue;
        } else {
            break;
        }
    }
    for (i = 0; i < read_size / scan_size; i++)
        process_scan(data + scan_size * i, channels, num_channels);
}
```

As we can see, after ring buffers initialization and enable, we attempt to open the `/dev/iio:deviceX` char device where we can get access to the desired ADC. Then, we start the loop where we can use the `poll()` system call to detect where some data are ready to be read and then we pass to collect them with `read()`.

Detecting a gas

In order to show a simple ADC usage (with a little help of a PWM source), we will see how we can detect a dangerous gas using an analogue sensor that is shown here:

The devices can be purchased at or
`http://www.cosino.io/product/mq-2-gas-sensor` by surfing the Internet.

We can get the datasheet of each GAS sensor at `http://gas-sensor.ru/p`
`df/combustible-gas-sensor.pdf`.

This sensor acts as a variable resistor according to the gas concentration, so they can be
easily read with a normal ADC. Looking carefully at the datasheet of the gas sensor, we can
see exactly how this sensors varies its internal resistance according to the gas concentration
(in reality, it depends on environment humidity and temperature too; but for an indoor
functioning, we can consider these values as constants). so if we put it in series with a
resistor and apply a constant voltage, we can get an output voltage that is proportional to
the actual gas concentration.

In the following diagram, there is a possible schematic where the gas sensor is connected to
3.3V power supply from the SAMA5D3 Xplained board and where the R_L resistor is formed
by three resistors of the same value of 6.8KΩ in order to have $R_L{\approx}20K\Omega$:

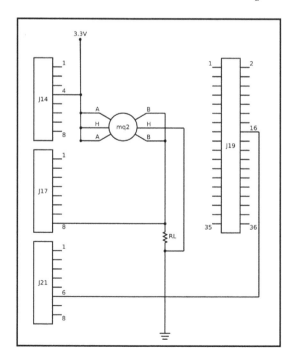

Note that the gas sensors have six pins labeled in pairs as **A**, **B**, and **H**. While the **A** and **B** pair pins are shortened, the **H** labeled pairs must be connected one end to the input voltage (3.3V in our case) and the other end to the **GND** (see the datasheet for further information).

Another important issue regarding these sensors is the calibration we should perform before using them. This last adjustment is very important. In fact, as reported in the MQ-2 datasheet, we read the following recommendation:

> *Resistance value of MQ-2 is difference to various kinds and various concentration gases. So, when using this components, sensitivity adjustment is very necessary. We recommend that you calibrate the detector for 1000 ppm liquified petroleum gas (LPG), or 1000ppm iso-butane (i-C_4H_{10}) concentration in air and use value of load resistance that (R_L) about 20K (5K to 47K) .*

This step can be done by replacing resistor R_L with a varistor and then fine-tuning its resistance. However, for simplicity, we can use a normal resistor of about 20KΩ.

The last note on the preceding circuitry is about the connection between pin *J19.16* and pin *J21.6*. This is because we're going to use a PWM signal to driver the sampling frequency of the ADC. In fact, we can image to use a PWM signal with a period of *T=0.5s* (half second) and a duty cycle of 50 percent. Then, using the ADC's external falling trigger (see the available list shown earlier), we can have a sampling rate of 2Hz (see Chapter 18, *Pulse-Width Modulation - PWM*, for further information regarding this devices).

OK, now, everything is in place, and we can set up the PWM as just stated. First of all, we need to enable the pwm0 device with the echo command:

```
root@a5d3:~# echo 0 > /sys/class/pwm/pwmchip0/export
```

Then, we have to write proper values into the files period and duty cycle (all values are in nanoseconds, and the duty cycle is specified as a time and not in percentage):

```
root@a5d3:~# echo 500000000 > /sys/class/pwm/pwmchip0/pwm0/period
root@a5d3:~# echo 250000000 > /sys/class/pwm/pwmchip0/pwm0/duty_cycle
```

Then, we only have to enable the PWM output:

```
root@a5d3:~# echo 1 > /sys/class/pwm/pwmchip0/pwm0/enable
```

OK, now, a 2Hz PWM signal should be present at the ADC's trigger pin, so we have to only correctly set up the ADC in order to use the hardware trigger:

```
root@a5d3:~# echo 1 >
    /sys/bus/iio/devices/iio\:device0/scan_elements/in_timestamp_en
```

```
root@a5d3:~# echo 1 >
    /sys/bus/iio/devices/iio\:device0/scan_elements/in_voltage7_en
root@a5d3:~/iio# ./generic_buffer -n f8018000.adc
                            -t f8018000.adc-dev0-external-falling
                            -l 20 -c 100
```

Finally, just use the `generic_buffer` utility we presented earlier. Instead of using the continuous trigger, we use the external falling trigger. By specifying the value `100` for the option argument `-c`, we decide to sample the sensor data for 100 samples, that is 50s.

Here is the output on my system:

```
root@a5d3:~/iio# ./generic_buffer -n f8018000.adc
                            -t f8018000.adc-dev0-external-falling
                            -l 20 -c 100
iio device number being used is 0
iio trigger number being used is 26478
/sys/bus/iio/devices/iio:device0 f8018000.adc-dev0-external-falling
804.931641 1478100875444651544
796.142578 1478100875944588271
803.466797 1478100876444588392
804.199219 1478100876944585786
792.480469 1478100877444585120
802.734375 1478100877944584210
799.804688 1478100878444583301
794.677734 1478100878944582816
799.072266 1478100879444581483
800.537109 1478100879944583119
796.875000 1478100880444578392
799.804688 1478100880944578331
801.269531 1478100881444580331
798.339844 1478100881944576088
867.919922 1478100882444575603
1676.513672 1478100882944574634
2184.814453 1478100883444573300
2302.001953 1478100883944572391
2330.566406 1478100884444570997
2334.960938 1478100884944573360
2310.791016 1478100885444569663
2277.832031 1478100885944568936
2243.408203 1478100886444571239
2215.576172 1478100886944565966
2190.673828 1478100887444564996
2167.968750 1478100887944564027
2146.728516 1478100888444563057
2123.291016 1478100888944562693
2105.712891 1478100889444562087
2079.345703 1478100889944560632
```

```
2057.373047 1478100890444559541
2033.935547 1478100890944558996
2011.230469 1478100891444557905
1987.792969 1478100891944556389
. . .
```

It may be possible that you may get this error in executing the `generic_buffer` utility:

```
root@a5d3:~/iio# ./generic_buffer -n f8018000.adc
               -t f8018000.adc-dev0-external-falling
               -l 20 -c 100
iio device number being used is 0
iio trigger number being used is 26478
/sys/bus/iio/devices/iio:device0 f8018000.adc-dev0-
external-falling
Failed to write current_trigger file
```

This is because the acquisition is still running. It may happen for several reasons, but if you are trying this test, the reason could be that `generic_buffer` has been stopped before the end by using, for instance, the *Ctrl + C* key sequence. In this case, the program didn't disable the acquisition, and so, the error. To solve the issue, we just need to disable the current running acquisition using this command line and then restart the program:

```
root@a5d3:~/iio# echo 0 > /sys/bus/iio/devices/iio\
:device0/buffer/enable
```

First of all, we can notice that looking at timestamps, the sampling intervals are quite regular (time is represented in nanoseconds). Then, we see that without any gas in the air, the raw value is around `800` (this value can be converted into a voltage as described earlier or in ppm according to the sensor's datasheet). However, when we approach the lighter to the sensor and then open it, the read values quickly move over `2000` and then slowly drop down when we close it.

The functioning is quite clear; however, for better readability of the read data, we can plot them using the `gnuplot` utility on the host PC with the command output:

```
$ gnuplot mq2.plot
        Rectangular grid drawn at x y tics
        Major grid drawn with lt 0 linewidth 1.000
        Minor grid drawn with lt 0 linewidth 1.000
        Grid drawn at default layer
```

Note that in order to execute this command, you need the `gnuplot` command, which can be installed using the usual command:

 # aptitude install gnuplot

Also, you can get further information on `gnuplot` on the *gnuplot homepage* at http://gnuplot.sourceforge.net.

The utility takes the `mq2.plot` file as its input. It defines the plotting directive as shown here:

```
set terminal png size 800,600 enhanced font "Helvetica,20"
set output 'mq2.png'
set xdata time
set autoscale
set nokey
set grid lw 1
show grid
set xlabel "\nTime"
set ylabel 'raw'
set format x "%.9f"
set xtics rotate
plot "mq2.log" using ($2/1000000000):($1) with lines
```

The `mq2.plot` file can be found in the `chapter_17/mq2.plot` file in the book's example code repository.

You should notice that the code, in the last command plot, refers to the `mq2.log` file, which must hold the data to be plotted. To create this file, we can simply copy and paste the `generic_buffer` output into the file, or we can use Bash's output redirection directive (remember to remove the first lines).

If the files are correctly made, your should get a plot similar to the following one:

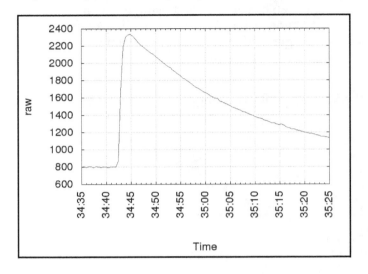

Summary

In this chapter, we saw ADC converters and their usage in a practical application, such as detecting dangerous gas using a proper gas sensor. We saw how to use them for a single analog-to-digital conversion as is and how to use them in continuous conversions driven by a software or hardware clock (or event) source.

In the next chapter, we'll see another important device class that can generate an analog output from a digital one, even if in a square waveform, useful to control several devices: PWM devices.

18
Pulse-Width Modulation - PWM

Using the **pulse-width modulation** (**PWM**) technique, we can encode a message into a pulsing signal (usually a square waveform) to generate an analog signal using a digital source as a microcontroller. Then, these messages can be used to control the power supplied to electrical motors or other electronics devices or, as we're going to show into this chapter, to control the position of a servo motor.

Using a few Bash commands, we'll see how an embedded developer can use PWM signal generators, available in GNU/Linux systems, to set a specific axis position of a servo motor.

What is a PWM device?

A PWM generator is a device that can generate a PWM signal according to its internal settings. The output of a PWM generator is just a sequence of pulse signals as a square waveform with well-defined characteristics:

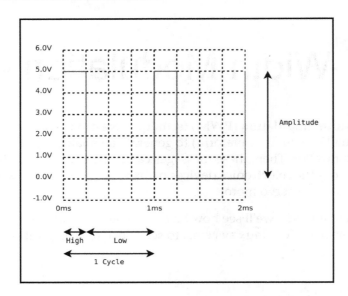

By referring to the preceding graph, where we have a simple PWM waveform, we can define the following parameters:

- **Amplitude (A)**: This is the difference between the maximum output value (y_{max}) and the minimum one (y_{min}).
- **Period (T)**: This is the duration of one cycle of the output square waveform.
- **Duty-cycle (dc)**: This is the ratio in percentage between the high state time (t_{high}) and the period (T).

In our example in the preceding graph, the amplitude is 5V (y_{max}=5V and y_{min}=0V), the period is 1ms (the wave is periodic, and it repeats itself every 0.001 seconds), and the duty-cycle is 25 percent (t_{high}=0.25ms and T=1ms).

You can find details about PWM at
https://en.wikipedia.org/wiki/Pulse-width_modulation.

The electrical lines

PWM generator lines are reported in the table here:

Name	Description
PWM output	The PWM output signal
GND	Common ground

PWMs on the BeagleBone Black

The BeagleBone Black has eight PWM generators available on expansion connectors, and their relative pins are summarized in this table:

PWM generator	PWM chip	PWM name	PWM output
ehrpwm0A	pwmchip0	pwm0	P9.22 (or P9.31)
ehrpwm0B	pwmchip0	pwm1	P9.21 (or P9.29)
ehrpwm1A	pwmchip2	pwm0	P9.14 (or P8.36)
ehrpwm1B	pwmchip2	pwm1	P9.16 (or P8.34)
ehrpwm2A	pwmchip4	pwm0	P8.19 (or P8.45)
ehrpwm2A	pwmchip4	pwm1	P8.13 (or P8.46)
ecappwm0			P9.42
ecappwm2			P9.28

Note that some pins may have their output lines multiplexed with another device, so they cannot be used without disabling the conflicting device.

Also, note that the last two PWM generators have no PWM chip or PWM name because they don't have a predefined DTS file to enable them. We warn you that we're not going to use these last two devices, so you will not find any suggestions for these devices in this book.

To enable PWM generators, we have to use one of these DTS files:

```
root@bbb:~# ls /lib/firmware/BB-*PWM*.dtbo
/lib/firmware/BB-PWM0-00A0.dtbo   /lib/firmware/BB-PWM2-00A0.dtbo
/lib/firmware/BB-PWM1-00A0.dtbo
```

The `BB-PWM0-00A0.dtbo` file refers to the generators named `ehrpwm0A` and `ehrpwm0B`, while `BB-PWM1-00A0.dtbo` refers to `ehrpwm1A` and `ehrpwm1B`, and `BB-PWM2-00A0.dtbo` to `ehrpwm2A` and `ehrpwm2B`.

As an example, let's enable the first PWMs couple using this command line:

```
root@bbb:~# echo BB-PWM0 > /sys/devices/platform/bone_capemgr/slots
bone_capemgr: part_number 'BB-PWM0', version 'N/A'
bone_capemgr: slot #5: override
bone_capemgr: Using override eeprom data at slot 5
bone_capemgr: slot #5: 'Override Board Name,00A0,Override Manuf,BB-PWM
bone_capemgr: slot #5: dtbo 'BB-PWM0-00A0.dtbo' loaded; overlay id #1
```

The related kernel messages are also reported for completeness.

Then, a new directory named `pwmchip0` should appear, as shown here:

```
root@bbb:~# ls /sys/class/pwm/
pwmchip0
```

PWMs on the SAMA5D3 Xplained

The SAMA5D3 Xplained has four PWM generators available on expansion connectors, and their relative pins are summarized in this table:

PWM generator	PWM chip	PWM name	PWM output
0	pwmchip0	pwm0	J19.16
1	pwmchip0	pwm1	J19.15 [*]
2	pwmchip0	pwm2	J19.18
3	pwmchip0	pwm3	J19.17 [*]

Note that pins marked with [*] are already enabled in the DTS, while the other two are not. So, a DTS modification is needed if these two pins are needed (refer to the *SAMA5D3 Xplained's User Guide* for further information).

PWM generators are already enabled by default in the DTS file, so the `pwmchip0` directory should already be present, as shown here:

```
root@a5d3:~# ls /sys/class/pwm/
pwmchip0
```

PWMs on the Wandboard

The Wandboard has no PWMs available on its expansion connectors.

PWM devices in Linux

Let's use the BeagleBone Black to see how a PWM device works (the steps that follow are almost the same for the SAMA5D3 Xplained and other GNU/Linux supporting these devices). We saw earlier that for each PWM generator, we have a well-defined directory in `/sys/class/pwm/`. In our case, we have the directory named `pwmchip0`. Then, by taking a look at its contents, we can find the following items:

```
root@bbb:~# ls /sys/class/pwm/pwmchip0/
device/    export    npwm      power/     subsystem/ uevent      unexport
```

You can notice that this representation is quite similar to the GPIO controllers we saw in the *GPIOs in Linux* section, in `Chapter 6`, *General Purposes Input Output signals – GPIO*. So, the `export` and `unexport` files are used to *export* and *unexport* the PWMs, respectively, while in `npwm`, we have the number of PWM lines we can manage within the PWM chip. As expected, in the command line here, we see that we can manage two PWM signals within the `pwmchip0` controller:

```
root@bbb:~# cat /sys/class/pwm/pwmchip0/npwm
2
```

To enable the first PWM line, we can use this command line:

```
root@bbb:~# echo 0 > /sys/class/pwm/pwmchip0/export
```

Then, in complete analogy with GPIOs, a new file appears:

```
root@bbb:~# ls /sys/class/pwm/pwmchip0/pwm0/
duty_cycle  enable  period  polarity  power  uevent
```

The `period` file defines the PWM signal's period in nanoseconds, while `duty_cycle` defines the duty-cycle by setting the high state time (t_{high}). In the end, the `enable` file is just used to enable the controller to generate the PWM wave. The command lines define a PWM signal with a period of 250ns and a duty-cycle of 50 percent ($t_{high}=125ns$):

```
root@bbb:~# echo 250 > /sys/class/pwm/pwmchip0/pwm0/period
root@bbb:~# echo 125 > /sys/class/pwm/pwmchip0/pwm0/duty_cycle
root@bbb:~# echo 1 > /sys/class/pwm/pwmchip0/pwm0/enable
```

With the `polarity` file, we can invert the waveform polarity (that is, by swapping the high state and low state) by writing the `inversed` string into it (`normal` is the default setting).

See the `Documentation/pwm.txt` file in Linux's tree repository for further information regarding the PWM interface.

Managing a servo motor

To show you how to use a PWM generator in order to manage a peripheral, we can use a servo motor. This is a really simple motor where we can set a specific gear position by setting a proper duty-cycle of the PWM signal (another example of how to use a PWM in order to generate a clock signal has been reported in the *Using an external controller* section, in Chapter 14, *Controller Area Network – CAN*, and the *Detecting a gas* section, in Chapter 17, *Analog-to-Digital Converters – ADC*).

In the following image, you can see the servo motor used in this example:

The device can be purchased at
`http://www.cosino.io/product/nano-servo-motor` or by surfing the
Internet.

The datasheet is at `http://hitecrcd.com/files/Servomanual.pdf`.

First of all, we've to setup the electrical connections. In the following diagram, the
correspondence between BeagleBone Black's pins and the servo motor's cables are shown:

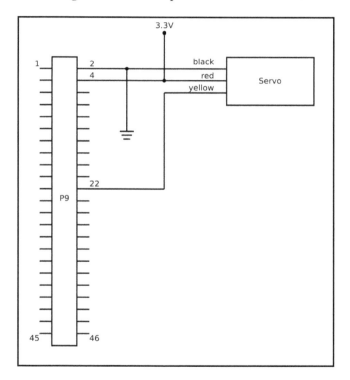

By taking a look at the datasheet, we can discover that the servo can be managed using a
periodic square waveform of 20ms period and a high state time (t_{high}) between 0.9ms and
2.1ms, with 1.5ms as (more or less) the center.

So, once connected, we can set the center position using the following settings:

```
root@bbb:~# echo 20000000 > /sys/class/pwm/pwmchip0/pwm0/period
root@bbb:~# echo 1500000 > /sys/class/pwm/pwmchip0/pwm0/duty_cycle
root@bbb:~# echo 1 > /sys/class/pwm/pwmchip0/pwm0/enable
```

Then, we can move the gear totally clockwise using this command:

```
root@bbb:~# echo 2100000 > /sys/class/pwm/pwmchip0/pwm0/duty_cycle
```

We can move it totally anticlockwise using this command:

```
root@bbb:~# echo 900000 > /sys/class/pwm/pwmchip0/pwm0/duty_cycle
```

Summary

In this chapter, you learned what a PWM signal is and how it can be easily generated using a PWM generator with few Bash commands. We also saw a practical example of how we can manage a servo motor using the sysfs interface that Linux offers to us to do this job.

In the next chapter, we're going to close this book by presenting a list of different kinds of devices that an embedded GNU/Linux developer may encounter in their professional life by explaining how they can easily manage them using our embedded kits.

19
Miscellaneous Devices

In this book, we've presented several device kinds, each of them divided in a well-defined class. However, for the sake of completeness, there are other peripherals we can use with our embedded kits that can fit in one of those classes, but they have not been discussed here for better readability. That's why, we decided to add this last chapter where we will present a list of additional peripherals we can encounter in a monitoring or controlling system.

Each presented device can be connected with the three embedded kits as described in the previous chapters according to their interfaces. However, we will present a possible circuitry for at least one kit, so you should refer to it to get useful information regarding the electronic connections to be done for the other kits.

Digital sensors

Digital sensors are devices that are capable of setting a GPIO input status in two possible states, *on* or *off*, according to the state of the measured entity. Then, these two states have to be converted into the corresponding logic *1* and *0* statuses with a proper circuitry.

Water sensor

A **water sensor** is a device capable of detecting the water presence near the circuitry by exploiting the water conductivity. In the following image, you can see one of the devices:

 The device can be purchased at
http://www.cosino.it/product/water-sensor or by surfing the Internet.

This is a really simple device that implements the circuitry in the following diagram, where the resistor (**R**) has been added to limit the current when the water closes the circuit:

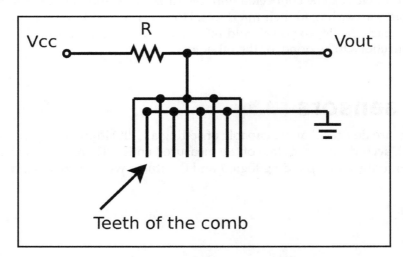

When a single drop of water *touches* two or more teeth of the comb in the schematic, the circuit is closed and the output voltage (Vout) drops from Vcc (logic *1*) to a value near 0V (logic *0*).

To test this device with our SAMA5D3 Xplained, we have to realize the simple circuitry shown here:

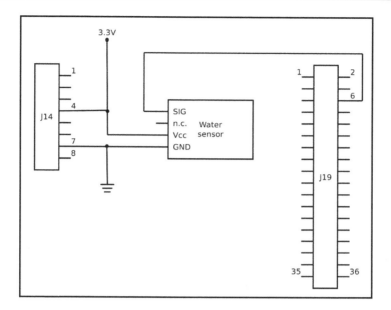

After all connections are in place, we have to enable pin *PB25*, which is connected with the *SIG* signal, as a GPIO input line with the following command (see the *GPIOs in Linux* section , in `Chapter 6`, *General Purposes Input Output signals – GPIO*):

```
root@a5d3:~# echo 57 > /sys/class/gpio/export
root@a5d3:~# echo in > /sys/class/gpio/pioB25/direction
```

Then, we can read the GPIO status when the sensor is in the water and when it is not using the following two commands:

```
root@a5d3:~# cat /sys/class/gpio/pioB25/value
0
root@a5d3:~# cat /sys/class/gpio/pioB25/value
1
```

Now, we're able to know when we're experiencing a water leakage around our device!

Infrared sensor

An **infrared sensor** is a device that is capable of detecting the infrared light. There are several types of infrared devices. However in this book, we will present phototransistors.

You can take a look at
https://en.wikipedia.org/wiki/Photodiode#Other_modes_of_operatio
n for more information on these devices.

The **phototransistor** we're going to use here is reported in the following figure (actually, the phototransistor is the device with the red dot; the other one is an infrared emitter, which is not presented here).

Note that the image shows only the top part of the above infrared devices. In reality, they look similar to a normal diode.

 The devices can be purchased at
http://www.cosino.io/product/infrared-emitter-detector or by
surfing the Internet.

The datasheet is available at
https://www.sparkfun.com/datasheets/Components/LTR-301.pdf.

The functioning of a phototransistor is reported in the diagram. When there is no **infrared light** (**IR**), the transistor is in its *off* state, and it acts as an open circuit, so the **Vout** is set to Vcc (logic *1*). However, when the infrared light arrives, the transistor switches to its *on* state, and the **Vout** drops to a value around 0V (logic *0*):

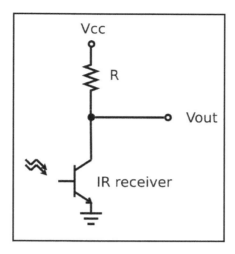

In the following diagram, you can see the connections with the SAMA5D3 Xplained that we need to do in order to use the sensor:

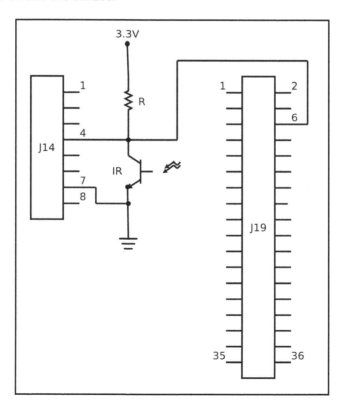

The IR is the transistor with the red dot, which has its collector at the longer pin, while the emitter at the shorter one. The resistor R is 6.8KΩ .

To test the functionality, we have to enable pin *PB25* as the GPIO input as in the previous section. However, now, we have to also set it sensible to the falling edge with the following command line (see the *GPIOs in Linux* section , in Chapter 6, *General Purposes Input Output signals – GPIO*):

```
root@a5d3:~# echo falling > /sys/class/gpio/pioB25/edge
```

Then, we can use the gpio-poll.php script we used in the *PHP* section, in Chapter 6, *General Purposes Input Output signals – GPIO* to wait on the select() system call for the GPIO status changed from high to low state due to IR detection. Here is the complete script where we've some changes at the beginning where the GPIOs stream is defined:

```php
#!/usr/bin/php
<?php
    define("gpio24", "/sys/class/gpio/pioB25/value");

    # Get the GPIOs streams
    $stream24 = fopen(gpio24, 'r');

    while (true) {
        # Set up stream sets for the select()
        $read = NULL;
        $write = NULL;
        $exept = array($stream24);

        # Wait for IRQs (without timeout)...
        $ret = stream_select($read, $write, $exept, NULL);
        if ($ret < 0)
            die("stream_select: error");

        foreach ($exept as $input => $stream) {
            # Read the GPIO status
            fseek($stream, 0, SEEK_SET);
            $status = intval(fgets($stream));

            # Get the filename from "/sys/class/gpio/gpioXX/value"
            $meta_data = stream_get_meta_data($stream);
            $gpio = basename(dirname($meta_data["uri"]));

            printf("$gpio status=$status\n");
        }
```

```
        }
?>
```

Now, to generate IR signals, we can use a normal TV remote pointed to the IR sensor. So, when we press a button, we should get the following output, where each state change is reported:

```
root@a5d3:~# ./gpio-poll.php
pioB25 status=1
pioB25 status=1
pioB25 status=1
pioB25 status=1
pioB25 status=0
pioB25 status=0
pioB25 status=1
pioB25 status=1
pioB25 status=1
pioB25 status=1
pioB25 status=0
pioB25 status=1
. . .
```

To stop the script, just hit *Ctrl+C*.

Analog sensors

Analog sensors are devices that are capable of returning an analog signal that is proportional to the measured entity. Then, the analog signal should be converted into a digital one using proper circuitry or, for simplicity, an AD.

Moisture sensor

A **moisture sensor** is a device that can change its internal resistance according to the wet intensity of the soil moisture:

The device can be purchased at
`http://www.cosino.io/product/moisture-sensor` or by surfing the
Internet.
The user guide of this device is available at
`http://seeedstudio.com/wiki/Grove_-_Moisture_Sensor.`

This device is quite similar to the water sensor presented in the preceding section since the functioning is still based on the water conductivity. However, its shape is different because we are interested to know the soil humidity level in place of the water present status.

The connections to the SAMA5D3 Xplained are reported in the following diagram:

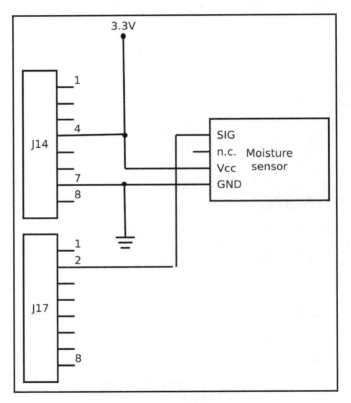

After all the connections are in place, we can read the moisture level in water (that is, the maximum moisture level) by putting the sensor into a cup of water and then executing the following command:

```
root@a5d3:~# cat /sys/bus/iio/devices/iio\:device0/in_voltage1_raw
1309
```

Then, we can read the moisture level in air (that is, the minimum moisture level) by removing the sensor from the water and then rerunning the preceding command in the following manner:

```
root@a5d3:~# cat /sys/bus/iio/devices/iio\:device0/in_voltage1_raw
0
```

So, higher the moisture level, higher is the returned value.

Pressure sensor

A pressure (or force) sensor is a device that can change its internal resistance when a pressure (or force) is applied. It is also known as a **force-sensitive resistor** (**FSR**).

 You can get more information at
https://en.wikipedia.org/wiki/Force-sensing_resistor.

In the following diagram, you can see one of these devices (pressure sensor):

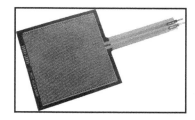

 The device can be purchased at
http://www.cosino.io/product/pressure-sensor or by surfing the Internet.

The user guide of this device is available at
https://www.pololu.com/file/download/fsr_datasheet.pdf?file_id=0
J383.

As explained earlier, this device can detect (and measure) a force acting on its active surface. In a few words, it can report a pressure intensity by varying its internal resistance. From the datasheet. we can discover that this resistance may vary from over 1 MΩ, when no force is present, to a few hundred ohms when a force is applied.

The connections needed to test the device with our SAMA5D3 Xplained are shown in the following figure:

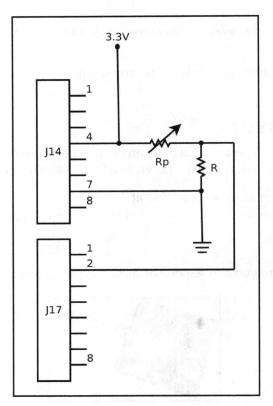

In the diagram, R is 6.8KΩ, where R_p is the pressure sensor's internal resistor, which is represented by a variable resistor.

The circuitry simply connects the pressure sensor with SAMA5D3 Xplained's ADC input *ain1* in such a way that when nothing is on the sensor we have that R_p gets a value very greater than R so we measure a value near 0V. On the other hand, when something is on the sensor, its internal resistance R_p drops to a few ohms, so we measure higher values to Vcc.

OK, if everything works well and we have nothing on the sensor, we should get the following output when we read from the ADC:

```
root@a5d3:~# cat /sys/bus/iio/devices/iio\:device0/in_voltage1_raw
0
```

However, if we simply try to put a finger on it and then re-read from the sensor, we get an higher value:

```
root@a5d3:~# cat /sys/bus/iio/devices/iio\:device0/in_voltage1_raw
3704
```

So, higher the pressure on the sensor, higher is the returned value.

Light sensor

A **light sensor** is a device that can detect the intensity of the light that reaches it. There are several kinds of light sensors, and in this chapter, we will present the ones named photoresistors. A **photoresistor** is a device that can change its internal resistance according to the incident light intensity. In other words, it exhibits photoconductivity: more light is present and less resistance is measured.

You can get more information on photoresistors at
https://en.wikipedia.org/wiki/Photoresistor.

Here is one of these devices:

The device can be purchased at http://www.cosino.io/product/photoresistoror by surfing the Internet.The user guide of this device is available at
https://www.sparkfun.com/datasheets/Sensors/Imaging/SEN-09088-datasheet.pdf.

This device functioning is quite similar to the pressure sensor presented earlier. So, even in this case, we can use the same circuitry as we did earlier to manage it with the SAMA5D3 Xplained board (you can just replace the pressure sensor with this light sensor).

Once all connections are in place, we can measure the normal light level intensity with the following command:

```
root@a5d3:~# cat /sys/bus/iio/devices/iio\:device0/in_voltage1_raw
2381
```

Now, we can verify that the internal resistance changes by first covering the sensor with a finger, or better, with a cup, and then re-reading from the ADC to get the following output:

```
root@a5d3:~# cat /sys/bus/iio/devices/iio\:device0/in_voltage1_raw
469
```

On the other hand, if we turn on a lamp over the sensor, we would get the following output:

```
root@a5d3:~# cat /sys/bus/iio/devices/iio\:device0/in_voltage1_raw
3685
```

So, higher the environment light, higher is the returned value from the ADC.

GSM/GPRS modem

A **GSM/GPRS modem** is a device used to establish communication between two computers using the GSM-GPRS system. **Global System for Mobile communication** (**GSM**) is an architecture used for mobile communication in most of the countries. On the other hand, **General Packet Radio Service** (**GPRS**) is an extension of GSM that enables higher data transmission rate. Usually, these devices are assembled together with power supply circuit and communication interfaces such as RS-232, USB, and so on.

In order to work, these devices require a **subscriber identity module** (**SIM**) card just like mobile phones to activate communication with the network, and once the SIM is inserted, they can perform the following main operations:

- Manage SMS messages.
- Do voice calls.
- Establish Internet connections.

To do their job, these devices use the **AT commands** to interact with a processor or controller, which are communicated through serial communication (or via a USB-emulated serial line). These commands are sent by the controller/processor, while the modem sends back the result after it receives a command.

For more information on the AT commands, you can take a look at `https://en.wikipedia.org/wiki/Hayes_command_set`.

The device we're going to evaluate with our **Wandboard** is the USB device shown here:

The device can be purchased at or `http://www.cosino.it/product/usb-gsmgprs-module-2` by surfing the Internet.

The AT commands list for this device is available at `http://simcom.ee/documents/SIM800H/SIM800%20Series_AT%20Comman d%20Manual_V1.09.pdf`.

You can now notice that this device has a non-standard USB connector, so we have to find a trick to connect it to our Wandboard. The *quick-and-dirty* solution can be in using a USB plug type. It is an adapter from an old USB device, soldered with male connectors, as shown in the following image, in such a way that we can plug each signal line in the desired input pin:

The needed connections are reported in the following diagram reporting the board's USB connector and the relative USB signals to be routed to the Wandboard:

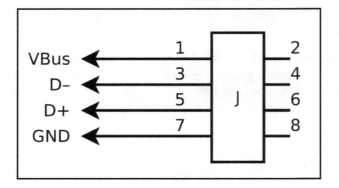

 The connector *pinout* can be retrieved at
https://en.wikipedia.org/wiki/USB in the **Pin out** box on the right.

If connections are done well, once we connect the device to the Wandboard's USB host port, we should get an output as follows:

```
usb 1-1: new full-speed USB device number 2 using ci_hdrc
usb 1-1: New USB device found, idVendor=0403, idProduct=6015
usb 1-1: New USB device strings: Mfr=1, Product=2, SerialNumber=3
usb 1-1: Product: FT230X Basic UART
usb 1-1: Manufacturer: FTDI
usb 1-1: SerialNumber: DN017HQF
usbcore: registered new interface driver usbserial
usbcore: registered new interface driver usbserial_generic
usbserial: USB Serial support registered for generic
usbcore: registered new interface driver ftdi_sio
usbserial: USB Serial support registered for FTDI USB Serial Device
ftdi_sio 1-1:1.0: FTDI USB Serial Device converter detected
usb 1-1: Detected FT-X
usb 1-1: FTDI USB Serial Device converter now attached to ttyUSB0
```

OK, the USB connection works, but now, we need some packages to manage our GSM, so let's install them using this command:

```
root@wb:~# aptitude install gsm-utils ppp libftdi-dev
```

Then, we have to download the code to manage the powering of the device. The commands to download the code and then compile it are shown here:

```
root@wb:~# git clone https://github.com/cosino/peripherals.git
root@wb:~# cd peripherals/WI400/
root@wb:~/peripherals/WI400# make
```

Once compiled, the new tool can be executed as reported in the following example:

```
root@wb:~/peripherals/WI400# ./wi400_ctrl -h
usage: wi400_ctrl [on | off]
```

You should notice that if executed without any arguments, the tool returns the current modem status:

```
root@wb:~/peripherals/WI400# ./wi400_ctrl
modem is off
```

If we execute the command in the serial console, most probably, we'll get the preceding output mixed with the kernel messages shown here, which also suggest to us that a new serial device is now present:

```
ftdi_sio ttyUSB0: FTDI USB Serial Device converter
now disconnected
ftdi_sio 1-1:1.0: device disconnected
ftdi_sio 1-1:1.0: FTDI USB Serial Device converter
usb 1-1: Detected FT-X
usb 1-1: FTDI USB Serial Device converter now attac
hed to ttyUSB0
```

This modem presents itself as a serial line over the USB bus (usually, the /dev/ttyUSB0 device). However, if we try to send some commands over such communication line, we'll get no response because the modem is turned off. So, let's turn it on:

```
root@wb:~/peripherals/WI400# ./wi400_ctrl on
modem is on
```

Now, the modem is ready, so we can try to talk with it by asking information regarding the SIM card we inserted before turning it on. To do this job, we can use the gsmctl tool, which has been designed to manage GSM devices. Here is t command to get as much information as possible from the modem:

```
root@wb:~# gsmctl -X -d /dev/ttyUSB0 ALL
```

Note that the command may take a while for answering. In any case, if we get the next answer, it means we have to insert a SIM card into the modem:

```
gsmctl[ERROR]: ME/TA error 'SIM not inserted' (cod
e 10)
```

While if we get the next message, then we have to supply the PIN number to unlock the SIM:

```
gsmctl[ERROR]: ME/TA error 'SIM PIN required' (cod
e 11)
```

In this last case, we can supply the requested PIN number with this command:

```
root@wb:~# gsmctl -X -d /dev/ttyUSB0
              -I "+CPIN=NNNN"
```

Here, in place of the NNNN string, we have to put the PIN number of our SIM card. Note that we can get a SIM busy error just after the PIN insertion. However, this is not an error, and we can verify that everything is OK just using the following command and obtaining the READY message:

```
root@wb:~# gsmctl -X -d /dev/ttyUSB0 PIN
<PIN0> READY
```

The output of the command is shown here:

```
root@wb:~# gsmctl -X -d /dev/ttyUSB0 ALL
<ME0>   Manufacturer: SIMCOM_Ltd
<ME1>   Model: SIMCOM_SIM800H
<ME2>   Revision: Revision:1308B02SIM800H32
<ME3>   Serial Number: 862950023936530
<FUN>   Functionality Level: 1
```

It could be possible that during this execution, we get the following error message:

```
gsmctl[ERROR]: expected ')' (at position 26 of std:
:string '(2,"I TIM","TIM","22201"),(1,"vodafone IT"
,"voda IT","22210"),(1,"22288","22288","22288"),,(0
-4),(0-2)')
```

This can safely be ignored.

Now, the GSM modem is operative, and we can send an SMS message with another tool designed for this purpose: gsmsendsms and the command to send an SMS with the Hello World! text is shown here, where you just need to replace the NNNNNNNNNNNN string with a proper phone number:

```
root@wb:~# gsmsendsms -X -d /dev/ttyUSB0 +NNNNNNNNNNNN 'Hello world!'
```

Another usage for this modem is to establish an Internet connection, but to do so, we have to use another tool, the **Point-to-Point Protocol** (**PPP**) daemon, which is held in the package named **ppp**.

Due to space reasons, we cannot explain what the PPP protocol is, so you can get more information on it at
https://en.wikipedia.org/wiki/Point-to-Point_Protocol.

Once installed, we have to configure it by adding a file named `myisp` (or any suitable name for our Internet Service Provider) in the `/etc/ppp/peers/` directory as follows:

```
# Set up the network's APN value.
connect "/usr/sbin/chat -v -f /etc/chatscripts/gprs -T my_APN_value"

# The GSM device
/dev/ttyUSB0

# Speed of the serial line.
115200

# Assumes that your IP address is allocated dynamically by the ISP.
noipdefault

# Try to get the name server addresses from the ISP.
usepeerdns

# Use this connection as the default route to the internet.
defaultroute

# Makes PPPD "dial again" when the connection is lost.
persist

# Do not ask the remote to authenticate.
noauth

# No hardware flow control on the serial link
nocrtscts

# No modem control lines
local

# Enable debugging messages
debug
```

 The file is stored in the `chapter_19/gsm/myisp` file in the book's example code repository.

You should modify the `my_APN_value` string with the right **Access Point Name (APN)** value according to their **Internet Service Provider (ISP)**.

Now, to verify that the connection is working correctly, before enabling it, we can set up a messages monitor using this command in another terminal:

```
root@wb:~# tail -f /var/log/syslog | grep pppd
```

In this manner, we can see all messages the pppd program (that is, the PPP daemon) sends to the logging system. OK, now, we can enable the connection using the following command:

```
root@wb:~# pon myisp
```

Then, on the messages monitor, we should see something like this:

```
pppd[10320]: pppd 2.4.6 started by root, uid 0
pppd[10320]: Script /usr/sbin/chat -v -f /etc/chatscripts/gprs -T ibox
.isp.it finished (pid 10321), status = 0x0
pppd[10320]: Serial connection established.
pppd[10320]: using channel 4
pppd[10320]: Using interface ppp0
pppd[10320]: Connect: ppp0 <--> /dev/ttyUSB0
```

These messages tell us that the GSM's serial port is now connected with the ppp0 interface and then, going forward in reading the messages, we should see these lines at the end:

```
pppd[10320]: local  IP address 10.69.201.218
pppd[10320]: remote IP address 10.64.64.64
pppd[10320]: primary  DNS address 10.205.41.16
pppd[10320]: secondary DNS address 10.204.57.104
pppd[10320]: Script /etc/ppp/ip-up started (pid 10329)
pppd[10320]: Script /etc/ppp/ip-up finished (pid 10329), status = 0x0
```

In these lines, we can easily read our new networking settings. In fact, if we use the ifconfig command (or ip, see *The net tools*, in chapter 12, *Ethernet Network Device – ETH*) as follows, we can verify that the ppp0 interface is up and running:

```
root@wb:~# ifconfig ppp0
ppp0      Link encap:Point-to-Point Protocol
          inet addr:10.69.201.218  P-t-P:10.64.64.64  Mask:255.255.255
.255
          UP POINTOPOINT RUNNING NOARP MULTICAST  MTU:1500  Metric:1
          RX packets:11 errors:0 dropped:0 overruns:0 frame:0
          TX packets:12 errors:0 dropped:0 overruns:0 carrier:0
          collisions:0 txqueuelen:3
          RX bytes:542 (542.0 B)  TX bytes:496 (496.0 B)
```

Also, our new Internet connection is working as expected, and for instance, we can use the `ping` command to the communication:

```
root@wb:~# ping www.google.com
PING www.google.com (216.58.214.132) 56(84) bytes of data.
64 bytes from fra16s06-in-f132.1e100.net (216.58.214.132): icmp_seq=1
ttl=50 time=641 ms
64 bytes from fra16s06-in-f132.1e100.net (216.58.214.132): icmp_seq=2
ttl=50 time=575 ms
64 bytes from fra16s06-in-f132.1e100.net (216.58.214.132): icmp_seq=3
ttl=50 time=533 ms
```

To stop the PPP daemon, we can simply use the `poff` command:

```
root@wb:~# poff
```

In the monitor, we should now read the next message, signaling the daemon ending:

```
pppd[10320]: Exit.
```

Smart card reader

A **smart card** and a **smart card reader** are complex devices that are used everywhere nowadays, starting from our credit cards to the smartphones. The term *smart card* implies a set of technologies, including integrated circuits, microprocessors, memories, antennas, and so on in the same integrated circuit to form a microchip that is the *heart* of a smart card. On the other hand, a *smart card reader* is complex device that can communicate with the smart card and save data on it or return data to a computer.

These devices can be used where the identification can be done by inserting a credit card (or something similar) somewhere for identification. These are not wireless.

You can get more information regarding the smart card world by taking a look at `https://en.wikipedia.org/wiki/Smart_card`.

The device we're going to evaluate with our Wandboard is the USB device reported here, which has a slot where the smart card can be inserted:

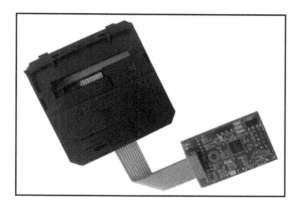

The device can be purchased at
http://www.cosino.io/product/smartcard-reader-isoiec-7816 or by surfing the Internet. The device is based on the chip Maxim 73S1215F, and its datasheet is available
at http://datasheets.maximintegrated.com/en/ds/73S1215F.pdf.

This device, as the GSM in the preceding section, has a non-standard USB connector, so we have to use a similar trick to get it connected to our Wandboard. Then, the electrical connections are the same as the ones shown earlier. Once we connect the device to the Wandboard's USB host port, we should get an output as shown here:

```
usb 1-1: New USB device found, idVendor=1862, idProduct=0001
usb 1-1: New USB device strings: Mfr=1, Product=2, SerialNumber=3
usb 1-1: Product: TSC12xxF CCID-DFU Version 2.10
usb 1-1: Manufacturer: Teridian Semiconductors
usb 1-1: SerialNumber: 123456789
```

OK, the connections are done, but now, we need some packages to manage our smart card reader. So, let's install them using the following command:

```
root@wb:~# aptitude install pcsc-tools pcscd libccid
```

Once finished, the `pcsc` tool is ready to work.

 You may take a look at
`http://ludovic.rousseau.free.fr/softwares/pcsc-tools/` for further
information on this tool.

Once installed, we have to execute the `pcsc_scan` command to try to detect connected
devices:

```
root@wb:~# pcsc_scan
PC/SC device scanner
V 1.4.23 (c) 2001-2011, Ludovic Rousseau <ludovic.rousseau@free.fr>
Compiled with PC/SC lite version: 1.8.11
Using reader plug'n play mechanism
Scanning present readers...
Waiting for the first reader...
```

 If we get the following error instead of the preceding output, we can try to
restart the daemon with the `/etc/init.d/pcscd restart` command
and then execute the `pcsc_scan` tool again:
SCardEstablishContext: Service not available.

OK, the daemon started correctly, but it still didn't recognize our device. In this case, we
have to patch the `/etc/libccid_Info.plist` configuration file as shown here:

```
--- /etc/libccid_Info.plist.orig       2016-10-24 17:48:15.956215450 +0000
+++ /etc/libccid_Info.plist      2016-10-24 17:51:50.106215475 +0000
@@ -377,6 +377,7 @@
            <string>0x08C3</string>
            <string>0x15E1</string>
            <string>0x062D</string>
+           <string>0x1862</string>
    </array>
        <key>ifdProductID</key>
@@ -652,6 +653,7 @@
            <string>0x0402</string>
            <string>0x2007</string>
            <string>0x0001</string>
+           <string>0x0001</string>
    </array>
        <key>ifdFriendlyName</key>
@@ -927,6 +929,7 @@
            <string>Precise Biometrics Precise 200 MC</string>
            <string>RSA RSA SecurID (R) Authenticator</string>
            <string>THRC Smart Card Reader</string>
+           <string>TSC12xxF Reader</string>
```

```
</array>
```

 The patch is stored in the
chapter_19/smartcard/add_TSC12xxF_reader.patch file in the
book's example code repository.

After all the modifications are in place, we have to restart the daemon, and then, the output
should change as shown here:

```
root@wb:~# /etc/init.d/pcscd restart
Restarting pcscd (via systemctl): pcscd.service.
```

Now, we can start the `pcsc_scan` command again, and the output should change as
follows:

```
root@wb:~# pcsc_scan
PC/SC device scanner
V 1.4.23 (c) 2001-2011, Ludovic Rousseau <ludovic.rousseau@free.fr>
Compiled with PC/SC lite version: 1.8.11
Using reader plug'n play mechanism
Scanning present readers...
0: TSC12xxF Reader (123456789) 00 00
1: TSC12xxF Reader (123456789) 00 01
2: TSC12xxF Reader (123456789) 00 02
3: TSC12xxF Reader (123456789) 00 03
4: TSC12xxF Reader (123456789) 00 04
Mon Oct 24 17:52:15 2016
Reader 0: TSC12xxF Reader (123456789) 00 00
  Card state: Card removed,
Reader 1: TSC12xxF Reader (123456789) 00 01
  Card state: Card removed,
Reader 2: TSC12xxF Reader (123456789) 00 02
  Card state: Card removed,
Reader 3: TSC12xxF Reader (123456789) 00 03
  Card state: Card removed,
Reader 4: TSC12xxF Reader (123456789) 00 04
  Card state: Card removed,
```

Great! Now, we can verify that the reader is working by inserting a card into the socket so
that the tool should print something as follows:

```
Mon Oct 24 17:55:47 2016
Reader 0: TSC12xxF Reader (123456789) 00 00
  Card state: Card inserted,
  ATR: 3B BE 11 00 00 41 01 38 00 00 00 00 00 00 00 00 01 90 00
ATR: 3B BE 11 00 00 41 01 38 00 00 00 00 00 00 00 00 01 90 00
```

```
+ TS = 3B --> Direct Convention
+ T0 = BE, Y(1): 1011, K: 14 (historical bytes)
   TA(1) = 11 --> Fi=372, Di=1, 372 cycles/ETU
      10752 bits/s at 4 MHz, fMax for Fi = 5 MHz => 13440 bits/s
   TB(1) = 00 --> VPP is not electrically connected
   TD(1) = 00 --> Y(i+1) = 0000, Protocol T = 0
-----
+ Historical bytes: 41 01 38 00 00 00 00 00 00 00 00 01 90 00
   Category indicator byte: 41 (proprietary format)

Possibly identified card (using /usr/share/pcsc/smartcard_list.txt):
3B BE 11 00 00 41 01 38 00 00 00 00 00 00 00 01 90 00
         ACS (Advanced Card System) ACOS-1
```

OK, the device is functioning. In fact, we've detected the card insertion/removal with the corresponding ATR identifier!

However, the `pcsc_scan` tool is not suitable for production, so let's try a more versatile Python program to better manage the card's reading. To do so, we have to install the **python-pyscard** and **python-daemon** packages with the usual commands, and then, we can consider the following code snippet:

```python
#
# Smart Card Observer
#

class printobserver(CardObserver):
    def update(self, observable, (addedcards, removedcards)):
        for card in addedcards:
            logging.info("->] " + toHexString(card.atr))
        for card in removedcards:
            logging.info("<-] " + toHexString(card.atr))

#
# The daemon body
#

def daemon_body():
    # The main loop
    logging.info("INFO waiting for card... (hit CTRL+C to stop)")

    try:
        cardmonitor = CardMonitor()
        cardobserver = printobserver()
        cardmonitor.addObserver(cardobserver)

        while True:
            sleep(1000000) # sleep forever
```

```
except:
    cardmonitor.deleteObserver(cardobserver)
```

 The complete code is stored in the
`chapter_19/smart_card/smart_card.py` file in the book's example
code repository.

The program defines a `cardmonitor` object and then adds its *observer* with the
`addObserver()` method in order to be called when a card is inserted or removed.

If executed, the program gives an output as shown here:

```
root@wb:~# ./smart_card.py
INFO:root:INFO waiting for card... (hit CTRL+C to stop)
```

Then, if we insert a card, we get the following output:

```
INFO:root:->] 3B BE 11 00 00 41 01 38 00 00 00 00 00 00 00 00 01 90 00
```

While when we extract it, the output changes:

```
INFO:root:<-] 3B BE 11 00 00 41 01 38 00 00 00 00 00 00 00 00 01 90 00
```

In this manner, we can detect each user action with the corresponding ATR parameter
involved.

 Note that implementation is very minimal since we limit our attention to
the ATR parameter, which cannot be used to uniquely identify a smart
card under all circumstances.

RFID reader

The evolution of smart cards is the **Radio-Frequency IDentification (RFID)** devices that
can be used to identify people or objects in a contactless form, starting from few centimeters
until several meters. The *RFID readers* and the corresponding *tags* (or *transponders*) are high-
technology radio devices that can exchange data with each other in order to accomplish
identification tasks.

You can get more information regarding the RFID world by taking a look at `https://en.wikipedia.org/wiki/Radio-frequency_identification`.

There are several classes of RFID readers according to the frequencies in which they work. Some of them are:

- RFID **low frequency** (LF) readers can be used where the identification tasks need no wires, but where the distance between the object to identify and the reader is no more than few centimeters. These devices are usually very simple as the ones we presented in `Chapter 7`, *Serial Ports and TTY Devices – TTY*. The reader is connected with the host by a serial port, and it simply returns a string each time a tag is detected.

- RFID **ultra high frequency** (UHF) readers can detect tags in a wireless mode like the LF reader, but at a distance of several meters. These devices can be more complex than the earlier ones, like the one we're going to use in this section. The reader still uses a serial connection to talk with the host, but it implements a more elaborate protocol to exchange data.

As a RFID UHF reader, we can use the following device that sends its data through a serial port at **TTL** 3.3V level:

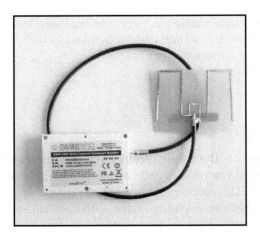

The device can be purchased at
`http://www.cosino.io/product/uhf-rfid-long-range-reader` or by surfing the Internet.

The product's information from the manufacturer is available at
`http://www.caenrfid.it/en/CaenProd.jsp?mypage=3&parent=59&idmod=818`.

The reader can be directly connected to our SAMA5D3 Xplained using these connections:

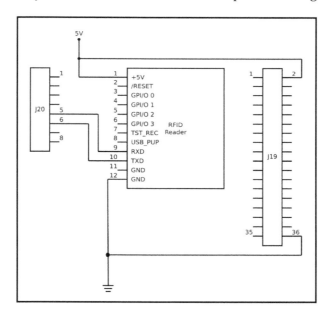

 Since the RFID reader used in this circuitry needs a high input current, we need to power up the SAMA5D3 Xplained board with an external power supply in order to have a properly functional system.

After all pins have been connected, the tag's data will be available at the `/dev/ttyS1` device, but to get them, we need extra software too. In fact, these readers require a special protocol to communicate with the host, so we need to install a special C library to do the trick.

We need to download, compile, and then install three libraries: **libmsgbuff**, **libavp,** and the **libcaenrfid**.

First of all, we need some prerequisite packages, so let's install them:

```
root@a5d3:~# apt-get install debhelper dctrl-tools
```

Now, we can start downloading the first library with the following command:

```
root@a5d3:~# git clone http://github.com/cosino/libmsgbuff.git
```

 A compressed archive of this package is stored in the
`chapter_19/rfid/libmsgbuff.tgz` file in the book's example code
repository.

Now, we have to enter the new directory `libmsgbuff` and execute the `autogen.sh`
command as shown here:

```
root@a5d3:~/libmsgbuff# ./autogen.sh
```

Then to compile the library we can use the command line below:

```
root@a5d3:~/libmsgbuff# ./debian/rules binary
. . .
dpkg-deb: building package `libmsgbuff0' in `../libmsgbuff0_0.60.0_arm
hf.deb'.
dpkg-deb: building package `libmsgbuff-dev' in `../libmsgbuff-dev_0.60
.0_armhf.deb'.
```

OK, now, the packages are ready, and we can install them using the `dpkg` command:

```
root@a5d3:~/libmsgbuff# dpkg -i ../libmsgbuff0_0.60.0_armhf.deb
                            ../libmsgbuff-dev_0.60.0_armhf.deb
. . .
Setting up libmsgbuff0 (0.60.0) ...
Setting up libmsgbuff-dev (0.60.0) ...
```

Now, it's the turn of the second library. The steps are the same as the earlier ones. First,
download the sources:

```
root@a5d3:~# git clone http://github.com/cosino/libavp.git
```

 A compressed archive of this package is stored in the
`chapter_19/rfid/libavp.tgz` file in the book's example code
repository.

Then, execute the `autogen.sh` script in the library's directory:

```
root@a5d3:~/libavp# ./autogen.sh
```

Then, start the compilation:

```
root@a5d3:~/libavp# ./debian/rules binary
...
dpkg-deb: building package `libavp0' in `../libavp0_0.80.0_armhf.deb'.
dpkg-deb: building package `libavp-dev' in `../libavp-dev_0.80.0_armhf
.deb'.
```

In the end, execute the `dpkg` command to install the packages:

```
root@a5d3:~/libavp# dpkg -i ../libavp0_0.80.0_armhf.deb
                            ../libavp-dev_0.80.0_armhf.deb
```

OK, for the last library, the procedure is similar, but with a little note. First, download the code and execute the `autogen.sh` script:

```
root@a5d3:~# git clone http://github.com/cosino/libcaenrfid.git
root@a5d3:~# cd libcaenrfid/
root@a5d3:~/libcaenrfid# ./autogen.sh
```

 A compressed archive of this package is stored in the `chapter_19/rfid/libcaenrfid.tgz` file in the book's example code repository.

Then, we need to create two new files for BeagleBone Black's architecture (which is named `armhf` in Debian). The commands are as follows:

```
root@a5d3:~/libcaenrfid# cp src/linux-gnueabi.c src/linux-gnueabihf.c
root@a5d3:~/libcaenrfid# cp src/linux-gnueabi.h src/linux-gnueabihf.h
```

Now, we can execute the usual package-generation command followed by the installation one as shown here:

```
root@a5d3:~/libcaenrfid# ./debian/rules binary
...
dpkg-deb: building package `libcaenrfid0' in `../libcaenrfid0_0.91.0_a
rmhf.deb'.
dpkg-deb: building package `libcaenrfid-dev' in `../libcaenrfid-dev_0.
91.0_armhf.deb'.
root@a5d3:~/libcaenrfid# dpkg -i ../libcaenrfid0_0.91.0_armhf.deb
                                 ../libcaenrfid-dev_0.91.0_armhf.deb
```

Well, at this point, the necessary libraries are in place, so we can compile our program to get access to the RFID UHF reader. A snippet of a possible implementation of the main() function is reported here:

```
int main(int argc, char *argv[])
{
    int i;
    struct caenrfid_handle handle;
    char string[] = "Source_0";
    struct caenrfid_tag *tag;
    size_t size;
    char *str;
    int ret;

    if (argc < 2)
        usage();

    /* Start a new connection with the CAENRFIDD server */
    ret = caenrfid_open(CAENRFID_PORT_RS232, argv[1], &handle);
    if (ret < 0)
        usage();

    /* Set session "S2" for logical source 0 */
    ret = caenrfid_set_srcconf(&handle, "Source_0",
                            CAENRFID_SRC_CFG_G2_SESSION, 2);
    if (ret < 0) {
        fprintf(stderr, "cannot set session 2 (err=%d)\n", ret);
        exit(EXIT_FAILURE);
    }

    while (1) {
        /* Do the inventory */
        ret = caenrfid_inventory(&handle, string, &tag, &size);
        if (ret < 0) {
            fprintf(stderr, "cannot get data (err=%d)\n", ret);
            exit(EXIT_FAILURE);
        }

        /* Report results */
        for (i = 0; i < size; i++) {
            str = bin2hex(tag[i].id, tag[i].len);
            if (!str) {
                fprintf(stderr,
                        "cannot allocate data (err=%d)\n", ret);
                exit(EXIT_FAILURE);
            }

            printf("%.*s %.*s %.*s %d\n",
```

```
                    tag[i].len * 2, str,
                    CAENRFID_SOURCE_NAME_LEN, tag[i].source,
                    CAENRFID_READPOINT_NAME_LEN,
                    tag[i].readpoint,
                    tag[i].type);

            free(str);
        }

        /* Free inventory data */
        free(tag);
    }

    caenrfid_close(&handle);

    return 0;
}
```

 The complete code is stored in the `chapter_19/rfid/rfid_uhf.c` file in the book's example code repository.

The program simply uses the `caenrfid_open()` function to establish a connection with the reader and then the `caenrfid_inventory()` function to detect the tags. The `caenrfid_set_srcconf()` function is used to set an internal special functioning (*session S2*) in order to avoid multiple readings of the same tag. In the internal `while` loop, we continuously repeat the inventory, and if there are some results to print (`size` greater than 0), we proceed to format the output to be printed accordingly to the tags data.

The program can be compiled with the `make` command and used as follows:

```
root@a5d3:~# ./rfid_uhf /dev/ttyS1
```

The program answers with no output if there are no tags near the reader's antenna, but if we approach some tags, we get something as follows:

```
root@a5d3:~# ./rfid_uhf /dev/ttyS1
e2801130200020d1dda500ab Source_0 Ant0 3
e280113020002861dd9100ab Source_0 Ant0 3
e280113020002491ddbc00ab Source_0 Ant0 3
e280113020002441ddbc00ab Source_0 Ant0 3
e2801130200024a1ddbc00ab Source_0 Ant0 3
e280113020002431ddbc00ab Source_0 Ant0 3
e280113020002801dd9100ab Source_0 Ant0 3
e2801130200028c1dd9100ab Source_0 Ant0 3
```

Z-Wave

The **Z-Wave technology** is oriented for the residential control and automation market, and its main goal is to minimize the power consumption because almost all Z-Wave devices work on battery. However, despite this fact, Z-Wave provides reliable and low-latency transmission of small data packets at data rates up to 100 kbit/s!

The Z-Wave communication protocol allows us, using a proper controller, to manage several home automation sensors and actuators in a wireless manner, so we don't need to modify our pre-existent plant. Also, we can easily add a power consumption measuring system or several environment sensors with a minor impact to the actual home layout.

For more information on Z-Wave, a good starting point is
`https://en.wikipedia.org/wiki/Z-Wave`.

Z-Wave controllers

There are several kinds of Z-Wave controllers. However, the most widely used are the ones on a USB dongle, such as the one shown in the following image:

The device can be purchased at
`http://www.cosino.io/product/usb-z-wave-controller` or by surfing the Internet.

A reference design is available at
`http://z-wave.sigmadesigns.com/wp-content/uploads/UZB_br.pdf`.

Once connected with BeagleBone Black's USB host port, we should get the following kernel messages:

```
usb 1-1: new full-speed USB device number 2 using musb-hdrc
usb 1-1: New USB device found, idVendor=0658, idProduct=0200
usb 1-1: New USB device strings: Mfr=0, Product=0, SerialNumber=0
cdc_acm 1-1:1.0: ttyACM0: USB ACM device
usbcore: registered new interface driver cdc_acm
cdc_acm: USB Abstract Control Model driver for USB modems and ISDN adapters
```

Looking at the third-last line, we can discover that the Z-Wave controller has been connected to the device file /dev/ttyACM0. So, the device is correctly connected, but to really test it, we need to install a proper management software. To do so, we can use an open source implementation of the Z-Wave protocol named **Open Z-Wave,** where we can find a lot of suitable software to test a Z-Wave network.

 The home page of the Open Z-Wave project is at http://www.openzwave.com.

With the following command, we can download the code we need in our prototype:

```
root@bbb:~# git clone https://github.com/OpenZWave/open-zwave
```

 A compressed archive of this package is stored in the chapter_19/zwave/open-zwave.tgz file in the book's example code repository.

Then, we need some extra packages to compile the necessary tools, so let's install them with one of the usual installation commands as shown here:

```
root@bbb:~# aptitude install libudev-dev libjson0
                            libjson0-dev libcurl4-gnutls-dev
```

Now, just enter the openzwave directory and simply use the make command as shown here:

```
root@bbb:~/open-zwave# make
```

 The compilation is quite slow, so be patient.

When finished, go back to the upper directory and download another repository with the following command:

```
root@bbb:~# git clone https://github.com/OpenZWave/open-zwave-control-panel
```

 A compressed archive of this package is stored in the chapter_19/zwave/open-zwave-control-panel.tgz file in the book's example code repository.

Then, after downloading, we have to install an extra package to proceed with the compilation, so let's use the aptitude command (or equivalent) again:

```
root@bbb:~/openzwave# aptitude install libmicrohttpd-dev
```

Now, enter the open-zwave-control-panel directory and modify Makefile as shown here:

```
--- Makefile.orig    2016-10-10 13:45:16.590209754 +0000
+++ Makefile    2016-10-10 13:46:43.660209764 +0000
@@ -34,15 +34,15 @@
 # for Linux uncomment out next three lines
 LIBZWAVE := $(wildcard $(OPENZWAVE)/*.a)
-#LIBUSB := -ludev
-#LIBS := $(LIBZWAVE) $(GNUTLS) $(LIBMICROHTTPD) -pthread $(LIBUSB) -
lresolv
+LIBUSB := -ludev
+LIBS := $(LIBZWAVE) $(GNUTLS) $(LIBMICROHTTPD) -pthread $(LIBUSB) -lresolv
 # for Mac OS X comment out above 2 lines and uncomment next 5 lines
 #ARCH := -arch i386 -arch x86_64
 #CFLAGS += $(ARCH)
 #LIBZWAVE := $(wildcard $(OPENZWAVE)/cpp/lib/mac/*.a)
-LIBUSB := -framework IOKit -framework CoreFoundation
-LIBS := $(LIBZWAVE) $(GNUTLS) $(LIBMICROHTTPD) -pthread $(LIBUSB) $(ARCH)
-lresolv
+#LIBUSB := -framework IOKit -framework CoreFoundation
+#LIBS := $(LIBZWAVE) $(GNUTLS) $(LIBMICROHTTPD) -pthread $(LIBUSB) $(ARCH)
-lresolv
 %.o : %.cpp
    $(CXX) $(CFLAGS) $(INCLUDES) -o $@ $<
```

Then, run the make command:

```
root@bbb:~/openzwave/openzwave-control-panel# make
```

When the compilation is finished, the `ozwcp` program should be available, so let's execute it using the command lines here:

```
root@bbb:~/open-zwave-control-panel# ln -s ../open-zwave/config .
root@bbb:~/open-zwave-control-panel# ./ozwcp -d -p 8080
2016-10-10 13:49:35.752 Always, OpenZwave Version 1.4.2277 Starting Up
webserver starting port 8080
```

Note that the `ln` command is just used once to create a proper link with the Open Z-Wave configuration directory `config`, which is located in the `open-zwave` directory.

If we get the following error in executing the program, it means that most probably, your web server is holding port `8080`, so we have to disable it:

Failed to bind to port 8080: Address already in use

Well, now, we should point the web browser on our host PC to the `http://192.168.7.2:8080` address to get the following screenshot:

OK, now, we have to enter the path name `/dev/ttyACM0` in the **Device name** field and then press the **Initialize** button to start the communication. If everything works well, we should see that a new device is listed in the **Devices** tab, as shown in the following screenshot:

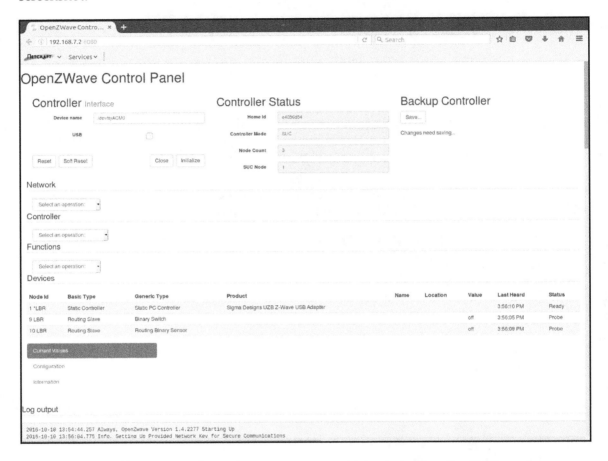

Now, the controller is up and running, so we can continue installing the Z-Wave slaves.

The Z-Wave wall plug sensor

The first Z-Wave slave is the wall plug shown in the following image:

 The device can be purchased at
`http://www.cosino.io/product/z-wave-wall-plug` or by surfing the
Internet.

A reference manual is available at
`http://www.fibaro.com/manuals/en/FGWPx-101/FGWPx-101-EN-A-v1.00.`
`pdf.`

The device is wireless, and once connected to a powered plug, it's self-powered, so we don't
need special connections to set it up. However, we need some home appliance connected to
it, as shown in the following image, for the power-consumption measurements:

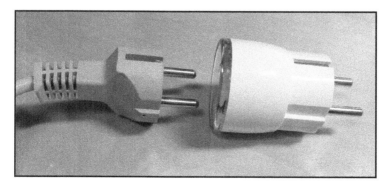

Now, to test this device and its communication with the controller, we can use the `ozwcp` program again. Just click on the **Select an operation** menu entry in the **Controller** tab, select the **Add Device** entry, and then press the **Go** button. On the left-hand side, we should see the **Add Device: waiting for a user action** message, so let's power up the device by putting it into a wall plug and then strike the button on the device in order to start the pairing procedure (like a bluetooth device does).

 Note that a newer version of this device doesn't require us to press the button to start the pairing procedure. It just starts automatically after the first plug.

If everything works well, a new device should appear in the**Devices** tab, as shown in the following screenshot:

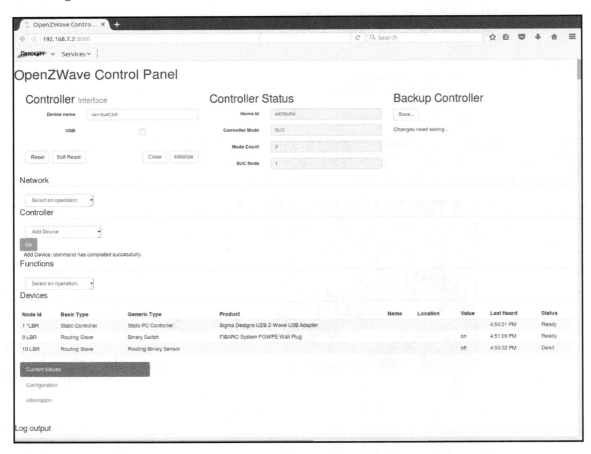

Now, we can change some device's settings by selecting the new device and then clicking on the **Configuration** option under the devices listing tab. A panel for settings similar to the following screenshot should appear:

The Z-Wave multi sensor

The second Z-Wave slave is the multi sensor shown in the following image:

The device can be purchased at
`http://www.cosino.io/product/z-wave-multi-sensor` or by surfing the
Internet.

A reference manual is available
at `http://aeotec.com/z-wave-sensor/47-multisensor-manual.html`.

To power the device, we can use four batteries or a USB cable connected as in the following
image. Then, to test the device and its communication with the controller, we can use again
the `ozwcp` program, so just click on the **Select an operation** menu entry in the **Controller**
tab and select the **Add Device** entry. Then, press the **Go** button in order to repeat a pairing
procedure again (the pairing button is the black button near the sensitivity regulator under
the battery pack cover):

Again, if everything works well, a new device should appear in the **Devices** tab, as shown in the following screenshot. We can change some device's settings by selecting the new device and then clicking on the **Configuration** option under the devices listing tab as shown in the screenshot here:

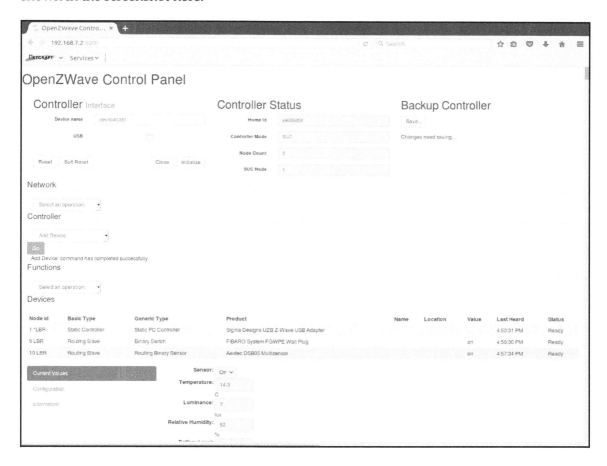

Summary

In this earlier chapter, we discovered a group of peripheral devices that can be connected with our embedded kits using a technique we presented in the previous chapters.

You should now have an idea of some basic examples of several computer peripherals that can be connected and used with a GNU/Linux-based embedded system.

Index

www.ingramcontent.com/pod-product-compliance
Lightning Source LLC
Chambersburg PA
CBHW081448050326
40690CB00015B/2716

* 9 7 8 1 7 8 6 4 6 1 8 0 3 *